Knitted Bears

Knitted Bears

Eight special friends
for you to knit and crochet

Claire Garland

NORTH LIGHT BOOKS

First published in North America
by North Light Craft
an imprint of F+W Publications, Inc.
4700 East Galbraith Road
Cincinnati, OH 45236
800-289-0963

First Published in Great Britain in 2008 by
New Holland Publishers (UK) Ltd.
London • Cape Town • Sydney • Auckland
Garfield House
86-88 Edgware Road
London W2 2EA
United Kingdom

ISBN-13: 978-1-60061-130-8
ISBN-10: 1-60061-130-3

Senior Editor **Emma Pattison**
Designer **John Garland**
Photography **John Garland**
Production **Marion Storz**
Editorial Direction **Rosemary Wilkinson**

10 9 8 7 6 5 4 3 2 1

Reproduction by Colour Scan Overseas Co., Singapore
Printed and bound by Craft Print International Ltd., Singapore

Note: Some of the projects in this book are unsuitable for children under 3 years of age
due to small parts. Always keep small or sharp objects (such as needles or buttons) away
from small children.

Contents

Introduction

Welcome to my special collection of eight quirky bear friends with their characteristic outfits. Each huggable, cuddly bear and their clothing are knitted or crocheted in a rainbow of colored and tactual textured yarn with colors and styles to reflect each bear's personality and charm.

The bears have each been given names and personal identities to further enhance the idea of knitting a friend. The hardest part is choosing which adorably soft and endearing little companion to begin with.

Have fun!

Claire

Blossom Boo

Delicate and genteel little Blossom Boo is a real girl's girl and doesn't like joining in with the rough-and-tumble of the boy's games. However, she loves playing with her friends, in her own dizzy, fluffy, pretty way. Oh, and she loves sugar—big time!

Blossom has a penchant for sweet things. She loves strawberries, cherries, and candied lemons, and, of course, ice cream!

Blossom Boo

Finished size

Completed toy measures approximately 17¾ inches (45 cm) tall by 14½ inches (37 cm) wide, arms outstretched.

Yarn

Bear: 50g light-worsted-weight (DK-weight) angora or mixed-fiber yarn in main color **MC**, hands and feet color **A** (*MC—Rowan Soft Baby shade 003 Princess, A—GGH Handknit Amelie shade 004 magenta*).

Fabric and extras

Felt: Scraps of terracotta colored felt for outer eyes.
Embroidery thread: Stranded cotton, for sewing on eyes, nose, and mouth.
Beads: 2 x 6 mm (¼ in.) Black Glass Pearls or similar.
Filling: Polyester toy filling.

Needles

Pair of US size 5 (3¾ mm) knitting needles.
Blunt-ended yarn sewing needle.
Embroidery sewing needle.

Gauge

20 sts and 36 rows to 4 inches (10 cm) measured over garter stitch, using US size 5 (3¾ mm) needles and yarn MC.

Front (knitted)

Front of Bear's body and head are worked in one piece from lower edge. Using US size 5 (3¾ mm) needles and yarn MC (main body color), cast on 8 sts, leaving a long tail end.

Next row (inc row) (RS) *K into front and back of st to inc one st–called **Kfb**—°rep from * to end. (16 sts)

Next row (inc row) (WS) Kfb, K to last st, Kfb. (18 sts)

Rep last row two times more, ending with a **WS** row. (22 sts)

Beg with a **RS** row, work 26 rows in g st, ending with a **WS** row.

Shape shoulders

Row 1 (dec row) (RS) K2tog, K to last 2 sts, K2tog. (20 sts)

Rep last row once more.

Shape neck

Next row (dec row) (RS) Bind off 3 sts at beg of row. (15 sts)

Next row (dec row) (WS) Rep last row once more. (12 sts)

Beg with a **RS** row, work straight in g st for 3 rows, ending with a **RS** row. **

Divide for front of face

Row 1 (dec row) (WS) K6, turn and work on these sts for Right Front. (6 sts) Work each side of the face separately.

Next row (inc row) (RS) Kfb, K to last st, Kfb. (8 sts)

Next row (WS) K to end. (8 sts)

Rep last 2 rows 5 times more, ending with a **WS** row. (18 sts)

Shape the nose

Next row (inc row) (RS) Kfb, K to end. (19 sts)

Next row (inc row) (WS) K to last st, Kfb. (20 sts)

Rep last 2 rows once more, ending with a **WS** row. (22 sts)

Beg with a **RS** row, work straight in g st for 6 rows, ending with a **WS** row.

Shape for the top of the nose

Next row (dec row) (RS) Bind off 6 sts, K to the end of row. (16 sts)

Next row (WS) K to end.

Next row (dec row) (RS) K2tog, K to end. (15 sts)

Rep last 2 rows once more ending with a **RS** row. (14 sts)

Next row (WS) K to end.

Next row (dec row) (RS) K2tog, K to last 2sts, K2tog. (12 sts)

Next row (dec row) (WS) *K2tog, rep from * to end. (6 sts)

Bind off.

Left Front

WS facing rejoin yarn to the inside edge of the right front and K row. (6 sts)

Next row (inc row) (RS) Kfb, K to last st, Kfb. (8 sts)

Next row (WS) K to end.

Rep last 2 rows 5 times more, ending with a **WS** row. (18 sts)

Shape the nose

Next row (inc row) (RS) K to last st, Kfb. (19 sts)

Next row (inc row) (WS) Kfb, K to end. (20 sts)

Rep last 2 rows once more, ending with a **WS** row. (22 sts)

Beg with a **RS** row, work straight in g st for 5 rows, ending with a **RS** row.

Shape for the top of the nose

Next row (dec row) (WS) Bind off 6 sts, K to the end of row. (16 sts)

Next row (RS) K to end.

Next row (dec row) (WS) K2tog, K to end. (15 sts)

Rep last 2 rows once more ending with a **WS** row. (14 sts)

Next row (RS) K to end.

Next row (dec row) (WS) K2tog, K to

last 2sts, K2tog. (12 sts)
Next row (dec row) (RS) *K2tog, rep from * to end. (6 sts)
Bind off.

Back (knitted)

Back of Bear's body and head are worked in one piece, from lower edge.

Using US size 5 (3¾ mm) needles and yarn MC (main body color), cast on 8 sts and work as for Front up to **. (12 sts)

Next row (WS) K to end.

Shape head

Next row (inc row) (RS) Kfb, K to last st, Kfb. (14 sts)

Next row (WS) K to end.

Rep last 2 rows 5 times more, ending with a **WS** row. (24 sts)

Beg with a **RS** row, work straight in g st for 16 rows, ending with a **WS** row.

Next row (dec row) (RS) K2tog, K to last 2sts, K2tog. (22 sts)

Next row (dec row) (WS) *K2tog, rep from * to end. (11 sts)
Bind off.

Arm (knitted)

Starting at the paw end, using US size 5 (3¾ mm) needles and yarn **A** (hands and feet color), cast on 7 sts, leaving a long tail end.

Next row (inc row) (RS) *Kfb, rep from * to end. (14 sts)

Beg with a WS row, work straight in g st for 23 rows, ending with a **WS** row.

Shape elbow

Next row (inc row) (RS) Change to yarn **MC**, Kfb, K to last st, Kfb. (16 sts)

Rep last row twice more, ending with

a RS row. (20 sts)

Next row (WS) K to end.

Next row (dec row) (RS) (K2tog) 3 times, K8, (K2tog) 3 times. (14 sts)

Beg with a WS row, work 19 rows in g st, ending with a **WS** row.
Bind off.

Make another arm in the same way.

Leg (knitted)

Starting at the paw end, using US size 5 (3¾ mm) needles and yarn **A** (hands and feet color) cast on 8 sts, leaving a long tail end.

Next row (inc row) (RS) *Kfb, rep from * to end. (16 sts)

Next row (inc row) (WS) Kfb, K to last st, Kfb. (18 sts)

Rep last row four times more, ending with a **WS** row. (26 sts)

Beg with a **RS** row, work 14 rows in g st, ending with a **WS** row.

Next row (dec row) (RS) Change to yarn **MC**, (K2tog) 5 times, K6, (K2tog)

5 times. (16 sts)

Beg with a WS row, work 55 rows in g st, ending with a **WS** row.
Bind off.

Make another leg in the same way.

Ear (knitted)

Using US size 5 (3¾ mm) needles and yarn **A** (hands and feet color), cast on 10 sts, leaving a long tail end.

Next row (WS) K to end.

Next row (inc row) (RS) *Kfb, rep from * to end. (20 sts)

Beg with a WS row, work 7 rows in g st, ending with a **WS** row.

Next row (dec row) (RS) K2tog, K6, (K2tog) twice, K6, K2tog. (16 sts)
Bind off.

Make another ear in the same way.

To make up

Press pieces lightly on wrong side, following instructions on yarn label.

Head, body, arms, legs, ears

Using blunt-ended yarn needle, matching yarn and mattress stitch for seams throughout, make up as Basic Bear (see page 106), but omit inner eyes.

Floaty spotted sundress

Finished size
Completed item measures 5⅛ inches (13 cm) long by 10 inches (25 cm) at waist.

Yarn
Sundress: 50g of finger-weight (4 ply) wool, or mixed-fiber yarn in main color **MC,** 1st stripe color **A,** small amount finger-weight (4 ply-weight) wool, or mixed-fiber yarn in hem color **B** (*MC—Opal Uni 4-ply shade mid blue, A—Opal Uni 4-ply shade grass green, B—Opal Uni 4-ply shade cream*).
Dots: Small amounts finger-weight (4 ply) angora, or mixed-fiber yarn in 4 different colors **C** (*Opal Uni 4 ply shades light pink, orange, hot pink, and chocolate*).
Short lengths fine yarn for tie and shoulder straps

Fabric and extras
Beads: 8 x 1 cm (½ in.) dia. plastic rings or similar.

Hook
Hook size US size E-4 (3.50 mm).
Blunt-ended yarn sewing needle.

Gauge
24 sts and 28 rows to 4 inches (10 cm) measured over double crochet using hook size US size E-4 (3.50 mm) and yarn **MC.**

Sun dress (crocheted)
Foundation chain Beg at the hem edge, using US size E-4 (3.50 mm) hook and yarn **B** (hem color), make 142CH.
Row 1 1dr in 3rd ch from hook, 1dr in each ch to end, turn. (140 sts)
Row 2 3CH, 1dr in each tr to end.
Rep last row once.
Fasten off yarn B.
Join on yarn **A** at beg of next row.
Row 4 1CH, 1SC in each tr to end. Turn.
Row 5 (dec row) 1CH, *Skip next sc, 1SC in each of next 13sc, rep from * to end. Turn. (130 sts)
Row 6 1CH, 1SC in each sc to end. Turn.
Rep last row ten times more.
Fasten off yarn **A.**
Next row (dec row) Join on yarn **MC,** 1CH, *Skip next sc, 1SC in each of next 12sc rep from * to end. Turn. (120 sts)
Next row 1CH, 1SC in each sc to end. Turn.
Rep last row 3 times more.
Next row and foll fifth row decrease 10 sts evenly across the row. (100 sts)
Work 4 rows sc.
Next row 1CH, *Skip next sc, 1SC in next sc, rep from * to end. Turn. (50 sts)

Next row 1CH, 1SC in each sc to end. Turn.
Rep last row three times more.
Fasten off.

To make up
Press piece lightly on wrong side, following instructions on yarn label.
Using blunt-ended yarn needle, matching yarn, and back stitch join row ends.
To make dots, using US size E-4 (3.50 mm) hook and yarn C (dots color), make 50CH for large dot, 35CH for medium dots, and 23CH for small dot. Fasten of each ch. Twist around to make a flat coil and sew in place onto the dress.
Beginning and ending at the front, weave a length of yarn in and out of the crochet at the bodice edge 1 sc row down from the top edge. Tie in a bow at the front.
To make halter neck straps, using US size E-4 (3.50mm) hook and two lengths of yarn make an 8-inch (20 cm) length of CH for each strap. Fasten off. Sew one end of each to the top of the dress—1 inch (2½ cm) each side of center front. Thread on the beads and tie at the back.

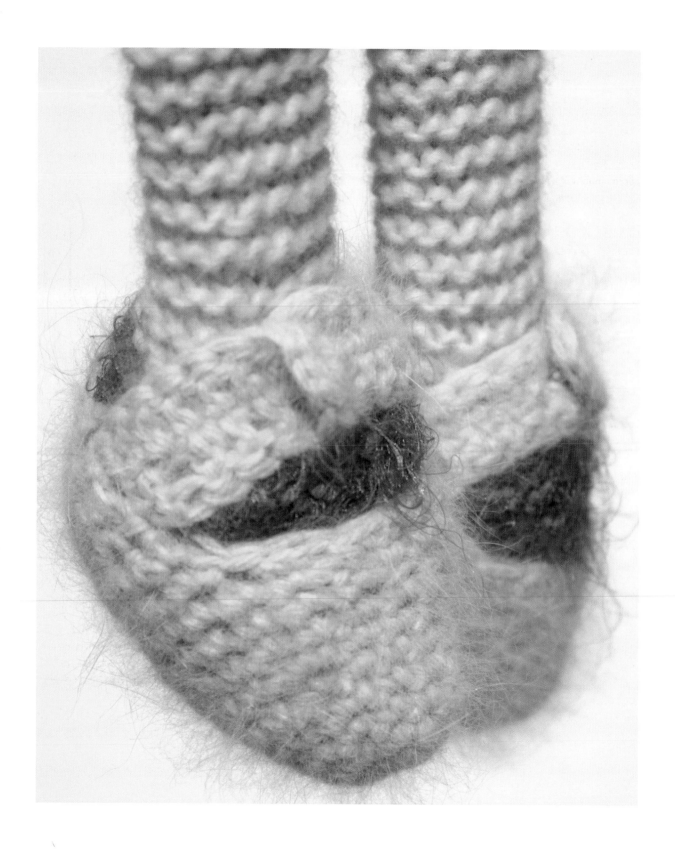

18 Blossom Boo

Best strap shoes

Finished size

Completed item measures approximately 3½ inches (9 cm) long by 6 inches (15 cm) max diameter.

Yarn

Shoes: Small amount light-worsted-weight (DK-weight) wool, cotton, or mixed-fiber yarn in main color **MC** (*Adriafil Angora Carezza angora / wool / nylon mix shade 82 cyan*).

Fabric and extras

Velcro: Small amount of Velcro for the shoe fastenings.

Hook

US size H-8 (5.00 mm) crochet hook
Blunt-ended yarn sewing needle
Embroidery sewing needle.

Gauge

16 sts and 17 rows to 4 inches (10 cm) measured over single crochet, using US size H-8 (5.00 mm) hook and yarn **MC**.

Shoe (crocheted)

Foundation chain Beg at the toe end, using US size H-8 (5.00 mm) hook and **MC**, make 4CH, leaving a long tail end. 1 Slip St in 1st ch to form a ring.
Round 1 1CH, 5SC in ring working over the long loose end, Sl St in 1st sc.
Round 2 1CH, 2SC in sl st of last round, 2SC in each 4sc, Sl St in 1st sc. (10 sc)
Round 3 1CH, 1SC in sl st of last round, 1SC in each sc, Sl St in 1st sc. (10 sc)

Round 4 1CH, 1SC in sl st of last round, 2SC in next sc, *1SC in next sc, 2SC in next sc, rep from * to end, Sl St in 1st sc. (15 sc)
Round 5 As round 3.
Round 6 1CH, 2SC in sl st of last round, 1SC in each of next 4sc, *2SC in next sc, 1SC in each of next 4sc, rep from * to end, Sl St in 1st sc. (20 sc)
Round 7 As round 3.
Round 8 1CH, 2SC in sl st of last round, 1SC in next 9sc, 2SC in next sc, 1SC in next 9sc, Sl St in 1st sc. (22 sc)
Cont to work as round 3–without shaping–twice more.

Side shaping

Row 1 1CH. 1SC in next 15sc. Turn. (15 sc)
Row 2 1CH, Skip 1st sc, 1SC in each of 14 sc, 1SC in 1ch. Turn. (15 sc)
Rep last row two times more.

Shape heel

Row 5 (Inc row) 1CH, 1SC in 1st sc, 1SC in each sc, ending 2SC in 1ch at edge, turn. (17 sc)
Rep last row two times more. (21 sc)
Fasten off.

Strap

Foundation chain Using US size H-8 (5.00 mm) hook and **MC**, make 5CH, leaving a long tail end.
Row 1 1SC in 2nd ch from hook, 1SC in each of 2ch, 5SC in last ch. Turn. Working back along other side of foundation ch, 1SC in each 3ch Turn. (11 sts)
Row 2 1CH, 1SC in each of 1st 5sc, 3SC in next sc, 1SC in each rem 5sc. (13 sts)
Fasten off.
Make another strap in the same way.

Shoes that you can fasten with one hand so that you can still keep hold of your ice cream are very important to Blossom Boo.

To make up

Using blunt-ended yarn needle, matching yarn, and back stitch for seam.

Sew up the back seam by joining finishing row with wrong sides facing. Turn out right way.

Stitch the straight edge of each strap to the upper edge of the shoe, approx 1 inch (2½ cm) from back seam.

Overlap the straps to about ¼ inch (6 mm) at the top of the shoe and sew velcro to each end.

Blossom's scarf is simply made using spare lengths of yarn on a knitting dolly (or make a cord with double pointed needles) until scarf measures approx 22 inches (56 cm). Bind off. Make another shoe in same way.

Acorn beanie

Finished size

Completed item measures 12 inches (30½ cm) diameter

Yarn

Beanie: Small amount worsted (Aran weight) wool or mixed-fiber yarn in main color **MC**. Small amount light worsted (DK weight) yarn in trim color **A**, (**MC**—RYC Cashsoft Aran shade 006 Bud, **A**—Adriafil Angora Carezza angora / wool / nylon mix shade Pink).

Hook

US H-8 (5.00 mm) crochet hook.

Gauge

13 sts and 15 rounds to 4 inches (10 cm) measured over single crochet using US H-8 (5.00 mm).

Beanie (crocheted)

Foundation chain Beg at top of crown, using US H-8 (5.00 mm) hook and yarn **MC** (main color), make 2CH.

Round 1 6SC in 2nd ch from hook.

Round 2 2SC in each 6sc. (12 sc)

Note: Before beg the next round, place a marker or short length of contrasting yarn across your crochet and up against the loop on the hook and above the working yarn. Work Round 3 then slip the marker out and place it at the beg of the next round and so on. The marker will indicate where each subsequent round starts.

Round 3 *1SC in next sc, 2SC in next sc, rep from * all around. (18 sc)

Round 4 1SC in each sc.

Round 5 *1SC in each of next 2sc, 2SC in next sc, rep from * all around. (24 sc)

Round 6 *1SC in each of next 3sc, 2SC in next sc, rep from * all around. (30 sc)

Round 7 As round 4.

Round 8 *1SC in each of next 4sc, 2SC in next sc, rep from * all around. (36 sc)

Round 9 * 1SC in each of 5sc, 2SC in next sc, rep from * all round. (42sc)

Shape side

Round 10 1SC in each next 42 sc. Rep last round once more. Fasten off yarn **MC** with Sl st in next sc. Weave in end.

Trim

Join on yarn **A** with sl st in sl st of last round.

Round 12 1SC in each sc all around.

Round 13 *Skip next sc, 1SC in each next 6sc, rep from *all round. (36 sc)

Round 14 1SC in each sc all round. Fasten off. Weave in end.

Pull up center loose end to close the ring, then thread this through to the right side to form a 'stem'. Trim to 1 inch (2½ cm).

Blossom Boo loves her cute Acorn Beanie hat—it keeps her warm & snug on cold days.

Doogs

A boystrous, fun, kick-a-ball-all-day kind of bear. Friends with all he meets and very popular. Nothing phases Doogs—he just shrugs it off! However, he doesn't like sitting down to eat; food is a waste of playing-with-the-ball time!

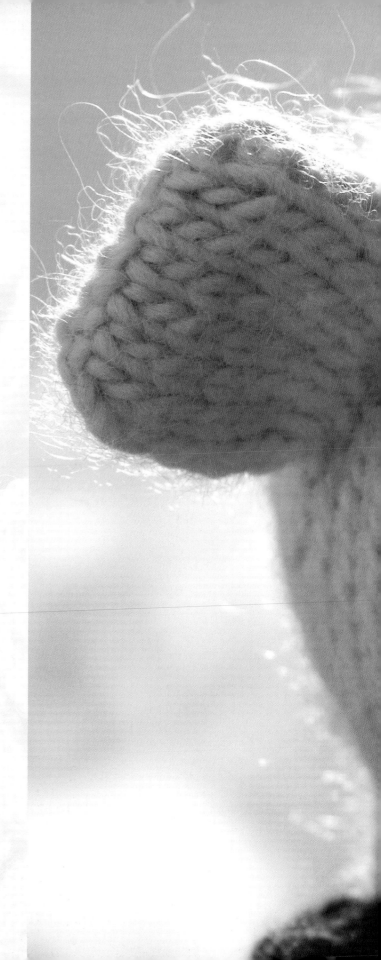

Embroidery thread: Stranded cotton, for sewing on eyes, nose, and mouth.
Beads: 2 x 6 mm (¼ in.) Black Glass Pearls or similar.
Filling: Polyester toy filling.

Needles
Pair of US size 5 (3¾ mm) knitting needles.
Blunt-ended yarn sewing needle.
Embroidery sewing needle.

Gauge
20 sts and 30 rows to 4 inches (10 cm) measured over stockinette stitch, using US size 5 (3¾ mm) needles and yarn **MC**.

Front, Back, Arms, and Ears
Work as Basic Bear (page 106).

To make up
Head, Body, Arms, Legs, and Ears
Make up as Basic Bear (page 106).

Egg Custard Dungarees

Finished size
Completed item measures approximately 14½ inches (36 cm) at waist by 8¾ inches (22 cm) long.

Yarn
Pants: 50g of US light-worsted-weight (DK-weight) all-seasons cotton yarn in main color **MC** *(Brown Sheep Company Cotton Fleece shade CW-620 Banana)*.

Doog's Dungarees are great for playing soccer and basketball in because they never fall down.

Doogs

Finished size
Completed toy measures approximately 20 inches (51 cm) tall by 17 inches (43 cm) wide, arms outstretched.

Yarn
Bear: 50g light-worsted-weight (DK-weight) 100% wool or mixed-sc yarn in main color **MC** *(Brown Sheep Company Worsted wool/mohair mix shade M-155 Lemon Drop)*.

Fabric and extras
Felt: Scraps of felt–sky blue for outer eyes, dark blue for inner eyes.

Waist edge and suspenders: Small amount of US light-worsted-weight (DK-weight) handknit cotton yarn in waist edge color **A** *(Rowan handknit Cotton shade 320 lemon yellow).*

Fabric and extras
Buttons: 2 x ¾ inches (2 cm).

Needles
Pair of US size 5 (3¾ mm) knitting needles.
Pair of US size 6 (4 mm) knitting needles.
Blunt-ended yarn sewing needle.
Embroidery sewing needle.

Gauge
20 sts and 26 rows to 4 inches (10 cm) measured over stockinette stitch using US size 6 (4 mm) needles and yarn **MC**.

Pants (knitted)
Left leg
Using US size 5 (3¾ mm) needles and yarn **A** (waist edge color), cast on 42 sts, leaving a long tail end.
Row 1 (RS) *K1, P1, rep from * to end.
Row 2 (WS) *P1, K1, rep from * to end.
Rep last 2 seed st rows once more, so ending with a **WS** row.
Next row (RS) Using US size 6 (4 mm) needles and yarn **MC** work in st for 14 rows so ending with a **WS** row.
Next row (dec row) (RS) K2 tog, K to last 2 sts, K2 tog. (40 sts)
Next row (dec row) (WS) P2 tog, P to last 2 sts, P2 tog. (38 sts)

This cool yet stylish striped sleeveless top in warm bulky knit yarn is perfect for playing ball.

Next row (dec row) (RS) K2 tog, K to last 2sts, K2 tog. (36 sts)
Next row (WS) P to end.
Rep last 2 rows once more, ending with a **WS** row. (34 sts)
Beg with a K row, work 6 rows in st st, ending with a **WS** row.
Next row (RS) Using US size 5 (3¾ mm) needles and yarn **A**, *K1, P1, rep from * to end.
Next row (WS) *P1, K1, rep from * to end.
Rep last 2 seed st rows once more, ending with a **WS** row. Bind off.

Right leg
Work as left leg.

Suspenders
Using US size 5 (3¾ mm) needles and yarn **A** (waist edge color), cast on 5 sts, leaving a long tail end.
Row 1 (RS) K1, *P1, K1, rep from * to end.
Rep last seed st row until the suspender measures 9½ inches (24 cm). Bind off.
Make another suspender in the same way.

To make up
Using blunt-ended yarn needle, matching yarn and backstitch for seams throughout, with **RS** facing sew legs seams. Turn one leg out the right way and slip inside the other leg so that **RS** are facing. Matching row ends sew front and back crotch seams. Turn out right way. Over sew the bind off end of each suspender to the back of the trouser setting them either side and ¼ inch (1 cm) away from the back seam. At the front of the trouser, cross the suspenders then pin approximately 1 inch (2½ cm) up from the cast on ends behind the front of the trouser setting them either side and 1¼ inch (3 cm) away from the seam. Sew a button to the front to hold each suspender in place.

Stylish Top

Finished size
Completed item measures approximately 6¾ inches (17 cm) wide by 5 inches (12½ cm) long.

Yarn
Top: 25g light-worsted-weight (DK-weight) wool, cotton or mixed-sc yarn in main color **MC** and 2nd stripe color **A** (*MC—Cottage Knits 100% Cotton Chenille shade 504 sky blue, **A** Frog Tree Bulky Alpaca shade 308 navy blue*).

Needles
Pair of US size 6 (4 mm) knitting needles.
Pair of US size 7 (4½ mm) knitting needles.
Blunt-ended yarn sewing needle.

Gauge
16 sts and 26 rows to 4 inches (10 cm) measured over stockinette stitch, using US size 7 (4½ mm) needles and yarn **MC**.

Top
Front and back alike
Using US size 6 (4 mm) needles and yarn **MC** (main body color), beg at the waist edge, cast on 23 sts, leaving a long tail end.
Next row (RS) K2, *P1, K2, rep from * to end.
Next row (WS) P2, *K1, P2, rep from * to end.
Rep last 2 rows 4 times more, so ending with a **WS** row. Change to yarn **A** (2nd stripe color.)
Using US size 7 (4½ mm) needles and yarn **A** (2nd stripe color), beg on a **RS** row g st 4 rows, ending with a **WS** row.
Next row (RS) Change to yarn **MC**, K to end.
Next row (WS) K to end.
Next row (RS) Change to yarn **A**, K to end.
Next row (WS) K to end.
Next row (RS) Change to yarn **MC**, K to end.
Next row (WS) K to end.
Shape for straps
Next row (RS) Change to yarn **A**, bind off 5 sts, K to end. (18 sts)
Next row (WS) Bind off 5 sts, K to end. (13 sts)
Next row (RS) K to end.
Next row (WS) K2 tog, K3, bind off 3 sts, K2, K2 tog. (8 sts).
Turn and work on 1st 4 sts for 1st (left front / right back) shoulder strap.

Beg on a **RS** row work 6 rows in g st, so ending with a **WS** row. Bind off.

Right front / left back shoulder strap
RS, rejoin yarn to rem 4 sts, beg on a **RS** row work 6 rows in g st, so ending with a **WS** row. Bind off.

To make up

Press pieces lightly on wrong side, following instructions on yarn label. Using mattress seam throughout, join shoulder straps and side seams. Weave in all ends.

Sneakers

Finished size

Completed item measures approximately 3 inches (7 cm) wide by 3½ inches (9 cm) long.

Yarn

Sneaker: 25g light-worsted-weight (DK-weight) wool, cotton or mixed-sc yarn in main color **MC**, 2 x 109 yards (10 m) wool tapestry skeins or any small amounts of worsted-weight (DK) yarn in sole color **A**, small amount finger-weight (4-ply) wool, cotton or mixed sc yarn plus 2 x 2 yards (2 m) lengths in laces color **B**, small amount light-worsted-weight (DK-weight) wool, cotton or mixed-sc yarn in color **C**, (*MC—Cottage Knits 100% Cotton Chenille shade 504 sky blue, A—Anchor Tapisserie shade 8442 deep berry, B—Jaeger Baby Merino shade cream, C—Frog Tree Chunky Alpaca shade 308 navy blue*).

Needles and hook

Pair of US size 6 (4 mm) knitting needles.
US size G-6 (4.00 mm) crochet hook.
Blunt-ended yarn sewing needle.

Gauge

22 sts and 23 rows to 4 inches (10 cm) measured over garter stitch using US size 6 (4mm) needles and yarn **MC**.

Sneaker upper (knitted)

Using US size 6 (4 mm) needles and yarn **MC** (main color), beg at the toe end cast on 2 sts, leaving a long tail end.

Next row (inc row) (RS) K into front and back of st to inc one st—called **Kfb**—twice. (4 sts)

Next row (inc row) (WS) K1, (Kfb) twice, K1. (6 sts)

Next row (RS) K to end.

Next row (inc row) (WS) K1, (Kfb) 4 times, K1. (10 sts)

Next row (RS) K to end.

Next row (inc row) (WS) K1, (Kfb) 8 times, K1. (18 sts)

Beg with a **RS** row work 4 rows in g st, ending with a **WS** row.

Upper shaping

Next row (dec row) (RS) K7, bind off 4, K6. (14 sts) Turn and work on last 7 sts for right upper.

Beg on a **WS** row, work 2 rows in g st, ending with a **RS** row.

1st eyelet

Next row (WS) K5, Yo, K2 tog. (7 sts)

Beg on a **RS** row, work 5 rows in g st, ending with a **RS** row.

Rep last 6 rows for 2nd eyelet, ending with a **RS** row.

3rd eyelet

Next row (WS) K5, Yo, K2 tog. (7 sts)

Next row (RS) K to end.

Heel shaping

Next row (dec row) (WS) K4, place rem 3 sts on a safety pin.

Working on 4 sts, beg on a **RS** row work 8 rows in g st, so ending with a **WS** row. Bind off.

Left upper

Next row (WS) Rejoin yarn to inner edge for left upper.

Beg on a **WS** row, work 2 rows in g st, ending with a **RS** row.

1st eyelet

Next row (WS) K2 tog, Yo, K5. (7 sts)

Beg on a **RS** row, work 5 rows in g st, ending with a **RS** row.

Rep last 6 rows for 2nd eyelet, ending with a **RS** row.

3rd eyelet

Next row (WS) K2 tog, Yo, K5. (7 sts)

Heel shaping

Next row (RS) K4, place rem 3 sts on a safety pin.

Working on 4 sts, beg on a **WS** row work 9 rows in g st, ending with a **WS** row. Bind off.

Join heel seam.

Cuff (knitted)

Using US size 6 (4 mm) needles and yarn **MC** (main color), **RS** facing, g st 3 sts from safety pin, pick up and K 4 sts to heel, 1 st at seam, 4 sts to 2nd set 3 sts on safety pin, g st 3 sts. (15 sts)

Next row (inc row) (WS) Kfb, K to last st, Kfb. (17 sts)

Rep last row 3 times more, ending with a **RS** row. (23 sts)

4th eyelet

Next row (WS) K2 tog, Yo, K19, Yo, K2 tog. (23 sts)

Beg on a **RS** row, work 2 rows in g st, ending with a **WS** row. Bind off.

Sole (knitted)

Using US size 6 (4 mm) needles and yarn **A** (sole color), beg at the toe end cast on 2 sts, leaving a long tail end.

Next row (inc row) (RS) (K into front and back of st to inc one st–called **Kfb**) twice. (4 sts)

Next row (inc row) (WS) K1, (Kfb) twice, K1. (6 sts)

Next row (RS) K to end.

Next row (inc row) (WS) K1, (Kfb) 4 times, K1. (10 sts)

Next row (RS) K to end.

Next row (inc row) (WS) K2, (Kfb) 6 times, K2. (16 sts)

Beg on a **RS** row, work 9 rows in g st, ending with a **RS** row.

Next row (dec row) (WS) K2 tog, K to last 2 sts, K2 tog. (14 sts)

Rep last row twice more. (10 sts)

Next row (RS) K to end.

Next row (dec row) (WS) K2 tog, K to last 2 sts, K2 tog. (8 sts)

Beg on a **RS** row work 3 rows in g st, so ending with a **RS** row.

Rep last 4 rows once more. (6 sts)
Bind off.

Ankle protector (crocheted)

Foundation chain Using US size G-6 (4.00 mm) hook and yarn **B**, make 3CH, leaving a long tail end. Slip St in 1st ch to form a ring.

Round 1 1 CH. 6SC into the ring, working over the long loose end. Ending Slip St into the top of 1ch.

Round 2 2SC into each of 6sc, ending Slip St into the top of 1 st sc of round. (12 sc)

Fasten off, pull the tail to close hole, and weave in tail end at center leaving finishing tail end free to sew onto the sneaker when complete.

Boot lace

Taking one 2 yard (2 m) length, bend in half, and tape two cut ends to a tabletop. Twist cord until it starts to twist in on itself; at this point bend the twisted yarn in half so that the end you are holding meets with the yarn that is taped down. The yarn will twist against itself; even out the twists with your fingers and knot the ends together. Finish off ends.

To make up

Press pieces lightly on wrong side, following instructions on yarn label. At outer ankle position over sew the ankle protector in place. **RS** facing backstitch sole to upper, joining toe end to toe end and easing along the row ends.

Lace up sneaker.

Crochet edge

Using US size G-6 (4.00 mm) hook join yarn **C** to back seam, inserting hook from upper through to the sole. Pinching the seam that joins the upper to the sole between the thumb and index finger of left hand, work 34SC, about ¼ inch (6 mm) apart all around the upper / sole seam. Slip St in 1st sc. Fasten off.

Make another sneaker in the same way.

Funky, chunky footwear for the coolest and hippest streetwise bear.

Fudge

Sweet tiny guy—the baby of the pack—kind and thoughtful and never in trouble. He only ever wants to help and join in, although this sometimes gets him stuck because he is so small and he can't climb as high or be as strong as the other bears. However, he does try.

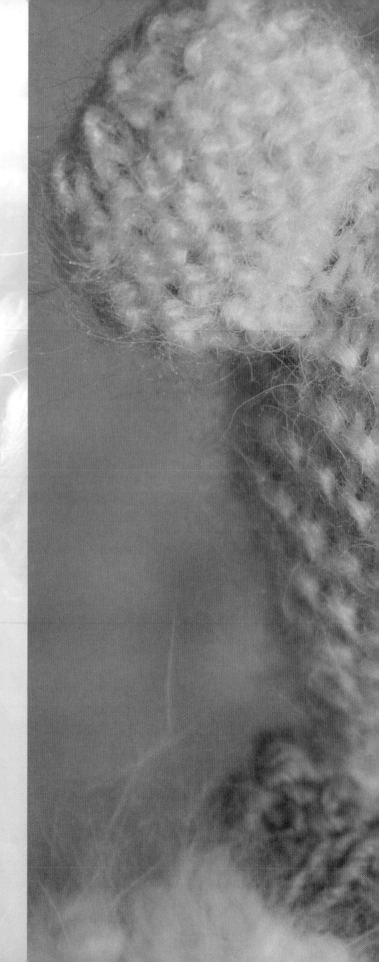

Fudge loves Birthdays—
this one's his second,
I hope he has a new
pair of socks!

Fudge

Finished size
Completed toy measures approximately 13 inches (33 cm) tall by 12½ inches (32 cm) wide, arms outstretched.

Yarn
Bear: 50g light-worsted-weight (DK-weight) angora or mixed-fiber yarn in main color **MC**, remnant nose color **A** (*MC—Bergere de France Doussine shade 233 38 peach, A—Adriafil Angora Carezza shade 87 mink*).

Fabric and extras
Felt: Scraps of felt for eyes (deep blue).
Embroidery thread: Stranded cotton, for sewing on eyes, nose, and mouth.
Beads: 3 x 6 mm (¼ in.) Black Glass Pearls or similar.
Filling: Polyester toy filling.

Needles
Pair of US size 5 (3¾ mm) knitting needles.
Blunt-ended yarn sewing needle.
Embroidery sewing needle.

Gauge
26 sts and 36 rows to 4 inches (10 cm) measured over garter stitch, using US size 5 (3¾ mm) needles and yarn **MC**.

Front (knitted)
Front of Bear's body and head are worked in one piece from lower edge. Using US size 5 (3¾ mm) needles and yarn **MC** (main body color), cast on 8 sts, leaving a long tail end.
Next row (inc row) (RS) *K into front and back of st to inc one st—called **Kfb**—rep from * to end. (16 sts)
Next row (inc row) (WS) Kfb, K to last st, Kfb. (18 sts)
Rep last row two times more, ending with a **WS** row. (22 sts)
Beg with a **RS** row, work 26 rows in g st, ending with a **WS** row.
Shape shoulders
Row 1 (dec row) (RS) K2tog, K to last 2 sts, K2tog. (20 sts)
Rep last row once more.
Shape neck
Next row (dec row) (RS) Bind off 3 sts at beg of row. (15 sts)

Next row (dec row) (WS) Rep last row once more. (12 sts)

Beg with a **RS** row, work straight in g st for 3 rows, ending with a **RS** row. **

Divide for front of face

Row 1 (dec row) (WS) K6, turn, and work on these sts for Right Front. (6 sts)

Work each side of the face separately.

Next row (inc row) (RS) Kfb, K to last st, Kfb. (8 sts)

Next row (WS) K to end. (8 sts)

Rep last 2 rows 5 times more, ending with a **WS** row. (18 sts)

Shape the nose

Next row (inc row) (RS) Kfb, K end. (19 sts)

Next row (inc row) (WS) K to last st, Kfb. (20 sts)

Adding different color for nose

Next row (inc row) (RS) Change to yarn **A**, Kfb, change to yarn **MC**, K end. (21 sts)

Next row (inc row) (WS) K to last st, change to yarn **A**, Kfb. (22 sts)

Beg with a **RS** row, work straight in g st for 6 rows, at the same time changing to color **A** for 4 sts at the beg of every **RS** row and at the end of every **WS** row, ending with a **WS** row.

Shape for the top of the nose

Next row (dec row) (RS) In color **A** bind off 3 sts, break yarn. In **MC** bind off 3 sts, K to the end of row. (16 sts)

Next row (WS) K to end.

Next row (dec row) (RS) K2tog, K to end. (15 sts)

Rep last 2 rows once more, ending with a **RS** row. (14 sts)

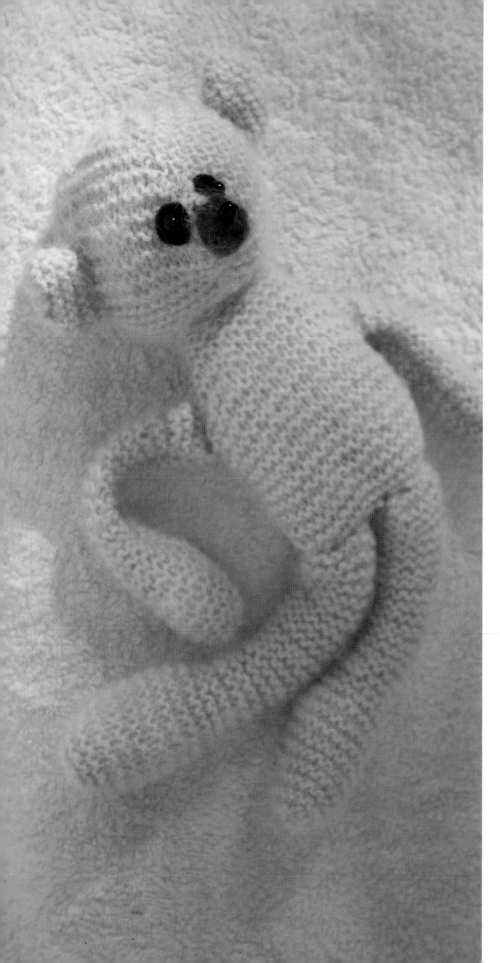

Next row (WS) K to end.
Next row (dec row) (RS) K2tog, K to last 2 sts, K2tog. (12 sts)
Next row (dec row) (WS) *K2tog, rep from * to end. (6 sts)
Bind off.

Left Front (knitted)

WS facing rejoin yarn to the inside edge of the right front and K row. (6 sts)
Next row (inc row) (RS) Kfb, K to last st, Kfb. (8 sts)
Next row (WS) K to end.
Rep last 2 rows 5 times more, ending with a **WS** row. (18 sts)
Shape the nose
Next row (inc row) (RS) K to last st, Kfb. (19 sts)
Next row (inc row) (WS) Kfb, K to end. (20 sts)
Adding different color for nose
Next row (inc row) (RS) K to last st, change to yarn **A**, Kfb. (21 sts)
Next row (inc row) (WS) Kfb, change to yarn **MC**, K to end. (22 sts)
Beg with a **RS** row, work straight in g st for 5 rows, at the same time changing to color **A** for 4 sts at the end of every **RS** row and at the beg of every **WS** row, ending with a **RS** row.
Shape for the top of the nose
Next row (dec row) (RS) In color **A** bind off 3 sts, break yarn. In **MC** bind off 3 sts, K to the end of row. (16 sts)
Next row (RS) K to end.
Next row (dec row) (WS) K2tog, K to end. (15 sts)
Rep last 2 rows once more, ending with a **WS** row. (14 sts)

Next row (RS) K to end.

Next row (dec row) (WS) K2tog, K to last 2 sts, K2tog. (12 sts)

Next row (dec row) (RS) *K2tog, rep from * to end. (6 sts)

Bind off.

Back (knitted)

Back of Bear's body and head are worked in one piece from lower edge. Using US size 5 (3¾mm) needles and yarn **MC** (main body color), cast on 8 sts and work as for Front up to **. (12 sts)

Next row (WS) K to end.

Shape head

Next row (inc row) (RS) Kfb, K to last st, Kfb. (14 sts)

Next row (WS) K to end.

Rep last 2 rows 5 times more, ending with a **WS** row. (24 sts)

Beg with a **RS** row, work straight in g st for 16 rows, ending with a **WS** row.

Next row (dec row) (RS) K2tog, K to last 2 sts, K2tog. (22 sts)

Next row (dec row) (WS) *K2tog, rep from * to end. (11 sts)

Bind off.

Arm (knitted)

Starting at the paw end, using US size 5 (3¾mm) needles and yarn **MC** (main body color), cast on 7 sts, leaving a long tail end.

Next row (inc row) (RS) *Kfb, rep from * to end. (14 sts)

Beg with a **WS** row, work straight in g st for 23 rows, ending with a **WS** row.

Shape elbow

Next row (inc row) (RS) Kfb, K to last st, Kfb. (16 sts)

Rep the last row two times more, ending with a **RS** row. (20 sts)

Next row K to end.

Next row (dec row) (RS) (K2tog) 3 times, K8, (K2tog) 3 times. (14 sts)

Beg with a **WS** row, work 19 rows in g st, ending with a **WS** row.

Bind off.

Make another arm in the same way.

Leg (knitted)

Starting at the paw end, using US size 5 (3¾mm) needles and yarn **MC** (main body color), cast on 8 sts, leaving a long tail end.

Next row (inc row) (RS) *Kfb, rep from * to end. (16 sts)

Next row (inc row) (WS) Kfb, K to last st, Kfb. (18 sts)

Rep last row four times more, ending with a **WS** row. (26 sts)

Beg with a **RS** row, work 14 rows in g st, ending with a **WS** row.

Next row (dec row) (RS) (K2tog) 5 times, K6, (K2tog) 5 times. (16 sts)

Beg with a **WS** row, work 37 rows in g st, so ending with a **WS** row.

Bind off.

Make another leg in the same way.

Ear (knitted)

Using US size 5 (3¾mm) needles and yarn **MC** (main body color), cast on 10 sts, leaving a long tail end.

Next row (WS) K to end.

Next row (inc row) (RS) *Kfb, rep from * to end. (20 sts)

Beg with a **WS** row, work 7 rows in g st, ending with a **WS** row.

Next row (dec row) (RS) K2tog, K6, (K2tog) twice, K6, K2tog. (16 sts)

Bind off.

Make another ear similar.

To make up

Press pieces lightly on wrong side, following instructions on yarn label.

Head and body

Using blunt-ended yarn needle, matching yarn, and mattress stitch for seams throughout, sew center front head seam that runs under the chin to the top of the head. Then sew the front to the back around the entire outer edge leaving the cast-on edges open. Cut out felt pieces for outer eyes using templates (see page 109). Using two strands of stranded cotton and an embroidery sewing needle, sew a bead to center of each eye and sew to head. (To make eye more secure, if you want, work short straight stitches around edge.)

Sew nose working a small upside-down triangle in satin stitch over two knitted stitches at the seam at the front of the nose, then work a line over one knitted stitch down from the point of the triangle, then work a small mouth, ¼ inch (6 mm) wide, across the bottom of the line, sew bead to tip of nose.

Sew remaining seam, leaving an opening for inserting filling. Insert filling, manipulating it to shape nose as shown. Sew up the gap to close.

Arms

Sew seam at back of each arm and around paw leaving the shoulder at the bind-off edges open. Then fill arm and paw lightly with toy filling. Sew remaining seam.

To position arms in place at the side seams of the body, overcast stitch each arm to the body at the bind-off edge, placing each arm four rows down from the neck, shaping with seam at underarm position.

Legs

Sew the bind-off edges and the seam at back of each leg and along paw, leaving the cast-on edge at the base of the paw open for stuffing. Then fill the paw with stuffing, leaving the leg free to dangle. At the bottom of the paw sew remaining seam.

To position legs on body, using matching yarn, overcast stitch each leg in place at the base of body, with leg seams facing toward back and leaving three clear knitted stitches between the legs at the center front.

Ears

RS facing, fold each ear in half and overcast stitch row ends together, then overcast stitch across cast on stitches.

Turn right sides out. With the overcast row ends at one side of ear, overcast stitch across bind-off stitches. Sew these edges to the sides of the head at the position shown in photograph.

Boaty all-in-one

Finished size

Completed item measures 4 inches (10 cm) long by 8¼ inches (21 cm) (arms outstretched).

Yarn

All-in-one: 50g of light-worsted-weight (DK-weight) angora or mixed-fiber yarn in main color **MC**, waist / cuff color **A**, small amount finger-weight (4 ply-weight) wool, or mixed-fiber yarn in collar color **B**, small amount light-worsted-weight (DK-weight) angora, or mixed-fiber yarn in pant color **C**, 2nd pant color **D** (*MC–Adriafil Angora Carezza angora / Wool / nylon mix shade 11 Cream, A–Bergere De France shade 237 631 Sharherazade, B–Uni Opal shade green, C–Adriafil Angora Carezza angora / wool / nylon mix shade 22 Blue, D–Adriafil Angora Carezza angora / wool / nylon mix shade 22 Pale yellow*).

Motif: Tiny amount finger-weight (4 ply) in boat hull yarn **E**, tiny amount finger-weight (4 ply) in boat sail yarn **F** (*E—RYC Luxury Cotton DK shade 252 Tang, F—Jaeger Baby Merino shade 95 Icing*).

Needles and hook

Pair of US size 2 (2¾ mm), US size 3 (3¼ mm) and US size 5 (3¾ mm) knitting needles.
Hook size US size E-4 (3.50 mm).
Blunt-ended yarn sewing needle.
Embroidery sewing needle.

Gauge

22 sts and 34 rows to 4 inches (10 cm) measured over stockinette stitch, using US size 5 (3¾ mm) needles and yarn **MC**.

Front (crocheted and knitted)

Foundation chain Beg at the waist edge, using US size E-4 (3.50 mm) hook and yarn **A** (waist edge / cuff color), make 20CH.
Row 1 (RS) 1SC in 2nd ch from hook, 1SC in each ch to end. Turn.
Row 2 1CH, skip first sc, 1SC in each sc, ending 1SC in 1ch. Turn.
Rep row 2 once more, so ending on a **RS** row. Fasten off.
With right side of crochet facing and using US size 5 (3¾ mm) needles, pick up and knit 20 sts along each sc of last row.
Beg with a **WS** row, work 7 rows in st st, ending with a **WS** row.
Add motif
Next row K8, change to yarn E (boat hull color), K4, change to **MC**, K8.
Next row P7, change to yarn E, P6, change to **MC**, P7.
Beg with a **RS** row, work 10 rows in st st, ending with a **WS** row.*
Shape neck
Next row (dec row) (RS) K8, bind off 4, K7. (16 sts)
Next row (dec row) (WS) P5, P2 tog, P1, turn, and work on these sts for Right Front Neck. (7 sts)
Next row (dec row) (RS) K1, Sl1, K1, Psso, K to end. (6 sts)
Next row (dec row) (WS) P to last 3 sts, P2 tog, P1. (5 sts)
Next row (dec row) (RS) K1, Sl1, K1,

Fudge 39

40 Fudge

Psso, K to end. (4 sts)

Beg with a **WS** row, work 3 rows in st st, ending with a **WS** row. Bind off.

Left front

WS facing, rejoin yarn to neck edge.

Next row (dec row) (WS) P1, P2 tog, P to end. (7 sts)

Next row (dec row) (RS) K to last 3 sts, Sl1, K1, Psso, K1. (6 sts)

Rep last 2 rows once more, ending with a **RS** row. (4 sts)

Beg with a **WS** row, work 3 rows in st st, ending with a **WS** row. Bind off.

Back (crocheted)

Using US size E-5 (3.00 mm) hook and yarn **A** (waist edge / cuff color), make 20CH and work as for Front, without adding in yarn E (boat hull color), up to *.

Beg with a **RS** row, work 6 rows in st st, ending with a **WS** row.

Next row (dec row) (RS) K5, bind off 10 sts, K4. (10 sts)

Left back

Next row (dec row) (WS) P2, P2 tog, P1. (4 sts) Bind off.

WS facing, rejoin yarn to neck edge.

Next row (dec row) (WS) P1, P2 tog, P2. (4 sts) Bind off.

Pants (crocheted)

Left pants leg

RS facing, beg at Center Front of waist edge, using US size E-4 (3.50 mm) hook join on yarn C (pants color) with sl st, 1CH, 1SC in each next 20ch along waist edge–along Left Front to Center Back. Turn.

Row 1 1CH, 1SC in each next 20sc. Turn. Fasten off.

Row 2 Join yarn D (2nd pants color), 1CH, 1DC in each 20 dc. Turn. Repeat row 1. Fasten off.

Right pants leg

RS facing, beg at Center Back of waist edge, using US size E-4 (3.50 mm) hook join on yarn C (pants color) with sl st, 1CH, 1SC in each next 20ch along waist edge–along Right Back to Center Front, Turn.

Row 1 1CH, 1SC in each next 20sc. Turn. Fasten off.

Row 2 Join on yarn D (2nd pants color), 1CH, 1SC in each 20 sc. Turn. Rep row 1. Fasten off.

Sleeve (knitted)

Beginning with the trim and using US size 3 (3¼ mm) needles and yarn **A** (waist/cuff color), cast on 7 sts, leaving a long tail end.

Beg with a **RS** row, work 32 rows in g st, ending with a **WS** row. Bind off. With right side of knitting facing and using hook size US size E-4 (3.50 mm) join yarn **MC** (main color) to top row end.

Row 1 Work 1SC into 1st cast-on st, 1 SC in every alt row end, and 1 SC in last cast-on st. Turn. (17 dc)

Row 2 1CH, skip 1st sc, 1SC in each sc, ending 1SC in 1ch, turn.

Rep last row 6 times more. Fasten off. Make another sleeve in the same way.

Boat sail (knitted)

Using US size 2 (2¾ mm) knitting needles and yarn D (boat sail color), cast on 7sts.

Next row (dec row) (RS) K2 tog, K to end. (6 sts)

Next row (WS) P to last 2 sts, P2 tog. (5 sts)

Rep last 2 rows twice more. (1 sts) Finish off.

Collar

RS facing, using US size 3 (3¼ mm) needles and yarn B (collar color), pick up and K22 sts evenly around neck.

Row 1 (WS) P1, * K2, P1, rep from * to end.

Row 2 (RS) K1, * P2, K1, rep from * to end.

Rep last 2 rows once more. Bind off knitwise.

To make up

Press pieces lightly on wrong side, following instructions on yarn label. Using blunt-ended yarn needle, matching yarn, and back stitch for crochet or mattress stitch for knitted seams, join inside leg, shoulder seams. Set in sleeves, placing center of head of sleeve to shoulder seam. Sew underarm seams and side seams. Work a French knot at one end of the hull. Sew the cast-on end of the sail to the center of the hull, referring to the photograph for position. In black thread, work a row of back st along the sewn-on end of the sail for mast.

Finished size

Completed item measures approximately 3½ inches (9 cm) long by 5¼ inches (13 cm) wide.

Yarn

Sock: Small amount finger-weight (4- ply weight) wool, cotton, or mixed-fiber yarn in first stripe color **MC**, second stripe color **A** (*MC–Jaeger Baby Merino shade 096 Marigold, A–Rowan 4-Ply Soft shade 389 Expresso*).

Needles and hook

Pair of US size 0 (2 mm) knitting needles
Blunt-ended yarn sewing needle.

Gauge

28 sts and 50 rows to 4 inches (10 cm) measured over stockinette stitch using US size 0 (2 mm) needles and yarn **MC**.

Sock (knitted)

Using US size 0 (2 mm) needles and yarn **MC** (1st stripe color), cast on 36 sts, leaving a long tail end.
Beg with a K row, work 4 rows in st st, change to yarn **A**, work 4 rows in st st. This forms the stripe patt.
Cont in stripe patt without shaping for 12 more rows, ending with a **WS** row and in yarn **MC**.

Shape top of foot

Break yarn, slip 9 sts onto a safety pin.
Using US size 0 (2 mm) needles, rejoin yarn **A** (2nd stripe color) K18, slip the last 9 sts onto a safety pin.
Beg with a **WS** row and keeping the

patt correct, work 19 rows in st st, ending with a **RS** row.
Then, in yarn **MC** only, shape toe as follows:
Next row (dec row) (RS) K2, K2 tog, K to last 4 sts, K2 tog, K2. (16 sts)
Next row (dec row) (WS) P2, P2 tog, P to last 4 sts, P2 tog, P4. (14 sts)
Next row (dec row) (RS) K2, (K2 tog) twice, K2, (K2 tog) twice, K2. (10 sts)
Next row (dec row) (WS) P2, (P3 tog) twice, P2. (6 sts). Bind off.

Back of sock

With US size 0 (2 mm) knitting needle in left hand, **WS** facing and row ends at the back of the sock meeting, slip 2 sets of 9 sts (2nd set first), off the safety pins onto the knitting needle, rejoin yarn **MC** and K row.
Beg with a P row, work 9 rows in st st, ending with a **WS** row.

Shape heel

Next row (dec row 1) (RS) K9, K2 tog, turn, and work on these sts.
Next row (dec row 2) (WS) Sl1, P1, P2 tog, P1, turn.
Next row (dec row 3) (RS) Sl1, K2, K2 tog, K1, turn.
Next row (dec row 4) (WS) Sl1, P3, P2 tog, P1, turn.
Next row (dec row 5) (RS) Sl1, K4, K2 tog, K1, turn.
Next row (dec row 6) (WS) Sl1, P5, P2 tog, P1, turn.
Next row (dec row 7) (RS) Sl1, K6, K2 tog, K2.
Next row (WS) P to end. (11 sts)
Change to yarn **MC** (1st stripe color), beg with a K row, st st 4 rows, change to yarn **A** (2nd stripe color) st st 4 rows. In yarn **MC** cont in st st for 5 rows.

Striped sock

Toe shaping
Next row (dec row) (WS) P4, P3 tog, P to end. (9 sts)
Next row (dec row) (RS) K2 tog, K to last 2 sts, K2 tog. (7 sts).
Bind off.

To make up

Weave in all ends.
Press piece lightly on wrong side, following instructions on yarn label.
Using blunt-ended yarn needle, matching yarn, and mattress stitch, sew back seam and along each side of the foot to join top to sole.
Make another sock, if you want!

Only one sock—the other is lost; socks always get lost!

Bilbry

Bilbry likes to be in charge, but he's not too bossy. (Well, not all of the time!) A really good listener he's very helpful and kind—he just doesn't take kindly to being told what to do...

Bilbry

Finished size

Completed toy measures approximately 20 inches (51 cm) tall by 17 inches (43 cm) wide, arms outstretched.

Yarn

Bear: 50g light-worsted-weight (DK-weight) wool, cotton or mixed-fiber yarn in main color **MC,** ear color **A** and hair color **B** (*MC—Brown Sheep Company Lambs Pride Worsted wool / mohair mix shade M-57 Brite Blue, A—shade M-10 Créme, B—RYC Cashsoft 4 ply shade 427 Dive*).

Fabric and extras

Felt: Scraps of felt–light olive green for outer eyes.
Embroidery thread: Stranded cotton, for sewing on eyes, nose, and mouth.
Beads: 2 x 6 mm (¼ in.) Black Glass Pearls or similar.
Filling: Polyester toy filling.

Needles

Pair of US size 5 (3¾ mm) knitting needles.
Blunt-ended yarn sewing needle.
Embroidery sewing needle.

Bilbry saves the day! Careful not to bump the ducks—careful not to damage Fudge's toy boat.

Gauge

20 sts and 30 rows to 4 inches (10 cm) measured over stockinette stitch, using US size 5 (3¾ mm) needles and yarn **MC**.

Front, Back, Arms, and Legs

Work as Basic Bear (page106).

Ear

Using US size 5 (3¾ mm) needles and yarn A (ear color), cont to work ear in rev st st as Marigold (page 82).

To make up

Head, Ears, Body, Arms, and Legs

Make up as Marigold (page 82). Cut eleven 3-inch (8-cm) lengths of yarn **B** and knot into top of head, between ears.

Red dungarees

Finished size

Completed item measures approximately 6¼ inches (16 cm) wide by 6¾ inches (17 cm) long (straps not included).

Yarn

Dungarees: 50g of light-worsted-weight (DK-weight) angora or mixed-fiber yarn in main color **MC,** tiny amount light-worsted (DK) yarn in pocket lining color **A** *(MC—Adriafil Angora Carezza angora / wool / nylon mix shade 17 Red, A—Adriafil Angora Carezza angora / wool / nylon mix shade 22 Blue).*

48 Bilbry

Fabric and extras

Buttons: 2 x ½ inch (12 mm) wooden buttons or similar.

Needles and hook

Pair of US size 5 (3¾ mm) knitting needles.
US size G-6 (4.00 mm) crochet hook.
Blunt-ended yarn sewing needle.

Gauge

23 sts and 29 rows to 4 inches (10 cm) measured over stockinette stitch, using US size 5 (3¾ mm) needles and yarn **MC**.

Trousers (knitted)

Pocket lining

Using US size 5 (3¾ mm) needles and yarn A (pocket lining color) cast on 8 sts, leaving a long tail end.
Beg with a K row, work st st for 10 rows, leave the sts on a safety pin and break yarn.

Right Leg

Beginning at the leg edge and using US size 5 (3¾ mm) needles and yarn **MC** (main color) cast on 42 sts, leaving a long tail end.
Beg with a K row work st st for 23 rows, ending with a **RS** row.

Insert pocket

Next row (WS) P26 sts, bind off 8 sts, P to end.
Next row (dec row) (RS) K2 tog, K6, with **WS** of pocket lining facing, slip the 8 pocket lining sts off the safety pin and onto the left needle, K the 8 sts of the pocket lining, K to last 2 sts, K2 tog. (40 sts)
Next row (dec row) (WS) P2 tog, P to last 2 sts, P2 tog. (38 sts)**.
Next row (dec row) (RS) K2 tog, K to end. (37 sts)
Next row (WS) P to end.
Rep last 2 rows once more. (36 sts)
Beg with a K row work in st st for 14 rows, ending with a **WS** row.
Bind off 10 sts, place marker for bib position, bind off rem sts.

Left leg

Beginning at the leg edge and using US size 5 (3¾ mm) needles and yarn **MC** (main color), cast on 42 sts, leaving a long tail end.
Beg with a K row, work st st for 24 rows, ending with a **WS** row.
Next row (dec row) (RS) K2 tog, K to last 2 sts, K2 tog. (40 sts)
Next row (dec row) (WS) P2 tog, P to last 2 sts, P2 tog. (38 sts)
Next row (dec row) (RS) K to last 2 sts, K2 tog. (37 sts)
Next row (WS) P to end.
Rep last 2 rows once more. (36 sts)
Beg with a K row, work in st st for 14 rows, ending with a **WS** row.
Bind off 26 sts, place marker here for bib positioning, bind off rem sts.

To make up

Using blunt-ended yarn needle, matching yarn, and backstitch for seams throughout, with **RS** facing sew legs seams. Turn one leg out the right way and slip inside the other leg so that **RS** are facing. Matching row ends sew front and back crotch seams. Using yarn A, sew down sides and base of pocket lining on **WS**.

Bib (crocheted)

With **WS** of center front of knitting facing and using US size G-6 hook (4.00 mm) and yarn **MC** (main color), join yarn at the right positional marker at the bind-off edge.
Row 1 (WS row) 1CH, 1SC in each of next 19 bind-off sts to next marker, turn.
Row 2 1CH, skip 1st sc, 1SC in each sc, to last sc, skip last sc, 1SC in 1ch. (19 sc)
Rep last row 6 times more (13 sc)
Fasten off.

Straps

Using US size 5 (3¾ mm) needles and yarn **MC** (main color), cast on 6 sts, leaving a long tail end.
Beg with a K row, work in st st for 8 rows, ending with a **WS** row.

Divide straps

Next row (RS) K3, turn, and work on these sts for right strap.
Beg with a P row, work in st st until strap measures 6 inches (15 cm)
Bind off.
Rejoin yarn to inner edge at rem 3 sts, K to end.
Beg with a P row, work in st st until strap measures 6 inches (15 cm)
Bind off.

To attach the straps

Over sew the cast-on end of the straps to the back of the dungarees, setting them evenly either side of the back seam. At the front, pin the bind-off edges of each strap end to each top corner of the bib; sew a button to the front to hold each strap in place.

Simple Notch Neck Sweater

Finished size
Completed item measures approximately 4 inches (10 cm) long by 11½ inches (29 cm) wide (arms outstretched)

Yarn
Sweater: 50g of light-worsted-weight (DK-weight) angora or mixed-fiber yarn in main color **MC** (*Louisa Harding Kashmir DK shade 02—baby blue*).

Fabric and extras
Button: 1 x ½ inch (1.5 cm).

Needles
Pair of US size 3 (3¼ mm) knitting needles.
Blunt-ended yarn sewing needle.

Gauge
24 sts and 35 rows to 4 inches (10 cm) measured over stockinette stitch, using US size 3 (3¼ mm) needles and yarn **MC**.

Sweater (knitted)
Back, Front, and Sleeves
This sweater is worked in one piece. Beg at the back waist edge and using US size 3 (3¼ mm) needles and yarn **MC** (main sweater color), cast on 26 sts, leaving a long tail end.
Beg with a **RS** row, work 4 rows in g st ending with a **WS** row.
Work 24 rows in st st, ending with a **WS** row.

Shape sleeves
Next row (inc row) (RS) Cast on 26 sts, K to end. (52 sts)
Next row (inc row) (WS) Cast on 26 sts, K4, P to last 4 sts, K4. (78 sts)
Next row (RS) K to end.
Next row (WS) K4, P to last 4 sts, K4.
Rep last 2 rows 7 times more, ending with a **WS** row.
Shape neck
Next row (dec row) (RS) K32, bind off 14, K to end, and work on these set of 32 sts for Left Sleeve, and Front.
Next row (dec row) (WS) K4, P to last 2 sts, P2 tog. (31 sts)
Next row (RS) Sl1, K to end.
Rep last 2 rows twice more. (29 sts)
Next row (WS) K4, P to end.
Beg with a K row and always keeping 4 knit sts at sleeve edge, work 6 rows in st st, so ending with a **WS** row.
Front notch opening
Next row (inc row) (RS) Cast on 8 sts, K to end. (37 sts)
Next row (WS) K4, P to end.
Beg with a K row, work 5 rows in st st, ending with a **RS** row.
Complete left sleeve
Next row (dec row) (WS) Bind off 26 sts, P to end. (11 sts)
Break yarn and leave rem Left Front 11 sts on a safety pin.
Right sleeve and front
With **WS** facing, rejoin yarn to 32 sts at the neck edge of Right Back, P to last 4 sts, K4 at sleeve edge, keeping 4 knit sts at the sleeve edge constant throughout.
Next row (dec row) (RS) K to last 2 sts, K2 tog tbl. (31 sts)
Next row (WS) P to last 4 sts, K4.

Rep last 2 rows twice more. (29 sts)
Beg with a K row, work 7 rows in st st, ending with a **RS** row.
Front opening
Next row (inc row) (WS) Cast on 8 sts, P to last 4 sts, K4. (37 sts)
Beg with a K row, work 7 rows in st st, ending with a **WS** row.
Complete right sleeve
Next row (dec row) (RS) Bind off 26 sts, K10, **RS** facing, slip 11 sts off the safety pin onto the left needle, Sl 1st st, K1, psso and knit st again, K across rem 10 sts. (22 sts)
Next row (inc row) (WS) P10, (Pfb) twice, P to end. (24 sts)
Next row (inc row) (RS) K11, (Kfb) twice, K to end. (26 sts)
Beg with a P row, work 19 rows in st st, ending with a **WS** row.
Beg with a RS row work 4 rows in g st so ending with a **WS** row.
Bind off.

To make up
Using blunt-ended yarn needle, matching yarn, and mattress stitch for seams throughout, matching row ends, sew sleeve seams and side seams. Catch front neck corners together and sew on button.

Bilbry 51

52 Bilbry

Ted Slip-on slippers

Finished size

Completed item measures approximately 2 inches (5 cm) wide by 3¼ inches (8cm) long.

Yarn

Slip-ons: 50g of light-worsted-weight (DK-weight) angora or mixed-fiber yarn in main color **MC**, tiny amount light-worsted (DK) yarn in bear muzzle color **A**, nose color **B**, trim color **C** (*MC—Adriafil Angora Carezza angora / wool / nylon mix shade 17 Red, A—Brown Sheep Company Lambs Pride Worsted wool / mohair mix shade M-10 Crème, B—scrap black light-worsted (DK) yarn, C—scrap gold / yellow light worsted (DK) yarn).*

Needles and hook

US size H-8 (5.00 mm) crochet hook. Blunt-ended yarn sewing needle.

Gauge

16 stitches and 20 rows to 4 inches (10 cm) measured over single crochet and yarn **MC**.

Slippers (crocheted)

Each slipper is worked in one piece, the sole is worked in rounds; the sides and heel are worked in rows.

Foundation chain: Beg at the toe end of the slipper, leave a long loose end and make 4CH. Join into a ring with a Sl st into the first ch.

Round 1: 1CH, 5SC into ring working over long loose end. Join with Sl st into 1st sc of round.

Round 2: 1CH, 2SC into 1st sc of last round (where the Sl st was worked). Work 2SC into each of rem 4sc. Sl st into 1st sc of round. (10 sc)

Round 3: 1 CH, 1SC into same place as Sl st of previous round. 1SC into each of rem sc. Join with Sl st into 1st sc of round. (10 sc)

Round 4: 1 CH, 1SC into the same place as Sl st of previous round. 2SC into next sc. *1SC into next sc, 2SC into the next sc, rep from * to end. Join with Sl st into 1st sc of round. (15 sc)

Round 5: As round 3.

Round 6: 1 CH. SC into same place as Sl st of previous round. 1SC into each of next 2sc. *2SC into next sc, 1SC into each of next 2sc, rep from * to end. Join with Sl st into 1st sc of round. (20 sc)

Round 7: As round 3.

Round 8: Make 1 CH, SC into same place as the Sl st of previous round. 1SC into each of next 4sc. *2SC into the next sc, 1SC into each of the next 4sc, rep from * to end. 1SC into last sc. Join with Sl st into the 1st sc of the round. (24 sc)

Round 9: Cont to work as round 3–without shaping, counting 24sc in every round–you may want to add a marker at the beginning of each round to aid with the counting–until the slipper measures 2 inches (5 cm).

Side shaping: Make 1 CH, 1SC into next 15sc, turn, 1 CH, work 1SC into next 15sc.

Now work back and forth in rows across these last 15sc.

Row 2: 1CH, 1SC into each sc to end, 1 sc into the end chain of the row. Turn. (16 sc)

Rep last row 3 times more. (19 sc)

Continue to work without shaping until slipper measures 3¼ inches (8 cm) long. Fasten off.

Ears

Foundation chain: Using yarn **MC**, make 2CH.

Round 1: 4SC into 2nd ch from hook. Join with Sl st in top of first sc of round.

Round 2: 1CH, 2SC into each sc. (8 sc) Fasten off.

Make another ear in the same way.

Muzzle

Foundation chain: Using yarn A, make 2CH.

Round 1: 4SC into 2nd ch from hook. Join with Sl st in top of first sc of round.

Round 2: 1CH, 2SC into the Sl st, 2SC each of the remaining 3sc. Join with Sl st into first sc of round. (8 sc)

Round 3: 1CH, work 1SC into Sl st, 1SC into each sc to the end. Join with Sl st into first sc of round. (8 sc)

Favorite bear shoes for cozy, bear toes and plenty of fun, fun, fun...

Round 4: 1CH, 2SC into Sl st, 1SC into next sc, *2SC into next sc, 1SC into next sc, rep from * to end. Join with Sl st into to first sc of round. (12 sc)

Round 5: 1 CH, work 1SC into Sl st, 1SC into each sc to end. (12 sc)

Round 6: 1 CH, 2SC into Sl st, 1SC into each of next sc, *2SC into next sc, 1SC into each of next 2sc, rep from * to end. Join with Sl st into first sc of round. (16 sc)

Round 7: 1 CH, 1SC into Sl st, 1SC into each dc to end. (16 dc)
Fasten off.

To make up
Sew up the back seam with wrong sides facing.

Sew muzzle to front of slippers. In the edging yarn C, starting at the back with the **RS** facing, work 1SC into each row end and 1SC in each st across front. Fasten off. Leave 1¼ inch (3 cm) ends at back as a trim. Sew ears to either side of muzzle.

Add facial features
Thread up yarn needle using yarn B, (nose color). Make four straight stitches close together across the top of the muzzle. Work a straight stitch mouth just beneath the nose. Work a French knot for each eye–either side of the muzzle.
Make another slip-on in the same way.

Bilbry loves to play with his friends and being wheeled along is so much fun!

Siss

Savvy Siss is fashionable, cool, and independent. A little vain, but a great friend to all her pals. She won't do the chores (although she must sometimes take her turn), but she will entertain. She loves telling jokes and singing songs—she has a fabulous voice—and she loves to shop!

Shop, shop, shop, a quick stop for a muffin and a hot chocolate, then shop some more...

Siss

Finished size
Completed toy measures approximately 20 inches (50 cm) tall by 18 inches (46 cm) wide, arms outstretched.

Yarn
Bear: 50g light-worsted-weight (DK-weight) angora, or mixed-fiber yarn in main color **MC** and ear color **A** (*MC—Brown Sheep Company Lambs Pride Worsted wool mohair mix shade M-10 Crème, **A**—shade M-57 Brite Blue*), plus small remnants for the flower slide (see individual project for details).

Fabric and extras
Felt: Scraps of felt—light olive green for outer eyes.
Embroidery thread: Stranded cotton, for sewing on eyes, nose, and mouth.
Beads: 2 x 6 mm (¼ in.) Black Glass Pearls or similar.
Filling: Polyester toy filling.

Needles and hook
Pair of US size 5 (3¾ mm) knitting needles.
US H-8 (5.00 mm) crochet hook.
Blunt-ended yarn sewing needle.
Embroidery sewing needle.

Gauge
20 sts and 30 rows to 4 inches (10 cm) measured over stocking stitch using US size 5 (3¾ mm) needles and yarn **MC**.

Front, Back, Arms, and Legs (knitted)
Using US size 5 (3¾ mm) needles and yarn **MC** (main body color), work as Basic Bear (page 106).

Ear (knitted)
Using US size 5 (3¾ mm) needles and yarn **A** (ear color)**,** cont to work as Basic Bear (page 106).

To make up
Head, Ears, Body, Arms, and Legs
Make up as Basic Bear (page 106) but note that K side of knitting is **RS** for ears but **WS** for all other pieces. Omit inner eyes.

Flower barrette (crochet)
Flower center
Foundation chain: Using flower center yarn (I used double strands, RYC Cashcotton 4-ply shade 905 Imp / tangerine), make 2CH.
Round 1: 4SC into 2nd ch from hook. Join with Sl st to top of first sc of round.
Round 2: 1CH, 2SC into Sl st, 2SC each of the rem 3sc. Join with Sl st into the first sc of round. (8 sc)
Round 3: 1CH, 1SC into Sl st, 1SC into each sc to the end. Join with Sl st into first sc of round. (8 sc)
Round 4: 1CH, 2SC into Sl st, 1SC into next sc, *2SC into next sc, 1SC into next sc, rep from * to end. Join with Sl st into to first sc of round. (12 sc)
Round 5: 1 CH, 1SC into Sl st, 1SC into each sc to end. Join with Sl st into first sc of round. (12 sc)
Round 6: 1 CH, 2SC into Sl st, 1SC into

next sc, *2SC into next sc, 1SC into next sc, rep from * to end. Join with Sl st into first sc of round. (18 sc)

Round 7: 1 CH, 1SC into Sl st, 1SC into each sc to end. (18 sc)

Fasten off.

Petal

Foundation chain: Using flower petal yarn (I used double strands, RYC Cashcotton 4-ply shade 901 Sugar / pale pink), make 2CH.

Round 1: 4SC into 2nd ch from hook. Join with Sl st to top of first sc.

Round 2: 1CH, 2SC into the Sl st, 2SC each of the rem 3sc. Join with Sl st into to first sc. (10 sc)

Fasten off.

Make 4 more petals. Sew each petal onto the Flower Center, radiating evenly around.

I then felted the flower by putting it into a sock and placing it in the washing machine on a hot setting then tumble drying and reshaping when it emerged. Sew the flower onto the head or attach onto a small hair barrette and slide it onto the head through a few knitted stitches.

Pink camisole and underpants

Finished size

Camisole: Completed item measures approximately 8 inches (20 cm) wide by 4 inches (10 cm) long.

Underpants: Completed item measures approximately 10¾ inches (27 cm) waist.

Yarn

Camisole and Underpants: 50g of light-worsted-weight (DK-weight) angora, or mixed-fiber yarn in main colour **MC** (*Bergere De France shade 237 631 Sherherazade*).

Fabric and extras

Ribbon: Length ⅒ inch (2 mm) narrow satin ribbon.

Needles

Pair of US size 2 (3 mm) knitting needles.

Blunt-ended yarn sewing needle.

Gauge

20 sts and 30 rows to 4 inches (10 cm) measured over stockinette stitch using US size 2 (3 mm) needles and yarn **MC**.

Camisole (knitted)

Front

Using US size 2 (3 mm) needles and yarn **MC** (main color), cast on 52 sts, leaving a long tail end.

Beg with a **RS** row, work g st for 8 rows, so ending with a **WS** row.

Proceed in patt as follows:

Next row (RS) K17, Yfd, K2 tog tbl, K1, K2 tog, Yfd, K8, Yfd, K2 tog tbl, K1, K2 tog, Yfd, K to end. (52 sts)

Next row (WS) P to end.

Next row (RS) K18, Yfd, Sl 1, K2 tog, Psso, Yfd, K10, Yfd, Sl 1, K2 tog, Yfd, K to end. (52 sts)

Next row (WS) P to end.

These four rows form the pattern.

Cont in patt until work measures 2¾ inches (7 cm) from beg, finishing at end of a P row.

Next row (RS) (K3 tog) 3 times, (K2 tog) 17 times, (K3 tog) 3 times. (23 sts)

Beg with a **WS** row, work g st for 4 rows, ending with a **RS** row.

Shape straps

Next row (WS) K6, bind off 11 sts, K to end.

Cont on each group of Strap sts as follows:

Work g st for 10 rows. Bind off.

Work back to match.

Underpants (knitted)

Front

Using US size 2 (3 mm) needles and yarn **MC** (main color), cast on 6 sts, leaving a long tail end.

Beg with a **RS** row, work g st for 2 rows, ending with a **WS** row.

Next row (inc row) (RS) *K into front and back of st to inc one st—called **Kfb**—, K to last st, Kfb. (8 sts)

Rep last row ten times more. (28 sts)

K1 row, ending with a **WS** row.

Proceed in patt as follows:

Next row (RS) K5, Yfd, K2 tog tbl, K1, K2 tog, Yfd, K8, Yfd, K2 tog tbl, K1, K2 tog, Yfd, K to end. (28 sts)

Next row (WS) P to end.

Next row (RS) K6, Yfd, Sl 1, K2 tog, Psso, Yfd, K10, Yfd, Sl 1, K2 tog, Psso, Yfd, K to end. (28 sts)

Next row (WS) P to end.

These four rows form the pattern.

Cont in patt until work measures 3¼ inches (8 cm) from beg.

Work 4 rows K1, P1 rib for waist edge.

Bind off in rib.

Back

Using US size 2 (3 mm) needles and

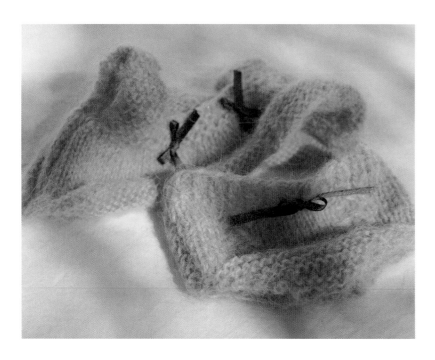

yarn **MC** (main color), cast on 6 sts, leaving a long tail end.

Beg with a **RS** row, work g st for 2 rows, ending with a **WS** row.

Next row (inc row) (RS) *K into front and back of st to inc one st—called **Kfb**—K to last st, Kfb. (8 sts)

Rep last row ten times more. (28 sts) K1 row ending with a **WS** row. Beg with a **RS** row, work g st until work measures 2¼ inches (6 cm) from beg. Work 4 rows K1, P1 rib for waist edge. Bind off in rib.

To make up

Press pieces lightly on wrong side, following instructions on yarn label.

Camisole: Using blunt-ended yarn needle, matching yarn, and backstitch for seams throughout, with **WS** facing, sew shoulder straps and side seams. Turn out the right way. Cut 2 x 5-inch (12 cm) lengths ribbon. Thread through center stitch at top of patt,

panels on front. Tie in a bow.

Knickers: Using blunt-ended yarn needle, matching yarn, and backstitch for seams throughout, with **WS** facing, sew gusset and side seams. Turn out the right way. Cut 1 x 5-inch (12-cm) length ribbon. Thread center through stitch at top of patt, panel on front. Tie in a bow.

Pretty pink slippers

Finished size

Completed item measures approximately 4¾ inches (12 cm) long

Yarn

Slippers: 50g of US light-worsted-weight (DK-weight) angora, or mixed-fiber yarn in main color **MC** *(Bergere De France shade 237 631 Sherherazade).*

Fabric and extras

Beads: 2 x 15 mm (½ in.) colored beads.

Needles and hook

Pair of US size 2 (3 mm) knitting needles.
Hook size US E-4 (3.50).
Blunt-ended yarn sewing needle.

Gauge

20 sts and 30 rows to 4 inches (10 cm) measured over stockinette stitch, using US size 2 (3 mm) needles and yarn **MC**.

Slippers (knitted and crocheted)

Right shoe

The shoe is worked both sides at the same time by beg at the bottom of the sole, then working along rows that will become shoe sides, at the same time increasing outward at the toe end—the cast on row becomes the sole seam.

Using US size 2 (3 mm) needles and yarn **MC** (main color), beg with the sole, cast on 36 sts, leaving a long tail end.

Shape sole sides and toe

Next row (inc row) (RS) Kfb, K15, Kfb, K2, Kfb, K15, Kfb. (40 sts)

Next row (WS) K to end.

Next row (inc row) (RS) Kfb, K16, Kfb, K4, Kfb, K16, Kfb. (44 sts)

Next row (WS) K to end.

Next row (inc row) (RS) Kfb, K17, Kfb, K6, Kfb, K17, Kfb. (48 sts)

Next row (WS) K to end.

Next row (inc row) (RS) Kfb, K18, Kfb, K8, Kfb, K18, Kfb. (52 sts)

Next row (WS) K to end.

Next row (inc row) (RS) Kfb, K19, Kfb, K10, Kfb, K19, Kfb. (56 sts)

Next row (WS) K to end.

Next row (inc row) (RS) Kfb, K20, Kfb, K12, Kfb, K20, Kfb. (60 sts)

Next row (WS) K to end.

Next row (inc row) (RS) K21, Kfb, K16, Kfb, K21. (62 sts)

Next row (WS) P to end.

Next row (inc row) (RS) K21, Kfb, K18, Kfb, K21. (64 sts)

Beg with a **WS** row, work g st for 8 more rows, so ending with a **RS** row.

Next row (WS) K11, place marker, K to end.

Next row (dec row) (RS) K36, Sl 1, K1, Psso. Turn and work on these sts only for top of shoe. (37 sts)

Top of shoe detail

Next row (WS) Sl 1, P8, P2 tog. Turn. (10 sts)

Next row (RS) Sl 1, K8, Sl 1, K1, Psso, Turn.

Rep last 2 rows seven times more.

Next row (WS) Sl 1, P8, P2 tog. Turn.

Next row (RS) Sl 1, K to end.

Next row (WS) K17, K2 tog, P8, Sl 1, K1, Psso, K17. (44 sts)

Next row (RS) Bind off 20 sts, K3, bind off 20 sts. Break yarn.

Front strap

Next row (WS) Rejoin yarn **MC** (main color). P4.

Beg with a **RS** row, work in st st until strap measures 3⅛ inches (8 cm). Bind off.

To make up

Press pieces lightly on wrong side, following instructions on yarn label. Using blunt-ended yarn needle,

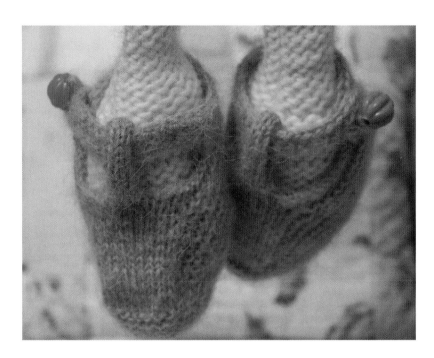

matching yarn, and backstitch for seams throughout. With **WS** facing, join row ends to form shoe back. Join the cast-on edge to form the sole. Turn out the right way. Loop in to **WS** front strap, sew bind-off row in place to edge at inside of upper. ******

Buttonhole strap

With right side of knitting facing and using hook size US size E-4 (3.50 mm) join yarn **MC** (main color) with a Sl st in knitted st at marker at shoe edge.

Row 1 1CH, then 1SC in each of next 22 knitted sts, make 23ch, turn.

Row 2 Skip first ch, 1SC in each of 22ch, 1sc in each of 22sc, turn. (44sc)

Make buttonhole

Row 3 1CH, 1SC in each sc to last 4sc, 3CH, skip 3sc, 1SC in last sc. Turn.

Row 4 1CH, 1SC in sc, 1SC in each of 3ch, 1SC in each of 40sc. Fasten off.

Left shoe

Using US size 2 (3 mm) needles and yarn **MC** (main color), work as for

Right Shoe to ******.

Buttonhole strap

With right side of knitting facing and using US size E-9 (3.50 mm) hook and yarn **MC** (main color) make 22ch, beg at marker at shoe edge. Work 22SC, turn.

Next row 1CH, 1SC in each SC, and CH to end. Turn. (44 sc)

Make buttonhole

Next row 1CH, 1SC in first sc, 3CH, skip 3sc, 1SC in each sc to end. Turn.

Next row 1CH, 1SC in each SC and CH to end.

Fasten off.

Sew on a button to each outer edge of shoe to correspond with buttonhole.

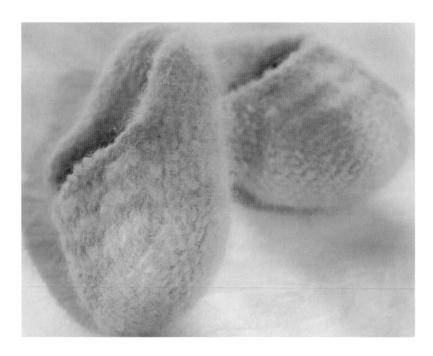

Striped espadrilles

Finished size
Completed item before felting measures approximately 5¼ inches (13½ cm) long, after felting measures approximately 4¾ inches (12 cm) long.

Yarn
Striped espadrilles: 50g US light-worsted-weight (DK-weight) angora or mixed-fiber yarn in main color **MC**, small amount US light-worsted-weight (DK-weight) wool or mixed-fiber yarn in 1st stripe color **A**, 2nd stripe color **B** *(MC—Brown Sheep Company Worsted wool / mohair mix shade M-155 Lemon Drop, A—Anchor Tappisserie shade 9282 acid yellow, B—Anchor Tappisserie shade 8014 light lemon).*

To make up
Weave in all ends.

Press piece lightly on wrong side, following instructions on yarn label. Using blunt-ended yarn needle, matching yarn, and mattress stitch, sew back seam and along each side of the foot to join top to sole.
Make another sock similar.

Needles
Pair of US size 5 (3¾ mm) knitting needles.
Blunt-ended yarn sewing needle.

Gauge
20 sts and 30 rows to 4 inches (10 cm) measured over stockinette stitch using US size 5 (3¾ mm) needles and yarn **MC**.

Striped espadrille (knitted)
The shoe is worked both sides at the same time by beg at the bottom of the sole, then working along rows which will become shoe sides, while increasing outward at the toe. The cast-on row becomes the sole seam. Using US size 5 (3¾ mm) needles and yarn **MC** (main color), beg with the sole, cast on 36 sts, leaving a long tail end.

Next row (WS) K to end.
Next row (inc row) (RS) K1, Yfd, K16, Yfd, (K1, Yfd) twice, K16, Yfd, K1. (41 sts)

Shape sole sides and toe
Next row (WS) K to end.
Next row (inc row) (RS) K2, Yfd, K16, Yfd, K2, Yfd, K3, Yfd, K16, Yfd, K2. (46 sts)
Next row (WS) K to end.
Next row (inc row) (RS) K3, Yfd, K16, Yfd, (K4, Yfd) twice, K16, Yfd, K3. (51 sts)
Next row (WS) P to end.
Next row (inc row) (RS) K4, Yfd, K16, Yfd, K5, Yfd, K6, Yfd, K16, Yfd, K4. (56 sts)
Next row (WS) P to end.
Beg with a **RS** row, work g st for 9 more rows, ending with a **RS** row.
Next row (WS) P to end.
Next row (dec row) (RS) K23, change to yarn **A** (1st stripe color), K9, Sl 1, K1, Psso. Turn and work on these 10 sts only for top of shoe.

Top of shoe detail
Next row (WS) Sl 1, P8, P2 tog, Turn. (10 sts)
Next row (RS) Change to yarn **B** (2nd stripe color), Sl 1, K8, Sl 1, K1, Psso, Turn.
Next row (WS) Sl 1, P8, P2 tog, Turn. (10 sts)
Next row (RS) Change to yarn **A**, Sl 1, K8, Sl 1, K1, Psso, turn.

Next row (WS) Sl 1, P8, P2 tog, turn. (10 sts)

Rep last 4 rows once more, then work first two of the four again, ending with yarn **B** on a **WS** row. With **RS** facing and yarn **MC**, bind off 17 sts of side, 10 sts of top and 17 sts of other side. Bind off.

Make another espadrille similarly.

To make up

Press pieces lightly on wrong side, following instructions on yarn label. Using blunt-ended yarn needle, matching yarn, and backstitch for seams throughout. With **WS** facing, join row ends at back of shoe to form shoe back. Join the cast-on edges to form the sole. Turn out the right way. Fold down the back of the shoe and hold in place with a couple of stitches.

Biba bear suit

Finished size

Completed item measures approximately 5¼ inches (31.5 cm) long (omitting straps).

Yarn

Bear suit: 50g Bulky weight (chunky weight) wool or mixed-fiber yarn in main color **MC**, small amount of Bulky weight (chunky weight) wool or mixed-fiber yarn in halter color **A** (*MC —Bergere de France Magic shade 232.991 Freon, A—Frog Tree Moss Green*) plus, small amounts yarn remnants for floral embellishments (see individual projects for details).

Needles and hook

Pair of US size 7 (4½ mm) knitting needles.

Hook size US size G-6 (4.00 mm).

Hook size US D-3 (3.00) for floral embellishments.

Blunt-ended yarn sewing needle.

Gauge

17 sts and 26 rows to 4 inches (10 cm) measured over stockinette stitch using US size 7 (4½ mm) needles and yarn **MC**.

Left leg (knitted)

Using US size 7 (4½ mm) needles and yarn **MC** (main color), cast on 48 sts, leaving a long tail end.

Beg with a **RS** row, work g st for 2 rows, ending with a **WS** row.

Next row (RS) K to end.

Next row (WS) P to end.

Rep last 2 rows once more, ending with a **WS** row.

Next row (dec row) (RS) K2 tog, K21, Sl1, K1, Psso, K21, K2 tog. (45 sts) Beg with a **WS** row, work st st for 3 rows, ending with a **WS** row.

Next row (dec row) (RS) K2tog, K19, Sl1, K1, psso, K20, K2tog. (42sts). Beg with a **WS** row, work 3 rows in st st, ending with a **WS** row.

Next row (dec row) (RS) K2 tog, K18, Sl1, K1, Psso, K18, K2 tog. (39 sts) Beg with a **WS** row, work st st for 3 rows, so ending with a **WS** row.

Next row (dec row) (RS) K2 tog, K16, Sl1, K1, Psso, K17, K2 tog. (36 sts) Beg with a **WS** row, work st st for 3 rows, ending with a **WS** row.

Next row (dec row) (RS) K2 tog, K15, Sl1, K1, Psso, K15, K2 tog. (33 sts) Beg with a **WS** row, work st st for 3 rows, ending with a **WS** row.

Next row (dec row) (RS) K2 tog, K13, Sl1, K1, Psso, K14, K2 tog. (30 sts) Beg with a **WS** row, work st st for 3 rows, ending with a **WS** row.

Next row (dec row) (RS) K2 tog, K12, Sl1, K1, Psso, K12, K2 tog. (27 sts)
Beg with a **WS** row, work st st for 3 rows, ending with a **WS** row.
Next row (dec row) (RS) K2 tog, K10, Sl1, K1, Psso, K11, K2 tog. (24 sts)
Beg with a **WS** row, work st st for 3 rows, ending with a **WS** row.
Next row (dec row) (RS) K11, Sl1, K1, Psso, K11. (23 sts)
Beg with a **WS** row, work st st for 3 rows, ending with a **WS** row.
Next row (dec row) (RS) K10, Sl1, K1, Psso, K11. (22 sts)
Beg with a **WS** row, work st st for 3 rows, ending with a **WS** row.
Next row (dec row) (RS) K10, Sl1, K1, Psso, K10. (21 sts)**
Break yarn and leave sts on a holder.

Right leg (knitted)

Using US size 7 (4½ mm) needles and yarn **MC** (main color), cast on 48 sts, leaving a long tail end.
Cont to work as Left leg up to **.
Join with Left leg
Next row (RS) K to end of row. With **RS** of Left leg facing, K across 21 sts of Left leg on holder. (42 sts)
Next row (RS) P to end.
Shape halter front
Next row (dec row) (RS) Change to yarn **A** (halter color), K2 tog, K to last 2 sts, K2 tog. (40 sts)
Next row (dec row) (WS) P2 tog, P to last 2 sts, P2 tog. (38 sts)
Next row (RS) K2 tog, K to last 2 sts, K2 tog. (36 sts)
Rep last 2 rows three times more, then work first of the rows again, ending with a **WS** row. (22 sts)

Next row (RS) K2 tog, K9, Turn.
Work on these 10 sts for left strap.
Left front divide
Next row (WS) P to end.
Next row (RS) K2 tog, K to last 2 sts, K2 tog. (8 sts)
Next row (WS) P to end.
Rep last row once. (6 sts)
Next row (RS) K to last 2 sts, K2 tog. (5 sts)
Beg with a **WS** row, work st st for 17 rows, ending with a **WS** row.**
Bind off leaving a long end for a trim.
With **RS** facing rejoin yarn to rem 11 sts.
Next row (RS) K9, K2 tog. (10 sts)
Next row P to end.
Next row (RS) K2 tog, K to last 2 sts, K2 tog. (8 sts)
Rep last 2 rows once more. (6 sts)
Work as for Left Strap. These straps tie at the back of the neck; alternately, knit to a shorter length and attach a piece of Velcro to each end as a securing device.

To make up

Press pieces lightly on wrong side, following instructions on yarn label. Using blunt-ended yarn needle, matching yarn, and backstitch for seams throughout. With **WS** facing, sew up inner seam. Sew up back seam to first decrease.

Large flower (crocheted)

Foundation chain Beg with the flower center using a finger-weight (4 ply) yarn (I used Opal Uni shade orange), and US D-3 (3.00) hook, make 5CH, join into a ring with Sl st in first ch.
Round 1 1CH, working over tail end,

12SC into ring. Fasten off and pull up the tail end to close the ring. Sew the center onto the front of one of the trouser legs.
Petal
Foundation chain Using a light or medium worsted weight (DK) yarn, (GGH Mystik shade 71 brown tweed), and US size G-6 (4.00 mm) hook, make 5CH, join into a ring with Sl st in first ch.
Round 1 1CH, working over tail end, 9SC into ring. Fasten off and pull up the tail end to close the ring.
Make four more petals. Sew petals around the flower center.

First small flower (crocheted)

Foundation chain Beg with the flower center using a finger-weight (4-ply) yarn (I used RYC Cashcotton 4-ply shade 900 Cream) and US D-5 (3.00) hook, make 6CH, join into a ring with Sl st in first ch.
Round 1 1CH, working over tail end, 15SC into ring. Fasten off and pull up the tail end to close the ring. Sew the center onto the front of same trouser leg.
Petal
1. Using the large eyed needle, thread up a 19¾-inches (50-cm) length of finger-weight (4-ply) yarn (I used Opal Uni 4-ply green) and secure at the back of the crocheted flower center.
2. Working into the flower center bring the needle through the crochet center—this will be the center of the first petal.
3. Bring the needle to the front and take a tiny stitch close to where the

needle first emerged. Leave the needle in the knitting. With your finger facing you, place the emerging thread over your left index finger.

4. Rotate your finger toward you. Keep the thread taut and looped over your index finger.

5. Take the tip of your finger under the working thread and then under the emerging thread, wrapping a loop around your finger.

6. Keeping the tension on the thread, place your fingertip on the point of the needle.

7. Slip the loop off your finger and onto the needle.

8. Slip the loop down the needle onto the fabric, pulling the fabric taut as you do so. This is your first cast-on stitch.

9. Work a second cast-on stitch in the same way, positioning it on the needle alongside the first.

10. Work 8 more cast-on stitches onto the needle.

11. Hold the cast-on stitches in your left hand. With your right hand, pull the needle and thread through the stitches.

12. To anchor the stitches, take the needle to the back of the center, close to where the needle last emerged.

13. Pull the thread through. Pull firmly but do not let the cast-on stitches disappear. Make six more petals in the same way, radiating them evenly around the flower center.

Second small flower (crocheted)

Foundation chain Beg with the flower center using a bulky weight (chunky weight) yarn (I used Bergere de France, Magic shade 232 Rosee / pale pink), and US G-6 (4.00) hook, make 3CH, join into a ring with a Sl st in first ch.

Round 1 1CH, working over tail end, 10SC into ring. Fasten off and pull up the tail end to close the ring. Sew the center onto the front of same trouser leg.

Petal

Using the large eyed needle, thread up a 19¾ inch (50 cm) length of finger-weight (4-ply) yarn (I used Opal Uni 4-ply magenta) and secure at the back of the crocheted flower center. Make six petals as for first small flower.

Summer breeze sweater

Finished size

Completed item measures approximately 14½ inches (37 cm) wide (arms outstretched) by 4¾ inches (12 cm) long.

Yarn

Sweater: 50g fingering-weight (4-ply) wool, or mixed-fiber yarn in main color **MC**, small amount medium weight 100% cotton yarn in sleeve color **A**, small amount of fingering-weight (4-ply) wool or mixed-fiber yarn in waist / neck color **B**, 1st stripe color C, 2nd stripe color D (*MC—RYC Cashcotton 4-ply shade 902 Pretty / light blue, A—Rowan Handknit Cotton shade 120 Orchid / pale pink, B –*
Rowan 4-Ply Soft shade 397 Teak / warm brown, C—Rowan 4-ply cotton dark yellow, D—Jaeger Baby Merino 4-ply shade 096 Marigold / tangerine).

Needles and hook

Pair of US size 5 (3¾ mm) knitting needles.
Blunt-ended yarn sewing needle.

Gauge

18 sts and 32 rows to 4 inches (10 cm) measured over stockinette stitch using US size 5 (3¾ mm) needles and yarn **MC**.

Front (knitted)

Beginning at the waist, using US size 5 (3¾ mm) needles and yarn **B** (waist / neck color), cast on 36 sts, leaving a long tail end.

Work 3 rows in g st, ending with a **RS** row.

Next row P to end.

Change to **MC** (main sweater color).

Shape sides

Row 1 (dec row) (RS) K1, K2 tog, K to last 3 sts, K2 tog, K1. (34 sts)

Beg with a **WS** row, work 3 rows in st st, ending with a **WS** row.

Change to C (1st stripe color).

Rep last 4 rows once more. (32 sts)

Change to **MC** (main sweater color).

Rep last eight rows once more, then the last 4 rows once more. (26 sts)

Shape raglan armholes

Change to D (2nd stripe color).

Next row (dec row) (RS) K1, K2 tog, K to last 3 sts, K2 tog, K1. (24 sts)

Next row (WS) P to end.

Rep last 2 rows twice more, ending with a **WS** row. (20 sts)

Neck Edge

Change to yarn **B**, beg with a **RS** row, work 7 rows in st, ending with a **RS** row. Bind off.

Back

Work as for front.

Sleeve (knitted)

Using US size 5 (3¾ mm) needles and yarn **A** (sleeve color), cast on 30 sts, leaving a long tail end.

Work 2 rows in g st, ending with a **WS** row.

Beg with a K row, work 20 rows in st st, ending with a **WS** row.

Shape raglan top

Row 1 (dec row) (RS) K1, K2tog, K to last 3 sts, K2tog, K1. (28 sts)

Next row P to end.

Rep last 2 rows six more times, ending with a **WS** row. (16 sts)

Shape raglan

Change to yarn D.

Next row (dec row) (RS) K1, K2 tog, K to last 3 sts, K2 tog, K1. (14 sts)

Next row (WS) P to end.

Rep last 2 rows twice more, ending with a **WS** row. (10 sts)

Neck Edge

Change to yarn **B**, beg with a **RS** row work 7 rows in st st, ending with a **RS** row. Bind off.

Make another sleeve in the same way.

To make up

Press pieces lightly on wrong side, following instructions on yarn label. Using blunt-ended yarn needle, matching yarn, and mattress stitch for seams throughout, sew the raglan seams. Join side and sleeve seams.

Dill

Cute and wide eyed, Dill is daring and stubborn—he won't go to bed, and when he's finally in bed he'll climb out of the window, down the tree outside the bedroom, into the kitchen, and straight to the refrigerator for some favorite chocolate milk!

Dill says "chocolate milk tastes so much nicer when you're not supposed to be having it." Like when you're supposed to be fast asleep in bed!

Dill

Finished size

Completed toy measures approximately 17 inches (43 cm) tall by 16 inches (41 cm) wide, arms outstretched.

Yarn

Bear: 50g light-worsted-weight (DK-weight) angora or mixed-fiber yarn in main color **MC**, second pattern color **A** *(MC—Adriafil Angora Carezza angora/ wool / nylon mix shade 82 Light Blue, A—Adriafil Angora Carezza angora/ wool / nylon mix shade 81 Yellow).*

Fabric and extras

Felt: Scraps of felt in 2 colors, mauve for outer eyes and olive green for eye irises.
Embroidery thread: Stranded cotton, for sewing on eyes, nose, and mouth.
Beads: 2 x ¼ inch (6 mm) Black Glass Pearls or similar.
Filling: Polyester toy filling.

Needles

Pair of US size 5 (3¾ mm) knitting needles.
Blunt-ended yarn sewing needle.
Embroidery sewing needle.

Gauge

26 sts and 36 rows to 4 inches (10 cm) measured over stockinette stitch, using US size 5 (3¾ mm) needles and yarn **MC**.

Front (knitted)

Front of Bear's body and head are worked in one piece.
Using US size 5 (3¾ mm) needles and yarn **MC** (main body color), cast on 8 sts, leaving a long tail end.
Next row (inc row) (RS) *K into front and back of st to inc one st—called *Kfb*—rep from * to end. (16 sts)
Next row (inc row) (WS) P into front and back of st to inc one st—called *Pfb*—P to last st, Pfb. (18 sts)
Next row (inc row) (RS) Change to yarn A (second patt color) Kfb, K to last st, Kfb. (20 sts)
Rep last P row once more, ending with a **WS** row. (22 sts)
Change to yarn **MC**, Beg with a K row, work 2 rows in st st, ending with a

WS row. Change to yarn **A** work 2 rows in st st—this stripe sequence forms the patt that is worked throughout. Work 22 rows more in st st, ending with a **WS** row.

Shape shoulders
Cont to work as Basic Bear following patt sequence (page 106).

To make up
Make up as Basic Bear (page106).

Pea green hoodie

Finished size
Completed hoodie measures approximately 4 inches (10 cm) long by 17¾ inches (45 cm) wide, arms outstretched.

Yarn
Hoodie: 25g light-worsted-weight (DK-weight) angora or mixed-fiber yarn in main color **MC**, sleeve color **A** (*MC—Bergere De France Ideal shade 259.771 Rouge, A Bergere De France Ideal shade 225.241 Chartreuse*).

Fabric and extras
Felt: Scrap of felt for "S".

Needles
Pair of US size 2 (3 mm) knitting needles.
Pair of US size 3 (3¼ mm) knitting needles.
Blunt-ended yarn sewing needle
Embroidery sewing needle.

Gauge
28 sts and 33 rows to 4 inches (10 cm) measured over stockinette stitch using US size 3 (3¼ mm) needles and yarn **MC**.

Body (knitted)
Back
Using US size 2 (3 mm) needles and yarn **MC** (main color), cast on 45 sts, leaving a long tail end.
Next row (RS) K1, *P1, K1, rep from * to end.
Next row (WS) P1, *K1, P1, rep from * to end.
Rep last 2 rows once more, ending with a **WS** row.
Change to US size 3 (3¼ mm) needles. Beg with a K row, work 16 rows in st st, ending with a **WS** row.

Shape armholes
Next row (dec row) (RS) Bind off 3 sts, K to end. (42 sts)
Next row (dec row) (WS) Bind off 3 sts at the beg of the row, P to end. (39 sts)**
Beg with a K row, work 12 rows in st st, ending with a **WS** row.

Shape shoulders
Next row (dec row) (RS) Cast off 5 sts, K to end. (34 sts)
Next row (dec row) (WS) Cast off 5 sts, P to end. (29 sts)
Rep last 2 rows once more, so ending with a **WS** row. (19 sts)
Bind off.

Front
Using US size 2 (3 mm) needles and yarn **MC** (main color), cast on 45 sts, leaving a long tail end.
Work as for Back up to **. (39 sts)

Beg with a K row, work 4 rows in st st, ending with a **WS** row.

Shape neck
Next row (RS) K15, turn, and work on these 15 sts for left neck.
Next row (dec row) (WS) P2, P2 tog, P to end. (14 sts)
Next row (dec row) (RS) K to last 4 sts, Sl1, K1, Psso, K2. (13 sts)
Rep last 2 rows once more and the last P row once more, ending with a **WS** row. (10 sts)
Beg with a K row, work 2 rows in st st, ending with a **WS** row.

Shape left shoulder
Next row (dec row) (RS) Bind off 5 sts, K to end. (5 sts)
Next row (WS) P to end.
Bind off.
RS facing, rejoin yarn to remaining 24 sts, bind off 9 sts, K to end. (15 sts)

Shape neck
Next row (dec row) (WS) P to last 4 sts, P2 tog, P2. (14 sts)
Next row (dec row) (RS) K2, K2 tog, K to end. (13 sts)
Rep last 2 rows once more and the last P row once more ending with a **WS** row. (10 sts)
Beg with a K row, work 3 rows in st st, ending with a **RS** row.

Shape right shoulder
Next row (dec row) (WS) Bind off 5 sts, K to end. (5 sts)
Bind off.

Sleeve (knitted)
Beg at the cuff end, using US size 3 (3¼ mm) needles and yarn **A** (sleeve color), cast on 31 sts, leaving a long tail end.

Dill 75

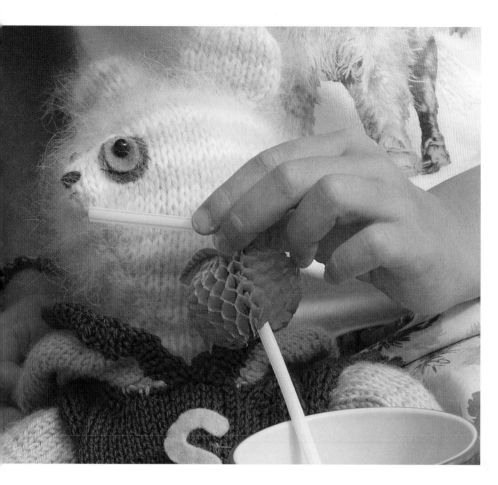

Beg with a **WS** row, work 3 rows in st st, ending with a **WS** row.

Next row (dec row) (RS) Sl1, K1, Psso, K to last 2 sts, K2 tog. (78 sts)

Rep last 4 rows 5 times more. (68 sts)

Beg with a **WS** row, work 9 rows in st st, ending with a **WS** row.

Shaping for top of hood

Next row (dec row) (RS) K32, (K2 tog) twice, K to end. (66 sts)

Next row (WS) P to end.

Next row (dec row) (RS) K31, (K2 tog) twice, K to end. (64 sts)

Rep last 2 rows once more, knitting to middle 4 sts and K2tog twice, ending with a **RS** row. (62 sts)

Next row (dec row) (WS) P29, (P2 tog) twice, P to end. (60 sts)

Next row (dec row) (RS) K28, (K2 tog) twice, K to end. (58 sts) Bind off.

Sometimes Dill won't do things he's supposed to do. When he decides he doesn't want to do something, a little persuasion can sometimes help...

To make up

Press pieces lightly on wrong side, following instructions on yarn label. Using blunt-ended yarn needle, matching yarn, and backstitch with **RS** tog for seams throughout, sew shoulder

Beg with a **RS** row work 10 rows in st, ending with a **WS** row.

Next row (inc row) (RS) K1, Yo, K to last st, Yo, K1. (33 sts)

Beg with a **WS** row, work 11 rows in st st, ending with a **WS** row.

Rep last 12 rows twice more, ending with a **WS** row. (37 sts)

Shape for top of sleeve

Next row (dec row) (RS) K2 tog, K to last 2 sts, K2 tog. (35 sts)

Next row (WS) P to end.

Rep last 2 rows twice more. (31 sts)

Next row (dec row) (RS) K2 tog, K to last 2 sts, K2 tog. (29 sts)

Next row (dec row) (WS) P2 tog, P to last 2 sts, P2 tog. (27 sts).

Bind off.

Make another sleeve in the same way.

Hood (knitted)

Using US size 2 (3 mm) needles and yarn **MC** (main color), cast on 82 sts, leaving a long tail end.

Next row (RS) K2, *P2, K2, rep from * to end.

Next row (WS) P2, *K2, P2, rep from * to end.

Rep last 2 rows once more, ending with a **WS** row.

Change to US size 3 (3¼ mm) needles and yarn **A** (sleeve color).

Next row (dec row) (RS) Sl1, K1, Psso, K to last 2 sts, K2 tog. (80 sts)

seams. Set in sleeves, placing center of head of sleeve to shoulder seam, then along bind-off edge of sleeve to decreased row edges at underarm. Sew underarm seams and side seams. Join back seam of hood. Sew the hood to the neck edge with cast-on edges of hood at center front neck and matching shaped row ends at neck with hood row ends—easing in fullness.

Draw a letter onto a piece of thin cardboard, cut around the letter, and use this template to transfer the shape onto a piece of felt. Cut out the felt shape and, using matching thread, sew it to the front of the hoodie.

Gauge

27 sts and 52 rows to 4 inches (10 cm) measured over garter stitch, using US size 3 (3¼ mm) needles and yarn **MC**.

Right leg (knitted)

Beginning at the leg edge and using US size 3 (3¼ mm) needles and yarn **MC** (Main color) cast on 42 sts, leaving a long tail end.

Beg with a **RS** row, work g st for 24 rows, ending with a **WS** row.

Center back and center front shaping

Next row (dec row) (RS) K2 tog, K to last 2 sts, K2 tog. (40 sts)

Rep last row once more. (38 sts)*

Center back shaping

Next row (dec row) (RS) K2 tog, K to end. (37 sts)

Next row (WS) K to end.

Rep last 2 rows twice more. (35 sts)

Beg with a **RS** row, work in g st for 10 rows, ending with a **WS** row.

Next row (RS) P to end.

Beg with a P row, work in st st for 2 rows, ending with a **RS** row. Bind off.

Left leg (knitted)

Beginning at the leg edge and using US size 3 (3¼ mm) needles and yarn **MC** (Main color) cast on 42 sts, leaving a long tail end.

Surfer's shorts

Finished size

Completed item measures approximately 3½ inches (9 cm) long by 11¼ inches (28 cm) around waist.

Yarn

Trousers: 50g finger-weight (4-ply weight) angora or mixed-fiber yarn in main color **MC** (Opal Sock Yarn shade 1193 Prisma).

Fabric and extras

19-inch (48-cm) length cord or narrow ribbon for the waist tie.

Needles

Pair of US size 3 (3¼ mm) knitting needles.
Blunt-ended yarn sewing needle.

Cont to work as Right Leg up to *. (38 sts)

Next row (dec row) (RS) K to last 2 sts, K2 tog. (37 sts)

Next row (WS) K to end.

Rep last 2 rows twice more. (35 sts) Beg with a **RS** row, work in g st for 10 rows, ending with a **WS** row.

Next row (RS) P to end.

Beg with a P row, work in st st for 2 rows, ending with a **RS** row. Cast off.

To make up

Using blunt-ended yarn needle, matching yarn, and backstitch for seams throughout, with **RS** facing, sew legs seams. Turn one leg out the right way and slip inside the other leg so that **RS** are facing. Matching row ends, sew seams. Turn in to **WS**, at the Purl row near the bind- off edge. Sew in place to form a channel at the waist. Thread cord through the channel and tie in place at the waist.

Socks

Finished size

Completed item measures approximately 5¼-inches (13-cm) high by 6-inches (15-cm) diameter.

Yarn

Socks: Small amount finger-weight (4-ply) wool, cotton, or mixed-fiber yarn in main color **MC**—1st stripe, **A**—2nd stripe (*MC—Adriafil Angora Carezza angora/ wool / nylon mix shade 18 Bordeaux, A—RYC Cashcotton 4-ply shade 905 Imp*).

Needles

Pair of US size 2 (3 mm) knitting needles.
Blunt-ended yarn sewing needle.

Gauge

24 sts and 32 rows to 4 inches (10 cm) measured over stockinette stitch, using US size 2 (3 mm) needles and yarn **MC**

Sock (knitted)

Using US size 2 (3 mm) needles and yarn **MC** (1st stripe color), cast on 36 sts, leaving a long tail end.

Beg with a K row, work 4 rows in st st, change to yarn **A**, work 4 rows in st st. This forms the stripe patt. Cont in stripe patt without shaping for 12 more rows, ending with a **WS** row and in yarn **MC**.

Shape top of foot

Break yarn, slip 1st 9 sts onto a safety pin. Using US size 2 (3 mm) needles, rejoin yarn **A** (2nd stripe color) K18, slip the last 9 sts onto a safety pin.

Beg with a **WS** row and keeping the patt correct, work 19 rows in st st, ending with a **WS** row.

Then, in yarn **MC** only, shape toe as follows:

Next row (dec row) (RS) K2, K2 tog, K to last 4 sts, K2 tog, K2. (16 sts)

Next row (dec row) (WS) P2, P2 tog, P to last 4 sts, P2 tog, P2. (14 sts)

Next row (dec row) (RS) K2, (K2 tog) twice, K2, (K2 tog) twice, K2. (10 sts)

Next row (dec row) (WS) P2, (P3 tog) twice, P2. (6 sts). Bind off.

Back of sock

With US size 2 (3 mm) knitting needle

in left hand, **WS** facing and row ends at the back of the sock meeting, slip 2 sets of 9 sts (2nd set first) off the safety pins onto the knitting needle, rejoin yarn **MC**, and K row.

Beg with a P row, work 9 rows in st st, ending with a **WS** row.

Shape heel

Next row (dec row 1) (RS) K9, K2 tog, turn, and work on these sts.

Next row (dec row 2) (WS) Sl1, P1, P2 tog, P1, turn.

Next row (dec row 3) (RS) Sl1, K2, K2 tog, K1, turn.

Next row (dec row 4) (WS) Sl1, P3, P2 tog, P1, turn.

Next row (dec row 5) (RS) Sl1, K4, K2 tog, K1, turn.

Next row (dec row 6) (WS) Sl1, P5, P2 tog, P1, turn.

Next row (dec row 7) (RS) Sl1, K6, K2 tog, K2.

Next row (WS) P to end. (11 sts)

Beg with a K row, cont in st st for 13 rows, ending with a **RS** row.

Toe shaping

Next row (dec row) (WS) P4, P3 tog, P to end. (9 sts)

Next row (dec row) (RS) K2 tog, K to last 2 sts, K2 tog. (7 sts). Bind off.

To make up

Weave in all ends.

Press piece lightly on wrong side, following instructions on yarn label.

Using blunt-ended yarn needle, matching yarn, and mattress stitch, sew back seam and along each side of the foot to join top to sole.

Make another sock in the same way.

Marigold

Motherlike, gentle, and kind, softly spoken Marigold takes good care of her friends. She loves nice things such as flowers, butterflies, fluffy white clouds, and sunshine, and she loves to bake. A cake a day keeps illness at bay!

generativity reflects a shift in focus from one close relationship (intimacy) to a broader concern with society as a whole.

Consistent with this idea, highly generative persons express high levels of commitment to assisting the next generation; they also show an integration between that commitment and a sense of agency (Mansfield & McAdams, 1996; see also de St. Aubin, McAdams, & Kim, 2004; McAdams, Diamond, de St. Aubin, & Mansfield, 1997). Once the quality of generativity emerges, it may continue through the rest of one's life (Zucker, Ostrove, & Stewart, 2002).

Adults who fail to develop this sense of generativity drift into stagnation. *Stagnation* is an inability or unwillingness to give of oneself to the future. These people are preoccupied with their own concerns. They have a self-centered or self-indulgent quality that keeps them from deeper involvement in the world around them. There's also evidence that an absence of generativity is related to poorer psychological well-being (Vandewater, Ostrove, & Stewart, 1997).

If there's a positive balance of generativity, the ego quality that emerges is care. *Care* is a widening concern for whatever you've generated in your life, be it children, something in your work, or something that emerged from your involvement with other people.

OLD AGE

The final stage is maturity, or old age. This is the closing chapter of people's lives. It's a time when people look back and review the choices they made and reflect on their accomplishments (and failures) and on the turns their lives have taken (see also Box 11.2). The crisis here is termed *ego integrity versus despair*. If you emerge from this review feeling that your life has had order and meaning, accepting the choices you made and the things you did, a sense of ego integrity emerges. This is a sense of satisfaction, a feeling that you wouldn't change much about your life.

The opposite pole of this conflict is despair: the feeling that your life was wasted. It's a sense of wishing you'd done things differently but knowing that it's too late. Instead of accepting your life's story as a valuable gift, there's bitterness that things turned out as they did.

Emerging from this life review with a sense of integrity creates the ego quality of *wisdom*. Wisdom involves meaning making and benevolence (Helson & Srivastava, 2002). It is an active concern with life and continued personal growth, even as one confronts the impending reality of death (see also Baltes & Staudinger, 1993; Kunzmann & Baltes, 2003).

THE EPIGENETIC PRINCIPLE

One more issue to address about Erikson's theory is that a given conflict is presumed to exist outside the stage in which it's focal. In the science of embryology, **epigenesis** is the process by which a single cell turns into a complex organism. For this process to occur requires a "blueprint" at the beginning, with instructions for all the changes and their sequencing. Erikson applied this idea to his theory, saying that there's a readiness for each crisis at birth. The core issue of each crisis is especially focal during a particular stage, but all of the issues are always there.

The principle of epigenesis has several implications. For one, as already indicated, it means your orientation to a particular crisis is influenced by the outcomes of earlier ones. It also means that in resolving the core crisis of any stage, you're preparing solutions (in simple form) for the ones coming later. As you deal in adolescence with the conflict between ego identity and role confusion, you're also

BOX 11.2 IS THERE A MIDLIFE CRISIS?

From Erikson's point of view, the last years of life are spent in review, examining choices that were made, values that were pursued, and passions that were abandoned. Erikson saw this review as coming late in life, after the opportunity to make changes has passed.

Others have also talked about a life review (Gould, 1980; Levinson, 1978; Stewart & Vandewater, 1999; Vaillant, 1977) but one that occurs earlier, around age 40 or so. Given its timing, the phenomenon is popularly referred to as the *midlife crisis*. It's a questioning of the decisions you've made over your adult years, the validity and worth of your goals, the adequacy of your life situation—nearly everything about your existence. It's a time of re-evaluation, but it's also a chance to change the way things are before it's too late. If you don't like your life, change it: remake decisions, rearrange your priorities, change careers, change your marriage (or leave it).

The notion of a midlife crisis rests partly on the typical course of life's major events in Western culture. It's common in the United States to finish college and take a job in one's early

20s and to marry and start raising a family in one's 20s and 30s. Depending on when the children are born, they're growing up and leaving home when the parents are in their 40s or early 50s. Around that time, it's also common to experience the death of one or both of one's own parents. Many changes of midlife are profound ones. Is it any wonder that they seem to cry out for a re-evaluation of life?

Another contributor to a crisis is cultural assumptions about the timing of these events. As a result, people do a certain amount of checking to see whether their lives are "on schedule." If you're in your mid-30s, are you making as much money as you're supposed to be? Are you in line for the career advancement you planned on? If you're nearing 40 with no children, you may hear the so-called biological clock ticking, telling you that you'll never have that experience if you don't hurry. Comparing your life against these markers of a "normal" life can produce a lot of soul searching.

Is there a midlife crisis? We're inclined to feel there's some truth to the idea. We know the feelings we've just written about. (We also know why one of us bought a motorcycle some years ago.) People do experience

regrets at midlife, and that does cause some people (though not all) to make life changes (Stewart & Vandewater, 1999).

Yet the evidence doesn't indicate that a real midlife crisis is all that common. Two longitudinal studies found little support for the idea in fairly large samples (Clausen, 1981; Haan, 1981). On the other hand, the participants in those studies lived through some very hard times—the Great Depression and World War II—and it's possible that having survived those experiences made them less likely to re-evaluate their choices and goals at midlife. Perhaps the midlife crisis is actually a baby-boomer phenomenon.

Alternatively, it may be that the midlife crisis isn't so much a matter of midlife as it is a reflection of a more consistent tendency to worry. This conclusion would fit with findings obtained by Costa and McCrae (1980) concerning life satisfaction over time. They found that satisfaction was relatively stable across a period of 10 years and that dissatisfaction related to the broad trait of neuroticism. Maybe, then, people who are inclined to worry do so throughout life, and it just happens to be more obvious at midlife.

moving toward handling the crisis of intimacy versus isolation. Finally, this principle means that crises aren't resolved once and for all. Your resolutions of previous conflicts are revisited and reshaped at each new stage of life (Whitbourne, Zuschlag, Elliot, & Waterman, 1992).

IDENTITY AS LIFE STORY

The sense of the epigenetic principle is well conveyed in some of the work of Dan McAdams. His work focuses partly on motivations that underlie personality (discussed in Chapter 5) and partly on the idea that people construct their identities as narratives, or life stories (McAdams, 1985, 1993, 2001). In his view, your story is never completed until the end of your life. It is constantly being written. Indeed, it's constantly under revision, just as your identity is constantly evolving.

As in any good book, the opening chapters of your narrative begin setting the stage for things that happen much later. Sometimes future events are foreshadowed; sometimes things that happen in early chapters create conditions that have to be reacted to later on. As chapters pile up, characters reinterpret events they experienced earlier or understand them in different ways. All the pieces eventually come together into a full and integrated picture, and the picture that results has qualities from everything that's happened throughout the story. McAdams thus sees the broad crisis of identity as one that continues to occupy each person throughout life (McAdams, 2001).

Of interest is how categories of narrative themes show up in many people's lives. McAdams and his colleagues have found that highly generative midlife adults often report life stories in which they had early advantages, became aware of the suffering of others, established a personal belief system that involved prosocial values, and committed themselves to benefiting society. McAdams calls these *commitment stories.* Often these commitment stories also contain *redemption themes,* in which a bad situation somehow is transformed into something good (McAdams, 2006; McAdams, Reynolds, Lewis, Patten, & Bowman, 2001). Indeed, the link from the sense of redemption to the quality of generativity appears quite strong (McAdams, 2006). Adults who are low in generativity sometimes have stories involving *contamination themes,* in which a good situation somehow turns bad.

LINKING ERIKSON'S THEORY TO OTHER PSYCHOSOCIAL THEORIES

Let's look back to the theories discussed earlier in this chapter to make a final point. Those theories represent contributions of their own. Yet in a sense, the fundamental theme of each is the same as that of the first crisis in Erikson's theory: basic trust versus basic mistrust. That's a big part of what security in attachment is about. It seems implicit in object relations theories. This issue is also the core of Erikson's own theory, providing the critical foundation on which the rest of personality is built.

Humans seem to need to be able to trust in the relationships that sustain our lives. In the minds of many theorists, that trust is necessary for adequate functioning. People who are deeply mistrustful of relationships or are constantly frightened about possibly losing relationships have lives that are damaged and distorted. The damage may be slight, or it may be significant. Avoiding such mistrust and doubt (or recognizing and overcoming it, if it's already there) seems a central task in human existence.

Assessment

Let's turn now to assessment from the psychosocial viewpoint. In general, assessment here is similar to that of the ego psychologists. There are two aspects of assessment, however, that are specific to this view.

OBJECT RELATIONS, ATTACHMENT, AND THE FOCUS OF ASSESSMENT

One difference concerns what's being assessed. The psychosocial approach places a greater emphasis than other approaches on assessing the person orientation to relationships.

There are several ways in which a person's mental model of relationships might be assessed. Relevant measures range from some that are open ended in nature (e.g., Blatt, Wein, Chevron, & Quinlan, 1979) to structured self-reports (e.g., Bell, Billington, & Becker, 1986). Some measures assess a range of issues pertaining to relationships (Bell et al., 1986). Others focus specifically on the attachments you have to other people in close relationships (e.g., Bartholomew & Horowitz, 1991; Carver, 1997a; Collins & Read, 1990; Griffin & Bartholomew, 1994; Simpson, 1990).

The object-relations measure of Bell et al. (1986) is a good illustration of content assessed from this viewpoint. It has four scales. The *alienation* scale measures a lack of basic trust and an inability to be close. People high on this scale are suspicious, guarded, and isolated, convinced that others will fail them. This resembles avoidant attachment. Another scale measures *insecure attachment,* which resembles the ambivalent pattern, a sensitivity to rejection and concern about being liked and accepted. The third scale, *egocentricity,* assesses narcissism, a self-protective and exploitive attitude toward relationships and a tendency to view others only in relation to one's own needs and aims. The final scale measures *social incompetence,* shyness and uncertainty about how to engage in even simple social interactions.

A different approach to assessment is the open-ended measure of Blatt et al. (1979). It has a coding system to assess the maturity of people's perceptions of social relations. This measure asks you to describe your mother and father. If you're at a low level of maturity, you tend to focus on how parents acted to satisfy your needs. Higher-level descriptions focus more on parents' values, thoughts, and feelings apart from your needs. At a very high level, the description takes into account internal contradictions in the parent and changes over time. This measure reflects a person's level of separation and individuation from the parent.

PLAY IN ASSESSMENT

Another facet of the psychosocial view on assessment reflects the emphasis on experiences of childhood as determinants of personality. As a result, this view deals with child assessment more than others. The assessment of children tends to emphasize the use of play as a tool. It's often said that children's play reveals their preoccupations (e.g., Axline, 1947, 1964; Erikson, 1963; M. Klein, 1935, 1955a, 1955b). Play lets them express their concerns in ways they can't do in words. Erikson (1963) devised a play situation using a specific set of toys on a table. The child is to imagine that the table is a movie studio and the toys are actors and sets. The child is to create a scene and describe what's happening. Other techniques use less structured settings, but elements almost always include a variety of dolls (e.g., mother, father, older person, children, baby). This permits children to choose characters that relate to their own concerns or preoccupations.

The play situation is projective, because the child imposes a story on ambiguous stimuli. It often has two objective characteristics, however. First is a *behavioral record.* This includes what the child says about the scene and a description of the scene and the sequence of steps taken to create it. Second, the face value of the child's behavior receives more attention than is usual in projectives. It isn't automatically assumed that the child's behavior has deeply hidden meanings.

Children often reveal their feelings through play.

Marigold

Finished size
Completed bear measures approximately 22 inches (56 cm) tall by 17 inches (43 cm) wide, arms outstretched.

Yarn
Bear: 50g light-worsted-weight (DK-weight) angora or mixed-fiber yarn in main color **MC** (*Adriafil Angora Carezza angora shade 85 orange*).

Fabric and extras
Felt: Scraps of felt for eyes (*mid-blue*).
Embroidery thread: Stranded cotton, for sewing on eyes, nose, and mouth.
Beads: 2 x 6 mm (¼ in.) Black Glass Pearls or similar.
Filling: Polyester toy filling.

Needles
Pair of US size 5 (3¾ mm) knitting needles.
Blunt-ended yarn sewing needle.
Embroidery sewing needle.

Gauge
20 sts and 30 rows to 4 inches (10 cm) measured over stockinette stitch, using US size 5 (3¾ mm) needles and yarn **MC**.

Front, Back, Arms, and Legs (knitted)
Work as Basic Bear (page 106).

Ear
Using US size 5 (3¾ mm) needles and yarn **MC** (main body color), cast on 10 sts, leaving a long tail end.
Next row (RS) Purl to end.
Next row (inc row) (WS) *K into front and back of st to inc one st—called **Kfb**—rep from * to end. (20 sts)
Beg with a P row, work 7 rows in rev st st, ending with a **RS** row.
Next row (dec row) (WS) K2tog, K6, (K2tog) twice, K6, K2tog. (16 sts)
Bind off.
Make another ear in the same way.

To make up
Head, Body, Arms, and Legs
Make up as Basic Bear (page 106) but omit inner eyes.

Ears
RS facing, fold each ear in half and overcast stitch row ends together, then overcast stitch across cast on stitches.
Turn right sides out. With the overcast row ends at one side of ear, overcast stitch across bind-off stitches. Sew these edges to the sides of the head referring to the photograph for position.

Buttercup cardigan

Finished size
Completed item measures approximately 12½ inches (32 cm) wide, arms outstretched, by 5¼ inches (13 cm) long.

Yarn
Cardigan: 50g light-worsted-weight (DK-weight) angora or mixed-fiber yarn in main color **MC** (*Rowan Soft Baby shade 008 Buttercup*)
Buttons: Tiny amount finger-weight (4-ply) yarn in button color yarn **A** (*Opal Uni 4-ply shade 1266 green*).

Needles and hook
Pair of US size 7 (4½ mm) knitting needles.
US size C-2 (2. 50mm) crochet hook.
Blunt-ended yarn sewing needle.

Gauge
19 sts and 27 rows to 4 inches (10 cm) measured over stockinette stitch, using US size 7 (4½ mm) needles and yarn **MC**.

Reminiscent of a soft summer's day, this cozy knitted cardigan is Marilgold's favorite— especially the tiny crocheted green daisy buttons.

Cardigan (knitted)
Left Front
Using US size 7 (4½ mm) needles and yarn **MC** (main color), cast on 20 sts, leaving a long tail end.
Cont in st st work button band patt as foll:
Next row (RS) K14, Yo, K2 tog, K1, Yo, K2 tog, K1. (20 sts)

Next row (WS) P to end.
Rep last 2 rows eight times more, ending with a **WS** row.
Shape armhole
Next row (dec row) (RS) K2, K2 tog, K to last 6 sts, Yo, K2 tog, K1, Yo, K2 tog, K1. (19 sts)
Next row (WS) P to end.
Rep last 2 rows four times more, ending with a **WS** row. (15 sts)
Shape front
Next row (dec row) (RS) K8, Yo, K2 tog, K1, Yo, (K2 tog) twice. (14 sts)
Next row (WS) P to end.
Next row (dec row) (RS) K7, Yo, K2 tog, K1, Yo, (K2 tog) twice. (13 sts)
Next row (WS) P to end.
Next row (dec row) (RS) K6, Yo, K2 tog, K1, Yo, (K2 tog) twice. (12 sts)
Next row (WS) P to end.

Next row (dec row) (RS) K5, Yo, K2 tog, K1, Yo, (K2 tog) twice. (11 sts)
Next row (WS) P to end.
Next row (dec row) (RS) K4, Yo, K2 tog, K1, Yo, (K2 tog) twice. (10 sts)
Next row (WS) P to end.
Bind off.
Right front
Using US size 7 (4½ mm) needles and yarn **MC** (main color), cast on 20 sts, leaving a long tail end.
Cont in st st working buttonhole band patt as foll:
Next row (RS) K1, K2 tog, Yo, K1, Yo, K2 tog, K to end. (20 sts)
Next row (WS) P to end.
Rep last 2 rows five times more, ending with a **WS** row.
1st buttonhole
Next row (RS) K1, K2 tog, (Yo) twice,

K1, K2 tog, K to end. (20 sts)
Next row (WS) P to end.
Next row (RS) K1, K2 tog, Yo, K1, Yo, K2 tog, K to end. (20 sts)
Next row (WS) P to end.
Rep last 2 rows once more, ending with a **WS** row.
Shape armhole
Next row (dec row) (RS) K1, K2 tog, Yo, K1, Yo, K2 tog, K to last 4 sts, K2 tog, K2. (19 sts)
Next row (WS) P to end.
2nd buttonhole
Next row (RS) K1, K2 tog, (Yo) twice, K1, K2 tog, K to last 4 sts, K2 tog, K2. (18 sts)
Next row (WS) P to end.
Next row (dec row) (RS) K1, K2 tog, Yo, K1, Yo, K2 tog, K to last 4 sts, K2 tog, K2. (17 sts)
Next row (WS) P to end.
Rep last 2 rows two times more, ending with a **WS** row. (15 sts)
Shape front
Next row (dec row) (RS) (K2 tog) twice, Yo, K1, K2 tog, Yo, K to end. (14 sts)
Next row (WS) P to end.
Rep last 2 rows 4 times more, ending with a **WS** row. (10 sts)
Bind off.
Back
Using US size 7 (4½ mm) needles and yarn **MC** (main color), cast on 30 sts, leaving a long tail end.
Beg with a **RS** row work 18 rows in st st, ending with a **WS** row.
Shape armholes
Next row (dec row) (RS) K2, K2 tog, K to last 4 sts, K2 tog, K2. (28 sts)
Next row (WS) P to end.

Rep last 2 rows four times more, ending with a **WS** row. (20 sts)

Beg with a **RS** row, work 8 rows in st st, ending with a **WS** row.

Next row (inc row) (RS) K6, K into front and back of st to inc one st—called *Kfb*—K1, turn, and work on these 9 sts only for right back.

Next row (inc row) (WS) P2, P into front and back of st to inc one st—called *Pfb*—P to end. (10 sts)

Bind off.

Rejoin yarn to rem 12 sts. Cast off 4 sts, Kfb, K to end. (9 sts)

Next row (inc row) (WS) P to last 3 sts, Pfb, P2. (10 sts)

Bind off.

Sleeve

Beg at the cuff end, using US size 7 (4½ mm) needles and yarn **MC** (main color), cast on 18 sts, leaving a long tail end.

Beg with a **RS** row, work 2 rows in st st, ending with a **WS** row.

Next row (RS) *K1, Yo, K2 tog, rep from * to end. (18 sts)

Next row (WS) P to end.

Rep last 2 rows once more, ending with a **WS** row.

Beg with a **RS** row, work 2 rows in st st, ending with a **WS** row.

Next row (inc row) (RS) Kfb, K to last st, Kfb. (20 sts)

A suitably pretty party dress—and there is always a party when Marigold makes chocolate cake...

Beg with a **WS** row work 9 rows in st st, ending with a **WS** row.

Next row (inc row) (RS) Kfb, K to last st, Kfb. (22 sts)

Beg with a **WS** row, work 5 rows in st st, ending with a **WS** row.

Shape armholes

Next row (dec row) (RS) K2, K2 tog, K to last 4 sts, K2 tog, K2. (20 sts)

Next row (WS) P to end.

Rep last 2 rows 4 times more, ending with a **WS** row. (12 sts)

Beg with a **RS** row, work 6 rows in st st, ending with a **WS** row.

Next row (dec row) (RS) K2 tog, K to last 2 sts, K2 tog. (10 sts)

Next row (dec row) (WS) P2 tog, P to last 2, P2 tog. (8 sts)

Bind off.

Make another sleeve in the same way.

Button (crochet)

Foundation chain Using US size C-2 (2.50 mm) hook and yarn **A**, make 3CH, leaving a long tail end. Slip St in 1st ch to form a ring.

Round 1 6SC into the ring, working over the long loose end.

Round 2 1SC into each SC.

Rep last row once more.

Fasten off.

Make another button in the same way.

To make up

Press pieces lightly on wrong side, following instructions on yarn label. Using blunt-ended yarn needle, matching yarn, and mattress stitch for seams throughout, sew shoulder seams. Set in sleeves placing center of head of sleeve to shoulder seam. Sew underarm seams and side seams. Position buttons on left front to correspond to buttonhole positions and sew center of each button in place.

Frilly party dress

Finished size

Completed item measures approximately 9 inches (23 cm) long by 11¾ inches (30 cm) all around waist.

Yarn

Dress: 50g light-worsted-weight (DK-weight) angora or mixed-fiber yarn in main color **MC**, 1st stripe color **A**, 2nd stripe color **B**, 3rd stripe color **C**, 4th stripe color **D**, *(MC—Rowan Soft Baby shade 002 Angel, A—Adriafil Angora Carezza angora shade 88 Amaranthe, B—RYC Luxury Cotton DK shade 252 Tang, C—RYC Luxury Cotton DK shade 251 Damsel, D—Berege de France Doussine shade 237.631 Sherherazade).*

Needles and hook

Pair of US size 7 (4½ mm) knitting needles.

US size H-8 (5.00 mm) crochet hook.

8 x 6 mm (¼ in.) pearly sequins

3 press studs.

Blunt-ended yarn sewing needle.

Embroidery sewing needle.

Gauge

18 sts and 24 rows to 4 inches (10 cm) measured over stockinette stitch using

US size 7 (4½ mm) needles and yarn **MC**.

Pattern note
Before stating to knit, thread sequins onto yarn. Use a fine sewing needle to thread the sequins onto a length of cotton thread, tie the ends of the thread to the yarn, and slide the sequins from the cotton thread down to the yarn. Continue in this way until the required number of sequins are threaded on the yarn.

Skirt (knitted and crocheted)
Beginning at the bottom edge and using US size 7 (4½ mm) needles and yarn **MC** (main color) cast on 100 sts, leaving a long tail end.

Row 1 (RS) *K1, P1, rep from * to end.

Row 2 (WS) *K1, P1, rep from * to end.

Beg with a **RS** row, work 30 rows in st st, ending with a **WS** row.

Next row (dec row) (RS) *K2 tog, rep from * to end. (50 sts)

Next row (WS) P to end.

Left back

Next row (RS) K9, turn, and work on these stitches only for left back.

Beg with a **WS** row, work 29 rows in st st, ending with a **WS** row.
Next row (RS) K1, *P1, K1, rep from * to end.
Rep last seed st row once more, so ending with a **WS** row.
Bind off.

Divide for left armhole

Next row (RS) Rejoin yarn to rem 41 sts, bind off 8 sts, K15, turn, and work on these sts for dress front. (16 sts)
Next row (WS) P to end.

Front

Beg with a **RS** row, work in the bead patt as follows:
Row 1 K7, Bead1, K1, Bead1, K to end.
Row 2 P to end.
Row 3 K5, Bead1, K5, bead1, K to end.
Row 4 P to end.
Row 5 K3, Bead1, K9, Bead1, K to end.
Row 6 P to end.
Row 7 K1, Bead1, K12, Bead1, K to end.
Beg with a **WS** row, work 11 rows in st st, ending with a **WS** row.
Next row (RS) *P1, K1, rep from * to end.
Next row (WS) *K1, P1, rep from * to end.
Bind off.

Divide for right armhole

Next row (RS) Rejoin yarn to rem 17 sts, bind off 8 sts, K8, turn, and work on these sts for right back. (9 sts)

Right back

Beg with a **WS** row, work 19 rows in st st, ending with a **WS** row.
Next row (RS) K1, *P1, K1, rep from * to end.

Rep last seed st row once more, ending with a **WS** row.
Bind off.

To make up

Using blunt-ended yarn needle, matching yarn, and mattress stitch for seams throughout, sew shoulders. Join back seam from bottom edge to dec row at waist. Attach 3 strands of yarn **MC** to the right opening at the neck, braid them together, then secure the ends to form a small buttonhole loop.
Using yarn D (4th stripe color) make a crochet button as before and sew it to the other side of the opening.

Crochet trim at hem

With **RS** of knitting facing and using crochet hook US size H-8 (5.00 mm) and yarn **A** (1st stripe color), join yarn to hem edge beg at the back seam.
Row 1 1CH (counts as 1st st), 1SC in each cast-on st to end, ss in 1ch. (101 sts)
Row 2 Change to yarn **B** (2nd stripe color), 1CH (counts as 1st st), 1SC in each sc to end, Sl st in 1ch. (101 sts)
Row 3 Change to yarn **C** (3rd stripe color), 1CH, * skip 1sc, 5TR in next sc, skip 1sc, 1SC in next dc, rep from * ending Sl st in 1ch.
Fasten off.

Crochet trim at Armholes

With **RS** of knitting facing and using crochet hook US size H-8 (5.00 mm) and yarn **B** (2nd stripe color) join yarn to armhole edge at underarm.
Row 1 1CH (counts as 1st st), 40SC evenly around armhole, Sl st in 1ch. (41 sts)

Row 2 1CH (counts as 1st st), 1SC in each sc to end. Sl st in 1ch. (41 sts)
Row 3 Change to yarn D (4th stripe color), 1CH, * skip 1sc, 5TR in next sc, skip 1sc, 1SC in next dc, rep from * ending Sl st in 1ch.
Fasten off.

Nice white socks

Finished size

Completed item measures approximately 3½ inches (9 cm) tall by 3 inches (7½ cm) at sole.

Yarn

Socks: Small amount finger-weight (4-ply) wool, cotton or mixed-fiber yarn in main color **MC** (*Jaeger Baby Merino shade 202 Snowdrop*).

Needles

Pair of US size 0 (2 mm) knitting needles.
Blunt-ended yarn sewing needle.

Gauge

30 sts and 48 rows to 4 inches (10 cm) measured over stockinette using US size 0 (2 mm) needles and yarn **MC**.

Sock (knitted)

Using US size 0 (2 mm) needles and yarn **MC**, cast on 36 sts, leaving a long tail end.
Row 1 (RS) Beg at the top of the sock, *K1, P2, rep from * to end.
Row 2 (WS) *K2, P1, rep form * to end.
Rep last two rib rows once more, ending with a **WS** row.

Beg with a K row, work 24 rows in st st, ending with a **WS** row.

Shape top of foot

Break yarn, slip 1st 9 sts onto a safety pin, using US size 0 (2 mm) needles, K18, slip the last 9sts onto a safety pin. Beg with a **WS** row, work 17 rows in st st, ending with a **WS** row.

Next row (dec row) (RS) K2, K2 tog, K to last 4 sts, K2 tog, K2. (16 sts)

Next row (dec row) (WS) P2, P2 tog, P to last 4 sts, P2 tog, P4. (14 sts)

Next row (dec row) (RS) K1, (K3 tog) 4 times, K1. (6 sts) Bind off.

Back of sock

WS facing and row ends meeting at the center, slip 2 sets 9 sts off the safety pins onto a US size 0 (2 mm) needle, with needle in left hand, rejoin yarn **MC** and K row.

Beg with a P row, work 9 rows in st st, ending with a **WS** row.

Shape heel

Next row (dec row 1) (RS) K9, K2 tog. Turn.

Next row (dec row 2) (WS) Sl1, P1, P2 tog, P1. Turn.

Next row (dec row 3) (RS) Sl1, K2, K2 tog, K1. Turn.

Next row (dec row 4) (WS) Sl1, P3, P2 tog, P1. Turn.

Next row (dec row 5) (RS) Sl1, K4, K2 tog, K1. Turn.

Next row (dec row 6) (WS) Sl1, P5, P2 tog, P1. Turn.

Next row (dec row 7) (RS) Sl1, K6, K2 tog, K1. Turn.

Next row (dec row 8) (WS) Sl1, P7, P2 tog. (10 sts)

Break yarn.

RS facing rejoin yarn **MC** and pick up

Marigold 89

90 Marigold

and K10 sts along row edge of 1st side of heel, K10 across heel, pick up and K10 sts along 2nd row edge of heel. (30 sts)

Sole of sock

Next row (WS) P to end.

Next row (dec row) (RS) K2 tog, K to last 2 sts, K2 tog. (28 sts)

Next row (WS) P to end.

Rep last 2 rows five times more, ending with a **WS** row. (18 sts)

Beg with a K row, work 8 rows in st st, ending with a **WS** row.

Shape toe

Next row (dec row) (RS) K2, Sl1, K1, Psso, K to last 4 sts, Sl1, K1, Psso, K2. (16 sts)

Next row (dec row) (WS) P2, P2 tog, P to last 4 sts, P2 tog, P2. (14 sts)

Rep last 2 rows twice more, ending with a **WS** row. (6 sts)

Bind off.

Make another sock in the same way.

To make up

Weave in all ends.

Press piece lightly on wrong side, following instructions on yarn label.

Using blunt-ended yarn needle, matching yarn, and mattress stitch, sew back seam and along each side of the foot to join top to sole.

Make another sock in the same way.

Pink Pumps

Finished size

Completed item measures approximately 3½ inches (9 cm) long by 6 inches (15cm) max diameter.

Yarn

Pump: Small amount light-worsted-weight (DK-weight) wool, cotton, or mixed-fiber yarn in main color **MC** and **A** (**MC**—*Rowan Soft Baby shade 003 Princess,* **A**—*Twilleys Freedom Cotton shade 010 lilac.*

Needles

Pair of US size 3 (3¼ mm) knitting needles.

Blunt-ended yarn sewing needle.

Gauge

24 sts and 32 rows to 4 inches (10 cm) measured over stockinette stitch, using US size 3 (3¼ mm) needles and yarn **MC**.

Pump (knitted)

Upper

Beginning at the toe end, using US size 3 (3¼ mm) needles and yarn **MC** (main color), cast on 5 sts, leaving a long tail end.

Next row (inc row) (RS) K1, (K into front and back of st to inc one st—called **Kfb)** 3 times, K1. (8 sts)

Next row (WS) K to end.

Next row (inc row) (RS) K1, (Kfb) 5 times, K2. (13 sts)

Next row (WS) K to end.

Next row (inc row) (RS) K3, (Kfb) 6 times, K4. (19 sts)

Beg with a **WS** row, work 15 rows in g st, ending with a **WS** row.

Shape upper opening

Next row (dec row) (RS) K8, bind off 3 sts, K7. (16 sts)

Turn and work on last 8 sts only for side.

Next row (WS) K to end.

Next row (dec row) (RS) K1, Sl1, K1, psso, K to end. (7 sts)

Rep last 2 rows twice more. (5 sts)

Beg with a **WS** row, work 11 rows in g st, ending with a **WS** row.

Bind off.

Rejoin yarn to rem set of 8 sts.

Next row (WS) K to end.

Next row (dec row) (RS) K to last 3 sts, Sl1, K1, psso, K1. (7 sts)

Rep last 2 rows twice more. (5 sts)

Beg with a **WS** row, work 11 rows in g st, ending with a **WS** row.

Bind off.

Sole

Using US size 3 (3¼ mm) needles and yarn **A** (sole color), cast on 3 sts, leaving a long tail end.

Next row (inc row) (RS) K1 (Yo, K1) twice. (5 sts)

Next row (WS) P to end.

Next row (inc row) (RS) K1, Yo, K to last 2 sts, Yo, K1. (7 sts)

Rep last 2 rows once more. (9 sts)

Beg with a P row, work 17 rows in st st, ending with a **WS** row.

Next row (dec row) (RS) K1, K2 tog, K to last 3 sts, K2 tog, K1. (7 sts)

Next row (WS) P to end.

Rep last 2 rows once more. (5 sts)

Next row (dec row) (RS) K1, K3 tog, K1. (3 sts)

Next row (WS) P to end.

Bind off.

To make up

Using blunt-ended yarn needle, matching yarn, and backstitch, sew up the back seam by joining bind off edges, finishing row with wrong sides facing. Turn out right way.

Ease the sole to fit the shoe upper and oversew in place.

Make another shoe in the same way.

Beads

Finished size
Completed bead measures approximately ¾ inch (1½ cm) diameter.

Yarn
Necklace: Remnants of light worsted-weight (DK-weight) or finger-weight 4-ply) yarn in assorted colors.

Needes and hook
US size E-4 (3.5 mm) crochet hook. Blunt-ended yarn sewing needle.

Gauge
No gauge is necessary for this project.

Bead (crocheted)
Foundation chain Using US size E-4 (3.50 mm) hook and any yarn, make 3CH, leaving a long tail end. Slip St in 1st ch to form a ring.
Round 1 1CH. 5SC into the ring, working over the long loose end. Ending Slip St into the top of 1st sc of round.
Fasten off. Pull the tail end leaving a tiny hole in the center of the ring— just large enough to be able to pass a needle and thread through.
Thread beads onto a length of yarn and tie around neck.

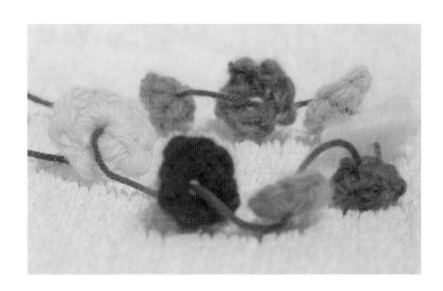

Marigold loves her pretty beads, and they can be worn as a necklace or a headress, too!

Lottie

Dancing mad and totally
obsessed with all things
ballet, Lottie is a real girly
girl—all sugary and sweet
with more than a hint of
bubblegum pink.

Fabric and extras
Felt: Scraps of felt for eyes *(cream)*.
Embroidery thread: Stranded cotton, for sewing on eyes.
Brown finger-weight (4-ply) yarn: for embroidering nose and mouth.
Filling: Polyester toy filling.

Needles
Pair of US size 5 (3¾ mm) knitting needles.
Blunt-ended yarn sewing needle.
Embroidery sewing needle.

Gauge
24 sts and 36 rows to 4 inches (10 cm) measured over stockinette stitch using US size 5 (3¾ mm) needles and yarn MC.

Note: This bear is suitable for a younger child under the age of three due to the fact that there are no beads that could come lose and cause choking. The same method of sewing on the eyes could be applied to all the bears in the book.

Front, Back, Arms, and Legs (knitted)
Work as Basic Bear (page 106).

Ear (knitted)
Noting that **P** side is **RS**, cont to work as Basic Bear (page 106).

To make up
Body, Arms, and Legs
Make up as Basic Bear (page 106).

Which little girl hasn't imagined what it would be like to be the twirling ballerina inside the jewelry box?

Lottie

Finished size
Completed toy measures approximately 17 inches (43 cm) tall by 15¾ inches (40 cm) wide, arms outstretched.

Yarn
Bear: 50g light-worsted-weight (DK-weight) angora or mixed-fiber yarn in main color **MC**, nose color **A** *(MC—Blue Sky Alpacas; Alpaca and Silk shade 30 rust).*

Head

Cut out felt pieces for outer eyes using template (see page 109). Using a length of brown finger-weight (4-ply) yarn work a French knot into the center of each felt piece. Use the tail of the yarn to join each eye to the head; either side of the nose. Using stranded cotton, work short stitches radiating around each felt eye to secure each eye onto the head.

Using a length of brown yarn and yarn needle, sew a nose working six straight stitches close together at the front of the nose, then work a small mouth, ¼ in (6 mm) wide, across the bottom of the seam, a little way under the nose.

Sew remaining seam, leaving an opening for inserting filling. Insert filling, manipulating it to shape nose as shown. Sew up the gap to close.

Ears

RS facing, fold each ear in half. Overcast stitch row ends together, then overcast stitch to join cast on and bind off stitches.

Turn right side out—**P** of knitting facing outward, sew up remaining row end. Bend ear around so that long seam joins. Backstitch along this edge to form the center of the ear. Sew onto the head at row end seams.

Ballet wrap

Finished size

Completed item measures 3½ inches (9cm) long by 10½ inches (27cm) wide (arms outstretched).

Yarn

Ballet wrap: 50g of finger-weight (4-ply) wool or mixed-fiber yarn in main color **MC,** *(MC—RYC Classic Cashcotton 4-ply shade 901 Sugar).*

Fabric and extras

Ribbon: 2 x 10¼ inches (26cm) lengths x ½ inch (12 mm) satin ribbon.
Embroidery thread: Stranded cotton, for sewing on ribbon.

Needles

Pair of US size 5 (3¾ mm) knitting needles.
Blunt-ended yarn sewing needle.
Embroidery sewing needle.

Gauge

24 sts and 29 rows to 4 inches (10cm) measured over stockinrette stitch using US size 5 (3¾ mm) needles and yarn MC.

Ballet wrap (knitted)

Back, front, and sleeves are worked in one piece.

Beg at the back, using US size 5 (3¾ mm) needles and yarn MC (main body color), cast on 26 sts, leaving a long tail end.

Beg on **RS,** work 5 rows in g st ending with a **RS** row.

Next row (WS) P to end.

Beg with a K row, work 6 rows in st st, ending with a **WS** row.

Shape back

Next row (inc row) (RS) Kfb, K to last st, Kfb. (28 sts)

Next row (WS) P to end.

Rep last 2 rows once more, ending with a **WS** row. (30 sts)

Shape sleeves

Next row (inc row) (RS) Cast on 20 sts at the beg of row, K to end. (50 sts)

Next row (inc row) (WS) Cast on 20 sts at the beg of row, P to end. (70 sts)

Next row (RS) K to end.

Next row (WS) K3, P to last 3 sts, K3. Rep last 2 rows 5 times, ending with a **WS** row.

Next row (RS) K to end.

Garter st detail across back of neck

Next row (WS) K3, P23, K18, P23, K3. Rep last 2 rows once more.

Next row (RS) K to end.

Divide for fronts

Next row (WS) K3, P23, K3, leave these sts on a holder for Left Front. Bind off 12 sts, K2, P23, K3. (29 sts on needle).

Right Front

Next row (RS) K to end. (29 sts)

Next row (WS) K3, P to last 3 sts, K3. Rep last 2 rows once more.

Shape front

Next row (inc row) (RS) K to last 3 sts, Kfb, K3. (30 sts)

Next row (inc row) (WS) K3, Pfb, P to last 3 sts, K3. (31 sts) Rep last 2 rows twice more. (35 sts)

Shape sleeve

Next row (RS) Bind off 20 sts, K10, Kfb, K3. (16 sts)

Next row (WS) K3, Pfb, P to end. (17 sts)

Next row (RS) K3, K2 tog, K to last 4 sts, Kfb, K3. (17 sts) Rep last 2 rows once more. (18 sts)

Next row (WS) K3, Pfb, P to end. (19 sts)

Next row (RS) K to last 4 sts, Kfb, K3. (20 sts)

Rep last 2 rows once more. (22 sts)
Next row (WS) K3, P to end.
Work 4 rows straight in g st.
Bind off.
Left Front
RS facing, rejoin yarn to rem 29 sts on holder.
Next row (RS) K to end. (29 sts)
Next row (WS) K3, P to last 3 sts, K3.
Rep last 2 rows once more.
Shape front
Next row (inc row) (RS) K3, Kfb, K to end. (30 sts)
Next row (inc row) (WS) K3, P to last 4 sts, Pfb, K3. (31 sts)
Rep last 2 rows twice more and last RS row once more. (36 sts)
Shape sleeve
Next row (WS) Bind off 20 sts k-wise, P11, Pfb, K3. (17 sts)
Next row (RS) K3, Kfb, K to end. (18 sts)
Next row (WS) P3, P2 tog tbl, P to last 4 sts, Pfb, K3. (18 sts)
Rep last 2 rows once more. (19 sts)
Next row (RS) K3, Kfb, K to end. (20 sts)
Next row (WS) P to last 4 sts, Pfb, K3. (21 sts)
Next row (RS) K3, Kfb, K to end. (22 sts)
Next row (WS) P to last 3 sts, K3.
Work 4 rows straight in g st. Bind off.

To make up
Sew end of one length of ribbon to first four st st row ends at Right Front. Sew the other length to the Left Front—same position.
Weave in all ends.
Press piece lightly on wrong side,

following instructions on yarn label. Using blunt-ended yarn needle, matching yarn, and mattress stitch, sew sleeve and side seams—leave a little of the seam along right side open to allow ribbon tie to be threaded through.

Headband

Yarn
Rose: Small amount finger-weight (4-ply) wool, cotton or mixed-fiber yarn in crocheted rose color **MC** (**MC**—*RYC Classic Cashcotton 4-ply shade 901 Princess*).

Needles and hook
US C-2 (2.50 mm) crochet hook.
Blunt-ended yarn sewing needle.
Embroidery sewing needle.

Fabric and extras
Ribbon: 9½ inches (24 cm) length gingham ribbon.
Embroidery thread: Stranded cotton, for sewing on ribbon.
Optional: Small buttons.

Rose (crocheted)
Foundation row Using yarn MC, make 17C. Turn.
Row 1 1DC in 5th ch from hook, *1CH, Sk next ch, (1DC, 1CH, 1DC) in next ch, rep from *. Turn.
Row 2 6DC in first ch sp, * 1SC in next ch sp, 6DC in next ch sp, rep from * to end, 1SC in turning ch. (17 shells)
Fasten off, leaving long tail end.

To make up
Fit the ribbon around the bear's head. Allowing for a turn up at each raw edge, cut to size. Turn in the ends and sew the band together at short ends.
Rose corsage
Thread needle with tail and weave to the bottom of last st. Starting at that end, roll first shell tightly to form the center bud: anchor at bottom of shell with 2 sts; roll rem strip to form rose, then secure by stitching in and out through layers of foundation ch at bottom of rose. Leave a long tail end to sew onto the ribbon band.

Tutu with twirly skirt

Finished size
Completed item measures 4 inches (10 cm) long by 5½ inches (14 cm).

Yarn
Tutu: 50g of light-worsted-weight (DK-weight) wool or mixed-fiber yarn in main color **MC** (**MC**—*RYC Classic Soft Lux shade 01 Pearl*)
Frilled skirt: Small amount of light-worsted-weight (DK-weight) wool or mixed-fiber yarn in skirt color **A** (**A**—*Louisa Harding Grace Silk and Wool shade 44 lilac*).

Needles and hook
Pair of US size 5 (3¾ mm) knitting needles.
US K-10½ (6.50 mm) hook.
Blunt-ended yarn sewing needle.

Gauge

20 sts and 32 rows to 4 inches (10 cm) measured over stockinette stitch using US size 5 (3¾ mm) needles and yarn MC.

Tutu (knitted)

Bodice

Worked in one piece.

Beg at the top of the bodice, using US size 5 (3¾ mm) needles and yarn MC (main color), cast on 30 sts, leaving a long tail end.

Beg on **RS** work 13 rows in st st, ending with a **RS** row.

Skirt

Next row (WS) P to end.

Next row (RS) *K1, kfb, rep from * to end. (45 sts)

Next row (WS) P to end.

Next row (RS) (K8, Kfb) five times. (50 sts)

Next row (WS) P to end.

Next row (RS) (K9, Kfb) five times. (55 sts)

Next row (WS) P to end.

Next row (RS) (K10, Kfb) five times. (60 sts)

Next row (WS) P to end.

Next row (RS) (K11, Kfb) five times. (65 sts)

Next row (WS) P to end.

Next row (RS) (K12, Kfb) five times. (70 sts)

Next row (WS) P to end.

Next row (RS) (K13, Kfb) five times. (75 sts)

Bind off, k-wise.

To make up

Thread needle with tail and sew up, working mattress stitch, along the center back seam at bodice back and skirt back.

Ruffled skirt (crocheted)

Foundation row Using yarn A and US K-10½ (6.50) hook, make 20CH, join into ring with Sl st in top of 1st ch.

Round 1 *1SC in next ch, 2SC in next ch, rep from * around. (30 dc)

Round 2 *1SC in each of next 2sc, 2SC in next sc, rep from * around. (40 sc)

Round 3 *1SC in each of next 3sc, 2SC in next sc, rep from * around. (50 sc)

Round 4 *1SC in each of next 4sc, 2SC in next sc, rep from * around. (60 sc)

Round 5 *1SC in each of next 5sc, 2SC in next sc, rep from * around. (70 sc)

Fasten off.

To make up

Weave in all ends. Slip the ruffled skirt over the tutu, stitch the ruffled skirt around the waist of the tutu bodice.

Lottie 101

102 Lottie

Ballet pumps

Finished size
Completed pump measures 3¼ inches (8 cm) long by 2 inches (5 cm) wide.

Yarn
Pumps: Small amount finger-weight (4-ply) wool or mixed-fiber yarn in main color **MC** (*MC—Jaeger Baby Merino 4 Ply shade 124 Dream*).

Needles and hook
US size C-2 (2.50 mm) crochet hook. Blunt-ended yarn sewing needle.

Fabric and extras
Ribbon: 33 inches (84 cm) length by ¾ inch (15 mm) satin ribbon.

Gauge
20 sts and 28 rows to 4 inches (10 cm) measured over single crochet using US size C-2 (2.50 mm) crochet hook and yarn MC.

Ballet pump (crocheted)
Worked in one piece.
Foundation row Beg at the toe of the pump, using US size C-2 (2.50 mm) hook and yarn MC (main color), make 2CH, join into ring with Sl st in top of 1st ch.
Round 1 Working over loose end, 6SC into ring.
Round 2 2SC in each dc. (12 sc)
Round 3 *1SC in each next sc, 2SC in next sc, rep from * to end. (18 sc)
Round 4 *1SC in each of next 2sc, 2SC in next sc, rep from * to end. (24 sc)
Round 5 *1SC in each of next 3sc, 2SC

in next sc, rep from * to end. (30 sc)
Round 6 1SC in each sc to end. (30 sc)
Rep last round six times more.
Shape sole
Next row 1SC in each next 20dc, 1CH, Turn.
Rep last row eight times more.
Next row * 1SC in each next 4sc, Sk next sc, rep from * to end. (16 sc)
Fold last row in half to form heel, join by working 1SC through both layers from top to bottom of the heel. Turn out to other side. Weave in all ends.

Make another ballet pump in the same way.
Cut the ribbon into two lengths. Fold each length in half and sew to the back of each pump.

Bear's Bears

Finished size

Completed toy measures approximately 17¾ inches (45 cm) tall by 13 inches (37 cm) wide, arms outstretched.

Yarn

Bear: Small amount light-worsted-weight (DK-weight) wool or mixed-fiber yarn in main color MC (a single skein of tapestry yarn will make one bear). If you wish to felt the bear use only natural fibers.

Fabric and extras

Embroidery thread: Stranded cotton, for sewing on eyes, nose, and mouth.
Filling: Polyester toy filling.

Needles

Pair of US size 5 (3¾ mm) knitting needles.
Blunt-ended yarn sewing needle.
Embroidery sewing needle.

Gauge

20 sts and 30 rows to 4 inches (10 cm) measured over stockinette stitch, using US size 5 (3¾ mm) needles and yarn MC.

Bear's body (knitted)

Front

Beginning at the bottom edge, cast on 6 sts, leaving a long tail end.
Next row (inc row) (RS) *K into front and back of st to inc one st—called *Kfb*—rep from * to end. (12 sts)
Beginning with a WS row, work 3 rows in st st, ending with a **WS** row.
Next row (inc row) (RS) *K3, Kfb, rep from * to end. (15 sts)
Beginning with a WS row, work 3 rows in st st, ending with a **WS** row.
Next row (dec row) (RS) *K1, K2tog, rep from * to end. (10 sts).
Next row (dec row) (WS) *P2tog, rep from * to end. (5 sts).
Bind off, leaving enough thread to sew up the seam.

Head (knitted)

Beginning with the neck edge, cast on 12 sts, leaving a long tail end.
Next row (dec row) (RS) K2 tog, K to last 2, k2 tog. (10 sts)
Next row (WS) P to end.
Rep last 2 rows four times more.
Bind off.

Nose (knitted)

Cast on 3 sts, leaving a long tail end.
Beginning with a RS row, work 3 rows in st st.
Break yarn, thread end through yarn needle, pass needle through 3 rem sts as you pull the knitting needle through and off the stitches. Weave end around edge of the square, pull up to gather into a ball-shaped nose.

Ear (knitted)

Beg at base of ear, cast on 5 sts, leaving a long tail end.
Next row (WS) P to end.
Next row (dec row) (RS) K2 tog, K1, k2 tog. (3 sts)
Next row (WS) P to end.
Break yarn, thread end through yarn needle, pass needle through 3 rem sts as you pull the knitting needle through sts. Pull up tight. Weave end over the row ends.
Make another ear similar.

Arm

Using US size 2 (2¾ mm) needles and yarn MC (main body color), cast on 3 sts, leaving a long tail end.
Work 6 rows in st st. Bind off.
Make another arm similar.

Leg (knitted)

Using US size 2 (2¾ mm) needles and yarn MC (main body color), cast on 4 sts, leaving a long tail end.
Work 10 rows in st st. Bind off.
Make another leg similar.

To make up

Body

Press piece lightly on wrong side, following instructions on yarn label. Fold the body with row ends together, RS facing. Using blunt-ended yarn needle, matching yarn, and backstitch, sew the bottom, across the cast-on stitches. Turn right side out. Join the row ends. Stuff the body through neck, gather up around neck edge, pull the gathers tightly to close gap, and fasten off.

Head

Fold the triangle with all points meeting at neck edge. From the points oversew up to top of head, leaving neck edge / cast-on row, open. The seam runs at the back of the head. Stuff the head through the neck. Run a row of gathering stitches around the neck edge. Gather up, then sew

the neck edge of head to neck edge
of body.

Nose

Sew the nose to the front of the head.

Ears

Attach the ear bottom to the top
corners of head.

Arms and legs

Join the arms and legs to the body.

Weave in all ends.
If you want, felt the bears by placing
in a sock and machine washing and
drying on a hot cycle. Reshape when
dry.
Sew two French knot eyes and a satin
stitch nose in black thread. Sew a
single stitch for the mouth.

Basic Bear

Finished size

For size of completed bear, see individual patterns.

Yarn

Bear: 50g light-worsted-weight (DK-weight) 100% wool or mixed-fiber yarn in main color **MC**
For specific yarns and yarn amounts, see individual patterns.

Fabric and extras

Felt: Scraps of felt for outer eyes and inner eyes.
Embroidery thread: Stranded cotton, for sewing on eyes, nose, and mouth.
Beads: 2 x 6 mm (¼ in.) Black Glass Pearls or similar.
Filling: Polyester toy filling
For specific fabric and thread colors, see individual patterns.

Needles

Pair of US size 5 (3¾ mm) knitting needles.
Blunt-ended yarn sewing needle.
Embroidery sewing needle.
For specific needles, see individual patterns.

Gauge

20 sts and 30 rows to 4 inches (10 cm) measured over stockinette stitch using US size 5 (3¾ mm) needles and yarn MC.
For specific yarn tensions, see individual patterns.

Front (knitted)

Front of Bear's body and head are worked in one piece from lower edge. Using US size 5 (3¾ mm) needles and yarn MC (main body color), cast on 8 sts, leaving a long tail end.
Next row (inc row) (RS) *K into front and back of st to inc one st—called **Kfb**—rep from * to end. (16 sts)
Next row (inc row) (WS) P into front and back of st to inc one st—called **Pfb**—P to last st, Pfb. (18 sts)
Next row (inc row) (RS) Kfb, K to last st, Kfb. (20 sts)
Rep last P row once more, ending with a **WS** row. (22 sts)
Beg with a K row, work 26 rows in st st, ending with a **WS** row.
Shape shoulders
Row 1 (dec row) (RS) K2 tog, K to last 2 sts, K2tog. (20 sts)
Row 2 (dec row) (WS) P2 tog, P to last 2 sts, P2tog. (18 sts)
Shape neck
Next row (dec row) (RS) Bind off 3 sts from the beg of row. (15 sts)
Next row (dec row) (WS) Rep last row once more. (12 sts)
Beg with a K row, work straight in st st for 3 rows, ending with a **RS** row.
**
Divide for front of face
Row 1 (dec row) (WS) P6, turn, and work on these sts for Right Front. (6 sts) Work each side of the face separately.
Next row (inc row) (RS) Kfb, K to last st, Kfb. (8 sts)
Next row (WS) P. (8 sts)
Rep last 2 rows 5 times more, ending with a **WS** row. (18 sts)
Shape the nose

Next row (inc row) (RS) Kfb, K to end. (19 sts)
Next row (inc row) (WS) P to last st, Pfb. (20 sts)
Rep last 2 rows once more, ending with a **WS** row. (22 sts)
Beg with a K row, work straight in st st for 6 rows, ending with a **WS** row.
Shape for the top of the nose
Next row (dec row) (RS) Bind off 6 sts, K to the end of row. (16 sts)
Next row (WS) P to end.
Next row (dec row) (RS) K2 tog, K to end. (15 sts)
Rep last 2 rows once more, ending with a **RS** row. (14 sts)
Next row (WS) P to end.
Next row (dec row) (RS) K2 tog, K to last 2 sts, K2 tog. (12 sts)
Next row (dec row) (WS) *P2 tog, rep from * to end. (6 sts) Bind off.
Left Front
WS facing, rejoin yarn to the inside edge of the right front and P row. (6 sts)
Next row (inc row) (RS) Kfb, K to last st, Kfb. (8 sts)
Next row (WS) P to end.
Rep last 2 rows 5 times more, ending with a **WS** row. (18 sts)
Shape the nose
Next row (inc row) (RS) K to last st, Kfb. (19 sts)
Next row (inc row) (WS) Pfb, P to end. (20 sts)
Rep last 2 rows once more, ending with a **WS** row. (22 sts)
Beg with a K row, work straight in st st for 5 rows, ending with a **RS** row.
Shape for the top of the nose
Next row (dec row) (WS) Bind off 6 sts, P to the end of row. (16 sts)

Next row (RS) K to end.

Next row (dec row) (WS) P2 tog, P to end. (15 sts)

Rep last 2 rows once more, ending with a **WS** row. (14 sts)

Next row (RS) K to end.

Next row (dec row) (WS) P2 tog, P to last 2 sts, P2 tog. (12 sts)

Next row (dec row) (RS) *K2 tog, rep from * to end. (6 sts) Bind off.

Back (knitted)

Back of Bear's body and head are worked in one piece, starting at bottom end, cast on 8 sts and work as for Front up to **. (12 sts)

Next row (WS) P to end.

Shape head

Next row (inc row) (RS) Kfb, K to last st, Kfb. (14 sts)

Next row (WS) P to end.

Rep last 2 rows 5 times more, ending with a **WS** row. (24 sts)

Beg with a K row, work straight in st for 16 rows, ending with a **WS** row.

Next row (dec row) (RS) K2 tog, K to last 2 sts, K2 tog. (22 sts)

Next row (dec row) (WS) *P2 tog, rep from * to end. (11 sts) Bind off.

Arm (knitted)

Starting at the paw end, cast on 7 sts, leaving a long tail end.

Next row (inc row) (RS) *Kfb, rep from * to end. (14 sts)

Beg with a P row, work straight in st st for 23 rows, ending with a **WS** row.

Shape elbow

Next row (inc row) (RS) Kfb, K to last st, Kfb. (16 sts)

Next row (inc row) (WS) Pfb, P to last st, Pfb. (18 sts)

Rep the last K inc row once more ending with a **RS** row. (20 sts)

Next row (WS) P to end.

Next row (dec row) (RS) (K2 tog) 3 times, K8, (K2 tog) 3 times. (14 sts)

Beg with a P row, work 19 rows in st st, ending with a **WS** row.
Bind off.

Make another arm in the same way.

Leg (knitted)

Starting at the paw end, cast on 8 sts, leaving a long tail end.

Next row (inc row) (RS) *Kfb, rep from * to end. (16 sts)

Next row (inc row) (WS) Pfb, P to last st, Pfb. (18 sts)

Next row (inc row) (RS) Kfb, K to last st, Kfb. (20 sts)

Rep last 2 rows once more, then the last P inc row once more, ending with a **WS** row. (26 sts)

Beg with a K row, work 14 rows in st st, ending with a **WS** row.

Next row (dec row) (RS) (K2 tog) 5 times, K6, (K2 tog) 5 times. (16 sts)

Beg with a P row, work 49 rows in st st, ending with a **WS** row.
Bind off.

Make another leg in the same way.

Ear (knitted)

Using US size 5 (3¾ mm) needles and yarn MC (main body color), cast on 10 sts, leaving a long tail end.

Next row (WS) P to end.

Next row (inc row) (RS) *Kfb, rep from * to end. (20 sts)

Beg with a P row, work 7 rows in st st, ending with a **WS** row.

Next row (dec row) (RS) K2tog, K6, (K2 tog) twice, K6, K2 tog. (16 sts)
Bind off.

Make another ear in the same way.

To make up

Press pieces lightly on wrong side, following instructions on yarn label.

Head and body

Using blunt-ended yarn needle, matching yarn, and mattress stitch for body seams, sew center front head seam that runs under the chin to the top of the head. Then sew the front to the back around the entire outer edge, leaving the cast-on edges open. Cut out felt pieces for outer eyes and inner eyes, using templates (see page 109). Using two strands of stranded cotton and an embroidery sewing needle, sew a bead to each inner eye then to center of outer eye. (To further secure inner eye, if desired, work short straight stitches around edge.)

Using two strands of stranded cotton and an embroidery sewing needle, sew nose working a small upside-down triangle in satin stitch over two knitted stitches at the seam at the front of the nose. Work a small mouth, ¼ inch (6 mm) wide, beneath the nose.

Sew remaining seam, leaving an opening for inserting filling. Insert filling, manipulating it to shape nose as shown. Sew up the gap to close.

Arms

With RS together, using backstitch, sew seam at back of each arm and around paw, leaving the shoulder at the bind-off edges open. Turn right sides out, then fill arm and paw lightly with toy filling. Sew remaining seam.

To position arms in place at the side seams of the body, using matching yarn, overcast stitch each arm to the body at the bind-off edge, placing each arm four rows down from the neck shaping with seam at underarm position.

Legs

With RS together, using backstitch sew the seam at back of each leg and along paw. Turn right sides out, then fill the paw only with stuffing, leaving the leg free to dangle.

To position legs on body, using matching yarn, overcast stitch each leg in place at the base of body, with leg seams facing toward back and leaving three clear knitted stitches between the legs at the center front.

Ears

RS facing, fold each ear in half and overcast stitch row ends together, then overcast stitch across cast on stitches.

Turn right sides out. With the overcast row ends at one side of ear, overcast stitch across cast off stitches. Sew these edges to the sides of the head at the position stated within the pattern.

The templates for the eyes below are at 100% (percent). See individual patterns for color use.

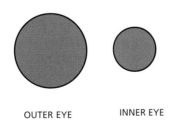

OUTER EYE   INNER EYE

Abbreviations

Knitting

Cont: continue

Dec: decrease

DK: double knit, refers to yarn type

Foll: following

G st: garter stitch, all knit rows

Inc: increase

K: Knit

Kfb: Knit into front of the stitch, then into the back, before completing the stitch

MC: main color

P: Purl

Patt: pattern

PFB: Purl into front of the stitch, then into the back, before completing the stitch

Psso: pass the slipped stitch over the top of the stitch just knitted

Rep: repeat

Rev st st: reverse stockinette stitch, where purl side is right side

RS: right side of knitting

Sl: slip the stitch onto the right needle without knitting it

St st: stockinette stitch, knit one row, purl one row

St/sts: stitch/stitches

Tbl: through the back loop of the stitch

Tog: together

WS: wrong side of knitting

Yfd: yarn forward; bring yarn to front in between the last stitch knitted and the next stitch to be knitted to increase one stitch

Yo: yarn over, wind yarn once over the needle before knitting the next stitch to increase one stitch

Crochet

Ch: chain

Ch sp: chain space

DC: double crochet; wrap yarn around hook, insert hook into stitch, wrap yarn around hook, draw hook through the stitch, wrap yarn around hook again and pull through 1st loop, wrap yarn around hook, pull through 1st two of remaining loops on hook, wrap yarn around hook, pull through two remaining loops on hook

Htr: half treble; wrap yarn around hook, insert hook into stitch, wrap yarn around hook, draw hook through the stitch, wrap yarn around hook again, and pull through all three loops on hook

Rem: remaining

Rep: repeat

SC: single crochet; insert hook into stitch, wrap yarn around hook, draw hook through the stitch, wrap yarn around hook, and pull through both loops on hook

Sk: skip next stitch

Index

Acknowledgments

May I extend my grateful thanks to all the team at New Holland, in particular Emma Pattison. Thanks Emma for seeing to everything and making the book the best it can be.
A very big thank you also to Rosemary Wilkinson for taking the Knitted Bears on board.

And thanks to my own little, but growing fast, bears—Harry, May, and James.

relationships (Bell et al., 1986). Others focus specifically on the attachments you have to other people in close relationships (e.g., Bartholomew & Horowitz, 1991; Carver, 1997a; Collins & Read, 1990; Griffin & Bartholomew, 1994; Simpson, 1990).

The object-relations measure of Bell et al. (1986) is a good illustration of content assessed from this viewpoint. It has four scales. The *alienation* scale measures a lack of basic trust and an inability to be close. People high on this scale are suspicious, guarded, and isolated, convinced that others will fail them. This resembles avoidant attachment. Another scale measures *insecure attachment,* which resembles the ambivalent pattern, a sensitivity to rejection and concern about being liked and accepted. The third scale, *egocentricity,* assesses narcissism, a self-protective and exploitive attitude toward relationships and a tendency to view others only in relation to one's own needs and aims. The final scale measures *social incompetence,* shyness and uncertainty about how to engage in even simple social interactions.

A different approach to assessment is the open-ended measure of Blatt et al. (1979). It has a coding system to assess the maturity of people's perceptions of social relations. This measure asks you to describe your mother and father. If you're at a low level of maturity, you tend to focus on how parents acted to satisfy your needs. Higher-level descriptions focus more on parents' values, thoughts, and feelings apart from your needs. At a very high level, the description takes into account internal contradictions in the parent and changes over time. This measure reflects a person's level of separation and individuation from the parent.

PLAY IN ASSESSMENT

Another facet of the psychosocial view on assessment reflects the emphasis on experiences of childhood as determinants of personality. As a result, this view deals with child assessment more than others. The assessment of children tends to emphasize the use of play as a tool. It's often said that children's play reveals their preoccupations (e.g., Axline, 1947, 1964; Erikson, 1963; M. Klein, 1935, 1955a, 1955b). Play lets them express their concerns in ways they can't do in words. Erikson (1963) devised a play situation using a specific set of toys on a table. The child is to imagine that the table is a movie studio and the toys are actors and sets.

The child is to create a scene and describe what's happening. Other techniques use less structured settings, but elements almost always include a variety of dolls (e.g., mother, father, older person, children, baby). This permits children to choose characters that relate to their own concerns or preoccupations.

The play situation is projective, because the child imposes a story on ambiguous stimuli. It often has two objective characteristics, however. First is a *behavioral record*. This includes what the child says about the scene and a description of the scene and the sequence of steps taken to create it. Second, the face value of the child's behavior receives more attention than is usual in projectives. It isn't automatically assumed that the child's behavior has deeply hidden meanings.

...veal their feelings through play.

generativity reflects a shift in focus from one close relationship (intimacy) to a broader concern with society as a whole.

Consistent with this idea, highly generative persons express high levels of commitment to assisting the next generation; they also show an integration between that commitment and a sense of agency (Mansfield & McAdams, 1996; see also de St. Aubin, McAdams, & Kim, 2004; McAdams, Diamond, de St. Aubin, & Mansfield, 1997). Once the quality of generativity emerges, it may continue through the rest of one's life (Zucker, Ostrove, & Stewart, 2002).

Adults who fail to develop this sense of generativity drift into stagnation. *Stagnation* is an inability or unwillingness to give of oneself to the future. These people are preoccupied with their own concerns. They have a self-centered or self-indulgent quality that keeps them from deeper involvement in the world around them. There's also evidence that an absence of generativity is related to poorer psychological well-being (Vandewater, Ostrove, & Stewart, 1997).

If there's a positive balance of generativity, the ego quality that emerges is care. *Care* is a widening concern for whatever you've generated in your life, be it children, something in your work, or something that emerged from your involvement with other people.

OLD AGE

The final stage is maturity, or old age. This is the closing chapter of people's lives. It's a time when people look back and review the choices they made and reflect on their accomplishments (and failures) and on the turns their lives have taken (see also Box 11.2). The crisis here is termed *ego integrity versus despair.* If you emerge from this review feeling that your life has had order and meaning, accepting the choices you made and the things you did, a sense of ego integrity emerges. This is a sense of satisfaction, a feeling that you wouldn't change much about your life.

The opposite pole of this conflict is despair: the feeling that your life was wasted. It's a sense of wishing you'd done things differently but knowing that it's too late. Instead of accepting your life's story as a valuable gift, there's bitterness that things turned out as they did.

Emerging from this life review with a sense of integrity creates the ego quality of *wisdom.* Wisdom involves meaning making and benevolence (Helson & Srivastava, 2002). It is an active concern with life and continued personal growth, even as one confronts the impending reality of death (see also Baltes & Staudinger, 1993; Kunzmann & Baltes, 2003).

THE EPIGENETIC PRINCIPLE

One more issue to address about Erikson's theory is that a given conflict is presumed to exist outside the stage in which it's focal. In the science of embryology, **epigenesis** is the process by which a single cell turns into a complex organism. For this process to occur requires a "blueprint" at the beginning, with instructions for all the changes and their sequencing. Erikson applied this idea to his theory, saying that there's a readiness for each crisis at birth. The core issue of each crisis is especially focal during a particular stage, but all of the issues are always there.

The principle of epigenesis has several implications. For one, as already indicated, it means your orientation to a particular crisis is influenced by the outcomes of earlier ones. It also means that in resolving the core crisis of any stage, you're preparing solutions (in simple form) for the ones coming later. As you deal in adolescence with the conflict between ego identity and role confusion, you're also

BOX 11.2 IS THERE A MIDLIFE CRISIS?

From Erikson's point of view, the last years of life are spent in review, examining choices that were made, values that were pursued, and passions that were abandoned. Erikson saw this review as coming late in life, after the opportunity to make changes has passed.

Others have also talked about a life review (Gould, 1980; Levinson, 1978; Stewart & Vandewater, 1999; Vaillant, 1977) but one that occurs earlier, around age 40 or so. Given its timing, the phenomenon is popularly referred to as the *midlife crisis*. It's a questioning of the decisions you've made over your adult years, the validity and worth of your goals, the adequacy of your life situation—nearly everything about your existence. It's a time of re-evaluation, but it's also a chance to change the way things are before it's too late. If you don't like your life, change it: remake decisions, rearrange your priorities, change careers, change your marriage (or leave it).

The notion of a midlife crisis rests partly on the typical course of life's major events in Western culture. It's common in the United States to finish college and take a job in one's early

20s and to marry and start raising a family in one's 20s and 30s. Depending on when the children are born, they're growing up and leaving home when the parents are in their 40s or early 50s. Around that time, it's also common to experience the death of one or both of one's own parents. Many changes of midlife are profound ones. Is it any wonder that they seem to cry out for a re-evaluation of life?

Another contributor to a crisis is cultural assumptions about the timing of these events. As a result, people do a certain amount of checking to see whether their lives are "on schedule." If you're in your mid-30s, are you making as much money as you're supposed to be? Are you in line for the career advancement you planned on? If you're nearing 40 with no children, you may hear the so-called biological clock ticking, telling you that you'll never have that experience if you don't hurry. Comparing your life against these markers of a "normal" life can produce a lot of soul searching.

Is there a midlife crisis? We're inclined to feel there's some truth to the idea. We know the feelings we've just written about. (We also know why one of us bought a motorcycle some years ago.) People do experience

regrets at midlife, and that does cause some people (though not all) to make life changes (Stewart & Vandewater, 1999).

Yet the evidence doesn't indicate that a real midlife crisis is all that common. Two longitudinal studies found little support for the idea in fairly large samples (Clausen, 1981; Haan, 1981). On the other hand, the participants in those studies lived through some very hard times—the Great Depression and World War II—and it's possible that having survived those experiences made them less likely to re-evaluate their choices and goals at midlife. Perhaps the midlife crisis is actually a baby-boomer phenomenon.

Alternatively, it may be that the midlife crisis isn't so much a matter of midlife as it is a reflection of a more consistent tendency to worry. This conclusion would fit with findings obtained by Costa and McCrae (1980) concerning life satisfaction over time. They found that satisfaction was relatively stable across a period of 10 years and that dissatisfaction related to the broad trait of neuroticism. Maybe, then, people who are inclined to worry do so throughout life, and it just happens to be more obvious at midlife.

moving toward handling the crisis of intimacy versus isolation. Finally, this principle means that crises aren't resolved once and for all. Your resolutions of previous conflicts are revisited and reshaped at each new stage of life (Whitbourne, Zuschlag, Elliot, & Waterman, 1992).

IDENTITY AS LIFE STORY

The sense of the epigenetic principle is well conveyed in some of the work of Dan McAdams. His work focuses partly on motivations that underlie personality (discussed in Chapter 5) and partly on the idea that people construct their identities as narratives, or life stories (McAdams, 1985, 1993, 2001). In his view, your story is never completed until the end of your life. It is constantly being written. Indeed, it's constantly under revision, just as your identity is constantly evolving.

As in any good book, the opening chapters of your narrative begin setting the stage for things that happen much later. Sometimes future events are foreshadowed; some-

times things that happen in early chapters create conditions that have to be rea later on. As chapters pile up, characters reinterpret events they experienced ea understand them in different ways. All the pieces eventually come together int and integrated picture, and the picture that results has qualities from everythin happened throughout the story. McAdams thus sees the broad crisis of identity that continues to occupy each person throughout life (McAdams, 2001).

Of interest is how categories of narrative themes show up in many p lives. McAdams and his colleagues have found that highly generative midlife often report life stories in which they had early advantages, became aware of t fering of others, established a personal belief system that involved prosocial and committed themselves to benefiting society. McAdams calls these *comm stories*. Often these commitment stories also contain *redemption themes*, in w bad situation somehow is transformed into something good (McAdams, McAdams, Reynolds, Lewis, Patten, & Bowman, 2001). Indeed, the link fro sense of redemption to the quality of generativity appears quite strong (McA 2006). Adults who are low in generativity sometimes have stories involving *a ination themes*, in which a good situation somehow turns bad.

LINKING ERIKSON'S THEORY TO OTHER PSYCHOSOCIAL THEORIES

Let's look back to the theories discussed earlier in this chapter to make a final Those theories represent contributions of their own. Yet in a sense, the fundar theme of each is the same as that of the first crisis in Erikson's theory: basic trust basic mistrust. That's a big part of what security in attachment is about. It implicit in object relations theories. This issue is also the core of Erikson's own t providing the critical foundation on which the rest of personality is built.

Humans seem to need to be able to trust in the relationships that sustain our In the minds of many theorists, that trust is necessary for adequate functioning. F who are deeply mistrustful of relationships or are constantly frightened about bly losing relationships have lives that are damaged and distorted. The damage be slight, or it may be significant. Avoiding such mistrust and doubt (or recogn and overcoming it, if it's already there) seems a central task in human existence.

Assessment

Let's turn now to assessment from the psychosocial viewpoint. In general, assess here is similar to that of the ego psychologists. There are two aspects of assessr however, that are specific to this view.

OBJECT RELATIONS, ATTACHMENT, AND THE FOCUS OF ASSESSMENT

One difference concerns what's being assessed. The psychosocial approach plac greater emphasis than other approaches on assessing the person orientation to tionships.

There are several ways in which a person's mental model of relationships m be assessed. Relevant measures range from some that are open ended in nature (Blatt, Wein, Chevron, & Quinlan, 1979) to structured self-reports (e.g., Billington, & Becker, 1986). Some measures assess a range of issues pertainin

Children ofte

Problems in Behavior, and Behavior Change

Given that psychosocial theorists focus on the nature of people's relationships, it's natural that they see problems as reflecting relationship difficulties. Here are three examples of how this approach applies to problems in behavior.

NARCISSISM AS A DISORDER OF PERSONALITY

One psychosocial view focuses specifically on **narcissism** as a disorder. Indeed, this disorder was the starting point for Kohut's work on the self. Pathological narcissism involves a sense that everyone and everything is an extension of the self or exists to serve the self. There's a grandiose sense of self-importance and need for constant attention. Narcissists show a sense of *entitlement,* of deserving others' adulation. As a result, they often exploit others.

Recall that Kohut said everyone begins life with a grandiose narcissism, which is tempered during development. Some people never escape it, however. To Kohut, inadequate mirroring by parents frustrates the narcissistic needs and prevents formation of an adequate self-structure (Kohut, 1977). Similarly, Kernberg (1976, 1980) said that narcissism arises from parental rejection. The child comes to believe that the only person who can be trusted (and therefore loved) is himself or herself. Fitting this picture, narcissists prefer romantic partners who are admiring over those who offer intimacy (Campbell, 1999). They're also less committed in their relationships, always on the lookout for someone better (Campbell & Foster, 2002).

Unmet narcissistic needs can cause a person to distort reality in several ways in an effort to satisfy those unmet needs. For example, narcissistic people are more likely to inflate their judgments of their own performances in various arenas of life than are less narcissistic people (John & Robins, 1994). If threatened by being told that someone else has outperformed them, they're more likely to put the other person down (Morf & Rhodewalt, 1993).

Narcissists may seem quite agreeable at first, but they wear on other people after a while (Paulhus, 1998). They are very responsive to opportunities for self-enhancement (Wallace & Baumeister, 2002). They love to take credit for successes but respond to failure or criticism with anger (Rhodewalt & Morf, 1998). Indeed, narcissists may erupt in extremes of rage if their desires are thwarted (Bushman & Baumeister, 1998; Stucke & Sporer, 2002) or they experience social rejection (Twenge & Campbell, 2003). This can be a real problem, because they are especially likely to view themselves as victims (McCullough, Emmons, Kilpatrick, & Mooney, 2003).

BASIC ANXIETY, VICIOUS CYCLES, AND NEUROTIC NEEDS

Another way of thinking about problems comes from ideas proposed by Karen Horney (see Box 11.3). Horney (1937, 1945) held that from childhood on, people have a sense of insecurity she called **basic anxiety.** This is a feeling of being abandoned, of being isolated and helpless in a hostile world. It can be minimized by being raised in a home where there's security, trust, love, warmth, and tolerance, but it's there in everyone.

Horney coined the term **vicious cycle** to refer to a pattern that basic anxiety often induces. Feeling insecure increases awareness of the need for love. If the need isn't met through whatever strategies are available (and often it isn't), the result is more anxiety and insecurity. Only if the need for affection is met is the cycle broken.

BOX 11.3 THE THEORIST AND THE THEORY

Karen Horney's Feminism

Karen Horney (pronounced "horn-eye") focused on general themes, such as the role of basic anxiety in behavior, but she also had much to say regarding the psychoanalytic view of women. She was a vocal critic of Freud, believing that he'd managed to get nearly everything wrong.

Recall that Freud believed a woman's life is deeply affected by the fact that she has no penis. According to him, women feel castrated and inferior, and they envy and resent men because of it. Horney came to a very different view (see Quinn, 1987). Her feelings of pleasure and pride in childbirth and motherhood led her to realize how shallow the comparable experiences of men were. Men play a minor role in creating and nurturing new life, and Horney came to think that this causes them to have a deep sense of inferiority. This idea was confirmed in her therapy experiences with men, who

gave considerable evidence of envying women's ability to have children.

One result of men's feelings of inferiority is an attempt to compensate through achievement. The world of business is an attempt to *create,* although such creations can never compare to creating a baby. Besides these efforts to compensate, men try to hide their inferiorities by disparaging and devaluing women. By denying women equal rights, men can hide from themselves the fact that they can never be as valuable to human society as women.

Horney argued forcefully that the tendency of women to feel inferior arises not from penis envy but from the cultural context in which they live. If women regard themselves as unworthy, it's because men have treated them that way for so long. It isn't penises that women want but the ability to participate as full members of society. (Horney was born in 1885, so keep in mind that the culture in which she lived was more restrictive than that of today.)

How did Freud feel about all this? He never responded directly to Horney's arguments, but late in life, he wrote something that probably was aimed in her direction: "We shall not be very greatly surprised if a woman analyst who has not been sufficiently convinced of the intensity of her own wish for a penis also fails to attach proper importance to that factor in her patients" (Freud, 1949/1940). To Freud, Horney's theory arose from her own penis envy.

Horney took many positions that anticipated and foreshadowed later developments in psychological theory and in Western culture more broadly. Her feminist stance was no exception. She did much to create the outline of a feminist agenda for the future. She argued that a woman's identity is not to be found in the mere reflection of her husband. Rather, a woman should seek her own identity by developing her abilities and pursuing a career. Truly, Karen Horney was a woman ahead of her time.

People develop strategies to combat basic anxiety. One is to strike back against people who abandon them. Another is trying to win back love by being submissive, never doing anything that could antagonize others. Another is growing an inflated self-concept to compensate for insecurity (as in narcissism). Yet another is seeking power over others to compensate for feelings of loss.

Horney (1942) believed the strategies people use to combat basic anxiety can become a fixed part of personality if they're used too much. She made a list of needs that are acquired by trying to deal with problem relationships (see Table 11.4). She called them **neurotic needs** because they aren't effective solutions to the problem. Instead, they often lead into vicious cycles.

Horney argued that these neurotic needs tend to result in three styles of acting, depending on whether the need moves you *toward* others, *away* from others, or *against* others (Horney, 1945, 1950). Neurotic needs for love and approval move you toward others but in clingy dependency (as in ambivalent attachment). Neurotic needs for independence and self-sufficiency move you away from others (as in the avoidant attachment pattern). Needs such as power and exploitation move you against others. As with all defenses, each can be useful but is problematic if it is used to an extreme. Indeed, extremes of the styles do relate to other measures of personality disorders (Coolidge, Moor, Yamazaki, Stewart, & Segal, 2001).

Table 11.4 Horney's List of Neurotic Needs (and a brief description of each). Each arises from overuse of various strategies of coping with anxiety. *Source:* Adapted from Horney, 1942, 1945.

Neurotic need for affection and approval	Having an indiscriminate wish to please others and live up to their expectations
	Having extreme sensitivity to any sign of rejection or unfriendliness
Neurotic need for a partner who will take over one's life	Feeling extremely afraid of being deserted and left alone
Neurotic need to restrict one's life within narrow borders	Being extremely undemanding, content with little, preferring to remain inconspicuous
Neurotic need for power	Craving power for its own sake, adoring strength and contempt for weakness
	May also be reflected in intellectual exploitation
Neurotic need to exploit others	Using others to your own advantage
Neurotic need for prestige	Basing your self-evaluation on public recognition
Neurotic need for personal admiration	Having an inflated picture of yourself and wishing to be admired for that, not for what you really are
Neurotic ambition for personal achievement	Wanting to be the very best and driving yourself to greater and greater achievements as a result of basic insecurity
Neurotic need for self-sufficiency and independence	Setting yourself apart from others, becoming a loner
	Refusing to be tied down to anyone or anything because of disappointment in attempts to find warm, satisfying relationships with people
Neurotic need for perfection and unassailability	Trying to make yourself impregnable and infallible
	Constantly searching for flaws in yourself so that they can be covered up before becoming obvious to others

Well-adapted people usually adopt one style at a time and shift from one to another flexibly as needed. This flexibility is the hallmark of good adaptation. People with problems rigidly adopt a single orientation, even in situations where one of the other styles might be more useful.

ATTACHMENT AND DEPRESSION

Another window on the nature of problems comes from the idea that an important cause of depression is interpersonal rejection, which has received a good deal of support (Blatt & Zuroff, 1992). Recall that the avoidant attachment pattern is also believed to be a product of neglectful or rejecting parenting, resulting in sadness, despair, and eventual emotional detachment (Carnelley, Pietromonaco, & Jaffe, 1994; Hazan & Shaver, 1994).

The avoidant attachment pattern has also been linked to development of emotional distress when under stress (Berant, Mikulincer, & Florian, 2001). Participants in this study were women who had found out two weeks earlier that their newborns had congenital heart disease. Those with avoidant (and those with anxious) attachment patterns were more distressed. Avoidant patterns also predicted further deterioration in emotional well-being a year later. Other research has also supported the idea that avoidant attachment is a risk factor for depression (Hankin, Kassel, & Abela, 2005).

It's been suggested that both the avoidant attachment pattern and the depression to which it relates can be passed from one generation to another. The argument is based on behavior, rather than genetics. The pattern you acquire as a child is the working model you bring to bear when you have children of your own. If you're an avoidant adult (due to parental rejection), and especially if you're a *depressed* avoidant adult, what kind of parent will you be? An emotionally distant one. You are likely to be experienced as a rejecting parent—not because you dislike your child but because you're so distant. Being emotionally unavailable, you may then create an avoidant child, just like you.

Thus, parents may transfer to the next generation precisely the attachment qualities that made them unhappy themselves. There's support for this line of reasoning on rejection and depression (Besser & Priel, 2005; Whitbeck et al., 1992). There's also evidence of transmission of an erratic pattern of adult behavior that may be tied to the ambivalent attachment pattern (Elder, Caspi, & Downey, 1986).

BEHAVIOR CHANGE

The process of therapeutic behavior change from the viewpoint of psychosocial theories reflects many of the themes we discussed for ego psychology. The techniques tend to focus on the here and now, and the person with the problem is seen as a collaborator in the therapeutic process.

Nevertheless, a few additional techniques were developed by people in the psychosocial tradition. For example, psychologists such as Erikson (1963), Virginia Axline (1947), and Melanie Klein (1955a, 1955b) developed **play therapy** techniques for use with children. These techniques give the child the opportunity to do as he or she wishes, without pressuring, intruding, prodding, or nagging. Under these conditions, children can have distance from others (if they are worried about being smothered by a too ever present parent) or can play out anger or the wish for closeness (if they're feeling rejected or unwanted). The playroom is the child's world. In it, children have the opportunity to bring their feelings to the surface, deal with them, and potentially change their working models of relationships and of the self in positive ways (Landreth, 1991).

Because object relations and self-theories emphasize the role of relationships in problems, they also emphasize relationships as part of the therapeutic process. Therapists try to provide the kind of relationship the patient needs so he or she can reintegrate problematic parts of the self. Healing is brought about by providing a successful experience of narcissism or attachment (almost a kind of re-parenting), replacing the earlier emotional failure.

These therapy techniques can be seen as representing a way of restoring to the person's life a sense of connectedness to others. By modifying the representations of relationships that were built in the past, they permit the developing of more satisfying relationships in the future. The optimism that this approach holds about being able to undo problematic experiences from the past is reflected in the saying "It's never too late to have a happy childhood."

Psychosocial Theories: Problems and Prospects

As was true of ego psychology, the psychosocial neoanalytic approach is home to many theorists. Although they had different starting points, there's a remarkable consistency in the themes behind their work. Each assumes that human relationships are the most important part of human life and that how relationships are managed is a core issue in personality. Each tends to assume that people develop working models of relationships in early experience, which then are used to frame new ones. Also implied is the idea that health requires a balance between being separate and being closely connected to someone (see also Helgeson, 1994, 2003; Helgeson & Fritz, 1999).

A strength of psychosocial theories is that they point us in directions that other theories don't. Thinking about personality in terms of attachment patterns, for example, suggests hypotheses that aren't readily derived from other viewpoints. Work based in attachment theory is leading to a better understanding of how personality plays out in social relations. This picture of this aspect of personality would very likely not have emerged without having the attachment model as a starting point. Furthermore, linking the themes of attachment to models of greater complexity, such as Erikson's, creates a picture of change and evolution across the life span that would be nearly impossible to derive from other viewpoints. The psychosocial viewpoint clearly adds something of great importance to our understanding of personality.

This is not to say that no unresolved issues remain for this approach. One important issue concerns a rather sharp clash between this view and the view of trait psychologists and behavior geneticists. Manifestations of adult attachment patterns correspond well to genetically influenced traits. Avoidants are essentially introverts, secures are extraverts, and anxious–ambivalents are high in neuroticism. Do these patterns result from parenting, or are they genetically determined? There are strong opinions on both sides of this question. It's a question that will surely continue to be examined closely.

Indeed, in considering the prospects of this viewpoint for the future, we should note explicitly that research on psychosocial approaches is continuing full speed. Indeed, adult attachment and related ideas represent one of the most active areas of research in personality psychology today. The recent flood of research on this topic shows no sign of abating (Mikulincer & Shaver, 2007; Rholes & Simpson, 2004). Research on the implications of attachment patterns for the life of the child—and the adult—promises to yield interesting new insights into the human experience. The prospects of this area of work seem very bright, as do the prospects for the approach more generally.

· SUMMARY ·

Psychosocial theories emphasize the idea that personality is intrinsically social and that the important issues of personality concern how people relate to others. Several psychosocial theories focus on early life. Mahler's object relations theory proposes that infants begin life merged psychologically with their mothers and that they separate and individuate during the first 3 years of life. How this takes place influences later adjustment.

Kohut's self psychology resembles object relations theory. He said humans have narcissistic needs that are satisfied by other people, represented as *selfobjects*. If the child receives enough mirroring (positive attention) from selfobjects (chiefly the mother), the sense of self develops appropriately. If there's too much mirroring, the child won't be able to deal with frustrations. If there's too little, the development of the self will be stunted.

Some of these ideas are echoed in the work of attachment theorists such as Bowlby and Ainsworth. Secure attachment provides a solid base for exploration. There are also patterns of insecure attachment (ambivalent and avoidant), which stem from inconsistent treatment, neglect, or rejection. There's increasing interest in the idea that infant attachment patterns persist and influence adult personality. There is now a great deal of work on this topic, assessing adult attachment in several ways. Although people do display diverse ways of relating across their social connections, a core tendency seems to exist. Adult attachment patterns influence many aspects of behavior, including how people relate to work activities and how they seek and give emotional support, as well as how they relate to romantic partners.

Another important theory of the psychosocial group is Erikson's theory of psychosocial development. Erikson postulated a series of crises from infancy to late adulthood, giving rise to ego strengths that influence one's ego identity: the consciously experienced sense of self. Erikson assumed that each crisis becomes focal at one stage but that each is present in a less obvious form throughout life.

The first crisis concerns the development of a sense of *basic trust*. The child then becomes concerned with control over its body and the sense of *autonomy* that comes with that. The next issue is *initiative,* as the child seeks to exercise its power. As children enter the school years, they begin to realize that the social environment demands being *industrious*. With adolescence, the child enters a new stage of life and has a crisis over *identity*. In young adulthood, identity issues give way to concern over *intimacy*. In adulthood, the person's concern is over *generativity*. Finally, in the last stage of life, people confront the *integrity* of their lives as a whole.

Assessment techniques from the psychosocial view are similar to those of ego psychology but focus more on relationships. This approach also leads to use of play for assessment with children. The psychosocial view of problems focuses on the idea that problems are rooted in relationship issues. Kohut suggested that pathological narcissism stems from inadequate childhood mirroring. Horney suggested that people suffer from basic anxiety, a feeling of being abandoned, isolated, and alone. People develop strategies to cope with this, but doing so can lead to a vicious cycle of increased anxiety. Strategies for dealing with basic anxiety often involve moving toward, away from, or against other people. Adaptive functioning involves flexibly shifting from one strategy to another as needed. Poor adjustment comes from rigid reliance on one strategy. Insecure attachment seems to create a risk for depression.

These theories approach therapy in ways similar to those of ego psychology, but there are additional variations. One of them is play therapy for children. Object relations and attachment theories also suggest that a relationship with a therapist is critical in permitting reintegration of the sense of self or establishing a sense of secure attachment.

· GLOSSARY ·

Attachment   An emotional connection to someone else.

Basic anxiety   A sense of insecurity, a feeling of being abandoned and isolated.

Ego identity   The overall sense of self that emerges from transactions with social reality.

Ego quality (ego strength or virtue)   The quality that becomes part of one's personality through successful management of a crisis.

Epigenesis   The idea (adopted from embryology) that an internal plan for future development is present at the beginning of life.

Identity commitment   The adoption of a specific identity.

Identity crisis   A time of intense exploration of alternative ways of viewing oneself.

Identity status   The condition of whether an identity crisis has occurred and whether an identity has been attained.

Life-span development   The idea that developmental processes continue throughout life.

Mirroring   The giving of positive attention and supportiveness to someone.

Narcissism   A sense of grandiose self-importance and entitlement.

Neurotic needs   Maladaptive needs that emerge from overuse of strategies to combat basic anxiety.

Object relations   An individual's symbolized relations to other persons (such as parents).

Play therapy   The use of play as a procedure for conducting therapy with children.

Psychosocial crisis (or conflict)   A period when some interpersonal issue is being dealt with and growth potential and vulnerability are both high.

Self psychology   Kohut's theory that relationships create the structure of the self.

Selfobject   The mental symbol of another person who serves functions for oneself.

Separation–individuation   The process of acquiring a distinct identity; separating from fusion with the mother.

Strange situation   A procedure used to assess the attachment pattern of infant to mother.

Symbiosis   A period in which an infant experiences fusion with the mother.

Transference   The viewing of other people through selfobject representations originally developed for parents.

Vicious cycle   A cycle of needing affection, failing to obtain it, and thereby increasing the need.

PART

6

The Learning Perspective

The Learning Perspective:
Major Themes and Underlying Assumptions

The experiences of life change us, and they do so in ways that are lawful and predictable. This is the central assumption of the learning perspective on personality. People have been interested in the processes of learning for a long time. At first, this interest was confined largely to those who studied lower animals. At first, this interest also focused primarily on small bits of behavior.

As knowledge grew, however, a tantalizing possibility began to take shape. The suspicion grew that the principles of learning might constitute the basic building blocks of behavior. All behavior. Not just the actions of rats in laboratory cages, but also the more complex actions of human beings in the world. *Personality,* from this point of view, is an accumulated set of learned tendencies. It's all the tendencies a person has learned over the course of a lifetime's experiences.

It's sometimes said that the basic metaphor of the learning perspective is the person as a white rat. In a sense, this is true, because many who take this perspective on behavior assume that learning processes are *universal,* that is, they are the same in virtually all animals. In that sense, a human being is nothing more than a very complex version of the rats and mice that occupy the attention (and the cages) of many scientists who study the learning process. This metaphor has been accepted by many of the learning theorists who've applied their findings to personality. The principles that they've focused on are discussed in Chapter 12.

Although this metaphor was useful as a starting place, many learning theorists ultimately came to believe that it's too simple. The processes of human learning began to appear more complex than they'd seemed at first. The result was the need for a more elaborated metaphor, along with more elaborate theories of learning. In the new metaphor, the human being is still a learner, but now a more self-directive learner and a learner whose knowledge can accumulate in great leaps, rather than just small increments. The learning is also seen as involving a set of cognitions, which play an important role themselves in behavior. The theories that draw on that expanded metaphor are discussed in Chapter 13.

The learning perspective on personality has also sparked something of a philosophical argument, which evolved and shifted as did the learning approach itself. In simple terms, the argument is about where behavior is *controlled*. Is behavior controlled from *within* the person, or is it controlled by events and processes *outside* the person? The analysis of behavior offered by the earliest learning theorists argued that behavior is shaped by external events, by stimuli and outcomes imposed from the environment. This assumption wasn't viewed with enthusiasm by everyone, perhaps partly because it doesn't offer a very flattering portrayal of human nature. More recently, many learning theorists have backed away from this assumption.

Nevertheless, one theme remains constant within the framework of the learning perspective across its two variants: Changes in behavior occur in predictable ways as a result of experience. By extrapolation, personality must also be susceptible to molding, grinding, and polishing by the events that form the person's unique and individual history.

Conditioning Theories

Lisa has a fondness for pastels. When asked why, she looks sort of blank and says she doesn't know, but she's felt that way at least since her eighth birthday, when she had the most wonderful surprise party, decorated all in pale pink, green, and violet.

Ann works hard at her job at the library. She bustles from meeting to meeting, smoothing disagreements among people she works with and making it easier for them to get their projects done. People express their appreciation in many ways—smiles, thanks, and last month a promotion to staff coordinator. The more signs she gets that she's doing a good job, the more enthusiasm she puts into each new morning.

W HY ARE these people the way they are? Why do people have the preferences they have? What makes one person put a lot of effort into her work when someone else doesn't? One answer is that these aspects of behavior, which contribute so much to the individuality of personality, are acquired through learning.

The beginnings of what would become the *learning perspective* on personality go back a long way. The puzzle of just how learning takes place—what the elements of the process are—intrigued scientists all over the world. The puzzle isn't fully solved even yet. For example, there remain disagreements about whether learning is one process that has several manifestations or whether there are several distinct processes (e.g., Locurto, Terrace, & Gibbon, 1980; Rescorla, 1987; Staats, 1996).

From the learning perspective, personality consists of all the tendencies you've learned during the experiences of your life. If personality is the residue of learning, then it's important to know how learning works. In this part of the chapter, we focus on broad principles of learning (for more see, e.g., B. Schwartz, 1989). For ease in presentation, we'll adopt the view implicitly taken by most people: that there are distinct types of learning that have their own rules. This chapter focuses on forms of learning called *conditioning.* Much of the work on these processes has used animals other than humans. Nonetheless, many people think these processes underlie the human qualities we know as *personality.*

Classical Conditioning

One of the early findings in the effort to understand learning was that responses could be acquired by associating one stimulus with another. This type of learning is called **classical conditioning**. It's sometimes also called *Pavlovian conditioning,* after the Russian scientist Ivan Pavlov, whose work opened the door to understanding it (e.g., Pavlov, 1927, 1955).

BASIC ELEMENTS

Classical conditioning seems to require two things. First, the organism must already respond to some class of stimuli reflexively. That is, the response must occur *reliably and automatically whenever the stimulus occurs*. A **reflex** thus is an existing connection between a stimulus and a response, such that the one causes the other to happen.

Consider some examples of reflexes from day-to-day experience. When you put something dry, acidic, or sour in your mouth (lemonade, tart candy), you start to salivate. When you see an object suddenly increase in size, as though it's approaching rapidly, you reflexively draw back. When skin near sexual organs is rubbed, you feel sexual excitement. When you touch a hot car door, you automatically yank your hand away. When someone smiles warmly at you, you automatically feel good. These reactions happen reflexively for most people. Some are innate and some are learned, but in each case, a stimulus leads directly and reliably to a particular response.

The second condition needed for classical conditioning is that the stimulus in the reflex has to become associated in time and place with another stimulus. The second stimulus is usually (though not always) *neutral* at first. That is, by itself it causes no particular response beyond being noticed. There aren't any special requirements for this stimulus. It can be pretty much anything—a color, a sound, an object, a person.

For clarity, people often describe classical conditioning in terms of several stages (see Figure 12.1). The first stage is the situation *before* conditioning happens. At this point, only the reflex exists—a stimulus causing an automatic response. This stimulus is termed the **unconditioned** or **unconditional stimulus (US)**. The response it touches off is called the **unconditioned** or **unconditional response (UR)**. The word *unconditional* here means there's no special condition required for the response to occur. It's automatic when the stimulus occurs (see Figure 12.1, A).

The second stage is when conditioning takes place. In this stage, the neutral stimulus occurs along with, or slightly before, the US (Figure 12.1, B). The neutral stimulus now gets a technical name: **conditioned** or **conditional stimulus (CS)**. We suggest two ways to keep track of what that means. First, this is the stimulus that's becoming *conditioned*. Second, a response occurs in the presence of this stimulus only under a specific condition: that the US be there as well. When the US comes, the UR

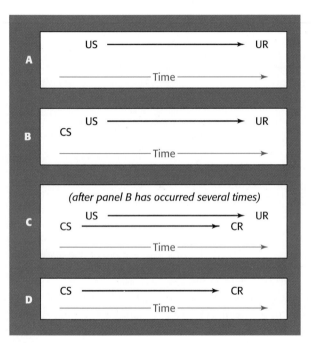

FIGURE 12.1

The various stages of a typical classical conditioning procedure (time runs left to right in each panel): (A) There is a pre-existing reflexive connection between a stimulus (US) and a response (UR). (B) A neutral stimulus (CS) is then paired repeatedly in time and space with the US. (C) The result is the development of a new response, termed a *conditioned response (CR)*. (D) Once conditioning has occurred, presenting the CS by itself will now lead to the CR.

Table 12.1 Illustrations of the Elements of Classical Conditioning in Two Common Research Procedures (A and B) in One Common Childhood Experience (C) and in One Common Adult Experience. Note that the elements are arranged here in terms of stimulus and the associated response, not in time sequence.

	US	UR	CS	CR
A.	Lemon juice in mouth	Salivation	Tone	Salivation
B.	Shock to foot	Pain	Light	Fear
C.	Ice cream in mouth	Pleasant taste	Sight of ice cream	Happiness
D.	Romantically enticing partner	Sexual arousal	Mood music	Sexual arousal

follows automatically, reflexively (and remember that it does so *whenever* the US is presented, whether something else is there or not).

When the US and the CS are paired frequently, something gradually starts to change (see Figure 12.1, C). The CS starts to acquire the ability to produce a response *of its own*. This response is termed the **conditioned** or **conditional response (CR)**. The CR is often very similar to the UR. Indeed, in some cases they look identical (Table 12.1, row A), except that the CR is less intense than the UR. In other cases, the two can be distinguished. There is, however, a key similarity: Specifically, if the UR has an unpleasant quality, so will the CR (Table 12.1, row B). If the UR has a pleasant quality, so will the CR (Table 12.1, rows C and D).

How does any of this apply to you? Let's go back to the examples used earlier to illustrate reflexes. Suppose you've started squandering your late evenings at a bar specializing in Italian wines and Sicilian folk music. Every time you take a sip of the very dry Chianti (US), your salivary glands pump like crazy (UR) because of the acidity. This reflexive event is surrounded by the strains of Sicilian folk songs (CS). Eventually, you may come to develop a salivation response (CR) to the music itself.

As another example, suppose that while in that little bar, you meet someone (US) who induces in you an astonishingly high degree of sexual arousal (UR). As you bask in candlelight, surrounded by green wine bottles, crimson wallpaper, and the soft strains of a Sicilian love song (all CSs), you may be acquiring a conditioned sexual response (CR) to those previously neutral features of the setting. Candlelight may never be the same again. The song you're hearing may gain a special place in your heart.

If you know that a US has occurred repeatedly along with a neutral stimulus, how do you know whether conditioning has taken place? To find out, present the CS by itself—without the US (see Figure 12.1, D). If the CS (alone) gets a reaction, conditioning has occurred. If there's no reaction, there's been no conditioning. Generally speaking, the more frequently the CS is paired with the US, the more likely conditioning is to occur. If a US is very strong, however—causing a very intense UR—conditioning may occur with only one pairing. For example, cancer patients undergoing chemotherapy often experience extreme nausea from the medication and develop very strong CRs to surrounding stimuli after only one exposure.

CLASSICAL CONDITIONING AS ANTICIPATORY LEARNING

It has been suggested that CRs represent anticipatory reactions (Rescorla, 1972; Zener, 1937). That is, although CRs are involuntary, they seem to reflect anticipation of, or preparation for, an impending US. Think of the earlier examples. If a tone sounds before lemon juice hits your mouth, the tone is a signal that the lemon will arrive shortly. The CR (salivation) prepares the surface of your mouth for the acidity of the lemon. If a child hears his father's steps coming up the stairs just before he gets a spanking, the steps signal the spanking and the reflexive pain. The CR (fear and perhaps trembling) reflect anticipation of the pain.

Another clue that CRs may involve anticipation comes from studies of timing. We said earlier that conditioning occurs through the more or less simultaneous presentation of the US and the CS. But conditioning is actually most effective if the CS slightly *precedes* the US (as in Figure 12.1). It's less effective if the two come at once. It's even *less* so if the CS comes *after* the US (e.g., Schneiderman & Gormezano, 1964; Spetch, Wilkie, & Pinel, 1981; Spooner & Kellogg, 1947). This also makes it look as though an anticipatory reaction is being developed.

Don't necessarily assume that the anticipatory reaction is a *conscious* anticipation of the US. The tone needn't evoke the image of lemon juice. The sound of steps needn't lead to an inference that a spanking is coming. By one sort of analysis, the CR is connected *to the CS itself,* not to an image of the US that comes to mind. The CS and the reaction to it are assumed to be bound together at this point, so the one reflexively produces the other.

On the other hand, today's learning theorists tend to see things a little differently (Mowrer & Klein, 2001). In particular, many accounts of classical conditioning now emphasize the idea that a link forms between the nervous system's representation of the US and its representation of the CS. (See Box 12.1 for more detail on some of the complexities of this view.) The link may not be represented in consciousness, but it is represented somewhere in the learning system. In this view, networks of links are formed among various stimuli through pairing, as well as from stimuli to responses.

Once conditioning has taken place, the CS–CR combination acts just like any other reflex. That is, once it's solidly there, this combination can serve as US and UR for another instance of conditioning (see Figure 12.2). Once soft candlelight has been conditioned to cause sexual arousal, candlelight itself can be used to condition arousal to other things, such as particular *meals* you eat by candlelight. This process is termed **higher-order conditioning.**

This process means that conditioning can be very pervasive. There are limitations, of course. The most potent USs are those that elicit very intense URs. The farther away you get from biological reflexes, the weaker the reflexes are, and the weaker is the conditioning.

DISCRIMINATION, GENERALIZATION, AND EXTINCTION IN CLASSICAL CONDITIONING

Classical conditioning provides a mechanism for new responses to become attached to neutral stimuli. Yet the CS almost never takes precisely the same form later as it did earlier. On the other hand, you do run across many stimuli later that are somewhat similar to the CS. What happens in these cases?

The answer comes through the concepts **discrimination** and **generalization.** *Discrimination* means telling things apart. More formally, it means responding differently to different stimuli. For example, suppose your experiences in the Sicilian wine bar have led you to associate candlelight, muted crimson wallpaper, and wine bottles (as CSs) with sexual arousal (as CR). If you entered a room that very closely resembled the bar (all other things being equal), you'd begin to feel a mellow glow (your CR). If you walked instead into a room with fluorescent lights and blue walls, that

BOX 12.1 WHAT'S GOING ON IN CLASSICAL CONDITIONING?

Classical conditioning has been part of psychology courses for decades. In most accounts, it's a process that was well mapped out early in the development of learning theory, and there's been little new to add since then. Not everyone agrees with this, however (Mineka & Zinbarg, 2006).

Classical conditioning is usually portrayed as a low-level process in which control over a response gets transferred from one stimulus to another because they occur close together in time. Robert Rescorla (1988) said that's not the way it is. He said conditioning concerns *relations* among events in the world. In his view, organisms use their experiences of relations between parts of the world to represent reality. Rescorla went on to say that the association in time and place isn't what makes conditioning take place. Rather, what's important is the information one stimulus gives about the other. To Rescorla, learning is a process by which the organism's representation of the world is brought into line with the actual state of the world. Organisms learn only when they're "surprised" by something that happens to them.

As a result, two stimuli experienced together sometimes don't become associated (Kamin, 1968). For example, consider two animals. One has had a series of trials in which a light (as a CS) has been paired with a shock (as a US). The other hasn't had this experience. Both then get a series of trials in which both the light and a tone (as *two* CSs) are paired with the shock. The second animal acquires a CR to the tone, but the first one doesn't. Apparently, the earlier experience with the light has made the tone redundant. Because the light already signals that the US is coming, there's no need to condition to the tone, and it doesn't happen.

In the same way, studies have found that cancer patients undergoing chemotherapy can be induced to form conditioned aversions to very specific foods, if an unusual food is given before chemotherapy (Bernstein, 1985). Doing this can make that specific food a scapegoat and prevent the conditioning of aversions to other foods, which otherwise is very common.

Rescorla also challenges other aspects of the traditional view. He argues against the assumption that classical conditioning is a slow process, requiring many pairings of stimuli. He says, in fact, that learning in five to six

trials is common. In summarizing his stance, Rescorla said that classical conditioning "is not a stupid process by which the organism willy-nilly forms associations between any two stimuli that happen to co-occur. Rather, the organism is better seen as an information seeker using logical and perceptual relations among events, along with its own preconceptions, to form a sophisticated representation of the world" (1988, p. 154).

Rescorla is not alone in believing that internal events are more important in conditioning than previously realized. An analysis with somewhat similar characteristics (but even more cognitive in certain respects) was proposed by Holyoak, Koh, and Nisbett (1989). Their model is based in part on ideas from cognitive psychology linked to the term *connectionism* (McClelland & Rumelhart, 1986). The most important characteristic of that model for the issue we're raising here is that it treats classical conditioning as rule learning.

The positions taken by Rescorla and by Holyoak et al. are clearly at odds with the point of view that's expressed in the body of this chapter. The views they express also herald a broad issue that is more prominent in the next chapter: the role of cognition in learning.

---

mellow glow would surely not emerge. You would *discriminate*, in your conditioned reactions, between the two sets of stimuli.

Now a harder question: What would happen if you walked into a room with muted lamplight, walls painted burgundy, and green glass vases? These aren't quite the stimuli that got linked to sexual arousal, but they're close. Here's where the process of *generalization* comes in. In all probability, you'd start to feel the glow, although it might not be as strong as in the first room. As shown in Figure 12.3, generalization from conditioned stimuli definitely takes place. The intensity of the reaction falls off, though, as the stimulus gets further and further removed from the original CS (Hovland, 1937; Moore, 1972). To put it differently, generalization begins to give way to discrimination, as the stimuli become more different from the initial CS. Discrimination and generalization thus are complementary.

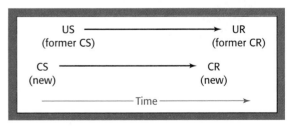

FIGURE 12.2

Once a link has been created between a CS and a CR by classical conditioning, that new reflex can serve as a US–UR pair for additional conditioning, termed *higher-order conditioning.*

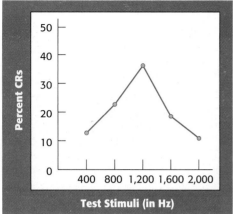

FIGURE 12.3
An illustration of generalization of a classically conditioned response to stimuli that are similar to the CS and of discrimination regarding stimuli that are less similar to the CS. The CS is a tone of 1,200 hertz (Hz). Tones that are similar to it (800, 1,600 Hz) elicit CRs—generalization. Tones that are less similar (400, 2,000 Hz) elicit fewer CRs—discrimination. *Source: Data from Moore, 1972, combined across two groups.*

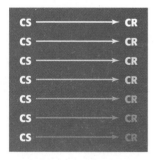

FIGURE 12.4
Extinction in classical conditioning. When a CS appears over and over without the US, the CR becomes progressively weaker and eventually disappears (or nearly does).

Another question: Do conditioned responses go away? Discussions of conditioning don't use words such as *forgetting*. CRs do weaken, however, by a process called **extinction.** This occurs when a CS comes repeatedly without the US (Pavlov, 1927). At first, the CS leads reliably to the CR (see Figure 12.4). Gradually, over repeated presentations, the CR grows weaker. The CR doesn't actually disappear, however. Even when a response stops in a given session, there's a spontaneous recovery the next day (Wagner, Siegel, Thomas, & Ellison, 1964). It is now believed that classical conditioning leaves a permanent record in the nervous system and that its effects can be muted but not erased (see Bouton, 1994, 2000).

EMOTIONAL CONDITIONING

As you may have realized already, a lot of the classical conditioning in humans involves responses with emotional qualities. That is, stimuli that most clearly cause reflexive reactions are those that elicit positive feelings (hope, delight, excitement) or bad feelings (fear, anger, pain). The term **emotional conditioning** is sometimes used to refer to classical conditioning in which the CRs are emotional reactions.

Conditioning of emotional responses is important to the learning view on personality. It's argued that the likes and dislikes—all the preferences that help define personality—arise through this process (De Houwer, Thomas, & Baeyens, 2001). Linking a neutral stimulus to a pleasant event creates a like (Razran, 1940; Staats & Staats, 1958). Linking a stimulus to an upsetting event creates a dislike (J. B. Watson & Raynor, 1920; see also Cacioppo & Sandman, 1981; Riordan & Tedeschi, 1983; Staats, Staats, & Crawford, 1962). In fact, just hearing someone describe a good or bad trait in someone else can link that trait in your mind to the person who's doing the describing (Skowronski, Carlston, Mae, & Crawford, 1998).

Different people experience different bits of the world and thus have different patterns of emotional arousal. Different people also experience the same event from the perspective of their unique "histories." As noted in Chapter 6, children from the same family experience the family differently (Daniels & Plomin, 1985). As a result, people can wind up with remarkably different patterns of likes and dislikes (see Box 12.2). Thus, emotional conditioning can play a major role in creating the uniqueness of personality (Staats & Burns, 1982).

Instrumental Conditioning

A second form of conditioning is called **instrumental conditioning.** (This phrase is often used interchangeably with *operant conditioning,* despite slight differences in meaning.) Instrumental conditioning differs in several ways from classical conditioning. For one, classical conditioning is *passive.* When a reflex occurs, conditioning doesn't require you to *do* anything—just to be there and be aware of other stimuli. Instrumental conditioning is *active* (Skinner, 1938). The events that define it begin with a behavior on your part (even if the behavior is the act of remaining still).

THE LAW OF EFFECT

Instrumental conditioning is a simple process, although its ramifications are widespread. The process goes like this: If a behavior is followed by a better or more satisfying state of affairs, the behavior is more likely to be done again later in a similar situation (see Figure 12.5, A). If a behavior is followed by a worse or less satisfying state of affairs, the behavior is less likely to be done again later (see Figure 12.5, B).

This simple description—linking an action, an outcome, and a change in the likelihood of future action—is the *law of effect* deduced by Thorndike a century ago (Thorndike, 1898, 1905). The law of effect is simple but profound. It provides a way to account for regularities in behavior. That is, any situation permits many potential acts (see Figure 12.5, C). Some acts come to occur with great regularity; others happen once and disappear, never to return. Others turn up occasionally but only occasionally. Why? Because some have been followed by satisfying outcomes, and others haven't.

One purpose of the business lunch is to associate your company and its products (as CSs) with the positive feelings produced by a good meal in a nice restaurant (as USs).

All the actions a person might do in a given situation can be seen as a **habit hierarchy,** a list of response potentials (N. E. Miller & Dollard, 1941). The order derives

Box 12.2 CLASSICAL CONDITIONING AND ATTITUDES

Where do attitudes come from? The answer provided in this chapter is that you develop attitudes by classical conditioning. A neutral stimulus (CS) begins to produce an emotional reaction (CR) after it's paired with a stimulus (US) that already creates an emotional reaction (UR). This approach holds that people acquire emotional responses to attitude objects (classes of things, people, ideas, or events) in exactly that way. If the attitude object is paired with an emotion-arousing stimulus, it comes to evoke the emotion itself. This response, then, is the basis for an attitude.

A good deal of evidence fits this depiction. Over 65 years ago, Razran (1940) presented several political slogans to people and had them rate how much they approved of each. Later, he presented the slogans again under one of three conditions: while the people were eating a free lunch, while they

were inhaling noxious odors, or while they were sitting in a neutral setting. Later on, they rated their approval of the slogans a second time. Slogans paired with a free lunch were now rated more positively than before. Slogans paired with unpleasant odors were now rated more negatively than before.

Many other studies have found similar results (De Houwer et al., 2001). Attitudes toward people can form the same way. Walther (2002) found that pairing photos of neutral persons with liked or disliked persons led to positive and negative attitudes, respectively, toward the neutral persons. These attitudes were also found to be resistant to extinction.

There's also the potential for higher-order conditioning here. Negative attitudes formed by associating a neutral person with a disliked person can produce further conditioning from that one to another neutral person (Walther, 2002). And think about the fact that words such as *good* and *bad* are tied

in most people's experience to positive and negative events (Staats & Staats, 1957, 1958) and thus probably cause emotional responses themselves. People use such words all the time around others, creating opportunities for higher-order conditioning.

A large number of studies have shown that classical conditioning *can* be involved in development of attitudes. They don't tell us whether attitudes *are* usually acquired this way. But events that arouse emotions are common in day-to-day life, which provides opportunities for conditioning to take place. For example, the business lunch is remarkably similar to Razran's experimental manipulation. It seems not at all unreasonable that classical conditioning may underlie many of people's preferences for persons, events, things, places, and ideas. Given that these preferences are important aspects of personality, conditioning would appear to represent an important contributor to personality.

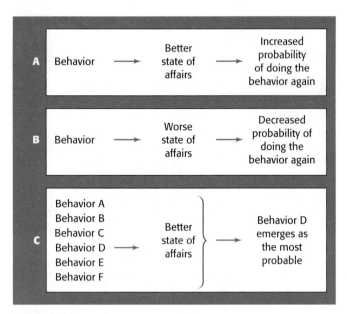

FIGURE 12.5
Instrumental conditioning: (A) Behavior that is followed by a more satisfying state of affairs is more likely to be done again. (B) Behavior that is followed by a less satisfying state of affairs is less likely to be done again. (C) This principle accounts for the fact that (over time and experiences) some behaviors emerge from the many possible behaviors as habitual responses that occur in specific situations.

from prior conditioning. Some responses are very likely, because they've often been followed by more satisfying states of affairs. Others are less likely, and others even less so. For example, in the cafeteria at noon, getting and eating lunch are very likely, working on coursework is less likely (though maybe not too far down the list), but taking off your clothes and reciting Shakespeare are very *un*likely. As another example, if you need to ask your parents for money, there are some tactics you'll use because they've worked in the past and others you've given up because they haven't worked. Habit hierarchies continually evolve, as the various actions you try are followed by either more or less satisfying states of affairs.

REINFORCEMENT AND PUNISHMENT

The term **reinforcer** has now replaced the phrase *satisfying state of affairs.* The term conveys the sense that it *strengthens* the tendency to do whatever act came before it. A *reinforcer* is anything that strengthens a behavioral tendency. Reinforcers can reduce biological needs (e.g., food or water) or satisfy social desires (e.g., smiles and acceptance). Some get their reinforcing quality indirectly (e.g., money). There's even evidence that visual sensations (seeing something you like) can act as reinforcers (Hayes, Rincover, & Volosin, 1980).

Different kinds of reinforcers have different names. A *primary reinforcer* is one that diminishes a biological need. A *secondary reinforcer* has acquired reinforcing properties by association with a primary reinforcer (through classical conditioning) or by virtue of the fact that it can be used to *get* primary reinforcers (Wolfe, 1936; Zimmerman, 1957).

The term **punisher** refers to unpleasant outcomes. Punishers reduce the tendency to do the behavior that came before them, although there's been controversy about how effective they are (Rachman & Teasdale, 1969; Solomon, 1964; Thorndike, 1933). Punishment can also be primary or secondary. That is, some events are intrinsically aversive (e.g., pain). Others are aversive because of associations with primary punishers.

Another distinction is also important, but a little tricky. When you think of reinforcement, what probably comes to mind are things you like—gifts, money, trips to fun places, CDs, and so on. When you think of punishment, you probably think of pain—being yelled at, slapped, or frowned at. In reality, however, both concepts are broader and more subtle than that.

Reinforcement always implies moving the person's "state of affairs" in a positive direction. But this can happen in two ways. The more obvious way is receiving the good things that come to mind as reinforcers (gifts, money). Receiving these things is termed **positive reinforcement**. *Positive* implies *adding* something good. When positive reinforcement occurs, the behavior that preceded it becomes more likely.

There's also a second kind of reinforcement called **negative reinforcement.** Negative reinforcement occurs when something *unpleasant* is *removed*. For instance, when your roommate stops playing his annoying *Polka Favorites* CD over and over, that might be a negative reinforcer for you. Removing something unpleasant moves the state of affairs in a positive direction—from unpleasant to neutral. It thus is reinforcing. Negative reinforcement can be just as potent as positive reinforcement. Whatever you did before your roommate's music stopped will become more likely in the future.

Punishment also comes in two forms. Most people think of punishment as adding pain, moving the state of affairs from neutral to negative. But sometimes punishment involves removing something good, changing from a positive to a neutral (thus less satisfying) state of affairs. This principle—punishing by withdrawing something good—underlies a tactic that's widely used to discourage unwanted behavior in children. It's called a **timeout,** short for "time out from positive reinforcement" (Drabman & Spitalnik, 1973; Risley, 1968). A timeout takes the child from whatever activity is going on to a place where there's nothing fun to do. Many find this practice appealing because it seems more humane than painful punishments such as spanking. In principle, however, a timeout creates a less satisfying state of affairs for the child and thus should have the same effect on behavior as any other punishment.

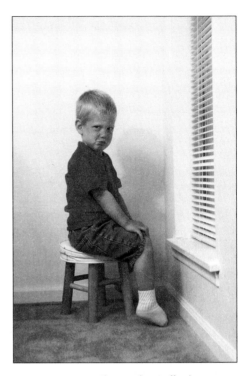

Timeout is an effective way of discouraging unwanted behavior in children.

A final issue here is that it's hard to specify how *satisfying* an outcome is (and thus how reinforcing it is). An outcome's value is determined partly by your situation. If you're starving, being handed a box of stale cheese puffs is a good outcome. If you've just had a great meal, the cheese puffs won't seem so good. In the same way, a truly starving man may not be impressed by a beautiful woman's overtures of sex, which in other circumstances would seem to him an *extremely* satisfying state of affairs.

This issue has led many people (though not all) to think of instrumental conditioning as a process that occurs primarily when the person has a motive to which the reinforcer relates (see Box 12.3). Indeed, many people use the term *instrumental* more broadly, going beyond the conditioning process per se. This broader use of the word implies *goal directed,* conveying the sense that the behavior is the instrument or tool by which a desired outcome is obtained.

DISCRIMINATION, GENERALIZATION, AND EXTINCTION IN INSTRUMENTAL CONDITIONING

Several ideas introduced in discussing classical conditioning also apply to instrumental conditioning, with slight differences in connotation. For example, *discrimination* still means responding differently in the presence of different stimuli. Here, however, the difference in response results from variations in prior reinforcement.

To understand how this kind of discrimination develops, imagine that when a stimulus is present, a particular action is always followed by a reinforcer. When the stimulus is absent, that action is *never* followed by a reinforcer. Gradually, the presence or absence of the stimulus gains an influence over whether the behavior takes place. It becomes a **discriminative stimulus,** a stimulus that turns the behavior on and off. You use the stimulus to discriminate among situations and thus among responses. Miller and Dollard (1941) called this a *cue function.* Behavior that's cued by discriminative stimuli is said to be *under stimulus control.*

Here's an illustration of discriminative stimuli that may be familiar. Imagine a high school class whose teacher is stiff and formal and doesn't tolerate play in class. The

Box 12.3   THEORETICAL CONTROVERSY

Do Motives Play a Role in Instrumental Conditioning?

As pointed out in the main text, you have to know an organism's present state to know what's reinforcing to it. There are, however, several ways to think about this.

Neal Miller and John Dollard (1941; Dollard & Miller, 1950), the first theorists to try to portray the full breadth of personality in terms of learning, held that the nature of reinforcement is intimately tied to motivation. Their view relied on Clark Hull's (1943) theory of motivation. Hull said that when an organism is deprived of a needed substance (e.g., food or water), it experiences an increase in **drive.** When drive goes up, it increases the tendency to emit behaviors high in the habit hierarchy. Sooner or later, you get what you've been deprived of. That causes drive to go back down. According to Miller and Dollard, *drive reduction constitutes reinforcement.*

In this view, to know what will reinforce a person, you need to know the person's needs or motives.

Not all conditioning theorists have agreed that motivational concepts are helpful here. An alternative view was posed by B. F. Skinner (e.g., 1953, 1974), who argued that the effort to explain behavior doesn't benefit from guessing about what's going on inside the organism. He was quite outspoken about his belief that concepts like motive, wish, desire—not to mention cognition—serve more to confuse the picture than to clarify it.

Skinner argued that use of terms such as *motive* and *wish* is often circular. That is, we often infer that people are motivated to do something by whether they do it. Skinner asked, Why not forget about the motive and simply analyze the acts? Indeed, Skinner felt that terms such as *drive* and *motive* are actually misleading, because they create the impression of an explanation while not really explaining anything.

Rather than talk about drives or needs, Skinner said, you should simply describe the stimulus conditions of deprivation versus satiation. *Deprivation* is a period of the absence of a consummatory behavior (for example, eating or drinking). *Satiation* is the end of a period of intense consummatory behavior. Both events are observable. Along with knowledge of prior reinforcement contingencies, they provide all the information necessary to predict behavior. This theoretical position is often called **radical behaviorism** because it represents a strict (thus radical) application of the idea that one shouldn't invent imaginary mechanisms when behavior can be accounted for by observable events (Baum, 2005; O'Donohue & Kitchener, 1999).

In sum, these two theoretical models agree in one respect and disagree in another. Both assume it's important to take the organism's present condition into account. But they take very different views on how to think about the organism's present condition.

---

teacher sometimes misses class due to illness. The substitute is relaxed and easygoing. In truth, he'd rather have a good time with the class than stick to the lesson plan. When he's there, cutting up is followed by reinforcement more often than when the regular teacher's there. The predictable result is that quiet prevails for the regular teacher, but the class turns into a party when the substitute's there. Because the shift occurs as a function of the teacher (the discriminative stimuli), the students' behavior is under stimulus control.

Earlier in this section, we mentioned the idea of a *habit hierarchy* (an ordering of the likelihood of doing various behaviors). We said that the hierarchy shifts constantly because of the ongoing flow of reinforcing (and nonreinforcing) events. It shifts constantly for another reason as well: Every change in situation means a change in cues (discriminative stimuli). The cues suggest what behaviors are reinforced in that situation. Thus, the shift in cues rearranges the list of behavior probabilities. Changing contextual cues can disrupt even very strong habits (Wood, Tam, & Guerrero Witt, 2005).

The concept of discriminative stimulus is important to reinforcement views of personality. It accounts for complexity in behavior. Very slight changes in the stimulus field dramatically alter behavior. As a traffic light turns green, people drive forward;

as the light turns red, they stop. As the clock reads 12:00, people leave their desks and go to lunch; as the clock reads 1:00, the same people return and start to work again. These differences in behavior are large in scope, but they're caused by extremely small changes in the surrounding array of stimuli.

The principle of generalization is also important here. It contributes a sense of continuity in behavior. As you enter a new setting and see objects and people you've never seen before, you respond easily and automatically. There are similarities between the new setting and previous discriminative stimuli. You generalize behaviors from the one to the other, and action flows smoothly forward. You may never have seen a particular style of spoon before, but you won't hesitate to use it on the soup. You may never have driven a particular make of car before, but if that's what the rental agency gives you, you'll probably be able to handle it.

The principle of generalization gives conditioning theorists a way to talk about traitlike qualities. A person should behave consistently across time and circumstances if discriminative stimuli stay fairly similar across the times and circumstances. Because key stimulus qualities often *do* stay the same across settings (even if other qualities differ greatly), the person's action tendency also stays the same across the settings. The result is that, to an outside observer, the person appears to have a set of internal traits. In this view, however, consistency of behavior depends on similarities of environments (an idea that's not too different from the discussion of consistency late in Chapter 4).

Extinction in instrumental conditioning occurs when a behavior that once led to a reinforcer no longer does so. As the behavior is done over and over—with no reinforcer—its probability drops. Eventually, it's barely there at all (though just as in classical conditioning there's a tendency for spontaneous recovery, causing some to believe that it hasn't gone away; Bouton, 1994; Rescorla, 1997, 1998). Thus, extinction is a way in which behavioral tendencies fade.

ALTERING THE SHAPE OF BEHAVIOR

The concepts of reward and punishment provide a way of talking about how behaviors become more or less likely to occur. Thus far, however, we haven't dealt with how a behavior changes in its form. Still missing is the concept of **shaping.**

Let's look first at shaping in the laboratory. Many times it's not practical to wait for a desired act and then reinforce it. Instead, reinforcement is first given for a rough *approximation* of the behavior, which then begins to occur more often. Gradually, you reinforce only closer and closer approximations of the desired act. This method is called **successive approximation.** Through it, the behavior of the organism comes to be very specific. That is, behavior is *shaped* in a particular direction. To characterize the process differently, the organism is learning a continually changing discrimination.

One might think of this as simply a convenient laboratory tactic, but much the same thing happens all the time outside the lab. Whether by chance or by design, general tendencies (e.g., going to school) are reinforced at first. These general tendencies then are channeled into more specific tendencies (e.g., studying political science) by shifts in patterns of reinforcement. This shaping can ultimately result in specific and highly specialized tendencies (attending law school, becoming a state representative). Shaping, then, provides a way to understand how behavior (indeed, personality) evolves continuously, with changing reinforcement patterns.

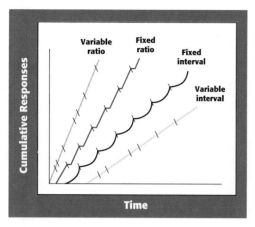

FIGURE 12.6

Behavioral tendencies created by four different types of reinforcement schedules, in which the total reinforcement across a long span of time is equivalent. Behavior is portrayed as *cumulative frequencies* of response, or responses summed across time. Each small mark on the line represents the occurrence of a reinforcer. As you can see, some reinforcement schedules produce higher and more consistent rates of behavior than others.

Source: Adapted from Reese, 1966.

SCHEDULES OF REINFORCEMENT

The issue of whether behavior tendencies stay or disappear is important in thinking about personality. Extinction helps us understand which behaviors persist and which do not, but it's not the only principle that matters. The persistence of an action tendency is also influenced by the *pattern* with which it's been reinforced in the past.

In reading about instrumental conditioning, people often assume that a reinforcement occurs every time the behavior occurs. But common sense and your own experience should tell you life's not like that. Sometimes reinforcements are frequent, but sometimes not. Variations in frequency and pattern are called *schedules of reinforcement*. A simple variation in schedules is between continuous and partial (or intermittent) reinforcement. In **continuous reinforcement,** the behavior is followed by a reinforcer *every single time.* In **partial reinforcement,** the behavior is followed by a reinforcer *less often than every time.*

There are many patterns of partial reinforcement. The reinforcer can come after a certain *number of occurrences* of the behavior (your teacher smiles and says "good" every fifth time you contribute to class discussion). This pattern is called a *ratio schedule.* The number involved can be large (every tenth time) or small (every second time). The numbers can be *fixed* (every fifth time exactly) or *variable* (randomly varying, but every fifth time on the average). The reinforcer may depend on the passage of some time as well as the occurrence of the behavior (a week has to pass since your teacher last smiled and said "good," but then he does it the very next time you contribute in class). This pattern is called an *interval schedule.* Intervals can also be fixed (exactly one week has to pass before your next contribution is rewarded) or variable (on the average, one week has to pass before your next contribution is rewarded).

Different schedules of reinforcement lead to different behavior tendencies across time. Figure 12.6 shows the tendencies associated with each type of schedule just described (adapted from Reese, 1966). The tendencies are described there in terms of cumulative frequencies of response—responses added up across time. Each small mark on the line represents the occurrence of a reinforcer.

A *fixed ratio schedule* causes a high rate of responding, with a brief pause immediately after reinforcement. This schedule is reflected in so-called piecework, in which a person is paid a fixed amount per unit of work (object assembled, basket of vegetables picked, and so on). A *variable ratio schedule* creates an even higher rate of response, without pauses after reinforcement. An example of a variable ratio is gambling, which pays off occasionally but unpredictably.

The *fixed interval schedule* produces a pronounced and reliable *scalloping* of the curve, a complete absence of behavior just after reinforcement, followed by a gradual renewal, which accelerates until the next reinforcer occurs. A good illustration of this schedule is the study behavior of students whose psychology course has exams at predictable intervals. They study most just before exams. This pattern also describes the behavior of the U.S. Congress, which passes most of its bills just before it adjourns (Weisberg & Waldrop, 1972).

Scalloping isn't apparent at all in the last schedule, the *variable interval schedule.* This one is characterized by consistent activity, as with the variable ratio schedule, but (in general) at a lower level of activity. An example of this schedule is the behavior of students whose instructor gives pop quizzes unexpectedly, rather than tests at predictable intervals.

THE PARTIAL REINFORCEMENT EFFECT

As you can see, reinforcement patterns can get complicated. What's most important, though, is that infrequent and unpredictable reinforcement affects behavior differently than reinforcement that's frequent and predictable. There are two differences. The first is that you acquire a new behavior faster when reinforcement is frequent than when it's not. Eventually, even infrequent reinforcement results in high rates of the behavior, but it may take a while.

The other effect is less intuitive but more important. It's often called the **partial reinforcement effect.** It shows up when reinforcement stops (see Figure 12.7). Take away the reinforcer, and a behavior built in by continuous reinforcement will go away quickly. A behavior built in by partial (less frequent) reinforcement will remain longer. It's more *resistant to extinction* (Amsel, 1967; Humphreys, 1939).

This effect isn't simply a matter of how easy or hard it is to tell when the extinction period is starting (Jenkins, 1962; Theios, 1962). Rather, there seems to be a subtle difference in what's conditioned in the first place (Amsel, 1967). In intermittent reinforcement, a nonreinforcement is actually becoming a discriminative stimulus that cues *persistence* (because if you keep trying, you eventually get a reinforcement). Nonreinforcement continues to act as a discriminative stimulus for a long time, even when the reinforcer's gone for good. When you start with continuous reinforcement, though, the link between nonreinforcement and persistence is never made. When the reinforcer goes away, nothing remains to keep the behavior going.

In the same vein, it has been argued that people learn to be industrious by receiving patterns of reinforcement that cause sensations of effort to become a cue for persistence (Eisenberger, 1992). Thus, instead of finding the experience of effort aversive, people find it rewarding. One can imagine a situation in which even a very aversive experience, such as fear, can become a discriminative stimulus for persistence. Such a case would represent a kind of "conditioned courage."

The partial reinforcement effect carries an important message: If you want a behavior to remain relatively persistent in someone, don't reinforce it all the time. In fact, the lower the rate of reinforcement (if it's enough to sustain the behavior), the stronger the link between the cue of nonreinforcement and persistence. Ironically, although this view emphasizes the importance of reinforcement in producing behavior, it also emphasizes the importance of *non*reinforcement during conditioning in *sustaining* behavior.

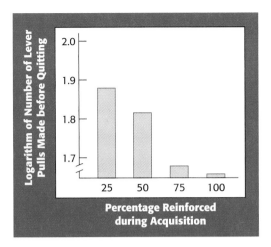

FIGURE 12.7

Effect of partial reinforcement and continuous reinforcement on persistence. Participants first played on a slot machine that paid off 25%, 50%, 75%, or 100% of the time. Then they were allowed to continue playing for as long as they liked, but they never again won. As can be seen, partial reinforcement leads to greater resistance to extinction. That is, the groups initially rewarded less than 100% of the time persist longer when all reward is removed. Moreover, the lower the percentage of partial reinforcement initially given, the greater the persistence. *Source: Adapted from Lewis & Duncan, 1956.*

Many personal superstitions are learned through a schedule of random partial reinforcement.

LEARNING "IRRATIONAL" BEHAVIOR

People who use conditioning principles often emphasize that the behavior need not *cause* the reinforcer for conditioning to occur. The behavior needs only to be *followed* by the reinforcer. Whatever behavior preceded the reinforcer is strengthened by the reinforcer's occurrence.

This relationship can lead to rather strange effects, as Skinner (1948) pointed out in a study of pigeons. Picture a bird in a cage, which gets a reinforcer (a bit of food) at a regular interval, regardless of what it's doing. Every reinforcer strengthens the behavior that preceded it. At first, because behavior is somewhat random, several behaviors are strengthened. Eventually, though, one action is reinforced often enough that it starts to predominate. Because it's more common, it now gets reinforced even more. The result is that the bird is now doing an entirely arbitrary behavior quite regularly.

Because the pigeon acts as though these specific actions are causing the reinforcer, Skinner called this *superstitious behavior*. He argued that seemingly irrational or senseless behaviors in people develop exactly the same way. Reinforcers occurred for reasons unrelated to the behavior, and they built the behavior in and shaped it into its present form. By the way, Skinner didn't assume that the pigeon was thinking about what caused the reinforcement, only that its behavior gave that outward appearance (see Box 12.4).

There's no difference between the process by which superstitious behaviors are acquired and the process by which any other behaviors are acquired. To call a behavior *irrational* (versus *adaptive*) is an observer's value judgment. To the conditioning

BOX 12.4 BEHAVIORISTS' VIEW OF THE ROLE OF THOUGHT IN CONDITIONING

Conditioning theorists hold that behavior tendencies are determined by reinforcement patterns. Most of them treat thought processes as irrelevant to this process (Rachlin, 1977). Although Skinner's pigeons may have *acted as though* they thought a particular action was producing the reinforcer, the appearance is illusory. Even if pigeons could think (which is questionable), their thoughts aren't behind the behavior. The reinforcement pattern is behind the behavior.

It's undeniable that people (unlike pigeons) talk and think. To conditioning theorists, however, these tendencies among humans simply reflect the fact that verbal behaviors (both overt speech and covert thought) become condi-

tioned in particular ways (e.g., Miller & Dollard, 1941). That is, people are conditioned to think in particular patterns and to talk in certain ways. But the real causes of all three phenomena—the behavior, the talk, and the thoughts—are the patterns of reinforcement.

Behaviorists try to avoid as much as possible using words such as *intention, thought, cognition,* and *consciousness* because they see them as unnecessary in explaining how people act (Baum, 2005; Skinner, 1987). Many behaviorists see the mental events that occur along with behavior and reinforcement as **epiphenomena,** phenomena with no causal role. They just happen alongside the behavior, or may even be caused by the behavior as subjective offshoots (cf. Rachlin, 1977). Skinner (1989) pointed out, in this regard, that

many words now used to describe mental states had their origins in descriptions of behavior. This history fits his contention that the behavior is what really matters.

This point of view has been more than a little controversial over the years. It hasn't been well received at all by people outside the behaviorist camp (see Catania & Harnad, 1988, for a wide-ranging discussion). Critics of the behaviorist position point out that a conditioning view has difficulty in accounting for a number of phenomena, including the emergence of language in children (Chomsky, 1959). This criticism has led some people to regard the conditioning view as incorrect. It led others more sympathetic to the learning perspective to modify the theories, a response that is taken up in the next chapter.

theorist, all behavior is acquired the same way—through reinforcement. On the other hand, there's a big difference between the situation just described and situations people normally encounter. Skinner had full control over the birds' environment. He could easily present reinforcers in a completely arbitrary pattern. In contrast, people's reinforcers more often follow particular behaviors for nonarbitrary reasons. These contingencies shape most human behavior into orderly patterns that only more rarely appear to be superstitious or irrational.

REINFORCEMENT OF QUALITIES OF BEHAVIOR

One final point about learning through instrumental conditioning: It's most intuitive to think that the reinforcer makes a particular *act* more likely in the future. However, there's evidence that what becomes more likely isn't always an act, but some *quality* of action (Eisenberger & Selbst, 1994). For example, reinforcing *effort* in one setting can increase *effortfulness* in other settings (Mueller & Dweck, 1998). Reinforcing accuracy on one task increases accuracy on other tasks. Reinforcing speed on one task increases speed elsewhere. Reinforcing creativity yields more creativity (Eisenberger & Rhoades, 2001). Reinforcing focused thought produces more focused thinking elsewhere (Eisenberger, Armeli, & Pretz, 1998). Reinforcing variability produces greater variability in behavior (Neuringer, 2004). Indeed, reinforcement can influence the process of selective attention (Libera & Chelazzi, 2006).

Thus, reinforcement can change not just particular behaviors but whole dimensions of behavior. This idea broadens considerably the ways in which reinforcement principles may act on human beings. It suggests that reinforcers act at many levels of abstraction. Indeed, perhaps many aspects of behavior at many different levels are reinforced *simultaneously* when a person experiences a more satisfying state of affairs. This possibility creates a far more complex picture of change through conditioning than was apparent in earlier parts of the chapter.

Assessment

From the view of conditioning theories, personality is the accumulation of a person's conditioned tendencies (Ciminero, Calhoun, & Adams, 1977; Hersen & Bellack, 1976; Staats, 1996). By adulthood, you have a wide range of emotional responses to various stimuli, which you experience as attitudes and preferences. You also have tendencies to engage in various kinds of actions in various kinds of settings. These tendencies differ from person to person in probability, resistance to extinction, and what discriminative stimuli cue them.

This view has at least three implications for personality assessment. Most simply, it suggests that assessment should focus on behavioral qualities, rather than cognitions. The assessment procedures suggested by this approach focus on observable aspects of emotional reactions or action tendencies, rather than on trying to obtain a general sense of what the person is like (Kanfer & Saslow, 1965).

A second implication stems from the idea that emotional responses are linked to specific CSs and that actions depend on discriminative stimuli (stimuli associated with reinforcement of the actions). This means that feelings and actions are tied to specific classes of situations or to cues within those situations. Thus, assessment should focus on specific classes of situations and specific responses, rather than on creating broad generalizations about the person.

Physiological responses provide one index of the intensity of emotional reactions.

A final implication is that there's no better form of assessment than observation. People can give self-reports of feelings and self-reports of act tendencies, but these may not be reliable or accurate. A better way to assess people's responses is to observe. Put the person in the situation you're interested in and let the person do or feel what comes naturally. Then measure what happens, as directly as possible, with as little interpretation as possible.

TECHNIQUES

This view of personality relates to two kinds of assessment techniques. One focuses on assessment of emotional responses; the other is broader in scope. The first, sometimes called **physiological assessment,** relies on the fact that emotional responses have several components. Besides subjective qualities, emotions also have physiological aspects (Cacioppo & Petty, 1983; Greenfield & Sternbach, 1972). When you experience an emotion (especially if it's intense), changes take place in your body: changes in muscle tension, heartrate, blood pressure, brain waves, sweat gland activity, and more. The changes can be thought of as internal behaviors.

These responses can be measured by devices called *physiographs.* The reactions thus are observable aspects of emotional experiences. More specifically, the degree of response can be taken as an index of the *intensity* of an emotional reaction. To illustrate, imagine yourself wired to a physiograph, which is collecting your body's responses. As you sit there, you are shown a series of stimuli that are possible sources of fear reactions: snakes, spiders, a view downward from the top of a tall building, and so on. Your body's responses reflect the intensity of any fear you have. An observer could conclude, for example, that you're scared of heights but not by snakes. All this can be assessed without a word from you. Your internal behavior gives all the information. Some think these procedures are quite useful in assessing problems such as posttraumatic stress disorder (Keane et al., 1998; Orr et al., 1998).

Physiological assessment is direct and objective, but it's also elaborate and technical. It tends to be used more in research than in clinical applications. A second technique can also be used to assess emotional responses, called **behavioral assessment** (Barlow, 1981; Haynes & O'Brien, 2000; Staats, 1996). It entails observing the person's overt behavior in situations of interest. Emotions such as fear can be assessed by behavioral indicators—trembling, paleness, avoidance, and so on. This technique can also be applied more broadly. It can be used to assess what kinds of activities people undertake, for how long, and in what patterns.

Behavioral assessment varies widely in how it's actually done. Sometimes the observer simply counts acts of specific types, checks possibilities from a prearranged list, or watches how far into a sequence of action a person goes before stopping (Lang & Lazovik, 1963; O'Leary & Becker, 1967; Paul, 1966). In other cases, the procedure is more elaborate, using automated devices to record how long the person being assessed engages in various behaviors.

For example, behavioral assessment of children often uses recorders with separate channels to keep track of the frequency and duration of activities such as talking, running, and sitting alone (Lovaas, Freitag, Gold, & Kassorla, 1965). The observer pushes a separate button that corresponds to each behavior category and continues holding for as long as that kind of behavior is being performed by the child whose behavior is being assessed.

These various techniques are useful but they have their drawbacks. Most obviously, they're elaborate and thus hard to use. Another problem is that different techniques don't always give the same results. The amount of behavioral avoidance in a situation—an index one might expect to be highly correlated with fear—doesn't always correspond well with self-reports of fear (Bernstein, 1973). Physiograph records may not fit well with either of these measures. Given this kind of disagreement, it's hard to know which measure represents the "real" fear level.

Problems in Behavior, and Behavior Change

If personality derives from classical and instrumental conditioning, then so does maladaptive behavior. People sometimes learn things that interfere with their lives. They sometimes fail to learn things that make life easier. This view suggests a basis for several kinds of personality problems along with ways of treating such problems. As a group, the treatment techniques are termed **behavior modification** or **behavior therapy** (Craighead, Kazdin, & Mahoney, 1981). These terms reflect the fact that the emphasis is on changing the person's actual *behavior*.

CLASSICAL CONDITIONING OF EMOTIONAL RESPONSES

One class of problems is emotional reactions that interfere with effective functioning. For example, people sometimes have intensely unpleasant anxiety when exposed to specific kinds of stimuli. Sometimes the anxiety is also inappropriate, because the same stimuli don't provoke comparable anxiety in other people.

Intense irrational fears are called **phobias.** The phobic person experiences fear whenever a particular stimulus is present and often becomes anxious just from thinking of it. Although a phobic reaction can become tied to virtually any stimulus, some phobias are more common than others. Common focal points for phobias are animals such as dogs, snakes, and spiders; closed-in spaces such as elevators; open or exposed spaces such as railings on high balconies; and germs and the possibility of infection.

The conditioning view assumes that phobic reactions are classically conditioned (though see Box 12.5). In this view, the person at some point must have experienced intense fear while in the presence of what's now the phobic stimulus (cf. Watson & Raynor, 1920). The previously neutral stimulus thereby took on the ability to provoke anxiety. The same principle presumably applies no matter what the feared stimulus is.

As an example, consider the plight of Allison, who nearly drowned in a boating accident three years ago. The intense fear she experienced became linked to a wide range of stimuli that had been neutral (even positive) for her—stimuli such as her father's boat, the lake she was on, and other aspects of the surroundings. Since this experience, Allison has been unable to walk out on a dock or step onto a boat without trembling violently and turning ghostly pale. She can't even drive near the lake without getting upset.

The conditioning view also leads to suggestions about how to treat phobias. Two ideas are important. The first is *extinction*. The anxiety reaction should weaken if the CS (the phobic stimulus) is presented repeatedly or for a long time without the US

BOX 12.5 ANOTHER VIEW ON PHOBIAS AND RESPONSES TO ANXIETY

A somewhat different view on the development of phobic behavior was suggested by Miller and Dollard. Their view used *instrumental conditioning* along with classical conditioning. Miller and Dollard assumed that people acquire new drives by classical conditioning from biologically built-in drives (N. E. Miller, 1948, 1951). Fear was seen as a learned drive that develops from pain. Once a fear drive is acquired, cues that arouse fear engage a drive to escape the fear. Remember that Miller and Dollard equated drive reduction with reinforcement. If you avoid or escape from whatever has cued fear, the drive goes down. This reinforces the avoidance or escape behavior, making the same behavior more likely next time.

Consider an example: Imagine there are two ways to get to class in the morning. The shorter, faster route requires you to go over a high, scary bridge, which makes you anxious. As you approach the bridge, fear mounts—and so does the drive to escape the fear. One day you decide to go the long way and avoid the bridge. As you head away from the bridge, your drive level goes down. The avoidance behavior is reinforced. As a result, you're more likely to avoid the shorter route in the future. If this occurs often, you'll have a phobia concerning the bridge.

Some stimuli that cause anxiety can't be avoided through overt behavior because the stimuli are internal—your thoughts. How can you reduce the fear if your own thoughts are creating it? The answer is simple: *Just don't think of whatever it is that's threatening you.* Successful "not-thinking" gets rid of the fear. It thereby causes a reduction in the drive, which reinforces the not-thinking tendency. In this way, Miller and Dollard accounted

in conditioning terms for the psychoanalytic phenomenon of repression. Repression is not-thinking. It occurs because doing it reduces the fear drive. Eventually, not-thinking happens before the threatening thought even comes to mind. Thus, the thought never becomes conscious.

The fact that Miller and Dollard's theory was able to deal with this psychoanalytic phenomenon wasn't just a curious sidelight. In fact, their theory was intended more generally as an explicit attempt to address psychoanalytic concepts through the principles of learning. This analysis of phobic behavior and repression is just one example of their efforts in that direction (see also J. S. Brown, 1948, 1957; N. E. Miller, 1944). As suggested by this example, it proved to be possible to use the language of learning to understand events that Freud and others had viewed in very different terms.

(whatever induced fear during conditioning). Oddly enough, by actively avoiding the phobic stimulus in their day-to-day activities, people such as Allison are actually preventing extinction from taking place.

The second important idea is that a *different* emotion can become conditioned to the *same* stimulus. If the new emotion is incompatible with fear, it will gradually come to predominate in place of the fear (a process termed **counterconditioning**). Although these ideas—extinction and counterconditioning—differ slightly from each other, in practice they lead to the same general sorts of therapeutic procedures.

One technique is **systematic desensitization.** People are first taught to relax thoroughly. This relaxation response is the *emotion* that's intended to take over for the anxiety. The therapist and the phobic person create an anxiety hierarchy—a list of situations with the feared stimulus, ranked by how much anxiety each creates (see Table 12.2). This hierarchy varies from person to person in what situations create the greatest fear.

In the desensitization process, you relax as fully as you can and then visualize a scene from the least threatening end of the hierarchy. The anxiety aroused by this image is allowed to dissipate. Then, while you continue to relax, you imagine the scene again. Do this sequence repeatedly, until the scene provokes no anxiety at all. Then move to the next level. Gradually, you're able to imagine increasingly threatening scenes without anxiety. Eventually, the imagined scenes are replaced by the actual feared stimulus. As the anxiety is countered by relaxation, you're able to interact more and more effectively with the stimulus that previously produced intense fear.

Table 12.2 An Anxiety Hierarchy Such as Might Be Used in Systematic Desensitization for One Type of Acrophobia (fear of heights). Each scene is carefully visualized while the person relaxes completely, working from the least threatening scene (at the bottom) to those that produce greater anxiety (toward the top).

Looking down from the top of the Empire State Building
Walking around the top floor of the Empire State Building
Looking out the window of a 12-story building
Looking over the balcony rail of a 4-story building
Looking out the window of a 4-story building
Looking up at a 30-story building from across a small park
Reading a story about the construction of a skyscraper
Reading a story that mentions being on top of the Statue of Liberty
Hearing a news story that mentions the tall buildings of a city
Seeing a TV news story in which tall buildings appear in the background

Systematic desensitization has proven very effective in reducing fear reactions, particularly fears that focus on a specific stimulus (e.g., Brady, 1972; Davison & Wilson, 1973). It works far more quickly than do many other therapies and thus is less expensive. The technique has been of enormous benefit to people with debilitating anxieties. How disruptive a phobia is, of course, depends on its focus. A fear of elephants wouldn't have too big an impact on most people's lives, but anxiety over entering stores with crowds of people can cripple your existence.

More recently, desensitization has been taken in a different direction. Many clinical researchers now use treatments in which the person is exposed to a more intense dose of the feared stimulus and endures it—while anxiety rises then gradually falls. The person is kept exposed to the feared stimulus well after the physical aspects of the anxiety have subsided. It seems that extinction occurs more quickly when the person is in a state of rest after the anxiety has fallen off. Such **exposure treatments** for phobias can sometimes be done in as little as one session (Öst, Ferebee, & Furmark, 1997). This sort of treatment has also proven to be superior for severe posttraumatic disorders (Foa & Meadows, 1997).

ADDITIONAL BENEFITS

Procedures such as these have secondary benefits. First, they've gone a long way to minimize the shame that people feel when their emotions hamper their actions. The learning perspective teaches people that having fear is no reason to be ashamed. Fear isn't a sign of a diseased personality. To the contrary, even irrational fears can result from ordinary events of life through the mechanism of classical conditioning.

Additional benefit can also come from learning techniques such as relaxation. These techniques are tools that people can apply more broadly any time they feel anxious or upset (Goldfried, 1971; Goldfried & Merbaum, 1973). The techniques thus promote effective functioning far beyond the therapy setting in which they're first learned.

Although the treatment of phobias provides a clear example of how the concepts of classical conditioning can be applied to problems, there are other examples. People often have conditioned responses of other emotions that they don't want to have, such as anger. Such undesired responses can be treated in the same way as fear: by extinguishing or counterconditioning the response.

It's hard to emphasize strongly enough how much the conditioning approach to phobias differs from approaches suggested by some other theoretical perspectives. For example, a psychoanalytic therapist (Chapter 9) wouldn't look for an instance of classical conditioning, but would try to uncover hidden conflicts from childhood. To the psychoanalyst, if it mattered at all what stimuli now elicit anxiety (and it might not), it would only be to suggest in a symbolic way what the real problem is. These approaches are quite different.

CLASSICAL CONDITIONING OF AVERSION

Classical conditioning in therapy is usually aimed at getting rid of conditioned responses. Sometimes, however, people want to *acquire* conditioned responses. These are cases in which people now have positive responses to stimuli they want to dislike and avoid. This would be a way to describe people who are trying to stop smoking or drinking (Cannon, Baker, Gino, & Nathan, 1986; Hackett & Horan, 1979). Stimuli related to those behaviors (liquor, cigarettes, and so on) are now tied to pleasant emotions. They would be easier to stay away from if they provoked *un*pleasant emotions.

Application of conditioning to this kind of situation is called **aversion therapy** (Rachman & Teasdale, 1969). The logic is much the same as that of counterconditioning, but the goal now is to condition a *negative* emotional response instead of a positive response. Doing this requires presenting the stimulus as a CS along with a US that produces a negative reaction. For example, nausea-inducing drugs are sometimes used as a US to be linked to the taste of liquor and cues for drinking (Cannon et al., 1986). Electric shock is used as a US to be linked to the touch of a cigarette (Powell & Azrin, 1968).

Aversive conditioning isn't as widely used as other behavior therapies, for several reasons. Some find the procedures objectionable, and some have raised questions about whether it's as effective as other procedures (Lichtenstein & Danaher, 1976; Powell & Azrin, 1968).

CONDITIONING AND CONTEXT

The point of using procedures based on extinction and counterconditioning is to replace an undesired response with a neutral response or a response opposite to the original one. However, there are some issues that complicate things. As noted earlier, it's now believed that extinction doesn't remove the original conditioning (Bouton, 1994, 2000). Rather, it creates a second conditioned response that dominates over the original one. Sometimes, though, the original response comes back. How might that be made less likely?

An important role is played by context. That is, the context of the original conditioning often differs from the context of the therapy. In effect, each context is a set of discriminative stimuli. People acquire a neutral response (via extinction) to the target stimulus in the therapy room. But when they return to the setting where the response was learned, the old response may reappear (Bouton, 2000). Why? Because the stimuli of the original setting *weren't there during the extinction*. As a result, they still link to CRs and serve as cues for behavior.

For the new response to predominate in the person's experience, one of two things must happen. First, the person can acquire the new response in a setting that resembles the setting where the old response was acquired. This will cause the new response to generalize to the original setting. Alternatively, the person can avoid the original setting. That's why many approaches to avoiding relapse emphasize staying away from settings resembling those where the original response was acquired.

As a concrete example, consider work on smoking relapse. Withdrawal from nicotine isn't the sole problem in quitting (Perkins, 1999). Relapse rates are as high as 60%, even if smokers get nicotine other ways (Kenford, Flore, Jorenby, & Smith, 1994). Many who quit smoking return to it well after the end of nicotine withdrawal (Brandon et al., 1990). Why? The smoking is linked by conditioning to particular contexts (after meals, after sex, or when drinking at social gatherings). The context itself remains a discriminative stimulus for smoking long after the craving for nicotine is gone (Carter & Tiffany, 1999).

Programs to quit smoking now emphasize efforts to extinguish responses to the cues linked to smoking. The contextual cues are presented alone, with no smoking. The hope is that the nonsmoking response will condition to those cues, and the person will thereby become resistant to relapse. Such programs have had only limited success (Conklin & Tiffany, 2002). Perhaps that's because they've used normative smoking cues, rather than personalized ones. Because everyone has a unique smoking history, individualizing the cues may promote better success (Conklin & Tiffany, 2001).

INSTRUMENTAL CONDITIONING AND MALADAPTIVE BEHAVIORS

Another set of problems in behavior relates to the principles of instrumental conditioning. The reasoning here stems from the idea that behavioral tendencies are built in by reinforcement. Indeed, tendencies can be acquired in ways that make them resistant to extinction.

How might this reasoning be applied to problems? Imagine that a certain behavior or class of behavior—throwing tantrums when you don't get your way—was reinforced at one period of your life because your parents gave in to them. The reinforcement strengthened the tendency to repeat the tantrums. If reinforced often enough and in the right pattern of partial reinforcement, the behavior will become both frequent and persistent.

Later, when you grow older, the behavior will become less appropriate. It won't be reinforced as often, although people may give in to it occasionally. (It's surprising how often people reinforce the exact behaviors they wish would stop.) Although the reinforcement will be rare, the behavior will continue (thanks to the partial reinforcement effect). The behavior will seem irrational to observers, but from the conditioning view, it will just be showing resistance to extinction.

The principles of instrumental conditioning suggest that the way to change undesired behavior is to change the patterns of reinforcement. The best approach would be to increase reinforcements after a desired (alternative) action. At the same time, reduce even further (if possible) any reinforcement of the undesired action. This should shape behavior toward greater adaptiveness or suitability. This approach is sometimes called **contingency management.**

An example comes from the literature of health psychology. Childhood obesity is a risk factor for serious health problems later on. It stems partly from habits such as watching TV instead of being active and partly from poor diet. Research has shown that reinforcing less sedentary activities causes both an increase in those activities and a decrease in the sedentary activities (L. H. Epstein, Saelens, Myers, & Vito, 1997). Similarly, reinforcing the choice of fruits and vegetables over snack foods causes an increase in the tendency to choose those healthy foods (Goldfield & Epstein, 2002).

Contingency management programs have also been used in efforts to keep people from drug and alcohol abuse. It can be used to shape undesired behavior in the direction of abstinence over time before quitting (Preston, Umbricht, Wong, & Epstein, 2001). It also can be useful in treating alcohol dependence (Petry, Martin, Cooney, & Kranzler, 2000) and in supporting abstinence from cocaine use (Higgins, Wong, Badger, Haug Ogden, & Dantona, 2000).

All of this is straightforward when it is easy to control the reinforcement. But sometimes reinforcement occurs in unexpected ways and places. For example, consider video games. People have the potential to learn a lot when they play video games. Why? Because the game often incorporates reinforcement for particular kinds of behavior in the game. It's been shown that playing games that reinforce violence in the game result in more violence and hostility outside the game (Carnagey & Anderson, 2005).

INSTRUMENTAL CONDITIONING OF CONFLICT

Another potential contributor to problems in personality is inconsistency in reinforcement. That is, a given act can be reinforced at some times and punished at other times. If the reinforcement and punishment occur in different settings, the person will learn a discrimination. But if they occur in the same setting (or if the cues for discrimination are hard to tell apart), the result is **conflict** (Dollard & Miller, 1950; N. E. Miller, 1944). That is, the reinforcement causes a tendency to do the behavior, and the punishment causes a tendency to not do it.

Whichever tendency is stronger is the one that will dominate. The fact that the other tendency is there, however, means there will be discomfort as the behavior is being done (or not done). If the situation is conflicted enough, the person may even learn to treat punishment as a discriminative stimulus for *doing* the behavior (if persistence is eventually followed by reinforcement). This person's behavior will appear especially irrational and can even be self-destructive, but it's a predictable result of inconsistent outcomes.

This issue is of special concern in childrearing, because parents can easily fall into the pattern of mixing reinforcement and punishment for the same behavior (e.g., sometimes punishing tantrums and sometimes giving in to them). It's interesting that many of the transitions of childhood that can be difficult for this reason are the transitions noted by Freud many years ago: weaning, toilet training, establishing power relationships between parent and child. Freud saw these situations as conflicted due to sexual pressures. But they also seem open to analysis in terms of inconsistent treatment by the parents.

INSTRUMENTAL CONDITIONING AND BIOFEEDBACK

Another use of instrumental conditioning concepts in therapy focuses on changing internal behaviors. The behaviors are usually small in scale—for example, muscle tensing that creates headaches or influences blood pressure, muscle cramping that produces pain in one's neck or lower back, and small muscle movements in areas that are paralyzed. As these examples imply, this therapy deals primarily with problems of pain or other conditions of ill health.

It was long thought that most internal behaviors of this type are outside voluntary control. Eventually, however, it was discovered that people could learn to control the internal actions through procedures thought to involve instrumental conditioning. The procedures as a group are called **biofeedback.**

Biofeedback training requires an internal behavior that's specific in one sense but vague in another. For example, you might be asked to raise the temperature of your hand, reduce muscle tension in your forehead, or lower your pulse rate. You aren't told *how* to do this, just to do it. While you try, you're attached to a machine that continuously tells you whether you're successful, by a signal light or tone. The light or tone (the biofeedback) acts as a reinforcer for whatever you did just before. The result is that people can learn to do very subtle internal behaviors through such training. Presumably, once the behavior is well learned, it will continue to occur even without the biofeedback.

This technique has been proposed as a way to treat physical problems that involve subtle muscle activity (Blanchard & Epstein, 1978). Many people, for example, can change their blood pressure during biofeedback, although this particular effect doesn't generalize well outside the training setting (Shapiro & Surwit, 1979). Biofeedback is also used as a treatment for many kinds of pain (Elmore & Tursky, 1981).

Conditioning Theories: Problems and Prospects

The conditioning view on personality has been particularly influential among two groups of psychologists: researchers who are actively involved in the experimental analysis of behavior in the laboratory and clinicians who received their training when behavior therapies were at their height of popularity. The conditioning view is attractive to these two groups for two different reasons, which in turn represent two strengths of this view of personality.

First, the conditioning viewpoint emerged—as had no other perspective before it—from the crucible of experimental research. The ideas that form this approach to behavior were intended to be subjected to close scrutiny, to be either upheld or disconfirmed through research. Many of the ideas have been tested thoroughly, and the evidence that supports them is substantial. This empirical base is important. Having a viewpoint on the nature of personality that can be verified by careful, objective observation is very satisfying to the researcher.

The second reason for the impact of conditioning ideas is the effectiveness of behavioral therapy techniques. Clinical psychologists found that many of people's problems in life can be treated with fairly simple procedures. With this realization, the clinicians began to look carefully at the principles behind the procedures. The learning perspective has taken on an aura of importance and credibility among this group of psychologists because of its good fit with these effective techniques of behavior change.

Although many psychologists find this viewpoint congenial, it also has its share of problems and criticisms. Some of the criticisms derive from a virtue we just named: the emphasis on research. More specifically, conditioning theorists have emphasized the study of laboratory animals. If the laws of learning are the same across different species, it makes no difference which animal they study. Many people, however, are wary of the assumption that underlies that strategy—that learning is the same across species. Indeed, skepticism on this point helped foster the development of a second generation of learning theories, discussed in Chapter 13.

A more subtle criticism concerns the researchers' tendency to simplify the situation under study. Simplification ensures experimental control. Having control helps clarify cause and effect. But it sometimes results in experimental situations that offer extremely few options for behavior. There's sometimes a nagging suspicion that the behavior occurred because there were so many pressures in its direction and so little chance to do anything *else*. What happens to behavior when the person leaves the laboratory? With more options, will the regularities still hold up?

This question turns out to be a very important one. Breland and Breland (1961) tried to use operant procedures to train animals. They were distressed to discover that reinforcers often were less powerful than animals' natural tendencies. For example, they tried to train a raccoon to pick up coins and put them into a "bank," but found it had a strong tendency to hold the coins and rub them together. The raccoon looked like a miser, but it was only trying to do what it would do with crayfish in its normal environment: rub them together to remove their shells. In the same way, pigs being trained to deposit wooden coins into a bank preferred to drop the coins, root them along the ground, and toss them into the air. The Brelands eventually questioned whether lab studies of conditioning really provide an accurate picture of behavior in normal environments. Perhaps the picture that's being conveyed is actually quite distorted.

Another problem with this view is that it isn't really so much a theory of personality as a view of the determinants of behavior. Some people think this view is too simplistic to provide a meaningful view of personality. The processes of learning presumably operate continuously in a piecemeal and haphazard fashion. The human experience, on the other hand, seems highly complex and orderly. How do the haphazard learning processes yield such an orderly product?

To put it another way, conditioning theories tell us a lot about how a specific behavior becomes more probable or less probable, but it doesn't tell us so much about the person who is doing the behavior. The processes in the theories are cold and mechanistic. There seems to be little place here for the subjective sense of personhood, little focus on the continuity and coherence that characterize the sense of self. In sum, to many people, this analysis of personality doesn't convey the subjective experience of what it means to *have* a personality. Perhaps the greatest challenge to the conditioning approach, then, is to convince skeptics that it accounts for the subjective qualities that seem so important to personality.

· SUMMARY ·

The conditioning approach to personality emphasizes two types of learning. In classical conditioning, a neutral stimulus (CS) is presented along with another stimulus (US) that already elicits a reflexive response (UR). After repeated pairings, the CS itself comes to elicit a response (CR) that's similar to the UR. The CR appears to be an anticipatory response that prepares for the US.

This basic phenomenon is modified by discrimination (different stimuli leading to different responses) and extended by generalization (different stimuli leading to similar responses). CRs fade if the CS is presented repeatedly without the US, a process termed *extinction*. Classical conditioning is important to personality primarily when the responses being conditioned are emotional reactions (emotional conditioning). Classical conditioning thus provides a basis for understanding people's unique preferences and aversions, and it provides a way of analyzing certain psychological problems, such as phobias.

In instrumental conditioning (a more active process), a behavior is followed by an outcome that's either positively valued or aversive. If the outcome is positively valued, the tendency to perform the behavior is strengthened. Thus, the outcome is called a *reinforcer*. If the outcome is aversive (a *punisher*), the tendency to perform the behavior is reduced. *Discrimination* in instrumental conditioning is responding in different ways to different situational cues; *generalization* is responding in a similar way to different cues; and *extinction* is the reduction of a behavioral tendency through nonreinforcement of the behavior. Behavior is shaped in new directions by reinforcing successively better approximations of the behavior you want eventually to occur. Reinforcers can occur in many patterns, termed *schedules*. The most important effect of variations in reinforcement schedules is that behavior learned by intermittent (partial) reinforcement is more persistent (under later conditions of nonreinforcement) than is a behavior learned by continuous reinforcement.

The conditioning approach holds that personality is the sum of the person's conditioned tendencies. Assessment, from this point of view, emphasizes the observation of various aspects of behavior tendencies as they occur in specific situations. Assessment can focus on people's physiological responses, their overt behaviors, or their reports of emotional reactions in response to different kinds of stimuli.

The conditioning approach assumes that problems in behavior are the result of the same kinds of conditioning processes as result in normal behavior. Classical conditioning can produce intense and irrational fears, called *phobias;* instrumental conditioning can produce behavior tendencies that persist even when they are no longer adaptive. These various problems can be treated by means of conditioning procedures, which collectively are termed *behavior therapy* or *behavior modification*. Systematic desensitization counterconditions fear reactions with relaxation. Other kinds of exposure treatments keep people focused on distressing situations until long after the burst of anxiety calms down. Aversion therapy conditions negative reactions in the place of positive reactions. The principles of instrumental conditioning underlie a variety of therapy techniques. In biofeedback training, people learn to engage in certain kinds of internal behavior for such goals as controlling pain.

· GLOSSARY ·

Aversion therapy The conditioning of an aversive reaction to what's now a positive stimulus.

Behavior modification (or **behavior therapy**) The changing of behavior therapeutically through conditioning processes.

Behavioral assessment An assessment made by observing a person's overt behavior.

Biofeedback The technique of learning to control an internal activity by instrumental conditioning.

Classical conditioning The pairing of a neutral stimulus with an unconditioned stimulus.

Conditioned (or **conditional**) **response (CR)** A response to the CS that's acquired by classical conditioning.

Conditioned (or **conditional**) **stimulus (CS)** A neutral stimulus that's paired with a US to become conditioned.

Conflict The simultaneous arousal of two incompatible behavioral tendencies.

Contingency management Programs in which reinforcement is increased for desired behaviors and withheld after undesired behaviors.

Continuous reinforcement A schedule in which reinforcement follows each instance of the behavior.

Counterconditioning The linking of an emotion to a stimulus that differs from the emotion the stimulus now causes.

Discrimination Responding in a different manner to different stimuli.

Discriminative stimulus A cue that controls the occurrence of behavior.

Drive A motivational state that increases behaviors that are high in the habit hierarchy.

Emotional conditioning Classical conditioning in which the CR is an emotional reaction.

Epiphenomena Phenomena that occur along with behavior but have no causal role in behavior.

Exposure treatments   Treatments in which people stay focused on the distressing topic until well after their anxiety reaction dissipates.

Extinction   In classical conditioning, the reduction of a CR by repeating the CS without the US; in instrumental conditioning, the reduction of a behavioral tendency by removing reinforcement.

Generalization   Responding in a similar manner to somewhat different stimuli.

Habit hierarchy   The ordering of a person's potential responses by their likelihood.

Higher-order conditioning   Event in which a former CS now acts as a US in a new instance of conditioning.

Instrumental conditioning   Conditioning in which a behavior becomes more likely because it is followed by a desirable event or less likely because it is followed by an undesirable event.

Negative reinforcement   The removal of an aversive stimulus.

Partial reinforcement   A schedule in which the behavior is reinforced less often than every time it occurs.

Partial reinforcement effect   The fact that a behavior acquired through partial reinforcement is resistant to extinction.

Phobia   An inappropriately intense fear of some specific class of stimuli.

Physiological assessment   The measuring of physiological aspects of emotional reactions.

Positive reinforcement   A reinforcement involving addition of a desired stimulus.

Punisher   An undesired event that weakens the behavior that came before it.

Radical behaviorism   The position that behavior should be explained solely on the basis of observable events.

Reflex   An event in which a stimulus produces an automatic response.

Reinforcer   An event that strengthens the behavior that came before it.

Shaping   Changing the nature of ongoing behavior by reinforcing a specific aspect of the behavior.

Successive approximation   Shaping by reinforcing closer approximations of the desired behavior.

Systematic desensitization   A therapeutic procedure intended to extinguish fear.

Timeout   A punishment in which a child is temporarily removed from an enjoyable activity.

Unconditioned (or **unconditional**) **response (UR)**   A reflexive response to an unconditioned stimulus.

Unconditioned (or **unconditional**) **stimulus (US)**   A stimulus that causes a reflexive (unconditioned) response.

CHAPTER 13

Social-Cognitive Learning Theories

"I was watching my 2-year-old the other day in the kitchen when he reached in and popped open the childproof latch on one of the cabinet doors, just like that, and reached in for a pan. I was so surprised I thought my teeth were gonna fall out. How do you suppose he figured out how to do that? Must've been from watching me, I guess."

"My job has changed a lot in the last year. The business has expanded really fast. In fact, the boss hasn't always had time to create new procedures for everything we do. We've had to make our own guesses about what would work. It hasn't been too bad, though. We seem to be guessing right most of the time. Sometimes you don't know if a decision was right until way later on, but that just makes it more interesting."

AS YOU saw in Chapter 12, the concepts of learning are powerful tools for analyzing behavior. The principles of conditioning account well for two large parts of human experience. They explain how attitudes and preferences seem to derive from emotional reactions. They also explain how behavior tendencies strengthen and fade as a result of good and bad outcomes.

Powerful as those theories are, however, they weren't completely accepted, even by everyone who believes learning is the key to personality. Some became disenchanted with conditioning theories because they ignore aspects of behavior that seem obvious outside the lab. For example, people often learn by watching one another. People often decide whether to do something by thinking about what would happen if they did it.

How can conditioning theories account for a baby's suddenly doing something complex that he'd never done before? How can they deal with the decision processes of a person trying to guess what to do in a specific situation at work? The conditioning theories don't seem wrong, exactly, but they seem incomplete. They explain some things well, but they don't cover it all.

From these dissatisfactions—and from the work to which they led—came what might be seen as another generation of learning theories. They provide a view of personality based in learning, but they emphasize mental events more than do the earlier theories. For this reason, they're often

Many of the important reinforcers affecting human
behavior are social in nature.

called *cognitive* learning theories. They also emphasize social aspects of learning more than was done
before. Thus, they're often called *social* learning
theories.

Elaborations on Conditioning Processes

Theorists of the newer learning approach didn't
abandon conditioning principles. Instead, they
began by elaborating on them. The easiest way to
start a discussion of the newer theories is with
those elaborations.

SOCIAL REINFORCEMENT

As social learning theory began to evolve, its theorists began to rethink the usefulness
of studying lower animals. Can human behavior be analyzed by studying laboratory
rats, or is it wiser to focus on people? What variables matter most in *human* learning?
Asking these questions led to a different view of *reinforcement.*

Many came to believe that reinforcement in human experience (beyond infancy,
at least) has little or nothing to do with physical needs. Rather, people are most
affected by **social reinforcers:** acceptance, smiles, hugs, praise, approval, interest, and
attention from others (Bandura, 1978; Kanfer & Marston, 1963; Rotter, 1954, 1982).
The idea that the important reinforcers for people are social is one of several senses
in which these learning theories are social (Brokaw &
McLemore, 1983; A. H. Buss, 1983; Turner, Foa, & Foa,
1971).

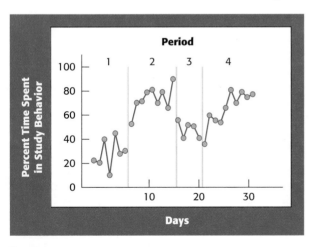

FIGURE 13.1
The effect of social reinforcement. This third-grade boy, whose
baseline level of studying in class was quite low (Period 1), was
systematically given attention and approval for studying. This
greatly increased his study behavior (Period 2). To see whether
the effect depended on social reinforcement, attention was
removed, which caused a decrease in studying (Period 3).
Reinstituting the social reinforcement (Period 4) caused a return
to a high rate of studying. *Source: Adapted from Hall et al., 1968.*

Here's an example of the power of social reinforcement. Hall, Lund, and Jackson (1968) examined
children who spent little time studying. After assessing
baselines, the researchers gave social reinforcement in
the form of attention and praise whenever a child
engaged in studying. Figure 13.1 shows the impact of
this procedure on one child. This child studied more
than twice as much when social reinforcement was
given than when it was not.

Emphasizing social reinforcement has a second
theoretical implication. In particular, social learning
theorists see no need to refer to *drives* in order to discuss reinforcement (e.g., Bandura, 1977a; Rotter, 1954,
1982). They say social reinforcers don't act via physical
need states. It isn't usually necessary, for example, that
the person being reinforced be in a state of deprivation.

A description of social reinforcement should also
mention **self-reinforcement.** This term has two meanings. The first is that people may give themselves
reinforcers after doing something they've set out to do

(Bandura, 1976; Goldiamond, 1976; Heiby, 1982). For example, you might reward yourself with a pizza for studying six straight hours, or you may get yourself a new piece of stereo equipment after a semester of good grades.

The second meaning of self-reinforcement derives more directly from the concept of social reinforcement. It's the idea that you react to your own behavior with approval or disapproval, much as you react to someone else's behavior. In responding to your actions with approval, you reinforce yourself. In responding with disapproval, you punish yourself. This sort of internal self-reinforcement and self-punishment plays an important role in social–cognitive learning theories of behavior and behavior change (Bandura 1977a, 1986; Kanfer, 1977; Kanfer & Hagerman, 1981; Mischel, 1973, 1979).

VICARIOUS EMOTIONAL AROUSAL

Another elaboration on conditioning comes from the fact that people can experience events vicariously—through someone else. Vicarious processes represent a second sense in which human learning is social. That is, vicarious processes involve two people: one to experience something directly, another to experience it indirectly.

One type of vicarious experience is **vicarious emotional arousal,** or empathy. This occurs when you observe someone feeling an intense emotion and you experience the same feeling yourself (usually less intensely). *Empathy* isn't the same as *sympathy,* a feeling of concern for someone else who's suffering (Gruen & Mendelsohn, 1986; Wispé, 1986). In empathy, you feel the same feeling, good or bad, as the other person (Stotland, 1969). Everyone can have this experience, but people differ in its intensity (Eisenberg et al., 1994; Levenson & Ruef, 1992; Marangoni, Garcia, Ickes, & Teng, 1995).

Examples of empathy are easy to point to (see also Box 13.1). When something wonderful happens to a friend, putting her in ecstasy, you feel happy yourself. Being

BOX 13.1 EMPATHY AND ALTRUISM

In this part of the chapter, we focus on the idea that vicarious processes influence learning. While we're talking about empathy, though, we'd like to point to another aspect of human behavior to which empathy is relevant: *altruism,* or helping. One general view on helping is that when you see someone else suffering, your empathy causes you to help. There are, however, different theories about *why* this happens.

A theory developed by Robert Cialdini and his colleagues (e.g., Cialdini, Schaller, Houlihan, Arps, Fultz, & Beaman, 1987) holds that empathy in this situation causes you to experience distress. One way to escape from the feelings is to do something to reduce the other person's suffering. In this view, empathy leads to helping as a way to reduce your *own* distress; the benefit to the other person is a side effect. A competing theory by Daniel Batson and his colleagues (Batson, 1990, 1991; Batson et al., 1988) holds that empathy creates a desire to relieve the suffering of the other person, plain and simple.

Which is right? The answer actually may be that *both* are right. There's evidence that exposure to someone else's distress provokes several different emotions, not just one (Batson, Fultz, & Schoenrade, 1987; Fultz, Schaller, & Cialdini, 1988). The feelings include distress, sadness, and sympathy for the other person. These different feeling qualities may well lead to very different motivations.

Despite some contradictory evidence (Batson, Bolen, Cross, & Neuringer-Benefiel, 1986; K. O. Smith, Keating, & Stotland, 1989), the data seem to suggest that empathic concern for someone else arouses a desire to ease that person's suffering and that this desire is separate from a desire to reduce one's own distress (Batson, 1990). The desire to reduce one's own distress also plays an important role, though, and may turn out to be the most important one (Maner, Luce, Neuberg, Cialdini, Brown, & Sagarin, 2002). No matter which pathway predominates, it's clear that empathy plays an important role in bringing people to each other's aid.

Empathy causes us to experience other's emotions. Others' grief elicits sadness from us and happiness elicits joy. As you look at this picture, you are probably beginning to feel the same emotions that the people in the picture are experiencing.

around someone who's frightened makes most people feel jumpy. Laughter is often contagious, even when you don't know what the other person is laughing at. There's even evidence that being around someone who's embarrassed can make you feel embarrassed too (R. S. Miller, 1987).

Experiencing vicarious emotional arousal doesn't *constitute* learning, but it creates an *opportunity* for learning. Recall the discussion of emotional conditioning from Chapter 12. Feeling an emotion in the presence of a neutral stimulus can cause that stimulus to become capable of evoking a similar emotion. It doesn't matter how the emotion is created. It's only necessary that it be *present*. The emotion can be caused by something you experience directly, but it can also arise vicariously. Thus, vicarious emotional arousal creates a possibility for classical conditioning. Such an event is called **vicarious classical conditioning.**

For example, in one procedure, participants simply watched a second person. A tone sounded (a neutral stimulus), and then the second person received an electric shock and grimaced. After a series of pairings of tone and shock, the observers began to react emotionally when the tone was sounded by itself (Berger, 1962; see also Bandura & Rosenthal, 1966; Vaughan & Lanzetta, 1980). This was true even though the observers never experienced pain directly. This appears to represent vicarious classical conditioning.

VICARIOUS REINFORCEMENT

Another vicarious process may be even more important. This one, called **vicarious reinforcement,** is very simple: If you observe someone do something that's followed by reinforcement, you become more likely to do the same thing yourself (Kanfer & Marston, 1963; Liebert & Fernandez, 1970). If you see a person punished after doing something, you're less likely to do it. The reinforcer or punishment went to the other person, not to you. But your own behavior is affected as though you'd received it yourself (see Figure 13.2).

This process is very important. It permits a lot of the trial and error of instrumental conditioning to take place secondhand. You don't have to "behave" all the time—just watch others behave and see what follows. Learning this way lets you learn about a lot of situations that other people are in, including some you'd rather not experience firsthand. Taking advantage of this can also save wear and tear on self-esteem, because you learn from other people's mistakes as well as their successes. Sometimes vicarious reinforcement even produces better learning than direct reinforcement does. Apparently, the vicarious situation lets you give "learning" some of the attention you'd normally devote to "behaving" (Berger, 1961; Hillix & Marx, 1960).

How do vicarious reinforcement and punishment influence people? Presumably, seeing someone be reinforced after a behavior leads you to infer you'd get the same reinforcer if you acted the same way (Bandura, 1971). If someone else is punished, you conclude the same thing would happen to you if you acted that way (Bandura, 1973; Walters & Parke, 1964). Often the inferences are more extensive. For example, you may limit your conclusion to situations that resemble the one you observed. To put it differently, you may learn *discriminations* vicariously. For instance, you may learn from observing others that talking in class leads to a scolding, but only in certain classes.

Note that the effect of vicarious reinforcement appears to involve developing an implicit (or even explicit) expectancy—that is, a mental model of links between acts and reinforcers. This is one case of a more general theme in the social–cognitive learning approach: the involvement of expectancies in learning. This theme comes up again later in the chapter.

SEMANTIC GENERALIZATION

We said the newer theories are more social and more cognitive than the earlier ones. So far, we've mostly focused on ways they're more social. Now let's consider ways they're more cognitive.

Another elaboration on the principles of conditioning came from looking more closely at the phenomenon of *generalization*—responding in a similar way to stimuli that are similar to (but not the same as) those for which conditioning has already taken place. Most animals generalize in response to varying lights or tones, but people can generalize in more interesting ways. They can do **semantic generalization,** which is generalization along a dimension of *meaning.* It's something people do often and take completely for granted.

Semantic generalization, just as any other generalization, can occur in both classical conditioning and instrumental conditioning (Diven, 1936; Maltzman, 1968). As an illustration of how it happens in classical conditioning, imagine a person who's been through a nasty divorce and now has negative emotional reactions to the mere mention of the word *divorce.* This person might well generalize this emotional reaction to semantically related words, such as *courtroom, lawyer, alimony,* and *breakup.*

Semantic generalization is explained by assuming that conditioning doesn't take place to a stimulus itself. Rather, it occurs toward cognitive elements that represent aspects of the stimulus. Semantic generalization occurs when there are mental associations to other words with related meanings. The theories discussed in this chapter assume this kind of elaborate mental structure. This is one of several senses in which they are *cognitive* learning theories.

RULE-BASED LEARNING

Another elaboration on conditioning is suggested by the idea that people can use instrumental learning to learn *rules,* rather than just to learn behaviors. Conditioning principles suggest that behavior tendencies build incrementally. Each reinforcer strengthens the tendency slightly. The longer the history of reinforcement, the stronger the tendency to behave in a certain way.

There are cases, though, that don't fit this picture. Perhaps the easiest illustration of how rules are used in human behavior comes from language acquisition. Language uses a large set of rules. For example, there are rules that specify how parts of a sentence are ordered and rules concerning how to create verb tenses and noun forms.

Early in life, children don't pay much attention to rules. They're focused on learning what specific words mean. As they get older and say things that are more

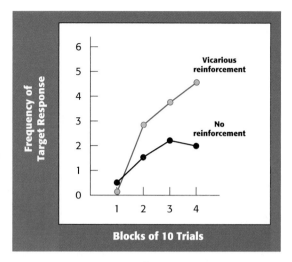

FIGURE 13.2
Effect of vicarious reinforcement. Participants were asked to say any word at random into a microphone whenever a signal was given. They also heard someone they thought was a co-participant say words periodically. In one condition, the experimenter reinforced the other voice by saying "good" every time it said a human noun. The measure of interest was how often the real participant said human nouns. As can be seen here, the reinforcement given to the other person caused a steady increase in the participants' tendency to do the same, despite the fact that they were never reinforced themselves. *Source: Adapted from Kanfer & Marston, 1963.*

complicated, they begin to use new word forms (e.g., new verb tenses), which they acquire word by word. At some point, though, children seem to realize that there are regularities to language, and they begin to use those regularities in their speech. A child may not be able to tell what the rule is, but the rule gets used when the child speaks. How do you know the child has learned a rule? You know because at this stage, the child sometimes *overregularizes*—uses the rule even where it doesn't apply (Marcus, 1996).

Consider the English rule for specifying past tense, which is to add *-ed* at the end (e.g., *cook* becomes *cooked*). There are many exceptions to this rule—verbs for which past tense is created a different way. For instance, *go* becomes *went, take* becomes *took, and break* becomes *broke*. Children use these irregular verb forms perfectly well when they first learn them. Apparently they memorize the words (which may involve an incremental conditioning process). The words are used correctly right up to the point where the rule starts to be used. At that point, the child applies the rule to every verb, even the irregular ones. As a result, the child now begins to make errors. A child who said "I went into the backyard" only a few weeks ago will now sometimes say "I goed into the backyard." This suggests that the child is acquiring a rule.

Once rule-based learning begins to take place, it becomes a pervasive feature of human learning. Past infancy, humans seem to respond to outcomes by learning implicit rules and conceptual principles. When you learn how to study for a psychology test, you're learning principles of preparing for tests in general. When you learn to drive, you're learning not just a set of movements, but a set of rules for creating forward motion, stopping, distancing from other cars, and so on. Whenever you've learned a rule, you can apply it to widely divergent new situations (e.g., preparing for an exam in a new course or driving in unfamiliar territory).

What, then, is the role of incremental conditioning in behavior? Perhaps incremental learning influences how a rule first emerges. That is, reinforcement processes may nudge you a little bit at a time in the right direction until you begin to identify a rule. When the rule comes into focus, concept learning takes over and the rate of learning increases.

EXPECTANCIES CONCERNING OUTCOMES

The learning theories in this chapter include a facet that can be viewed in either of two ways. It might be an elaboration on conditioning theories, or a step away from conditioning. This facet provides another sense in which these theories are cognitive. Specifically, the theories assume that people hold *expectancies* about whether given behaviors will lead to desired outcomes (Rotter, 1954). This expectancy, then, is an important determinant of what the person does.

This concept is often discussed along with a view on motivation termed *expectancy–incentive theory*. (We touched on this view in Chapter 5.) **Incentives** are values that goals have for the person. Incentives don't necessarily depend on deprivation. The concept thus differs from the concept of drive. **Expectancies,** here, are implicit judgments about the likelihood that a given behavior will attain the goal. Predicting behavior, from this view, requires you to take into account both incentives and expectancies (Feather, 1982).

The idea that people hold expectancies and that expectancies influence action wasn't new when it was absorbed into social learning theory (e.g., Brunswik, 1951; Lewin, 1951b; Postman, 1951; Tolman, 1932). But an emphasis on expectancies (in one form or other) is a cornerstone of this approach to personality (Rotter, 1954; see also Bandura, 1977a, 1986; Kanfer, 1977; Mischel, 1973).

BOX 13.2 THEORETICAL CONTROVERSY: HOW DOES LEARNING TAKE PLACE?

We've treated the principles of social–cognitive learning theories as elaborations on conditioning theories. Our aim has been to show how the various changes can be inserted into the picture of the learning process that was drawn in Chapter 12. Some of the modifications, however, raise questions about the concepts that they seem at first to embellish. This box briefly explores two such questions (see also Brewer, 1974).

The Role of Awareness

The first concerns the role of *awareness* in conditioning. It's long been assumed that conditioning is automatic (cf. Skinner, 1953). There's reason to suspect, though, that it involves cognition. For example, several studies seem to indicate that people show little or no classical conditioning from repeated pairings of stimuli unless they realize the stimuli are correlated (Chatterjee & Eriksen, 1962; Dawson & Furedy, 1976; Grings, 1973). On the other side of the coin, sometimes just expecting an aversive event (as a US) can produce conditioned responses to other stimuli

(Bridger & Mandel, 1964; Spacapan & Cohen, 1983). There's also evidence that people change their behavior in response to reinforcers only when they've become aware of what's being reinforced (Dulany, 1968; Spielberger & DeNike, 1966).

Extinction may also involve cognition. After classical conditioning of a fear response, a statement that the painful US will no longer be given sometimes eliminates fear of the CS (Bandura, 1969; Grings, 1973). Classical conditioning is supposed to be automatic, independent of thought. It's supposed to link stimuli directly with responses. But effects such as these suggest that expectations may play an important role (Bandura, 1986).

The Concept of Reinforcement

The second issue concerns the concept of *reinforcement*—and, by implication, the very nature of instrumental conditioning. Conditioning theorists say *reinforcers* are events that strengthen the tendency to do the behavior that preceded them. Yet Bandura (1976, 1977a), a prominent social learning theorist, explicitly rejected this sense of the reinforcement concept, while continuing to use the term *reinforcement*

(see also Bolles, 1972; Brewer, 1974; Rotter, 1954).

If reinforcers don't strengthen action tendencies, what do they do? Bandura said they do two things: In providing information about outcomes, they lead to hypotheses (expectancies) about what actions work in what settings. They also provide the potential for future motivational states through mental anticipation of the reinforcer in the future. In the same way, Henderlong and Lepper (2002) argued that praise enhances motivation by linking outcomes to causes that are controllable. Many people would agree that these various functions are important. But do the functions really constitute *reinforcement* in any meaningful sense? If not, do they actually belong in the process of instrumental conditioning?

The two issues addressed here—the nature of reinforcement and the role of awareness in conditioning—raise a far broader question: If reinforcement doesn't strengthen response tendencies and if conditioning isn't really conditioning, then just how strong a conceptual connection remains between the social–cognitive learning theories and the conditioning theories from which they grew?

Let's be sure we're clear about how this view differs from the conditioning approach (see also Box 13.2). Conditioning views assume that reinforcement has a direct effect on the probability of the behavior. They *don't* assume that mental representations (expectancies) matter. In the social–cognitive theories, people think over the available evidence—past outcomes, the situation they now confront—and judge the likelihood of the desired outcome. These expectancy judgments then influence behavioral choices (e.g., Kirsch, 1985).

Theorists disagree about exactly what kinds of expectancies matter. Major theories have been proposed concerning two specific types of expectancies. These ideas are described, in the order they were developed, in the next two sections.

LOCUS-OF-CONTROL EXPECTANCIES

The first idea was developed by Julian Rotter (1954, 1966) from his observations of people in therapy. Rotter's observations led him to this conclusion: Given the same event, different people learn different things. More specifically, some people learn from reinforcement, just as the principle of instrumental conditioning says. Others seem not to learn anything at all.

As an illustration, imagine two college freshmen, Bert and Ernie, who are shy and have trouble making conversation with women. Each goes to the university guidance center for help. The therapist provides suggestions for topics of conversation, ways to make the conversation move along, and so on. After some practice, the therapist asks each young man to go out and have a conversation with an attractive young woman who works in the next office.

In each case, the woman's response is pleasant and positive. Bert returns to the therapist and says, "I did what you suggested, and she seemed to like me. I'm going to remember those suggestions from now on, because they really seem useful." Ernie returns and says, "I did what you suggested. She acted friendly. Why? I don't know." Bert's response looks like instrumental learning: If something works well enough to be reinforced, it tends to be done again. But what sense does Ernie's response make?

Rotter became convinced that people differ from each other in the extent to which they see a cause-and-effect link between their behaviors and the reinforcers that follow. Rotter believed, as do most social learning theorists, that instrumental learning requires seeing that connection. Because some people (like Bert) see a link between behavior and reinforcer, the reinforcer affects their behavior. People who don't see a link (like Ernie) react haphazardly to reinforcers. Instrumental conditioning, for these people, isn't straightforward at all.

The phrase used in discussing this idea is **locus of control** (Rotter, Seeman, & Liverant, 1962; Rotter, 1966, 1990). *Locus* means "place." People termed *internals* (internal locus of control) see reinforcers as controlled from within, by their own actions. People termed *externals* (external locus of control) see reinforcers as controlled by things outside themselves, things other than their own actions. Although locus of control is a continuous dimension, it's often described by its endpoints. Because the terms *internal* and *external* are so commonly used to refer to the two orientations, the concept is referred to with the letters *I–E*.

This dimension has been studied both in experiments and in individual-difference research. In experiments, temporary locus of control is created by telling some people that task outcomes are caused by skill (internal) and telling other people that they're caused by chance (external). In one early study, Phares (1957) found that people with skill instructions used their outcomes as a guide to likely future outcomes. This is just what should occur from instrumental conditioning. It didn't occur, though, among those who were told their outcomes were based on luck (see also Holden & Rotter, 1962; Walls & Cox, 1971).

A huge body of evidence has also accumulated on individual differences in locus of control (Lefcourt, 1976; Phares, 1976). People with an internal locus of control adjust their expectancies upward after success and downward after failure. Externals often shift their expectancies in the direction *opposite* to the prior outcome. These differences in how people learn have important implications for other more elaborate behaviors, including such areas as academic achievement (Findley & Cooper, 1983).

Most research on this topic has used Rotter's measure (1966) of locus of control, but this scale has been criticized on several grounds. For one, it measures only generalized expectancies, not specific ones. It also mixes perceptions of control over personal outcomes with perceptions of control over government and so on (cf. Gurin, Gurin, Lao, & Beattie, 1969; Mirels, 1970). Finally, there is more diversity among externals than internals, because there are many different ways to have an external control orientation (Hersch & Scheibe, 1967).

These criticisms led to new measures (Lefcourt, 1981). Several people created measures that focus selectively on one domain of behavior at a time (Lefcourt, Martin, Fick, & Saleh, 1985; Lefcourt, Von Baeyer, Ware, & Cox, 1979; Paulhus, 1983; Paulhus & Christie, 1981; Wallston & Wallston, 1978, 1981). Another effort has been to separate causal influences from one another. For example, Levenson's (1973, 1981) scale distinguishes between chance factors and powerful others as external causes of outcomes.

Although the locus-of-control concept has been influential, a theoretical question has been raised about it. Recall the underlying rationale: Instrumental learning requires seeing a link between action and outcome. Rotter (1966) assumed that this link requires an internal locus of control. Others, however (e.g., Weiner, Heckhausen, Meyer, & Cook, 1972), challenged that view, noting that much of the relevant evidence confounds two qualities.

Consider the experiments described earlier, in which task outcomes were said to be based on either luck or skill. These two labels differ in the locus of the cause, but they also differ in other ways. Skill is a *stable* causal force, whereas chance is more *variable*. Which dimension influences change in expectancy: locus or stability? Research tends to favor stability (e.g., Diener & Dweck, 1978; McMahan, 1973; Meyer, 1980; Weiner et al., 1972; Weiner, Nierenberg, & Goldstein, 1976).

This raises broader questions about the meaning of the locus-of-control literature more generally. For example, does the I–E personality scale similarly confound locus with stability? This question hasn't been answered. It's been suggested, though, that the I–E scale confounds locus of causality with confidence about the outcomes, with internals being more confident than externals (Carver, 1997b). This would suggest that expectancies about good outcomes in the future may be what matters, rather than the perceived locus of cause.

EFFICACY EXPECTANCIES

A second variation on the theme of expectancies also derives partly from clinical experience. Albert Bandura (1977b) argued that people with problems generally know exactly what actions are needed to reach the outcomes they want. Just knowing what to do, however, isn't enough. You also have to be confident of your ability to *do* the behavior. This confidence about having the ability to carry out a desired action is what Bandura terms **efficacy expectancy,** or **self-efficacy.** To Bandura, when therapy works, it's because the therapy has restored the person's sense of efficacy, or confidence in the ability to carry out actions that earlier were troublesome.

The concept of efficacy expectancy draws conceptually on a variety of earlier sources, including White's discussion (1959) of competence motivation (outlined in Chapter 10). White believed the competence motive is central to human behavior. Bandura argues more specifically that a sense of personal efficacy is needed for people to strive consistently (see also Box 13.3).

Efficacy expectancy differs from internal locus of control, despite superficial similarities. In principle, people with internal locus of control see both good and bad outcomes as depending on their own actions. In principle, they don't necessarily feel they have the competence to act in effective ways. In theory, they're just as likely to view bad outcomes as showing they're bad at what they're trying to do. For example, Joe has an internal locus of control. He believes that getting good grades relates

BOX 13.3   THE THEORIST AND THE THEORY

Bandura Stresses Personal Agency but Also Appreciates the Role of Chance

Albert Bandura has made many contributions to the learning perspective on personality, having done pioneering work on observational learning and the effects of social reward. More recently, he has argued forcefully for the importance of feelings of personal efficacy. Yet this theorist who places such emphasis on personal agency has also been outspoken in pointing to the role of chance encounters in people's lives, including his own.

Bandura was born in 1925 in a small town in northern Alberta, Canada, the son of wheat farmers of Polish descent. His town's school had only two teachers and a handful of students, but it gave him a good enough start to send him to college at the

University of British Columbia. There, sharing a ride to class with several other students, he had a chance encounter that would change his life. His friends, mostly pre-med and engineering students, had very early classes. Lacking anything better to do at that early hour, Bandura decided to kill time by taking a psychology course. He liked it so much that he decided to make psychology his career (Evans, 1989).

A similar chance encounter gave Bandura a special interest in *clinical* psychology. During a summer spent as a laborer, filling potholes in the Alaskan highway in the Yukon, he found himself in the company of an odd assortment of characters, people who had fled to the remote North for a variety of unsavory reasons. This chance exposure to a range of bizarre individuals caused Bandura to develop an appreciation for the minor "psychopathology of everyday life," which

continued to spark his interest for years thereafter.

A third chance encounter is especially notable (Bandura, 1982b). While a graduate student, he went one day to play golf with a friend. By chance, they found themselves playing behind two attractive young women. The two twosomes became a foursome for the rest of the round, and one of the women later became Bandura's wife. As Bandura (1982b) wrote, without this chance encounter "it is exceedingly unlikely" the two of them would ever have met.

Surely this story isn't unique. Many lifelong relationships begin with improbable and unforeseen encounters. Indeed, Bandura's point was how often life is influenced in dramatic and critical ways by chance events. It's somewhat ironic, though, that chance encounters played such an important role in determining the life goals of this theorist whose belief in human self-agency came to be so strong.

directly to his preparing for exams. He also believes he doesn't know how to prepare for exams. Thus, it's possible for someone with an internal locus of control to have low expectancies of personal efficacy.

What about the person with an external locus of control? This one is a little trickier. In a sense, the concept of self-efficacy seems less relevant to these people at all. If their outcomes depend on the whims of fate or powerful people around them, efficacy isn't much of an issue. One might argue that the absence of a sense of personal control implies a low sense of personal efficacy. On the other hand, Bandura sometimes treats a belief in the efficacy of external agents (such as medications) as equivalent to belief in one's own personal efficacy. This suggests that even externals can have high efficacy expectancies if they see themselves as lucky or well connected.

Research on Bandura's concept began by focusing on changes associated with therapy and quickly expanded to examine a wide range of other topics (Bandura, 1986, 1997). Here are some examples: Brown and Inouye (1978) found that people with high self-efficacy were more persistent on problems than people with lower efficacy perceptions. Wood and Bandura (1989) found that self-efficacy influenced how business students performed in a management task. Manning and Wright (1983) found that efficacy perceptions predicted the ability to control pain during childbirth (see also Litt, 1988). Cozzarelli (1993) found that efficacy perceptions predicted adjustment to the experience of abortion. Bauer and Bonano (2001) found that efficacy perceptions predicted less grief over time among persons adapting to bereave-ment. Efficacy expectancies have also been shown to predict whether drug users stay clean during the year after treatment (Ilgen, McKellar, & Tiet, 2005). There's even evi-dence that acquiring a sense of efficacy can have a positive influence on immune function (Wiedenfeld, O'Leary, Bandura, Brown, Levine, & Raska, 1990).

Beyond these direct associations, perceptions of efficacy may underlie the posi-tive effects found for other variables. For example, efficacy perceptions may be a pathway by which social support gives people a sense of well-being (Major et al., 1990). There's also evidence that self-esteem and optimism operate through percep-tions of efficacy (Major, Richards, Cooper, Cozzarelli, & Zubek, 1998).

Observational Learning

As we said earlier, many aspects of social learning theory can be viewed as elabora-tions on the concepts of classical and instrumental conditioning. There is, however, at least one part of social learning theory that leaves the conditioning concepts behind, suggesting a completely different basis for learning. This part is called **observational learning.** Two people are involved in this process, providing yet another basis for the term *social learning theory*.

Observational learning takes place when one person performs an action and another person observes the act and thereby acquires the ability to repeat it (Bandura, 1986; Flanders, 1968). For such an event to represent observational learning unam-biguously, the behavior should be one the observer doesn't already know. At a minimum, the behavior should be one the observer hadn't previously associated with the context in which it's now occurring.

Observational learning allows people to pack huge amounts of information into their minds quickly. This makes it very important. Observational learning occurs as early as the first year of life (Meltzoff, 1985). What's most remarkable about it is how simple it is. It seems to require little more than the observer's noticing and under-standing what's going on.

This last statement requires several qualifications, which help to give a better sense of what observational learning is (see Table 13.1). First, observational learning requires the observer to *pay attention* to the model (the person being observed). If attention isn't given to the right aspect of the model's behavior, the behavior won't be encoded well enough to be remembered.

This principle has several implications. For one, it means that observational learn-ing will be better with some models than others. Models that draw attention for some reason—from their power or attractiveness—are most likely to be effective. The role of attention also means that some *acts* are more likely to be encoded than others. Acts that are especially noticeable have more impact than acts that aren't (cf. McArthur, 1981; Taylor & Fiske, 1978). Other variables that matter here are the observer's capa-bilities, intentions, and concentration. For instance, if an observer is distracted by music while viewing a model, he may miss entirely what she's doing.

A second important set of processes in observational learning concern *retention* of what's observed. In one way or another, what's been observed has to be represented in memory (which makes this a cognitive as well as a social sort of learning).

Two strategies of coding predominate. One is *imaginal coding,* or creating a mental picture of what you're seeing. The other is *verbal coding,* or creating a description to

Table 13.1 Four Categories of Variables (and specific examples of each) That Influence Observational Learning and Performance. *Source:* Adapted from Bandura, 1977a, 1986.

Attention for Encoding	Characteristics of the model:
	    Is the model attractive or powerful or an expert?
	Characteristics of the behavior:
	    Is the behavior distinctive, clear, and simple?
	Characteristics of the observer:
	    Is the observer motivated to attend and capable of attending?

Retention	Use of imagery as an encoding strategy Use of language as an encoding strategy Use of mental rehearsal to keep in memory
Production	Observer's capacity to produce necessary responses Observer's prior experience with overall behavior Observer's prior experience with components of behavior

Performance	Consequences to the model:
	    Is the model rewarded or punished, or are there no consequences?
	Consequences to the observer:
	    Is the observer rewarded or punished, or are there no consequences?

yourself of what you're seeing. Either strategy can produce a memory that can later be used to repeat the behavior (Bandura & Jeffery, 1973; Bandura, Jeffery, & Bachicha, 1974; Gerst, 1971). Mental rehearsal (repeating the mental picture or description) also helps retention (Jeffery, 1976).

Once an action's in memory, one more thing is needed for the act to occur. Specifically, you have to translate what you observed into a form you can *produce* in your own actions. How successful you are depends partly on whether you already know some of the components of the act. It's easier to reproduce a behavior if you have the skills that underlie it or know some of the action involved in it. That's why it's often so easy for experienced athletes to pick up a new sport. They often already know movements similar to those used in the new sport.

The importance of having components available also applies to the encoding process (see W. Johnson & Kieras, 1983). For example, if you already know names (or have good images) for components of the modeled activity, you have to put less into memory. If you have to remember every little thing, it gets harder to keep straight. Think of the difference in complexity between the label *Sauté one onion* (or *Remove the brake pad assembly*) and the set of physical acts the label refers to. Now think about how much easier it is to remember the label than the sequence of acts. Using the label as mental shorthand simplifies the task for memory. But you can do this only if you know what the label refers to (see the cartoon).

SHOE by Jeff MacNelly

Having readily available summary labels for action sequences greatly simplified the task of storing things in memory. *Reprinted by permission: Tribune Media Services.*

ACQUISITION VERSUS PERFORMANCE

Observational learning permits fast learning of complicated behaviors. Given what we've just discussed, it also seems to be a case of "the more you already know, the easier it is to learn." An important distinction needs to be made, however, between the *acquisition* of a behavioral potential and the *performance* of the behavior. People don't always repeat the actions they see. In fact, people learn a great deal of actions that they never do.

To know whether observational learning will result in behavior, we need to know something else. We need to know what reinforcement or punishment the person expects the behavior to lead to (Bandura, 1977a, 1986). A good illustration of the distinction between acquisition and performance comes from an early study of children by Bandura (1965). Children saw a five-minute film in which an adult model performed a series of distinctive aggressive acts toward an inflated doll. The model accompanied each act with verbalizations, each associated with one aggressive behavior. For example, as he pounded the doll on the head with a mallet, he said, "Sockeroo—stay down."

At this point, three experimental conditions were created using three versions of the film. In one condition, another adult entered the picture, praised the model as a "strong champion," and said his excellent performance deserved a special treat. He then gave the model some candy, making it clear that it and the social approval were both conse-

quences of the aggressive acts. In a second condition (the no-consequence control group), this final scene was simply omitted. In a third condition, this scene was replaced by one in which the second adult came in and punished the model for the aggressive actions. In this condition, the model was called a "big bully" and was spanked by the other person, who made it clear that the punishment resulted from the aggressive acts.

After seeing one of these three films, each child in the study was taken to an observation room that held a wide range of toys. Among the toys was an inflated doll identical to the one in the film. The child was left alone for 10 minutes. Hidden assistants noted whether the child did any of the previously modeled aggressive acts. The number of acts the child did was the measure of spontaneous *performance*.

Ten minutes later, the experimenter returned. At this point, the child was offered an incentive (fruit juice and picture stickers) to show the experimenter as many of the previously viewed aggressive acts as the child could remember. The number of behaviors correctly shown was the measure of *acquisition*.

The results of this study are very instructive. The top line in Figure 13.3 shows how many acts children

Many complex behaviors are acquired by children through observational learning.

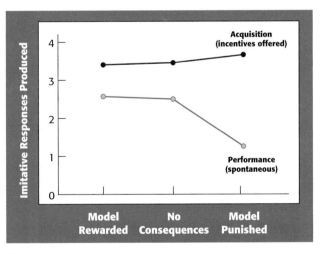

FIGURE 13.3

Acquisition and performance. Participants observed a model display a series of aggressive acts that led to reward, no consequences, or punishment. Participants then had an opportunity to imitate the model spontaneously (performance). Finally, they were asked to demonstrate what they could remember of the model's behavior (acquisition). The study showed that reinforcement of the model played no role in acquisition but did influence spontaneous performance. *Source: Adapted from Bandura & Walters, 1963.*

reproduced correctly in the three experimental conditions, when given an incentive to do so (the measure of acquisition). It's obvious there isn't a trace of difference in acquisition. Reinforcement or punishment for the model had no impact here.

Spontaneous performance, though, shows a different picture. The outcome for the model influenced what the observers did spontaneously. As in many studies (Thelen & Rennie, 1972), the effect of punishment was greater than the effect of reward, although other evidence shows that both can be effective in this sort of situation (e.g., Kanfer & Marston, 1963; Liebert & Fernandez, 1970; Rosekrans, 1967).

In conclusion, vicarious reinforcement influences whether people spontaneously do behaviors they've acquired by observation. This effect is the same as in any instance of vicarious reinforcement. It thus reflects vicarious instrumental learning. In contrast, reinforcement to the model has no influence on acquisition of the behavioral potential. Thus, observational learning and instrumental learning are distinct processes.

Observational learning is a powerful process in human learning (and in the learning of some other animals; Zentall, Sutton, & Sherburne, 1996). Its power and its value to personality development lie in the fact that it allows huge amounts of information to be added to a person's behavioral repertoire quickly. It's much faster than shaping through instrumental conditioning or even vicarious instrumental conditioning. On the other hand, observational learning doesn't determine which acts occur in which situations (motivational and reinforcement variables seem to do that). Rather, it's a way for behavior potentials to be acquired for use. To paraphrase Bandura (1977a), once the ability to engage in observational learning emerges (in infancy), it's virtually impossible to prevent people from learning what they see.

Manifestations of Cognitive and Social Learning

The processes described thus far provide a set of tools for analyzing behavior. To indicate how broadly they can be used, the next sections describe two areas in which the processes play central roles (see also Box 13.4). The various processes get tangled up with one another in both areas. Nevertheless, they can be distinguished conceptually, and we'll do so as we go along.

MODELING AND SEX-ROLE ACQUISITION

Sex roles are behavior patterns that people in a given culture see as more appropriate in one sex than the other (cf. Bussey & Bandura, 1999; Deaux & Lewis, 1984; Eagly, 1987; Eagly & Wood, 1999). As with all roles, sex roles are expectations about how to act. American society has a fairly stereotyped set of sex roles, though their content is always evolving somewhat.

Children learn about sex roles early in life. This knowledge is acquired by several processes discussed in this chapter. Some information comes from explicitly stated rules ("Little girls don't play tackle football" or "Little boys don't wear dresses"). Observational learning also plays a role (Sears, Rau, & Alpert, 1965). Sons who watch their fathers shaving and working with wrenches encode how to do those things. Daughters who watch their mothers do housework and cook encode how to do those things.

But wait a minute. Don't children watch both parents? Shouldn't boys and girls learn the same things by observational learning? Yes and no. Certainly, both boys and girls do encode a lot of information about activities of both sexes. But there's some

BOX 13.4 MODELING AND DELAY OF GRATIFICATION

Social–cognitive learning theories emphasize that people's acts are determined by cognitions about potential outcomes of their behavior (Kirsch, 1985). This emphasis returns us to the concept of **self-control,** the idea that people sometimes restrain their own actions.

Self-control is an idea we considered at length in Chapter 10. As noted there, people often face the choice of getting a desired outcome immediately or getting a better outcome later on. The latter choice—delay of gratification—isn't all that easy to make. Imagine that after saving for four months, you have enough money to go to an oceanside resort for two weeks. You know that if you saved for another 10 months, you could take the trip to Europe you've always wanted. One event is closer in time. The other is better, but getting it requires more

self-control. Ten more months with no vacation is a long time.

As we noted earlier, many variables influence people's ability to delay. Especially relevant to this chapter is the role played by *modeling* (Mischel, 1974). Consider a study by Bandura and Mischel (1965) of fourth- and fifth-graders who (according to a pretest) preferred either immediate or delayed reward. Children of each preference were put into one of three conditions. In one, the child saw an adult model make a series of choices between desirable items that had to be delayed and less desirable ones that could be had immediately. The model consistently chose the opposite of the child's preference. Children in the second condition read about the model's choices. In the third condition (a control group), there was no modeling.

All the children were given a series of delay-of-gratification choices just afterward and again a month later. Seeing a model who chose immediate rewards

made delay-preferring children more likely to choose immediate reward. In the same manner, seeing a model who chose delayed rewards made immediate-preferring children more likely to delay. These effects were maintained a month later. Similar effects were shown among 18- to 20-year-old prison inmates who'd had only weak tendencies to delay gratification before being exposed to models showing strong preference for delay (Stumphauzer, 1972).

How do models exert this influence on self-control? Presumably through vicarious reinforcement. In the Bandura and Mischel (1965) study, for example, the model vocalized reasons for preferring one choice over the other. The statements imply that the model felt reinforced by his choices (see also Bandura, Grusec, & Menlove, 1967; Mischel & Liebert, 1966; Parke, 1969). Thus, people obtain information from seeing how others react to experiences and use that information to guide their own actions.

---

evidence that a discrimination is made even in encoding. Why? There's evidence that children prefer and identify more with same-sex adults (Maccoby & Wilson, 1957; Mischel, 1970; Stevenson, Hale, Hill, & Moely, 1967). People also presumably attend more to models they like than to models they don't like, which means more encoding.

A far greater contributor to sex-role behavior, however, is the subtle web of social reinforcement, both direct and vicarious. Children are rewarded for attending to, and acting like, adults and children of their own sex. Little Tommy gets more approval when watching Daddy change the oil in the car than when watching Mommy put on her makeup. Little Suzy is treated the opposite way. Given these patterns of reinforcement, Tommy and Suzy spend more time watching the activities of one adult than the other. They also probably see those activities differently in terms of relevance to themselves.

Even if they prefer models of their own sex, children undoubtedly learn a lot of opposite sex-role behavior. But remember the acquisition–performance distinction. At an early age, children see which actions are gender appropriate and spontaneously perform mostly those appropriate to their gender (Bussey & Bandura, 1984). Why? They've been led to anticipate certain reward and punishment contingencies (Fagot, 1977; Raskin & Israel, 1981). Suzy may be praised and cuddled after putting on makeup, but Tommy won't (nor will the message be lost on Mikey, if he happens to be observing).

There's one question about gender roles that's been debated, even argued over: Why is the content of the roles what it is? The evolutionary view (discussed in Chapter 6) gave one answer. Another answer is that the qualities of the roles depend on cultural contexts. Wood and Eagly (2002) summarized evidence that where cultures differ in pressures, the nature of gender roles also differs across cultures.

Though live models are important in the acquisition of sex roles (and other behavior), in the modern world, **symbolic models** are also important. Indeed, their influence is pervasive. Symbolic models are figures on TV, in movies, magazines, books, and so on. The actions they portray—and the patterns of reinforcement around those actions—can have a big impact on both acquisition and performance of observers. If TV portrays women as weak and silly, then observers learn that weakness is feminine behavior. If TV portrays men as hiding their emotions, then observers learn that masculinity means not showing feelings.

In the social learning view, there's nothing magic about what behaviors define sex roles. Indeed, this point of view would see all roles as a little arbitrary. Given that there's something of value in each sex role, many wonder whether there may be virtue in encouraging people to have the positive qualities of both roles. Having both so-called masculine qualities (e.g., assertiveness) and feminine qualities (e.g., gentleness, sympathy) has been called **androgyny** (S. L. Bem, 1974, 1975; Kaplan & Bean, 1976; Kaplan & Sedney, 1980). It's been suggested that such diversity makes people more adaptable and flexible (Taylor & Hall, 1982).

MODELING OF AGGRESSION AND THE ISSUE OF MEDIA VIOLENCE

Another topic to which social–cognitive learning theories have been applied is symbolic models in aggression. This topic is particularly sensitive, given the level of violence in TV programs and movies. All the ways models influence observers are implicated here, to one degree or another (C. A. Anderson et al., 2003). At least three processes have been proposed, and there is a lot of support for all of them.

First, people who observe innovative aggressive techniques (live or on film) can and do acquire the techniques as behavior potentials by observational learning. That is, observational learning *does* occur wherever it *can* occur (Geen, 1998; Heller & Polsky, 1975). This principle looms large as producers strive to make movies seem new and different every year. A common source of novelty is new methods for inflicting pain on others.

Second, observing violence that is permitted, condoned, or even rewarded helps promote the belief that aggression is an appropriate way to deal with conflict or disagreement. Vicarious reinforcement thus increases the likelihood that viewers will use such tactics themselves. (By implication, this is also why some people worry about the level of sex on TV and in movies.)

When it's suggested that violence is reinforced in the media, a common reply is that the "bad guys" in TV and movie stories get punished. Note two things, though. First, the punishment usually comes late in the story, after aggression has produced a lot of short-term reinforcement. As a result, aggression is linked more closely to reinforcement than to punishment. Second, the actions of the heroes usually are also aggressive, and these actions are highly reinforced. From that, there's a clear message that aggression is a good way to deal with problems.

Does viewing "acceptable" aggression make people more likely to use aggression in their own lives when they're annoyed? The overwhelming majority of the evidence says yes. Whether the model is live (e.g., Baron & Kempner, 1970) or symbolic (e.g., Bandura, 1965; Liebert & Baron, 1972), exposure to aggressive models increases the aggression of observers.

The final point to be made here is more diffuse. It's that repeated exposure to violence *desensitizes* observers to human suffering. The shock and upset that most people would associate with acts of extreme violence are extinguished by repeated exposure to violence. The police chief of Washington, DC, was quoted in 1991 as saying, "When I talk to young people involved with violence, there's no remorse, . . . no sense that this is morally wrong." Exposure to violence in video games can produce a similar desensitizing effect (Bartholow, Sestir, & Davis, 2005).

Evidence of desensitization comes from several sources (e.g., Cline, Croft, & Courrier, 1973; Geen, 1981; Thomas, Horton, Lippincott, & Drabman, 1977). The results of one study are shown in Figure 13.4 (Thomas et al., 1977, Experiment 1). Participants were attached to a machine that measured emotional reactions as "bumps" of arousal. They first watched a videotape of either an exciting volleyball championship or a violent program. As can be seen in Figure 13.4, A, the tapes (overall) were equally arousing. Later, participants briefly viewed what they thought was a real confrontation resulting in physical violence. As Figure 13.4, B, shows, those who'd seen the violent TV show reacted less to this than did the other group. Watching the TV violence apparently made them less sensitive to real-life violence.

This process has long-term consequences that are profoundly worrisome. As people's emotional reactions to violence become extinguished, being victimized (and also victimizing others) is seen as an ordinary part of life. It's hard to study the impact of this process in its full scope. The effects are pervasive enough, however, that they represent a real threat to society.

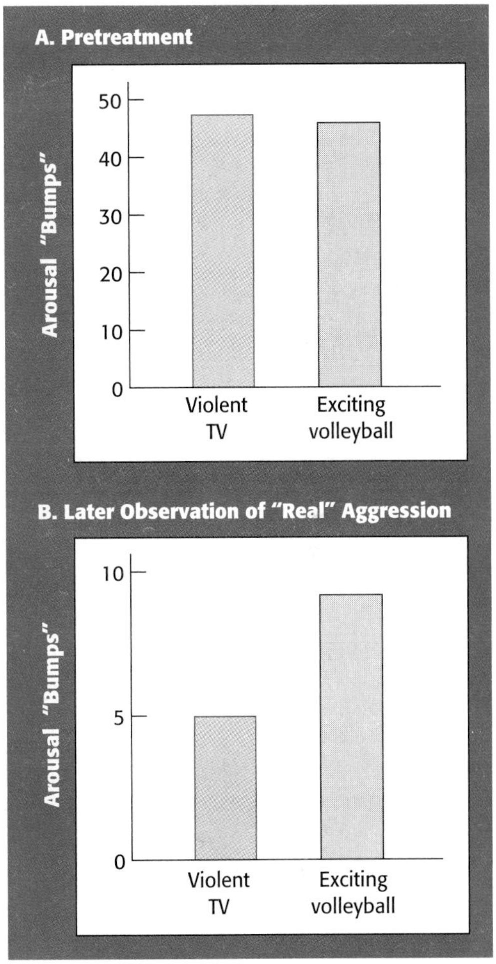

FIGURE 13.4
Habituation to aggression by viewing aggression. (A) Participants watched a videotape of either an exciting volleyball championship or a violent TV program, which were equally arousing (as measured by arousal bumps). (B) When seeing an apparently real confrontation that resulted in physical violence, participants who had watched the violent TV reacted less to this aggression than did the other group. Presumably watching the TV violence made them less sensitive to later real-life violence. *Source: Adapted from Thomas, Horton, Lippincott, & Drabman, 1977, Experiment 1.*

Assessment

Let's turn now to assessment. This section addresses the social–cognitive learning view on assessment in very general terms. The goal is to make explicit some of the logical threads that underlie it.

Three issues are important. The first is that self-report devices are widely used to assess personality from this view, as opposed to behavioral observation. Recall that the cognitive view of learning emphasizes the role of thoughts in behavior. Given that, it's only natural to take people's reports of their tendencies to act in various ways and to experience various kinds of thoughts and feelings as being appropriate and useful sources of information.

The second issue concerns what variables are measured. Given the assumption that cognitive processes influence behavior, assessment from this view tends to focus on *experiential* variables. That is, instead of charting actions, assessments frequently ask people how they feel in certain situations or what kinds of thoughts go through their minds in those situations (see Table 13.2). Particularly important are people's

Table 13.2 Assessing People's Psychological Experiences in Difficult Exam Situations. The first set of items (answered on scales ranging from "Strong agreement" to "Strong disagreement" examines emotional reactions to the exam; the second set examines cognitions that can interfere with test performance. *Source:* Items from Morris, Davis, & Hutchings, 1981. Copyright 1981 by the American Psychological Association. Adapted by permission of the author.

Emotionality	I feel my heart beating fast.
	I am so tense that my stomach is upset.
	I have an uneasy, upset feeling.
	I am nervous.
	I feel panicky.
Worry	I feel regretful.
	I am afraid that I should have studied more for this test.
	I feel that others will be disappointed in me.
	I feel I may not do as well on this test as I could.
	I do not feel very confident about my performance on this test.

expectancies: expectancies of control, expectancies of coping, and expectancies of personal efficacy. This emphasis should be no surprise, because expectations are regarded as so important in this view of behavior.

A third issue is also implicit in the last paragraph. Assessment in the social–cognitive learning view tends to emphasize responses to *specific* categories of situations. This emphasis actually applies throughout the learning perspective on personality. It reflects the fact that behavior can vary greatly from one situation to another. The social–cognitive learning view differs from the conditioning view, however, in its emphasis on *personal views* of situations, rather than *objective definitions* of situations (e.g., Mischel, 1973). One person sees a philosophy class as a chance to learn something new; another person sees the same class as a threat to his grade-point average. This approach says it's people's representations that determine how they act. This must be taken into account in assessment.

Problems in Behavior, and Behavior Change

Let's now turn to problems in behavior from the social–cognitive learning view and some of the treatment procedures that derive from this view. Again, the discussion combines concepts from conditioning theories with concepts that are more cognitive and social in nature.

CONCEPTUALIZING BEHAVIORAL PROBLEMS

As noted in Chapter 12, principles of conditioning suggest that inappropriate emotions such as fear result from classical conditioning. Similarly, inappropriate behavioral tendencies result from reinforcement patterns. The social–cognitive learning approach suggests further contributors, using three key principles: vicarious conditioning, expectancies, and observational learning.

Thinking about vicarious processes suggests two changes to earlier analyses. First, you don't have to have direct experience with a stimulus to develop an emotional response (such as fear) toward it. You can acquire emotional responses vicariously. Second, your patterns of action can be influenced by watching outcomes that other people experience. Vicarious reinforcement can build in a behavior, even if the behavior isn't desirable. Vicarious punishment can reduce your tendency to do a behavior, even if the behavior is actually adaptive.

All these effects may be viewed as mediated in part by expectancies (see Bandura, 1986). If you *expect* to experience strong fear in high places, you'll avoid high places. If you *expect* to get social approval for bullying someone else, you may do it. If you *expect* to be rejected by someone, or to do badly on an exam, or even to do badly at "life" (Scheier & Carver, 1992), you may not try. These expectations can develop from direct experience, from vicarious experience, from things that other people tell you, or from putting two and two together in your own head.

No matter how expectations are acquired, they can have powerful effects on your actions and feelings. Negative expectations can cause you to stop trying, thereby making success impossible. The conviction that success won't come leads to a pattern of low motivation and reduced effort that's sometimes called **learned helplessness** (see Box 13.5).

A final source of behavior problems, in the social learning view, is more specific. Problems sometimes reflect **skill deficits.** A person with a skill deficit is literally unable to do something that's necessary or desirable. Some skill deficits reflect deficits in observational learning. That is, in some cases, people never had good models to learn from. Without being able to learn how to do important things (such as cooking, taking notes in class, dancing, and many others), people can have gaps in the ability to function.

Note that having a skill deficit can influence the development of expectations. People who know they lack particular skills come to anticipate bad outcomes when the skills are relevant. (For example, people who see themselves as lacking social skills come to expect the worst in social situations.) People who do have the relevant skills may come to view the situations as being under their personal control (Lefcourt et al., 1985).

Modeling-Based Therapy for Skill Deficits

It will be no surprise to discover that *modeling* plays an important role in the therapy techniques identified with the social–cognitive learning viewpoint. Techniques involving modeling have been used in two areas: skill deficits and emotion-based problems.

When people lack specific types of adaptive behaviors, they can often add the skills by observing good models. The model is put in the situation for which the skill is lacking and makes an action appropriate to the situation. The observer (the person in therapy) is then encouraged to repeat the action. This repetition can be overt (action), or it can be covert (mentally practicing the action). Indeed, the modeling can also be covert, with the subject being told to imagine someone else doing a particular behavior within a particular scenario (Kazdin, 1975).

In principle, modeling can be used to supply missing skills any place there are deficits. Research on this subject, however, commonly focuses on such areas as basic social skills (e.g., La Greca & Santogrossi, 1980; La Greca, Stone, & Bell, 1983; Ross, Ross, & Evans, 1971) and assertiveness (Goldfried & Davison, 1976; Kazdin, 1974, 1975; McFall & Twentyman, 1973; Rosenthal & Reese, 1976). *Assertiveness* is acting to make sure your rights aren't violated while also not violating someone else's rights. It can be hard to know just how to respond to a problem situation in a manner that's

BOX 13.5   HELPLESSNESS: CASE STUDY OF A THEORY

The concept of learned helplessness originated in the finding that exposure to painful and unavoidable shocks made it harder for dogs to learn an avoidance or escape response when that response became possible (Overmier & Seligman, 1967; Seligman & Maier, 1967). This finding led to a flood of research on humans. The typical procedure looks at effects of prolonged failure on later performances. Extensive failure often has an adverse—sometimes devastating—impact on later performance (e.g., Hiroto & Seligman, 1975; I. W. Miller & Norman, 1979; Roth, 1980). This has implications for analyzing problems such as depression (Abramson, Metalsky, & Alloy, 1989; Abramson, Seligman, & Teasdale, 1978).

The evolution of theories of helplessness makes an interesting case study. It's particularly interesting when taken in combination with the issue discussed in Box 13.2—the relationship between conditioning and social–cognitive learning theories. The first explanation for the effect was based, somewhat loosely, on conditioning principles. Exposure to unavoidable shock results in learning that an outcome (removal of pain) isn't contingent on behavior (avoidance effort). The result is a reduction in effort, to the point where the animal no longer tries at all.

Indeed, the term *learned helplessness* was coined because the animal looked as though it had learned it was helpless to avoid the shocks. In conditioning terms, the pretreatment extinguished the attempt to escape. Thus, the animal doesn't do any escape behavior when it actually would work.

As analogous research was done on people, however, the theory became progressively more cognitive. Explanations of helplessness in humans typically rely on expectations of future noncontingency (Abramson et al., 1978) or expectations of being unable to control outcomes (Wortman & Brehm, 1975). In simple terms, the person develops (temporarily) the idea that good outcomes can't be obtained because they're not related to his or her actions.

More recent analyses of helplessness have included additional cognitive processes. Several analyses have emphasized attributional variables as a way of discussing how the expectation of bad outcomes develops (Abramson et al., 1978; I. W. Miller & Norman, 1979; Roth, 1980). Vicarious and verbal–symbolic processes also appear to play an important role here. For example, watching someone else experience noncontingency (particularly someone you think has the same ability as you) can produce behavioral impairments in you (Brown & Inouye, 1978; DeVellis, DeVellis, & McCauley,

1978). These various effects appear to indicate that the *cognition* of uncontrollability is critical to helplessness, rather than actual uncontrollability.

As if these weren't cognitive enough, another approach added yet another layer of thought processes. This approach (Frankel & Snyder, 1978; M. L. Snyder, Stephan, & Rosenfield, 1978) holds that people do poorly after prolonged failure because the failure threatens their self-esteem. That is, rather than risk further confirmation that they can't do the task, they stop trying. The withdrawal of effort creates a face-saving attribution while at the same time (ironically) causing the poor outcome they'd been afraid of in the first place (Frankel & Snyder, 1978).

Thus, a phenomenon identified in the animal conditioning lab was extended to human behavior. In doing this, however, theorists who pursued the phenomenon have increasingly invoked cognitive processes as a way of accounting for it. Doing so raises several questions: Do the same processes apply to human helplessness as apply to helplessness in other species? One probably wouldn't want to argue that dogs stop trying to escape because they're concerned about their self-esteem. But what about the other processes—expectancies and attributions? At the moment, there's no clear answer to this question.

---

properly assertive. But observing a model who illustrates appropriate responses (combined with a little practice, to make sure you can do the same thing) can make a big difference.

In therapies dealing with skill deficits, observational learning is often intermingled with vicarious reinforcement. There are cases, though, in which one or the other seems most relevant. In some cases, people literally don't know what to do in a given situation. Observational learning is most relevant here, because it provides new responses. In other cases, it's not so much that people don't know what to do, but that they have doubts about whether doing it will work. In these cases, vicarious reinforcement seems to play a larger role.

MODELING AND RESPONSES TO FEAR

In discussing modeling and fear-related behavior problems, a distinction is made between two kinds of models: those who exhibit mastery and those who exhibit coping (e.g., Meichenbaum, 1971). A **mastery model** seems to be completely without fear regarding what the person in therapy fears. This model presumably creates vicarious extinction of the conditioned fear, as the observer sees that the model experiences no distress.

In contrast, a **coping model** is one who initially displays fear, but overcomes the fear and eventually handles the situation. The effect of this model presumably depends on the fact that the model is in the *same situation* as the observer but is (noticeably) able to overcome the fear by active effort. This effect seems more cognitive than that of the mastery model. Although the evidence isn't entirely consistent, coping models seem more

Seeing someone else cope successfully with something that you fear can help you develop the ability to cope successfully yourself.

effective than mastery models in therapy for reducing fears (Kornhaber & Schroeder, 1975; Meichenbaum, 1971). This effectiveness attests to the powerful role that cognitive processes can play in coping with fear.

Another distinction to be made here is between modeling in which the observer just observes and **participant modeling,** in which the model (often the therapist) performs the behavior in front of the other person, who then repeats it. Participant modeling usually involves a lot of verbalization, instruction, and personalized assurance from the model. It takes more of the therapist's time, but it's more powerful as a behavior change technique (e.g., Bandura, 1982a; Bandura, Adams, & Beyer, 1977).

In a typical case of modeling therapy for a specific fear, a model approaches, engages, and deals with the feared stimulus. While doing so, the model describes the feelings that develop and the mental strategies that are being used to cope. Then the observer tries to do the same thing—first with the therapist's help and then alone. This procedure is effective at reducing fears and increasing coping in a variety of domains. These include fears aroused by animals such as dogs and snakes (Bandura et al., 1977; Bandura, Grusec, & Menlove, 1967; Bandura & Menlove, 1968); by surgery, injections, and dental work (Melamed & Siegel, 1975; Melamed, Weinstein, Hawes, & Katin-Borland, 1975; Vernon, 1974); and by test taking (Cooley & Spiegler, 1980; Malec, Park, & Watkins, 1976; Sarason, 1975).

THERAPEUTIC CHANGES IN EFFICACY EXPECTANCY

The research just outlined indicates that models who display an ability to cope with difficulties can help people to overcome their own fears. But how does it happen? Bandura (1977b) says these effects illustrate a broader principle behind behavior change. He says that when therapy is effective (through whatever technique), it works by increasing the person's sense of efficacy for a given class of situations. In his view, when a model shows an ability to overcome a fear, it helps give observers a sense that they can also overcome their fears. This enhanced perception of personal efficacy, then, results in greater effort and persistence.

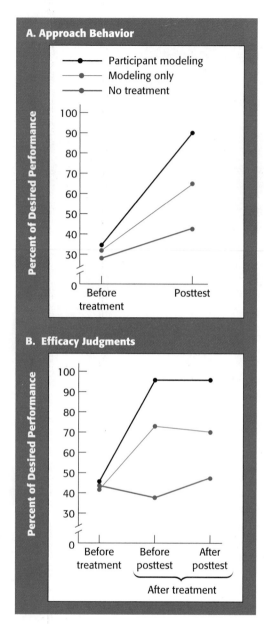

A. Approach Behavior

- Participant modeling
- Modeling only
- No treatment

Percent of Desired Performance

100
90
80
70
60
50
40
30
0

Before treatment   Posttest

B. Efficacy Judgments

Percent of Desired Performance

100
90
80
70
60
50
40
30
0

Before treatment   Before posttest   After posttest

After treatment

FIGURE 13.5
(A) Level of approach toward a feared stimulus and (B) self-efficacy judgments. Both behavior and efficacy perceptions were assessed before therapy (left side of each panel) and afterward (right side of each panel). Efficacy perceptions were assessed both before and immediately after the behavioral posttest.
Source: Adapted from Bandura, Adams, & Beyer, 1977.

These ideas, which were introduced earlier in the chapter, have been tested in many studies of the therapy process (e.g., Avia & Kanfer, 1980; Bandura et al., 1977; Bandura, Adams, Hardy, & Howells, 1980; Bandura & Schunk, 1981; DiClemente, 1981; Gauthier & Ladouceur, 1981). As an illustration, consider an early experiment by Bandura et al. (1977), in which people with an intense fear of snakes received one of three treatments. In a participant-modeling condition, they saw a therapist perform a series of increasingly scary actions with a live snake. Then, with the therapist's assistance, they tried the same actions. In a modeling-only condition, participants saw a model but didn't practice the activities. Those in a control condition had no therapy at all.

Participants were tested both before and after therapy on a behavioral avoidance test. This required trying a range of actions with the snake without assistance. Participants also rated their expectations for being able to perform each of the acts in the avoidance test. They made these ratings at three times: after the behavioral pretest and both before and after the behavioral posttest. This self-report constituted a measure of perceived self-efficacy.

Figure 13.5, A, shows that participant modeling had a better impact on behavior than did modeling without practice, which had a better impact than no treatment. These differences in behavior were paralleled by differences in efficacy statements (see Figure 13.5, B). Moreover, both approach outcomes generalized (particularly for the participant-modeling group) to a snake that looked distinctly different from the snake used during treatment.

In Bandura's view, results such as these make several points (Bandura, 1986, 1997). The broadest is that change in efficacy expectancy can mediate behavior change. That is, the behavior changes *because* of a change in the expectancy. Two other points concern factors that determine efficacy perceptions. Notice that the expectancy ratings in this study changed most among people who had an opportunity to show themselves that they could cope (the participant-modeling group). This fits with Bandura's belief that *performance accomplishments* are the strongest influence on efficacy perceptions.

The study also demonstrates a second influence on efficacy perceptions, however: *vicarious experiences*. That is, the modeling-only group outperformed the control group and also reported greater efficacy. Vicarious consequences don't have as strong an impact as personal outcomes, but they definitely play a role. Bandura (1977b) also holds that *verbal persuasion* and *emotional arousal* can influence efficacy perceptions.

Although Bandura's view is very influential, it's also had some criticism. (Commentaries, both pro and con, can be found in Rachman [1978].) Most of the discussion bears on whether efficacy perceptions are causes or consequences of behavior, but there are also other issues. For example, increasing efficacy perceptions is not useful for everyone. Some prefer to place responsibility for changing their behavior elsewhere (Burger, 1989; Chambliss & Murray, 1979). This leads to the question of which is critical: perceptions of personal efficacy, or expectations that desired outcomes will occur (Carver & Scheier, 1986, 1998).

SELF-INSTRUCTIONS AND COGNITIVE–BEHAVIORAL MODIFICATION

One last approach to therapy we'll note here is called **cognitive–behavioral modification** (Meichenbaum, 1971, 1972, 1977; Meichenbaum & Goodman, 1971). This approach assumes that problems stem from ineffective and disruptive cognitions that slip into people's minds. People often tell themselves that problems are bigger or less resolvable than they really are—or even that they can't cope. The expectation of a bad outcome causes them not to try. The goal of cognitive–behavioral therapies is to get the person to recognize cases of maladaptive thinking and make suitable adjustments.

This process involves teaching the person to identify stimuli that bring out negative cognitions. Then the therapist and client develop substitute cognitions designed to be adaptive (see Table 13.3). These cognitions emphasize three strategies: (1) break the problem situation into concrete components, each of which can be mastered by itself; (2) acknowledge that problem emotions (e.g., anxiety or anger) may exist, but be determined not to let them overwhelm you; and (3) redirect yourself to the actions that have to be done to manage the situation effectively, instead of worrying about how well you'll do.

One more set of self-statements is used after the coping attempt is done. These statements emphasize that progress is incremental: If you didn't do as well as you hoped this time, you'll do better next time. This sort of self-statement helps prevent people from becoming discouraged (from developing negative expectations). Once these mental statements are laid out and learned, the person practices using them when confronting the problem that's being dealt with.

Cognitive–behavioral therapies often focus on specific problems, such as test anxiety (Meichenbaum, 1972), anger (Novaco, 1978), physical pain (Turk, 1978), and

Table 13.3 Examples of Coping Statements Used in Cognitive Therapy. The purpose of the therapy is to train people to engage in effective self-instructions such as these, rather than fill their minds with negative thoughts when engaged in a stressful or fear-inducing activity. *Source:* From Meichenbaum, 1974.

Preparing for the Stressor
What exactly do you have to do?
You can develop a plan to deal with it.
Don't worry—worry won't help anything.
No negative self-statements—just think rationally.

Confronting and Coping with the Stressor
One step at a time—you can handle the situation.
This anxiety is what the doctor said you would feel. It's a reminder to use your coping exercises.
Don't try to eliminate fear totally—just keep it manageable.
When fear comes, just pause.
Keep the focus on the present—what is it you have to do?

After the Coping Attempt
It's getting better each time you use the procedures.
You can be pleased with the progress you're making.

children's impulsiveness (Meichenbaum & Goodman, 1971). It should be obvious, though, that it's easy to generalize to other kinds of stressful experiences. For example, one study found that teaching coping skills to handle test anxiety resulted in lowered anxiety, improved academic performance, and higher levels of a generalized sense of self-efficacy (R. E. Smith, 1989). The term **stress inoculation** is sometimes used to refer to the process of training people to use these techniques not just for one problem but for a broad range of stressful events (Meichenbaum, 1985).

Social-Cognitive Learning Theories: Problems and Prospects

The social–cognitive learning view on personality has been influential in personality psychology over a period of several decades. Some of the reasons for its influence are the same as those noted earlier for the conditioning view. That is, the concepts of this approach have been tested extensively in research and have generally been supported. Similarly, cognitive–behavioral therapy techniques have been shown to be very effective for many kinds of problems.

The social–cognitive learning approach also gains extra benefits from having addressed problems confronted by the conditioning approach. A criticism of the conditioning approach mentioned in Chapter 12 is that research on conditioning usually involves drastically simplified laboratory situations. This criticism is far less applicable to the social–cognitive learning approach. People working from it have examined behavior in very diverse settings and contexts.

Another criticism of the conditioning view is that it seems to have little place for the sense of *personhood,* the continuity and coherence that characterize the sense of self. This criticism is also less applicable to the social–cognitive learning theories. Concepts such as the sense of personal efficacy have a great deal to do with that sense of personhood, even if the focus is on only a limited part of the person at any given time. The idea of evaluating oneself with respect to the attainment of desired incentives also evokes the sense of personhood.

A problem remaining for both learning viewpoints concerns the relationship between the two. The two approaches to learning that are described in Chapters 12 and 13 are split by a disagreement so fundamental that it's hard to know how a single perspective can be welded from the pieces. We minimized this issue while presenting the theoretical principles, but it deserves examination.

The problem is this: In explaining behavior, the conditioning approach restricts itself to events that are observable. Behavioral tendencies are explained from patterns of prior experiences and present cues. Nothing else is needed. If cognitions exist, they are irrelevant—foam on the stream of behavior, shaped by the same forces as shape behavior, but not important in causing behavior. The social–cognitive learning approach is in direct opposition to this view. Expectations cause behavior. Actions follow from thinking, rather than occur in parallel with thinking.

This latter characterization fits more with the introspections that most people have about their own lives. As noted earlier, however, treating cognitions as causes of behavior may mean rejecting some of the most fundamental tenets of the conditioning approach. In the more cognitive view, classical and instrumental conditioning aren't necessarily incremental processes occurring outside awareness; they depend on expectancies and mental models. Reinforcement is seen as providing information about future incentives, instead of acting directly to strengthen behavioral tendencies.

The emphasis on expectancies and other cognitions isn't the only area of conflict between approaches. Social–cognitive learning theorists agree with conditioning theorists that reinforcement is necessary to maintain behavior (despite holding a view of reinforcement that differs drastically from that of conditioning theorists). But sometimes a behavior occurs with no obvious reinforcer. In such a case, theorists may assert that the behavior is being supported by self-reinforcement. The appeal to self-reinforcement is far from satisfying, both to conditioning theorists and to people who stand outside the learning perspective. If self-reinforcement accounts for behavior *sometimes*, why not *all the time*? Why is external reinforcement *ever* necessary? How do you decide when it's needed and when it isn't?

One challenge for the evolution of the thinking of the social–cognitive learning theorists is to determine how—or whether—their ideas can be reconciled with the principles of conditioning. Are the newer theories extrapolations from the previous theories, or are they fundamentally different? Can they be merged, or are they competitors for the same theoretical niche? That is, some people would say the newer version of the learning perspective should simply *replace* the conditioning version—that the conditioning view was wrong, that human learning simply doesn't occur that way.

Some people have abandoned the effort at integration and simply stepped away from the issue altogether. For example, in recent years, Bandura has dropped the word *learning* from the phrase he uses to characterize his theory. He now calls it *social–cognitive theory* (Bandura, 1986). This raises the question of whether his current ideas (as opposed to his earlier ideas) should be seen as belonging to the learning perspective on personality at all.

Bandura's change of label reflects a more general trend among people who started out within the social learning framework. Many of these people have been influenced in the past 30 years by the ideas of cognitive psychology. Many people who used to call their orientation to personality a *social learning view* now would hedge. Some of them would now give their orientation a different label, one that would be more likely to include terms such as *cognitive* and *self-regulation*. There has been a gradual fraying of the edge of the social learning approach, which blends with the cognitive self-regulation theories. This overlap will become more apparent in later chapters.

This blurring and shifting between bodies of thought raises a final question for the social–cognitive learning approach: Will this approach retain its identity as an active area of work in the years to come, or will it disperse and have its themes absorbed by other viewpoints?

· SUMMARY ·

Dissatisfactions with the conditioning approach led to development of another generation of learning theories. They're called *cognitive* because they emphasize the role of thought processes in behavior, and *social* because they emphasize the idea that people often learn from one another. Several aspects of these theories can be thought of as *elaborations* on conditioning principles, although close examination of the elaborations raises questions about the validity of those conditioning principles.

These elaborations include an emphasis on the role of social reinforcement (rather than other sorts of reinforcement) in shaping behavior. Social reinforcers such as acceptance and approval can also be applied to oneself. Because humans have the capability for empathy (vicariously aroused emotions), we can experience classical conditioning vicariously. We can also experience reinforcement and punishment vicariously, causing shifts in action tendencies on the basis of someone else's outcomes. Functions such as *discrimination* and *generalization* are broadened in these theories to include such phenomena as semantic generalization. This view also holds that human learning is not always incremental. That is, we often learn rules and then apply them to new situations.

A fundamental principle that seems to underlie many aspects of human learning is that expectancies concerning upcoming events and outcomes play an important part in determining our responses. Specific theorists have also focused on two additional kinds of expectancy. Rotter holds that people who expect their outcomes to be determined by their actions (*internals*) learn from reinforcers but that people who expect their outcomes to be unrelated to their actions (*externals*) do not. Bandura holds that perceptions of personal efficacy or competence determine whether a person will persist when in stressful circumstances.

One portion of this approach to personality stands as completely distinct from conditioning principles: the process of acquiring behavior potentials through *observational learning*. This process requires only that an observer attend to a model (who is displaying a behavior), retain some memory of what was done (usually a visual or verbal memory), and have the component skills to be able to reproduce what was modeled. This process of acquisition is not directly influenced by reinforcement contingencies, although reinforcement can have an indirect effect by influencing how much attention is paid to the model. On the other hand, spontaneous performance of the acquired behavior is very much influenced by perceptions of reinforcement contingencies. It's easy to see the importance of the various processes of social–cognitive learning in many domains, including the acquisition of sex-role behavior, the tendency to be aggressive, and strategies that are used to delay gratification.

Personality assessment within this framework emphasizes the use of self-report devices. Many of these instruments are designed to measure subjective qualities such as feelings, cognitions, and expectancies (consistent with the emphasis placed on these qualities as determinants of behavior). There is also a growing emphasis on assessment within the context of the person's own definitions of situations.

Problems in behavior can develop through both vicarious and direct learning. Problems also result when people haven't had the opportunity to learn needed behaviors from models. Therapy techniques based on the social–cognitive learning approach often involve modeling procedures, whether as an attempt to remedy skill deficits through observational learning or as an attempt to show the utility of coping skills through vicarious reinforcement. Such techniques seem most effective when subjects overtly engage in the behaviors under the therapist's guidance, which led Bandura to suggest that improvement is mediated by a growing sense of efficacy. Other therapies emphasize the idea that people often hurt themselves by saying things to themselves that are negativistic. These therapies teach people to stop these negative self-statements and substitute self-statements that emphasize active, effective coping.

· GLOSSARY ·

Androgyny   The condition of having both masculine and feminine qualities.

Cognitive–behavioral modification   A therapeutic technique that attempts to change behaviors by changing thought patterns.

Coping model   A model that displays fear but ultimately handles it.

Efficacy expectancy   Confidence of being able to do something successfully.

Expectancy   Judgment about how likely a specific behavior is to attain a goal.

Incentive   The desirability of an outcome.

Learned helplessness   A state of low motivation and effort following extensive exposure to lack of control.

Locus of control   A dimension of believing that one's outcomes are caused by oneself or by external forces.

Mastery model   A model that displays no fear.

Observational learning   Acquiring the ability to do a new behavior by watching someone else do it.

Participant modeling   The act of practicing a behavior that's hard for oneself while using the therapist as model.

Self-control   The regulation and sometimes restraint of one's own activities.

Self-efficacy   Confidence of being able to do something successfully.

Self-reinforcement   The approval one gives to oneself for one's own behavior.

Semantic generalization   Generalization along a dimension of meaning.

Sex role   The behaviors associated more with members of one sex than the other.

Skill deficit   The absence or insufficiency of a needed behavior or skill.

Social reinforcer   Praise, liking, acceptance, or approval received from someone else.

Stress inoculation   A therapy to develop the ability to cope with a broad range of stressors.

Symbolic models   Models in print, movies, TV, and so on.

Vicarious classical conditioning   Conditioning in which the unconditioned response occurs via empathy.

Vicarious emotional arousal   The tendency to feel someone else's feelings along with them; also called *empathy*.

Vicarious reinforcement   An event in which a reinforcement experienced by someone else has a reinforcing effect on one's own behavior.

CHAPTER 14

Humanistic Psychology: Self-Actualization and Self-Determination

Julia spends most of her waking hours doing things for others. She talks often with her mother, whose life never goes smoothly and who always wants more from Julia than she can give. Julia sometimes feels as though she's being drawn into quicksand, but she never complains. Then there's Eric, a guy she used to date. Eric's life is a mess, and he often calls her late at night for advice. Although she needs her sleep, she never refuses him a sympathetic ear. Julia always seems to be setting her own life aside for the benefit of others. It's as though she thinks she's unworthy as a person unless she does so. Deep inside, a small voice says she's wrong about that (but she's usually too busy to hear). And sometimes, just sometimes, she has the feeling that a different destiny awaits her, if she could only free herself to find it.

THE EXPERIENCE of being human is mysterious and challenging. You have events, feelings, thoughts, and choices that are different from those of any other person who ever has lived or ever will live. You are continuously "becoming," evolving from a simpler version of yourself into a more complex version. It's sometimes mystifying, because you don't always understand why you feel what you're feeling. But the fact that the life you're living is your own—a set of sensations that belongs to you and nobody else—makes the experience also vivid and compelling.

How does your self know *how* to "become"? As you evolve over your lifetime, how do you still remain yourself? Why do you sometimes feel as though part of you wants to grow in one direction and another part wants to grow in another direction? Why do you still have the sense of being an integrated person even when things pull in different ways inside you? What makes this experience of being human so special? These are among the questions asked by theorists whose ideas form the phenomenological perspective on personality. In this chapter, we examine some of the answers they've given.

The subject of this chapter is sometimes referred to with the phrase **humanistic psychology,** or the *human potential movement* (Schneider, Bugental, & Pierson, 2001). These terms reflect the idea that everyone has the potential for growth and development. *No one* is inherently bad or unworthy. A goal of humanistic psychology is to help people realize this about themselves, so they'll have the chance to grow.

Self-Actualization

An important figure in humanistic psychology was Carl Rogers. His ideas provide a way to talk about how potential is realized and how that can fail to happen. In Rogers's view, the potential for positive, healthy growth expresses itself in everyone if there are no strong opposing influences. This growth is termed **actualization.** Actualization is a tendency to develop capabilities in ways that *maintain or enhance the organism* (Rogers, 1959).

In part, the actualizing tendency is reflected physically. For example, your body actualizes as your immune system kills disease organisms. Your body actualizes when it grows bigger and stronger. The actualizing principle also applies to personality. When it promotes maintenance or enhancement of the self, it's called **self-actualization.** Self-actualization moves you toward more autonomy and self-sufficiency. It enriches your life experiences and enhances creativity. It promotes **congruence,** *wholeness or integration* within the person, and it minimizes disorganization or incongruence.

We all have a strong need to experience positive regards from others, to feel wanted, appreciated, and respected.

Rogers believed that the actualizing tendency is part of human nature. This is also reflected in another term he used: the **organismic valuing process.** This phrase refers to the idea that the organism automatically evaluates its experiences to tell whether they are enhancing actualization. If they aren't, the organismic valuing process creates a nagging sense that something isn't right.

Rogers used the phrase **fully functioning person** to describe someone who is self-actualizing. Such people are open to experiencing their feelings and are not threatened by them, no matter what the feelings are. Fully functioning people trust the feelings. They are also open to experiencing the world. Rather than hide from it, they immerse themselves in it. The result is that the fully functioning person lives a life filled with meaning, challenge, and excitement but also a willingness to risk pain. The fully functioning person isn't a particular *kind of person.* It's a *way of functioning* that can be adopted by anyone who chooses to live that way (see Box 14.1).

THE NEED FOR POSITIVE REGARD

Self-actualization isn't the only big influence on human behavior, however. People also are motivated to be accepted and to have the love, friendship, and affection of others—particularly others who matter to them (called *significant others*). Rogers referred to this acceptance with the term **positive regard.**

BOX 14.1 THE THEORIST AND THE THEORY

Carl Rogers as a Fully Functioning Person

Although Carl Rogers apparently didn't consciously draw on his own life in developing his theory, his life certainly embodied all the theory's principles. Rogers lived a life characterized by a willingness to change and an openness to experience. Several times, he left the security of the familiar and moved in new directions, using only his intuitions and feelings as guides. Rogers was very much the fully functioning, self-actualizing person his theory describes.

Rogers was born in Oak Park, Illinois, in 1902, the middle child in a large family. His parents were conservative and devoutly Christian. During college, he decided to pursue a life in the ministry. At the same time, he also

participated in a six-month-long religious conference in China. This trip had a profound effect on him. The exposure to religious leaders from different cultures changed his thinking about religious issues. He began to entertain the possibility that all he had believed might be wrong. Rogers wrote to his parents, announcing his independence from their religious views, fully realizing the emotional cost that such an act would incur.

Rogers took his degree in history and then continued pursuing his remaining interest in religion, while also taking courses in psychology. After a while, though, he abandoned the path of religion forever to focus on psychology. After earning his doctorate, he took his first job in Rochester, New York. There, two experiences greatly influenced his thinking. First, clinical experience made it apparent that psychoanalytic therapy,

which dominated the group in which he worked, was often ineffective. Second, he recognized vast disagreements among his senior colleagues about how to deal with specific cases. In short, conventional wisdom didn't seem to be working, and the authorities couldn't agree about what to do. To Rogers, it was time to go it alone and develop his own way of treating problems.

In 1939, Rogers published the first of his books on the therapeutic technique he'd developed. This led to a series of academic appointments at several universities. In his later years, he left the familiar confines of academia and set out once again to make a change. The latter part of his career took place at the Western Behavioral Sciences Institute in California, where he pursued a developing interest in group therapies, and at the Center for Studies of the Person.

Positive regard can come in two ways, and the difference is important. Affection given without special conditions—with "no strings attached"—is called **unconditional positive regard.** Sometimes, though, affection is given only if certain conditions are satisfied. The conditions vary from case to case, but the principle is the same: I'll like you and accept you, but only if you act in a particular way. This is called **conditional positive regard.** Much of the affection that people get in their day-to-day lives is conditional.

Another phrase used here is **conditions of worth.** These are the conditions under which the person is judged to be worthy of positive regard. When people act to conform to a condition of worth, they're doing so not because the act is *intrinsically* desirable, but to get positive regard from other people (see the cartoon at right).

Rogers argued that after years of having conditions of worth applied to us by people around us, we start to apply

SHOE by Jeff MacNelly

People sometimes attempt to impose conditions of worth on other people.
Reprinted by permission: Tribune Media Services.

them to *ourselves* (Sheldon & Elliot, 1998). We give ourselves affection and acceptance only when we satisfy those conditions. This pattern of self-acceptance (and self-rejection) is called **conditional self-regard.** Conditional self-regard makes you behave so as to fit the conditions of worth you're applying to yourself (Crocker & Wolfe, 2001).

Conditions of worth and conditional regard have an important effect: *Changing your behavior, values, or goals to gain acceptance can interfere with self-actualization.* Because self-actualizing is more important than fulfilling conditions of worth, it should get first priority. But the need for positive regard is so salient that its influence is often felt more keenly.

Let's consider a couple of examples to see how these motives can conflict with each other. Joel is a young man who's decided to give up a possible career in music because his father needs help in the family business. In doing this, Joel is responding to conditions of worth imposed by his family. Bowing to those conditions of worth, however, may mean denying something that's important inside him, something that's truly a part of who he is.

The same kind of conflict is experienced by Julia, the woman described in the chapter opening. Recall that Julia spends much of her time and energy giving of herself to others. Her actions, however, seem driven by a need to prove she's worthy as a human being. She seems to be applying conditions of worth to herself. By trying to live up to them, Julia prevents herself from hearing the voice of self-actualization and from growing in her own way.

Finally, Mary feels a strong desire for a career, but her parents want her to marry and raise a family. If her parents won't fully accept her unless she bends to their wishes, they're creating a condition of worth for her. Accepting this condition may interfere with her self-actualization. Remember, though, that conditions of worth aren't always imposed from outside. It's possible that Mary's desire for a career may itself be a condition of worth, a self-imposed condition (just like Julia's need to prove her worthiness by giving to others). Mary may have decided she won't accept herself as a complete person unless she has a career.

It can be very hard to distinguish a true desire from a condition of worth (Janoff-Bulman & Leggatt, 2002). What defines a condition of worth is that it's a *precondition for acceptance,* either self-acceptance or acceptance by others. A condition of worth is always coercive: It pushes you into doing things. Whenever such conditions are applied, they can prevent self-actualization. There's also evidence that when parents place such conditions on their children, the result is resentment and lower well-being (Assor, Roth, & Deci, 2004).

CONTINGENT SELF-WORTH

Jennifer Crocker and her colleagues have conducted a good deal of research on the idea that people place such conditions of worth on themselves (Crocker & Knight, 2005; Crocker & Park, 2004; Crocker & Wolfe, 2001). People who use their performance in some domain of life as a precondition for self-acceptance are said to have **contingent self-worth** (which means essentially the same as conditional self-regard). Conditions of worth come in many forms. Some people are demanding about their academic performance and others about their appearance.

Contingencies can be motivating, in some ways. People who impose an academic condition of worth study more than other people; people who impose an appearance-based condition of worth exercise more and shop for clothes more than other people (Crocker, Luhtanen, Cooper, & Bouvrette, 2003). When a failure happens in some domain, though, it's more upsetting for those who have a contingency in that domain than for those who do not. And the failure can then result in loss of motivation for those who failed to meet the contingency.

Consistent with the view expressed by Rogers, holding oneself to these conditions has costs. It is stressful and disrupts relationships (Crocker & Knight, 2005).

Perhaps most important, it keeps you focused on that particular condition of worth instead of letting you grow freely in self-actualization.

Self-Determination

The ideas of Rogers are echoed in a more recent theory of **self-determination** proposed by Ed Deci (Deci, 1975) and developed by Deci and Richard Ryan (1980, 1985, 1991, 2000; Ryan, 1993; Ryan & Deci, 2001; see also Vallerand, 1997). Deci and Ryan believe that having a life of growth, integrity, and well-being means satisfying three needs. The needs are for autonomy (self-determination), competence, and relatedness. Research confirms that people in general do see these needs as being most important (Sheldon, Elliot, Kim, & Kasser, 2001).

This theory began with the idea that behavior can reflect several underlying dynamics. Some actions are *self-determined,* done because the actions have intrinsic interest or value to you. Other actions are *controlled,* done to gain payment or to satisfy some pressure. A behavior can be controlled even if the control occurs entirely inside your own mind. If you do something because you know you'd feel guilty if you didn't do it, you're engaging in controlled behavior.

Whether behavior is controlled or self-determined can have several consequences. One of them concerns how long you'll stay interested in the activity. People stay interested longer when their actions are self-determined. There's a lot of evidence that promising rewards for working on activities can undermine people's interest in them (Deci, Koestner, & Ryan, 1999). The effect has been found in children as well as adults. In children, it's been called "turning play into work" (Lepper & Greene, 1975, 1978).

It's not the reward itself that does this. What matters is whether people see their actions as self-determined. Telling people they're going to be paid for something often seems to make them infer that their behavior isn't self-determined. As a result, they lose interest.

Sometimes, though, the presence of reward increases motivation instead of undermining it (Elliot & Harackiewicz, 1994; Harackiewicz, 1979; Henderlong & Lepper, 2002). Why? Because reward has two aspects (Deci, 1975). It has a *controlling* aspect, telling you your actions aren't self-determined. It can also have an *informational* aspect, telling you something about yourself. If a reward tells you you're competent, it increases your motivation (Eisenberger & Rhoades, 2001; Koestner, Zuckerman, & Koestner, 1987). It's even possible for a reward to promote a sense of autonomy, under the right conditions (Henderlong & Lepper, 2002). If the reward implies a condition of worth, however, or if it implies you're acting only for the reward, then the controlling aspect stands out and your motivation falls off.

Deci and Ryan believe that people want to feel a sense of autonomy in everything they do. In this view, accomplishments such as doing well in your courses are satisfying only if you feel a sense of self-determination in them. If you feel forced or pressured to do those things, then you'll be less satisfied (Flink, Boggiano, & Barrett, 1990; Grolnick & Ryan, 1989). Indeed, pressuring *yourself* to do well can also reduce motivation (Ryan, 1982). This fits the idea that people can impose conditions of worth on themselves.

INTROJECTION AND IDENTIFICATION

Deci and Ryan and their colleagues have used several more terms in describing controlled and self-determined behavior. *Introjected regulation* happens when a person treats a behavior as a "should" or an "ought." That is, the person does the behavior to avoid guilt or to gain self-approval. You've taken the behavior up but not really accepted it as your own. If you try to do well in a class so you won't feel guilty about wasting your parents' money, that's introjected behavior. Introjected behavior is controlled, but the control is being exerted from inside. If you try to do well so your parents won't look down on you, that's also controlled, but it's not introjected because the control is outside you.

In *identified regulation,* the person has come to hold the behavior as personally meaningful and valuable. If you try to do well in a class because you believe learning the information is important to your growth, that's identified regulation. Identified regulation is self-determined. It's not quite as self-determined as intrinsically motivated behavior (for which the interest is naturally there), but it's close. In general, as people mature, they regulate less by introjected values and more by identified (autonomous) values (Sheldon, 2005).

These ideas have many applications. For example, think about what you want out of life. There's evidence that wanting financial success (which generally reflects controlled behavior) relates to poorer mental health, whereas wanting community involvement relates to better mental health (Kasser, 2002; Kasser & Ryan, 1993). Of course, *why* the person has the aspiration is also important (Carver & Baird, 1998). Wanting community involvement for controlling reasons (e.g., because it will make people like you) is bad. Wanting financial success for truly self-determined reasons (because the process itself is intrinsically enjoyable) can be good.

The pressures that lead to introjected regulation stem from the desire to be accepted by others or to avoid a sense of guilt over doing things you think others won't like. This fits with Rogers's belief that the desire for positive regard can disrupt self-actualization. A lot depends on whether significant others place conditions of worth on you. Restrictive parenting produces adults who value conformity instead of self-direction (Kassner, Koestner, & Lekes, 2002).

Having a sense of autonomy also seems to foster further autonomy. In one research project, medical students who thought their professors were supportive of their own autonomy became even more autonomous in their learning over time (Williams & Deci, 1996). They also felt more competent in the skills they were learning, and they acted toward others in ways that supported the others' autonomy.

NEED FOR RELATEDNESS

Deci and Ryan also hold that people have an intrinsic need for relatedness (Baumeister & Leary, 1995). At first glance, it might seem that the need for relatedness should conflict with the need for autonomy. However, Deci and Ryan's definition of *autonomy* doesn't mean being separate from others and thus low in relatedness. It means having the sense of free self-determination (Deci & Ryan, 1991, 2000). Real relatedness doesn't conflict with this.

Several studies have confirmed that autonomy and relatedness can exist side by side. One project found across several studies that autonomy and relatedness were complementary: Each related independently to well-being (Bettencourt & Sheldon, 2001). Another study found that a measure of behaving autonomously was tied to *more* relatedness, in the form of having open and positive communication with significant others. People who regulated their lives in a controlled way were the ones who interacted defensively with others (Hodgins, Koestner, & Duncan, 1996). Yet other research has found that being autonomous promotes the use of relationship-maintaining coping strategies and positive responses in discussing the relationships

(Knee, Patrick, Vietor, Nanayakkara, & Neighbors, 2002). The result is less defensive-ness and more understanding responses to conflict (Knee, Lonsbary, Canevello, & Patrick, 2005).

Support for autonomy is a powerful force. When relationship partners are sup-portive of autonomy, the relationship is experienced as being better and richer (Deci, La Guardia, Moller, Scheiner, & Ryan, 2006). The relationship also feels better to you when you support your *partner's* autonomy (Deci et al., 2006).

Still, the need for relatedness has some resemblance to the need for positive regard. Why, then, doesn't it interfere with self-actualization? The answer seems to be that Deci and Ryan's conception of relatedness implies a genuine connection to others, an unconditional acceptance rather than a connection based on pressure and demand. It might be more accurate to equate this need to a need for *unconditional* regard.

SELF-CONCORDANCE

Self-determination theory has important implications for thinking about the goals people pursue in their lives. Elsewhere in this book, you will read about personality being expressed in the goals people take up (for example, Chapter 17). But goals are not equal in what they're about or in their contributions to well-being. The key is that it's good to pursue goals that are **self-concordant,** or consistent with your core values (Sheldon & Elliot, 1999). You care more about such goals. You'll also benefit more from attaining them than from attaining goals that don't connect to your core values. Support for this reasoning comes from several sources (Brunstein, Schultheiss, & Grässmann, 1998; Sheldon & Elliot, 1999; Sheldon & Kasser, 1998).

There's even evidence that pursuit of self-concordant goals can create a longer-term spiral of benefit (Sheldon & Houser-Marko, 2001). When you try to reach self-concordant goals, you try harder, you have more satisfying experiences, and you attain better well-being. This experience promotes greater motivation for the next self-concordant goal, and the cycle continues.

FREE WILL

Humanistic psychologists emphasize the idea that people have freedom to decide for themselves how to act, what to become. Rogers believed that people are free to choose whether to act in self-actualizing ways or to accept conditions of worth. Deci and Ryan believe that people are exerting their will when they choose to act in self-determined ways.

The concept of *free will* is interesting and controversial. It's nearly impossible to know for sure whether we have free will, but people certainly seem to *think* they do. One reflection of this belief is called **reactance** (Brehm, 1966; Brehm & Brehm, 1981). Reactance happens when you expect to have a particular freedom and you see the freedom as being threatened. The result is an attempt to regain or reassert that freedom. There are lots of examples. Young children who've been told they can't do something want to do it all the more. In the same way, "playing hard to get" can create more attraction. The best illustration of

When we are prevented from doing something that we want to do, our desire to do that activity increases even more.

reactance, however, may be what's often said when one person is pressuring another: "Don't tell me what to do!" A substantial literature supports the idea that reactance leads to reassertion of freedom (Brehm & Brehm, 1981).

Although people think they have free will, research raises questions about it. Wegner and Wheatley (1999) set up a situation in which pairs of people together moved a computer mouse (as if using a Ouija board). One person (who was actually part of the experiment) caused the mouse to stop at particular moments, so the cursor fell on specific objects on the computer screen. Through complicated procedures, the researchers caused the true participant to think of the object on which the cursor stopped, either just before or after the stop occurred. If the thought about the object came just before the stop (which, remember, was caused by the other person), the participant reported having stopped there intentionally. This and other evidence led Wegner (2002) to suggest that free will is an illusion. This issue, of course, will continue to be debated.

The Self and Processes of Defense

Let us now turn to the concept of *self*. Rogers is sometimes called a *self theorist,* because he stressed the importance of the self. As did many theorists, he assumed that the self doesn't exist at birth but that infants gradually differentiate self from nonself. As the person grows, the self becomes more elaborate and complex. It never reaches an end state but continues to evolve.

Rogers used the term *self* in several ways. Sometimes, he used it to refer to the subjective awareness of being (Rogers, 1965). At other times, he used it interchangeably with *self-concept.* The self-concept is the set of qualities a person views as being part of himself or herself (much like the concept of *ego identity;* Chapter 11). Many distinctions can be made among the elements of the self-concept. One of them is between the actual (or real) self and the ideal self. The **ideal self** is an image of the kind of person you want to be. The **actual self** is what you think you're really like.

Recall that self-actualizing is supposed to promote congruence. *Congruence* means "fitting closely together." One kind of congruence is between the actual and ideal selves. In particular, as self-actualization takes place, it creates a closer fit between the actual and the ideal. It leads you to become more like the self you want to be.

A second kind of congruence that's also important is between the actual self and experience. That is, the experiences you have in life should fit with the kind of person you think you are. For example, if you think you're a kind person and you find yourself doing something that's insensitive and unkind, there's an incongruity between self and experience. If you think you're a smart person but find yourself doing poorly in a course, there's an incongruity between self and experience. Self-actualization should tend to promote a closer congruence here, as well.

INCONGRUITY, DISORGANIZATION, AND DEFENSE

Incongruence is disorganization, a fraying of the unitary sense of self. You don't always know it consciously, but the organismic valuing process notes it automatically. Rogers said that incongruence—either a perceived gap between real and ideal or experiencing something that doesn't fit your self-image—leads to anxiety.

The experience of incongruence can also make people vulnerable to yet further problems. Low self-esteem (incongruity between actual and ideal self) leads people to underestimate how much their significant others care for them (Murray, Holmes, & Griffin, 2000; Murray, Holmes, Griffin, Bellavia, & Rose, 2001). This misperception can cause them to react poorly to their partners. They feel pessimistic about the relationship and may act in ways that are not genuine. Ultimately, the relationship is less likely to flourish.

It isn't always possible to have complete congruence. Rogers assumed, though, that people defend themselves against even the *perception* of incongruence to avoid the anxiety it creates. Defenses against perceptions of incongruity form two categories, which aren't so different from some of the defenses addressed by psychoanalytic theory (Chapter 9).

One kind of defense involves *distortion of experience*. Rationalization is such a distortion, creating a plausible but untrue explanation for why something is the way it is. Another distortion occurs when you see an event as being different from the way it really is. For instance, if you say something that makes someone else feel bad, you may protect yourself by believing that the other person wasn't really bothered.

The second kind of defense involves *preventing threatening experiences from reaching awareness*. Denial—refusing to admit to yourself that a situation exists or an experience took place—serves this function. A woman who ignores overwhelming evidence that her boyfriend is unfaithful to her is engaging in denial.

You can also prevent an experience from reaching awareness indirectly, by not letting yourself be in a situation where the experience would be *possible*. By taking steps to prevent it from occurring, you prevent its access to consciousness. This is a subtle defense. For example, a person whose self-image is threatened by sexual feelings among attractive strangers may avoid going to the beach or to a nightclub, thereby preventing the experience from occurring.

SELF-ESTEEM MAINTENANCE AND ENHANCEMENT

Defenses act to maintain and enhance the congruity or integrity of the self. Another way to put it is that defenses protect and enhance self-esteem (though see Box 14.2). The idea that people go out of their way to protect self-esteem has been around for a long time. It's been an active area of study under several labels, including self-evaluation maintenance, self-affirmation, ego defensiveness, and egotism (e.g., Darley & Goethals, 1980; M. L. Snyder, Stephan, & Rosenfield, 1976, 1978; Steele, 1988; Tesser, 1986, 1988; Tesser & Campbell, 1983).

It's often said that two conditions are required for concerns to arise about maintaining (or enhancing) self-esteem (Snyder et al., 1978). First, an event must take place that's attributable to you. An event that's outside your control is not relevant to you. Second, the event must be good or bad, thereby having a potential connotation for self-esteem.

What happens when there's a threat to self-esteem? Just as Rogers argued, people either distort perceptions or keep them out of awareness. If self-esteem is threatened, people minimize the negativity of the event, thus distorting their perceptions. Alternatively, they try to prevent the event from being attributed to permanent qualities of the self, thereby denying its relevance.

Let's consider a couple of examples. A common threat to self-esteem is failure. Failure (academic, social, or in another domain) can make most of us feel inadequate. What do people do when they fail? They make excuses (C. R. Snyder & Higgins, 1988). They blame the failure on things beyond their control. They attribute the failure to task difficulty, to chance, to other people, or (in a bind) to a lack of effort

Box 14.2 How Can You Manage Two Kinds of Congruence Simultaneously?

This section of the chapter discusses how people protect or enhance their self-image to defend against perception of incongruence between the actual self and the ideal self. Don't forget, though, that another kind of incongruence—between the self and experience—is also distressing. Unfortunately, there are circumstances when the desire to avoid one kind of incongruity can plunge you right into the other.

What kind of circumstance would do that? An example is suggested by the work of William Swann and his colleagues on what they call *self-verification* (e.g., Swann, 1987, 1990). The principle behind this research is that once people have an idea of what they're like, they want to have that self-concept confirmed by other people's reactions to them. That is, people want their experience to be congruent with their self-concept. For example, if you think you're a good athlete, you want others to think so too. If you think you're shy, you want others to realize it. It may seem odd, but the desire to verify beliefs about yourself extends even to beliefs that are unflattering

(Swann, Wenzlaff, & Tafarodi, 1992). If you think you're homely, you'd rather have someone else agree than say the opposite.

But there's a problem. For the person who holds a negative self-view, there's a built-in conflict between self-verification and self-protection. *Self-verification* is trying not to have incongruity between one's self and one's experience. *Self-protection* is trying not to be aware of incongruity between one's desired self and actual self. Attempts to diminish the two incongruities can pull a person in opposite directions.

Swann and his colleagues argue that both of these forces operate in everyone. Which one dominates at a given moment depends on your options. Keep in mind that most people's self-concept contains both positive and negative qualities (Swann, Pelham, & Krull, 1989). Suppose, then, you had the chance to obtain information about yourself (from another person or from a personality test). Would you prefer to get information about what you view as your best quality or about what you view as your worst? Given this option, most people

prefer to learn about something they view as desirable. This fits the self-protection tendency.

But suppose you know that the quality about which you can get information is one you think is negative. Would you rather get information that says you're good in that quality or that says you're bad? The answer obtained by Swann, Pelham, and Krull (1989) is that if the information is about a quality people perceive as negative, they tend to seek unfavorable information.

In sum, the self-protection and self-enhancement tendency seems to influence where people look (and don't look) when they consider relations between their actual and desired selves. We prefer to look at favorable self-aspects. Once we're looking at some self-aspect in particular, though, the self-verification tendency influences the kind of information we focus on. We want information that confirms our view of who we are—that fits our experienced self to our actual self. In each case, the effect is to enhance perceptions of congruence, consistent with the ideas proposed by Rogers.

(e.g., Bradley, 1978; Snyder et al., 1976, 1978). This happens whether the event is as trivial as failure on a laboratory task or as profound as the experience of divorce (Gray & Silver, 1990). Blaming something else creates distance between the failure and you. Given enough distance, the failure doesn't threaten your self-esteem.

When you experience success, on the other hand, you have the chance to *enhance* your self-esteem. You can do this by ascribing the success to your abilities (Agostinelli, Sherman, Presson, & Chassin, 1992; Bradley, 1978; Snyder et al., 1976, 1978; Taylor & Brown, 1988). Indeed, there's even evidence that people think that their positive personal qualities are under their own control, allowing them to claim credit for being the way they are (Alicke, 1985).

A person can also protect self-esteem after a failure by distorting perceptions another way. As we said earlier, an event is relevant to self-esteem only if it has an impact that's either good or bad. You can be self-protective, then, by minimizing the event's impact. Making a bad impression on someone isn't a problem if that person isn't worth bothering with. Doing poorly on a test doesn't matter if the test isn't important or valid. People who are told they did poorly on a test say exactly that: It's not so important and not so valid (Greenberg, Pyszczynski, & Solomon, 1982).

SELF-HANDICAPPING

Distorting perceptions of bad outcomes maintains self-esteem. But so does denial to awareness. One way to deny access to awareness is called **self-handicapping** (e.g., Arkin & Baumgardner, 1985; Higgins, Snyder, & Berglas, 1990; Jones & Berglas, 1978; Jones & Pittman, 1982). Self-handicapping is acting to create the very conditions that tend to produce a failure. If you have a test tomorrow, it's self-handicapping to party all night instead of studying. If you want to make a good impression on someone, it's self-handicapping to show up drunk or drenched in sweat.

Why would you do this to yourself? If you want to reach a goal, why create conditions that make it harder? The theory is that failing to attain a goal is a threat to self-esteem. You can't really fail, though, if success is prevented by circumstances beyond your control. If such conditions exist, the stigma of failing goes away. If you fail the test or make a poor impression, well, *no one* could do well under those conditions. So it wasn't really a failure. Thus, you've prevented the awareness of failing. Note that for this strategy to be successful, you need to be *unaware of using it*. If you realize you're setting up barriers for yourself, the barriers won't have the same psychological meaning.

Self-handicapping may be common, but it's not a good strategy. People who tend to self-handicap cope poorly with stress (Zuckerman, Kieffer, & Knee, 1998). Indeed, self-handicapping and maladjustment reinforce each other (Zuckerman & Tsai, 2005). In addition, if people think you're self-handicapping, they will react negatively to you (Hirt, McCrea, & Boris, 2003). And don't forget that self-handicapping helps create the very failure it was intended to protect against.

STEREOTYPE THREAT

A concept that has similarities to the ideas we've been discussing is called **stereotype threat.** It was first proposed and studied by Claude Steele and his colleagues (Pronin, Steele, & Ross, 2004; Steele, 1997; Steele & Aronson, 1995). It begins with the fact that some social groups are stereotyped in ways that lead to expectations of poor performances of some sort. For example, the negative stereotype of African Americans includes an expectation that they will perform poorly on intellectual tasks. The negative stereotype of women includes an expectation that they will perform poorly on math tests. The negative stereotype of elderly people includes an expectation that they will perform poorly on memory tasks. Members of these groups can be threatened by being viewed through the stereotype, rather than as individuals. This sense of being prejudged occupies the person's mind and promotes negative thinking (Cadinu, Maass, Rosabianca, & Kiesner, 2005). All of this can interfere with performance, thus confirming the stereotype.

What may be even worse, however, is what may occur if this happens frequently. Steele (1997) argued that the person begins to disidentify with the behavioral domain in which the threat is occurring, or stops caring about it. This protects self-esteem by denying that the experience is relevant to the self. Failure doesn't matter if the test isn't important. But disidentification also has bad consequences. As does self-handicapping, it makes poor performance more likely (due to withdrawal of effort). Further, disidentification ultimately causes people to stop caring about

Box 14.3 The Theorist and the Theory

Abraham Maslow's Focus on the Positive

Abraham Maslow focused his work almost exclusively on the positive side of human experience. He was interested in what caused some people to achieve greatness in their lives and to succeed where others failed. He cared about issues of personal growth and the realization of human potential. It's clear that these interests were influenced by events in his own life.

Maslow was born in 1908 in Brooklyn, New York, the oldest of seven children of Russian–Jewish immigrants. His home life definitely did not foster personal growth. His father thought little of him and even publicly ridiculed his appearance. This led young Maslow to seek out empty cars whenever he rode the subway, sparing others the sight of him. If Maslow's father treated him badly, his mother was worse. Because the family was

poor, she kept a lock on the refrigerator to keep the children out, feeding them only when she saw fit. Maslow once characterized her as a "cruel, ignorant, and hostile figure, one so unloving as to nearly induce madness in her children" (Hoffman, 1988, p. 7).

Maslow later said that his focus on the positive side of personality was a direct consequence of his mother's treatment of him. It was a "reaction formation" to the things his mother did and the qualities she represented (Maslow, 1979, p. 958). Thus, from a life begun in hardship came a determination to understand the best in human experience.

Maslow entered college intending a career in law, but he quickly became disenchanted because law focuses so much on evil and so little on good. He turned to psychology. According to Maslow, that was when his life really started. His doctoral work, done under the direction of well-known primate researcher Harry Harlow, focused on how dominance is established among

monkeys. Thus, even while conducting animal research, Maslow was interested in what sets exceptional individuals off from others who are less special.

Maslow shifted this research interest to humans during the period surrounding World War II. New York in the 1930s and 1940s was a gathering place for some of the greatest intellectuals of Europe who were escaping from Nazi Germany. Maslow was quite taken with several of these individuals and tried to find out everything he could about them. In this search to understand how these people came to be exceptional, Maslow was sowing the seeds of more formal work he would conduct later on.

Maslow was deeply moved by the suffering and anguish caused by World War II. He vowed to devote his life to proving that humans were capable of something better than war, prejudice, and hatred. He proceeded to do just that, by studying the process of self-actualization.

important areas of endeavor in which they may actually have considerable skill (Bergeron, Block, & Echtenkamp, 2006).

Self-Actualization and Maslow's Hierarchy of Motives

Another theorist who emphasized the importance of self-actualization was Abraham Maslow (1962, 1970). He was interested in the qualities of people who seem to get the most out of life—the most fully functioning of persons, the healthiest and best adjusted. He spent most of his career trying to understand how they were able to be so complete and so well adapted (see Box 14.3).

As part of this effort, Maslow eventually came to examine motivation and how diverse motives are organized. His view of motivation was very different from the view discussed in Chapter 5. Maslow came to view human needs as forming a hierarchy (Maslow, 1970), which is often portrayed as a pyramid (see Figure 14.1). He pointed out that needs vary in their immediacy and power. Some are extremely primitive, basic, and demanding. Because they're so fundamental, they form the base of the pyramid. These needs are *physiological*—pertaining to air, water, food, and so on—things obviously necessary for survival.

The qualities at the next higher level are also necessary for survival but are less demanding. These are *safety and* (physical) *security* needs—shelter from the weather, protection against predators, and so on. Maslow considered this second class of needs to be less basic than the first class because they require satisfaction less frequently. You need to get oxygen every few seconds, water every few hours, food once or twice a day. But once you've found an apartment, you have physical shelter for quite a while (as long as you pay the rent). If both your apartment and your air supply became inaccessible, you'd surely try to regain the air first and worry about the apartment later.

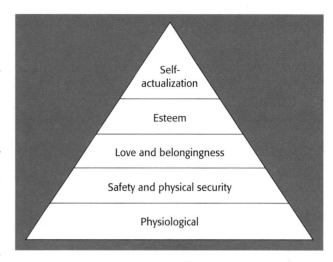

At the next level of the hierarchy, the needs begin to have more social qualities. The level immediately above safety needs is the category of *love and belongingness*. Here the needs are for companionship, affection, and acceptance from others (much like the need for positive regard). Needs of this type are satisfied through interaction with other people.

Higher yet on the pyramid are *esteem* needs: needs bearing on evaluation (and self-evaluation). Esteem needs include the need for a sense of mastery and power and a sense of appreciation from others (Leary & Baumeister, 2000). Notice that this differs from acceptance and affection in the last paragraph. *Acceptance* may not be evaluative. *Appreciation* is. You're appreciated and esteemed for some quality or qualities that you possess. The need for appreciation thus is more elaborate than the need for acceptance.

At the top of the hierarchy stands *self-actualization*. Maslow used this term much as Rogers did to mean the tendency to become whatever you're capable of becoming—to extend yourself to the limits of your capacities. This, to Maslow, is the highest of human motives.

The pyramid is a visual analogue for Maslow's core assumptions. He assumed that low-level needs are more primitive and more demanding than needs higher on the hierarchy. As noted earlier, the need for air is more demanding than the need for shelter. Maslow's assumption was broader than that, however. He also assumed that the need for physical shelter is more demanding than the need to have a sense of being accepted, and that the need for a sense of belonging is more demanding than the need to be appreciated or powerful. Maslow thus held that the power of the motive force weakens as you move up the pyramid. On the other hand, as you move up, the needs are also more distinctly human and less animalistic.

Thus, Maslow saw a trade-off between the constraints of biology and the uniqueness of being human. We have needs that make us different from other creatures. Self-actualization is the highest and most important. But we can't escape the motives we share with other creatures. Those needs are more powerful when they're unsatisfied than the needs that make us special.

In general, people must deal with the needs they have at lower levels of the pyramid before they can attend to higher needs. Two implications follow. First, if a need begins to develop at a lower level while you're trying to satisfy a higher one, the lower-level need can cause you to be pulled away from the higher-level one. Your attention, in effect, is pulled downward, and you're forced to do something about the lower need (see Wicker, Brown, Wiehe, Hagen, & Reed, 1993).

FIGURE 14.1
Maslow's theoretical hierarchy of needs. Needs lower on the hierarchy are more demanding and animalistic. Needs higher on the hierarchy are more subtle, but more distinctly human. *Source: Based on Maslow, 1970.*

The second implication concerns how people move up through this set of needs. It may be precisely the freeing of your mind from the demands of low-level needs that lets you be attuned to the very quiet voice of self-actualization. Remember, the further up the pyramid you go, the more subtle and less survival related is the motive. Self-actualization, the highest motive, is the last to be taken into account. Only when the other needs are quieted can this one be attended to.

The steps on the hierarchy also differ from each other in one more sense. Maslow said that motives low on the pyramid are **deficiency-based motives,** whereas those high on the pyramid (particularly self-actualization) are **growth-based motives** (Maslow, 1955). That is, lower needs arise from deprivation. Satisfying such needs means escaping unpleasant conditions. Self-actualization, in contrast, is more like the distant call of your still-unrealized potential as a person. Satisfying this need isn't a matter of avoiding an unpleasant state. Rather, it's the seeking of growth (see also Sheldon et al., 2001).

Finally, compare Maslow's ideas to those of Rogers. Recall that Rogers emphasized two motives: the self-actualizing tendency and the need for positive regard (affection and acceptance). It's possible to see a similarity between those ideas and Maslow's more elaborate structure (see Figure 14.1). The bottom two levels of Maslow's pyramid refer to needs that Rogers ignored. Rogers focused on social needs, which for Maslow begin at the third level. Maslow assumed, as did Rogers, that the need for acceptance could be more demanding than the need for self-actualization. The structure of the pyramid clearly implies that people can be distracted from self-actualization by the need for positive regard.

The intermediate level of Maslow's pyramid—esteem needs—can be viewed as an elaboration on the need for positive regard. Esteem needs seem similar in many ways to Rogers's conditions of worth. The two theorists differed in how they saw this motive. To Rogers, bowing to conditions of worth is bad. To Maslow, esteem needs are part of being human, although less important than the need to self-actualize. The two agreed, however, that this need can get in the way of self-actualization. In sum, despite the fact that each theorist had unique ideas about personality, their theoretical views also have much in common.

CHARACTERISTICS OF FREQUENT SELF-ACTUALIZERS

The concept of self-actualization is, in many ways, the most engaging and intriguing of the ideas of these theorists. Although Maslow painted a broad picture of human motives, self-actualization most fully absorbed his interest and imagination. He devoted much of his career to studying it.

According to Maslow, everyone has the potential to self-actualize, and everyone has an intrinsic desire to become more and more the person that he or she is capable of being. Because self-actualization is so diffuse a quality, it can appear in virtually any kind of behavior. It isn't just the painter, musician, writer, or actor who can be self-actualizing. It's any person who's in the process of becoming more congruent, more integrated, more complete as a person.

Despite the belief that every person has this potential, Maslow also recognized that some people self-actualize more than others. To better understand the process, he sought out people who displayed self-actualizing properties often. He worked hard to describe these people, in part because self-actualization is such a hard concept to grasp. By describing them, he hoped to help others recognize self-actualizing experiences in their own lives.

Table 14.1 Characteristics of Self-Actualizers. *Source:* Based on Maslow, 1968.

Self-actualizing people . . .
- are *efficient* and accurate *in perceiving* reality
- are *accepting* of themselves, of other people, and of nature
- are *spontaneous* in thought and emotion, natural rather than artificial
- are *problem centered*, or concerned with eternal philosophical questions
- are *independent* and *autonomous* when it comes to satisfactions
- have a continued *freshness of appreciation* of ordinary events
- often experience so-called *oceanic feelings*, a sense of oneness with nature that transcends time and space
- *identify with* all of *humanity* and are democratic and respectful of others
- form *deep ties* but *with only a few persons*
- *appreciate*, for its own sake, the *process* of doing things
- have a *philosophical*, thoughtful, nonhostile *sense of humor*
- have a childlike and fresh *creativity and inventiveness*
- maintain an inner *detachment from* the *culture* in which they live
- are sufficiently *strong*, independent, and guided by their own inner visions that they sometimes appear *temperamental* and even *ruthless*

Maslow came to believe that frequent self-actualizers share several characteristics (Maslow, 1962, 1968). Here are a few of them (for a more complete list, see Table 14.1): Self-actualizers are *efficient* in their perception of reality. That is, their experience is in extra-sharp focus. Self-actualizers can spot the confused perceptions of others and cut through tangles. People who frequently engage in self-actualization are also *accepting*. They accept both themselves and others. Their self-acceptance isn't smug self-promotion. Self-actualizers realize they're not perfect. They accept themselves *as they are*, imperfections and all. They also accept the frailties of people around them, as a part of who those people are.

Another characteristic of the self-actualizer is a mental *spontaneity*. This is reflected in a creativity without artificiality. This is often linked to a fresh appreciation of life, an excitement in the process of living. The idea that creativity relates to self-actualization has received research support. In one study (Amabile, 1985), writers were led to think about the act of creation either from the view of extrinsic incentives (thus lower on Maslow's hierarchy) or from qualities intrinsic to the act itself (by implication, self-actualization). They then wrote poems. Judges later rated the creativity of the poems. Those written after thinking about external incentives were lower in creativity than those written from the self-actualizing orientation.

The self-actualizing person is often said to be *problem centered*, but this phrase is a little misleading. The word *problem* here refers to enduring questions of philosophy or ethics. Self-actualizers take a wide view, consider universal issues. Along with this goes an independence from their own culture and immediate environment. The self-actualizer lives in the universe, and only secondarily in this apartment, city, or country. Frequent self-actualizers know relationships require effort. They have deep ties because relationships matter to them, but the ties are often limited to a very few others.

Toward the end of his life, Maslow made a distinction between these people and another kind of self-actualizers (Maslow, 1971), whom he called **transcendent self-actualizers.** These people are so invested in self-actualization that it becomes the most precious aspect of their life. They are more consciously motivated by universal

Box 14.4 SELF-ACTUALIZATION AND *YOUR* LIFE

By now you've read a lot about the concept of self-actualization, and it may all sound pretty abstract. To get a more concrete feel for the idea, try spending a few minutes thinking about how it applies to your own life.

For example, think about how Maslow's hierarchy of needs pertains to your current existence. Which level of the hierarchy dominates your day-to-day experiences? Are you mostly concerned with having a sense of belonging to a social group (or perhaps a sense of acceptance and closeness with a particular person)? Is the need to feel valued and respected what you're currently focused on? Or are you actively trying to grow as close as possible to the blueprint hidden inside you that holds the secret of your possibilities?

Now think back to your junior year of high school and what your life was like back then. What were your needs and concerns during that period? Since then, has your focus moved upward on the hierarchy or downward, or are you focused at about the same level?

Here's another question: Think about your current mission in life, the goal that gives your life focus and provides it meaning. Where did it come from? Did it get passed down to you by your parents (or someone else)? Or does it come from deep inside you? How *sure* are you that your goal is your own and not someone else's assignment for you, a condition of worth? How sure are you that it isn't an assignment you've given *yourself*? What would it feel like to spend the rest of your life doing "assignments"?

Another question: You can't always do what you want. Everyone knows that. Sometimes you *have* to do things. But how much of the time? How much of your time—how much of your *self*—should be used up doing your duty, being obedient to conditions of worth, before you turn to your other needs? How dangerous is it to say to yourself that you'll do these assignments—these duties—for a while, just for a little while, and that after a few weeks or months or years, you'll turn to the things you

really want? How sure are you that you won't get in a rut and come to see the assignments as the only reality in life? How sure are you that you'll be able to make the decision to turn to your own self-actualization, years down the road, when it's become such a habit to focus on fulfilling conditions of worth?

Not every experience in life is self-actualizing. Even people who self-actualize extensively get stalled sometimes and have trouble with it. When *you* find yourself unable to self-actualize, what's preventing it? What barriers to growth do you confront from time to time? Are they the demands of other needs? Do they stem from your relationships with your parents and family? With your friends? Or are they barriers you place in front of yourself?

Obviously, these questions aren't easy to answer. You can't expect to answer them in just a few minutes. People spend a lifetime trying to answer them. But these questions are important, and thinking about them for a little while should give you a more vivid sense of the issues raised by the phenomenological approach.

---

values or goals outside themselves (such as beauty, truth, and unity). They're more holistic about the world, seeing the integration of all its elements. There's a transcendence of the self, so that self-actualization almost becomes "universe-actualization." All of experience seems sacred to these people. They see themselves as the tools by which capabilities are expressed, rather than the owners of the capabilities. From this characterization comes the term *transpersonal* ("beyond the person"). This term is sometimes used to refer to this way of viewing human potential (see also Box 14.4).

PEAK EXPERIENCES

In trying to describe the process of self-actualization, Maslow also focused on moments in which self-actualization was clearly occurring. Remember, not every act involves self-actualization, even for a person who self-actualizes a great deal. Maslow used the term **peak experiences** to refer to moments of intense self-actualization.

In peak experiences, people have a sense of being connected with the elements of their surroundings. Colors and sounds seem crisper. There's a sharper clarity in perceptions (see Privette & Landsman, 1983). There's also a loss of the sense of time as the experience flows by. The feelings associated with the peak experience are often those of awe, wonder, or even ecstasy. The peak experience tends to take you outside yourself. You aren't thinking about yourself but rather are experiencing whatever you're experiencing as fully as possible.

Peak experiences *can* occur in a passive way (for instance, in examining a great work of art). Usually, though, they occur when people are engaged in action (Czikszentmihalyi, 1975; Privette & Landsman, 1983). Indeed, there's evidence that they happen more during work than during leisure (Czikszentmihalyi & LeFevre, 1989). The person having a peak experience is so immersed in an activity that the activity seems to "become" the person. The term **flow** is also used for such experiences (Czikszentmihalyi, 1990; Czikszentmihalyi & Czikszentmihalyi, 1988).

We should re-emphasize that it's not necessary that the activity involve artistic creation or any such thing. What's important isn't *what's* being done but rather *how* it takes place. If you're completely immersed in it, if it's stretching you as a human being, it can be a peak experience.

Peak experiences occur when a person is deeply engaged in a demanding activity and fully caught up in the moment. Imagine how this football player feels while scoring this touchdown.

Existential Psychology: Being and Death

So far, we've focused on several ideas: that people have a natural tendency toward growth, that people can exert free will to change the course of their lives, that people defend against perceptions of incongruence and try to prevent them from arising, and that the motive to grow is at the peak of a hierarchy of motives. However, there's another side to growth and human potential: The possibilities of self-actualization have a cost. They bring responsibilities.

This is one message of another group of phenomenological psychologists called **existential psychologists.** The term *existential* is related to the word *existence*. It pertains to a philosophical view which holds that existence is all anyone has. Each person is alone in an unfathomable universe. This view stresses that each person must take responsibility for his or her choices in life. This view fits the phenomenological orientation in emphasizing the importance of the individual's experience of reality.

THE EXISTENTIAL DILEMMA

A concept that's central to the existentialist view is **dasein.** This German word is often translated as "being in the world." This phrase is used to imply the totality of a person's experience of the self as an autonomous, separate, and evolving entity (Binswanger, 1963; Boss, 1963; May, 1958). The term *dasein* also emphasizes that humans have no existence apart from the world and that the world has no meaning apart from the people in it.

To the existentialists, the basic issue in life is that life inevitably ends in death, which can come at any time (Becker, 1973). Death is the one event no one escapes, no matter how self-actualizing his or her experiences are. Awareness of the inevitability of death provokes *angst*—dread, anguish far deeper than the anxiety experienced over incongruity. There exist only being and not-being, and we constantly face the polarity between them.

How should you respond to this realization? To the existentialists, this is the key question in life. The choice is to retreat into nothingness or to have the courage to *be*. At its extreme, the choice is whether or not to commit suicide, thus avoiding the absurdity of a life that will end in death anyway. To kill oneself is to choose nothingness. But nothingness can also be chosen in less extreme ways. People can choose not to act authentically, not to commit themselves to the responsibilities and goals that are part of who they are. They can drift, go along with some crowd. When people fail to take responsibility for their lives, they're choosing nothingness.

What's involved in the choice to be? To the existentialists, life has no meaning unless you create it. Each person with the courage to do so must assign meaning to his or her existence. You assign meaning to your life by acting authentically, by being who you are. The very recognition of the existential dilemma is an important step to doing this. As May (1958, p. 47) put it, "To grasp what it means to exist, one needs to grasp the fact that he might not exist."

Exercising this freedom isn't easy. It can be hard to find the way to knowing who you are, and it can be hard to stare death in the face. It's often easier to let other people decide what's right and just go along. Existential psychologists believe, though, that all persons are responsible for making the most of every moment of their existence and fulfilling that existence to the best of their ability (Boss, 1963; Frankl, 1969; May, 1969). This responsibility is inescapable, and it's not to be taken lightly.

Although people are responsible for their choices, even honest choices aren't always good ones. You won't always deal perfectly with the people you care about. You'll sometimes lose track of your connection to nature. Even if your choices are wise, you'll still have **existential guilt** over failing to fulfill your possibilities. This guilt is strongest when a person who's free to choose fails to choose. But people who are aware are never completely free of existential guilt, because it's impossible to fulfill every possibility. In realizing some of your capabilities, you prevent others from being expressed. Thus, existential guilt is inescapable. It's part of the cost of being.

EMPTINESS

The existentialists also focus on the problem of emptiness in life. They are concerned that people have lost faith in values (May, 1953). Many people no longer have a sense of worth and dignity. This is partly because they've found themselves powerless to influence forces such as government and big business. The planet warms, and we do nothing to stop it. Businesses need multibillion dollar bailouts, and we're stuck with the bill. The leaders of our country commit us to wars without justifying them, or even declaring them as wars, and we bear the consequences.

When people lose their commitment to a set of values, they experience a sense of emptiness and meaninglessness. When people feel this way, they turn to others for answers. The answers aren't there, however, because the problem is really within the person. This illustrates once again the existentialist theme that you must be responsible for your own actions and that truth can come only from within and from your actions.

TERROR MANAGEMENT

Some of the ideas of existential psychology are reflected in *terror management theory* (Greenberg, Pyszczynski, & Solomon, 1986). This theory begins with the idea that an awareness of one's eventual death creates existential angst, or terror (Becker, 1973). People respond to the terror by trying to live lives of meaning and value. This much matches what we said about existential psychology.

Terror management theory goes on to suggest, however, that people often don't define the meaning of life on their own. Rather, they use a process of social and cultural consensus. This means that group identity plays an important role in how people affirm the value of their lives. Reminders of mortality lead people to be more protective of their own cultural values (Greenberg, Solomon, & Pyszczynski, 1997). By weaving themselves into a meaningful cultural fabric, a fabric that will last long after they're gone, they affirm their own value as human beings.

People respond to reminders of mortality by holding more closely to their social fabric.

This theory has led to a great deal of research over the past two decades (Greenberg et al., 1997). Some of these studies have shown that making people aware of their mortality causes them to become more favorable toward those who uphold their worldview and more negative toward those who don't. This *mortality salience* also makes people adhere more to cultural norms themselves. Americans become more patriotic; jihadists become more devoted to their cause (Pyszczynski, Solomon, & Greenberg, 2002). Mortality salience can make people act more altruistically—for instance, by supporting charities (Jonas, Schimel, Greenberg, & Pyszczynski, 2002)—but only if the charities connect to their own culture.

Much of the research on this topic examines how people affirm their cultural worldview after being reminded of their mortality. However, at least one study has looked at how people affirm values of the self (McGregor, Zanna, Holmes, & Spencer, 2001, Study 4). After a mortality salience manipulation, participants completed a measure of identity seeking and an assessment of their goals for the immediate future. Those whose mortality had been brought to mind stood higher on the measure of identity seeking than others. They also reported intending to work at projects that were more self-consistent than were the projects reported by others.

Terror management theory leads to a number of other interesting ideas. One is that terror management is the reason people view themselves as separate from other animals. To think of yourself as an animal is to be reminded of your death, because all animals die. Consistent with this idea, making mortality salient causes people to have more disgust in response to animals and to favor more strongly the idea that humans are distinct from other animals (Goldenberg, Pyszczynski, Greenberg, Solomon, Kluck, & Cornwell, 2001).

This view also has implications for sexuality (Goldenberg, Pyszczynski, Greenberg, & Solomon, 2000). Sex is one more reminder of your animal nature. That may be one reason many people are nervous about sex: It reminds them of their mortality. People sidestep this reminder in many ways. They ascribe aesthetic value to the sex act. They create romance around it to distract themselves from its animal qualities (Florian, Mikulincer, & Hirschberger, 2002). They create cultural standards of beauty that are idealized and symbolic. In doing so, the *animal* is transformed to the *spiritual*.

People struggle against existential terror in many ways. According to terror management theory, propping up self-esteem can establish a sense of one's value and stave off existential angst (Pyszczynski, Greenberg, Solomon, Arndt, & Schimel, 2004). Recent research has added the idea that confronting mortality motivates people to form close relationships (Mikulincer, Florian, & Hirschberger, 2003). In fact, the push toward affiliation may be even more important than the affirmation of cultural values (Wisman & Koole, 2003).

As we said, this theory has prompted a great deal of research, extending in many directions. For present purposes, however, let's link it back to existentialism. The research makes it clear that reminding people of their eventual death makes them try to affirm the value of their lives. People do this mostly (though not entirely) by embracing the values of the culture in which they live. Only a little evidence indicates that people try to create their own personal meanings. Does this mean that for most people, the response to existential angst is to let other people decide what's right and just go along? Surely this would dismay the existential psychologists. It may simply mean, though, that values are naturally defined more by groups than the existentialists realized.

Assessment

A basic issue in personality assessment is how to go about it. Various views suggest different approaches to the process. This view suggests yet another one.

INTERVIEWS IN ASSESSMENT

Phenomenological psychologists are less tied than other psychologists to the structure of specific measuring instruments. To them, assessment isn't a process of having a person respond to a set of stimuli. It's a process of finding out *what the person is like*. Given this view, they are very much at home with interviewing as an assessment technique. The interview offers maximum flexibility. It lets the person being assessed say whatever comes up. It lets the interviewer follow stray thoughts and ask questions that might not otherwise occur. It lets the interviewer get a subjective sense of what that person is like from *interacting* with him or her.

Finding out what a person is like in this way requires empathy. After all, the interviewer is trying to enter the other person's private world. Empathy isn't automatic. It requires sensitivity to small changes. As an interviewer, you must repeatedly check the accuracy of your sensing to make sure you haven't taken a wrong turn. (Empathy isn't important just for interviewing, by the way. Rogers saw it as important to doing therapy and to being a fully functioning person.)

An extensive interview produces a lot of information. One way to evaluate this information is called **content analysis**. This involves grouping the person's statements in some way and seeing how many statements are in each group. For example, in an interview Susan said two things about herself expressing self-approval, eighteen expressing self-disapproval, and fifteen that were ambivalent. One might infer from this that Susan isn't very satisfied with herself.

This tactic can also be used to assess progress in therapy. For example, in a second interview after three months of therapy, Susan made five statements that expressed approval of herself, five that expressed disapproval, and eight that were ambivalent. One implication might be that Susan is now less negative about herself than before.

The flexibility that makes interviews useful also creates problems. Unless an interview is highly structured, it's hard to compare one with another. If Jane expresses more self-disapproval than Sally, is it because Jane dislikes herself more than Sally? Or did the interviewer just happen to follow up a particularly bothersome aspect of Jane's self-image? If Susan expresses less self-disapproval after therapy than before, is it because she's become more satisfied with herself or because the interviewer failed to get into self-critical areas in the second interview?

It's also clear that what a person says in an interview can vary as a function of other things. For example, people are more self-disclosing to an interviewer who has good rapport with them (Jourard, 1974). In fact, small differences in an interviewer's verbal behavior can produce large differences in what people say. Thus, many see the interview as primarily a tool for getting informal impressions, rather than for conducting a full assessment.

MEASURING THE SELF-CONCEPT BY Q-SORT

assess. Theorists discussed in
sess the self-concept.
ept is called the **Q-sort** (e.g.,
many variations on this proves giving the person a large
f-evaluative statements, as in
gs. The person doing the Q-
2). At one end are just a few
end are just a few cards with
esent gradations between the

n a given pile (Figure 14.2).
not like me, neither) and then
o look hard at the statements
ptive. By comparing qualities,
ffers in this respect from rating
let the person say that all the
en in a Q-sort.
according to how you think
t more complex information.
to what they were like earlier
l the two match. Differences

ures.

erson.

I am optimistic.	
I express my emotions freely.	I make strong demands on myself.
I understand myself.	I get along easily with others.
I am lazy.	I often feel driven.
I am generally happy.	I am self-reliant.
I am moody.	I am responsible for my troubles.

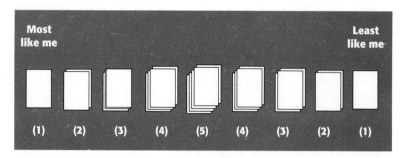

Most like me

(1)　(2)　(3)　(4)　(5)　(4)　(3)　(2)　(1)

Least like me

FIGURE 14.2
In the Q-sort procedure, you sort a set of cards containing descriptive statements into a row of piles. At one end of the row might be the card containing the single statement that's most like you, at the other end the card containing the single statement that's least like you. The other piles of cards represent gradations between these two points. As you can see from the numbers in parentheses in this example, the piles toward the middle are permitted to have more cards in them than the piles closer to the end points. Thus, you're forced to decide which items really are very much like and unlike yourself.

between the two reflect changes in self-concept over time. It's also possible to sort for the ideal self (the kind of person you want to be). Then you can look to see how much difference or similarity there is between the ideal and the actual. Similarity reflects *congruence,* the closeness between your ideal self and your perceived self.

MEASURING SELF-ACTUALIZATION

A second content for personality assessment is suggested by the emphasis on self-actualization. Given this emphasis, it would seem desirable to measure the degree to which people have characteristics of frequent self-actualization.

The Personal Orientation Inventory (POI) was developed for this purpose (Shostrom, 1964, 1974; see also Knapp, 1976). The POI consists of paired statements. People choose the one from each pair they agree with more. The POI has two major scales. One, called *time competence,* reflects in part the degree to which the person lives in the present, as opposed to being distracted by the past and future. As the word *competence* hints, though, it also has a more complex meaning. Time-competent people are able to effectively tie the past and future with the present. They sense continuity among these three aspects of time.

The second scale assesses a tendency to be *inner directed* in the search for values and meaning. Self-actualizers are believed to have a stronger tendency toward inner direction in determining their values than people who are less self-actualizing. It's been found that scores on the POI improve after group therapy (Dosamantes-Alperson & Merrill, 1980).

Jones and Crandall (1986) developed another measure of self-actualization. Their scale has four factors, reflecting self-direction, self-acceptance, acceptance of emotions, and trust and responsibility in interpersonal relations. As with the POI, there's evidence that scores on this scale change after group therapy (Crandall, McCown, & Robb, 1988).

MEASURING AUTONOMY AND CONTROL

Yet another quality that's important to the viewpoints presented in this chapter is the extent to which a person's actions tend to be *autonomous* versus *controlled.* A number of self-report measures exist to assess this difference among people. One measure assesses the extent to which people generally tend to function in a self-determined way in their lives (Sheldon, Ryan, & Reis, 1996). This measure of general self-determination can give a broad sense of a person's behavior across multiple domains. It's been used, for example, to show that people high in general self-determination have harmony between their needs and goals (e.g., Thrash & Elliot, 2002).

Several other measures focus on how people behave in some specific domain of life. For example, Ryan and Connell (1989) developed a measure of children's academic behavior and prosocial behavior. The items ask children why they do various things and provide potential reasons that had been chosen to reflect controlled or autonomous motivation. In another project, Black and Deci (2000) developed a measure to ask college students their reasons for learning things in their courses. Again, options are provided for reasons that are controlled and reasons that are autonomous. Another such measure was devised to assess the motives underlying religious behavior (Ryan, Rigby, & King, 1993).

Problems in Behavior, and Behavior Change

How are problems in living conceptualized in this view? Recall that fully functioning people are attuned to the actualizing tendency and experience a sense of
coherence and consistency. They're not trying to live up to conditions of worth.
They're being who they are. To Rogers (and others), lack of congruity within the self
creates psychological problems. (For supporting evidence of various kinds, see Deci
and Ryan [1991]; Higgins [1990]; and Ryan, Sheldon, Kasser, and Deci [1996].)

To Rogers, incongruity (between experience and self-concept or within the
self-concept) is experienced as anxiety (though see Box 14.5 for a more complex
view). Anxiety is a signal from the organismic valuing process that the self is
disorganized. Although we have ways to protect the self from such threats (discussed
earlier in the chapter), anxiety can occur. This is especially likely if the person focuses
too much on conditions of worth and acts in ways that interfere with self-
actualization. If incongruities get large, the person will act in ways that are labeled
neurotic. If they get extreme enough, the person will act in ways that are labeled as
psychotic.

When the holistic self is threatened by uncertainty, the person becomes not just
more distressed but more rigid (McGregor et al., 2001). This seems to be an effort to
hold onto the self that existed before. People faced by an incongruity in one self-aspect

Box 14.5 Self-Discrepancies and Emotions

Rogers believed that incongruity of any sort creates anxiety. This belief is challenged by work done by Tory Higgins (1987) and his colleagues, who say the situation is more complicated.

Higgins says that three aspects of self need to be taken into account, not just two: the *actual*, the *ideal*, and the *ought* selves. To Higgins, the ideal self is what you wish for yourself, the self to which you aspire. The ought self is defined by duty or obligation. An *ought* is something you feel compelled to be, rather than desire to be. An ought sounds very much like a condition of worth. Higgins refers to ideals and oughts as **self-guides,** because they serve as comparison points for the actual self and as guides for behavior.

Higgins assumes, as did Rogers, that incongruities between the self-guides and the actual self produce negative feelings. Unlike Rogers, however,

Higgins distinguishes between two feelings, which come from two different kinds of incongruities. Specifically, Higgins holds that discrepancies between the actual and *ideal* selves cause feelings of sadness and dejection. Discrepancies between the actual and *ought* selves cause feelings of anxiety.

Studies have consistently supported this reasoning (e.g., Higgins, Bond, Klein, & Strauman, 1986; Strauman, 1989; Strauman & Higgins, 1987). In most studies, self-concept is assessed by having people list 10 attributes they think contribute to their actual selves, 10 they think contribute to their ideal selves, and 10 they think contribute to their ought selves. The extent of discrepancy between the actual and ideal is computed by counting the number of matches on the two lists and the number of opposites. A similar procedure is used to assess discrepancy between the actual and ought selves. Either in the same session or at another time, subjects also report their

moods, including feelings of depression and feelings of anxiety.

The usual finding is that the extent of actual–ideal discrepancy relates uniquely to depression but not anxiety. The extent of actual–ought discrepancy relates uniquely to anxiety but not depression. These results are especially impressive in light of the fact that depression and anxiety tend to occur together. In fact, many psychologists have viewed them as different facets of the same thing. Being able to distinguish between them is no small feat.

It's also of interest that the ought self seems to be linked conceptually to the notion of conditions of worth. That is, an ought is an obligation, a duty. The ideal self, in contrast, isn't tied to conditions of worth. This body of research, then, suggests a variation on the position taken by Rogers. Incongruities that derive from failures to meet conditions of worth lead to anxiety. Incongruities that derive from a failure to self-actualize are reflected in dejection.

stress their certainty about other things, apparently trying to compensate for what's been threatened. They become more zealous or extreme in their beliefs and personal values. In fact, McGregor et al. (2001) suggested that this is what happens in the terror management responses discussed earlier in the chapter.

The process of therapy, to Rogers, is essentially the process of reintegrating a partially disorganized self. This involves reversing the processes of defense to confront the discrepancies between the elements of the person's experience. Doing so isn't easy, however.

Rogers believed that an important condition must be met before such changes can occur. Specifically, the conditions of worth that distorted the person's behavior in the past must be taken away. The person still needs positive regard, but it must be *unconditional*. Only then will the person feel able to confront the discrepancies. Removing the conditions of worth will allow the person to focus more fully on the organismic valuing process, the quiet inner voice that knows what's good and what's bad for you. This, in turn, allows a reintegration of the self. Consistent with this is evidence that people are less defensive when they're accepted for who they are than when they're accepted in an evaluative, conditional way (Arndt, Schimel, Greenberg, & Pyszczynski, 2002; Schimel, Arndt, Pyszczynski, & Greenberg, 2001).

Unconditional positive regard, then, is a key to therapy. But it's a complex key. For unconditional regard to be effective, it must be given *from the person's own frame of reference*. That is, it means acceptance for who *you* think you are. Someone who knows nothing about you or your feelings can't give meaningful acceptance. This is a second reason it's important for a therapist to be empathic. The first was that empathy is necessary to get an adequate sense of what the client is like. The second is that it's necessary if the therapist is to show unconditional positive regard for the client in a way that will facilitate reintegration of the client's personality.

There's one more potential problem here. Sometimes people undertake therapy to satisfy someone's conditions of worth for them. It stands to reason that people who are trying to make changes for autonomous reasons will do better than people trying to make similar changes to satisfy conditions of worth. In at least one domain of change—weight loss—there's evidence that this is so. In one study, people who lost weight for autonomous reasons lost more and kept it off longer than those who did it for less autonomous reasons (Williams, Grow, Freedman, Ryan, & Deci, 1996).

CLIENT-CENTERED THERAPY

There are several humanistic approaches to therapy (Cain & Seeman, 2002). The one that's best known, developed by Rogers (1951, 1961; Rogers & Stevens, 1967), is called **client-centered therapy,** or **person-centered therapy.** As the phrase implies, the client takes responsibility for his or her own improvement. Recall Rogers's belief that the tendency toward actualizing is intrinsic. If people with problems can be put in a situation in which conditions of worth are removed, they should naturally reintegrate themselves. This is a bit like the rationale for putting a bandage on a wound. The bandage doesn't heal the wound, but by maintaining a sterile environment, it helps the natural healing process take place.

In person-centered therapy, the therapist displays empathy and unconditional positive regard. This lets the client escape temporarily from conditions of worth and begin exploring aspects of experience that are incongruent with the self. Throughout, the therapist remains nondirective and nonevaluative, showing no emotion and giving no advice. The therapist's role is to *remove* the pressure of conditions of worth. By avoiding evaluative comments (e.g., saying that something is good or bad), the effective therapist avoids imposing additional conditions of worth.

Rather than be evaluative, the therapist tries to help clients gain a clear perspective on their own feelings and experiences. In general, this means reflecting back to the client, in slightly different ways, things the client is saying so the client can re-examine them from a different angle. There are two variations on this procedure.

The first is called **clarification of feelings.** Part of what the client does in the therapy session is emotional, expressing feelings about things, either directly in words or indirectly in other ways. As feelings are expressed, the therapist repeats those expressions in different words. The purpose here is to make the client more aware of what his or her true feelings are. Simply being reminded of the feelings can help this to happen.

A moment's reflection should confirm the usefulness of this technique. Feelings are often fleeting. When people express feelings in their words or actions, they often fail to notice them. Moments later, they may be unaware of having had them. If the feelings are threatening, people actively defend against recognizing them. The process of reflecting feelings back to the client allows the nature and the intensity of the feelings to become more obvious to the client. This puts the client into closer touch with the experience.

The second kind of reflection in person-centered therapy is more intellectual and less emotional. It's called **restatement of content**. This is equivalent to what was just described but in terms of the *ideas* in the client's statements—the cognitive content of what the client says.

Is client-centered therapy effective? It can be (M. L. Smith & Glass, 1977). Studies of this technique have focused primarily on changes in self-image. There's evidence that people do change their pictures of themselves after client-centered therapy, so that their perceived self becomes more congruent with their ideals (e.g., Butler & Haigh, 1954; Truax & Mitchell, 1971).

BEYOND THERAPY TO PERSONAL GROWTH

To humanistic psychologists, therapy isn't a special process of fixing something that's wrong and then forgetting about it. Rather, it's on a continuum with other life experiences. In this view, a person who's living life to the fullest should always engage in more or less the same processes as occur in therapy. These processes provide a way for people who have average lives—or even very good lives—to further enrich their experiences and to self-actualize even more completely.

Rogers's view of the ideal way of life is captured in the phrase *fully functioning person*. He believed that personal growth throughout life should be a goal for everyone. Growth requires the same conditions as those needed for effective therapy. Growth requires that the people with whom you interact be genuine and open, with no holding back and no putting up false fronts. It requires empathic understanding together with unconditional positive regard. This view on growth is similar to Maslow's view on self-actualization: Growth isn't a goal that's reached once and cast aside. It's a way of living to be pursued throughout your lifetime.

Humanistic Theories: Problems and Prospects

The humanistic view is regarded by many as an intuitively *accessible* approach to personality. The intuitive appeal of this view derives partly from its emphasis on the uniqueness and validity of each person's experience. Indeed, this view treats each person's subjective experience as being of primary importance. This emphasis on personal experience fits well with what many people bring to mind when they think of the word *personality,* especially when they think of their *own* personality. For this reason, this viewpoint feels comfortable and commonsensical to many people.

This viewpoint also has at least two other virtues. First, it represents an optimistic and positive view of human nature. Humanistic psychologists such as Rogers, Maslow, Deci, and Ryan have argued strenuously that people are intrinsically good—naturally motivated to be the best they can be. According to this view, that motive will be expressed in everyone, as long as other circumstances don't interfere too much.

This optimistic outlook on humanity is also reflected in a practical virtue of the humanistic view. This view emphasizes the importance of fully experiencing and appreciating your own reality and maintaining close contact with your own feelings. This emphasis provides a strategy for living that many people have used to enrich their lives. The benefits sometimes have come through formal therapy. But remember that many phenomenologists assume there's no real distinction between therapy and the more ordinary "course corrections" that are part of normal living. Thus, the move toward personal enrichment has come for many people in informal ways. It's been sort of a self-guided exploration of how to make one's life better.

Although humanistic psychology certainly has virtues, it has had problems as well. One problem in the past was a lack of precision. It was hard to generate research from the theories. For example, consider self-actualization. To study self-actualization, you need to know the areas of life to which the actualizing tendency is relevant for each person you're studying. But actualization occurs in different ways within different people. In theory, it might be necessary to study as many types of behavior as there are people being studied.

This difficulty was a serious one. However, more recent humanists have taken many steps to overcome it. Deci and Ryan and their co-workers, who share many orienting assumptions with earlier humanists, have devised hypotheses that can be tested readily and in a straightforward manner. Findings from research on topics such as self-determination provide powerful support for many assumptions of the humanistic viewpoint.

A second set of criticisms of humanistic psychology aims at a quality that was just described as a virtue: its optimistic, positive view of human nature. This view is sometimes criticized as arbitrary, naïve, sentimental, and romantic. Some believe it has no basis other than the theorists' belief that people are inherently good. Not everyone believes that all people are inherently good (Baumeister & Campbell, 1999).

The idea that everyone's self-actualization should be encouraged is also criticized. Some say that if this principle were carried to its extreme, it would require that everyone be encouraged to live life to the fullest, regardless of the consequences for anyone else. The result of such unrestrained self-expression would be chaos. Such a way of life would create serious conflict whenever one person's self-actualization somehow interfered with someone else's self-actualization, which certainly would happen.

It's also worth noting that the optimistic overtones that permeate so much of humanistic psychology are largely missing from the writings of the existentialists. Whereas humanists such as Rogers and Maslow emphasized the fulfilling quality that can come from making your own way in the world, the existentialists emphasize that doing this is hard and can be very painful. Living honestly means confronting harsh realities and absurdities and rising above them. This picture is very different from the one painted by Rogers and Maslow. It can be difficult to reconcile the warm and glowing optimism of the one view with the angst of the other.

Another point of contention about this view on personality concerns the concept of free will. Humanists tend to assume that people can decide for themselves what to do at any point in their lives. Others regard this conception of free will as a convenient fiction, an illusion that is misleading at best. Surely people act as though they *think* they have free will. But how to demonstrate the *existence* of free will has never been an easy problem to solve. Indeed, as noted earlier, there's now evidence for the position that the perception of will is illusory (Bargh & Ferguson, 2000; Wegner, 2002).

What, then, are the prospects for this approach to personality? Although many questions remain to be answered, the future of this way of thinking seems a great deal brighter than it did two decades ago. Several areas of vigorous and enthusiastic research activity have opened up seams of knowledge bearing on assumptions made years earlier by the pioneers of humanism. Topics such as self-determination, stereotype threat, terror management, and self-discrepancies are all being actively explored. The development and exploration of these sorts of ideas are a source of considerable encouragement for the future prospects of this approach.

· SUMMARY ·

The theorists of this chapter emphasize that people have an intrinsic tendency toward self-actualization. *Self-actualization* is the tendency to develop your capabilities in ways that maintain or enhance the self. This tendency promotes a sense of congruence, or integration, within the person. Its effectiveness is monitored by the organismic valuing process.

People also have a need for *positive regard,* acceptance and affection from others. Positive regard may be unconditional, or it may be conditional on your acting in certain ways. These conditions of worth mean that the person is held worthy only if he or she is acting in a desired manner. Conditions of worth, which can be self-imposed as well as imposed by others, can cause you to act in ways that oppose self-actualization.

Self-determination theory focuses on the difference between behavior that's self-determined and behavior that's controlled in some fashion. People enjoy activities more if they feel they're doing them from intrinsic interest instead of extrinsic reward. People whose lives are dominated by activities that are controlled are less healthy than people whose lives are self-determined.

Many theorists of this group assume that people have free will. This is a very hard idea to test, but people do seem to think they have free will. Studies of reactance have shown that people resist threats to freedoms they expect to have. Other research has questioned whether free will is illusory, though.

Behavior that opposes the actualizing tendency creates *disorganization* in the sense of self. Disorganization can be reduced by two kinds of defenses. You can distort perceptions of reality to reduce the threat, or you can act in ways that prevent threatening experiences from reaching awareness (for example, by ignoring them). Use of these defenses is seen in the fact that people blame their failures on factors outside themselves but take credit for their successes. People also engage in self-handicapping strategies, creating esteem-protective explanations for the possibility of failure before it even happens. Use of self-handicapping is paradoxical because it increases the likelihood of failure.

Maslow elaborated on the idea of self-actualization by proposing a hierarchy of motives, ranging from physical needs (most basic) to self-actualization (at the top). Basic needs are more demanding than higher needs, which (being more subtle) can affect you only when the lower needs are relatively satisfied. Maslow's intermediate levels appear to relate to the need for positive regard, suggesting why it can be hard to ignore the desire for acceptance from others.

Existential psychologists point out that with freedom comes the responsibility to choose for yourself what meaning your life has. The basic choice is to invest your life with meaning or to retreat into nothingness. When people are reminded of their own mortality, they try harder to connect to cultural values. Even if people try to find meaning, they can't escape existential guilt. No life can reflect all the possibilities it holds, because each choice rules out other possibilities.

This view on personality uses many assessment techniques, including both interviews and self-reports. Regarding content, it emphasizes the self-concept, self-actualization, and self-determination. One way to assess self-concept is the *Q-sort,* in which a set of items is sorted into piles according to how much they apply to oneself. Different "sorts" can be compared with each other for additional information.

From this perspective, problems derive from *incongruity.* Large incongruity is reflected as neurosis; when even more extreme, the result is psychosis. Therapy is a process of reintegrating a partly disorganized self. For reintegration to occur, the client must feel a sense of unconditional positive regard. In *client-centered therapy,* people are led to refocus on their feelings about their problems. The (nonevaluative) therapist simply helps clients to clarify their feelings. In this viewpoint, the processes of therapy blend into those of ordinary living, with the goal of experiencing continued personal growth.

· GLOSSARY ·

Actual self   One's self as one presently views it.

Actualization   The tendency to grow in ways that maintain or enhance the organism.

Clarification of feelings   The procedure in which a therapist restates a client's expressed feelings.

Client-centered therapy (also called **person-centered therapy**)   A type of therapy that removes conditions of worth and has clients examine their feelings.

Conditional positive regard   Affection that's given only under certain conditions.

Conditional self-regard   Self-acceptance that's given only under certain conditions.

Conditions of worth   Contingencies placed on positive regard.

Congruence   An integration within the self and a coherence between the self and one's experiences.

Content analysis   The grouping and counting of various categories of statements in an interview.

Contingent self-worth   Self-acceptance that's based on performance in some domain of life.

Dasein   "Being in the world"; the totality of one's autonomous personal existence.

Deficiency-based motive   A motive reflecting a lack within the person that needs to be filled.

Existential guilt   A sense of guilt over failing to fulfill all of one's possibilities.

Existential psychology   The view that people are responsible for investing their lives with meaning.

Flow   The experience of being immersed completely in an activity.

Fully functioning person   A person who's open to the experiences of life and who's self-actualizing.

Growth-based motive   A motive reflecting the desire to extend and elaborate oneself.

Humanistic psychology   A branch of psychology emphasizing the universal capacity for personal growth.

Ideal self   The personal values to which one aspires.

Organismic valuing process   The internal signal that tells whether self-actualization is occurring.

Peak experience   A subjective experience of intense self-actualization.

Positive regard   Acceptance and affection.

Q-sort   An assessment technique in which descriptors are sorted according to how much they apply to oneself.

Reactance   A motive to regain or reassert a freedom that's been threatened.

Restatement of content   A procedure in which a therapist rephrases the ideas expressed by a client.

Self-actualization   A process of growing in ways that maintain or enhance the self.

Self-concordance   Pursuing goals that are consistent with one's core values.

Self-determination   Deciding for oneself what to do.

Self-guides   Qualities of the self one desires to be (ideal) or feels compelled to be (ought).

Self-handicapping   Creating situations that make it hard to succeed, thus enabling avoidance of self-blame for failure.

Stereotype threat   Having a negative perception of the self because of feeling prejudged.

Transcendent self-actualizers   People whose actualization goes beyond the self to become more universal.

Unconditional positive regard   Acceptance and affection with "no strings attached."

Personal Constructs

Rachel and Jerry are sitting in the lounge taking a break from studying. They're talking about a new movie they've both just seen, and they're disagreeing loudly about how good it was (or wasn't). Rachel thinks the plot was subtly intricate and that there was a delicate tension throughout. Jerry thinks there wasn't any plot at all and that the film could not possibly have moved more slowly. At this point, Susan joins them and chimes in with her opinion. She didn't see the nuances of plot that Rachel saw, but she points out that the film had a lot of symbolism. Jerry just shakes his head in disbelief.

THE SAME physical world exists for everyone. An oak tree growing across the street is the same object when *you* look at it as when *anyone else* looks at it. A building stands there—brick and mortar—and no matter who's looking at it, its nature doesn't change. Physical reality is, after all, physical reality.

But people's experience of the world isn't based entirely on physical reality. Rachel, Jerry, and Susan saw the same film, but their experiences weren't even remotely the same. That's potentially true of all experiences. For example, consider again that oak across the street. You might look at it and sense a graceful product of nature's mysteries. Someone else may glance at the same tree and see a source of shade on a hot day. Another person might see a nuisance, a tall thing covered with leaves that soon will have to be raked. A fourth person may see a source of hardwood for furniture. The physical reality is the same for all, but the *experience* of it can vary widely from person to person.

This is also true in experiencing ourselves, the people around us, the actions we engage in, and the events of our lives. Consider John, a student who works extra hard at his courses, spending weekends in the library instead of partying. John sees his actions as an effort to learn as much as he can, about as many things as he can, while he has the chance. John's father sees these actions as an effort to establish a good record, thereby getting a good start toward a high-paying job. To one of John's professors, the pattern is an effort to compensate for feelings of inferiority. Dan, a casual friend, sees mindless compulsiveness. Susan, an even more casual friend, thinks it's silly to study so much and sees John as an incredibly dull person.

How is it that people have such different experiences when exposed to the same reality? Where do these differences in interpretation come from? Some psychologists answer these questions by saying that *physical reality* isn't the same as *human experience*. It's merely the raw material. No one can examine all the raw material available—no one has the time. No one can deal with *just* raw material, either. You have to impose organization on it, create order from the chaos. So each person *samples* the raw material and constructs a personal vision of how reality is organized. These mental representations then provide the basis for future perceptions, interpretations, and actions (Jussim, 1991).

It might even be said that *personality* consists of the organization of mental structures through which the person views reality (or which the person imposes on reality). This is essentially the position taken by George Kelly, whose ideas are the subject of this chapter (Kelly, 1955; for reviews, see Adams-Webber, 1979; Bannister, 1970, 1985; Bonarius, Holland, & Rosenberg, 1980; Mancuso & Adams-Webber, 1982).

Kelly is considered part of the phenomenological perspective because he emphasized the uniqueness of each person's subjective worldview. As you read about his ideas, you'll see some similarity to themes of Chapter 14, such as the idea that people choose for themselves how to think and act. But in many ways, Kelly's ideas also foreshadow a cognitive view that began to form nearly two decades later (discussed in Chapter 16). It may be useful to think of Kelly's theory as a bridge between the phenomenological perspective and a newer perspective that hadn't yet come into being.

Personal Constructs and Personality

Kelly argued that the best way to understand personality is to think of people as *scientists*. This view was also being promoted at about the same time by Fritz Heider (1958), an early cognitive theorist in social psychology. Just as scientists do, all of us have a need to predict events and to understand things that happen around us. Just as scientists, all of us develop theories of reality.

The need for prediction is basic to life. It shows up in every aspect of behavior. Think about it. You're making a prediction about the nature of the world every time you turn on a faucet and expect water to come out. You test a prediction whenever you turn a doorknob (expecting the door to open) or eat (expecting not to get sick). In truth, it's hard to think of any action that doesn't involve an implicit prediction about how reality is organized. Most of these predictions are made automatically and unconsciously, but they're predictions nonetheless.

Because so much of human life is social, the desire for predictability is especially important in social events. Every time you look at someone's expression and use it as a guide to his or her feelings, you're predicting social reality. Virtually all social encounters—even those as simple as buying something at a store—involve many implicit assumptions and predictions. In order to choose our own actions, we need to interpret other people's actions.

Each person responds to this need to predict by constructing a personal view of the world and how it works. This personal view, or theory, is a guide to predicting and interpreting future events. In Kelly's terms, people generate a set of **personal constructs** and impose them on reality. In his view, people don't experience the world directly. Rather, they know the world through the lens of their constructs. This is the essence of Kelly's "fundamental postulate" of human behavior: that people's behavior, thoughts, and feelings are determined by the constructs they use to anticipate or predict events.

BOX 15.1   APPRAISAL AND STRESS

Kelly's assertion that personal constructs determine how people see the world is echoed in a number of other theories. An example is a theory of psychological stress developed by Richard Lazarus, Susan Folkman, and their colleagues (e.g., Lazarus, 1966; Lazarus & Folkman, 1984). You certainly have an intuitive understanding of what the word *stress* means. However, the precise nature of stress has been hard to agree on. Lazarus took a very cognitive view of it, which fits nicely with many of the ideas discussed in this chapter.

Lazarus argues that the experience of stress involves three processes. The first, **primary appraisal,** is the process of perceiving an impending threat. The next, **secondary appraisal,** is the process of determining what to do (of the many things that might be done) to deal with the threat. The third element,

coping, is doing whatever's been chosen. It should be obvious that this analysis relies extensively on the concept of appraisal. *Appraisal* is weighing and evaluating the meaning of the raw material of one's perceptions. The word *appraisal,* in fact, is similar in meaning to the word *construal.*

Lazarus has always emphasized that the two appraisal processes rely heavily on the person's representation of reality. As a result, many kinds of stress can easily be said to be in the mind of the beholder, rather than in the outside world. That is, perceiving a threat (versus no threat) is largely a matter of how people construe the situations they're in. A bustling city street may seem absolutely harmless to one person, enticing to another, and fraught with peril to someone else.

Similarly, how people choose to respond to a threat will depend partly on how they construe various actions. For one person, walking away from a threat means losing face or looking

foolish. For another person, the same response means being efficient and not wasting energy. In both cases, personal interpretations are crucial determinants of what people experience and how they act in response to a given event.

It's also assumed that people often *reinterpret* the meanings of events, either while they are taking place or after they occur. These reappraisals can be induced by changes in the situation or by changes in the constructs the person brings to bear on the situation. In some cases, called **defensive reappraisal,** the act of reappraising seems calculated to produce the best possible construal, even if it's unrealistic. In other cases, however, the reappraisal seems to be more a matter of finding an interpretation that fits the event well. This emphasis on people's ability to reorganize their interpretations of stressors is similar to the philosophical orientation that Kelly called *constructive alternativism.*

Kelly saw constructs as important because he believed all events in life are open to multiple interpretations (see also Box 15.1). Kelly used the term **constructive alternativism** as a label for this idea and for the further assumption that people decide for themselves what constructs to apply to events. Kelly held that people can always alter their experiences, even looking back on them, by construing them in different ways.

We should perhaps say something about the meaning of the word *event* before going on. Kelly used this word to refer broadly to virtually anything in a person's experience. We'll use it the same way here. *Event* can refer to objects, people, feelings, experiences, or physical events. We should also say something about the word *construe.* This word refers to mental processes that range from perception to understanding and interpretation. It's a broader word than any of these, encompassing all of them. It's also a more specific word, in the sense that it implies actively taking a point of view.

USING CONSTRUCTS

Applying a construct to an event is slightly more complex than it might seem at first. The process is similar to the way a scientist uses a theory. That is, when you apply a construct, you *hypothesize* (implicitly) that it will fit an event. Then you *test* the hypothesis by applying the construct and predicting something. If your prediction is *confirmed,* the construct applies and you retain it as useful. If your prediction is *disconfirmed,* you may rethink when to apply the construct, you may revise the construct, or you may even abandon it. Constructs that predict events most of the time have a high degree of **predictive efficiency.**

To illustrate, Ann believes that some men see women as unique individuals, with their own distinct qualities, whereas other men see women as stereotypes. When meeting and first talking with Jim, she construes him as a man who views women as individuals. She's about to test this construal by making the implicit prediction that he'll be interested in her weekend activity: motocross racing. If Jim is interested or impressed, her prediction will be confirmed. If he recoils in horror, her prediction will be disconfirmed. If the latter occurs, something about how Ann applies the construct, or something about the construct itself, may require revision.

Kelly's starting point was that people use their constructs to predict and antici-pate events. He expanded on this basic idea by making a set of more focused statements, called *corollaries,* about constructs and how they're used. Here are several of them.

CONSTRUCTS ARE BIPOLAR

Kelly assumed that constructs are bipolar. That is, a construct consists of a pair of opposing characteristics. Examples are *friendly versus unfriendly* and *stable versus change-able.* The pole you're applying to the event you're construing is the **emergent pole.** If you view a person as friendly, you're applying your friendliness construct, with *friendly* as the emergent pole.

The end of the construct that's *not* being actively applied to the event is the **implicit pole.** The implicit pole is just as important as the emergent pole in defining the construct's nature. It's meaningless to think of someone as *friendly* unless you have an implicit recognition that it's possible for people to be *unfriendly.* Thus, both ends are involved in defining the construct, even though it's easy to lose track of that.

Kelly believed that constructs are *dichotomous* as well as *bipolar.* That is, he believed that people use constructs in a yes-or-no manner, not as vary-ing on a continuum. Kelly admitted that people see gradations, but he had a way to deal with that (Kelly, 1955). He assumed that gradations arise from an array of interrelated dichotomous con-structs. The array makes finer and finer distinc-tions, as one dichotomous decision leads to another one, at a lower level (see Figure 15.1).

For example, consider the construct *long versus short.* You can use it as a dichotomy, then repeat the process over and over again. It's as though you decide how long something is in a quick series of steps. First you decide if it's basically long or short. Assume you decide it's long. That throws out half the scale (the right half of Figure 15.1). Then you decide whether it's long or not among the gener-ally long. That decision then reduces the range by half again, and you make another decision within whichever part is left. If you do this often enough, the decisions become so fine grained that the result is equivalent to a continuum.

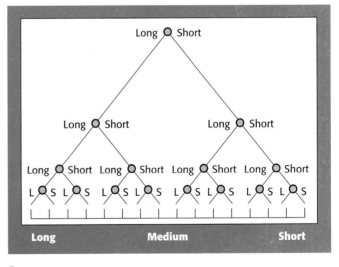

FIGURE 15.1
A dichotomous decision, repeated several times across ever-finer units, creates a set of possibilities that duplicates the range of varia-tion along a continuum. The simple set of decisions illustrated here yields 16 gradations. Given a few more decisions, the result would be indistinguishable from a continuously varying scale.

Consistent with Kelly's general view, there's evidence that people tend to polarize their perceptions—particularly social perceptions—seeing the world in black-and-white terms. For example, when people are in different groups, they tend to think of the two groups in terms of *us versus them* (Tajfel & Turner, 1986). In the same way, people who are very committed to a partner in a close relationship tend to polarize their perceptions by devaluing potential alternative partners (D. J. Johnson & Rusbult, 1989).

THE ROLE OF RECURRENCES

Constructs reflect qualities that *recur* in a person's experience, that show up repeatedly. It's rare for a construct to emerge on the basis of a single event. Constructs evolve over time and across repeated experiences. Developing a construct from a series of events is complicated by the fact that no two events are exactly alike, even if they're from the same family of events. Think, for instance, of filling your car at a gas station. The experience is somewhat the same each time, but it's not identical from one time to another.

The fact that constructs are based on recurring elements makes good sense from the view we began with—that people try to anticipate events according to a personal theory. The kind of theory that's most sensible to invent would be one that's been useful in construing *many* events, not just a few. It follows, then, that constructs should be based on *recurring* themes or qualities.

RANGE AND FOCUS OF CONVENIENCE

Although recurrences are important, it's also important to recognize that most constructs won't be useful *everywhere*. A few can be used widely, for instance, *good versus bad*. But most are more limited in scope, and some apply only narrowly. For example, *friendly versus unfriendly* can be applied to fewer events than *good versus bad*. *Supportive versus not supportive* can be applied to even fewer. *Willing to lend class notes versus unwilling to lend class notes* applies to still fewer. The set of events for which a construct is useful is called its **range of convenience**. This range is wide for some constructs, narrow for others.

When people try to apply a construct to events outside its range of convenience, predictive efficiency usually drops. For example, the range of convenience of the construct *happy versus sad* includes people, some animals, songs, many social events, and maybe such things as skies and flowers. It would be harder to apply that construct to events such as stones or spaghetti. The result of *trying* to apply it to such events will likely be a lack of predictive efficiency. In general, it's not too often that people try to apply a construct to events that fall outside its range of convenience.

A construct's range of convenience isn't permanently fixed, however, because sometimes you *do* apply it outside its range of convenience and it works. The **permeability** of a construct is the degree to which its range of convenience can be spread to include new events. A construct that's permeable lets new types of events be added into its range of convenience fairly easily. One that's impermeable is more rigid and less likely to absorb new events into its range of convenience.

Another term pertaining to a construct's applicability is its **focus of convenience**: the events for which the construct is *most* predictive. A construct's focus of convenience is some narrower *portion* of its range of convenience.

For example, consider the constructs *sociable versus unsociable* and *polite versus impolite,* and situations where you might apply them. If you wanted to guess how many people Jane will talk to at a party, you'd probably be better off using the construct of *sociability* than *politeness.* This event falls within the range of convenience of both, but talking to people at a party is almost the essence of sociability. It's clearly in its focus of convenience. If you wanted to predict how Jane would reply to a surly store clerk, the *sociability* construct might work. But you'd probably do better predicting from *politeness.* Its focus of convenience is events that involve role-based behavior and specific social conventions. Both the party and the store clerk interaction are within the *range* of convenience of each construct. But differences in *focus* of convenience make one construct more useful than the other for each type of event.

ELABORATION AND CHANGE IN CONSTRUCT SYSTEMS

As indicated earlier, people's constructs evolve across time and experience. Change can come in several ways. If a construct continues to predict events well, it becomes more refined. If it predicts in new and interesting ways, it grows.

Kelly gave names to these two kinds of changes. **Definition** occurs during ordinary use of a construct. It involves applying the construct in a familiar way to an event it's very likely to fit. Applying it this way allows it to become more explicit or possibly more refined and precise. For example, people often squeeze avocados to tell whether they're ripe. The construal *ripe* implies a prediction of what you'll find when you cut the avocado open. Repeated application of this technique lets you refine your sense of how much softness implies perfect ripeness.

The other kind of elaboration, called **extension,** involves using the construct to predict or construe an event it hasn't been applied to before. This use has more potential for error, given the unfamiliarity, but it also provides the potential for elaboration. If the construct predicts well in unfamiliar territory, it thereby proves more broadly useful than was obvious before. This outcome adds more information than does definition. As an example, a person who's familiar with avocados but not cantaloupes may apply the squeeze technique to decide whether a cantaloupe is ripe. If the prediction made this way is accurate, the *ripeness* construct has been extended.

The idea of extension relates to two ideas we just discussed: permeability and range of convenience. Constructs that are *permeable* can be applied to new events more easily than those that are less permeable. Thus, they're more capable of change by the extension process.

Both extension and definition are important processes. Indeed, both are necessary. They differ in important ways, though. In general terms, definition is the *safer* of the two, whereas extension is potentially the more *informative* of the two.

Which process is more likely to occur depends on several factors. Some people are chronically more likely than others to go out on a limb and apply a construct in new ways, as extension requires. Indeed, some people make a habit of seeking out opportunities to engage in extension (see also Box 15.2). On the other hand, people don't normally do this throughout their construct systems at once. That is, doing definition in some domains is a way of creating a sense of security. You then can risk trying extension in some other domain.

Temporary factors probably also influence whether definition or extension occurs. For instance, being upset or anxious (maybe because of a wrong prediction) may inhibit extension. Having been made uncertain about one thing, you may want to be very certain about other things (McGregor, Zanna, Holmes, & Spencer, 2001). In contrast, boredom may lead to extension (Sechrest, 1977). Knowing which will occur at any moment may require knowing whether the person is motivated toward security or adventure at that moment.

Box 15.2 The Theorist and the Theory

George Kelly, Conceptual Pioneer

Just as individuals must elaborate and extend their construct systems, so must theorists. George Kelly was a theorist who was always willing to shift his construct system in directions that felt right to him, no matter what anyone else thought. His ideas moved along paths not yet traveled by personality theorists. He displayed a true pioneering spirit in his work, a pioneering spirit that had a counterpart in his personal history.

Kelly was born in 1905 on a farm in Kansas. When he was 4, his parents uprooted the family to move to Colorado to homestead a parcel of land (Thompson, 1968). Homesteading was a risky life in the best of circumstances, and the circumstances the Kellys confronted weren't the best. The land they'd claimed had no water. As a result, they soon moved back to Kansas. Still, their westward migration reflected considerable independence of spirit. This spirit is also shown in Kelly's theoretical independence.

Two other experiences in Kelly's life also appear to be reflected directly in the theory he developed. The first occurred while he was teaching at a junior college in Iowa. His duties there included being drama coach. The fact that Kelly held this role is interesting for two reasons. First, it may well have helped sensitize him to the elusive nature of objective reality and the importance of the person's private understanding in creating a personal reality. Second, Kelly later developed a form of therapy in which the client is asked to enact a role, as if in a play. It seems likely that the idea for this technique, which is described later in the chapter, derived in part from Kelly's experiences with acting.

The other noteworthy experience occurred when Kelly was on the faculty at Fort Hays State College in Kansas. While there, he developed a traveling clinic to serve public schools by helping teachers deal with problem children. Kelly made two observations during this period that influenced his later thinking. First, he discovered that inventing an unusual explanation for a client's problem often caused improvement. It didn't seem to matter what the explanation was, as long as it had two qualities: It had to account for the facts as the client understood them, and it had to suggest the usefulness of looking at the situation in a different way. If people could be made to look at their situation differently, they seemed to improve. Second, Kelly discovered that the problems teachers were reporting often said more about the teachers than the students. That is, what defined the problem was the way the teacher was construing the child's behavior, not the child's actual behavior. Both observations were strongly reflected in Kelly's theory.

Evolution of a construct system through definition and extension is growth. By implication, at least, both stem from people's choices about how to use constructs. Sometimes, though, circumstances *force* changes on people. Such changes can be disruptive. If you encounter a very unusual event, you don't have constructs readily available to interpret it. If an existing construct is used and fails badly, or if the person feels an absence of *any* construct to apply, the result can be abrupt change in the construct system. We'll consider the question of forced change later in the chapter when we take up the question of how to think about problems in adjustment.

Organization among Constructs

The personal construct is the basic unit of analysis in this theory. But constructs don't rattle around loose in people's minds, to be applied piecemeal. Kelly assumed that each person's constructs are interrelated in an organized fashion. He argued that constructs form a hierarchy. Some are at low (*subordinate*) levels of abstraction, and others at higher (*superordinate*) levels, subsuming or taking in the more basic ones (see also Epstein, 1983). For example, *good versus bad* may subsume *generous versus stingy*, *friendly versus unfriendly*, and *broken versus unbroken*. *Good versus bad* thus is superordinate to the others.

Earlier in the chapter, we described how a hierarchy of constructs could create a sense of continuous variability on a dimension. In the example we used to illustrate that idea (construal of length), the same fundamental quality was dichotomized at each decision point. What we're talking about now is a little different. The qualities at the different levels relate to one another, but they aren't the same.

Is the hierarchical arrangement that you have among your constructs permanent? No. The organization is retained only if it has predictive efficiency. One common change is in what specific subordinate constructs a specific superordinate construct includes. For example, Alice's *friendly versus unfriendly* construct used to subsume *polite versus impolite*. She eventually grew to see these two as not being related. In her new organization, *politeness* relates instead to constructs such as *manipulative versus not manipulative*.

Organizations among constructs can be even more fluid than that. In principle, it's possible for two constructs to *reverse* places, so that the subordinate one becomes superordinate and vice versa. For instance, Judy's *loving versus not loving* used to be a broad construct that encompassed a number of others, such as *accepting versus rejecting,* which was more specific. Over time and experience, though, she came to see the sense of *acceptance* as broader. Her viewpoint shifted so that *loving* was encompassed by *acceptance*. She now has a different organization, in which the relationship between constructs has reversed (see Figure 15.2).

Organizations among constructs play a role in individual differences in personality. Assume for a moment that two people have similar sets of constructs but different *organizations* among them (see Figure 15.2). These two people would be quite different from each other in how they view and relate to the world.

There's one last point to make about these hierarchies: At any given moment, the organization constrains your construals and actions. In particular, using a given superordinate construct dictates which subordinate constructs you're most likely to use in more fine-grained construals of the event. That is, any superordinate construct subsumes *some* lower-level ones but not others. Using a superordinate construct channels you toward subordinate constructs that fall under it and away from those that don't. This, in turn, greatly influences the character of your subsequent impressions.

For example, Julie walks up to David after class, converses for a few minutes, and then asks whether he wants to study with her for their upcoming test. If David initially construes Julie as a *student,* he's likely to apply constructs that are under *student* in his hierarchy as he further construes her behavior. He may filter her conversation to judge how much she knows and decide from that whether the proposed study session would be useful. However, if David initially construes Julie as an *attractive woman,* he'll apply different constructs to the same aspects of her behavior. He may see her conversation as a sign of interest, the offer to study together as a ploy to get to know him better, and the study session as a step toward intimacy.

INDIVIDUALITY OF CONSTRUCTS

Thus far, our discussion of constructs and their organization has largely disregarded the word *personal.* However, that word was every bit as important to Kelly as the word

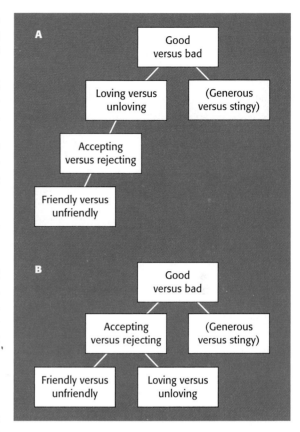

FIGURE 15.2
Two potential hierarchies of constructs held by one person at two different times (or by two different people), incorporating the same constructs but organized differently. In organization A, *loving versus unloving* subsumes *accepting versus rejecting,* which in turn subsumes *friendly versus unfriendly.* In B, *accepting versus rejecting* subsumes both *friendly versus unfriendly* and *loving versus unloving.* Someone with organization B would hold *acceptance* as fundamental and as implicit both in *friendliness* and in *loving,* which are distinct. Someone with organization A would treat *loving* as fundamental and as implicit in *acceptance,* which in turn is implicit in *friendliness.*

People have a need to understand and predict events around them. People differ greatly from each other, however, in how they interpret any given event.

construct. Kelly emphasized that each person's understanding of reality is separate from everyone else's. Each person's construct system is unique.

It's easy to be misled on this point by the fact that people usually can find words for their constructs and different people even use the same words. However, words don't always mean precisely the same thing to one person as to another. Perhaps the easiest illustration is the deceptively simple statement *I love you.* This sentence can have a vast number of meanings, depending on who's saying it to whom and the psychological context in which it's being said.

Indeed, even when two people think they agree about the meaning of a single word, it's impossible to be sure they do. For example, you say something is *red,* and I agree with you: It's red. But is your experience of redness, your construal of it, exactly the same as mine or even close to mine? Who can know? In principle, the same problem occurs in all experience. And that is precisely Kelly's point about people's constructs. Even if the words are the same, the constructs are probably not. Indeed, Kelly emphasized that constructs are *preverbal.* People can have a hard time representing their constructs, even to themselves, except as raw experience (Kelly, 1969; see also Riedel, 1970).

If all of our constructs are potentially so different, how do we ever communicate? How do we ever get along with one another? The answer, in part, is that your constructs don't *totally* diverge from those of other people. Remember, constructs are retained only if they have predictive efficiency. If they fail to predict adequately, you modify or discard them and form new ones. By the time you're an adult, you've tested your constructs quite a bit. So has everyone else. There has to be *some* similarity between your construct system and the systems of other people, or they wouldn't have been maintained for so long.

Nevertheless, construct systems do differ enough that there's plenty of potential for disagreement. How then do people find a sense of harmony with each other? How do they even get to know each other? In Kelly's view, the process of getting to know other people is partly (perhaps largely) a matter of testing your constructs against theirs. If you find you agree about what constructs apply to various events, you feel comfortable with each other. To put it another way, people with similar construct systems see the same things when they look at the world. That similarity of views is reassuring and forms the basis of a friendship. From this view, you form relationships with other people by jointly assessing similarities in construct systems (see Duck, 1973, 1977; Duck & Allison, 1978; Klion & Leitner, 1991; Tesser, 1971).

Both the use of constructs in forming impressions of other people and the fact that different people use different constructs are nicely illustrated in research by Higgins, King, and Mavin (1982). Participants were asked to write down the traits of several specific friends (Study 1) or the traits of several specific types of people (Study 2). The traits that a given person wrote down frequently (Study 1) or wrote down first (Study 2) were taken as representing important constructs for that person, because they were so accessible in memory.

Several days later, in what was portrayed as a separate study, each participant read a description of a target person written especially for him or her. The description included some of the participant's important (accessible) constructs and some that were less important (less accessible). After doing another task (to interfere with memory), the participants wrote their impressions of the target person. Then they tried to recall the description they'd read. As expected, the participants' impressions were influenced by the constructs that were important to them personally, and they tended to disregard the other ones (see Figure 15.3). Indeed, they had a harder time even recalling the unimportant ones. Apparently, then, different people do rely on different mental dimensions in construing others.

SIMILARITIES AND DIFFERENCES BETWEEN PEOPLE

In Kelly's view, people are psychologically similar to each other if their systems of constructs are similar. Two people need not have gone through the same events to have similar constructs. Nor will two people who do experience the same events necessarily have similar constructs. A given construct can emerge from a thousand different events, and any event can be construed in many different ways. What makes people resemble each other is similarity in their *patterns of construals*—however the patterns arise—not similarity in their "learning histories" (see also Gilovich, 1990).

To Kelly, this principle applies to differences and similarities between persons and also to those between cultures. People from a given culture typically share a physical environment and manner of upbringing, but Kelly thought this was of secondary importance. To him, the essence of a culture is a similarity in how people construe experiences (Kelly, 1962).

Research appears to support the idea that cultural differences relate to variations in people's constructs (Triandis et al., 1984). Participants in this research made judgments about what kinds of behavioral elements occur in different kinds of social interactions. Analyzing the judgments made by each participant revealed something of the constructs applied by that person to social situations. Comparisons from one person to another indicated that people from the same culture shared elements of their construct systems. These similarities were *not* shared as widely across the different cultures.

ROLE TAKING

Much of life involves social interaction. If people have different construct systems, how do they interact? According to this theory, a social interaction entails an elaborate set of processes. It involves an attempt by each person to construe some part of the construct system held by the other. In other words, to really interact with someone else requires you to try to understand and anticipate how that person is understanding and anticipating reality. This is what Kelly meant by **role taking** with respect to another person.

When in a role, you're especially interested in understanding how the other person views *your* role. What does the person expect of you? What constructs is the person using to predict your behavior? If you can answer these questions in your own mind, you can act in ways that the other person can interpret within his or her construct system.

Is it possible to take roles effectively if your construct system differs from those of the other people involved? Yes and no. Role taking is more complete and effective if you construe the other person's construct system in more or less the way it actually

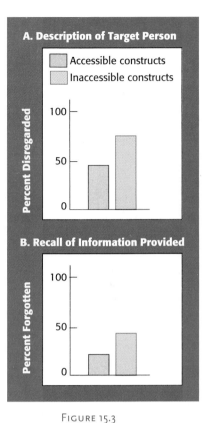

FIGURE 15.3
Each participant received a description of a target person that was made up of several accessible constructs (ones that the participant used spontaneously) and several inaccessible constructs (ones that the participant didn't use spontaneously). (A) In writing impressions of their target people later on, participants gave a lot of weight to the accessible constructs that had been mentioned and tended to disregard the others. (B) Indeed, participants were even less able to remember the inaccessible constructs when asked to recall the initial descriptions of their target people. *Source: Adapted from Higgins, King, & Mavin, 1982, Experiment 1.*

exists. But it's not the entire construct system that matters. The effectiveness of your role taking depends mainly on how accurately you construe the other person's construal of *your* role.

Evidence that people work to get pictures of each other's roles when interacting comes from research on how people try to establish common ground in a conversation. For example, an expert has to use different terms when talking with a novice than when talking with another expert. The expert also must decide how much detail to convey. But this decision isn't made just once. The expert has to continue to judge whether the novice is following the expert, and adjust further, if necessary. This continued adjustment does occur in people's conversations (Isaacs & Clark, 1987). Furthermore, it's an interactive process between those conversing. People who overhear the conversation don't grasp the common ground as clearly as the people in it (Schober & Clark, 1989).

We enact many roles in the course of our lives. Not all are important or have more than superficial impact. The role of store customer, for instance, matters little to most of us most of the time. Other roles, however, are extremely important, even central to our lives. These roles, which Kelly termed **core roles,** are major determinants of our sense of identity. Examples are occupational and professional roles, the roles of parent and child, close friend, lover, and so on. Whether any of these actually *is* a core role depends on the person, of course.

Because core roles are important, failing to perform them adequately can have adverse consequences. Kelly said that failing to enact a core role in the way it's construed by another person produces guilt. **Guilt** thus is an awareness of a disparity between your actions and the actions you see as fitting the other's expectations for your role. This definition of guilt is similar in some respects to Rogers's discussion of *conditions of worth* (Chapter 14), in which people feel uncomfortable when they fail to live up to others' expectations for them.

PERSONAL CONSTRUCTS AND BEHAVIORAL CONSISTENCY

Back in Chapter 4, we addressed in some detail the issue of behavioral consistency. We noted there that people are apparently less consistent in their actions than seemed implied by early trait views of personality. This evidence led to the emergence of an *interactionist* position, in which personality and situational forces are seen as joint determinants of behavior.

The personal construct viewpoint allows us to address this issue in a way that's very similar to the context-dependent view of traits presented toward the end of Chapter 4 (and also discussed in Chapter 16). It says that to predict a person's behavior in any given situation, we need to know how the person *construes* the situation. An individual will act in a consistent way across situations to the degree that the situations are construed in similar ways.

This idea sounds a little like the principle of generalization from the learning perspective. Where it differs from generalization is its emphasis on the personal. It doesn't matter whether the situations look the same or different to an outside *objective* observer. What matters is whether the person who's behaving

An effective communicator presents ideas in terms the listener can understand.

perceives the situations as similar. Similar construals of situations should yield cross-situational consistency. Divergent construals should yield less consistency.

Research by Lord (1982) found support for this idea. Participants described what characteristics would go into being *conscientious* in each of six common situations (e.g., keeping good lecture notes, keeping an orderly closet). These descriptions were done using a variation on the Q-sort method described in Chapter 14. These Q-sorts produced profiles of how the participant viewed the characteristics of each situation. The profiles were then compared with one another (for each participant) to assess their similarity.

Participants' actual conscientiousness was rated by an observer later in six situations corresponding closely to those the participant had rated. Participants' level of conscientiousness proved to be most consistent across the situations that they'd construed in similar terms. Behavior was less consistent across situations that they'd construed in divergent terms.

Assessment

We've focused in this chapter on the idea that personality is defined by the constructs that a person uses in dealing with the world. Personality assessment from this viewpoint likewise emphasizes assessment of the constructs the person uses.

KELLY'S ROLE CONSTRUCT REPERTORY TEST

In thinking about how to get an accurate view of another person's system of constructs, Kelly confronted a dilemma: It's useless to do behavioral observation, because a given behavior might stem from the use of any of several constructs. But asking people to describe their constructs isn't satisfactory either, for several reasons.

First, although we've given names to constructs throughout the chapter, constructs aren't always easy to label. As noted earlier, many are intuitive or preverbal. They exist in a private experiential form that can't be expressed. Second, people aren't used to describing their constructs. As a result, they may not do a good job at communicating what they mean, even if they can pin it down. Finally, the words that people choose to describe constructs are often so open to interpretation that it's hard to get clear, specific meanings from what's being said.

Faced with these problems, Kelly tried to devise a strategy for getting at people's constructs indirectly. Rather than have people verbalize their constructs, he had them engage in construals. Across repeated construals, the nature of the construct system should begin to reveal itself. Kelly called his procedure the Role Construct Repertory Test, a name that's usually shortened to **Rep Test.** As implied by the longer title, this test often (although not always) focuses on constructs used to perceive aspects of people and their roles.

The Rep Test involves the use of a printed grid (see Figure 15.4). In this grid, significant people in your life (who have different roles) are listed at the heads of columns. The rows are used to specify a set of comparisons and construals to make. In taking the test, you begin by reading a definition for each role that's being used and deciding who in your life best fits that definition. Then you write that person's name on the grid next to the role label, not using any person's name twice.

Then you start with the construals. For each row, you're asked to think about the people listed in three specific columns (marked by circles in the figure). More

Sort no.	Yourself 1	Mother 2	Father 3	Spouse 4	Pal 5	Rejecting person 6	Pitied person 7	Attractive person 8	Emergent Pole	Implicit Pole
1						○	○	○		
2	○			○	○					
3	○						○	○		
4				○	○			○		
5	○	○	○							
6		○	○				○			
...										
n		○		○		○				

FIGURE 15.4

Example of the sort of grid used in the Rep Test. You begin by filling in the names of the people who play various roles in your life in the slanted sections across the top. Then you conduct a series of comparisons among sets of three people at a time, deciding how two of them are similar to each other in a way that makes them different from the third. (See the text for a more complete description.)

Source: From Kelly, 1955. Reproduced with permission of Gladys Kelly.

precisely, you are to think of an important characteristic that makes two of those three people similar to each other and different from the third. Once you've decided, you mark the two that are similar and write a word or phrase in the column headed "Emergent Pole" to indicate how the two are alike. In the column headed "Implicit Pole," you indicate how the third person is different. Next you look at the people (roles) in the other columns, decide whether they fit the emergent pole of the construct or the implicit pole, and mark each accordingly. When you've done one row, you go to the next, repeating the whole process row by row.

As you go through the rows, you're generating a list of constructs. These aren't the only constructs you have. But since the people listed across the top are people who play important roles in your life, the constructs that come up are probably important in your construals of people. Several of the comparisons in the Rep Test are of interest in their own right. Consider line 3 in Figure 15.4, where you're asked to think about yourself, an attractive person, and a pitied person. Which of the two will you see as more like yourself and why? This comparison reveals something about your feelings toward yourself and also what aspect of yourself comes easily to mind.

The roles listed in Figure 15.4 represent only a few of the roles in the full Rep Test. Furthermore, people doing this test also usually do many construals, thus providing a much larger base of information. This procedure has also been adapted to assess construals of other sorts of events, such as social issues (Epting, 1972), occupations (Shubsachs, 1975), and situations (Krieger, Epting, & Leitner, 1974; Neimeyer & Neimeyer, 1981).

Though the Rep Test is useful, it also has limitations. As noted earlier, people's constructs can't always be verbalized. The Rep Test tries to get around this by asking people to actively construe people and to use whatever construct naturally comes to mind to say what makes people similar or different. This strategy only partly handles the problem, though, because the person still has to provide a label for the construct.

This requirement creates two potential problems. The first is the ordinary problem of whether the word used to identify the construct means the same thing to one person as to another. The second problem is that being asked repeatedly to label your constructs may create a bias in what constructs you use while doing the test. Specifically, you may be inclined to report only constructs that are easy to verbalize, even if those aren't the most important constructs in your mind (cf. Shubsachs, 1975). Thus, even the Rep Test may be susceptible to the problems inherent in just asking people to describe their construct systems.

Problems in Behavior, and Behavior Change

The importance of personal constructs in personality is also stressed in considering the nature of problems and what's involved in the process of therapy (see also Neimeyer, 1985).

PERSONAL CONSTRUCTS AND PSYCHOLOGICAL DISTRESS

In Kelly's view, normal human functioning involves successfully anticipating and interpreting events. Problems in behavior thus involve problems in interpreting or predicting events.

Such difficulties can arise for several reasons. One possibility is confronting events that differ drastically from any previously experienced. Because of this lack of experience, you may not have constructs that seem relevant. The event, in effect, is beyond your ability to grasp it. Another possibility is that you may be trying to construe the event with a construct with poor predictive efficiency for that situation.

Kelly said that when people don't have adequate constructs, they feel uncertain and helpless. He labeled this experience **anxiety.** If the event is outside the available construct system, people sometimes even have trouble grasping why they're experiencing anxiety.

How often do people experience events that differ greatly from their prior experiences?

Experiences unlike any you have had before are hard to absorb, because you lack constructs for them.

Perhaps more often than you might imagine. Think back to your first week at college, for example. That period is often filled with experiences that differ enough from what people knew before to make them wonder what's going on. Perhaps you even felt concern or apprehension. The same feelings can occur for someone entering a new job (Van Maanen, 1973, 1975), being hospitalized for an illness, or having her first child (Deutsch, Ruble, Fleming, Brooks-Gunn, & Stangor, 1988). In fact, anytime you do *anything* for the very first time, it can be unsettling, just because it's the first time and you don't know exactly what to expect.

As more extreme cases, consider the experiences of people involved in disasters, such as hurricanes, fires, and earthquakes. It's often said that such experiences are traumatic precisely because they are so unlike anything the people have ever gone through before. Consequently, the people have no constructs to interpret the events or anticipate their consequences. Think about people in the midst of divorce, victims of crime, and those who win huge sums of money. These people are suddenly experiencing things that prior events in their lives haven't prepared them for. Part of the difficulty in living through these events is the very lack of constructs available for use in anticipating their consequences and implications.

It's unpleasant to discover that your constructs are inadequate to deal with events. Even worse, however, are events that suggest that important aspects of your construct system may be completely *wrong* and that major change is necessary (cf. Leitner & Cado, 1982). The more central the construct that's challenged, the more extensive the change that's necessary and the greater the problem. The sense of an imminent major change in one's fundamental construct system is termed **threat.** The experience of threat is much the same as that of anxiety but more extreme. Both arise from poor prediction from the construct system. In threat, however, the failure is more massive and fundamental.

DEALING WITH ANXIETY AND THREAT

Reducing anxiety (or threat) is straightforward in principle, though it can be more difficult in practice. One way is to generate a new construct. This response to poor prediction may be the major source of new constructs across a person's lifetime (see also Box 15.3). The other way to deal with threat or anxiety is to modify an existing construct so the experience can be successfully construed through it. If the event can then be construed with predictive efficiency, the anxiety or threat should evaporate.

As noted earlier in the chapter, sometimes you can modify a construct by extending its range of convenience. Doing this means saying, in effect, that the new experience really isn't totally new. It has similarities to other experiences you've had; you just didn't notice it before.

Sometimes this doesn't work, though, and you have to change the construct in a bigger way. Making one change may even require more changes. Why? Recall that

BOX 15.3   RECONSTRUCTING YOUR WORLD AFTER A TRAUMATIC EVENT

Minor adversity strikes everyone on occasion—getting a test score that's a point short of the grade you wanted, finding a ticket on your car window after shopping just a little too long, or coming down with the flu the day before spring break. Most people's constructs allow them to interpret and understand such minor inconveniences (e.g., "Stuff happens"). But what about a traumatic event—being diagnosed with a life-threatening illness, being raped or beaten, or hearing that members of your family were just killed in a car accident?

Traumatic events are harder to integrate into one's world view than minor events, for many reasons. For one, traumatic events often are sudden and unexpected. Moreover, traumatic events often create irreversible, long-lasting problems for the future. By their very nature, traumatic events suggest a world that's unpredictable and uncontrollable (Tedeschi & Calhoun, 1995). They can undermine the most basic assumptions people hold about themselves and their world (e.g., Horowitz, 1986; Janoff-Bulman, 1992).

Kelly's theory suggests that people who experience a traumatic event will struggle to create new constructs for interpreting it. That's also what more recent theorists say. Tedeschi and Calhoun (1995) argue that a traumatic event partly destroys the person's worldview. They also say that the event thereby initiates a potential for growth. The shattering of one worldview prompts an effort to construct a new more meaningful one. Others have taken similar positions (e.g., Davis, Nolen-Hoeksema, & Larson, 1998; Taylor, 1983; Thompson & Janigian, 1988).

Research has even begun to show that making sense of traumatic events can help people adjust and move forward. For example, Thompson (1985) studied people whose homes were severely damaged by fire. Those who found a positive meaning in the event coped best with it. Thompson found similar effects among people who suffered a stroke (Thompson, 1991). Other research has shown that finding positive aspects of having cancer seems to help people cope with it (Andrykowski, Brady, & Hunt, 1993; Stanton et al., 2002; Taylor, Lichtman, & Wood, 1984; Tomich & Helgeson, 2002), though the data are not com-

pletely consistent (Tomich & Helgeson, 2004).

These and other studies have begun to establish a link between psychological well-being and the capacity to understand and find meaning in traumatic events (for review, see Helgeson, Reynolds, & Tomich, 2006). It's even possible that finding meaning may promote physical health. Bower, Kemeny, Taylor, and Fahey (1998) examined immune functioning and mortality among HIV-positive gay men who had recently experienced the AIDS-related death of a partner or close friend. Men who found meaning in the death showed better immune functioning during the months afterward compared to those less able to find meaning. Those who found meaning also had a lower rate of AIDS-related mortality during that period. Conceptually similar results have been reported by Tomich and Helgeson (2002) in a study of physical functioning among breast cancer patients. Although there are inconsistencies in the literature (Helgeson et al., 2006), it may be that finding meaning not only enhances well-being after a traumatic event, but it also helps keep people alive.

your construct system forms a hierarchy. Subordinate constructs contribute to and help define high-level ones. When you change your sense of what one construct means to you, you're rearranging some of the connections in your hierarchy, maybe even a lot of connections.

Sometimes the problem isn't that you don't have a construct to use but that you're continuing to use a construct that's outlived its usefulness. Sometimes you're treating a construct as though it has a broader range of convenience than it actually has. The result in each of these cases is unsuccessful anticipation of new events. Again, the solution is to reorganize your construct system. In the latter case, the reorganization means restricting the construct's range of convenience. If your construct has really outlived its usefulness, though, you're back to having to come up with a new one.

From the personal construct view on personality, the distress that goes with poor prediction of events is the primary symptom of problems. This is what leads a person to seek help. Keep in mind that the construct system is the essence of personality from this point of view. The process of therapy is one of assisting people in elaborating or altering their construct system to improve its predictive efficiency (see Epting, 1980; Fransella, 1972). Better prediction will result in less anxiety, distress, and dissatisfaction.

FIXED-ROLE THERAPY

What kinds of therapeutic procedures help attain this goal? Keep in mind that there's no perfect construct system that people should adopt to be adjusted to reality. Everyone has a personal view of the world. Each person must evolve an arrangement of constructs that will be functional from his or her personal viewpoint. The goal of therapy is to facilitate evolution of the construct system in its own way.

Kelly believed the best way to promote evolution of the construct system is to have the person change outward behavior. This will force the person to generate unusual construals of events that result. The procedure Kelly developed for doing this is called **fixed-role therapy**. In this procedure, the client enacts the role of a hypothetical person. This person is carefully crafted to have certain characteristics that the client wants. This fixed-role character is even given a name, to provide a sense of identity to the role.

The therapeutic process begins with an assessment in which the client completes a self-characterization or self-description. On the basis of this, the therapist develops a role for the client to enact. The role is a composite of some of the client's positive characteristics and of some characteristics the client feels are lacking.

The use of a composite role has several benefits. Building in some familiar characteristics helps make the role easier to adopt because it keeps the role from being entirely alien. Building pre-existing *positive* qualities into it helps to create a sense of confidence in your ability to enact the role, and it strengthens the use of constructs that contribute to those positive qualities.

When the fixed role has been established, you're asked to enact it for a while. The idea is not to adopt the role as a permanent part of your personality but just to enact it for some period. This instruction means there's little risk involved, which takes some of the pressure off. If you aren't happy with how something goes, you can look at the experience as just a bit of acting that needs more polishing, not as a failure. It often happens, however, that after a while, the client stops thinking of the role as a role and starts to think of it as a natural part of himself or herself (Collier & Callero, 2005).

Enacting this fixed role forces the client to construe events in ways that differ from those used previously. For example, Luke sees himself as shy and passive and interpersonally inadequate. Luke might be asked to take on the role of a person who's quiet but "deep," a person whom others find interesting and stimulating but who doesn't always show those characteristics openly because he's more interested in learning something from others than in showing his own strengths. He's a person who has a pronounced but subtle influence on others, so that people don't always realize they're being influenced until later on.

Notice that this role (which is adapted from Kelly, 1955, p. 121) is a composite of Luke's self-image and characteristics that he sees himself as lacking. The role incorporates quietness (which Luke now has) but recasts it within a general effectiveness in interpersonal interaction. In order to enact this role, Luke must construe his behavior in ways that differ from his previous view of himself. He must construe his quietness as a positive act of benefiting from others, rather than as a sign of passivity and inadequacy. In this way, he's rearranging his system of constructs. As he enacts this role over time, he should gradually reorganize his construct system, modifying constructs at some points and perhaps developing new ones at other points. The result should be a system with a high degree of predictive efficiency that permits him to live a more satisfying life than he did before.

Personal Construct Theory: Problems and Prospects

Personal construct theory shares a couple of strengths with the humanistic theories described in Chapter 14. Its emphasis on the uniqueness and validity of each person's experience fits with the emphasis those theories place on the importance of subjective experiences. Similarly, the principle of constructive alternativism suggests a basis for assuming that people tend toward being better over time. That is, people can always reconstrue events in more and more functional ways.

The personal construct view places less of an emphasis on will than does the humanistic orientation. Although in principle you're free to determine for yourself how to construe the present, past experiences have a big influence on present construals. When people make drastic reorganizations of how they view the world, they don't do so easily or without strain. It remains an open question, then, how free people actually are from their past.

Perhaps the greatest strength of this view on personality is one that was wholly unanticipated by its author. As you'll see in the next chapter, Kelly's intuitions foreshadowed several themes that would re-emerge later on from very different sources. These ideas came from cognitive psychology, not personality, and returned to personality only through a circuitous path. Kelly's view, however, was much more idiographic than the newer cognitive view (recall his emphasis on the idea that constructs are personal). This idiographic emphasis humanizes the ideas in a way that the newer views don't usually do.

One historic problem of personal construct psychology is that it's not terribly conducive to research. There is a cadre of personality psychologists who are devoted to personal construct psychology, and there are journals devoted to personal construct psychology. But the group who takes this view is relatively small in number.

What are the prospects for this view on personality? We've continued to include it in this book largely because of its status as a forerunner of cognitive theories. The extent to which this is true is quite remarkable. In some ways, it is this convergence of lines of thought that provides a continuing basis for interest in personal construct psychology. Lacking an active research literature of its own, however, personal construct psychology is beginning to acquire the patina of ideas that are primarily of historical interest. It appears to be on its way to fading from the scene, perhaps becoming a footnote in the discussion of newer cognitive models.

· SUMMARY ·

Kelly believed that people have a fundamental need to predict the events that they experience. They do so by developing a system of personal constructs, which they use to interpret or construe new events. *Constructs* are derived from recurring elements in one's experience, but because they're developed separately by each person, each person's system of constructs is unique. *Constructive alternativism* is the idea that any event, for any person, is open to multiple interpretations and that people decide for themselves how to construe each event.

People implicitly evaluate their constructs over time in terms of *predictive efficiency,* or the degree to which the constructs allow the person to interact successfully with the world. Kelly treated constructs as bipolar and dichotomous. Each construct under use has an *emergent pole,* the end of the conceptual dimension that is being applied to the event being construed. The *implicit pole* of the construct is the end not being applied. A construct's *range of convenience* is the range of events to which it can be applied meaningfully. Its *focus of convenience* is the range of events for which it is optimally predictive.

Constructs can be refined by actively using them in familiar ways (a process called *definition*) and can be elaborated by using them in unfamiliar ways (a process called *extension*). Changes in one's construct system can also be induced by situations in which one finds oneself without adequate constructs to interpret an event. Constructs are organized in a hierarchical system of inclusiveness. This organization is not permanent, however, just as the constructs themselves are not permanent. How long any aspect of the construct system remains stable depends on its predictive efficiency.

Kelly held that constructs are unique to each person, despite the fact that they're often illustrated by familiar words. The fact that each person's constructs are potentially different from those of other people raises questions about how people can interact effectively. In Kelly's view, getting to know other people means testing one's own constructs against theirs. People are similar to the extent their construct systems are similar. Interpersonal interaction in this viewpoint involves the taking of a role with respect to some other person. *Role taking* entails construing how the other person is construing you in your role. *Core roles* are those roles that are particularly important to one's sense of identity.

Assessment from Kelly's viewpoint is done by the Rep Test, which assesses the constructs that people use in construing their role relations and other aspects of their experience. Kelly's viewpoint on problems in self-management was that people experience *anxiety* when events fall outside the range of convenience of their construct systems, and they experience *threat* when they anticipate a major reorganization of important aspects of their construct systems because of poor predictive efficiency. Kelly developed *fixed-role therapy* as a way of getting people to engage in behaviors that they would not ordinarily engage in, for the purpose of developing different ways of construing events in their lives.

· GLOSSARY ·

Anxiety   The response to inability to impose a construct adequately on an event one is experiencing.

Constructive alternativism   The idea that any event can be construed in many ways.

Coping   The effort to handle a threat by executing whatever response has been chosen.

Core roles   The roles that are central to one's life, contributing to one's identity.

Defensive reappraisal   The process of defining a threat out of existence.

Definition   The applying of a construct in a familiar way, causing its refinement.

Emergent pole   The end of a construct that's being applied to the event being construed.

Extension   The applying of a construct to an unfamiliar event in an attempt to increase its range of convenience.

Fixed-role therapy   A therapy in which the client enacts a role that differs somewhat from his or her current self-perception.

Focus of convenience   The range of applicable events for which a construct has the best prediction.

Guilt   The sensing of a discrepancy between one's acts and another's role expectations for oneself.

Implicit pole   The end of the construct that isn't being applied to the event being construed.

Permeability   The degree to which a construct extends to events to which it hasn't yet been applied.

Personal construct   A mental representation used to interpret events.

Predictive efficiency   The degree to which a construct can be applied successfully to events.

Primary appraisal   The process of perceiving a threat in the environment.

Range of convenience   The range of events for which a construct is useful.

Rep Test   A test used to identify a person's major constructs.

Role taking   The process of construing how another person construes oneself.

Secondary appraisal   The process of determining how to respond to a threat.

Threat   The perception of an impending reorganization of one's construct system.

The Cognitive Self-Regulation Perspective

The Cognitive Self-Regulation Perspective: Major Themes and Underlying Assumptions

The human nervous system is a vast and elaborate network of tiny cells that communicate continuously with each other. These cells relay information from one place to another throughout your life, whether you're awake or asleep. This network has been compared to many things over the decades, including a network of telephone lines, a paper-shuffling bureaucracy, and a computer. As computer functions were extended to control autonomous agents, some came to think that a *robot* metaphor is better than a *computer* metaphor, because human lives are filled with actions aimed at reaching goals. To some psychologists, it doesn't seem outlandish to ask whether human beings pursuing those goals are not perhaps the ultimate "guided missiles."

Theories that relate these metaphors to personality aren't as well developed as theories with longer histories. Nonetheless, this way of thinking does seem to have at least a few implications for personality. Those implications are described in Chapters 16 and 17.

The ideas presented in these chapters rest implicitly on three assumptions. The first is that understanding behavior means understanding how people deal with the information that surrounds them. *Information* is a pretty vague term, but its meaning is fairly intuitive. Look around the room. You're surrounded by sights and sounds and maybe by other people doing things. Each of these is a source of information. The information comes in tiny bits, but you don't experience it that way. You see *walls,* not just patches of color. You hear a *song,* not unconnected bits of noise. You have an *impression* of your roommate, not just a collection of facts. To have these broader experiences, you integrate and organize the bits of information the world provides you.

A second assumption is that the flow of life consists of an elaborate web of decisions. Some of them are conscious, but far more occur outside your awareness. Your personality is reflected partly in the flow of decision making in your mind. It's reflected in the biases that follow from the sort of mental organization you have and how you use it. The flow of implicit decisions is more unpredictable than people used to think. The realization of this has led to some reworking of theories about cognitive processes. This, in turn, also has implications for thinking about personality. Despite these changes, some theorists think that human thought is a continuing stream of implicit decisions at many levels.

These two assumptions underlie some of the ideas presented in Chapter 16. There, we describe theories about how the mind is organized and how personality is thus structured. The ideas described there focus on how events are represented in memory and how memories guide your experience of the world. How all this complexity is organized and used is an important issue from the cognitive vantage point.

A third assumption behind this perspective on personality is that human behavior is goal directed. This idea represents a view of motivation, albeit somewhat different from the motive view that was considered in Chapter 5. The idea that goals underlie behavior is consistent with the robotics metaphor. A robot has a purpose (or several) that it's trying to fulfill. It often has some kind of representation of its goal, and it tries to move toward that representation.

A self-regulation view on personality assumes that people do much the same—take up (or create) goals and try to move toward them. To be sure they're moving in the right direction, people monitor their progress. From this idea comes the term *self-regulation*. In this view, human action is continually aimed at attaining some goal or other. Life is a never-ending stream of sensing, checking, and adjusting—an ever-continuing process of moving within a network of self-defined goals. This idea provides part of the basis of Chapter 17.

These two chapters are more interconnected than were the pairs of chapters on any other perspective besides psychoanalysis. The ideas in these two chapters aren't so much *alternative* views as *interrelated* views. One set of ideas tends to flow into the other. Chapter 16 focuses on the person's mental world; Chapter 17 focuses on how this mental world is reflected in actions.

Contemporary Cognitive Views

Don and Sandy have been shopping for a house. Some options were easy to discard: one was way too much money, one was right next to a gas station, one was ugly. Others were harder. They're getting to be good at noticing things they care about. They've started making a brief list of the pros and cons of each, sure that by doing that they'll make a rational choice. Last month, though, they went to a house on Forest Hills Drive. It's smaller than they wanted, needs more work than they wanted, doesn't have the pool they wanted. But something about it seemed exactly right. Almost at once they decided to buy it, and now it's their home.

ONE TOPIC in cognitive psychology is how people represent their experiences mentally. Another is how people make decisions. Hundreds of studies have examined these processes, and many theories have been proposed to account for them. The picture of how such processes work has also influenced how theorists think about personality.

Aspects of the picture are startlingly similar to ideas proposed much earlier by George Kelly, described in Chapter 15. Kelly never saw himself as a cognitive theorist. In fact, he actively distanced himself from that idea (Neimeyer & Neimeyer, 1981). Study of cognitive processes in personality stemmed mostly from other lines of thought (Bruner, 1957; Heider, 1958; Koffka, 1935; Köhler, 1947; Lewin, 1951a). In fact, in what came to be called the "cognitive revolution" in psychology, Kelly was pretty thoroughly ignored. Yet aspects of today's cognitive view of personality greatly resemble his ideas.

For example, cognitive theorists view people as implicit scientists who try to predict the world, as did Kelly. But there's a different slant on *why*. Today's view is that you're surrounded by more information than you can use. You can't check every bit, so you don't try (Gigerenzer & Goldstein, 1996). Instead, you impose an organization. You use partial information to make inferences about the rest (J. R. Anderson, 1991; Nisbett & Ross, 1980). This saves mental resources (Macrae, Milne, & Bodenhausen, 1994). That's important, because you usually have several things on your mind at once, and you *need* those resources. You can save resources this way, though, only if you can predict events fairly well.

Representing Your Experience of the World

Cognitive theorists are interested partly in how people organize, store, and retrieve memories of their experiences. How do we do these things?

SCHEMAS AND THEIR DEVELOPMENT

People impose order from recurrences of similar qualities across repeated events. In doing so, they form **schemas,** mental organizations of information (also called *knowledge structures*). Schemas are (roughly) categories. Sometimes the sense of category is explicit, but sometimes it's only implicit. Schemas can include many kinds of elements, including perceptual images, abstract knowledge, feeling qualities, and information about time sequence (Schwarz, 1990).

Most views assume that schemas include information about specific cases, or **exemplars,** and also information about the more general sense of what the category is. Thus, for any given category (e.g., football players), you can bring to mind specific examples. You can also bring to mind a sense of the category as a whole (a typical football player). This sense of the category as a whole is captured in an idealized best member of the category, often called its **prototype.** In some theories, this is the best *actual* member you've found so far. In other theories, it's an *idealized* member, an average of those you've found so far.

The word *category* tends to imply that there's a definition for what the schema does and does not include, but that's not always so. Features of the category all contribute to its nature, but often they aren't necessary. For example, your *bird* schema probably includes the idea that birds fly. But some birds don't fly (e.g., chickens and penguins). This means flying can't be a defining feature of birds, though flying does make an animal more likely to be a bird. The term **fuzzy set** has been used to convey the sense that the schema is defined in a fuzzy way by a set of criteria that are relevant but not necessary (Lakoff, 1987; Medin, 1989). The more criteria that are met by an exemplar, the more likely it will be seen as a category member. But if there's no *required* criterion, members can vary a lot in the attributes they do and don't have.

Theories about schemas differ, but all of them treat schemas as having an organizing quality. They integrate meaning. An *event* is a collection of people, movements, objects in use, and so on. But unless you have a sense of what the event's *about,* it might just as well all be random. In the same way, the attributes of an *object* are just a collection of bits unless you have an overriding sense of what the object *is.* The schema, in effect, is the glue that holds the bits of information together.

Once schemas are developed, they're used to recognize new experiences. You identify new events by quickly (and mostly unconsciously) comparing them to existing schemas (J. R. Anderson, 1976, 1985; Medin, 1989; Rosch & Mervis, 1975; E. E. Smith, Shoben, & Rips, 1974). If the features of the new event resemble an existing schema, the new stimulus is recognized as "one of those." This is how we recognize objects and events. Each new perception is based partly on incoming information and partly on what you've got as schemas (Jussim, 1991).

EFFECTS OF SCHEMAS

Schemas have several effects. First, they make it easy to put new information into memory. It's as though the schema were made of Velcro. Once a schema's been evoked, new information sticks to it easily. But what information sticks depends on what schema you use. The schema tells where in the experience to look for information. Specifically, you look for information that relates to the schema. A change in schemas changes what you look for. As a result, you notice different things. Having different goals in mind can change what schema is used. For example, Don and Sandy in the chapter opening looked at houses as potential buyers. They noticed and remembered things about appliances and room layouts. If they'd looked at houses as potential burglars, they'd instead have noticed such things as jewelry, TVs, and stereos (R. C. Anderson & Pichert, 1978).

These schema-based biases can be self-perpetuating. That is, schemas tell you more than where to look. They also suggest what you're going to find. You're more likely to remember what *confirms* your expectation than what doesn't. This can make the schema more solid in the future and thus more resistant to change (Hill, Lewicki, Czyzewska, & Boss, 1989).

Another effect of schemas follows from the fact that information is often missing from events. If a schema is evoked, it gives you additional information from *memory*. You assume that what's in the schema is true of the new (schema-related) event, because it's been true in the past. For example, if you hear about Joe doing laundry, you're likely to assume he put soap in the washer, even if that's not mentioned. In fact, you may even believe later you'd been told that when you hadn't (Cantor & Mischel, 1977). Something you assume is true unless you're told otherwise is called a **default**. A second effect of schemas, then, is to bring default information from memory to fill gaps.

SEMANTIC MEMORY, EPISODIC MEMORY, AND SCRIPTS

Schemas are organizations among memories. But memories are organized in several ways (Tulving, 1972). **Semantic memory** is organized by meaning. It comprises categories of objects and concepts. For example, most people have a schema for *boats,* with images of what boats look like and words that describe their nature. This schema often incorporates feeling qualities as well, if the person thinks of boats as a source of either fun or danger.

A second type of organization, **episodic memory,** is memory for events, or *episodes.* It comprises memory for your experiences in space and time (Tulving, 1993). In episodic memory, elements of an event are strung together as they happened (Freyd, 1987). Some episodes are long and elaborate—for example, going to high school. Others are brief—for example, a screech of tires on pavement, followed by crashing metal and tinkling glass. A brief event can be stored both by itself and as a part of a longer event (e.g., a car crash may have been a vivid episode in your experience of high school).

Scripts refer to well-defined sequences of behavior that tell us what to expect and what to do in certain situations, such as going to a wedding.

If you experience enough episodes of a given type, a schema for that class of episodes starts to form. This kind of schema is often called a **script** (Schank & Abelson, 1977). Scripts are prototypes of event categories. They're used partly to perceive and interpret common events, such as going to the hardware store, mowing the lawn, and so on. A script provides a perception with a sense of duration and a sense of flow and change through the event. As with all schemas, scripts have defaults, things you assume to be true.

For example, read this description: "John went to a new Thai restaurant last night. He had chicken curry, spicy. After paying his bill, he went home." You understood this description by using your *dining out* script. Your defaults added a lot of details to what you read. You probably assumed John drove to the restaurant (although you might have assumed he walked). You probably assumed he ordered the chicken before he ate it, rather than snatching it off someone else's table. And you probably assumed that the bill he paid was for his dinner, not for broken dishes. In all these cases, you supplied information to fill in gaps in the story. Scripts allow a lot of diversity, but each has a basic structure. Thus, when you encounter a new variation on it, you easily understand what's going on.

It's easy to distinguish between semantic and episodic memory, but most experience is coded both ways at once. For example, conceptual categories (semantic) develop through repeated exposure to regularities in experiences (episodic). If a young child tries to play with several animals and has varying degrees of success, it may help lead the child to discover that dogs and cats are two different categories of animals.

In recent years, theorists have become more aware of the important role that feelings play in schemas. The involvement of feelings has many implications. For example, having a feeling can evoke particular schemas (Niedenthal, Halberstadt, & Innes-Ker, 1999). Feeling qualities seem especially likely to be part of schemas when the feeling is one of threat (Crawford & Cacioppo, 2002). Presumably, this is because sensing threat is so important for survival that we preferentially code information about it.

SOCIALLY RELEVANT SCHEMAS

Soon after cognitive psychologists began to study categories, personality and social psychologists began to study how these processes apply to socially meaningful stimuli. This came to be called **social cognition** (Fiske & Taylor, 1984; Higgins & Bargh, 1987; Kunda, 1999; Macrae & Bodenhausen, 2000; Schneider, 1991; Wyer & Srull, 1986). People form categories of all sorts of socially meaningful things—for example, people, gender roles, environments, social situations, types of social relations, emotions, and the structure of music.

People differ in how readily they develop schemas (Moskowitz, 1993; Neuberg & Newsom, 1993). People also differ in the content and complexity of their schemas. This comes partly from the fact that people have different amounts of experience in a given domain. For example, some people have elaborate mental representations of the diversity among wines; others know only that some wine is red and some is white.

SELF-SCHEMAS

A particularly important schema is the one you form about yourself (Greenwald & Pratkanis, 1984; Markus, 1977; Markus & Wurf, 1987; T. B. Rogers, 1981), called the **self-schema.** This term is a little like *self-concept,* but it's also a little different. The self-schema, like any schema, makes it easier to remember things that fit it. It provides you with a lot of default information. It also tells you where to look for new information. Your self-schema can even bias your recall, twisting your recollections so they fit better with how you see yourself now (Ross, 1989).

Does the self-schema differ from other schemas? Well, it seems to be larger and more complex (Rogers, Kuiper, & Kirker, 1977). This makes sense, because you've probably spent more time noticing things about yourself than about anything else in the world. It incorporates both trait labels and information about concrete behaviors (Fekken & Holden, 1992; Schell, Klein, & Babey, 1996), and it has more emotional elements than other schemas (Markus & Sentis, 1982). There are questions, though, about whether the self-schema is truly special. Features that seem special in it are also present in other well-developed schemas (Greenwald & Banaji, 1989; Karylowski, 1990). Perhaps it seems special only because it's so well developed.

The self-schema is more complex than other schemas, and individuals' self-schemas differ in complexity (Linville, 1987). Some people keep their different self-aspects distinct from each other. Each role these people play, each goal they have, each activity they do has its own place in their self-image. These people are high in **self-complexity.** Other people's self-aspects are less distinct. Everything blends together. These people are low in self-complexity.

This difference has interesting implications. For people low in self-complexity, feelings relating to a bad event in one aspect of life tend to spill over into other aspects of the sense of self (Linville, 1987). Having trouble in a course may make you also feel bad about your social life. This doesn't happen as much for people higher in self-complexity, apparently because the separations and boundaries they have between self-aspects prevent it (see also Niedenthal, Setterlund, & Wherry, 1992; Showers & Ryff, 1996).

In the same way, thinking of oneself in a contextualized way—even temporarily—can dampen emotional reactions to a specific failure. In one study (Mendoza-Denton, Ayduk, Mischel, Shoda, & Testa, 2001), people who had been led to think of themselves in terms of particular classes of situations ("I am _____ when _____") were less affected emotionally by bad outcomes than those who were led to think of themselves in broader terms ("I am _____").

How do people acquire (or fail to acquire) complexity in the self-schema? It may be partly a matter of how much you think about yourself. Nasby (1985) found that people who say they think about themselves a lot have self-schemas with more complexity and detail than people who say they think about themselves less. Presumably, the very process of thinking about yourself causes more growth and articulation of the self-schema.

Another way of viewing self-complexity is to think of the self as a *family* of self-schemas, rather than one (e.g., Markus & Nurius, 1986). In a sense, you're a different person when you're in different contexts (Andersen & Chen, 2002; Swann, Bosson, & Pelham, 2002). You make different assumptions about yourself. You attend to different aspects of what's going on. When you go from your friends at college to your parents at home, it's as though you're putting aside one schema about yourself and taking up another one.

Self-schemas also vary in other ways. Markus and her colleagues (e.g., Markus & Nurius, 1986) suggest that people have diverse images of themselves. People have selves they expect to become, selves they'd like to become (Hewitt & Genest, 1990), and selves they're afraid of becoming (Carver, Lawrence, & Scheier, 1999). People have disliked selves (Ogilvie, 1987) and selves they think they ought to be (Higgins, 1987, 1990). These various **possible selves** can be brought to bear as motivators because they provide goals to approach or to avoid.

Entity versus Incremental Schemas

Another variation in self-schemas is in how much stability people assume. An easy example of this is how people think of their abilities (Dweck & Leggett, 1988).

To some people, an ability is an *entity*. It's something you have more of or less of, but it doesn't change. To other people, an ability is something you can *increment*, or increase through experience. (Once you establish one or the other of these views, you tend to maintain it [Robins & Pals, 2002].)

Both views reflect coherent schemas about ability, but the two views lead to different experiences. When people have an entity view, performing a task is about *proving* their ability. If they do poorly, they're distressed and want to quit. When people have an incremental view, performing a task is about *extending* their ability. If they do poorly, they see it as a chance to increase the ability.

Are these views really schemas? They do seem to act in ways schemas do. For example, they guide people's search for new information (Plaks, Stroessner, Dweck, & Sherman, 2001). When people hold an entity view, they attend to (and remember) cues of consistency. When people hold an incremental view, they attend to (and remember) cues of change.

People who hold an incremental view of ability treat setbacks as challenges for future improvements.

ATTRIBUTION

An important aspect of experiencing events is judging their causes. Inferring a cause tells you whether it was intentional or accidental. It also tells you something about how likely it is to occur again. Inferring the cause of an event is called **attribution** (Heider, 1944, 1958). People do this spontaneously, without even knowing they're doing it (Hassin, Bargh, & Uleman, 2002). Attribution has been studied extensively, and several principles have been identified.

One principle is that people tend to judge events they experience (as actors) differently from events they see or hear about (as observers). *Observers* tend to assume that other people's behavior reflects their personality (Jones & Nisbett, 1971). *Actors*, however, tend to see the same acts as caused by the situation. Thus, the same action can be seen in very different ways by two people. For example, if *you* are late for an appointment, *I* may think it's because you're irresponsible. If *I* am late, I may think it's because things out of my control slowed me down.

The process of making attributions relies partly on schemas about the nature of social situations (Read, 1987). Default values from those schemas help you make inferences beyond the information that's present (Carlston & Skowronski, 1994). And (as in other contexts) using different schemas causes people to make different inferences about the causes of events.

Another important aspect of attribution is the interpretations that people make for good and bad outcomes—successes and failures. Success and failure can have many causes, but work has focused on four causes: ability, effort, task difficulty, and luck or chance factors. The best-known analysis of this kind of attribution is that of Bernie Weiner (1979, 1986, 1990).

Weiner points out that these causes can be placed on a dimension of *locus of causality:* Either the cause is *internal,* part of yourself (ability, effort), or it's *external,* outside

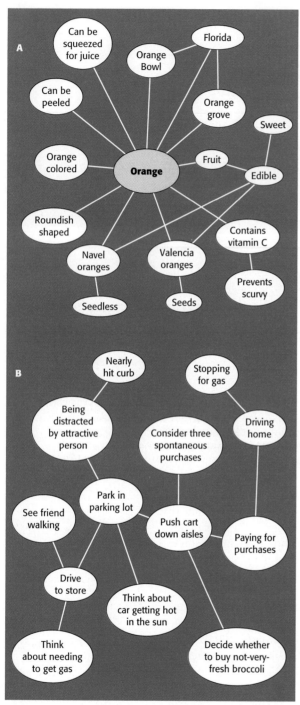

FIGURE 16.1

(A) Part of the network of semantic associations surrounding the concept *orange.* (B) Part of the network of episodic memories surrounding the event *going to the grocery store for broccoli, strawberries, and beer.*

yourself (chance factors, task difficulty, powerful others). Causes also vary in *stability*. Some seem fairly stable (ability), whereas others vary from one time to another (effort). In general, people tend to interpret their successes as having internal stable causes—specifically, their ability. (Note that this enhances self-esteem, as suggested in Chapter 14.) People generally tend to see their failures as caused by relatively *unstable* influences, such as bad luck or too little effort.

On the other hand, there are also individual differences in attributional tendencies, which can have big effects. If you see failure as caused by unstable factors, there's no need to worry about the future. That is, since the cause is unstable, the situation probably won't be the same next time. If the cause is stable, though, the picture is quite different. If you failed because you don't have ability or because the world is permanently against you, you're going to face that same situation next time and every time. Your future will hold only more failure. Your behavior, thoughts, and feelings can be deeply affected by that. Seeing stable and permanent reasons for bad life outcomes relates to depression (e.g., Abramson, Alloy, & Metalsky, 1995; Abramson, Metalsky, & Alloy, 1989; Abramson, Seligman, & Teasdale, 1978; Weiner & Litman-Adizes, 1980) and even sickness and death (e.g., Buchanan, 1995; Peterson, 1995).

Activation of Memories

We've talked about schemas from several angles now. Do schemas just pile up on top of each other in memory? Certainly not. One view is that memories form a vast network (see Figure 16.1). **Nodes,** or areas of storage, are linked if they have some logical connection. Some connections are semantic, linking attributes that contribute to a category (Figure 16.1, A). Others are episodic, linking attributes that form an event (Figure 16.1, B). Bits of information that have a lot to do with each other are strongly linked. Bits of information that don't have much to do with each other are not as strongly linked. In this view, knowledge is an elaborate web of associations of different strengths among a huge number of nodes of information. (Don't think about distance between nodes, by the way, only strength of association; distance isn't part of this picture.)

When a memory node is activated, the information it contains appears in consciousness. A node can be activated by an intentional search (e.g., think of your phone number) or in other ways. As one node becomes active, *partial* activation spreads to other nodes that are related to it. The stronger the relation, the greater the spread. Partial activation makes it easier for the related area to come all the way to consciousness. That is, because it's already partly activated, it takes less of a boost to make it fully active.

To use the examples in Figure 16.1, thinking of an orange partially activates related semantic nodes. Thinking of an orange tends to remind you of navel oranges, the color and flavor of oranges, orange trees, maybe the Orange Bowl. Since orange groves and the Orange Bowl are both in Florida, you may be slightly reminded of Florida, as well. In the same way, thinking about a bit of an episode partially activates related nodes. Thinking about being in the parking lot tends to remind you vaguely of the person you saw there, which in turn may remind you of the fact that you almost lost control over your driving and ran up over the curb.

These examples involve *partial* activation. The memory may not make it all the way to consciousness without another boost from somewhere. But it's more likely to get there than it was before. An extra boost sometimes comes from another source (e.g., seeing someone who looks a little like the person in the parking lot or hearing the song that was on the radio while you were parking). Given that extra boost, the node becomes active enough for its content (the image of the person) to pop into awareness. If the node hadn't already been partially active, the boost wouldn't have been enough.

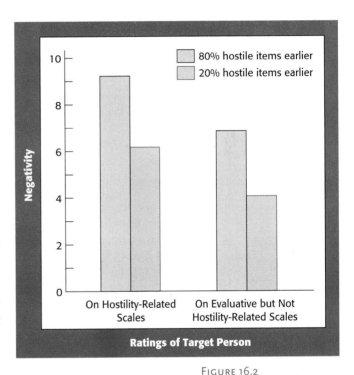

FIGURE 16.2
Effects of priming. Participants read a set of items, 80% of which (or 20% of which) contained words related to *hostility*. Later, in what they thought was a different experiment, they read an ambiguous portrayal of a target person and rated him on two sets of scales: some pertaining to hostility and others evaluative but not directly related to hostility. Reading a larger number of hostile words caused the target person to be seen as more hostile and as less pleasant. *Source: Adapted from Srull & Wyer, 1979, Experiment 1, immediate condition.*

PRIMING AND THE USE OF INFORMATION

The idea that partial activation causes easier access to memories has led to a technique called **priming.** Priming is activating a node of information in a task that comes before the task of interest starts. This technique was first used to study two questions. One is whether the same information is more accessible later on. That is, after priming, it takes a while for the activation to fade. This would leave the node more accessible than before, until the activation is gone. The other is whether *related* information becomes more accessible after the priming.

The answer to both questions is yes. For example, Srull and Wyer (1979) had people do a task in which they read words related to hostility. Later, in what was presented as a different study, they were more likely to see an ambiguously portrayed person as hostile (see Figure 16.2). They rated the person more negatively on other evaluative terms, as well, suggesting a spread of activation to related areas of memory.

These effects occur only if the primed information can plausibly be applied to the later event (Higgins & Brendl, 1995). If you prime *dishonest,* it won't influence your judgments of *athletic* ability. On the other hand, priming seems to activate the full dimension, not just the end that's primed (Park, Yoon, Kim, & Wyer, 2001). If you prime *honest* and then present a target that might be *dishonest,* people are more likely to see dishonesty. (This fits Kelly's idea, discussed in Chapter 15, that constructs are bipolar dichotomies.)

The technique of priming makes use of the fact that events can make information more accessible. But people also differ in what categories are usually accessible for them (Bargh, Lombardi, & Higgins, 1988; Higgins, King, & Mavin, 1982; Lau, 1989). The most accessible categories are the ones they *use* the most. Thus, *chronic* accessibility reflects people's readiness to use particular schemas in seeing the world (Bargh & Pratto, 1986). Finding out about what schemas are chronically accessible in a particular person, then, can provide information about how that person sees the world.

As an example, children who grow up in poor neighborhoods are more likely than other children to be exposed to violence. This exposure may lead them to develop social schemas with violent themes. These schemas should be very accessible for children from such neighborhoods and thus likely to be used. Consistent with this, children from low-income neighborhoods see more hostile intent in ambiguous actions than do other children (Brady & Matthews, 2006; Chen & Matthews, 2001).

Nonconscious Influences on Behavior

We've been talking about ways in which information moves from memory to consciousness and is then used in various ways. However, a line of research by John Bargh and his colleagues (e.g., Chartrand & Bargh, 1996; Fitzsimons & Bargh, 2004) has made it very clear that information does not have to reach consciousness in order to influence what happens next.

In this work, research participants receive **subliminal** primes—that is, primes outside their awareness. These subliminal primes often have the same effect as do more overt primes. For example, people who have the goal of forming an impression pay attention to different things than people who have the goal of memorizing. Activating these goals subliminally has the same effect as activating them overtly (Chartrand & Bargh, 1996). As another example, goals are often linked to particular relationships (e.g., your father may be linked in your mind with doing well on your exams). It appears that priming the relationships outside awareness activates the related goal, which you then set about pursuing unconsciously (Fitzsimons & Bargh, 2003). There's also evidence that subliminally priming an emotion causes judgments of subsequent stimuli to take on that emotional quality (Ferguson, Bargh, & Nayak, 2005).

The findings of this work are fascinating. They represent an important reason for a renewed interest in the processes of the unconscious (Hassin, Uleman, & Bargh, 2005). This view of the unconscious is very different from that of Freud (described in Chapter 8). Yet it holds (as did Freud) that the impact of forces that operate outside awareness can be quite pronounced.

When you think carefully about what priming is, you realize that it happens constantly in life (Carver & Scheier, 2002). Whenever you hear something, read something, think something, or watch something, it makes the corresponding parts of your memories active. This, in turn, causes partial activation in related areas and will leave residual activation in the areas that are now active. That can have a wide range of subtle effects on behavior (see also Box 16.1).

Box 16.1 What's in a Name?

Priming is a funny process. It happens all the time, though people don't realize it. And it can have some very unexpected effects on people's behavior. For example, consider your name. Your name is part of your self-schema. For most of us, our name marks family ties. But does your name have a broader impact on your life? Beyond the fact that some people are teased for having unusual names, most people would probably say no.

Studies have shown, however, that people's names may be involved with important life decisions. Pelham, Mirenberg, and Jones (2002) reported 10 studies of people's names and how they related to where the people lived and what their businesses were. Five studies found that people were more likely to live in places whose names resembled their own than would

happen by chance. For example, men named *Jack* live in Jacksonville in a greater proportion than in, say, Philadelphia. There are more than *twice* as many men named *Louis* in Louisiana than would be expected by chance. Women named *Virginia* are extra likely to move to Virginia but not to Georgia, whereas the reverse is true of women named *Georgia*.

It's not just where people live. It's also what they do. People tend to have jobs that have the same first initial as their own names. *Sheri's* odds of owning a *salon* are greater than chance but not *Carol's. Carol* is more likely to own a *candle* shop. People named *Thompson* have a greater than chance involvement in the *travel* business.

Pelham and his colleagues have also examined these effects in other areas of life (see Pelham et al. [2002]). In the 2000 presidential campaign, people whose last names start with *B*

were more likely to give to the *Bush* campaign, and those whose last names start with *G* were more likely to give to *Gore*. People are also more likely to marry other people whose names resemble their own (J. T. Jones, Pelham, Carvallo, & Mirenberg, 2004).

Why do these things happen? The explanation is that most people have positive feelings about themselves as part of the self-schema. The positive feelings are evoked by anything that reminds them of themselves. This happens even if the reminding is very slight and even if it's unconscious. In effect, if you're named *Ken* and you live in Kentucky, you're surrounded by primes to your self-schema. People may gravitate slightly to anything that evokes that warm sense of self. We don't know if there's a *Ken* in Kentucky who owns a *kennel* and is married to a woman named *Karen*. But if there is, we'd bet he's a very contented man.

Connectionist Views of Mental Organization

For the most part, the way we've been discussing cognition thus far reflects a view in which cognition concerns symbol processing. That view dominated cognitive psychology for many years. In the mid-1980s, however, another view emerged, which is now having an impact on how we think about personality. This other view of cognitive processes has several labels, including *parallel distributed processing* (McClelland, Rumelhart, & PDP Research Group, 1986), *neural networks* (Anderson, 1995; Levine & Leven, 1992), and, perhaps most common, **connectionism** (J. L. McClelland, 1999).

This view uses neuronal processes, rather than computer processes, as a metaphor for cognitive processes. Because the nervous system processes information simultaneously along many pathways, parallel processing is one of its key features. This view also holds that representations aren't centralized in specific nodes. Rather, a representation exists only in a pattern of activation of an entire network of neurons.

Connectionists describe cognition in terms of networks of simple neuronlike units, in which *processing* means passing activations from one unit to another (see Figure 16.3). Each activation can be either excitatory or inhibitory. Thus, it either adds to or subtracts from the total of the unit to which it serves as input. Each unit sums its inputs (pluses and minuses) and passes the total onward. Energy passes in only one direction for each connection, as in neurons. But connections are often assumed in which activation goes from a "later" unit back to an "earlier" one, which is also true

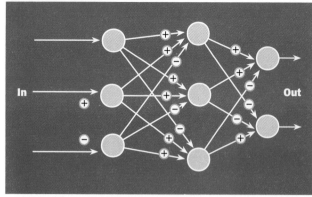

FIGURE 16.3

Example of a connectionist network. The network consists of units that receive and send activation, with two connections (printed in color) that feed activation back to "earlier" units. A given activation can be either excitatory (+) or inhibitory (−). Each unit receives activation from all the units that project to it and sends activation to all the units that it projects to.

Source: Adapted from Carver & Scheier, 1998.

of neurons. The network reacts to an input with a pattern of activity. This activity goes through the network's layers starting on the input side, through whatever elaborate connections exist, to the output side. The pattern that emerges on the output side is the response to the input.

The pattern of activations in the network is updated repeatedly—potentially very often. Gradually, the system "settles" into a configuration and further updates yield no more change. A common way to view this is that the system *simultaneously satisfies multiple constraints* that the units place on each other (Thagard, 1989). For example, if there are two units that inhibit each other, they can't both be highly active at the same time. Each is trying to constrain the other's activity. One of them eventually inhibits the other enough to keep it from being active. Diverse constraints settle out during the repeated updating of activations. The process is complicated, but here's the bottom line: The parallel constraint satisfaction process creates the greatest organization and coherence it can across the network, given the constraints.

The literature of connectionism in cognitive psychology is large and growing rapidly (e.g., J. A. Anderson, 1995; Dawson, 2005; Elman, 2005; Seidenberg, 2005; Smolensky, Mozer, & Rumelhart, 1996; Wendelken & Shastri, 2005). Several authors have also tried to indicate why these ideas are useful for other areas of psychology, including personality (Caspar, Rothenfluh, & Segal, 1992; Kunda & Thagard, 1996; Overwalle & Siebler, 2005; Read & Miller, 1998, 2002; Read, Vanman, & Miller, 1997; Schultz & Lepper, 1996; Smith, 1996).

One interesting application is to social perception and decision making (Read et al., 1997; Thagard & Millgram, 1995). These phenomena involve selecting one possibility from among two or more. When you view an ambiguous figure (see Figure 16.4), you perceive one or the other possibility, not a blend of the two. The perception of one or the other pops into mind. In the same way, when you make a decision, you pick one option. You don't usually get to blend options. Again, even if you're trying to be rational, it's often the case that an answer seems to pop into your mind. Think back to Don and Sandy in the chapter opening, who were trying to find a house they liked. They were being rational and orderly, but a decision just suddenly appeared.

How would connectionists analyze such an experience? They would say the experience is being constructed from bits of input. The bits activate units in the network, and the units place constraints on each other. Activations get transferred from unit to unit, around and around. As the activation pattern is updated over and over, some constraints get stronger over cycles, and some get weaker. The network as a whole settles into a pattern. The pattern is the perception or the decision. Although there may be many cycles, the time involved can be very short. Subjectively, the pattern (perception or decision) emerges as a final product, sometimes abruptly.

These processes can create influences in multiple directions. That is, decisions are made from fitting bits of evidence together despite their constraints on one another. Once a decision has been reached, however, there's also an influence back on your evaluation of the evidence, making it more coherent with the decision (Simon, Snow, & Read, 2004).

Something that's interesting about these networks is that it can be very hard to tell ahead of time how they will settle out. The pattern of constraints can be intricate. Constraints may relate to each other in ways that aren't obvious. The network doesn't care about the "big picture." That's not how it works. Each unit just keeps sending out activations as a function of how active *it* is. In the pushing and pulling, perceptions and decisions can emerge that seem irrational. And they aren't rational, in a sense. The decision about buying a house isn't the algebraic sum of the ratings of the good and bad points of each house. It's more interwoven. This aspect of the connectionist approach in particular makes it feel very different from the symbolic approach.

Another thing that's interesting is that often these networks are very stable, but sometimes they reorganize abruptly (Read & Miller, 2002). In many cases, if you change one part of the input, nothing much changes. Reverberations from the change are dampened in the network. Sometimes, though, change in one part of the input is critical. If the effects of that small change are amplified instead of dampened, there can be profound reverberations over cycles, producing a drastic reorganization. Thus, if you're looking at a figure such as the one in Figure 16.4, it can suddenly reorganize and become the alternate image. These ideas have been used to discuss how the self-concept is sometimes resistant to and sometimes responsive to information from outside (Nowak, Vallacher, Tesser, & Borkowski, 2000).

FIGURE 16.4
An example of an ambiguous figure. This image can be seen either as a young woman turning aside or as an old woman with a protruding nose and chin. Although your perception can easily shift from one to the other, you don't see a blend of images.
Source: Adapted from Boring, 1930.

DUAL-PROCESS MODELS

Cognitive psychologists wrestled for some time with differences between the symbol-processing approach and the connectionist approach. In the end, several turned to the idea that cognition involves two kinds of thought, rather than one. Smolensky (1988) argued that a *conscious processor* is used for effortful reasoning and following of programs of instructions and that an *intuitive processor* manages intuitive problem solving, heuristic strategies, and skilled or automatic activities using connectionist processes. This view has also been expressed in several other **dual–mode models** in cognitive psychology (De Neys, 2006; Holyoak & Spellman, 1993; Sloman, 1996).

When doing controlled processing, the mind in effect says, "Find a rule, apply it to the situation, carry out its logical steps of inference and action, and make decisions as needed. If no rule is available, use whatever's closest." When the mind is in connectionist mode, the settling process goes on until the elements shake out and a pattern emerges. The activity of this mode fits the experience of insight: A pattern appears suddenly where none was before.

The idea that people experience the world through two different modes of processing also appears in the literature of personality. Depictions of two modes of processing bear a very strong resemblance to an argument made some time ago by Seymour Epstein (1985, 1990, 1994). Epstein's *cognitive–experiential self-theory* assumes we experience reality through two systems. The *rational system* operates mostly consciously, uses logical rules, and is fairly slow. This is the symbolic processor that we think of as our rational mind. The *experiential system* is intuitive. It's a "quick and dirty" way of assessing and responding to reality. It relies on shortcuts and information that's readily available. It functions automatically and quickly.

Epstein believes that both systems are always at work and that they jointly determine behavior. Each can also be engaged to a greater degree by circumstances. For example, asking people to give strictly logical responses to hypothetical events tends to place them in the rational mode. Asking them how they would respond if the events happened to them tends to place them in the experiential mode (Epstein, Lipson, Holstein, & Huh, 1992). The more emotionally charged a situation is, the more thinking is dominated by the experiential system.

In Epstein's view, the experiential system resulted from eons of evolution. It dominates when speed is needed (as when the situation is emotionally charged). You can't be thorough when you need to act fast (for example, to avoid danger). Maybe you can't even wait to form an intention. The rational system is more recent in origin. It provides a more cautious, analytic, planful way of proceeding. That also has advantages, of course, when there is enough time and freedom from pressure to think things through.

More recently, the dual-process idea has emerged several more times in forms that are very similar to this (for review see Carver, 2005). Metcalfe and Mischel (1999) proposed there is a "hot" system that's emotional, impulsive, and reflexive. It operates in a connectionist manner. There is also a "cool" system that is strategic, flexible, slower, and unemotional. This line of thought was derived in part from a long line of research on delay of gratification (see Box 16.2). But it obviously applies more broadly.

A different application of this idea is to the anger that arises in response to rejection. In a study by Ayduk, Mischel, and Downey (2002), students recalled a situation in which they had been rejected or excluded. After bringing that situation to mind,

Box 16.2 DELAY OF GRATIFICATION

The Role of Cognitive Strategies

Several previous chapters have discussed the ability to delay gratification—to wait a while for something good. From a psychoanalytic view (Chapter 8), this is a matter of the ego holding the id in check until the time is right to fulfill its desires. From the view of ego psychology (Chapter 10), traits of ego control and ego resiliency determine self-restraint. From the view of the learning perspective (Chapter 13), whether a person delays or not depends on the reward structure of the situation and the behavior of salient models.

The cognitive point of view suggests yet another angle on the process of delaying gratification. Specifically, an important influence on delay of gratification is the mental strategies people use (Kanfer, Karoly, & Newman, 1975; Mischel, 1974, 1979). *What* people think about—and *how* they think about it—can make delays easier or harder.

Early work showed that preschoolers would wait 10 times longer for a desired food if it wasn't visible than if it was (Mischel & Ebbesen, 1970). On the other hand, delays were easier to tolerate if pictures of the rewards were present (Mischel & Moore, 1973). Later research showed these effects could be changed by varying how children *thought* about the desired object. Thinking about consummatory aspects of a food, such as its taste, made it nearly impossible for children to delay (Mischel & Baker, 1975). In contrast, attending to qualities of the food that weren't related to eating made it possible for children to tolerate delay quite easily (see also Kanfer et al., 1975; Moore, Mischel, & Zeiss, 1976; Toner & Smith, 1977).

Research on how these self-control strategies evolve shows that there's a natural progression over time (Mischel, 1979). At first, children attend to aspects of the reward that are most appealing (such as taste), which doesn't help (Yates & Mischel, 1979). Eventually, they begin to generate cognitive strategies to keep these thoughts from their awareness. The result is increased self-restraint. As Mischel (1990) pointed out, it's not what's in front of the children that matters but what's going on in their heads. The same is true for adults (Trope & Fishbach, 2000, 2005). This research thus reinforces one of Mischel's major theoretical points: the importance of people's mental strategies in determining their behavior.

some were told to focus on the feelings and sensations they'd experienced, and others were told to focus on the arrangement of people, objects, and lighting in the event. Then they wrote down what they had thought and felt while recalling the experience. Those who had taken a "cool" stance on the situation reported less anger and hurt than did the others.

The dual-process idea has also emerged in a number of other places. For example, Lieberman, Gaunt, Gilbert, and Trope (2002) looked at attributions that are relatively effortful versus those that are automatic (because they'd been made over and over). As did Epstein, they assume that the reflexive system is attuned to pressured and emotional demands of the world and that it acts very quickly. The other system uses symbolic logic and is slower. As did Epstein, they believe that both systems are always at work and that each can be induced to dominate by variations in the situation. After reviewing findings from several sources, Lieberman et al. (2002) concluded that the consciously controlled and automatic versions of attribution are managed by different parts of the brain.

These dual-process models resemble some ideas from Chapter 7. We said there that behavior sometimes reflects automatic impulses and sometimes the oversight of a temperament of constraint or effortful control. Controlled behavior seems restrained and socialized. Behavior dominated by automatic processing can be impulsive and may seem unsocialized. Those ideas resemble the dual-process models described here. The focus here is a little different, however: the idea that personality may have two cognitive modes with different "feels." One mode is clearly recognizable as *thinking*. The other is more like intuitive *reacting* (see also Kuhl, 2000).

Many people have believed thinking is more important and more a part of personality. But intuitive reacting may be a far more potent influence on behavior than most people realize (see also Toates, 2006). The dual-mode theories outlined here all assume that it's harder for the effortful process to dominate over the automatic process when the person's mind is relatively full (e.g., when you're trying to do two things at once). Similarly, the automatic process tends to take over when the situation is emotional or pressured. Being cognitively busy and being pressured or emotionally aroused applies to a good proportion of most people's lives.

EXPLICIT AND IMPLICIT KNOWLEDGE

Another body of research on mental representations also seems to fit a dual-mode view of cognition. This research examines the idea that people have both **explicit knowledge** (which is accessible on demand) and **implicit knowledge** (which isn't). To put it differently, implicit knowledge is the existence of automatic mental associations we aren't really aware of.

A topic that helped lead to the emergence of this line of thought concerns prejudices and how they're represented in the mind. Many people believe they aren't prejudiced against minorities—that they treat all people equally well. It turns out, though, that many of these same people have stronger mental links from these minorities to the semantic quality *bad* than from the minorities to *good* (Greenwald, McGhee, & Schwartz, 1998). These links are called *implicit associations,* because they are measured quite indirectly (usually through a set of reaction-time trials) and because people are unaware of the links.

The discovery of implicit attitudes has led to a much larger exploration of explicit knowledge of various kinds, including implicit theories of the self (Beer, 2002) and implicit self-esteem (DeHart, Pelham, & Tennen, 2006; Greenwald, Banaji, Rudman,

Farnham, Nosek, & Mellott, 2002). Implicit self-esteem has been found to relate to negative feeling states in day-to-day life, independent of any role of explicit self-esteem (Conner & Barrett, 2005). It is of considerable interest that *implicit* self-esteem is not very highly correlated with *explicit* self-esteem (the self-esteem that's reported on self-report scales). The same is often true of attitudes. There's evidence that both implicit and explicit attitudes of various types relate to behavior, but often to different aspects of behavior (Asendorpf, Banse, & Mücke, 2002).

Why aren't these two aspects of knowledge closely related? One possibility follows from the view that much of implicit knowledge comes from simple association learning—classical and instrumental conditioning—whereas explicit knowledge comes from verbal, conceptual learning. Perhaps the experiences that provide associative and verbal knowledge about the self (or anything else) are more separate than people have often assumed. For example, a child may be harshly treated by parents but told verbally that he is a wonderful boy. These two sources of experience don't agree well with each other. Over time, this would lead to different knowledge at the implicit (associative) and explicit (verbal) levels.

It might follow from this that the implicit knowledge starts forming earlier in life than explicit knowledge. That is, conditioning begins very early. Conceptual and verbal learning develop somewhat later. Consistent with this line of thought, negative implicit attitudes toward minorities are displayed as early as age 6; egalitarian explicit attitudes emerge at about age 10, but the implicit attitudes remain as they were (Baron & Banaji, 2006).

In introducing this topic, we said that implicit and explicit attitudes may relate to dual-mode models of cognition. It seems possible that what we are referring to here as *implicit knowledge* is the same sort of associative system that others have termed an *experiential* or *reflexive* or *intuitive system*. The *explicit knowledge* would seem to be more related to a *rational, deliberative system*. Fitting that picture, there is evidence that controlled processes are what help people override automatic tendencies to stereotype others (Payne, 2005) and react to cues of stigma (Pryor, Reeder, Yeadon, & Hesson-McInnis, 2004).

Broader Views on Cognition and Personality

Much of the cognitive view of personality concerns specific mental processes that underlie personality. This work tends to be tightly focused on particular issues. As a result, the cognitive approach is very fragmented (Funder, 2001). Attempts have been made, however, to make more integrative statements about cognition and personality. Two of the most influential statements were made by Walter Mischel, a theorist with a huge influence on today's cognitive view (see also Box 16.3). Interestingly, these statements were made nearly a quarter century apart.

COGNITIVE PERSON VARIABLES

As is true of many who now hold a cognitive view on personality, Mischel earlier was identified with the *cognitive–social learning* view. The theoretical statement he made in 1973 represents a transition between Mischel the learning theorist and Mischel the cognitive theorist. He proposed that an adequate theory of personality must take into account five classes of cognitive variables in the person, all of which are influenced by learning. Given these criteria, Mischel gave them the long name of *cognitive–social learning person variables*. He intended them to take the place of traits (Mischel, 1990).

BOX 16.3 THE THEORIST AND THE THEORY

Mischel and His Mentors

Professional mentors influence their students in many ways. Most obviously, they impart a set of skills and a way of looking at the world, which the students then apply to domains of their own choosing. Sometimes, however, there's more to it than that. Sometimes an imprint on the mind of a student reverberates for a long time in his or her work. The student absorbs the essence of the mentor's view and recasts it in a new and more elaborated form. This seems to be the case in the career of Walter Mischel.

Mischel was born in Vienna in 1930 and lived within walking distance of Sigmund Freud's house. When he was 9, his family fled to New York to escape Nazism. Mischel grew up in New York and became a social worker, using Freud's theory of personality. His enthusiasm for psychoanalysis waned, however, when he tried to apply it to juvenile offenders in New York's Lower East Side. After a time, Mischel set off to continue his studies at Ohio State University.

There, he came under the influence of two psychologists who were already making a mark on personality psychology: George Kelly and Julian Rotter. Kelly's ideas (described in Chapter 15) emphasized the importance of personal constructs. Rotter's ideas (described in Chapter 13) concerned the importance of people's expectations in determining their behavior. Both Kelly and Rotter were also skeptical about a purely dispositional approach to personality.

Mischel's work has incorporated all three of these themes, although he has also taken each theme in direc- tions of his own. For example, as dis- cussed in Chapter 4, Mischel (1968) sparked a huge controversy in per- sonality psychology over the question of whether behavior has enough cross-situational consistency to war- rant believing in dispositions. He spent much of his career focusing on issues in the cognitive–social learning perspective, including the role played by various kinds of expectancies. In the past three decades, his views have become increasingly cognitive, leading to what some see as a reso- lution of the controversy he sparked in 1968. As we noted at the start of this chapter, the emergence of today's cognitive view on personality has roots in several places other than Kelly's ideas. Surely, however, one reason for the emergence of this cognitive view is the impact that Kelly the mentor had on the young Walter Mischel.

One class of variables is the person's *competencies,* the skills that one develops over life. Just as people develop skills for manipulating the physical world, they develop social skills and problem-solving strategies, tools for analyzing the social world. These competencies are much like what was discussed in Chapter 10 in the context of the idea that the ego functions to promote better adaptation.

Different people have different patterns of competencies, of course. Some people have the ability to empathize with others, some have the skill to fix brakes, some have the ability to make people laugh, and some have the ability to make people follow them into danger. Situations also vary in what competencies they call for (Shoda, Mischel, & Wright, 1993). Thus, different situations provide opportunities for differ- ent persons to take advantage of.

The second class of variables is *encoding strategies and personal constructs.* This covers schemas, as well as what Kelly said about the unique worldview that each person develops. You construe events and people differently, depending on the schema you're using. (You look at the house one way if you're a potential buyer, another way if you're a potential burglar.) It's not the objective situation that determines how you react, but how you construe it. Two people react to a situation differently because they literally experience it differently.

Encoding strategies are ways of seeing the world. But to know what people will *do* in that world, you also need to know their *expectancies.* One type of expectancy is the anticipation that one event typically is followed by another. For example, hearing a siren is often followed by seeing an emergency vehicle. Seeing dark clouds and hearing thunder are often followed by rain. Expectancies about what's connected to what provide continuity in experience. A second type of expectancy is *behavior-outcome expectancy,* the belief that particular acts typically lead to particular outcomes. These are much like the outcome expectancies in Bandura's social–cognitive learning theory (discussed in Chapter 13). Entering a restaurant (behavior) usually is followed by being greeted by a host or waiter (outcome). Being friendly to others (behavior) is usually followed by friendly responses (outcome). Typing the right codes into an ATM (behavior) usually leads to receiving money (outcome). If the expectancies you have match reality, your actions will be effective. If you've learned a set of behavior-outcome expectancies that don't fit the world, you'll be less effective.

Expectancies begin to specify what people do: People do what they think will produce outcomes. The fourth part of the puzzle is knowing what outcomes the person wants to produce, the person's *subjective values.* These values are what cause people to use their expectancies in action. If the available outcome isn't one the person cares about, the expectancies won't matter.

The fifth set of variables Mischel (1973) discussed is what he called *self-regulatory systems and plans.* People set goals, make plans, and do the various things that need to be done to see that the plans are realized in action. This covers a lot of ground. Since Mischel proposed his five categories, this category has taken on something of a life of its own. In part for this reason, we'll talk about it separately in Chapter 17.

PERSONALITY AS A COGNITIVE–AFFECTIVE PROCESSING SYSTEM

Mischel and Shoda (1995) proposed a model that extends and elaborates Mischel's earlier statement. (We discussed the Mischel and Shoda model briefly in Chapter 4.) They described what they called a *cognitive–affective processing system.* The linking of *cognitive* to *affective* in this label reflects the recognition that emotion plays a key role in much of cognitive experience.

Mischel and Shoda said that people develop organizations of information about the nature of situations, other people, and the self. These schemas are more complex in one sense than what we've described thus far. Specifically, Mischel and Shoda said that they have a kind of *if . . . then* property, a conditional quality. Saying someone is aggressive doesn't mean you think the person is aggressive every moment. It means you think he or she is more likely than most people to be aggressive in a certain class of situations.

Evidence from several sources supports this view. For example, in describing others, we often use *hedges,* conditions under which we think the others act a particular way (Wright & Mischel, 1988). This suggests that people normally think in conditional terms about each other. In fact, the better you know someone, the more likely you are to think in conditional terms about him or her (Chen, 2003).

Mischel and Shoda said that people also think conditionally about themselves. That is, each person's behavior also follows an *if . . . then* principle. Schemas to construe situations include information about appropriate actions in those situations (Carver & Scheier, 1981). Norms are mentally represented as links between settings and the behaviors that relate to those settings (Aarts & Dijksterhuis, 2003). If a situation is identified that's linked to a particular behavior, then that behavior will tend to occur (*if . . . then*).

In this view, individuality arises from two sources. First, people differ in the accessibility of their various schemas and the cues that evoke the schemas. Thus, different schemas are likely to pop up for different people in a given setting. People literally perceive different things in the same situation. Second, people differ in their *if . . . then* profiles. When a schema is active, the person will act in ways that fit it. But that may mean different actions for different people.

For example, some people will view an ambiguous remark made by another person as a rejection, some as a provocation, some as an indication that a "power play" is underway, and some as an indication that the other person was out too late last night and is hung over. If Marty sees a power play—even if no one else in the room does—he erupts in bluster and bravado. If he doesn't see it that way, he doesn't do that. Ed is also sensitive to power plays, but he has a different *if . . . then* link: If Ed sees a power play, he gets very quiet and starts looking for cues about who's likely to win. Thus, even if Ed and Marty identify the same situation—a power play—they will act quite differently from each other.

To predict consistency of action, then, you need to know two things. First, you need to know how the person construes the situation (which depends on the person's schemas and their accessibility). Second, you need to know the person's *if . . . then* profile. In this view, the unique profile of *if . . . then* relations is seen as a *behavioral signature* for a person's personality (Shoda, Mischel, & Wright, 1994). Indeed, these profiles of *if . . . then* relations may in some sense *define* personality (Mischel, Shoda, & Mendoza-Denton, 2002). These profiles are relatively stable over time (Shoda et al., 1994) and thus account for temporal consistency in behavior. Consistency over time, of course, is a key element in conceptions of personality.

This line of thought has been applied by Andersen and Chen (2002) to the core social relationships in a person's life. They argue that we develop schematic knowledge of people who are significant to us early in life. When we encounter new people who resemble one of those significant people enough to activate that schema, it evokes the *if . . . then* profile associated with that significant person. You act more like the version of yourself that you displayed to that significant other.

This general viewpoint on behavior suggests that schemas are deeply interconnected to one another. Schemas about what people are like relate to schemas about the nature of situations. Both of these are tied to schemas for acting. Although you may focus on one of these at a time, the use of one implicitly involves the use of the others as well (Shoda et al., 1989).

Consistent with this line of thought, there's evidence that some of the same brain structures are involved in perception–cognition and related actions. For instance, certain neurons that are active when a monkey *does* an action are also active when the monkey *sees* the same action being done (Gallese, 2001; Rizzolatti, Fogassi, & Gallese, 2002). They are often called **mirror neurons.** Similar evidence has also been found in humans (Buccino et al., 2001). Later work extended the finding to sound. Neurons that are active when the monkey does or sees the action are also active when the monkey *hears* sounds associated with that action (Kohler, Keysers, Umiltà, Fogassi, Gallese, & Rizzolatti, 2002). Such findings have led to the idea that perceptual memories may actually be organized in terms of potentials for action (Fadiga, Fogassi, Gallese, & Rizzolatti, 2000).

Assessment

From the cognitive viewpoint, personality assessment emphasizes assessing people's mental structures. There are many ways to assess mental pictures of reality (e.g., Merluzzi, Glass, & Genest, 1981) called **cognitive assessment** techniques. They range from interviews and self-reports to *think-aloud protocols,* in which people say what comes into their minds while doing an activity. A variation on this is *experience sampling,* which is more intermittent.

THINK-ALOUD, EXPERIENCE SAMPLING, AND SELF-MONITORING

The technique used is often determined by the nature of the event of interest. For example, think-aloud approaches are used to assess cognition during problem solving (Ericsson & Simon, 1993). They're aimed at finding out what thoughts occur at various stages of problem solving. The intent is to examine such questions as which strategies are effective and which aren't and how the strategies of experts and novices differ (Simon & Simon, 1978).

Experience sampling (or thought sampling) typically has somewhat different purposes. This technique has people report at certain times what they've been thinking and doing. Sometimes the reports are made at scheduled times, and sometimes people are randomly paged and asked to report (e.g., Gable, Reis, & Elliot, 2000; Hormuth, 1990; Laurenceau, Barrett, & Pietromonaco, 1998; Pietromonaco & Barrett, 1997). This procedure lets you sample across a wide range of events in the person's day. That way, you can find out what cognitions and emotions go along with which kinds of events. The result is a clearer picture of what various events feel like to the people who are taking part in them.

For example, Csikszentmihalyi and Csikszentmihalyi (1988) paged people at irregular intervals and had them record their activities, thoughts, and feelings. As noted in Chapter 14, a focus of that work was on optimal experience. There were several interesting findings: Positive feelings relate mostly to *voluntary* actions, not things people *have* to do. Satisfaction, freedom, alertness, and creativity relate to events in which people's attention is tightly focused on what they're doing (Csikszentmihalyi, 1978). Interestingly, positive feelings of immersion are very likely during work (see also Table 16.1).

More recent research has extended experience sampling methodology into many new domains. Further, it's now common to collect people's reports of their thoughts and feelings on hand-held computers (Gable et al., 2000; Laurenceau et al., 1998; Pietromonaco & Barrett, 1997). This makes collecting these sorts of cognitive assessments extremely easy. This technique is now being used to study ideas from a wide variety of theoretical perspectives.

Table 16.1 Activities Producing Positive Feelings of Immersion. Positive feelings of being deeply and pleasantly involved in one's activities are tied to a wide range of activities. People were given descriptions that expressed such feelings and were asked to indicate one context in which they themselves had had similar experiences in their own lives. *Source:* Adapted from Csikszentmihalyi, 1982.

Activity Named	Percentage of People Naming It
Work activities (working, being involved in challenging problems at work)	31
Hobbies and home activities (cooking, singing, photography, sewing, etc.)	22
Sports and outdoor activities (golf, dancing, swimming, etc.)	18
Social activities (spending time with spouse or children, parties, vacationing)	16
Passive attending activities (listening to music, reading, watching TV)	13

Another technique, termed *event recording* or *self-monitoring,* focuses not on particular moments of the day but on particular classes of events. This technique has you record instances of specific event types (Ewart, 1978; Mahoney, 1977; Nelson, 1977). You note the particular behavior, emotion, or thought pattern, and record information about what was going on at the time (e.g., the time of day, whether you were with others or alone, what the situation was). Doing this lets you see regularities in the contexts that surround particular thoughts and emotions. You get a better understanding of what schemas you're automatically using.

CONTEXTUALIZED ASSESSMENT

Another aspect of the cognitive view on assessment is the idea that personality should be assessed for specific classes of contexts. This element is shared with the cognitive–social learning view. Several studies indicate that doing this adds important information.

Research on this issue by Wright and his colleagues has focused on assessment of children with problems. In one study (Wright, Lindgren, & Zakriski, 2001), teachers rated boys on two measures. One was a commonly used measure of problem behaviors (aggression and social withdrawal) that didn't identify the context in which they happen. The other measure assessed how often the behaviors occur *in response to specific situations*. The broad measure was able to distinguish aggressive children from others but didn't distinguish between two groups of boys whose aggression occurred in very different contexts. Thus, the contextualized measure provided fine-grained information that the other did not.

In another study (Wright, Zakriski, & Drinkwater, 1999), children were observed in a residential setting over a six-week period. Elaborate recordings were made of their behaviors and the contexts in which they occurred. Each child was also rated on the measure of problem behaviors that ignores context. Each child was classified by the latter measure as being an *externalizer* (displaying behaviors such as aggression), an *internalizer* (displaying behaviors such as social withdrawal), a *mixed case,* or *not a clinical case* (i.e., not fitting a diagnosis).

The behavioral signatures of these groups differed in ways that could not have been predicted by the global ratings. When teased or threatened by a peer, externalizers tended to hit and boss, whereas internalizers whined and withdrew. Outside these specific situations, these groups of children didn't differ behaviorally from children who had no problem diagnosis. The mixed cases didn't do any of these things in response to teasing, but they did tend to both hit and withdraw socially when a peer simply talked to them. Again, contextualized assessment gave much more information about those being assessed (see also Wright & Zakriski, 2003).

DIAGNOSTIC CATEGORIES AS FUZZY SETS

The cognitive approach has one more implication concerning assessment that differs completely from anything we've said thus far. This point isn't about assessment methods but about the result of some assessments. In particular, it concerns how clinicians organize their knowledge about the nature of people's problems.

People with psychological problems aren't just one big group. They fit into several diagnostic categories based on symptoms. Categories once had defining characteristics. If a person had all of a specific set of qualities, he or she was in that category. Otherwise, he or she wasn't. An alternative strategy is suggested by a view on the nature of categories discussed earlier, in which categories don't have explicit definitions. Rather, the category is a fuzzy set, made up of a set of features that category members often have but sometimes don't. In the same way, a diagnostic category may be a collection of features that are *often* present in exemplars of that category *but not always* (Cantor, Smith, French, & Mezzich, 1980).

Using the old strategy, if a person generally fits a diagnostic category but lacks a specific feature, the psychologist would hesitate to place the person in that category. With the newer strategy, the psychologist may be more willing to do so. Under this strategy, fit to the category is determined by the *proportion* of features that fit that category. This approach emphasizes the idea that diagnosis is probabilistic, rather than exact (Cantor et al., 1980).

Problems in Behavior, and Behavior Change

The focus on cognitive structure that's been so apparent throughout this chapter is also involved in how this view conceptualizes psychological problems and therapeutic behavioral change.

INFORMATION-PROCESSING DEFICITS

One implication of the cognitive view is that some problems reflect deficits in basic cognitive or memory functions: attending, extracting and organizing information, and so on. For example, people with schizophrenia need more time than other people to recognize stimuli such as letters (Miller, Saccuzzo, & Braff, 1979; Steronko & Woods, 1978). It isn't clear whether this implies a deeper problem or whether it bears only on perceiving. Just by itself, however, this problem would account for some of the difficulty a schizophrenic person has in life.

Another simple idea is that there's a limit on attentional capacity. If you pay too much attention to things other than what you're trying to do, you become less efficient at what you're trying to do. Using attention elsewhere can also make it hard to learn. For example, anxiety takes up attention. For that reason alone, being anxious can make it harder to process other things (Newman et al., 1993; Sorg & Whitney, 1992). People with test anxiety or social anxiety thus become less efficient when their anxiety is aroused. A related argument has been used to explore deficits related to depression (Conway & Giannopoulos, 1993; Kuhl & Helle, 1986).

Some styles of *deploying* attention may also create problems (Crick & Dodge, 1994). For example, children who are overly aggressive don't attend to cues of other children's intentions (Dodge, 1986; Dodge & Crick, 1990). As a result, they often misjudge others' intentions and act aggressively. Indeed, they often strike out preemptively (Hubbard, Dodge, Cillessen, Coie, & Schwartz, 2001). This may also be true of violent adults (Holtzworth-Munroe, 1992).

Why do people deploy their attention in ineffective ways? Their *schemas* lead them to do so. Recall that one effect of schemas is to tell you where to look for information in a new event: You look for information that fits the schema. Thus, a biased or faulty schema can bias the search for cues, which can lead to misinferences and inappropriate actions.

DEPRESSIVE SELF-SCHEMAS

A broad implication of the cognitive view is that many problems stem from schemas that interfere with effective functioning in more complex ways. This reasoning has been applied to several problems, most notably depression. Theorists hold that people sometimes develop ideas about the world that are inaccurate or distorted, which lead to adverse effects (e.g., Beck, 1976; Ellis, 1987; Meichenbaum, 1977; Young & Klosko, 1993). Aaron Beck (1972, 1976; Beck, Rush, Shaw, & Emery, 1979) is one theorist who thinks that depression and other problems follow from such distortions. In effect, people with these problems use faulty schemas to interpret events. They rely on negative preconceptions (their schemas) and ignore information that's available in the environment (though see Box 16.4).

In Beck's view, the inaccurate schemas are used quickly and spontaneously. They produce a stream of what he calls **automatic thoughts.** These automatic thoughts (e.g., "I can't do this," "What's the point of trying?," "Everything's going to turn out wrong") influence feelings and behaviors. The pattern has a run-on quality, because the negative feelings lead to more use of negative schemas, which in turn leads to more negative affect (cf. Nolen-Hoeksema, Morrow, & Frederickson, 1993; Wenzlaff, Wegner, & Roper, 1988). Indeed, just expecting emotional distress makes distress more likely (Kirsch, 1990; Kirsch, Mearns, & Catanzaro, 1990).

People who are prone to depression or anxiety seem to rely too much on information in memory and rely too little on the reality of the situation. This creates problems because the self-schemas of these people are negative (Kuiper & Derry, 1981; Segal, 1988). When people use the negative schemas, they naturally expect bad outcomes. They don't look at the situation with an open mind but attend to and encode the worst side of what's happening (Gotlib, 1983).

Box 16.4 Theoretical Controversy

Whose Perceptions Are Distorted, Anyway?

Beck's theory of depression is based on the premise that people who get depressed make a variety of cognitive distortions. He sees these distortions as leading to depressed feelings and to other symptoms of depression. However, research has raised questions about who's doing more distorting: people who are depressed or people who aren't.

In one research program bearing on this question (Alloy & Abramson, 1988), participants were presented a series of problems. For some, there was a connection between their responses and the outcome of the problem. For others, there was no relation between response and outcome. The measure of interest was participants' estimates of the degree to which their responses had controlled the outcomes.

The results were surprising. The researchers found that depressed persons were in fact fairly *accurate* in their judgments. People who weren't depressed, on the other hand, tended to overestimate the control they'd had over good outcomes that in reality were random. No one was surprised that the depressed and nondepressed groups differed. What was surprising was that the *depressed* persons apparently had the better grip on reality.

Another study made a similar case, using very different procedures (Lewinsohn, Mischel, Chaplin, & Barton, 1980). Participants were observed in social interaction and were rated on several dimensions by observers. The participants also rated themselves. The results revealed that people who weren't depressed saw themselves in a better light than the observers did. People who were depressed saw themselves pretty much as the observers saw them. Again, the depressed participants had a better grasp on reality than did the nondepressed.

What are the implications of these findings for Beck's theory of depression? In answering this question, it's important to keep in mind that depressed people *did* differ from nondepressed people in the expected direction. Thus, Beck's argument that depression involves distortion—*in comparison with other people*—still holds. What was startling was that this distortion resulted in greater, rather than less, accuracy. Thus, if Beck's theory about depression is correct, it seems to need one additional assumption: that the perceptions of nondepressed people incorporate a rosy and unrealistic glow of optimism. A number of people have, in fact, come to precisely that conclusion (Taylor & Brown, 1988; Weinstein, 1989).

Beck uses the term **cognitive triad** to refer to negative thinking about the self, the world, and the future. Depressed people also use other distortions. They *overgeneralize* in a negative way from a single bad outcome to their overall sense of self-worth (Carver, 1998; Carver, La Voie, Kuhl, & Ganellen 1988; Hayes, Harris, & Carver, 2004). They make *arbitrary inferences,* jumping to negative conclusions when there isn't evidence for them (Cook & Peterson, 1986). They *catastrophize,* anticipating that every problem will have a terrible outcome. And they interpret bad outcomes as *permanent* (Abramson et al., 1978; Abramson et al., 1989). The result of all this is a low sense of self-worth and hopelessness for the future (Haaga, Dyck, & Ernst, 1991; J. E. Roberts, Gotlib, & Kassel, 1996; J. E. Roberts & Monroe, 1994).

A few paragraphs back, we said that Beck views the use of negative mental structures as automatic. This argument has taken on new overtones in recent years in light of the emerging idea that implicit and explicit aspects of the self compete for influence on behavior (described earlier in the chapter). This emerging idea suggests that the negative mental structures are in a part of the brain that's different from the part guiding conscious, effortful action. The negative patterns may have come from conditioning or just become automatic over the years. Regardless, in the dual-mode view they influence behavior unless overridden by a more effortful process.

This is much the argument that Beevers (2005) has made about vulnerability to depression. Specifically, a person with negative associations in the implicit self is likely to often be subject to negative feelings. This person needs to make an effortful corrective process to counter those negative associations in the implicit self. If that effortful process doesn't occur, the implicit self maintains control over the person's experiences and depression is more likely.

COGNITIVE THERAPY

In Beck's view, therapy should get the person to put faulty schemas aside and build new ones. People must learn to recognize automatic self-defeating thoughts and substitute other self-talk for them. This is termed **cognitive restructuring** or **reframing.** They should also try to focus on the information in the situation and rely less on preconceptions. To put it differently, these people should become more *controlled* in processing what's going on and less *automatic* (cf. Barber & DeRubeis, 1989; Kanfer & Busemeyer, 1982).

The procedures used for changing faulty schemas and their consequences are known broadly as **cognitive therapies** (Beck, 1976, 1991; Beck et al., 1979; DeRubeis, Tang, & Beck, 2001). There are several different techniques. A surprising one is getting people to go ahead and do things they expect (unrealistically) to have bad consequences. If the bad outcome doesn't happen, the people are thereby led to re-examine—and perhaps change—their expectations.

More generally, people are encouraged to view their thought patterns as hypotheses to be tested, instead of as certainties. They're also encouraged to go ahead and test the hypotheses. For example, if you're a person who thinks a single failure means you can't do anything right, you might be told to examine your skills in other domains immediately after a failure. If you're a person who thinks everyone will despise you if you do anything wrong, you might be told to test this assumption by being with friends the next time you do something wrong.

Even a small amount of this sort of "reality testing" can have a large impact on how people view themselves. In one study (Haemmerlie & Montgomery, 1984), students with strong social anxiety were given a simple treatment for it. The treatment was having a conversation with a member of the opposite sex who'd been told to initiate conversation topics, use the pronoun *you* fairly often, and avoid being negative. These *biased interactions* were held twice, a week apart, for about an hour each time. The result was a large reduction in signs of anxiety (see Figure 16.5).

Contemporary Cognitive Theories: Problems and Prospects

Some psychologists find the cognitive view on personality exciting. Others find it less so. It's seen by many as disorganized and not yet mature (Funder, 2001). Those who find it interesting acknowledge that it has many loose ends. Some critics of this view, on the other hand, think it's a passing fad, a misguided effort to graft a very different part of psychology someplace it just doesn't belong.

One criticism of the cognitive view has been that some who use it took the *computer* metaphor too literally. Knowing how a computer does something doesn't necessarily tell us anything about how people do the same thing. There may be dozens of ways to get a computer to do something, but there's no assurance that any of them is even remotely the same as the way a person does it. One response to this is that the computer metaphor has been a useful tool, even if it's hard to know how far to press the analogy. When the metaphor is taken in its general form, rather than as a precise blueprint, it yields interesting suggestions about human thought. Many of these suggestions have been supported in research.

Another criticism of the cognitive view is that it's nothing more than a transplantation of cognitive psychology into the subject of personality. What's gained by knowing that a person's knowledge is schematically organized? What does it tell you about personality to know that these knowledge structures can be brought into use by priming them?

One answer is that these aspects of the mind's functioning do seem to have important implications for the kinds of day-to-day behaviors we usually think of in terms of personality. People absorb new experiences in terms of their current understanding of the world. Thus, it's useful to know what biases are created by their current understanding (i.e., schemas). How people interpret their experiences is also influenced by the goals they have in mind. Because different people have different goals, they experience events in very different ways.

The fact that people's construals can be influenced by priming is of special interest, partly because it relates to an idea of Freud's but with a very different spin. The idea is that people do things for reasons they're unaware of. Priming studies show that this definitely does happen, but the reason need not reside in the psychoanalytic unconscious. The process may be far more superficial (and for that reason less ominous). But because it's superficial, it may also be far more common than previously realized (Bargh & Chartrand, 1999; Carver & Scheier, 2002; Hassin et al., 2005).

The broadest answer to criticisms of the cognitive view, however, may be this: The cognitive viewpoint on personality is part of a broad attempt to understand the

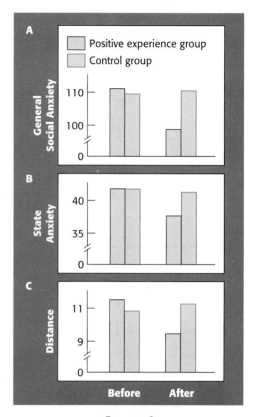

FIGURE 16.5
Scores before and after on three measures among socially anxious men who engaged in unpressured positive conversations with a woman on two different occasions compared with scores of men who did not do so. The measures are (A) self-rated general social anxiety, (B) self-rated state anxiety (taken while in the presence of an attractive woman), and (C) distance from the woman while engaged in a cooperative task. The pleasant experiences improved participants' scores on all these variables. *Source: Adapted from Haemmerlie & Montgomery, 1984.*

operating characteristics of the mind. A better understanding of those characteristics can't help but illuminate important aspects of personality. From this view, the intrapersonal functioning of personality is a reflection of the complexities of the mind and its workings. It's not possible to fully understand the former without understanding the latter.

· SUMMARY ·

The cognitive orientation to personality considers how people attend to, process, organize, encode, store, and retrieve information. *Schemas* are mental organizations of information that develop over experience and are used to identify new events. Some think schemas organize around prototypes (best members); some say that schemas have fuzzy, or inexact, definitions. Schemas make new events easy to remember. They also provide default information to fill in the gaps of events. Schemas can represent concepts (in semantic memory) and events (in episodic memory). Each aspect of memory holds *exemplars* and *generalities*. Stereotypic event categories are called *scripts*.

Social cognition refers to cognitive processes bearing on stimuli relevant to social behavior. People develop schematic representations of many kinds of socially relevant categories. People also develop *self-schemas,* representations of themselves. The self-schema is more elaborate than other schemas, but it seems to follow the same principles. The self-schema may have several facets (e.g., possible selves). Some social schemas imply permanence (entity); some imply potential for change (incremental).

Many psychologists view *memory* as a vast set of content nodes, linked to each other by various associations. Activating one node in memory causes partial activation of related nodes (*priming*), causing that information to become more accessible. Priming can even happen outside awareness. Connectionist models view memory in terms of patterns in overall networks. A given pattern reflects the satisfaction of many constraints simultaneously. This view applies nicely to social perception and decision making. Some theorists believe there are two distinct kinds of thought processes: one quick, intuitive, and connectionist, the other slower, rational, and linear. Research on implicit attitudes suggests that people have knowledge at two levels, which may correspond to the two modes of thought processes.

Broad statements on cognitive views of personality emphasize the importance of people's schemas, encoding strategies, personal competencies, expectancies about how things are related in the world, values or incentives, and self-regulatory systems. People's behavior is seen as following *if . . . then* contingencies, in which the *if* describes a situation and the *then* describes a behavioral response. In this view, personality is a profile of these contingencies, forming a unique "behavioral signature" for each person.

Assessment from this viewpoint is the process of determining the person's cognitive tendencies and contents of consciousness. Cognitive assessment techniques include think-aloud procedures, thought sampling, and monitoring of the occurrence of particular categories of events. These procedures give a clearer idea of what sorts of thoughts are coming to mind in various kinds of situations, typically situations that are problematic. Also important is the idea that assessment be contextualized, to capture the person's *if . . . then* contingencies.

Problems in behavior can come from information-processing deficits (e.g., difficulty encoding, ineffective allocation of attention). Problems can also arise from development of negative self-schemas. In this view, depression results from various kinds of cognitive distortions, all of which cause events to seem more unpleasant or as having more negative implications than is actually true. *Cognitive therapy* involves, in part, attempting to get people to stop engaging in these cognitive distortions and to develop more adaptive views of the events that they experience. This may entail correcting automatic, intuitive processes through oversight from consciousness, effortful processes.

· GLOSSARY ·

Attribution   The process of making a judgment about the cause (or causes) of an event.

Automatic thoughts   Self-related internal dialogue that often interferes with behavior.

Cognitive assessment   Procedures used to assess cognitive processes and contents of consciousness.

Cognitive restructuring or **reframing**   The process of taking a different and more positive view of one's experience.

Cognitive therapy   Procedures aimed at reducing cognitive distortions and the resulting distress.

Cognitive triad   Negative patterns of thinking about the self, the world, and the future.

Connectionism   An approach to understanding cognition based on the metaphor of interconnected neurons.

Default   Something assumed to be true until one learns otherwise.

Dual-mode models   Models assuming two different modes of cognition—one effortful, one automatic.

Episodic memory   Memory organized according to sequences of events.

Exemplar   A specific example of a category member.

Fuzzy set   A category defined by a set of attributes that aren't absolutely necessary for membership.

Implicit knowledge   Associations between things in memory that are not directly accessible.

Mirror neurons   Neurons that are active both when perceiving an action and when doing the action.

Node   An area of memory that stores some element of information.

Possible self   An image of oneself in the future (expected, desired, feared, etc.).

Priming   The process of activating an element in memory by using the information contained in it.

Prototype   The representation of a category in terms of a best member of the category.

Schema   An organization of knowledge in memory.

Script   A memory structure used to represent a highly stereotyped category of events.

Self-complexity   The degree to which one's self-schema is differentiated and compartmentalized.

Self-schema   The schematic representation of the self.

Semantic memory   Memory organized according to meaning.

Social cognition   Cognitive processes focusing on socially meaningful stimuli.

Subliminal   Occurring too fast to be consciously recognized.

Self-Regulation

As Susan awakes, thoughts come to mind about the presentation she's to give this morning. While dressing, she rehearses the points she intends to make. She catches herself skipping too quickly from one to another and makes a mental note to slow down in the middle section so she doesn't leave anything out. For the twentieth time, she retraces her logic, looking for flaws. She wants this to be perfect—to nail down the recommendation for law school she's going to ask her professor for next week. She has planned what to wear to make the impression she wants to make, and just before leaving, she checks her appearance in the hall mirror. A little poking and rearranging of her hair, and she turns to go. As she opens the door, she runs a mental checklist of what she needs to have with her—notes for her presentation, money, purse, keys, and—oh, yeah—the photos she said she'd show Carolyn. Grab the photos. Check to see that the door's locked. Check to be sure there's enough gas in the car. Check to see if there's enough time to take the scenic route to campus. And she's off. "Good," Susan thinks. "Things are going just the way I want them to. Everything's right on track."

P EOPLE SHIFT from one task to another as the day proceeds, yet there's usually coherence and continuity as well. Your days are usually planful (despite disruptions and impulsive side trips) and include many activities. How do you move so easily from one thing to another, keep it all organized, and make it all happen? These are some of the questions behind this chapter.

The approach to personality discussed here uses several metaphors. One of them is *person as robot* (also know by the more formidable label *autonomous artificial agent*). The growth of robotics has influenced the way some people think about human nature (Brooks, 2002; Dawson, 2004; Fellous & Arbib, 2005). As more has been learned about how to get machines to do things, the suspicion has arisen that some of the ideas involved may help us understand how people do things.

The easiest way to start exploring these ideas is to think of them as a view of *motivation*. Much of this chapter focuses on how people adopt, prioritize, and attain goals. In some ways, these functions resemble what was discussed in Chapter 5 as *motives*.

From Cognition to Behavior

As we continue, it will also help to keep in mind the cognitive view of personality discussed in Chapter 16. The general view that people have an organized network of memories is assumed here, too. Now, though, the focus is on how the cognitions and memories result in behavior.

SCHEMAS AND ACTIONS

As noted in Chapter 16, the schemas people use to understand events often include information about behavior. You use this information to recognize what other people are doing. But you also use information from memory to guide the *making of behavior*. Information in schemas helps you decide what to do in the class of situation the schema represents (Burroughs & Drews, 1991; Dodge, 1986). For example, just as the *dining out* script lets you understand someone else's evening, it also reminds you what actions to take if *you* are dining out—order before you're served and pay the bill before you leave.

What's the relation between the information used to recognize acts and the information used to do acts? It's not clear whether one schema serves two purposes or whether there are two parallel forms—one for understanding and one for doing (Petri & Mishkin, 1994). However, there does at least seem to be overlap. As noted in Chapter 16, it's been found that certain neurons (so-called *mirror neurons*) are active both when an action is being watched and when the same action is being done (Gallese, 2001; Rizzolatti, Fogassi, & Gallese, 2002). This suggests a very strong link between thinking and doing.

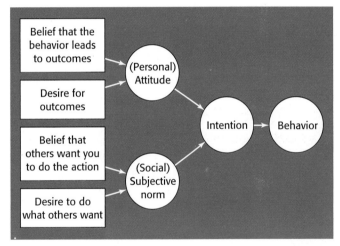

INTENTIONS

Sometimes a situation evokes a schema that provides guidelines for action. Often, though, actions follow from intentions. An important question, then, is, How are intentions formed? Icek Ajzen and Martin Fishbein (Ajzen, 1985, 1988; Ajzen & Fishbein, 1980) say the process uses a kind of mental algebra creating an action probability. If the probability is high enough, an intention is formed to do the act.

According to Ajzen and Fishbein, when people are deciding whether to do something, they weigh several kinds of information (see Figure 17.1). They think about the action's likely outcome and how much they want it. For example, you might think that spending money on a Caribbean trip over spring break would result in a lot of fun, and you really want that fun. The outcome and its desirability merge to form an **attitude** about the behavior. Because it stems from your own wants, your attitude is your *personal orientation* to the act.

Two other kinds of information pertain to the act's *social* meaning to you. One kind of information is whether people who matter to you want you to do the action. You might think about your parents, who don't want you to take the trip (they want

FIGURE 17.1
Foundations of intentions. The belief that an act will produce a particular outcome and the personal desirability of the outcome merge to form an *attitude* (a personal orientation to the act). The belief that other people want you to do the act and the desire to go along with their wishes merge to form a subjective *norm* (a social orientation to the act). The attitude and the subjective norm are weighted in forming the *intention*. The intention then influences the *behavior*. *Source: Adapted from Ajzen, 1988.*

you to come home instead). Or you might think about your friends, who think the trip is a great idea. The other element is how much you want to please the people you're thinking about. How much do you want to please your parents, or at least stay on their good side? How much do you want to go along with your friends' wishes? What the other people in your mind want you to do and how much that matters to you merge to form a **subjective norm** about the action.

The intention derives from both the attitude and the subjective norm. If both favor the behavior, you'll form a strong intention to do it. If both oppose the behavior, you'll form a strong intention *not* to do it. Things are more complex when the attitude and subjective norm conflict. Sometimes you want an outcome, but you know your parents (or your friends) don't want you to do the behavior. In this case, which intention you form depends on which matters more: satisfying yourself or satisfying your parents (or friends).

GOALS

Underlying what we've said so far is the idea that behavior is directed toward *goals.* Schemas suggest behaviors to do. Forming an intention means setting up a goal to attain. The idea that human experience is organized around goals has been discussed a lot in the past two decades (e.g., Austin & Vancouver, 1996; E. S. Elliott & Dweck, 1988; Freund & Baltes, 2002; Pervin, 1983, 1989). Diverse terms have been used, including *life tasks* (Cantor & Kihlstrom, 1987), *personal strivings* (Emmons, 1986), *current concerns* (Klinger, 1987), and *personal projects* (Little, 1989), but the core theme is much the same. The theme is that people's goals energize their activities, direct their movements, and even provide meaning for their lives (Baumeister, 1989).

All these constructs assume both overall goals and subgoals. That is, any life task can be achieved in many ways. The way you choose depends on other aspects of your life. Strategies that are used to pursue life tasks also differ from one person to another (Langston & Cantor, 1989). For example, someone who's relatively shy will have different strategies for making friends than a person who's more outgoing.

In this view, the self is made up partly of goals and organizations among them. Indeed, there's evidence that traits derive their meaning from the goals to which they relate (Read, Jones, & Miller, 1990; B. W. Roberts & Robins, 2000). Goals and aspirations certainly vary from person to person. Yet there is evidence that goals have a coherent set of relations to each other among persons from diverse cultures. That is, goals come together in a two-dimensional circumplex in which some are compatible with each other and some are in conflict (Grouzet et al., 2005). One dimension ranges from intrinsic to extrinsic goals (see Figure 17.2); the other ranges from goals pertaining to the physical self to goals involving self-transcendence. (Both dimensions are consistent with ideas discussed in Chapter 14.)

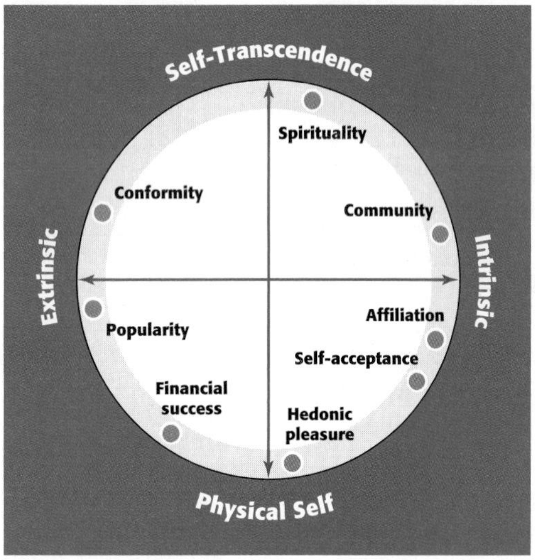

FIGURE 17.2
Circumplex formed by relationships among diverse goals, across 15 cultures. Goals vary along the dimension of intrinsic versus extrinsic and separately along the dimension of concerning the physical self versus transcending the self. *Source: Based on Grouzet et al., 2005.*

GOAL SETTING

Many goals specify intended and desired actions but don't imply any standard of excellence. The goal of going water skiing on a hot afternoon doesn't necessarily imply a goal of excellence (though it might). Forming an intention to go to the grocery store creates a guide for behavior, but it's not really very challenging.

On the other hand, performance level is clearly an issue in some areas. In many activities, the goal isn't just to perform; it's to do *well*. An example is taking a college course. For many people, the goal isn't just completing the course, it's getting a good grade. Another example is business performance. The goal isn't just to survive, but to thrive. One question that arises in such contexts is this: Does setting a particular goal level influence how well you do?

Yes. Setting higher goals leads to higher performance (Locke & Latham, 1990). This is true when high goals are compared to easy goals, and it's also true when they're compared to the goal of "Do your best." Apparently, most people don't take "Do your best" literally. It's taken as "Try to do reasonably well." Thus, it leads to poorer performance than does setting a specific high goal.

Why do higher goals lead to better performance? There are three interrelated reasons. First, setting a higher goal causes you to *try* harder. For example, you know you won't solve 50 problems in 10 minutes unless you push yourself. So you start out pushing yourself. Second, you're more *persistent*. A brief spurt of effort won't do; you'll have to push yourself the entire time. Third, high goals make you *concentrate* more, making you less susceptible to distractions. In all these respects, setting a lower goal causes people to ease back a little.

The positive effect of setting high goals is well documented, but it has a very important limitation. In particular, if you're given a goal that's totally unrealistic, you won't adopt it. You won't try for it. If you don't adopt it, it's as if the goal doesn't exist. The key, then, is taking up a goal that's high enough to sustain strong effort but not so high that it's rejected instead of adopted.

IMPLEMENTATION INTENTIONS AND THE IMPORTANCE OF STRATEGIES

In describing goals, we noted that typically there are *subgoals,* or strategies related to them. Peter Gollwitzer and his colleagues (Brandstätter, Lengfelder, & Gollwitzer, 2001; Gollwitzer, 1999; Gollwitzer & Brandstätter, 1997) have made a similar distinction between two kinds of intentions. A **goal intention** is the intent to reach a particular outcome. An **implementation intention** concerns the how, when, and where of the process. It's the intention to take specific actions when encountering specific circumstances. This linking of context to action is what we described as *if . . . then* links in Chapter 16 (Mischel & Shoda, 1995). Some *if . . . then* links are habitual and well learned (Brandstätter & Frank, 2002). Sometimes, though, they need to be formed consciously for specific intended paths of behavior.

Implementation intentions are more concrete than goal intentions. They serve the goal intentions. They're important because they help stop problems that can arise in getting the behavior done. Often people fail to fulfill goal intentions because they haven't decided how to go about doing so. An implementation intention, being concrete and specific, takes care of that. Sometimes people fail to act because they're distracted and brief opportunities pass them by. Having an implementation intention helps you recognize the opportunity quickly and act on it (Brandstätter et al., 2001). Sometimes people fail to act because they're worn out. Having an implementation intention helps you overcome the lack of energy (Webb & Sheeran, 2003). Forming an implementation intention to do something hard (e.g., writing an assigned paper over Christmas break) greatly increases the likelihood of actually doing it (Gollwitzer & Brandstätter, 1997).

On the other hand, the implementation intention by itself doesn't seem to be enough. You also have to have a strong and active goal intention (Sheeran, Webb, &

Gollwitzer, 2005). In fact, implementation intentions help more if the goal fits with your sense of self than if it doesn't (Koestner, Lekes, Powers, & Chicoine, 2002).

Implementation intentions make a link between a situational cue and a strategy for moving toward the goal. Another body of work also shows the importance of having such links. It derives from the concept of *possible self*. As described in Chapter 16, possible selves are broad images of the person you think you might become. For a desired possible self to influence behavior, you also have to have strategies to attain it (Oyserman, Bybee, & Terry, 2006; Oyserman, Bybee, Terry, & Hart-Johnson, 2004). If the strategies are not already there to be used, effort needs to be spent in creating them.

DELIBERATIVE AND IMPLEMENTAL MINDSETS

Goal intentions and implementation intentions matter. But forming intentions and doing the actions they entail are different processes. People do them with different mindsets (Heckhausen & Gollwitzer, 1987). Forming an intention requires weighing possibilities, thinking of pros and cons, and juggling options. This is called a **deliberative mindset** because the person is deliberating the decision to act. It is relatively unbiased, careful, and cautious in the service of making the best choice (Taylor & Gollwitzer, 1995).

Once the intention has been formed, actually doing the behavior entails a different mindset. People no longer deliberate. Now it's all about doing. This is called an **implemental mindset** because it focuses on implementing the intention to act. This mindset is optimistic and minimizes potential problems in the service of trying as hard as possible to carry out the action (Taylor & Gollwitzer, 1995). Generally, it fosters persistence (Brandstätter & Frank, 2002).

There's evidence that these two mindsets may use different areas of the brain. Lengfelder and Gollwitzer (2001) studied patients with frontal-lobe damage and patients with damage in other areas. They found those with frontal damage were impaired in deliberating. However, if they were provided with *if . . . then* implementation intentions, they weren't impaired at acting. This suggests that the planning is done in the frontal cortex, whereas the handling of the action is done elsewhere.

Self-Regulation and Feedback Control

We've discussed behavioral schemas, intentions, the use of goals, the impact of lofty goals, and the importance of having strategies. But once a goal is set and an intention formed, what ensures that the behavior you *actually do* is the one you *set out to do*? This question brings us to the concept of *feedback control* (Carver & Scheier, 1981, 1998; MacKay, 1963, 1966; Miller, Galanter, & Pribram, 1960; Powers, 1973; Scheier & Carver, 1988; Wiener, 1948).

FEEDBACK CONTROL

A **feedback loop** has four parts (see Figure 17.3). The first is a value to self-regulate toward: a *goal, standard of comparison,* or *reference value* for behavior. (All of these mean the same thing here.) These can come from many places and can exist at many levels of abstraction. For example, they can be plans, intentions, possible selves, or strategies.

The second element is a perception of your present behavior and its effects. This just means noting what you're doing and the effect it's having. Often this is just a flicker of awareness, sensing in a vague way what you're doing. Sometimes it means thinking carefully about what you've been doing over a longer period. Sometimes people literally watch what they're doing (e.g., at dance studios). Although it's easiest to talk about it in terms of *thinking,* this function (as a function) doesn't require consciousness (Bargh & Ferguson, 2000).

These perceptions are compared with the goal by an element termed a **comparator.** If you're doing what's intended, there's no discrepancy between the two, and you continue as before. If your behavior *differs* from what you intended, though, a final process kicks in. This process changes the behavior, adjusts it to bring it more in line with your intention. (For a subtle theoretical issue pertaining to this viewpoint, see Box 17.1.)

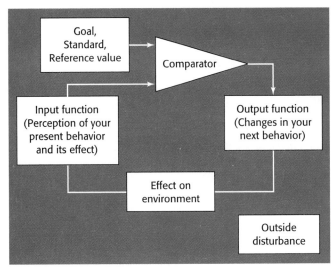

FIGURE 17.3
Diagram of a discrepancy-reducing feedback loop, which shows the basic processes presumed to underlie self-corrective behavioral self-regulation in both artificial and living systems.

The word *feedback* is used because when you adjust the action, the result is "fed back" in the form of a new perception, which is rechecked against the reference value. This loop is also called a *control system,* partly because each event in the loop depends on the result of a previous one. Thus, each prior event controls the next one.

The feedback idea has several implications. For one, it assumes that behavior is purposeful (as do the goal concepts discussed earlier). In this view, virtually all behavior involves trying to conform to some reference value. Life is a process of forming goals and intentions (broad and narrow, short term and long term) and adjusting behavior to match them, using feedback perceptions to tell whether you're doing as you've intended.

According to this logic, self-regulation is continuous and never ending. Every change in output changes current conditions. The new condition has to be checked against the goal. In addition, goals are often dynamic—evolving over time. For example, think of the goal of doing well in school, or making a particular impression on someone (and maintaining it), or taking a vacation trip. You do well in school not by going to a particular end point but by doing well at many tasks over time. You take a vacation trip not by leaving and coming back but by doing activities that constitute vacationing. There's a continuous interplay between adjusting your action and moving forward to the next phase of an evolving goal.

As we said about goals, referring to something as a *standard* here means only it's the value used as a guide. It doesn't necessarily mean a standard of excellence (though it can). Think of a student who's regulating study behavior around the goal of making a C in a course by looking over class notes the night before the exam but not much more. The *structure* of this behavior (setting a goal, checking, and adjusting as needed) is exactly the same as that of a student who's trying to make an A. They're just using two different comparison values.

In order for feedback control to occur, people need to monitor what they are currently doing.

Box 17.1 THEORETICAL ISSUE

Feedback versus Reinforcement

It's long been known that people doing tasks benefit from knowing the results of their last efforts (Locke & Latham, 1990; Schmidt, 1988). But this evidence is interpreted differently by different people. According to the view under discussion, knowledge of results is *feedback*, which people can use to adjust their behavior. It's sometimes argued, however, that the feedback is actually a *reinforcer* (Kulhavy & Stock, 1989). That's a rather different view of what's going on.

What's the role of reward and punishment in the self-regulation view? People whose work is discussed in this chapter don't entirely agree. Some see reward, particularly self-reward, as

important. For example, Bandura (1986) holds that the self-reward or self-praise that a person engages in after attaining a desired goal is a crucial aspect of self-regulation.

On the other side of the disagreement, we've argued that this concept isn't needed (Carver & Scheier, 1981, 1990). In our view, it doesn't add anything to say that the person engages in self-praise after goal attainment. Although self-praise may occur, it's only a reaction to an event; the *event* is what matters. The crucial events, in this view, are the goal attainment and the person's realization of how the goal was reached.

The concept of reinforcement comes from learning theory. In thinking about this issue, it's of interest that learning theorists have long argued about the role of reinforcement in learning. Tolman (1932) believed that

reward—even to a laboratory rat—doesn't stamp anything in but just provides information that the animal can learn from. Specifically, the animal learns what leads to what, by experiencing the events in association with one another. Tolman said rewards and punishments aren't necessary for learning, but they can draw attention to aspects of the learning situation that are particularly relevant.

It's also been found that a simple social reinforcer such as saying "good" has more impact if you've been led to believe that the person saying "good" does so only rarely (Babad, 1973). Presumably, this is because events that are rare provide more information than events that are common. That finding joins with Tolman in suggesting that it may be the *informational value* of the reinforcer that matters, not the reinforcer itself.

SELF-DIRECTED ATTENTION AND THE ACTION OF THE COMPARATOR

Does human behavior follow the pattern of feedback control? One source of evidence is studies of the effects of self-directed attention. It's been argued that when you have a goal or intention in mind, directing your attention toward yourself engages the comparator of the loop that's managing your behavior (Carver & Scheier, 1981, 1998).

In some studies of self-directed attention, participants are exposed to things that remind them of themselves (e.g., an audience, a TV camera, or a mirror that shows their image). In other studies, researchers measure the strength of people's natural tendency to be self-reflective (Fenigstein, Scheier, & Buss, 1975; Trapnell & Campbell, 1999).

The idea that self-directed attention engages a comparator leads to two kinds of predictions. First, self-focus should increase the tendency to compare goals with current behavior. It's hard to study that, but here's an indirect way. Create a situation in which people can't make a mental comparison between a goal and behavior without getting some concrete information. Put people in that situation, then measure how much they seek the information. Presumably, more seeking of the information implies more comparison. In several studies based on this reasoning, self-focused persons sought comparison–relevant information more than less self-focused persons (Scheier & Carver, 1983).

If self-directed attention engages a comparator, something else should happen as well: Behavior should be regulated more closely to the goal. It does. As an illustration, people in one project (Carver, 1975) said they either opposed or favored the use of punishment as a teaching tool. Later, all of them had to punish someone for errors in learning. All were told to use their own judgment about how much punishment to use. Only those who were self-aware actually did so. Many other studies also show that self-focus leads to goal matching, ranging quite widely in the standards of comparison evoked for use.

HIERARCHICAL ORGANIZATION

These studies suggest that feedback processes might be involved in behavior. But a feedback loop is pretty simple. How do you actually get behavior out of it? One answer is that feedback loops may exist in layers. William Powers (1973) argued that this type of organization is what makes physical action possible. Others have made related arguments (e.g., Broadbent, 1977; Gallistel, 1980; Rosenbaum, 1987, 1990; Toates, 2006; Vallacher & Wegner, 1987).

The notion of a **feedback hierarchy** assumes there are both high-level and low-level goals that relate to each other. You have the goal of being a particular possible self, but you may also have the goal of having clean clothes to wear and the goal of making it to your psychology class on time. How do these things fit together? Recall the structure of the feedback loop from Figure 17.3. Powers says that in a hierarchy, the *behavioral output* of a high-level loop consists of setting a goal for a lower-level loop (see Figure 17.4). High-level loops don't "behave" by physical actions but by providing guides to the loops below them. Only the very lowest loops actually create physical acts, by controlling muscle groups (Rosenbaum, 1987, 1990, 2005). Each layer receives feedback appropriate to its level of abstraction.

The levels proposed by Powers that are most relevant to personality are shown in Figure 17.4. At the top are very abstract qualities he called **system concepts.** An example is the broad sense of ideal self people try to maintain. Richard, the person whose behavior is outlined in Figure 17.4, is trying to live up to his desired self-image. Doing this resembles the experience of self-actualization (Chapter 14). It promotes the sense of personal wholeness and integration.

People don't just go out and *be* their ideal selves, though. Trying to attain that ideal self means trying to live in accord with the **principles** it specifies. Thus, Powers called the next level *principle control.* Principles are broad guidelines. They specify broad qualities of behavior, which can be displayed in many ways. When they're active, principles help you decide what activities to start and what choices to make as you do them (Verplanken & Holland, 2002). Principles tend to correspond to traits.

As Figure 17.4 shows, Richard's ideal self includes a principle corresponding to *thoughtfulness.* This principle can be used as a guide for many kinds of action, including taking this opportunity to buy flowers. As another example, the principle of *honesty* would lead a person to ignore an opportunity to cheat on an exam. The principle of

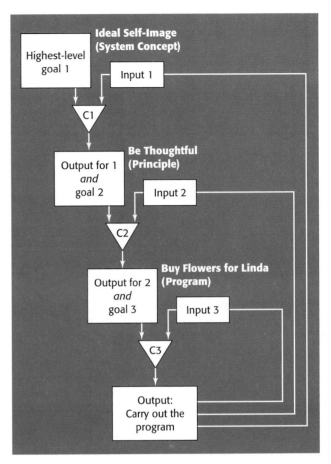

FIGURE 17.4
Diagram of a three-level hierarchy of feedback systems. This diagram shows the "cascade" of control that flows from higher-level loops to lower-level ones. High-level loops set the goals for the loops directly below them. The levels of control illustrated here are those at the top of the hierarchy proposed by Powers (1973). The diagram shows a cross-section of the behavior of a man who is actively attempting to (1) match his self-perceptions to his idealized self by (2) following the principle of *thoughtfulness,* which is being manifested (3) in the programmatic activity of buying flowers for his wife.

Calvin and Hobbes
by Bill Watterson

Though principles often have overtones of goodness and morality, that need not be the case. Principles can also be self-serving. What's necessary is that a principle must be abstract enough to apply to many kinds of behavior.

Calvin and Hobbes copyright Watterson. Distributed by Universal Press Syndicate. Reprinted with permission. All rights reserved.

frugality would lead a person to choose a moderately priced restaurant over an expensive one.

What defines something as a *principle* is its abstractness and broad applicability, not its social appropriateness. Thus, expedience is a principle, even though it's not socially desirable (see the cartoon). Knowing only that something is a principle doesn't tell what direction it pulls behavior. For example, it's been shown that different principles can lead people either to support affirmative action or to oppose it (Reyna, Henry, Korfmacher, & Tucker, 2005).

Just as people don't go out and *be* their ideal selves, they don't just go out and *do* principles. Principles act by specifying **programs** (or by specifying decisions within programs; see Figure 17.4). A program resembles a script (Schank & Abelson, 1977). It specifies a general course of action but with many details left out. Enacting a program (or script) thus requires you to make choices within a larger set of possibilities. Programs, in effect, are strategies.

The principle of *thoughtfulness* led Richard to enter the program of buying flowers. This program is partly specified: Stop at the florist, pick out flowers, and pay for them. But which flowers he gets will depend on what's available; he can pay with cash or a credit card; and he may or may not have to put money into a parking meter.

Two more things about this example: Both stem from the fact that there are several ways to conform to this principle. First, Richard might have chosen another program—making Linda a special dinner or washing her car. Entering any of these programs would conform to the same principle. Second, matching the principle of *thoughtfulness* didn't require *entering* a program; the principle might have come into play *during* a program. For example, if Linda had told him to buy flowers on his way home, he'd be buying flowers anyway. The *thoughtfulness* principle might have become active in the midst of the buying-flowers program, leading him to decide to buy Linda's favorite flower, even though it's out of season and therefore expensive.

Much of what people do in their day-to-day lives seems programlike, or scriptlike. Most of the intentions you form in an average day involve programs. Doing the laundry, going to a store or the movies, studying for an exam, fixing lunch, trying to get noticed by that person in class—all of these are programs. They all have general courses of predictable acts and subgoals, but exactly what you do at a given point can vary, depending on the situation.

Most likely, there are well-learned links between many principles and the programs to which they pertain. Connections between programs and lower levels of control are probably

Much of what we do in our day-to-day lives, such as grocery shopping, has a programlike or scriptlike character.

even stronger. For example, there's evidence that when a person has a goal in mind that concerns travel, it automatically activates information about a plausible and common way to get there (Aarts & Dijksterhuis, 2000).

ISSUES CONCERNING HIERARCHICAL ORGANIZATION

Several questions come up when people think about hierarchies. For example, are all the levels active all the time? Not necessarily. People can go for a very long time without thinking about their ideal selves. Behavior often is guided for long periods by programs. To put it differently, lower levels may sometimes be *functionally superordinate*.

That's probably what happens when people do the routine "maintenance" activities of life: buying groceries, washing dishes, driving to school. At such times, people may often lose all sight of higher-order goals. Note also that programs inherently require decisions. That in itself may cause them to be attended to more often than other levels. It's interesting that when people describe themselves, they tend to describe things they *do,* rather than what they *are* (McGuire & McGuire, 1986). This suggests that the program level may be especially salient to people.

When low levels are functionally superordinate, it's almost as though the higher layers were disconnected. But the disconnect is rarely permanent. Goals at high levels can be affected by things that happen while lower levels are in charge. The effect can be either good or bad. A program (buying shoes on sale) can help you match a principle (frugality), even if that's not why you're doing it (you just liked the shoes). A program can also create a problem, if it violates the principle. For example, many health-conscious people have a principle of eating lowfat foods. But if they get caught up in the action at a party (with lower levels in charge), they may eat lots of greasy food, which they will later regret.

We said earlier that goals can be achieved in diverse ways. Any specific act can also be done in the service of diverse principles. For example, Richard in Figure 17.4 could have been buying flowers not to be thoughtful but to be manipulative—to get on Linda's good side. The same motions would occur, but they'd be aimed at a very different higher-order goal.

Another point is that people often try to match several values at once—at the *same level*. Sometimes the values are compatible (being frugal while being conscientious). In other cases they're less so (being frugal while dressing well; getting good grades while having a very active social life). In such cases, matching one value creates a problem for the other (Emmons & King, 1988; Emmons, King, & Sheldon, 1993). This defines **goal conflict.**

EVIDENCE OF HIERARCHIES

Is behavior organized hierarchically? Work by Robin Vallacher and Dan Wegner suggests that it is (Vallacher & Wegner, 1985, 1987). They began by asking how people view their actions, a process called **action identification.** Any behavior can be identified in a wide variety of ways. For example, taking class notes can be identified as "sitting in a room and making marks on paper with a pen," "taking notes in a class," "trying to do well in a course," or "getting an education." Some identities are concrete; others more abstract. How you think about your actions presumably says something about the goals you're using in your behavior.

Vallacher and Wegner held that people generally tend to see their actions in as high level a way as they can. Thus, you're more likely to see your student behavior as "attending classes," "getting an education," or "listening to a lecture" than as "walking into a building, sitting down, and listening to someone talk." But if a person starts to struggle in regulating an act at the high level, he or she retreats to a lower-level identity for the action. In terms of the previous section, difficulty at a high level causes a lower level to become functionally superordinate. Using that lower-level identity, the person irons out the problem. As the problem is resolved, the person tends to drift again to a higher-level identification.

For example, if you're in class taking notes and having trouble understanding the lecture, you may stop thinking of your behavior as "taking helpful notes" and start thinking of it as "writing down as much as I possibly can so I can try to figure it out later." If the lecture gets easier to follow after a while, you may be able to start thinking of your behavior in more abstract terms again.

EMOTIONS

How does the self-regulation view treat emotions? Long ago, Herb Simon (1967) argued that emotions are *crucial*. People often have several goals in place at the same time, which they have to pursue sequentially (e.g., you go to a gas station, then stop for lunch, then drive to the beach, where you study for an exam while getting some sun, and then you go home and do some laundry if there's time). The order of doing things is partly a matter of priorities—how important each goal is to you at the time.

Priorities are subject to rearrangement. Simon argued that emotions are an internal call to rearrange. *Anxiety* is a signal that you're not paying enough attention to personal well-being (an important goal) and you need to do so. *Anger* may be a signal that your autonomy (another goal that people value) needs to have a higher priority.

Implicit in this analysis is that progress toward many goals is monitored outside awareness, as you focus on one goal at a time. If a problem arises for some goal, emotion pertaining to it arises. If the problem gets big enough, the emotion becomes intense enough to interrupt what you're doing. For example, look back at the goals described two paragraphs earlier. If you had decided to put off buying gas until after doing the other things, you might start to feel anxious about maybe being stranded at the beach with an empty gas tank. If the anxiety got strong enough, you'd change your mind (reprioritize) and stop for the gas after all.

Simon's theory fits the idea that emotions are produced by a system that monitors "how well things are going" toward attaining goals (Carver & Scheier, 1990, 1998). When progress is going well, you feel good. When it's going *really* well, you feel joy, even ecstasy. When things are going poorly, on the other hand, negative feelings arise: frustration, anxiety, or sadness. If you're actually losing ground, the negative feelings intensify. In all these cases, the emotion is a subjective readout of how well you're doing regarding that goal.

Evidence fitting this comes from several studies. For example, Hsee and Abelson (1991, Experiment 2) put people in hypothetical situations where they'd bet money on sports events. Each viewed a display showing progress toward winning—at different rates—and indicated how satisfied he or she would be with each event. Of special interest are events in which the starting and ending points were identical but the rate of change differed. Participants liked the faster change better than the slower one.

Feelings have implications for action. As suggested by Simon (1967), when something is going badly and negative feelings arise, you engage more effort toward the goal the feeling relates to. If you're behind at something and feeling frustrated, you try harder. If you're scared of something, you try harder to get away from it. How positive feelings affect action is less clear. It's been argued, though, that they also affect priorities (Carver, 2003). When you feel good about some goal, you can "coast" a little on that one and check to see if anything else needs your attention. This would allow the priority of another goal to rise.

EFFECTS OF EXPECTANCIES: EFFORT VERSUS DISENGAGEMENT

Until the last section, the focus of this chapter has been mostly on behavior when no major difficulties arise. However, things don't always work so well. People often encounter obstacles when they try to carry out their intentions and attain their goals. What happens then?

As we just said, obstacles cause negative feelings. If the obstacles are serious, they also tend to disrupt effort—sometimes briefly, sometimes longer. This can occur before you start (if you anticipate trouble) or while you're acting (if snags arise along the way). The interruptions remove you temporarily from the action and lead you to judge how likely you are to reach your goal, given the situation you're in.

Expectancy of success is a concept idea that's come up in other chapters. We discussed it in the motive viewpoint (Chapter 5). We also discussed it in social learning theory (Chapter 13) and in Mischel's cognitive view (Chapter 16). The expectancy concept actually provides a major link between learning models and cognitive self-regulation models.

The way expectancies function in self-regulation models is essentially the same as in the other theories. Confidence of overcoming obstacles leads people back into self-regulatory effort. With enough doubt, however, people are more likely to **disengage**, or reduce their effort toward goal attainment. Perhaps they will even abandon the goal altogether, temporarily or permanently (Klinger, 1975; Kukla, 1972; R. A. Wright, 1996).

Effort is a continuum. It can be useful, though, to think of variations in effort as forming a rough dichotomy (see Figure 17.5). Think of it as the question of whether you keep trying or quit. In many cases, people have only those two options. This view of the impact of expectancies lets the person who's walked into a corner back out of it and take up another goal (Wrosch, Dunne, Scheier, & Schulz, 2006; Wrosch, Scheier, Carver, & Schulz, 2003).

Different people emphasize different facets of expectancies. We've focused on confidence versus doubt of attaining desired outcomes, rather than the *reasons* the confidence or doubt exists (Carver & Scheier, 1998). Bandura, in contrast (described in Chapter 13), stresses self-efficacy expectancy: believing one has the personal capability of doing the action that needs to be done. Whatever variation you prefer, there's evidence that expectancies play an important role in determining how hard people try and how well they do. People who are confident about reaching their goals (or who hold perceptions of high efficacy) are more persistent and perform better than doubtful people. They do better in many ways (see also Box 17.2).

For example, consider a study of women who were learning to protect themselves against sexual assault (Ozer & Bandura, 1990). They learned skills for self-defense and verbal techniques to deal with dangerous situations. At several points, they rated their confidence that they could do both the physical maneuvers and the verbal tactics. They also rated their confidence that they could turn off thoughts about sexual

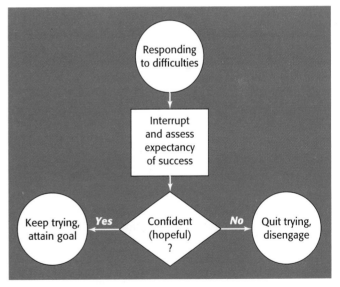

FIGURE 17.5
When people confront difficulties in moving toward their goals, they sometimes interrupt their efforts to assess the likelihood of succeeding. Sufficient confidence leads to renewed efforts; sufficient doubt leads to giving up. All responses seem ultimately to fall into one of these two classes.

BOX 17.2   CONFIDENCE ABOUT LIFE

Effects of Generalized Optimism

In the main text, we say that expectancies are an important determinant of people's behavior. The expectancies considered there are mostly specific ones: confidence versus doubt about making a desired impression, achieving an academic goal, or carrying out a specific strategy. However, just as people have both specific and general goals, people also have both specific and generalized expectancies. What's been known for centuries as *optimism* is generalized confidence; what's been known as *pessimism* is generalized doubt—not about one specific outcome but about life in general (Scheier & Carver, 1992; Scheier, Carver, & Bridges, 2001). This generalized confidence is very traitlike. It's quite stable over time and seems genetically influenced (Plomin et al., 1992).

Optimism, as a dimension of personality, has been studied for a long

while, and a lot is known about it (Scheier et al., 2001). People who are optimistic about life are better liked than pessimists (Carver, Kus, & Scheier, 1994). Probably for that reason, they're better at forming social networks when they go to a new environment (Brissette, Scheier, & Carver, 2002). They are also better in relationships, because they are more supportive of their partners in resolving conflicts (Srivastava, McGonigal, Richards, Butler, & Gross, 2006).

Much of the research on optimism deals with its influences on how people deal with stressful situations (Scheier et al., 2001). Optimists deal better with adversity than pessimists, whether experiencing a missile attack (Zeidner & Hammer, 1992) or confronting cancer (Carver et al., 1993; Stanton & Snider, 1993) or heart disease (Scheier et al., 1989). They have less distress, are more focused on moving forward, and are less likely to withdraw from their usual activities (Carver, Lehman, & Antoni, 2003). They seem more prepared to accept

the reality of the stressful experience (Carver et al., 1993). They don't stick their heads in the sand and ignore threats to their well-being. They attend to risks in their lives but only if the risk concerns a serious problem and also pertains to them (Aspinwall & Brunhart, 1996).

Most of what is known about optimism concerns people's actions and their subjective emotional experiences. At least a little research has gone beyond that, however, looking at people's physical responses to adversity. For example, Scheier et al. (1999) found that after major heart surgery, pessimists were more likely than optimists to require rehospitalization. Optimists literally healed better. Other recent studies have related optimism to lower risk of cancer death (Allison, Guichard, Fung, & Gilain, 2003) and cardiovascular death (Giltay, Kamphuis, Kalmijn, Zitman, & Kromhout, 2006). The idea that this personality trait may have pervasive health benefits is now being actively investigated.

---

assault. The key outcome was ratings of the extent to which they took part in (or avoided) activities outside the home.

The results were complex, but a broad theme runs through them. The sense of confidence was very important. The women's confidence that they could use their new coping skills related to perceptions of less vulnerability and ultimately to behavior. In sum, confidence in diverse areas helped the women cope more effectively with their social world.

PARTIAL DISENGAGEMENT

We've distinguished sharply here between effort and giving up. Sometimes, though, the line blurs. Sometimes a goal can't be attained, but another one can be substituted for it (Freund & Baltes, 2002; Wrosch et al., 2003). For example, a man who enjoys sports becomes wheelchair bound. He can't play football, but he can turn to sports that don't require using his legs.

Sometimes disengagement involves only scaling back from a lofty goal in a given domain to a less demanding one. This is disengagement in the sense that the person is giving up the first goal while adopting the lesser one. It's more limited in the sense that it doesn't entail leaving the domain. This partial disengagement keeps you engaged in the domain you had wanted to quit. By scaling back, giving up in a small way, you keep trying to move ahead, thus *not* giving up in a larger way.

We should stress that whether giving up is bad or good depends on the context (Wrosch et al., 2006; Wrosch et al., 2003). In some cases, disengagement is bad. It's a poor way of coping with the difficulties of life. These are cases where being persistent would pay off in success. In such cases, the goal shouldn't be abandoned so easily.

On the other hand, it's often necessary to give up or defer goals when circumstances make it hard or impossible to reach them. For example, it's senseless to hold onto a lost love who will never return. Giving up sometimes is the right response. But when it *is* the right response, it sometimes doesn't happen. In this case, the failure to disengage leads to continuing distress. We return to this point later on, when we consider problems in behavior.

Further Themes in Self-Regulation

The chapter thus far has presented a relatively straightforward picture in which people form intentions and then shift to a mode of implementing the intentions and which may go well or poorly. We've talked a little about the fact that people have goals at various levels of abstraction and the fact that people have many goals at once (and thus many semi-autonomous feedback loops going at the same time). Here, we bring up three complications to this picture.

APPROACH AND AVOIDANCE

The chapter to this point has been based on the idea that self-regulation involves moving toward goals. An issue that came up in other chapters also comes up here. Specifically, not all actions involve *approach*. Some involve *avoidance*. By this, we don't mean disengaging from a desired (approach) goal. We mean actively trying to get away (or stay away) from a threat. Because no word seems quite parallel to *goal* for the thing you try to avoid, we've sometimes called it an *antigoal* (Carver & Scheier, 1998).

Discussion of the motivation view on personality (Chapter 5) noted that two opposite motives can underlie the same action. As an example, you can try to perform well at a task (action) either to approach success or to avoid failure. Those motives aren't the same (and sometimes the behavior isn't quite the same either). Virtually anything you think about doing can be viewed in terms of either *making* one thing happen or *preventing* something else from happening (E. T. Higgins, 1997). The same issue arises in this chapter.

As it happens, there is a category of feedback processes that enlarges discrepancies, rather than reducing them. That seems to provide a basis for a self-regulatory model of avoidance. It is clear, as well, that emotions are involved both when trying to approach and trying to avoid. In either case, you can be doing well or doing poorly. Thus, the self-regulatory model has a place for both kinds of processes, approach and avoidance. In the interest of minimizing confusion, though, we will not talk much more about the avoidance function here (see Carver & Scheier, 2007).

INTENTION-BASED AND STIMULUS-BASED ACTION

The chapter thus far has also focused mostly on behavior that is intentional: behavior that starts with the setting of goals. However, there is a good deal of evidence that not all behavioral self-regulation happens that way. Some behavior—maybe a lot of it— is cued by stimulus qualities that the person encounters.

Early hints of this phenomenon came from studies intended to show that interpretive schemas were closely linked to specifications for action. These studies used

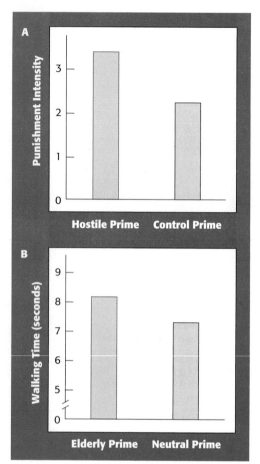

FIGURE 17.6

Effects of priming an interpretive schema on behavior related to that schema.
(A) People who had been exposed to hostile content in a sentence-formation task gave punishments of greater intensity in a later task than people exposed to less hostile content. (B) People who had been exposed to elements of the elderly stereotype in a sentence-formation task took longer to walk to the elevator when leaving the experiment than people exposed to neutral words. *Sources: Panel A is based on data from Carver et al., 1983, Study 2; Panel B is based on data from Bargh et al., 1996, Experiment 2.*

priming techniques to activate schemas and found influences on overt behavior. In one case, people had to form sentences from scrambled sets of words (Carver, Ganellen, Froming, & Chambers, 1983). For some people but not others, the word sets had hostile content. Later, all had to punish someone else while teaching a concept. Those who'd read the words with hostile content gave stronger punishment than did the others (see Figure 17.6, A).

Another study used a similar task to prime the stereotype of the elderly (Bargh, Chen, & Burrows, 1996). Some people read many words pertaining to the stereotype; some did not. All then received credit for participation. The question of interest was how long it took them to walk down the corridor on their way out. Those exposed to the stereotype of the elderly walked more slowly, as though they themselves were old (see Figure 17.6, B).

The interpretation of these effects goes like this: To form sentences from the words, you have to understand the words. Understanding the words requires activating nodes of meaning in memory. This activation spreads to nodes bearing on *behavior.* This quality then emerges in the person's own behavior (Bargh, 1997). In fact, the link goes both ways: Acting in a way that fits a stereotype brings that stereotype to mind for use in later perception (Mussweiler, 2006).

Findings such as these are part of a large and growing literature on automaticity (some of which was mentioned in Chapter 16; see also Moors & De Houwer, 2006). Much of this work has been done by John Bargh and his colleagues (Bargh, 1997; Bargh & Chartrand, 1999; Bargh & Ferguson, 2000; Dijksterhuis & Bargh, 2001). Many studies now show clearly that goals can be activated (and people pursue them) with no knowledge that it's happening (for review see Bargh & Williams, 2006). Indeed, some of the studies show that goals can be activated by subliminal stimuli.

Although it's impressive to see how people's minds can be tricked by various sorts of priming, the more important message is that automaticity is important in behavior. Indeed, it's been argued that habitual actions occur in much the same way as the priming effects: Situations activate goals that are associated with them, and behavior follows the goals automatically (Aarts & Dijksterhuis, 2000). Similarly, categories of people activate specific responses that are well learned to that group, and behavior follows automatically (Jonas & Sassenberg, 2006).

Nonetheless, the idea that behavioral qualities can be activated and slide into the ongoing flow of behavior without your awareness is, in some ways, startling. Your actions can be affected by things you hear on the radio or read in the paper, by conversations you have, by random stimuli you encounter—and *you don't even know it.* This idea provides an interpretation of modeling effects (Chapter 13), in which people repeat things they observe others do (Carver et al., 1983). People mimic, without realizing it, the postures and gestures of their partners in interactions (Chartrand & Bargh, 1999). The pervasiveness of such effects leads some people to ask whether behavior is best seen as *directed* or as *self-organizing* (Carver & Scheier, 2002; Vallacher & Nowak, 1997; Vallacher, Read, & Nowak, 2002).

Can both be right? Certainly. In Chapter 16, we described dual-mode models of cognition. One mode is said to use connectionist, associationist processes and the other, symbolic processes. The first mode is characterized as *intuitive,* whereas the second is characterized as *rational.* It seems reasonable to suggest that the dual-process models can also help reconcile how intentions and automaticity both influence action (Bargh & Williams, 2006; Kuhl, 2000; Rothbart, Ellis, Rueda, & Posner, 2003; Strack & Deutsch, 2004).

The interpretation goes like this. The intuitive system functions automatically. When a stimulus happens to cue an action quality, that action quality slips into the behavioral stream. It seems likely that the action quality has to be either simple or well learned for this to happen. That is, the intuitive system is capable of handling fairly complicated events (Kuhl, 2000), but its capacities derive from associations. It's good at being impulsive and quickly responsive, but it's not good at thinking things through.

The rational system, in contrast, is brought into play when you form an intention, or set a goal purposefully. When this system is in charge, behavior is self-regulated in an effortful, top-down manner. It is effortful, planful (Eisenberg et al., 2004). Its purpose is to handle situations that *have* to be thought through, because no automatic cue-driven response is ready to go. Being organized to think things through, however, makes it slower to act (Keller, Wascher, Prinz, Waszak, Koch, & Rosenbaum, 2006).

In talking about the cognitive view in Chapter 16, we noted that people have a natural tendency to conserve mental resources while thinking, because they have many things on their minds at once. The same principle is true here. Being able to do something with little thought is extremely useful, because it lets you think about other things at the same time as you're doing whatever you're doing (Wood, Quinn, & Kashy, 2002).

SELF-REGULATION AS SELF-CONTROL

Another issue that should receive attention is that acts of *self-regulation* sometimes (though not always) entail *self-control.* That is, sometimes people act to restrain behavior aimed at one goal to make it possible to attain another goal. Self-control always represents a case of conflict, because the goals are incompatible.

Situations entailing self-control arise in a great many circumstances, and the conflicts in question apply to very important practical problems (see Part VI in Baumeister & Vohs, 2004). This situation exists, for example, in the context of dieting. The dieter is motivated by hunger to eat and is motivated to restrain eating. The same conflict arises in circumstances surrounding substance abuse and domestic violence. People who are effective at self-control employ a variety of strategies to counteract temptations that keep them from gaining the long-term goal (Trope & Fishbach, 2000, 2005).

Discussions of self-control failure (Baumeister & Heatherton, 1996) tend to portray the situations as involving a relatively automatic tendency to act in one way that is opposed by a planful and effortful tendency to restrain the act. The action that is being inhibited is often characterized as an *impulse,* a desire that would automatically be translated into action unless it is controlled (perhaps in part because this action is habitual, perhaps in part because it is more primal). Once again, this seems to have overtones of the two-mode models. Consistent with this, there is evidence that identifying an action in high-level terms makes it easier to disregard immediate outcomes in favor of delayed outcomes (Fujita, Trope, Liberman, & Levin-Sagi, 2006).

Assessment

The self-regulation view on personality is fairly new. It's been far more theoretical than applied. Nevertheless, it offers a few suggestions concerning personality assessment.

ASSESSMENT OF SELF-REGULATORY QUALITIES

The view described in this chapter emphasizes the existence of several processes in human experience. This emphasis suggests it may be useful to measure individual differences in self-regulatory processes (Williams, Moore, Pettibone, & Thomas, 1992).

For example, *private self-consciousness* (Fenigstein et al., 1975) is a tendency to be self-reflective—to think about your feelings, motives, actions, and so on. (The term *self-conscious* here doesn't mean "embarrassment," just "self-focus.") It may follow that people high in self-consciousness are careful and thorough self-regulators (maybe even obsessive–compulsive ones). They notice it if their actions don't match their intentions, and they adjust accordingly. People with less self-consciousness are more random and less guided in their behavior (see also Box 17.3). Consistent with this, self-consciousness relates to conscientiousness from the five-factor model (Trapnell & Campbell, 1999). There's even evidence that those high in self-consciousness are more prone to engage in self-regulation that's automatic and nonconscious (Hull, Slone, Meteyer, & Matthews, 2002).

BOX 17.3   REDUCTION OF SELF-REGULATION

Deindividuation and Alcohol

Elsewhere in the chapter, we described how self-focused attention causes better self-regulation toward salient standards. If greater self-focus makes behavior *better* regulated, it follows that reduced self-focus causes behavior to be *more poorly* regulated. But what does this mean? It doesn't mean the person stops behaving altogether. It means the behavior is more likely to fluctuate, to become less carefully thought out and more responsive to cues of the moment.

Two bodies of research have studied the effects of reduced self-awareness. Their origins are different, but the effects are strikingly similar. One set of studies concerns deindividuation. The other concerns alcohol.

Deindividuation is an experience people have when they become immersed in a group. In so doing, they can lose their sense of personal identity. They are more likely to use obscenities (Festinger, Pepitone, & Newcomb, 1952), to be aggressive (Prentice-Dunn & Rogers, 1980, 1982), and to engage in childish and uninhibited acts. There's evidence that deindividuation involves loss of self-focus (Diener, 1979; Mullen, 1986; Prentice-Dunn & Rogers, 1982, 1989). It's easy to see the effects as reflecting poor self-regulation regarding programs and principles that normally guide behavior. Thus, there's a tendency to act impulsively, to respond to cues of the moment rather than to use well-thought-out plans. Behavior becomes a string of spontaneous sequences, rather than a pattern guided by higher-order values.

These effects of deindividuation are remarkably similar to some of the effects of alcohol. People who've been drinking are often inappropriately aggressive and overly responsive to cues of the moment. Alcohol is widely regarded as a releaser of inhibitions, and it's sometimes used intentionally for that purpose. As a group, the behavioral effects of alcohol seem to reflect a loss of careful self-regulation. As with deindividuation, the result seems to be a string of sequences of spontaneous acts, rather than carefully planned activity.

Furthermore, the behavioral effects of alcohol and deindividuation seem to have at least one process in common. Alcohol appears to act (at least partly) by reducing self-awareness (Hull, 1981; Hull & Rielly, 1986) and executive function (Giancola, 2004). As this happens, you stop monitoring your values and intentions. Your behavior becomes more disorganized, impulsive, and fragmented. Thus, two distinct sets of phenomena—deindividuation and alcohol intoxication—can be interpreted by a single principle. Both seem to involve interference with a process that underlies the normal self-regulation of behavior.

Note that self-focus by itself is relatively content free. That is, its self-regulatory effect is largely unrelated to the goal being used. Thus, an athlete who's self-conscious should be sure to work out. A self-conscious biology major should be sure she's up to date in her biology reading. A self-conscious musician should focus closely on moving toward the music-related goals he's set for himself.

Trapnell and Campbell (1999) distinguished two aspects of self-consciousness. They think two motives underlie it: curiosity (which is a growth-oriented motive) and the desire to probe negative feeling states (which ultimately is a safety-seeking motive, if the source of the feelings can be isolated). They created a measure called the Rumination–Reflection Questionnaire, to focus separately on these motives. *Rumination* items refer to being unable to put something behind you. *Reflection* items refer to being fascinated and inquisitive. Not surprisingly, reflection relates to openness to experience, and rumination relates to neuroticism.

Another self-regulatory function that might be useful to assess is whether people tend to view their behavior in high-level or lower-level terms. Vallacher and Wegner (1989) developed a measure called the Behavior Identification Form for that purpose. They argued that people with similar traits can differ greatly from each other if they think of their goals at different levels. People who identify their actions at high levels tend to look at the "big picture," whether they're socializing, studying, or making music. People who identify their actions at lower levels tend to focus more on the "nuts and bolts" of what's going on, no matter the domain.

ASSESSMENT OF GOALS

We don't mean to imply that the content of behavior doesn't matter to this viewpoint. As we said earlier, the self-regulation view emphasizes *goals*. It would seem useful, from this view, to assess people's goals and how they're organized (Emmons, 1986; Pervin, 1983). One might even want to assess what sort of "possible selves" the person has in mind (Markus & Nurius, 1986). Knowing what goals are salient to a person might be more informative than knowing other aspects of what the person is "like."

An example of this is the technique Emmons (1986) used to assess personal striving. He asked people to describe their recurring personal goals in four areas: work/school, home/family, social relationships, and leisure/recreation. People were to think about their own intentions and goals and not to compare themselves with other people. Within these guidelines, they were free to write down any striving that seemed important to them. This produced an individualized picture of the goal values that occupied the person's mind over a given span of time.

Problems in Behavior and Behavior Change

Given how new the self-regulation point of view is, one might expect it to have had little or no impact on understanding either problems or therapy. This isn't so, however (see J. C. Hamilton, Greenberg, Pyszczynski, & Cather, 1993; Ingram, 1986; Merluzzi, Rudy, & Glass, 1981). Self-regulation models have made a number of suggestions about those topics (see also Box 17.4).

PROBLEMS AS CONFLICTS AMONG GOALS AND LACK OF STRATEGY SPECIFICATIONS

The hierarchical model suggests several ways for problems to arise (Carver & Scheier, 1990, 1998). The simplest way stems from the idea of a deeply rooted conflict between

BOX 17.4   REGULATING WITH THE WRONG FEEDBACK

A central theme of this chapter is that people act and then check to see whether they're doing what they intended to do. Just how fundamental is this principle? Research from health psychology suggests that feedback matters so much that people will seek it out and rely on it even when it doesn't tell them anything. They'll rely on it even when they're *told* it doesn't tell them anything. They'll rely on it even though relying on it creates *problems.*

Consider people being treated for hypertension, or high blood pressure (Baumann & Leventhal, 1985; Meyer, Leventhal, & Gutmann, 1985). People with hypertension have no reliable symptoms, yet most quickly come to believe they can isolate symptoms of it. Indeed, the longer they're in treatment, the more likely they are to think so. In one study, more than 90% of those in treatment for more than three months

claimed to be able to tell (Meyer et al., 1985).

Can they? By and large, no. In another study (Baumann & Leventhal, 1985), self-reports of elevated blood pressure were well correlated with self-reports of symptoms and self-reported moods. But they were virtually unrelated to actual elevation.

Unfortunately, people with hypertension use their symptoms as a guide to whether their blood pressure's up. They then make important decisions on the basis of those symptoms. In particular, they use the symptom to tell them whether to take their medication. If they think their blood pressure isn't up (because the symptom isn't there), they don't take the medication. If they feel no symptoms, they often drop out of treatment altogether. This can lead to serious medical problems—all because the people are relying on faulty feedback to guide their actions.

This example concerns a physical problem, rather than a psychological

one. But the same pattern can also be seen in cases where people misinterpret others' reactions to them or rely on the wrong kinds of cues. If you take someone's frown as a sign of rejection when really he's remembering he forgot to put the cat out, you may behave in ways that create problems for you, rather than help you attain your desired ends.

These examples also illustrate how much people rely on feedback to guide behavior. If the people with hypertension perceive a present state (symptom) that is discrepant from their standard (no symptoms), they act to reduce the discrepancy (take their medication). They're using feedback, just as the self-regulation approach says people do all the time. One view of such phenomena is that people *need* feedback. The natural tendency to use feedback is so strong that people will continue to do so even when the feedback they're using is actually unrelated to what they're trying to control.

goals. Conflict occurs when a person is committed to two goals that can't be attained easily at the same time (being a successful attorney while being a good wife and mother; having a close relationship while being emotionally independent). You may alternate between the goals, but this can be exhausting and distressing (Emmons & King, 1988). It requires a lot of effort to keep the conflict from re-emerging. Another solution is to decide that one goal contributes more to your higher-order values than the other and trim back investment in the other one.

A second idea suggested by the hierarchical model is that people sometimes want abstract goals but lack the know-how to reach them. If specifications from level to level are missing, self-regulation falls apart. Thus, many people want to be "fulfilled," "successful," or "well liked"; many even have more specific goals, such as "not arguing with my wife" or "being more assertive," but don't know strategies to attain them. They can't specify the concrete behavior that would move them in the right direction, so they can't make progress and are distressed. For things to be better, the strategies need to be built in (Oyserman et al., 2006).

PROBLEMS FROM AN INABILITY TO DISENGAGE

A third source of problems stems from the idea that people who expect failure quit trying. As noted earlier, sometimes this is the right response. (When you realize you've forgotten your money, you quit shopping.) Sometimes, though, it can't be done easily. Some goals are very hard to give up, even if you have grave doubts about reaching them. Examples are doing well in your chosen work and having a fulfilling relationship with another person. Why is it so hard to give them up? The hierarchical view says it's because these goals are high in your hierarchy (thus, central to your self) or represent paths to those higher goals. Sometimes abandoning a concrete goal means giving up on the person you want to be.

When people have serious doubts about attaining important goals, they show a predictable pattern. They stop trying, but soon confront that goal again. For example, having decided to give up on having a fulfilling relationship, you see a movie about relationships, which reminds you that you want one. Having given up trying to get along with a co-worker, you find you're assigned to work on a project together. Having given up on your calculus assignment, you see it's time for calculus class. Deep doubt about reaching an important goal can lead to a repeated cycle of sporadic effort, doubt, distress, disengagement, and reconfronting the goal.

Generally, when people fail at something, they want to ignore it, put it behind them, and move on. After a failure, most people avoid self-focus; after a success, they seek it out. Seeking self-focus here presumably means focusing on the *success*. Avoidance of self-focus presumably means trying to avoid thinking about the *failure*. Pyszczynski and Greenberg (1985, 1987) found, however, that people who are depressed show the *opposite* pattern: They are more likely to self-focus after a *failure* than after a success. What's going on? Apparently, depressed people have trouble giving up goals. Given a failure, they hang onto the goal, even if it wasn't important. They also let success slide by without enjoying it.

It's not always bad to keep thinking about a failure. It can motivate you to try harder next time (if there is a next time). Sometimes it leads to ideas about how to do things differently next time (Martin & Tesser, 1996). But Pyszczynski and Greenberg (1985, 1987) argued that it's dangerous to do this when the failure can't be undone (see also Wrosch et al., 2003). When people lose a big source of self-worth and focus too long on trying to regain it, major distress results. Doing this too often turns it into a habit. Focusing on failure and ignoring success not only maintains depressive symptoms, but it also makes the pattern self-perpetuating.

A similar point was made by Susan Nolen-Hoeksema and her colleagues, who argued that people who are prone to depression focus much of their attention on their sad feelings. This rumination acts to prolong the depressed state (Nolen-Hoeksema, Morrow, & Frederickson, 1993; Nolen-Hoeksema, Parker, & Larson, 1994).

SELF-REGULATION AND THE PROCESS OF THERAPY

Control-process ideas have also been used by several theorists in addressing therapy issues. Fred Kanfer and his colleagues (e.g., Kanfer & Busemeyer, 1982; Kanfer & Hagerman, 1985; Kanfer & Schefft, 1988; see also Semmer & Frese, 1985) have depicted therapy in a way that's quite compatible with the self-regulatory ideas presented throughout this chapter, as well as with the cognitive principles discussed in Chapter 16.

One point these researchers have made is that much of human behavior isn't well monitored consciously but is cued automatically and habitually. This is a point that was made early in this chapter and has been made by many cognitive theorists as well (e.g., Beck, 1972, 1976; Dodge, 1986; Semmer & Frese, 1985). Therapy is partly an effort to break down the automaticity. The person must engage in more controlled or monitored processing of what's going on. Doing this should yield responses that are more carefully thought out.

Does this mean that people dealing with problems must spend the rest of their lives carefully monitoring their actions? Some think so (Kirschenbaum, 1987). To avoid lifelong monitoring, therapy must provide a way to make the desired responses automatic in place of the problem responses. How do you do that? Presumably, it's an issue of how thoroughly coded the links are in memory. New responses become automatic by building them into memory very redundantly. This makes them more likely to be used later, when the person is on "automatic pilot." Techniques that are in widespread use—such as imagery, role-play, and practicing therapeutic changes in real-life situations—probably do exactly this.

Another point made by Kanfer and Busemeyer (1982) is that the process of therapy is itself a dynamic feedback system. It's a series of stages in which clients repeatedly use feedback, both from therapy sessions and from actions outside therapy, to adjust their movement through a long-term plan of change. The goals and issues that guide the process of changing behavior also keep changing. As you proceed, you must keep checking to make sure the concrete goals you're working toward support your higher-order goals.

THERAPY IS TRAINING IN PROBLEM SOLVING

A point that's been made by many people is that therapy is not just for the present. It should make the person a better problem solver, more equipped to deal with problems in the future (Nezu, 1987; Schefft & Lehr, 1985). Being able to generate choices and select the best ones are important skills, whether you get them through therapy or on your own.

A useful way to create choices is called **means–end analysis** (Newell & Simon, 1972). You start by noting the difference between your present state and your desired state (the *end*). Then you think of an action that would reduce the difference (a *means*). At first, the things that come to mind are abstract, involving large-scale goals. You then examine each large step and break it into subgoals. If you keep breaking things down long enough, the means–end path becomes complete and concrete enough to get you from here to there. You've created a strategy.

This line of thought has been used in a program designed to help low-income, African American middle school students develop an academic identity (Oyserman, Terry, & Bybee, 2002). Students in this program had trouble creating possible selves that involved school as a pathway to adulthood. Oyserman et al. developed a small-group intervention to do that. They gave students the experience of developing academic possible selves. Moreover, it tied those possible selves to strategies for achieving desired short-term goals and extended them to adult self-images. The program emphasized the solving of everyday problems, breaking them down by means–end analysis. The result was that the students bonded more strongly to school.

It's good to have goals broken down enough to be concrete and specified. On the other hand, it's also possible to specify things too much. In particular, following too rigid a timetable can cause you to lose motivation. People seem to do best when they have flexibility. By being able to choose when to try to move forward, they can recognize better when certain kinds of efforts are counterproductive. They're also able to be "opportunistic," or take advantage of unexpected opportunities (Hayes-Roth & Hayes-Roth, 1979).

Finally, it's important to seek accurate feedback about the effects of your actions. If you get accurate feedback, you don't have to make perfect choices. If you make continual adjustments from the feedback you get, you keep moving in the right direction. This principle, which is basic to the self-regulation approach, yields an important kind of freedom—the freedom from having to be right the first time.

Self-Regulation Theories: Problems and Prospects

As is true of the cognitive view, there have been mixed reactions to the self-regulation view on personality. It shares loose ends and unanswered questions with the cognitive view, and it has some of its own. It remains unclear whether these are fatal problems or just gaps to be filled.

One criticism of this view derives from the *robotics* metaphor. Critics say that artificial systems can't possibly be good models for human behavior. Humans have free will and make their own decisions. Robots have to rely on the programs they've been given.

One response to this criticism is that it rests on the assumption that people have free will, and not everyone shares that assumption (Bargh & Ferguson, 2000; Wegner, 2002). Further, the behavior of so-called *intelligent* artificial systems moves further every year in the direction of what looks suspiciously like self-determination (Brooks, 2002). It seems clear that how humans and artificial systems resemble and differ from each other will continue to be debated well into the future. But as the behavior of artifacts becomes more and more personlike, the debate will likely focus on increasingly subtle points.

Another response is that the robotics metaphor isn't the only one applicable to this line of thought. Electronic examples are often used to illustrate the principle of feedback control, but the feedback concept wasn't invented by engineers. It was devised to account for functions of the body (Cannon, 1932). The robotics metaphor may not always feel appropriate to living systems, but the feedback principle itself was devised precisely *for* living systems.

Another criticism sometimes made of this approach (even within the physiological metaphor) is that a model based on feedback principles is merely a model of **homeostasis** (literally, "steady state"). Homeostatic mechanisms exist to control body temperature, the levels of various elements in the blood, and many other physical parameters of the body. But how much sense does it make to think this way about something we know is always *changing*? Human behavior isn't about steady states. Doesn't the self-regulation view imply that people should be immobile and stable, or just do the same thing over and over?

Actually, no. People do regulate some things in a recurrently homeostatic way—for example, the amount of affiliation they engage in across time (O'Connor & Rosenblood, 1996)—but not always. As we noted earlier, many goals are dynamic (e.g., going on a vacation trip, having an interesting conversation with someone). Being dynamic doesn't make them any less goal-like. It just means that the whole process of matching the behavior to the goal must be dynamic as well. If the goal is to create a flow of experiences, rather than a state, then the qualities of behavior being monitored will also have this changing quality. So there's no contradiction between the fact that humans keep changing what they're doing and the idea that behavior occurs within a system of feedback control.

Greater difficulty is posed by another criticism aimed at the hierarchical model—that it fails to deal effectively with the homunculus problem. *Homunculus,* a term once used to explain how people act, refers to a hypothetical tiny man who sits inside your head and tells you what to do. That explains *your* behavior. But who tells the *little man* what to do? If people are just fancy robots, what tells the person what to do? Where do the highest goals come from, the ones that specify all the lower goals?

One response is that cognitive models typically assume an executive system that coordinates other activities, makes decisions, and so on. The executive is manifest in subjective experience as consciousness. The executive presumably has control over many other systems and thus in some ways is the analogue of the homunculus. This reasoning is plausible, but it isn't altogether satisfying.

Another response is that people have built-in goals of survival, personal coherence, and so on. These goals are vague enough that they rarely appear in consciousness, but they're pervasive enough that they constantly influence in subtle ways people's decisions about what goals to take up. Thus, behavior is being guided by values that are built into the organism but that aren't always apparent to the person. This line of reasoning is plausible too, but it's also less than fully satisfying. The homunculus problem thus remains a real one.

Another criticism of the self-regulation view (as well as the cognitive view of Chapter 16) is similar to a criticism made of the learning perspective: All this seems too much a description from the outside looking in. There's too little feel of what it means to *have* a personality. This view describes the "self-regulation of behavior," but what does it really say about personality? This approach emphasizes structure and process, rather than content. For this reason, some see the ideas as dealing with an empty shell, programmed in ways that aren't well specified, for purposes and goals that are largely arbitrary (e.g., Deci & Ryan, 2000).

There is some merit to this criticism. We note, however, that these ideas weren't devised to focus directly on *personality.* Rather, they were intended to focus on issues that stand at a slight tangent from personality. Although the ideas don't form a full theory of personality, they provide a window on the nature of human experience that seems to have some implications for personality. Will these ideas evolve into a more complete picture of personality? It's too early to know.

Despite these criticisms, the self-regulation view on personality has proven to have merit. It's had heuristic value, suggesting new places to look for information about how things work. Indeed, it makes some predictions that aren't intuitively suggested by other views. This value alone makes it likely that it will be around for a while. Only the test of time and further study will tell whether this approach will continue to emerge as a viable perspective on personality.

· SUMMARY ·

In self-regulation models, behavior is sometimes specified by interpretive schemas, if an interpretation is closely tied to an action quality. Sometimes actions follow from intentions. *Intentions* are products of a mental algebra in which personally desired outcomes and social considerations are weighed to yield an intent to act or not act.

Theory concerning self-regulation emphasizes *goals.* The goals underlying behavior have a variety of labels, including *life tasks, personal strivings, personal projects,* and *current concerns.* This view treats the structure of the self as an organization among goals. Some goals are fairly neutral, but others imply a standard of excellence. In the latter case, setting higher goals results in higher performances. This is because committing oneself to a more demanding goal focuses one's efforts more fully. If the goal is too high, though, people don't adopt it.

Some intentions concern attaining end goals; others are about implementing action plans to reach those end goals. The latter are important for ensuring that behavior actually gets done. Implementation intentions constitute linking of strategies to the contexts in which the person wants to engage them. Intentions are formed in a deliberative mindset, but once the person starts to pursue them, the person is in an implementational mindset.

Once a goal for behavior has been evoked, *self-regulation* reflects a process of feedback control. A reference value (or goal) is compared against present behavior. If the two differ, behavior is adjusted, leading to a new perception and comparison. Given that many goals are dynamic and evolving, this view emphasizes that self-regulation is a never-ending process. A single feedback loop is too simple to account for the diversity in people's actions alone, but complexity is provided by the fact that feedback systems can be organized in a hierarchy, in which one system acts by providing reference values to the system directly below it. The concept of hierarchy accounts for the fact that a goal can be attained by many kinds of actions, and also the fact that the same action can occur in service to diverse goals.

Emotions have been viewed within this framework as calls for reprioritizing one's goals. Emotions are also viewed as giving a subjective reading of how well you're progressing toward a goal. Emotions thus convey important information that has a strong influence on behavior.

When a person encounters obstacles in his or her efforts, self-regulation is interrupted and the person considers whether success or failure is likely. If the expectancies are positive enough, the person will keep trying; if not, the person may disengage from the effort and give up. Disengagement is sometimes the adaptive response, but people sometimes give up too quickly. Sometimes disengagement is only partial—goal substitution or scaling back. This keeps the person engaged, in one way, while disengaging in another.

Although much of this chapter concerns conformity to goals, self-regulation models also include discussions of avoidance. *Avoidance* means creating distance instead of conformity. Another issue is that some behavior occurs via intentions but some actions are triggered fairly automatically, even without the person's awareness. This difference between sources of influence is sometimes dealt with by dual-process models resembling those discussed in Chapter 16. An *intuitive* system promotes behaviors that are triggered by cues of the moment; a *rational* system promotes behaviors that are thought out and intentional. Self-regulation sometimes entails self-control: the prevention of behavior with one goal in service to another more important goal.

Assessment, from this view, is partly a matter of assessing individual differences in self-regulatory functions, such as self-reflectiveness or the level of abstraction at which people view their goals. This view also suggests the value of assessing goals themselves. There are several ways to conceptualize problems from this view. One possibility focuses on conflict between incompatible goals; another points to a lack of specification of midlevel behavioral reference values to guide behavior. Another emphasizes that people sometimes are unable to disengage from behaviors that are necessary for the attainment of higher-order goals. There's evidence that people who are depressed display an exaggerated inability to disengage.

Just as behavior can be construed in terms of self-regulatory systems, so can the process of behavior change induced by therapy. People in therapy use feedback from decisions they've put into practice to make further decisions. They monitor the effects of changes in behavior to determine whether the changes have produced the desired effects. One long-term goal of therapy is to make people better problem solvers through techniques such as *means–end analysis,* so that they can make their own adjustments when confronting new problems.

· GLOSSARY ·

Action identification   The way one thinks of or labels whatever action he or she is performing.

Attitude   A personal evaluation of the desirability of an action.

Comparator   A mechanism that compares two values to each other.

Deliberative mindset   A careful mindset that is used while deciding whether to take an action.

Disengage   To cease and put aside self-regulation with regard to some goal.

Feedback hierarchy   An organization of feedback loops, in which superordinate loops act by providing reference values to subordinate loops.

Feedback loop   A self-regulating system that maintains conformity to some comparison value.

Goal conflict   An attempt to self-regulate toward two incompatible goals at the same time.

Goal intention   The intention to attain some particular outcome.

Homeostasis   Regulation around a constant steady state.

Implemental mindset   A positively biased mindset used while implementing an intention to act.

Implementation intention   The intention to take specific actions in specific contexts.

Means–end analysis   The process of creating a plan to attain an overall goal (end) by breaking it into successively more concrete goals (means).

Principle   A broad, abstract action quality that could be displayed in any of several programs.

Program   A guideline for the actions that take place in some category of events (as a script).

Subjective norm   A person's impression of how other people value an action.

Subliminal stimuli   Stimuli presented too quickly to be consciously recognized.

System concept   A very abstract guide for behavior, such as an ideal sense of self.

Personality in Perspective

Overlap and Integration

Six blind men from Indostan heard of a creature called an *elephant*. They went to determine its nature. One of them bumped into the elephant's side and concluded that elephants resemble walls. A second encountered a tusk and decided elephants are like spears. The third, grasping the wriggling trunk, decided that elephants are similar to snakes. Wrapping his arms around one of its legs, the fourth concluded that elephants resemble trees. The fifth felt a floppy ear and surmised that an elephant is a type of fan. Coming upon its tail, the sixth decided that elephants are like ropes.

Each of these men was sure his investigation had led him to the truth. And, indeed, each man was partly right. But each was partly wrong, as well.

—Hindu fable

I N T H E preceding chapters, you encountered a series of viewpoints on the nature of personality. Each was rooted in its own assumptions about how best to view human nature. Each had its own way of thinking about how people function. Each had its own view of the sources of individual differences, as well as their meaning and importance. Each approach also had its drawbacks, places where things were left unexplained or even unexamined.

In writing about these perspectives on personality, we tried to give you a sense of what each was like from inside that perspective. In so doing, we tended to emphasize what makes each approach special, distinct from other approaches. The views do differ in important ways, and some points of conflict seem hard to resolve. For example, how can you reconcile the belief that people have free will (from the phenomenological perspective) with the belief that behavior is determined by patterns of prior outcomes (from the learning perspective) or the belief that behavior is determined by internal forces (from the psychoanalytic perspective)?

Our emphasis on the uniqueness of each theory may have led you to see the theories as being quite different from one another. The diversity may even have led you to wonder whether the theorists were describing the same *creature* (as would be true for anyone listening to the blind men describe the elephant). The diversity of ideas in earlier chapters raises questions: Do the various perspectives have anything in common? Is one perspective right, or better than the others? If so, which one? In this chapter, we consider these questions.

SIMILARITIES AMONG PERSPECTIVES

Psychoanalysis and Biology: Evolutionary Psychology and the Structural Model

Psychoanalysis and Evolutionary Psychology: Fixations and Mating Patterns

Psychoanalysis and Conditioning

Psychoanalysis and Self-Regulation: Hierarchy and the Structural Model

Psychoanalysis and Cognitive Processes

Social Learning and Cognitive Self-Regulation Views

Neoanalytic and Cognitive Self-Regulation Perspectives

Maslow's Hierarchy and Hierarchies of Self-Regulation

Self-Actualization and Self-Regulation

Dispositions and Their Equivalents in Other Models

RECURRENT THEMES, VIEWED FROM DIFFERENT ANGLES

Impulse and Restraint

Individual versus Group Needs

COMBINING PERSPECTIVES

Eclecticism

An Example: Biology and Learning as Complementary Influences on Personality

WHICH THEORY IS BEST?

SUMMARY

426 PART NINE: PERSONALITY IN PERSPECTIVE

Do the theories you've read about have anything in common? Yes. The first part of this chapter describes several commonalities we think are interesting. You certainly noticed some of them already, but others are more subtle and harder to spot. We also consider a couple of key issues that many different theories address, albeit from different angles.

The question of which view is *best* or *right* is harder to answer. One answer is that even big differences among theories may not mean that one is right and the others are wrong. It often happens that some issue, or some element of personality, seems very important from the view of one theory but is less important or even irrelevant from the view of another theory. As with the blind men, one theory grapples closely with an issue, but another theory doesn't even touch on it. To borrow Kelly's phrase, each theory has a *focus of convenience* that differs from that of any other theory.

Perhaps, then, various perspectives on personality are facets of a bigger picture. From this point of view, the perspectives would complement, rather than contradict, each other. Each may have some truth, but none by itself has the whole truth. The idea that the perspectives are facets of a broader picture is developed more fully in the last part of the chapter.

Similarities among Perspectives

Let's first consider some specific similarities among the views described earlier in the book. We won't point to every similarity. Rather, we will simply give you a sense of some of the connections that can be made.

We begin with commonalities between psychoanalysis and other views. Psychoanalysis is a natural starting point. It's been around for a very long time. Some people regard it as the only really comprehensive theory of personality ever devised. For both of these reasons, it's a natural comparison point for every other approach.

On the other hand, psychoanalysis is also a particularly *unusual* theory. This suggests it may be hard to find similarities between it and other approaches. As we noted earlier in the book, even neoanalytic theories, which *derive* from psychoanalysis, don't seem to share a lot with it. Nonetheless, there are several similarities worth noting. In fact, parallels have been suggested between psychoanalysis and at least three other perspectives: the biological, learning, and cognitive self-regulation perspectives.

PSYCHOANALYSIS AND BIOLOGY: EVOLUTIONARY PSYCHOLOGY AND THE STRUCTURAL MODEL

How does psychoanalysis relate to the biological approach? Freud was strongly influenced by Darwin's view of evolution, a fact that's often overlooked. Psychoanalytic theory is about beings that are deeply concerned with biological necessities: survival and reproduction. Attaining these goals is critical, because that's what biological life is all about. It should be no surprise, then, that the core of personality focuses on them. On the other hand, because humans live in a dangerous world, it's necessary to deal with complexities imposed by reality. Because we live in groups, it's eventually important to deal with another issue as well: the fact that people other than us also have needs.

This is the general line of thought that lies behind an attempt by Leak and Christopher (1982) to interpret some of Freud's ideas from the framework of evolutionary psychology. They noted that the evolutionary view sees behavior as self-serving (with one exception, to which we turn momentarily). This self-serving quality in the biological view resembles the selfish nature of Freud's concept of the id. The id is primitive and single minded about its desires. It represents the self-interested animal that our genes make us as those genes try to continue their existence.

The id isn't rational; nor are the genes. Freud tied rationality to the ego, a mechanism to mediate between id and reality. Leak and Christopher (1982) suggested that the genes also need some help in dealing with some of the complexities of reality. They argued that the cortex of the brain evolved to serve this purpose. Evolution of the cortex in the species would parallel evolution of the ego in the person. Both structures—cortex and ego—permit greater planfulness and care in decision making. Both are adaptations that foster survival.

What about the superego? This is the trickiest part of Leak and Christopher's (1982) argument. To view the superego in evolutionary terms requires one more idea. Specifically, survival isn't only an individual matter. Humans evolved as highly social beings, living and surviving in groups. Because we're so interdependent, we sometimes do better in the long run by letting group needs override personal needs in the short run. As noted in Chapter 6, it's been argued that people in groups evolved mechanisms for inducing, even forcing, reciprocal altruism (Trivers, 1971). A genetic mechanism to do this would enhance the adaptive success of the group.

In psychological terms, evolving such a mechanism looks like developing a capacity to have a superego. Thus, having a superego confers an evolutionary advantage. People who adopt the values of their social group and conform to those values will be accepted as members of the group. They will be more likely to get the benefits that follow from group membership (for example, having other members take care of you if you're sick). These benefits have survival value.

In sum, Leak and Christopher (1982) suggested that the ego (conscious rationality) is a behavioral management system, for which the id and the superego provide motivation. There are two types of motivation—selfish and group related—with adaptive value. The id adapts to the physical environment, where competition for resources is intense and selfish. The superego is the tendencies that evolved in response to pressures from group living.

PSYCHOANALYSIS AND EVOLUTIONARY PSYCHOLOGY: FIXATIONS AND MATING PATTERNS

We see one more similarity between psychoanalytic and evolutionary views, one that's quite different from the points made by Leak and Christopher. Think back to the Oedipal conflict and the fixations that can emerge from it. Fixation in the phallic stage for a male is said to cause an exaggerated attempt to show that he hasn't been castrated. He does this by having sex with as many women as possible and by seeking power and status. Female fixation in this stage involves a seductiveness that doesn't necessarily lead to sex.

These effects look remarkably similar to the mating strategies that evolutionary psychologists argue are part of our species. Recall from Chapter 6 the idea that men and women have different reproductive strategies due to differing investment in offspring (Trivers, 1972). The male mating tactic is to create the appearance of power and status and to mate as frequently as possible. The female tactic is to appear highly desirable but to hold out for the best mate available. These tactics have strong echoes in the fixations just described. We can't help but wonder whether Freud noticed a phenomenon that's biologically based, and ascribed psychodynamic properties to it in order to fit it better into his theory.

PSYCHOANALYSIS AND CONDITIONING

Now consider psychoanalysis and the learning perspective. We noted a relationship in Chapter 12, in passing, while discussing Miller and Dollard's (1941) effort to describe personality in terms of conditioning. In doing that, they were trying to translate psychoanalytic concepts into the ideas of learning. Thus, there's a built-in link between aspects of Freud's theory and Miller and Dollard's theory.

Of particular relevance is Miller and Dollard's (1941) analysis of repression. This concept is important in psychoanalysis and it therefore was something of a focus for Miller and Dollard. They saw *repression* as a conditioned tendency not to think about things that are distressing. By not thinking about them, you avoid the pain. Escaping the pain reinforces the tendency not to think. It thereby builds this tendency in more completely. In this way, Miller and Dollard accounted for a phenomenon that's central to the psychodynamic view, using very different language.

Though it may not be obvious, development of the not-thinking tendency also is a special case of extinction. That is, learning *not to think* means that the tendency *to think* is getting weaker. If you're learning not to think about a distressing topic, whatever stimulus formerly cued the thought no longer does so. Thus, the conditioned response (thinking) is extinguishing. It's only one more step to suggest that there may be a connection between *all* instances of extinction and repression, or *anticathexis.*

Freud said an anticathexis uses energy to keep an impulse or thought out of consciousness. If the restraining force isn't strong enough, the response leaks out. Recall that in Chapter 12, we described a phenomenon called *spontaneous recovery after extinction.* This recovery means that the behavioral tendency is still there. This in turn suggests that, at some level, extinction may involve creating an active restraint. Because a restraint presumably requires energy, it may be the same as an anticathexis.

Thinking about *anticathexes* in conditioning terms leads us to consider *cathexes* as well. We noted in Chapter 8 that psychoanalytic theory distinguishes between id cathexes and ego cathexes. An *id cathexis* is binding energy in an activity or object that satisfies a need. An *ego cathexis* doesn't satisfy a need directly. Rather, it binds energy in an object or activity that's *associated* with the satisfying of a need.

There's a similarity between these ideas and conditioning concepts. *Primary reinforcers* in operant conditioning are things that directly satisfy a need (e.g., food or water). Obtaining a primary reinforcer might be equivalent to having an id cathexis. *Secondary reinforcers* are stimuli *associated* with primary reinforcers or which provide a way to *get* primary reinforcers. Getting (or anticipating) a secondary reinforcer seems similar to forming an ego cathexis.

A final similarity between conditioning and psychoanalytic views concerns the role of the unconscious in determining behavior. To behaviorists, behavior stems from prior conditioning. Conditioning occurs outside consciousness. In effect, this says that behavior results from unconscious influences. In this particular learning view, people do things for reasons they may not be aware of. This is consistent with one of Freud's beliefs. Obviously, Freud had different dynamics in mind. Nonetheless, it's a potentially important link between the views.

PSYCHOANALYSIS AND SELF-REGULATION: HIERARCHY AND THE STRUCTURAL MODEL

The psychoanalytic approach to personality also has certain similarities to the cognitive self-regulation approach. One similarity derives from the notion of a self-regulatory hierarchy. The behavioral qualities involved range from very limited movements through organized sequences to abstract higher-level qualities. As pointed out in Chapter 17, attention can be diverted from the higher levels. When this happens, behavior is more spontaneous and responsive to cues of the moment. It's as though low-level action sequences, once triggered, run off by themselves. In contrast to this impulsive style of behavior, actions being regulated according to higher-order values (programs or principles) have a more carefully managed character.

Aspects of this description hint at similarities to Freud's three-part view of personality. Consider the spontaneity and responsiveness to situational cues in the self-regulation model when high-level control isn't being exerted. This resembles certain aspects of id functioning. An obvious difference is Freud's assumption that id impulses are primarily sexual or aggressive. The self-regulation model, in contrast, makes no such assumption. It's worth noting, though, that alcohol intoxication and deindividuation, which seem to reduce control at high levels (Chapter 17), often lead to sexual and/or destructive activity.

The link between id processes and low-level control is a bit tenuous. In contrast, there's quite a strong resemblance between program control in the self-regulation approach and ego functioning in the psychoanalytic approach. Program control involves planning, decision making, and behavior that's pragmatic, as opposed to either impulsive or principled. These qualities also characterize the ego's functioning.

Levels higher than program control resemble, in some ways, the functioning of the superego. Principle control, in some cases at least, induces people to conform to moral principles. Control at the highest level involves an effort to conform to your idealized sense of self. These efforts resemble, in some respects, the attempt to fit your behavior to the principles of the ego ideal and to avoid a guilty conscience for violating these principles.

The fit between models at this high level isn't perfect, partly because not all principles are moralistic. Yet here's a question: Why did Freud focus on morality and ignore other kinds of ideals? Was it perhaps because morality was so prominent an issue in his society at that time? Maybe the superego is really the capacity to follow rules *in general,* rather than just moral rules. If this were so—if the superego actually pushed behavior toward *other* principles as well as moral ones—the similarity between models would be even greater.

PSYCHOANALYSIS AND COGNITIVE PROCESSES

Several links exist between psychoanalytic themes and ideas from cognitive psychology (e.g., Westen, 1998). Matthew Erdelyi (1985) has even suggested that Freud's theory was largely a theory of cognition. Indeed, he said that Freud was straining toward an analogy between mind and computer but never got there because the computer didn't exist yet.

Erdelyi (1985) argued that cognitive psychologists essentially reinvented many psychodynamic concepts. For example, Freud assumed a process that keeps threats out of awareness. This is similar in some ways to the filtering process by which the mind preattentively selects information to process more fully. Freud's concept of ego becomes executive control processes. The strength of a cathexis is the amount of

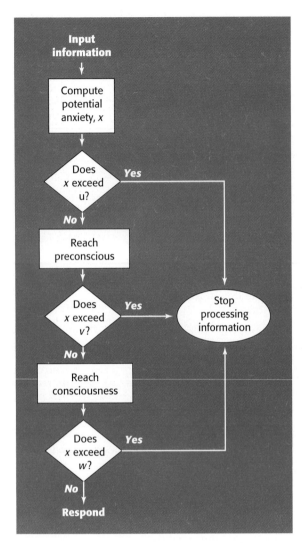

FIGURE 18.1

An information-processing picture of repression and denial. Input information (top)—whether perceptual or from a suppressed memory—is judged preattentively for its anxiety-inducing value. Then come a series of implicit decisions. First, does the anxiety the information would create (x) exceed a criterion of *unbearability* (u)? If so, processing stops; if not, the material goes to a memory area corresponding to the preconscious. Next, does the predicted anxiety exceed a *serious discomfort* criterion (v)? If so, processing ceases and the information stays in memory; if not, the information moves to consciousness. The final decision is whether to acknowledge openly the information that's now conscious, depending on whether the anxiety from doing so will exceed a final criterion (w). This sequence provides for information never to be stored in memory, to be stored but not reach consciousness, to reach consciousness but be suppressed, or to be acknowledged openly. *Source: Adapted from Erdelyi, 1985.*

attention devoted to something. The topography of the mind becomes a matter of levels of processing, and distortions become biases in processing.

As an example of Erdelyi's (1985) approach, consider repression and denial (see also Paulhus & Suedfeld, 1988). When ideas, desires, or perceptions arise that are threatening, repression and denial prevent them from reaching consciousness. This reaction can occur before a threatening stimulus is even experienced, a phenomenon termed **perceptual defense**, or it can involve forgetting an event after it's been experienced. Erdelyi argued that these reflect a sequence of information-processing decisions (see Figure 18.1).

Information is partially analyzed preattentively. This may yield an implicit estimate of how much anxiety would arise if the information reached awareness. If the estimate exceeds a threshold, processing stops and the information never goes further. If the estimate is lower than the threshold, the information goes to a memory area corresponding to the preconscious. Similar decisions are made at other stages, with lower and lower criteria for moving to the next level of processing. This model treats repression, response suppression, and self-deception more generally as reflecting checks at several stages of information processing.

As implied by this description, today's cognitive view assumes that much of the mind is unconscious. Indeed, the study of unconscious processes is a very active area of work (Bargh, 1997; Hassin, Uleman, & Bargh, 2005). Today's cognitive view tends to equate *consciousness* with *attention*. Events that are unconscious are those that get little or no attention.

There are several reasons an event might get little attention. It may be tagged preattentively as having too much potential for anxiety. Or it might occur in a part of the nervous system that attentional processes can't reach. Many cognitive scientists think of the nervous system as a set of special-purpose components, only some of which can be examined consciously (Gardner, 1985). Thus, the basic "wiring" of the system renders some aspects of experience inaccessible.

Sometimes events are unconscious because some behaviors are highly preprogrammed and automatic. Acts that are automatic require little or no monitoring. Highly automated sequences can be triggered by stimuli that are noted by the nervous system at some level but never reach consciousness (Bargh, 1997; Norman, 1981). Even elaborate actions drop mostly out of awareness as they become routine (which all experienced drivers discover at one time or other, as they arrive at home with no memory of how they got there).

These descriptions obviously differ in important ways from Freud's treatment of the unconscious. Only Erdelyi's (1985) example involving preattentive estimates of anxiety implies the sort of process that Freud assumed. All these ideas, however, suggest ways in which information can fail to reach consciousness.

Another body of work has linked cognitive processes to the psychoanalytic concept of *transference*. Transference occurs when a person in therapy displaces emotional reactions onto the therapist. Presumably, these reactions were initially stimulated by significant others in the person's earlier life. Recent studies provide a cognitive explanation for such a turn of events (Andersen, Glassman, Chen, & Cole, 1995; Glassman & Andersen, 1999).

Specifically, the schemas people have of significant others seem chronically to be partially active (thus accessible). As with other instances of partial activation, this makes it easier for the schema to emerge and be used in perceiving and interpreting other stimuli. As a result, you may view many people through the lens of that schema and not even realize it. If someone does something that reminds you vaguely of your mother's way of inducing guilt, you may use your *mother* schema and perceive that person as like your mother.

Indeed, when such schemas pop up, self-aspects relating to those significant others emerge as well (Hinkley & Andersen, 1996). Thus, if someone tends to induce guilt as your mother did, you may react just as you did to your mother (e.g., by becoming irrationally angry), even if the reaction isn't appropriate to the present situation. All this can happen in therapy, or anywhere.

Highly programmed acts, such as walking, can occur with little awareness. This suggests a possible point of contact between cognitive self-regulation ideas and psychodynamic theory.

SOCIAL LEARNING AND COGNITIVE SELF-REGULATION VIEWS

As newer theories were created over the years, personality psychologists were often influenced by ideas that were being used in other areas of psychology. Indeed, this cross-fertilization has been very common. Among the sources of ideas for personality psychologists during the past several decades were learning psychology and cognitive psychology. To a considerable extent, people who sampled from these sources sampled from both, rather than just one.

One result of this pattern is a set of similarities between the social–cognitive learning approach (Chapter 13) and the cognitive self-regulation approaches (Chapters 16 and 17). One of these similarities is also shared with Kelly's personal construct theory (Chapter 15). These approaches have diverse histories, but their central concepts resemble one another more than just a little. Indeed, as you may have noticed, the work of several people pertains not just to one of these views but to two or more of them.

One area of overlap concerns the importance these approaches ascribe to cognitive processes in creating representations of the world and the self. Differences among theories on this issue stem largely from the fact that each has different *reasons* for emphasizing cognition. In discussing cognition from the social learning approach, Mischel (1973) said that if we want to understand learning, we have to look at people's mental representations of stimuli, not the stimuli themselves. People learn from what *they* think is there, not what an outsider sees. The way the stimuli are mentally represented and transformed determines how people will respond to them (see also Bandura, 1977a, 1986).

From the learning perspective, these statements emphasize that human learning is more complicated than it seems. An event doesn't lead automatically to conditioning that's the same for everyone. From the learning perspective, such statements are qualifications on theories of learning. They say to other learning theorists that the *person* has to be considered in analyzing learning. That's the point of such statements— *when they're made from the learning perspective.*

When embedded in Kelly's theory of personal constructs or today's cognitive view on personality, however, ideas about the role of cognition take on a broader life. From these views, cognitive processes are central to understanding *everything* about personality. When Mischel (1973) takes the cognitive view on personality, he focuses not on the subtleties of learning but on how people organize their understanding. Note the difference of emphasis. In the cognitive view, the idea that people *organize* their experience is a key principle regarding the essence of personality. Learning per se is more peripheral, and it may even be disregarded altogether. Cognitive processes are also critical to the self-regulation view on personality, although once again there's a slight difference of emphasis. The focus in the self-regulation approach is mostly on the role cognitions play in *creating behavior.*

Another similarity between the social learning and cognitive self-regulation views concerns expectancies. (Indeed, expectancies also appear in the need-and-motive approach, and they're implicit in ego psychology.) All these approaches see expectancies as determinants of how hard people try to do things. Many people—Rotter (1954, 1966), Bandura (1977a, 1986), Kanfer (1977), Kirsch (1985, 1990), Mischel (1973, 1979), Carver and Scheier (1981, 1990, 1998), and others—have argued that people hold expectancies about the effects their actions are likely to have and whether they can do things they want to do. These expectations can influence how hard a person tries and what the person learns from an event.

The social learning and cognitive self-regulation approaches also resemble each other in the structure they assume underlies behavior. (Kelly's theory becomes less relevant here, because Kelly didn't say much about behaving, as opposed to construing.) The social learning view says people have *incentives,* which draw them forward into action. Incentives function the same as *goals,* a concept that plays a key role in the self-regulation perspective. Indeed, other perspectives also have constructs that serve a comparable role (see Table 18.1).

There is, however, one important difference of emphasis here between the learning and self-regulation views. It concerns the concept of *reinforcement.* The social learning view uses this concept explicitly. The concept is basic to the principle of instrumental learning. As we noted in Chapter 13, however, one social learning theorist—Bandura—has consistently used the concept differently than did earlier theorists. To Bandura, reinforcers create mental representations of future incentives.

Table 18.1 Comparable Behavioral Concepts Taken from Four Perspectives on Personality.

Concept	Theoretical Perspective
Incentive	Social learning
Goal, reference value	Self-regulation
Motive	Need and motive
Ego cathexis	Psychoanalytic

They cause people to learn expectancies about what actions are useful in what situations. But reinforcers don't directly increase the tendency to do the acts that preceded them. The way Bandura used this concept raises questions about whether its meaning is compatible with that assumed by other learning theorists.

Keep in mind, though, that Bandura stands with one foot in the learning perspective and one in the cognitive self-regulation perspective. His view on reinforcement may reflect Bandura the self-regulation theorist more than Bandura the learning theorist. As we noted in Chapter 17, self-regulation theorists are divided on reinforcement as a concept. Some say that people self-reinforce after success. Others see the concept of self-reinforcement as less useful.

This may be a point where theorists' personal histories influenced how their theories were constructed. Most self-regulation theorists who assume a role for self-reinforcement began their work in the learning perspective. Only gradually did they identify with the emerging cognitive self-regulation view. Perhaps they retained a role for self-reinforcement from a psychological inertia, because it represented a comfortable tie to the past. It's also of interest that those theorists are more likely to talk about *self-reinforcement* than *external reinforcement* (e.g., Kanfer, 1977). It's the person's own goal representations that matter, after all. Only *you* can decide whether your goal's been met. Thus, self-reinforcement, rather than external reinforcement, is at the heart of these discussions.

To others, introducing self-reinforcement as a concept simply raises questions. Certainly, people often feel pride after success and sadness after failure. But do these reactions create the learning? Or are they just emotional reactions to informational events, with the latter being what really matters? This is an issue that's not been settled in the self-regulation perspective (or, to some extent, even in the learning perspective; see Timberlake, 1993; Viken & McFall, 1994).

NEOANALYTIC AND COGNITIVE SELF-REGULATION PERSPECTIVES

The learning and cognitive self-regulation perspectives arose in academic psychology, with an emphasis on controlled research. Early neoanalytic psychology, in contrast, derived mostly from the clinical experiences of the theorists. Despite this difference, there's a surprising convergence among these views (cf. Westen, 1991).

Consider, for example, a series of conceptual similarities between self-regulation ideas and Adler's ideas. Recall that Adler saw people as motivated by feelings of inferiority, which make them strive for superiority. He referred to the continual struggle for greater competence as a great upward drive. As we said in Chapter 10, he believed that feelings of inferiority cause healthy people to work throughout life toward greater integration and perfection.

Adler also believed that people establish long-term goals for their lives. He called this the principle of *fictional finalism*. This term conveys the sense that people are motivated by views of their final outcomes and that those views are invented, or fictional. Future goals are always fictional in the sense that they aren't yet real. People act, however, as though they're headed toward these end points and use them as guides for their efforts. To Adler, these future-oriented goals (which he also called *guiding self-ideals*) are more important determinants of behavior than are events in the person's past.

These ideas resemble ideas from the cognitive self-regulation perspective in two ways. First, Adler's thinking placed considerable emphasis on goals, which are also a cornerstone of the self-regulation view of personality. Indeed, Adler's fictional life plans seem quite similar to the possible selves discussed by Markus and her colleagues.

The other similarity relates to the structure of people's strivings. Adler's account resembles the self-regulation approach in one way here, while differing from it in another. The similarity is Adler's belief that changes in behavior are prompted by discrepancies between where you are and where you want to be. When a person notices an *inferiority* (as Adler called it), he or she tries to overcome it. The structure of this process is very similar to that of the feedback loop described in Chapter 17. The difference is that Adler emphasized the role of subjective feelings of inferiority. The self-regulation model doesn't assume such feelings. It simply assumes that when goals have been set, the person tries to meet them.

MASLOW'S HIERARCHY AND HIERARCHIES OF SELF-REGULATION

There are also similarities between elements of the phenomenological perspective and the cognitive self-regulation perspective. We noted earlier a strong thematic resemblance between Kelly's theory of personal constructs and today's cognitive theories. But this isn't the only similarity. Consider Maslow's hierarchy of motives (Chapter 14). There are at least two similarities between that hierarchy and the self-regulation hierarchy.

First, Maslow conceived of the motive qualities at the top of the hierarchy as more abstract and subtle, but also as more integrative, than those at lower levels. The levels of the hierarchy of control also have this character. Second, Maslow saw the lower motives as more demanding than the higher ones, in the sense that a deficit or a problem lower in the hierarchy draws the person's attention to it and forces him or her to deal with it. Similarly, in at least one version of the control hierarchy, if a problem develops at a low level, attention is brought to that level in an attempt to resolve the problem.

There are, however, differences between these views as well. The biggest difference concerns the *content* of the hierarchies. Maslow's analysis was explicitly an analysis of *motives* intended to incorporate both biological needs and psychological motives. The control hierarchy, in contrast, focuses on the structure of *action* with goals that relate to qualities of behavior. This difference means that the two hierarchies are very different at their low levels. Maslow's hierarchy points to survival needs; the other hierarchy points to muscle movements.

At higher levels, though, the two hierarchies are more similar. The highest level of control in the self-regulation view seems roughly equivalent to the concept of self-actualization used by Maslow and Rogers. There's still one difference, however. Woven through the writings of Maslow and Rogers on this topic is the sense that self-actualization is something that happens *to* you, if you can free yourself from the demands of motives at lower levels and just let yourself sense what your body is saying is right for you. It shouldn't involve an effort. If you're *trying* to self-actualize, you probably *aren't* self-actualizing.

The nature of self-regulation in the control hierarchy is ambiguous in that regard. It's by no means clear that such high-level self-regulation is free of effort. On the other hand, the nature of the goal at the highest level—an ideal self that relates to the many principles in force at the next lower level—is quite diffuse. It's so diffuse, in fact, that it isn't too hard to imagine that self-regulation toward it might also feel diffuse. Thus, the subjective experience of self-regulation at the highest level might *not* feel effortful in the same way as does self-regulation at lower levels.

SELF-ACTUALIZATION AND SELF-REGULATION

Two other similarities between the self-actualization view and the self-regulation view of personality go beyond Maslow's hierarchy. One similarity is that both viewpoints use concepts corresponding to idealized and experienced qualities of self. The labels *real self* and *ideal self* are explicit in the phenomenological view of Rogers. The sense of an idealized self is also one value at the top of the control hierarchy, as is the experienced actual self that's compared with it.

The comparison process itself is also similar between the approaches. Rogers emphasized that people compare their current selves with their ideal selves and that they experience anxiety when there's incongruity between them. The comparison between a sensed condition and a standard, or reference point, is also intimately involved in the self-regulation perspective, not only with respect to an ideal self but at all levels of the hierarchy.

DISPOSITIONS AND THEIR EQUIVALENTS IN OTHER MODELS

Another resemblance among theories brings us full circle to an idea with which we began this book. We started with the concept of *dispositions,* and we now return to it. As we noted in Chapter 1, a major theme of personality psychology is how people differ from one another, not just temporarily but in an enduring way. This theme is the basis for the dispositional perspective on personality. Dispositions take a variety of forms: traits, enduring motive qualities, and (in a biological extension of this view) inherited temperaments.

The essence of dispositions, if not the concept itself, is also prominent in at least two more views on personality. The psychoanalytic view assumes that people derive stable personality qualities from childhood psychosexual crises. The neoanalytic view holds that early experiences influence personality in other ways. Erikson assumed that childhood psychosocial crises shape adult personality, and object relations and attachment theories make similar assumptions.

These theories differ regarding the source of dispositions. Yet the theories share two assumptions: that something is stamped or etched into the individual early in life and that this characteristic continues to influence the person from then on. The disposition has been viewed as a biological temperament, a transformation of sexual drives, a reflection of a psychosocial crisis, a learned motive quality, and simply a trait. Yet all these theories treat the disposition as having an enduring impact on the person's life experiences. This similarity among approaches, which is often overlooked, is not a trivial one.

Indeed, the disposition concept also has a place in other views. For example, one version of the learning approach assumes that people differ in locus of control, which helps determine how and what people learn. One aspect of the self-regulation approach assumes that people vary in the disposition to be self-reflective and thus carefully self-regulated. In both of these cases (and others as well), it's assumed that individual differences are stable dispositions that influence a broad range of the person's experiences.

Recurrent Themes, Viewed from Different Angles

Our emphasis in the preceding section was on the notion that certain ideas in one theoretical perspective resemble ideas from another perspective. We also want to note another kind of similarity across perspectives: a similarity in the issues the theories consider. We said earlier in this chapter that different theories often address different issues. That's true. But at least a couple of issues recur across a surprisingly wide range of perspectives.

IMPULSE AND RESTRAINT

One of these issues concerns what seems to be a basic distinction between *impulse* and *restraint*. This issue has been part of personality psychology for a long time, but it has become even more prominent in recent years. The issue is often introduced in the context of delay of gratification, where a choice must be made between a small reward now and a larger reward later. We've discussed the phenomenon of delay of gratification from several viewpoints: psychoanalysis (where we said the ego restrains the id's impulses), ego psychology (where we described variations in ego control and ego resiliency), social learning theory (where we considered effects of models), and the cognitive view (where the focus was on mental images that can foster restraint).

But the issue of impulse versus restraint is far broader than that. In some ways, it's fundamental to personality. As a result, its broader manifestations emerge in many views of personality:

- It's there in trait psychology, in which a trait of conscientiousness is assumed to be defined partly by self-discipline and deliberation (McCrae & Costa, 1987). Indeed, another trait theory treats constraint as a basic dimension of personality (Tellegen, 1985).
- It comes up in temperament theories, where some argue that constraint is in fact a basic temperament (Clark & Watson, 1999) and others argue for a similar temperament that's been called *effortful control* (Rothbart et al., 2003).
- It's found in biological process models, where an argument is made that approach and avoidance systems are joined by a system that concerns restraint versus impulsiveness (Carver & Miller, 2006; Depue & Spoont, 1986; Eysenck & Eysenck, 1976; Zuckerman, 2005).
- It's a core issue in psychoanalysis concerning the balance between the id's desires in many domains and the ego's restraint over how and when those desires are met.
- It emerges in neoanalytic theories, where ego control (ranging from overcontrol to undercontrol) is a key dimension of personality (J. H. Block & J. Block, 1980).
- It's there in cognitive theories, in the form of a contrast between rational and experiential systems (Epstein, 1994) and in a contrast between "hot," incentive-related cognition and "cool," restrained cognition (Metcalfe & Mischel, 1999).
- It also appears in self-regulation theories, in the distinction between deliberative and implemental mindsets (Heckhausen & Gollwitzer, 1987).

Impulse versus restraint has emerged in the past decade as a key issue in several areas of personality psychology (Carver, 2005). Indeed, this issue is one influence that's led a number of people to think about cognitive processing as occurring in two modes (as described in Chapter 16). In these theories, the management of behavior is seen as subject to two layers of influence, which may use two different parts of the brain. One system provides an automatic, intuitive, superficial, and fast way of interacting with the world. It's believed to have evolved earlier. The other system provides a rational, deliberative, but slower way of interacting with the world. It's believed to be of more recent origin.

The question of how and why a person chooses to act quickly versus hold back from acting is basic. It's no wonder that many theories say something about this question. This issue undoubtedly will remain a focus of interest for many people in the years ahead.

INDIVIDUAL VERSUS GROUP NEEDS

Another fundamental issue concerns the competing pressure of individualistic self-interest versus the needs arising from being involved in groups (or couples). In many specific cases, this issue is tangled up with the issue of action versus restraint. This is because the needs of other people are often what urges restraint on one's own impulses. Conceptually, however, it's a separate issue.

Earlier in this chapter, we noted that psychoanalytic theory and evolutionary psychology both confront the contrast between these pressures. In psychoanalysis, the ego deals with the immediate demands of both social and physical reality and the superego deals with other, more complex, aspects of social needs. In evolutionary psychology, people have individualistic needs—survival, competition for mates. But they also have group-based needs—cooperation with one's mate and with the larger society.

This distinction between individualistic and social goals also appears in other approaches. In trait psychology, it emerges in two places. One is the trait of *agreeableness,* which concerns maintaining positive relations with others. People high on this dimension are attuned to mutual well-being; those lower on the dimension are unconcerned with others' interests. The distinction also emerges in the trait of *extraversion*. Extraverts want to have social impact. Introverts are less concerned with group involvement and follow more individualistic paths.

In the motive approach, this issue shows up in the motives to achieve and exert power versus to affiliate and attain intimacy. The issue is also in the biological process approach in unsocialized sensation seeking, with its disregard of others' needs. It's in the social version of the neoanalytic approach, in the issue of separation–individuation versus merger. And it's in the self-actualization approach in the balance between the self-actualizing tendency and the need for positive regard from other people.

In all these cases, people confront the need to balance the two competing pressures. Both pressures are important but in different ways. Given all this attention from theorists of so many different perspectives, this issue appears to be critically important in human experience.

Combining Perspectives

As should now be apparent, similarities do exist between seemingly unrelated approaches to personality. These similarities may, in time, allow integration of the approaches. It's probably safe to say, though, that most personality psychologists view that as a distant goal. One reason is the sheer size and complexity of the job.

Theorists do sometimes try to integrate across boundaries. For example, Cattell (1985) tried to merge psychoanalytic elements of the id, ego, and superego with physiological qualities of temperament and cognitive variables such as expectancy, all in a factor-analytic framework. It's hard, however, to fit all the pieces together in a way that people can use easily.

Theorists such as Eysenck and Zuckerman have tried to integrate across two or three perspectives. In describing Eysenck's work in earlier chapters, we treated it as two sets of ideas with separate focuses of convenience. Some of them are biological, dealing with brain function (and to some extent the heritability of differences). Others form a hierarchical model of relations among acts, habits, traits, and supertraits. Though we presented the ideas as separate, Eysenck viewed them as an integrated model with multiple facets. Zuckerman (1991, 1994, 2005) has made a similar kind of statement, binding together—in a single model—trait, inheritance, and biological-process views.

ECLECTICISM

Another option, exercised by many psychologists, is to take an *eclectic approach* to personality. This involves drawing useful ideas from many theories, rather than being tied to just one or two. Essentially, it means saying that different ideas are useful for different purposes and that there may be no approach that's best for all purposes. To understand a phenomenon, you may need to look at it from the angle of a theory that focuses on it, rather than a theory that doesn't. As Scarr (1985, p. 511) put it, "There is no need to choose a single lens for psychology when we can enjoy a kaleidoscope of perspectives."

This sort of approach suggests that views of personality from the various perspectives may be mutually supportive. It may not be necessary to integrate them into a single set of constructs or principles. As we said earlier, the focus of convenience of one theory differs from that of any other theory. By taking bits of theory across several focuses of convenience, perhaps we can obtain a more well-rounded picture of what personality really is.

Thus, many personality psychologists today accept the idea that personality was shaped by evolutionary pressures. Most assume there are inherited temperaments and that the processes by which personality is reflected are biological. Several ideas from psychoanalytic theory are also widely accepted—for example, that determinants of behavior are sometimes outside awareness and that mechanisms exist within the mind that protect us from things we don't want to deal with. Many personality psychologists accept the idea that early experiences have a big impact on what people are like. (Indeed, there's even evidence from the learning lab that associations conditioned first to a stimulus are more permanent than associations conditioned later; Bouton, [1994].) Obviously, learning has an impact on personality. People do seem to organize records of the experiences of their lives in idiosyncratic ways. We may well have an inner voice of self-actualization. Behavior may even reflect the operation of feedback loops.

All of these ideas may be true or only some of them. All of them may be useful or only some of them. Many psychologists pick and choose bits from various perspectives and use them where they seem reasonable. The choice among the available elements is an individual one.

AN EXAMPLE: BIOLOGY AND LEARNING AS COMPLEMENTARY INFLUENCES ON PERSONALITY

Perhaps the simplest illustration of an eclectic approach is that psychologists almost universally acknowledge the importance to personality of both biology and learning. Everyone does this: people who focus on biology, people who focus on learning, and people who focus on some other part of personality. Early learning theorists claimed the mind is a "blank slate," on which any kind of personality can be sketched. It's clear, though, that this isn't true. There are biological constraints on learning.

A key point is that some associations are learned more easily than others. A term used to describe this is **preparedness.** This term implies that organisms are prepared to condition certain links more easily than others (Öhman & Mineka, 2001; Seligman & Hager, 1972). Preparedness isn't all or nothing. It's a dimension of ease versus difficulty in learning connections. Presumably, this is biologically influenced.

For example, if you get sick to your stomach, you could, in theory, develop a conditioned aversive response toward any number of stimuli. If conditioning depended only on association between stimuli, you should condition aversions to *all* neutral stimuli that are present. However, in reality, you're more likely to develop an aversion to a *flavor* experienced just before getting sick than to other stimuli (Garcia & Koelling, 1966). Apparently the links are just easier to create in the nervous system for some pairs of events than others.

Both biological and learning principles are needed to understand fully the phenomenon of preparedness—such as the biological readiness that chimps and people show in learning to use tools.

Preparedness also seems to be involved in instrumental learning. That is, some kinds of actions are easier for animals to learn than others, even if the same reward follows both. Rats learn more quickly to avoid a foot shock by jumping than by pressing a bar (Wickelgren, 1977). Pigeons quickly learn to peck a spot to obtain food, but it's hard to get them to learn to *refrain* from pecking to get food.

Just as it's clear the mind is not a blank slate, it's also clear that the expression of most biological tendencies depends on experience. Earlier in the book, we talked about *diathesis-stress models,* in which a particular kind of stress produces a problem only if the person also has a particular vulnerability (which might be biological, though it doesn't have to be). Such models are widely accepted. One reason for this acceptance is that twin studies of disorders show two things at once: that serious disorders such as schizophrenia are genetically influenced and that genes aren't everything. That is, if you are the monozygotic twin of someone with schizophrenia, your chances of being schizophrenic are elevated but still less than 100%. If genes were all that mattered, the figure would be 100%.

Thus, an eclectic acceptance of both biology and learning as important influences on personality seems well founded. Perhaps other combinations will prove in the future to be similarly well founded.

Which Theory Is Best?

As we said just earlier, one answer to the question of which theory is best is that *no* theory is perfect, and you may benefit from using bits and pieces of many theories. We should point out, though, that this question is sometimes answered another way. This answer returns us to a point we made in the book's opening chapter. We think it provides a fitting way to end, as well.

Over a century ago, William James wrote that a theory must account reasonably well for the phenomena that people experience as real, but to be successful, a theory must do more than that. James wrote (1890, p. 312) that people will believe those theories which "are most interesting, those which appeal most urgently to our aesthetic, emotional, and active needs." Put more simply, the theory that's best is the one you *like* best. The one that's best—for you—is the one that appeals to you most, the one you find most interesting and engaging. Edward Tolman (1959, p. 152) also put it pretty simply: "I have liked to think about psychology in ways that have proved congenial to me. . . . In the end, the only sure criterion is to have fun. And I have had fun."

· SUMMARY ·

Although various perspectives on personality differ from one another in important ways, they also resemble one another in important ways. The psychoanalytic perspective is similar to at least three alternative views. First, ideas about biological evolution in the species parallel Freud's ideas about the evolution of personality in the individual. That is, in each case, a primitive force (the genes, the id) needs another force to help it deal with reality (the cortex, the ego), and eventually it also needs a force to keep it in contact with the social world (inherited sensitivity to social influence, the superego). Second, one branch of the conditioning view was devised to create a link between psychoanalytic concepts and the language of learning. Third, the psychoanalytic view and the cognitive self-regulation view resemble each other in two ways. The notion of a hierarchy of control echoes psychoanalytic theory's three components of personality. Work on cognition has also developed concepts that resemble, in some ways, those postulated years earlier by Freud.

A substantial overlap exists between the social learning and the cognitive self-regulation viewpoints. They share an emphasis on mental representations of the world (as does Kelly's theory of personal constructs), although the theories have somewhat different rationales for the emphasis. They also have similar views of the importance of people's expectancies and similar views on the basic structure of behavior.

A similarity also exists between self-regulation ideas and Adler's neoanalytic theory. Both assume that behavior is aimed at reducing discrepancies, and both emphasize the importance of people's long-term goals. The notion of a hierarchy in self-regulation also suggests a similarity between that view and the phenomenological view, especially Maslow's. Although the lower levels of Maslow's motive hierarchy deal with motives that are ignored in the control hierarchy, at their upper levels, the models resemble each other more closely. The principle of self-actualization also resembles the self-regulation model in the concepts of ideal and actual self and the desire for congruity between them.

Another similarity among approaches concerns the concept of disposition. Obviously, this construct is central to the dispositional perspective. It's also important in the psychoanalytic and neoanalytic views. In all these cases (and by implication in others as well), the assumption is made that people have qualities that endure over time and circumstances and that influence their behaviors, thoughts, and feelings.

Although the various theories differ in their focus, certain issues do seem to recur across many of them. This represents another kind of similarity among the theories. One issue that many different theories address is the polarity between impulse versus restraint. Indeed, this issue has become increasingly prominent in recent years. Another is the competing pressures of individual self-interest and communal interest.

Thus, there are areas of overlap among theories. Yet the theories also differ. Which theory, then, is right? One answer is that *all* the perspectives seem to have something of value to offer. Many psychologists prefer an *eclectic position,* taking elements and ideas from several views, rather than just one. At a minimum, people who operate within the framework of a given theory must take into account the limitations imposed by other views. For example, temperament theorists believe much of personality is determined by genetics, but they also assume that temperaments are modified by learning. Learning theorists believe that personality is a product of a learning history, but it's clear that some kinds of learning are easier than others. Perhaps the future will see greater emphasis on this eclecticism, the sharing of ideas from one perspective to another.

· GLOSSARY ·

Perceptual defense   Responding to screen out a threatening stimulus before it enters awareness.

Preparedness   The idea that some conditioning is easy because the animal is biologically prepared for it to happen.

Aarts, H., & Dijksterhuis, A. (2000). Habits as knowledge structures: Automaticity in goal-directed behavior. *Journal of Personality and Social Psychology, 78,* 53–63.

Aarts, H., & Dijksterhuis, A. (2003). The silence of the library: Environment, situational norm, and social behavior. *Journal of Personality and Social Psychology, 84,* 18–28.

Abramson, L. Y., Alloy, L. B., & Metalsky, G. I. (1995). Hopelessness depression. In G. M. Buchanan & M. E. P. Seligman (Eds.), *Explanatory style* (pp. 113–134). Hillsdale, NJ: Erlbaum.

Abramson, L. Y., Metalsky, G. I., & Alloy, L. B. (1989). Hopelessness depression: A theory-based subtype of depression. *Psychological Review, 96,* 358–372.

Abramson, L. Y., Seligman, M. E. P., & Teasdale, J. D. (1978). Learned helplessness in humans: Critique and reformulation. *Journal of Abnormal Psychology, 87,* 49–74.

Adams, G. D., & Fastnow, C. (2000, November 10). *A note on the voting irregularities in Palm Beach, Florida.* Retrieved from http://madison.hss.cmu.edu

Adams, G. R., & Shea, J. A. (1979). The relationship between identity status, locus of control, and ego development. *Journal of Youth and Adolescence, 8,* 81–89.

Adams-Webber, J. R. (1979). *Personal construct theory: Concepts and applications.* New York: Wiley.

Adler, A. (1917). *Study of organ inferiority and its psychical compensation.* New York: Nervous and Mental Diseases Publishing.

Adler, A. (1927). *Practice and theory of individual psychology.* New York: Harcourt, Brace, & World.

Adler, A. (1929). *The science of living.* New York: Greenberg.

Adler, A. (1930). Individual psychology. In C. Murchison (Ed.), *Psychologies of 1930.* Worcester, MA: Clark University Press.

Adler, A. (1931). *What life should mean to you.* Boston: Little, Brown.

Adler, A. (1956). *The individual psychology of Alfred Adler: A systematic presentation of selections from his writings.* H. L. Ansbacher & R. R. Ansbacher (Eds.). New York: Basic Books.

Adler, A. (1958). *What life should mean to you.* New York: Capricorn Books. (Originally published, 1931)

Adler, A. (1964). *Social interest: A challenge to mankind.* New York: Capricorn Books. (Originally published, 1933)

Agostinelli, G., Sherman, S. J., Presson, C. C., & Chassin, L. (1992). Self-protection and self-enhancement biases in estimates of population prevalence. *Personality and Social Psychology Bulletin, 18,* 631–642.

Ahadi, S., & Diener, E. (1989). Multiple determinants and effect size. *Journal of Personality and Social Psychology, 56,* 398–406.

Ainsworth, M. D. S. (1983). Patterns of infant–mother attachment as related to maternal care. In D. Magnusson & V. Allen (Eds.), *Human development: An interactional perspective.* New York: Academic.

Ainsworth, M. D. S., Blehar, M. C., Waters, E., & Wall, T. (1978). *Patterns of attachment.* Hillsdale, NJ: Erlbaum.

Ajzen, I. (1985). From intentions to actions: A theory of planned behavior. In J. Kuhl & J. Beckmann (Eds.), *Action control: From cognition to behavior.* New York: Springer-Verlag.

Ajzen, I. (1988). *Attitudes, personality, and behavior.* Chicago: Dorsey.

Ajzen, I., & Fishbein, M. (1980). *Understanding attitudes and predicting social behavior.* Englewood Cliffs, NJ: Prentice-Hall.

Alexander, R. (1979). *Darwinism and human affairs.* Seattle: University of Washington Press.

Alicke, M. D. (1985). Global self-evaluation as determined by the desirability and controllability of trait adjectives. *Journal of Personality and Social Psychology, 49,* 1621–1630.

Allen, J. J., Iacono, W. G., Depue, R. A., & Arbisi, P. (1993). Regional electroencephalographic asymmetries in bipolar seasonal affective disorder before and after exposure to bright light. *Biological Psychiatry, 33,* 642–646.

Allen, L. S., & Gorski, R. A. (1992). Sexual orientation and the size of the anterior commissure in the human brain. *Proceedings of the National Academy of Sciences of the U.S.A., 89,* 7199–7202.

Allison, P. J., Guichard, C., Fung, K., & Gilain, L. (2003). Dispositional optimism predicts survival status 1 year after diagnosis in head and neck cancer patients. *Journal of Clinical Oncology, 21*(3), 543–548.

Alloy, L. B., & Abramson, L. Y. (1988). Depressive realism: Four theoretical perspectives. In L. B. Alloy (Ed.), *Cognitive processes in depression* (pp. 223–265). New York: Guilford.

Allport, G. W. (1937). *Personality: A psychological interpretation.* New York: Holt.

Allport, G. W. (1961). *Pattern and growth in personality.* New York: Holt, Rinehart, & Winston.

Almagor, M., Tellegen, A., & Waller, N. G. (1995). The Big Seven model: A cross-cultural replication and further exploration of the basic dimensions of natural language trait descriptors. *Journal of Personality and Social Psychology, 69,* 300–307.

Amabile, T. M. (1985). Motivation and creativity: Effects of motivational orientation on creative writers. *Journal of Personality and Social Psychology, 48,* 393–399.

Amsel, A. (1967). Partial reinforcement effects on vigor and persistence: Advances in frustration theory derived from a variety of within-subject experiments. In K. W. Spence & J. T. Spence (Eds.), *The psychology of learning and motivation* (Vol. 1). New York: Academic.

Anastasi, A. (1988). *Psychological testing* (6th ed.). New York: Macmillan.

Andersen, S. M., & Chen, S. (2002). The relational self: An interpersonal social-cognitive theory. *Psychological Review, 109,* 619–645.

Andersen, S. M., Glassman, N. S., Chen, S., & Cole, S. W. (1995). Transference in social perception: The role of chronic accessibility in significant-other representations. *Journal of Personality and Social Psychology, 69,* 41–57.

Anderson, C., John, O. P., Keltner, D., & Kring, A. M. (2001). Who attains social status? Effects of personality and physical attractiveness in social groups. *Journal of Personality and Social Psychology, 81,* 116–132.

Anderson, C. A., Berkowitz, L., Donnerstein, E., Huesmann, L. R., Johnson, J. D., Linz, D., Malamuth, N. M., & Wartella, E. (2003). The influence of media violence on youth. *Psychological Science in the Public Interest, 4,* 81–110.

Anderson, J. A. (1995). *An introduction to neural networks.* Cambridge, MA: MIT Press.

Anderson, J. R. (1976). *Language, memory and thought.* Hillsdale, NJ: Erlbaum.

Anderson, J. R. (1985). *Cognitive psychology and its implications* (2nd ed.). New York: Freeman.

Anderson, J. R. (1991). The adaptive nature of human categorization. *Psychological Review, 98,* 409–429.

Anderson, J. W. (1988). Henry Murray's early career: A psychobiographical exploration. *Journal of Personality, 56,* 138–171.

Anderson, R. C., & Pichert, J. W. (1978). Recall of previously unrecallable information following a shift in perspective. *Journal of Verbal Learning and Verbal Behavior, 17,* 1–12.

Andrykowski, M. A., Brady, M. J., & Hunt, J. W. (1993). Positive psychosocial adjustment in potential bone marrow transplant recipients: Cancer as a psychosocial transition. *Psycho-oncology, 2,* 261–276.

Andrzejewski, M. E., Spencer, R. C., & Kelley, A. E. (2006). Dissociating ventral and dorsal subicular dopamine D_1 receptor involvement in instrumental learning, spontaneous motor behavior, and motivation. *Behavioral Neuroscience, 120,* 542–553.

Archer, J. (2006). Testosterone and human aggression: An evaluation of the challenge hypothesis. *Neuroscience and Biobehavioral Reviews, 30,* 319–345.

Archer, J., & Coyne, S. M. (2005). An integrated review of indirect, relational, and social aggression. *Personality and Social Psychology Review, 9,* 212–230.

Ardrey, R. (1966). *The territorial imperative.* New York: Dell.

Arkin, R. M., & Baumgardner, A. H. (1985). Self-handicapping. In J. H. Harvey & G. Weary (Eds.), *Attribution: Basic issues and applications.* New York: Academic.

Arndt, J., Schimel, J., Greenberg, J., & Pyszczynski, T. (2002). The intrinsic self and defensiveness: Evidence that activating the intrinsic self reduces self-handicapping and conformity. *Personality and Social Psychology Bulletin, 28,* 671–685.

Arnett, P. A., Smith, S. S., & Newman, J. P. (1997). Approach and avoidance motivation in psychopathic criminal offenders during passive avoidance. *Journal of Personality and Social Psychology, 72,* 1413–1428.

Asendorpf, J. B., Banse, R., & Mücke, D. (2002). Double dissociation between implicit and explicit personality self-concept: The case of shy behavior. *Journal of Personality and Social Psychology, 83,* 380–393.

Asendorpf, J. B., & van Aken, M. A. G. (1999). Resilient, overcontrolled, and undercontrolled personality prototypes in childhood: Replicability, predictive power, and the trait-type issue. *Journal of Personality and Social Psychology, 77,* 815–832.

Asendorpf, J. B., & Wilpers, S. (1998). Personality effects on social relationships. *Journal of Personality and Social Psychology, 74,* 1531–1544.

Aserinsky, E., & Kleitman, N. (1953). Regularly occurring periods of eye motility, and concomitant phenomena during sleep. *Science, 118,* 273.

Ashton, M. C., Lee, K., & Goldberg, L. R. (2004). A hierarchical analysis of 1,710 English personality-descriptive adjectives. *Journal of Personality and Social Psychology, 87,* 707–721.

Ashton, M. C., Lee, K., Perugini, M., Szarota, P., de Vries, R. E., Di Blas, L., Boies, K., & De Raad, B. (2004). A six-factor structure of personality-descriptive adjectives: Solutions from psycholexical studies in seven languages. *Journal of Personality and Social Psychology, 86,* 356–366.

Ashton, M. C., Lee, K., & Son, C. (2000). Honesty as the sixth factor of personality: Correlations with Machiavellianism, primary psychopathy, and social adroitness. *European Journal of Personality, 14,* 359–368.

Aspinwall, L. G., & Brunhart, S. N. (1996). Distinguishing optimism from denial: Optimistic beliefs predict attention to health threats. *Personality and Social Psychology Bulletin, 22,* 993–1003.

Assor, A., Roth, G., & Deci, E. L. (2004). The emotional costs of parents' conditional regard: A self-determination theory analysis. *Journal of Personality, 72,* 47–88.

Atkinson, J. W. (1957). Motivational determinants of risk-taking behavior. *Psychological Review, 64,* 359–372.

Atkinson, J. W., & Birch, D. (1970). *The dynamics of action.* New York: Wiley.

Atkinson, J. W., Heyns, R. W., & Veroff, J. (1954). The effect of experimental arousal of the affiliation motive on thematic apperception. *Journal of Abnormal and Social Psychology, 49,* 405–410.

Atkinson, J. W., & McClelland, D. C. (1948). The projective expression of needs II. The effect of different intensities of the hunger drive on thematic apperception. *Journal of Experimental Psychology, 38,* 643–658.

Atkinson, J. W., & Raynor, J. O. (Eds.). (1974). *Motivation and achievement.* Washington, DC: V. H. Winston.

Austin, J. T., & Vancouver, J. B. (1996). Goal constructs in psychology: Structure, process, and content. *Psychological Bulletin, 120,* 338–375.

Avery, R. R., & Ryan, R. M. (1988). Object relations and ego development: Comparison and correlates in middle childhood. *Journal of Personality, 56,* 547–569.

Avia, M. D., & Kanfer, F. H. (1980). Coping with aversive stimulation: The effects of training in a self-management context. *Cognitive Therapy and Research, 4,* 73–81.

Avila, C. (2001). Distinguishing BIS-mediated and BAS-mediated disinhibition mechanisms: A comparison of disinhibition models of Gray (1981, 1987) and of Patterson and Newman (1993). *Journal of Personality and Social Psychology, 80,* 311–324.

Axelrod, R., & Hamilton, W. D. (1981). The evolution of cooperation. *Science, 211,* 1390–1396.

Axline, V. M. (1947). *Play therapy.* Boston: Houghton Mifflin.

Axline, V. M. (1964). *Dibs: In search of self.* Boston: Houghton Mifflin.

Ayduk, O., Mischel, W., & Downey, G. (2002). Attentional mechanisms linking rejection to hostile reactivity: The role of "hot" versus "cool" focus. *Psychological Science, 13,* 443–448.

Babad, E. Y. (1973). Effects of informational input on the "social deprivation-satisfaction effect." *Journal of Personality and Social Psychology, 27,* 1–5.

Badner, J. A., & Gershon, E. S. (2002). Meta-analysis of whole-genome linkage scans of bipolar disorder and schizophrenia. *Molecular Psychiatry, 7,* 405–411.

Bailey, J. E., Argyropoulos, S. V., Lightman, S. L., & Nutt, D. J. (2003). Does the brain noradrenaline network mediate the effects of the CO_2 challenge? *Journal of Psychopharmacology, 17,* 252–259.

Bailey, J. M., Dunne, M. P., & Martin, N. G. (2000). Genetic and environmental influences on sexual orientation and its correlates in an Australian twin sample. *Journal of Personality and Social Psychology, 78,* 524–536.

Bailey, J. M., Gaulin, S., Agyei, Y., & Gladue, B. A. (1994). Effects of gender and sexual orientation on evolutionarily relevant aspects of human mating psychology. *Journal of Personality and Social Psychology, 66,* 1081–1093.

Bailey, J. M., & Pillard, R. C. (1991). A genetic study of male sexual orientation. *Archives of General Psychiatry, 48,* 1089–1096.

Bailey, J. M., Pillard, R. C., Neale, M. C., & Agyei, Y. (1993). Heritable factors influence sexual orientation in women. *Archives of General Psychiatry, 50,* 217–223.

Bain, A. (1859). *The emotions and the will.* London, England: Longman.

Baldwin, M. W., Keelan, J. P. R., Fehr, B., Enns, V., & Koh-Rangarajoo, E. (1996). Social-cognitive conceptualization of attachment working models: Availability and accessibility effects. *Journal of Personality and Social Psychology, 71,* 94–109.

Balmary, M. (1979). *Psychoanalyzing psychoanalysis: Freud and the hidden fault of his father.* Baltimore, MD: Johns Hopkins University Press.

Baltes, P. B., & Staudinger, U. M. (1993). The search for a psychology of wisdom. *Current Directions in Psychological Science, 2,* 75–80.

Bandura, A. (1965). Influence of models' reinforcement contingencies on the acquisition of imitative response. *Journal of Personality and Social Psychology, 1,* 589–595.

Bandura, A. (1969). *Principles of behavior modification.* New York: Holt, Rinehart, & Winston.

Bandura, A. (1971). Vicarious and self-reinforcement processes. In R. Glaser (Ed.), *The nature of reinforcement.* New York: Academic.

Bandura, A. (1973). *Aggression: A social learning analysis.* Englewood Cliffs, NJ: Prentice-Hall.

Bandura, A. (1976). Self-reinforcement: Theoretical and methodological considerations. *Behaviorism, 4,* 135–155.

Bandura, A. (1977a). Self-efficacy: Toward a unifying theory of behavioral change. *Psychological Review, 84,* 191–215.

Bandura, A. (1977b). *Social learning theory.* Englewood Cliffs, NJ: Prentice-Hall.

Bandura, A. (1978). The self system in reciprocal determinism. *American Psychologist, 33,* 344–358.

Bandura, A. (1982a). The psychology of chance encounters and life paths. *American Psychologist, 37,* 747–755.

Bandura, A. (1982b). Self-efficacy mechanism in human agency. *American Psychologist, 37,* 122–147.

Bandura, A. (1986). *Social foundations of thought and action: A social cognitive theory.* Englewood Cliffs, NJ: Prentice-Hall.

Bandura, A. (1997). *Self-efficacy: The exercise of control.* New York: Freeman.

Bandura, A., Adams, N. E., & Beyer, J. (1977). Cognitive processes mediating behavioral change. *Journal of Personality and Social Psychology, 35,* 125–139.

Bandura, A., Adams, N. E., Hardy, A. B., & Howells, G. N. (1980). Tests of the generality of self-efficacy theory. *Cognitive Therapy and Research, 4,* 39–66.

Bandura, A., Grusec, J. E., & Menlove, F. L. (1967). Vicarious extinction of avoidance behavior. *Journal of Personality and Social Psychology, 5,* 16–23.

Bandura, A., & Jeffery, R. W. (1973). Role of symbolic coding and rehearsal processes in observational learning. *Journal of Personality and Social Psychology, 26,* 122–130.

Bandura, A., Jeffery, R., & Bachicha, D. L. (1974). Analysis of memory codes and cumulative rehearsal in observational learning. *Journal of Research in Personality, 7,* 295–305.

Bandura, A., & Menlove, F. L. (1968). Factors determining vicarious extinction of avoidance behavior through symbolic modeling. *Journal of Personality and Social Psychology, 8,* 99–108.

Bandura, A., & Mischel, W. (1965). Modification of self-imposed delay of reward through exposure to live and symbolic models. *Journal of Personality and Social Psychology, 2,* 698–705.

Bandura, A., & Rosenthal, T. L. (1966). Vicarious classical conditioning as a function of arousal level. *Journal of Personality and Social Psychology, 3,* 54–62.

Bandura, A., & Schunk, D. H. (1981). Cultivating competence, self-efficacy, and intrinsic interest through proximal self-motivation. *Journal of Personality and Social Psychology, 41,* 586–598.

Bandura, A., & Walters, R. (1963). *Social learning and personality development.* New York: Holt, Rinehart, & Winston.

Bannister, D. (Ed.). (1970). *Perspectives in personal construct theory.* London, England: Academic.

Bannister, D. (1985). *Issues and approaches in personal construct theory.* London, England: Academic.

Barash, D. P. (1977). *Sociobiology and human behavior.* New York: Elsevier.

Barash, D. P. (1986). *The hare and the tortoise: Culture, biology, and human nature.* New York: Penguin.

Barash, D. P. (2001). *Revolutionary biology: The new, gene-centered view of life.* London, England: Transaction.

Barber, J. P., & DeRubeis, R. J. (1989). On second thought: Where the action is in cognitive therapy for depression. *Cognitive Therapy and Research, 13,* 441–457.

Barch, D. M. (2004). Pharmacological manipulation of human working memory. *Psychopharmacology, 174,* 126–135.

Bargh, J. A. (1997). The automaticity of everyday life. In R. S. Wyer, Jr. (Ed.), *Advances in social cognition* (Vol. 10, pp. 1–61). Mahwah, NJ: Erlbaum.

Bargh, J. A., & Chartrand, T. L. (1999). The unbearable automaticity of being. *American Psychologist, 54,* 462–479.

Bargh, J. A., Chen, M., & Burrows, L. (1996). Automaticity of social behavior: Direct effects of trait construct and stereotype activation on action. *Journal of Personality and Social Psychology, 71,* 230–244.

Bargh, J. A., & Ferguson, M. J. (2000). Beyond behaviorism: On the automaticity of higher mental processes. *Psychological Bulletin, 126,* 925–945.

Bargh, J. A., Gollwitzer, P. M., Lee-Chai, A., Barndollar, K., & Trötschel, R. (2001). The automated will: Nonconscious activation and pursuit of behavioral goals. *Journal of Personality and Social Psychology, 81,* 1014–1027.

Bargh, J. A., Lombardi, W. J., & Higgins, E. T. (1988). Automaticity of chronically accessible constructs in person X

situation effects on person perception: It's just a matter of time. *Journal of Personality and Social Psychology, 55,* 599–605.

Bargh, J. A., & Pratto, F. (1986). Individual construct accessibility and perceptual selection. *Journal of Experimental Social Psychology, 22,* 293–311.

Bargh, J. A., & Williams, E. L. (2006). The automaticity of social life. *Current Directions in Psychological Science, 15,* 1–4.

Barkow, J. H., Cosmides, L., & Tooby, J. (1992). *The adapted mind: Evolutionary psychology and the generation of culture.* New York: Oxford University Press.

Barlow, D. H. (Ed.). (1981). *Behavioral assessment of adult disorders.* New York: Guilford.

Barnier, A. J., Levin, K., & Maher, A. (2004). Suppressing thoughts of past events: Are repressive copers good suppressors? *Cognition and Emotion, 18,* 513–531.

Baron, A. S., & Banaji, M. R. (2006). The development of implicit attitudes: Evidence of race evaluations from ages 6 and 10 and adulthood. *Psychological Science, 17,* 53–58.

Baron, R. A. (1974a). The aggression-inhibiting influence of heightened sexual arousal. *Journal of Personality and Social Psychology, 30,* 318–322.

Baron, R. A. (1974b). Sexual arousal and physical aggression: The inhibiting influence of "cheesecake" and nudes. *Bulletin of the Psychonomic Society, 3,* 337–339.

Baron, R. A. (1979). Heightened sexual arousal and physical aggression: An extension to females. *Journal of Research in Personality, 13,* 91–102.

Baron, R. A., & Bell, P. A. (1977). Sexual arousal and aggression by males: Effects of type of erotic stimuli and prior provocation. *Journal of Personality and Social Psychology, 35,* 79–87.

Baron, R. A., & Kempner, C. R. (1970). Model's behavior and attraction toward the model as determinants of adult aggressive behavior. *Journal of Personality and Social Psychology, 14,* 335–344.

Baron, R. A., & Richardson, D. R. (1994). *Human aggression* (2nd ed.). New York: Plenum.

Barrett, L. F., Williams, N. L., & Fong, G. T. (2002). Defensive verbal behavior assessment. *Personality and Social Psychology Bulletin, 28,* 776–788.

Barron, F. (1953). An ego-strength scale which predicts response to psychotherapy. *Journal of Consulting Psychology, 17,* 327–333.

Bartholomew, K., & Horowitz, L. M. (1991). Attachment styles among young adults: A test of a four-category model. *Journal of Personality and Social Psychology, 61,* 226–244.

Bartholow, B. D., & Anderson, C. A. (2001). Effects of violent video games on aggressive behavior: Potential sex differences. *Journal of Experimental Social Psychology, 38,* 283–290.

Bartholow, B. D., Sestir, M. A., & Davis, E. B. (2005). Correlates and consequences of exposure to video game violence: Hostile personality, empathy, and aggressive behavior. *Personality and Social Psychology Bulletin, 31,* 1573–1586.

Batson, C. D. (1990). How social an animal? The human capacity for caring. *American Psychologist, 45,* 336–346.

Batson, C. D. (1991). *The altruism question: Toward a social-psychological answer.* Hillsdale, NJ: Erlbaum.

Batson, C. D., Bolen, M. H., Cross, J. A., & Neuringer-Benefiel, H. E. (1986). Where is the altruism in the altruistic personality? *Journal of Personality and Social Psychology, 50,* 212–220.

Batson, C. D., Dyck, J. L., Brandt, J. R., Batson, J. G., Powell, A. L., McMaster, M. R., & Griffitt, C. (1988). Five studies testing two new egoistic alternatives to the empathy–altruism hypothesis. *Journal of Personality and Social Psychology, 55,* 52–77.

Batson, C. D., Fultz, J., & Schoenrade, P. A. (1987). Distress and empathy: Two qualitatively distinct vicarious emotions with different motivational consequences. *Journal of Personality, 55,* 19–39.

Bauer, J. J., & Bonanno, G. A. (2001). I can, I do, I am: The narrative differentiation of self-efficacy and other self-evaluations while adapting to bereavement. *Journal of Research in Personality, 35,* 424–448.

Bauer, J. J., McAdams, D. P., & Sakaeda, A. R. (2005). Interpreting the good life: Growth memories in the lives of mature, happy people. *Journal of Personality and Social Psychology, 88,* 203–217.

Baum, W. M. (2005). *Understanding behaviorism: Behavior, culture, and evolution.* Oxford, England: Blackwell.

Baumann, L. J., & Leventhal, H. (1985). "I can tell when my blood pressure is up, can't I?" *Health Psychology, 4,* 203–218.

Baumann, N., Kaschel, R., & Kuhl, J. (2005). Striving for unwanted goals: Stress-dependent discrepancies between explicit and implicit achievement motives reduce subjective well-being and increase psychosomatic symptoms. *Journal of Personality and Social Psychology, 89,* 781–799.

Baumeister, R. F. (1989). The problem of life's meaning. In D. M. Buss & N. Cantor (Eds.), *Personality psychology: Recent trends and emerging directions* (pp. 138–148). New York: Springer-Verlag.

Baumeister, R. F. (1994). The crystallization of discontent in the process of major life changes. In T. F. Heatherton & J. L. Weinberger (Eds.), *Can personality change?* (pp. 281–297). Washington, DC: American Psychological Association.

Baumeister, R. F. (2002). Ego depletion and self-control failure: An energy model of the self's executive function. *Self and Identity, 1,* 129–136.

Baumeister, R. F., Bratslavsky, E., Muraven, M., & Tice, D. M. (1998). Ego depletion: Is the active self a limited resource? *Journal of Personality and Social Psychology, 74,* 1252–1265.

Baumeister, R. F., & Campbell, W. K. (1999). The intrinsic appeal of evil: Sadism, sensational thrills, and threatened egotism. *Personality and Social Psychology Review, 3,* 210–221.

Baumeister, R. F., & Heatherton, T. F. (1996). Self-regulation failure: An overview. *Psychological Inquiry, 7,* 1–15.

Baumeister, R. F., & Leary, M. R. (1995). The need to belong: Desire for interpersonal attachments as a fundamental human motivation. *Psychological Bulletin, 117,* 497–529.

Baumeister, R. F., & Vohs, K. D. (Eds.). (2004). *Handbook of self-regulation: Research, theory, and applications.* New York: Guilford.

Beck, A. T. (1972). *Depression: Causes and treatments.* Philadelphia: University of Pennsylvania Press.

Beck, A. T. (1976). *Cognitive therapy and the emotional disorders.* New York: International Universities Press.

Beck, A. T. (1991). Cognitive therapy: A 30-year retrospective. *American Psychologist, 46,* 368–375.

Beck, A. T., Rush, A. J., Shaw, B. F., & Emery, G. (1979). *Cognitive therapy of depression: A treatment manual.* New York: Guilford.

Becker, E. (1973). *The denial of death.* New York: Free Press.

Beer, J. S. (2002). Implicit self-theories of shyness. *Journal of Personality and Social Psychology, 83,* 1009–1024.

Beevers, C. G. (2005). Cognitive vulnerability to depression: A dual process model. *Clinical Psychology Review, 25,* 975–1002.

Bell, M., Billington, R., & Becker, B. (1986). A scale for the assessment of object relations: Reliability, validity, and factorial invariance. *Journal of Clinical Psychology, 42,* 733–741.

Belmont, L., & Marolla, F. A. (1973). Birth order, family size, and intelligence. *Science, 182,* 1096–1101.

Bem, D. J., & Allen, A. (1974). On predicting some of the people some of the time: The search for cross-situational consistencies in behavior. *Psychological Review, 81,* 506–520.

Bem, S. L. (1974). The measurement of psychological androgyny. *Journal of Consulting and Clinical Psychology, 42,* 155–162.

Bem, S. L. (1975). Sex role adaptability: One consequence of psychological androgyny. *Journal of Personality and Social Psychology, 31,* 634–643.

Benet, V., & Waller, N. G. (1995). The Big Seven factor model of personality description: Evidence for its cross-cultural generality in a Spanish sample. *Journal of Personality and Social Psychology, 69,* 701–718.

Benet-Martínez, V., & John, O. P. (1998). Los Cinco Grandes across cultures and ethnic groups: Multitrait multimethod analyses of the Big Five in Spanish and English. *Journal of Personality and Social Psychology, 75,* 729–750.

Benjamin, J., Li, L., Patterson, C., Greenberg, B. D., Murphy, D. L., & Hamer, D. H. (1996). Population and familial association between the D4 dopamine receptor gene and measures of novelty seeking. *Nature Genetics, 12,* 81–84.

Bentler, P. M. (1990). Comparative fit indexes in structural models. *Psychological Bulletin, 107,* 238–246.

Berant, E., Mikulincer, M., & Florian, V. (2001). Attachment style and mental health: A 1-year follow-up study of mothers of infants with congenital heart disease. *Personality and Social Psychology Bulletin, 27,* 956–968.

Berenbaum, S. A., & Hines, M. (1992). Early androgens are related to childhood sex-typed toy preferences. *Psychological Science, 3,* 203–206.

Berg, I. A. (Ed.). (1967). *Response set in personality assessment.* Chicago: Aldine.

Bergeman, C. S., Chipuer, H. M., Plomin, R., Pedersen, N. L., McClearn, G. E., Nesselrode, J. R., Costa, P. T., Jr., & McCrae, R. R. (1993). Genetic and environmental effects on openness to experience, agreeableness, and conscientiousness: An adoption/twin study. *Journal of Personality, 61,* 159–179.

Berger, S. M. (1961). Incidental learning through vicarious reinforcement. *Psychological Reports, 9,* 477–491.

Berger, S. M. (1962). Conditioning through vicarious instigation. *Psychological Review, 69,* 450–466.

Bergeron, D. M., Block, C. J., & Echtenkamp, B. A. (2006). Disabling the able: Stereotype threat and women's work performance. *Human Performance, 19,* 133–158.

Bergmann, M. S. (1980). Symposium on object relations theory and love: On the intrapsychic function of falling in love. *Psychoanalytic Quarterly, 49,* 56–77.

Berkowitz, L., & Alioto, J. T. (1973). The meaning of an observed event as a determinant of its aggressive consequences. *Journal of Personality and Social Psychology, 28,* 206–217.

Bernhardt, P. C., Dabbs, J. M., Jr., Fielden, J., & Lutter, C. (1998). Testosterone changes during vicarious experiences of winning and losing among fans at sporting events. *Physiology and Behavior, 65,* 59–62.

Bernstein, A., Newman, J. P., Wallace, J. F., & Luh, K. E. (2000). Left-hemisphere activation and deficient response modulation in psychopaths. *Psychological Science, 11,* 414–418.

Bernstein, D. A. (1973). Situational factors in behavioral fear assessment: A progress report. *Behavior Therapy, 4,* 41–48.

Bernstein, I. L. (1985). Learning food aversions in the progression of cancer and its treatment. *Annals of the New York Academy of Sciences, 443,* 365–380.

Berry, D. S., & Miller, K. M. (2001). When boy meets girl: Attractiveness and the five-factor model in opposite-sex interactions. *Journal of Research in Personality, 35,* 62–77.

Bertrand, S., & Masling, J. M. (1969). Oral imagery and alcoholism. *Journal of Abnormal Psychology, 74,* 50–53.

Besser, A., & Priel, B. (2005). The apple does not fall far from the tree: Attachment styles and personality vulnerabilities to depression in three generations of women. *Personality and Social Psychology Bulletin, 31,* 1052–1073.

Bettelheim, B. (1982). Reflections: Freud and the soul. *New Yorker, 58,* 52–93.

Bettencourt, B. A., & Sheldon, K. (2001). Social roles as mechanisms for psychological need satisfaction within social groups. *Journal of Personality and Social Psychology, 81,* 1131–1143.

Binswanger, L. (1963). *Being-in-the-world: Selected papers of Ludwig Binswanger.* New York: Basic Books.

Bjork, J. M., Dougherty, D. M., Moeller, F. G., & Swann, A. C. (2000). Differential behavioral effects of plasma tryptophan depletion and loading in aggressive and nonaggressive men. *Neuropsychopharmacology, 22,* 357–369.

Bjorklund, D. F., & Pellegrini, A. D. (2002). *Origins of human nature: Evolutionary developmental psychology.* Washington, DC: American Psychological Association.

Black, A. E., & Deci, E. L. (2000). The effects of instructors' autonomy support and students' autonomous motivation on learning organic chemistry: A self-determination theory perspective. *Science Education, 84,* 740–756.

Blackburn, R. (1968a). Emotionality, extraversion and aggression in paranoid and non-paranoid schizophrenic offenders. *British Journal of Psychiatry, 115,* 1301–1302.

Blackburn, R. (1968b). Personality in relation to extreme aggression in psychiatry offenders. *British Journal of Psychiatry, 114,* 821–828.

Blanchard, E. B., & Epstein, L. H. (1978). *A biofeedback primer.* Reading, MA: Addison-Wesley.

Blanchard, R. (2004). Quantitative and theoretical analyses of the relation between older brothers and homosexuality in men. *Journal of Theoretical Biology, 230,* 173–187.

Blanchard, R., Cantor, J. M., Bogaert, A. F., Breedlove, S. M., & Ellis, L. (2006). Interaction of fraternal birth order and handedness in the development of male homosexuality. *Hormones and Behavior, 49,* 405–414.

Blanck, R., & Blanck, G. (1986). *Beyond ego psychology: Developmental object relations theory.* New York: Columbia University Press.

Blatt, S. J., Wein, S. J., Chevron, E., & Quinlan, D. M. (1979). Parental representations and depression in normal young adults. *Journal of Abnormal Psychology, 88,* 388–397.

Blatt, S. J., & Zuroff, D. C. (1992). Interpersonal relatedness and self-definition: Two prototypes for depression. *Clinical Psychology Review, 12,* 527–562.

Block, J. (1977). Advancing the science of personality: Paradigmatic shift or improving the quality of research? In D. Magnusson & N. S. Endler (Eds.), *Personality at the crossroads: Current issues in interactional psychology* (pp. 37–63). Hillsdale, NJ: Erlbaum.

Block, J. (1982). Assimilation, accommodation, and the dynamics of personality development. *Child Development, 53,* 281–295.

Block, J. (1995). A contrarian view of the five-factor approach to personality assessment. *Psychological Bulletin, 117,* 187–215.

Block, J. (2001). Millennial contrarianism: The five-factor approach to personality description 5 years later. *Journal of Research in Personality, 35,* 98–107.

Block, J. (2002). *Personality as an affect-processing system: Toward an integrative theory.* Mahwah, NJ: Erlbaum.

Block, J., & Block, J. H. (2006). Venturing a 30-year longitudinal study. *American Psychologist, 61,* 315–327.

Block, J., & Kremen, A. M. (1996). IQ and ego-resiliency: Conceptual and empirical connections and separateness. *Journal of Personality and Social Psychology, 70,* 349–361.

Block, J., von der Lippe, A., & Block, J. H. (1973). Sex-role and socialization patterns: Some personality concomitants and environmental antecedents. *Journal of Consulting and Clinical Psychology, 41,* 321–341.

Block, J. H. (1961). *The Q-sort method in personality assessment and psychiatric research.* Springfield, IL: Charles C. Thomas.

Block, J. H. (1973). Conceptions of sex role: Some cross-cultural and longitudinal perspectives. *American Psychologist, 28,* 512–526.

Block, J. H. (1979). Another look at sex differentiation in the socialization behaviors of mothers and fathers. In F. L. Denmark & J. Sherman (Eds.), *Psychology of women: Future directions for research.* New York: Psychological Dimensions.

Block, J. H., & Block, J. (1980). The role of ego-control and ego-resiliency in the organization of behavior. In W. A. Collins (Ed.), *Development of cognition, affect, and social relations* (Minnesota symposia on child psychology, Vol. 13, pp. 39–101). Hillsdale, NJ: Erlbaum.

Bocklandt, S., Horvath, S., Vilain, E., & Hamer, D. H. (2006). Extreme skewing of X chromosome inactivation in mothers of homosexual men. *Human Genetics, 118,* 691–694.

Bogg, T., & Roberts, B. W. (2004). Conscientiousness and health-related behaviors: A meta-analysis of the leading behavioral contributors to mortality. *Psychological Bulletin, 130,* 887–919.

Bolger, N., & Zuckerman, A. (1995). A framework for studying personality in the stress process. *Journal of Personality and Social Psychology, 69,* 890–902.

Bolles, R. C. (1972). Reinforcement, expectancy, and learning. *Psychological Review, 79,* 394–409.

Bonarius, H., Holland, R., & Rosenberg, S. (Eds.). (1980). *Personal construct theory: Recent advances in theory and practice.* London, England: Macmillan.

Booth, A., & Dabbs, J. M., Jr. (1993). Testosterone and men's marriages. *Social Forces, 72,* 463–477.

Borgatta, E. F. (1964). The structure of personality characteristics. *Behavioral Science, 12,* 8–17.

Boring, E. G. (1930). A new ambiguous figure. *American Journal of Psychology, 42,* 444–445.

Borkenau, P., Riemann, R., Angleitner, A., & Spinath, F. M. (2001). Genetic and environmental influences on observed personality: Evidence from the German observational study of adult twins. *Journal of Personality and Social Psychology, 80,* 655–668.

Borkenau, P., Riemann, R., Angleitner, A., & Spinath, F. M. (2002). Similarity of childhood experiences and personality resemblance in monozygotic and dizygotic twins: A test of the equal environments assumption. *Personality and Individual Differences, 33,* 261–269.

Bornstein, R. F., & Masling, J. (1985). Orality and latency of volunteering to serve as experimental subjects: A replication. *Journal of Personality Assessment, 49,* 306–310.

Borsboom, D., Mellenbergh, G. J., & van Heerden, J. (2004). The concept of validity. *Psychological Review, 111,* 1061–1071.

Boss, M. (1963). *Psychoanalysis and Daseinsanalysis.* New York: Basic Books.

Bottome, P. (1939). *Alfred Adler: A biography.* New York: Putnam's.

Botwin, M. D., & Buss, D. M. (1989). Structure of act-report data: Is the five-factor model of personality recaptured? *Journal of Personality and Social Psychology, 56,* 988–1001.

Bouchard, T. J. (2004). Genetic influence on human psychological traits. *Current Directions in Psychological Science, 13,* 148–151.

Bouchard, T. J., Jr., Lykken, D. T., McGue, M., Segal, N. L., & Tellegen, A. (1990). Sources of human psychological differences: The Minnesota study of twins reared apart. *Science, 250,* 223–228.

Bouton, M. E. (1994). Context, ambiguity, and classical conditioning. *Current Directions in Psychological Science, 3,* 49–53.

Bouton, M. E. (2000). A learning theory perspective on lapse, relapse, and the maintenance of behavior change. *Health Psychology, 19,* 57–63.

Bower, J. E., Kemeny, M. E., Taylor, S. E., & Fahey, J. L. (1998). Cognitive processing, discovery of meaning, CD4 decline, and AIDS-related mortality among bereaved HIV seropositive men. *Journal of Consulting and Clinical Psychology, 66,* 979–986.

Bowlby, J. (1969). *Attachment and loss: Vol. 1, Attachment.* New York: Basic Books.

Bowlby, J. (1988). *A secure base: Parent–child attachment and healthy human development.* New York: Basic Books.

Boyatzis, R. E. (1973). Affiliation motivation. In D. C. McClelland & R. S. Steele (Eds.), *Human motivation: A book of readings.* Morristown, NJ: General Learning Press.

Bradburn, N. M., & Berlew, D. E. (1961). Need for achievement and English industrial growth. *Economic Development and Cultural Change, 10,* 8–20.

Bradley, G. W. (1978). Self-serving biases in the attribution process: A reexamination of the fact or fiction question. *Journal of Personality and Social Psychology, 36,* 56–71.

Brady, J. P. (1972). Systematic desensitization. In W. S. Agras (Ed.), *Behavior modification: Principles and clinical applications.* Boston: Little, Brown.

Brady, S. S., & Matthews, K. A. (2006). Effects of media violence on health-related outcomes among young men. *Archives of Pediatric Adolescent Medicine, 160,* 341–347.

Bramel, D., Taub, B., & Blum, B. (1968). An observer's reaction to the suffering of his enemy. *Journal of Personality and Social Psychology, 8,* 384–392.

Brandon, T. H., Tiffany, S. T., Obremski, K. M., & Baker, T. B. (1990). Postcessation cigarette use: The process of relapse. *Addictive Behaviors, 15,* 105–114.

Brandstätter, H. (1983). Emotional responses to other persons in everyday life situations. *Journal of Personality and Social Psychology, 45,* 871–883.

Brandstätter, V., & Frank, E. (2002). Effects of deliberative and implemental mindsets on persistence in goal-directed behavior. *Personality and Social Psychology Bulletin, 28,* 1366–1378.

Brandstätter, V., Lengfelder, A., & Gollwitzer, P. M. (2001). Implementation intentions and efficient action initiation. *Journal of Personality and Social Psychology, 81,* 946–960.

Branje, S. J. T., van Lieshout, C. F. M., & van Aken, M. A. G. (2004). Relations between big five personality characteristics and perceived support in adolescents' families. *Journal of Personality and Social Psychology, 86,* 615–628.

Breedlove, S. M. (1992). Sexual dimorphism in the vertebrate nervous system. *Journal of Neuroscience, 12,* 4133–4142.

Breedlove, S. M. (1994). Sexual differentiation of the human nervous system. *Annual Review of Psychology, 45,* 389–418.

Brehm, J. W. (1966). *A theory of psychological reactance.* New York: Academic.

Brehm, S. S., & Brehm, J. W. (1981). *Psychological reactance: A theory of freedom and control.* New York: Academic.

Breland, H. M. (1974). Birth order, family constellation, and verbal achievement. *Child Development, 45,* 1011–1019.

Breland, K., & Breland, M. (1961). The misbehavior of organisms. *American Psychologist, 16,* 681–684.

Brennan, K. A., Clark, C. L., & Shaver, P. R. (1998). Self-report measurement of adult attachment: An integrative overview. In J. A. Simpson & W. S. Rholes (Eds.), *Attachment theory and close relationships* (pp. 46–76). New York: Guilford.

Brenner, C. (1957). *An elementary textbook of psychoanalysis.* Garden City, NY: Doubleday.

Brewer, W. F. (1974). There is no convincing evidence for operant or classical conditioning in adult humans. In W. B. Weimer & D. S. Palermo (Eds.), *Cognition and the symbolic processes.* Hillsdale, NJ: Erlbaum.

Bridger, W. H., & Mandel, I. J. (1964). A comparison of GSR fear responses produced by threat and electric shock. *Journal of Psychiatric Research, 2,* 31–40.

Briggs, S. R. (1989). The optimal level of measurement for personality constructs. In D. M. Buss & N. Cantor (Eds.), *Personality psychology: Recent trends and emerging directions* (pp. 246–260). New York: Springer-Verlag.

Brissette, I., Scheier, M. F., & Carver, C. S. (2002). The role of optimism in social network development, coping, and psychological adjustment during a life transition. *Journal of Personality and Social Psychology, 82,* 102–111.

Britt, T. W., & Shepperd, J. A. (1999). Trait relevance and trait assessment. *Personality and Social Psychology Review, 3,* 108–122.

Broadbent, D. E. (1977). Levels, hierarchies, and the locus of control. *Quarterly Journal of Experimental Psychology, 29,* 181–201.

Broadbent, E., Petrie, K. J., Alley, P. G., & Booth, R. J. (2003). Psychological stress impairs early wound repair following surgery. *Psychosomatic Medicine, 65,* 865–869.

Brody, N. (Ed.). (1987). Special issue on the unconscious. *Personality and Social Psychology Bulletin, 13,* 293–429.

Brokaw, D. W., & McLemore, C. W. (1983). Toward a more rigorous definition of social reinforcement: Some interpersonal clarifications. *Journal of Personality and Social Psychology, 44,* 1014–1020.

Brooks, R. A. (2002). *Flesh and machines: How robots will change us.* New York: Pantheon.

Brown, I., Jr., & Inouye, D. K. (1978). Learned helplessness through modeling: The role of perceived similarity in competence. *Journal of Personality and Social Psychology, 36,* 900–908.

Brown, J. S. (1948). Gradients of approach and avoidance responses and their relation to level of motivation. *Journal of Comparative and Physiological Psychology, 41,* 450–465.

Brown, J. S. (1957). Principles of intrapersonal conflict. *Journal of Conflict Resolution, 1,* 135–154.

Bruhn, A. R., & Schiffman, H. (1982). Prediction of locus of control stance from the earliest childhood memory. *Journal of Personality Assessment, 46,* 380–390.

Bruner, J. S. (1957). On perceptual readiness. *Psychological Review, 64,* 123–152.

Brunstein, J. C., & Maier, G. W. (2005). Implicit and self-attributed motives to achieve: Two separate but interacting needs. *Journal of Personality and Social Psychology, 89,* 205–222.

Brunstein, J. C., Schultheiss, O. C., & Grässmann, R. (1998). Personal goals and emotional well-being: The moderating role of motive dispositions. *Journal of Personality and Social Psychology, 75,* 494–508.

Brunswik, E. (1951). The probability point of view. In M. H. Marx (Ed.), *Psychological theory.* New York: Macmillan.

Buccino, G., Binkofski, F., Fink, G. R., Fadiga, L., Fogassi, L., Gallese, V., Seitz, R. J., Zilles, K., Rizzolatti, G., & Freund,

H. J. (2001). Action observation activates premotor and parietal areas in somatotopic manner: An fMRI study. *European Journal of Neuroscience, 13,* 400–404.

Buchanan, A., Brock, D. W., Daniels, N., & Wikler, D. (2000). *From chance to choice: Genetics and justice.* New York: Cambridge University Press.

Buchanan, G. M. (1995). Explanatory style and coronary heart disease. In G. M. Buchanan & M. E. P. Seligman (Eds.), *Explanatory style* (pp. 225–232). Hillsdale, NJ: Erlbaum.

Buller, D. J. (2005a). *Adapting minds: Evolutionary psychology and the persistent quest for human nature.* Cambridge, MA: MIT Press.

Buller, D. J. (2005b). Evolutionary psychology: The emperor's new paradigm. *Trends in Cognitive Sciences, 9,* 277–283.

Burger, J. M. (1989). Negative reactions to increases in perceived personal control. *Journal of Personality and Social Psychology, 56,* 246–256.

Burnstein, E., Crandall, C., & Kitayama, S. (1994). Some neo-Darwinian decision rules for altruism: Weighing cues for inclusive fitness as a function of the biological importance of the decision. *Journal of Personality and Social Psychology, 67,* 773–789.

Burroughs, W. J., & Drews, D. R. (1991). Rule structure in the psychological representation of physical settings. *Journal of Experimental Social Psychology, 27,* 217–238.

Bursik, K. (1991). Adaptation to divorce and ego development in adult women. *Journal of Personality and Social Psychology, 60,* 300–306.

Bushman, B. J. (2002). Does venting anger feed or extinguish the flame? Catharsis, rumination, distraction, anger, and aggressive responding. *Personality and Social Psychology Bulletin, 28,* 724–731.

Bushman, B. J., & Baumeister, R. F. (1998). Threatened egotism, narcissism, self-esteem, and direct and displaced aggression: Does self-love or self-hate lead to violence? *Journal of Personality and Social Psychology, 75,* 219–229.

Bushman, B. J., Baumeister, R. F., & Phillips, C. M. (2001). Do people aggress to improve their mood? Catharsis beliefs, affect regulation opportunity, and aggressive responding. *Journal of Personality and Social Psychology, 81,* 17–32.

Buss, A. H. (1983). Social rewards and personality. *Journal of Personality and Social Psychology, 44,* 553–563.

Buss, A. H., & Plomin, R. (1975). *A temperament theory of personality development.* New York: Wiley-Interscience.

Buss, A. H., & Plomin, R. (1984). *Temperament: Early developing personality traits.* Hillsdale, NJ: Erlbaum.

Buss, D. M. (1984). Toward a psychology of person-environment correlation: The role of spouse selection. *Journal of Personality and Social Psychology, 47,* 361–377.

Buss, D. M. (1985). Human mate selection. *American Scientist, 73,* 47–51.

Buss, D. M. (1988). The evolution of human intrasexual competition: Tactics of mate attraction. *Journal of Personality and Social Psychology, 54,* 616–628.

Buss, D. M. (1989). Sex differences in human mate preferences: Evolutionary hypotheses tested in 37 cultures. *Behavioral and Brain Sciences, 12,* 1–49.

Buss, D. M. (1991). Evolutionary personality psychology. *Annual Review of Psychology, 42,* 459–491.

Buss, D. M. (1994a). *The evolution of desire: Strategies of human mating.* New York: Basic Books.

Buss, D. M. (1994b). The strategies of human mating. *American Scientist, 82,* 238–249.

Buss, D. M. (1995). Evolutionary psychology: A new paradigm for psychological science. *Psychological Inquiry, 6,* 1–30.

Buss, D. M. (2001). Cognitive biases and emotional wisdom in the evolution of conflict between the sexes. *Current Directions in Psychological Science, 10,* 219–223.

Buss, D. M. (Ed.). (2005a). *The handbook of evolutionary psychology.* New York: Wiley.

Buss, D. M. (2005b). *The murderer next door: Why the mind is designed to kill.* New York, Penguin.

Buss, D. M., Gomes, M., Higgins, D. S., & Lauterbach, K. (1987). Tactics of manipulation. *Journal of Personality and Social Psychology, 52,* 1219–1229.

Buss, D. M., Larsen, R. J., Westen, D., & Semmelroth, J. (1992). Sex differences in jealousy: Evolution, physiology, and psychology. *Psychological Science, 3,* 251–255.

Buss, D. M., & Schmitt, D. P. (1993). Sexual strategies theory: An evolutionary perspective on human mating. *Psychological Review, 100,* 204–232.

Buss, D. M., & Shackelford, T. K. (1997). From vigilance to violence: Mate retention tactics in married couples. *Journal of Personality and Social Psychology, 72,* 346–361.

Bussey, K., & Bandura, A. (1984). Influence of gender constancy and social power on sex-linked modeling. *Journal of Personality and Social Psychology, 47,* 1292–1302.

Bussey, K., & Bandura, A. (1999). Social cognitive theory of gender development and differentiation. *Psychological Review, 106,* 676–713.

Butcher, J. N. (Ed.). (1996). *International adaptations of the MMPI-2: Research and clinical applications.* Minneapolis: University of Minnesota Press.

Butcher, J. N., Dahlstrom, W., Graham, J., Tellegen, A., & Kaemmer, B. (1989). *Manual for administering and scoring the MMPI-2.* Minneapolis: University of Minnesota Press.

Butler, J. M., & Haigh, G. V. (1954). Changes in the relation between self-concepts and ideal concepts consequent upon client-centered counseling. In C. R. Rogers & R. F. Dymond (Eds.), *Psychotherapy and personality change: Coordinated research studies in the client-centered approach.* Chicago: University of Chicago Press.

Byrne, D., McDonald, R. D., & Mikawa, J. (1963). Approach and avoidance affiliation motives. *Journal of Personality, 31,* 21–37.

Cacioppo, J. T., Gardner, W. L., & Berntson, G. G. (1999). The affect system has parallel and integrative processing components: Form follows function. *Journal of Personality and Social Psychology, 76,* 839–855.

Cacioppo, J. T., & Petty, R. E. (1980). The effects of orienting task on differential hemispheric EEG activation. *Neuropsychologia, 18,* 675–683.

Cacioppo, J. T., & Petty, R. E. (1982). The need for cognition. *Journal of Personality and Social Psychology, 42,* 116–131.

Cacioppo, J. T., & Petty, R. E. (1983). *Social psychophysiology.* New York: Guilford.

Cacioppo, J. T., & Petty, R. E. (1984). The need for cognition: Relationship to attitudinal processes. In R. P. McGlynn, J. E. Maddux, C. Stoltenberg, & J. H. Harvey (Eds.), *Social perception in clinical and counseling psychology.* Lubbock: Texas Tech Press.

Cacioppo, J. T., Petty, R. E., Feinstein, J. A., & Jarvis, W. B. G. (1996). Dispositional differences in cognitive motivation: The life and times of individuals varying in need for cognition. *Psychological Bulletin, 119,* 197–253.

Cacioppo, J. T., Petty, R. E., Kao, C. F., & Rodriguez, R. (1986). Central and peripheral routes to persuasion: An individual difference perspective. *Journal of Personality and Social Psychology, 51,* 1032–1043.

Cacioppo, J. T., Petty, R. E., & Morris, K. J. (1983). Effects of need for cognition on message evaluation, recall, and persuasion. *Journal of Personality and Social Psychology, 45,* 805–818.

Cacioppo, J. T., & Sandman, C. A. (1981). Psychophysiological functioning, cognitive responding, and attitudes. In R. E. Petty, T. M. Ostrom, & T. C. Brock (Eds.), *Cognitive responses in persuasion.* Hillsdale, NJ: Erlbaum.

Cadinu, M., Maass, A., Rosabianca, A., & Kiesner, J. (2005). Why do women underperform under stereotype threat? Evidence for the role of negative thinking. *Psychological Science, 16,* 572–578.

Cain, D. J., & Seeman, J. (Eds.). (2002). *Humanistic psychotherapies: Handbook of research and practice.* Washington, DC: American Psychological Association.

Cameron, O. G., Abelson, J. L., & Young, E. A. (2004). Anxious and depressive disorders and their comorbidity: Effect on central nervous system noradrenergic function. *Biological Psychiatry, 56,* 875–883.

Campbell, D. T. (1960). Recommendations for the APA test standards regarding construct, trait, and discriminant validity. *American Psychologist, 15,* 546–553.

Campbell, D. T., & Fiske, D. W. (1959). Convergent and discriminant validation by the multitrait-multimethod matrix. *Psychological Bulletin, 56,* 81–105.

Campbell, W. K. (1999). Narcissism and romantic attraction. *Journal of Personality and Social Psychology, 77,* 1254–1270.

Campbell, W. K., & Foster, C. A. (2002). Narcissism and commitment in romantic relationships: An investment

model analysis. *Personality and Social Psychology Bulletin, 28,* 484–495.

Cannon, D. S., Baker, T. B., Gino, A., & Nathan, P. E. (1986). Alcohol-aversion therapy: Relation between strength of aversion and abstinence. *Journal of Consulting and Clinical Psychology, 54,* 825–830.

Cannon, W. B. (1932). *The wisdom of the body.* New York: Norton.

Cantor, N., & Kihlstrom, J. F. (1987). *Personality and social intelligence.* Englewood Cliffs, NJ: Prentice-Hall.

Cantor, N., & Mischel, W. (1977). Traits as prototypes: Effects on recognition memory. *Journal of Personality and Social Psychology, 35,* 38–48.

Cantor, N., Smith, E. E., French, R., & Mezzich, J. (1980). Psychiatric diagnosis as prototype categorization. *Journal of Abnormal Psychology, 89,* 181–193.

Caporeal, L. R. (2001). Evolutionary psychology: Toward a unifying theory and a hybrid science. *Annual Review of Psychology, 52,* 607–628.

Carey, G. (2003). *Human genetics for the social sciences.* Thousand Oaks, CA: Sage.

Carey, G., Goldsmith, H. H., Tellegen, A., & Gottesman, I. I. (1978). Genetics and personality inventories: The limits of replication with twin data. *Behavior Genetics, 8,* 299–313.

Carlston, D. E., & Skowronski, J. J. (1994). Savings in the relearning of trait information as evidence for spontaneous inference generation. *Journal of Personality and Social Psychology, 66,* 840–856.

Carnagey, N. L., & Anderson, C. A. (2005). The effects of reward and punishment in violent video games on aggressive affect, cognition, and behavior. *Psychological Science, 16,* 882–889.

Carnelley, K. B., Pietromonaco, P. R., & Jaffe, K. (1994). Depression, working models of others, and relationship functioning. *Journal of Personality and Social Psychology, 66,* 127–140.

Carroll, L. (1987). A study of narcissism, affiliation, intimacy, and power motives among students in business administration. *Psychological Reports, 61,* 355–358.

Carter, B. L., & Tiffany, S. T. (1999). Meta-analysis of cue reactivity in addiction research. *Addiction, 94,* 327–340.

Carter, C. S. (1998). Neuroendocrine perspectives on social attachment and love. *Psychoneuroimmunology, 23,* 779–818.

Carver, C. S. (1975). Physical aggression as a function of objective self-awareness and attitudes toward punishment. *Journal of Experimental Social Psychology, 11,* 510–519.

Carver, C. S. (1997a). Adult attachment and personality: Converging evidence and a new measure. *Personality and Social Psychology Bulletin, 23,* 865–883.

Carver, C. S. (1997b). The Internal–External scale confounds internal locus of control with expectancies of positive outcomes. *Personality and Social Psychology Bulletin, 23,* 580–585.

Carver, C. S. (1998). Generalization, adverse events, and development of depressive symptoms. *Journal of Personality, 66,* 609–620.

Carver, C. S. (2003). Pleasure as a sign you can attend to something else: Placing positive feelings within a general model of affect. *Cognition and Emotion, 17,* 241–261.

Carver, C. S. (2004). Negative affects deriving from the behavioral approach system. *Emotion, 4,* 3–22.

Carver, C. S. (2005). Impulse and constraint: Perspectives from personality psychology, convergence with theory in other areas, and potential for integration. *Personality and Social Psychology Review, 9,* 312–333.

Carver, C. S., & Baird, E. (1998). The American dream revisited: Is it *what* you want or *why* you want it that matters? *Psychological Science, 9,* 289–292.

Carver, C. S., Ganellen, R. J., Froming, W. J., & Chambers, W. (1983). Modeling: An analysis in terms of category accessibility. *Journal of Experimental Social Psychology, 19,* 403–421.

Carver, C. S., Kus, L. A., & Scheier, M. F. (1994). Effects of good versus bad mood and optimistic versus pessimistic outlook on social acceptance versus rejection. *Journal of Social and Clinical Psychology, 13,* 138–151.

Carver, C. S., LaVoie, L., Kuhl, J., & Ganellen, R. J. (1988). Cognitive concomitants of depression: A further examination of the roles of generalization, high standards, and self-criticism. *Journal of Social and Clinical Psychology, 7,* 350–365.

Carver, C. S., Lawrence, J. W., & Scheier, M. F. (1999). Self-discrepancies and affect: Incorporating the role of feared selves. *Personality and Social Psychology Bulletin, 25,* 783–792.

Carver, C. S., Lehman, J. M., & Antoni, M. H. (2003). Dispositional pessimism predicts illness-related disruption of social and recreational activities among breast cancer patients. *Journal of Personality and Social Psychology, 84,* 813–821.

Carver, C. S., & Miller, C. J. (2006). Relations of serotonin function to personality: Current views and a key methodological issue. *Psychiatry Research, 144,* 1–15.

Carver, C. S., Pozo, C., Harris, S. D., Noriega, V., Scheier, M. F., Robinson, D. S., Ketcham, A. S., Moffat, F. L., & Clark, K. C. (1993). How coping mediates the effect of optimism on distress: A study of women with early stage breast cancer. *Journal of Personality and Social Psychology, 65,* 375–390.

Carver, C. S., & Scheier, M. F. (1981). *Attention and self-regulation: A control-theory approach to human behavior.* New York: Springer-Verlag.

Carver, C. S., & Scheier, M. F. (1986). Functional and dysfunctional responses to anxiety: The interaction between expectancies and self-focused attention. In R. Schwarzer (Ed.), *Self-related cognitions in anxiety and motivation.* Hillsdale, NJ: Erlbaum.

Carver, C. S., & Scheier, M. F. (1990). Principles of self-regulation: Action and emotion. In E. T. Higgins & R. M. Sorrentino (Eds.), *Handbook of motivation and cognition: Foundations of social behavior* (Vol. 2, pp. 3–52). New York: Guilford.

Carver, C. S., & Scheier, M. F. (1998). *On the self-regulation of behavior.* New York: Cambridge University Press.

Carver, C. S., & Scheier, M. F. (2002). Control processes and self-organization as complementary principles underlying behavior. *Personality and Social Psychology Review, 6,* 304–315.

Carver, C. S., & Scheier, M. F. (2007). Feedback processes in the simultaneous regulation of action and affect. In J. Y. Shah & W. L. Gardner (Eds.), *Handbook of motivation science.* New York: Guilford.

Carver, C. S., & White, T. L. (1994). Behavioral inhibition, behavioral activation, and affective responses to impending reward and punishment: The BIS/BAS scales. *Journal of Personality and Social Psychology, 67,* 319–333.

Caspar, F., Rothenfluh, T., & Segal, Z. (1992). The appeal of connectionism to clinical psychology. *Clinical Psychology Review, 12,* 719–762.

Caspi, A., Elder, G. H., Jr., & Bem, D. J. (1987). Moving against the world: Life-course patterns of explosive children. *Developmental Psychology, 23,* 308–313.

Caspi, A., Elder, G. H., Jr., & Bem, D. J. (1988). Moving away from the world: Life-course patterns of shy children. *Developmental Psychology, 24,* 824–831.

Caspi, A., & Herbener, E. S. (1990). Continuity and change: Assortative marriage and the consistency of personality in adulthood. *Journal of Personality and Social Psychology, 58,* 250–258.

Caspi, A., McClay, J., Moffitt, T. E., Mill, J., Martin, J., Craig, I. W., Taylor, A., & Poulton, R. (2002). Role of genotype in the cycle of violence in maltreated children. *Science, 297,* 851–854.

Caspi, A., Roberts, B. W., & Shiner, R. L. (2005). Personality development: Stability and change. *Annual Review of Psychology, 56,* 453–484.

Cassidy, J., & Shaver, P. R. (Eds.). (1999). *Handbook of attachment: Theory, research, and clinical applications.* New York: Guilford.

Catania, A. C., & Harnad, S. (Eds.). (1988). *The operant behaviorism of B. F. Skinner: Comments and consequences.* New York: Cambridge University Press.

Cattell, H. E. P. (1993). Comment on Goldberg. *American Psychologist, 48,* 1302–1303.

Cattell, R. B. (1947). Confirmation and clarification of primary personality factors. *Psychometrica, 12,* 197–220.

Cattell, R. B. (1965). *The scientific analysis of personality.* Baltimore: Penguin.

Cattell, R. B. (1978). *The scientific use of factor analysis.* New York: Plenum.

Cattell, R. B. (1979). *Personality and learning theory, Volume 1. The structure of personality in its environment.* New York: Springer-Verlag.

Cattell, R. B. (1985). *Human motivation and the dynamic calculus.* New York: Praeger.

Cattell, R. B., Eber, H. W., & Tatsuoka, M. M. (1977). *Handbook for the 16 personality factor questionnaire.* Champaign, IL: IPAT.

Cattell, R. B., & Kline, P. (1977). *The scientific analysis of personality and motivation.* New York: Academic.

Cervone, D. (1997). Social-cognitive mechanisms and personality coherence: Self-knowledge, situational beliefs, and cross-situational coherence in perceived self-efficacy. *Psychological Science, 8,* 43–50.

Cervone, D. (2004). The architecture of personality. *Psychological Review, 111,* 183–204.

Chambliss, C. A., & Murray, E. J. (1979). Efficacy attribution, locus of control, and weight loss. *Cognitive Therapy and Research, 3,* 349–354.

Chamorro-Premuzic, T., & Furnham, A. (2003). Personality predicts academic performance: Evidence from two longitudinal university samples. *Journal of Research in Personality, 37,* 319–338.

Chance, S. E., Brown, R. T., Dabbs, J. M., Jr., & Casey, R. (2000). Testosterone, intelligence and behavior disorders in young boys. *Personality and Individual Differences, 28,* 437–445.

Chaplin, W. F., Phillips, J. B., Brown, J. D., Clanton, N. R., & Stein, J. L. (2000). Handshaking, gender, personality, and first impressions. *Journal of Personality and Social Psychology, 79,* 110–117.

Chapman, L. J. (1967). Illusory correlations in observational report. *Journal of Verbal Learning and Verbal Behavior, 6,* 151–155.

Chartrand, T. L., & Bargh, J. A. (1996). Automatic activation of impression formation and memorization goals: Nonconscious goal priming reproduces effects of explicit task instructions. *Journal of Personality and Social Psychology, 71,* 464–478.

Chartrand, T. L., & Bargh, J. A. (1999). The chameleon effect: The perception–behavior link and social interaction. *Journal of Personality and Social Psychology, 76,* 893–910.

Chassin, L., Flora, D. B., & King, K. M. (2004). Trajectories of alcohol and drug use and dependence from adolescence to adulthood: The effects of familial alcoholism and personality. *Journal of Abnormal Psychology, 113,* 483–498.

Chatterjee, B. B., & Eriksen, C. W. (1962). Cognitive factors in heart rate conditioning. *Journal of Experimental Psychology, 64,* 272–279.

Chen, E., & Matthews, K. A. (2001). Cognitive appraisal biases: An approach to understanding the relation between socioeconomic status and cardiovascular reactivity in children. *Annals of Behavioral Medicine, 23,* 101–111.

Chen, S. (2003). Psychological-state theories about significant others: Implications for the content and structure of significant-other representations. *Personality and Social Psychology Bulletin, 29,* 1285–1302.

Chomsky, N. (1959). Review of *Verbal behavior* by B. F. Skinner. *Language, 35,* 26–58.

Christensen, A. J., Ehlers, S. L., Wiebe, J. S., Moran, P. J., Raichle, K., Ferneyhough, K., & Lawton, W. J. (2002). Patient personality and mortality: A 4-year prospective examination of chronic renal insufficiency. *Health Psychology, 21,* 315–320.

Church, A. T. (Ed.). (2001). Introduction: Culture and personality [Special issue]. *Journal of Personality, 69,* 787–801.

Church, A. T., & Burke, P. J. (1994). Exploratory and confirmatory tests of the big five and Tellegen's three- and four-dimensional models. *Journal of Personality and Social Psychology, 66,* 93–114.

Cialdini, R. B., Schaller, M., Houlihan, D., Arps, K., Fultz, J., & Beaman, A. L. (1987). Empathy-based helping: Is it selflessly or selfishly motivated? *Journal of Personality and Social Psychology, 52,* 749–758.

Ciminero, A. R., Calhoun, K. S., & Adams, H. E. (Eds.). (1977). *Handbook of behavioral assessment.* New York: Wiley.

Claridge, G. S. (1967). *Personality and arousal.* New York: Pergamon.

Clark, L. A., Kochanska, G., & Ready, R. (2000). Mothers' personality and its interaction with child temperament as predictors of parenting behavior. *Journal of Personality and Social Psychology, 79,* 274–285.

Clark, L. A., & Watson, D. (1999). Temperament: A new paradigm for trait psychology. In L. A. Pervin & O. P. John (Eds.), *Handbook of personality: Theory and research* (2nd ed., pp. 399–423). New York: Guilford.

Clark, R. A., & McClelland, D. C. (1956). A factor-analytic integration of imaginative and performance measures of the need for achievement. *Journal of General Psychology, 55,* 73–83.

Clark, R. D., & Hatfield, E. (1989). Gender differences in receptivity to sexual offers. *Journal of Psychology and Human Sexuality, 2,* 39–55.

Clark, W. R. (1996). *Sex and the origins of death.* New York: Oxford University Press.

Clausen, J. A. (1981). Men's occupational careers in the middle years. In D. H. Eichorn, J. A. Clausen, N. Haan, M. P. Honzik, & P. H. Mussen (Eds.), *Present and past in middle life* (pp. 321–351). New York: Academic.

Cleare, A. J., & Bond, A. J. (1995). The effect of tryptophan depletion and enhancement on subjective and behavioural aggression in normal male subjects. *Psychopharmacology, 118,* 72–81.

Cleare, A. J., & Bond, A. J. (1997). Does central serotonergic function correlate inversely with aggression? A study using D-fenfluramine in healthy subjects. *Psychiatry Research, 69,* 89–95.

Cline, V. B., Croft, R. G., & Courrier, S. (1973). Desensitization of children to television violence. *Journal of Personality and Social Psychology, 27,* 360–365.

Cloninger, C. R. (1987). A systematic method of clinical description and classification of personality variants: A proposal. *Archives of General Psychiatry, 44,* 573–588.

Cloninger, C. R. (1988). A unified biosocial theory of personality and its role in the development of anxiety states: A reply to commentaries. *Psychiatric Developments, 2,* 83–120.

Clower, C. E., & Bothwell, R. K. (2001). An exploratory study of the relationship between the Big Five and inmate recidivism. *Journal of Research in Personality, 35,* 231–237.

Coccaro, E. F., Kavoussi, R. J., Cooper, T. B., & Hauger, R. L. (1997). Central serotonin activity and aggression: Inverse relationship with prolactin response to *d*-fenfluramine, but not CSF 5-HIAA concentration, in human subjects. *American Journal of Psychiatry, 154,* 1430–1435.

Cohen, A. R. (1957). Need for cognition and order of communication as determinants of opinion change. In C. I. Hovland (Ed.), *The order of presentation in persuasion.* New Haven, CT: Yale University Press.

Cohen, A. R., Stotland, E., & Wolfe, D. M. (1955). An experimental investigation of need for cognition. *Journal of Abnormal and Social Psychology, 51,* 291–294.

Cohen, D., Nisbett, R. E., Bowdle, B. F., & Schwarz, N. (1996). Insult, aggression, and the Southern culture of honor: An "experimental ethnology." *Journal of Personality and Social Psychology, 70,* 945–960.

Cohen, S. (2005). The Pittsburgh common cold studies: Psychosocial predictors of susceptibility to respiratory infectious illness. *International Journal of Behavioral Medicine, 12,* 123–131.

Cohen, S., Doyle, W. J., Turner, R. B., Alper, C. M., & Skoner, D. P. (2003). Emotional style and susceptibility to the common cold. *Psychosomatic Medicine, 65,* 652–657.

Cohen-Bendahan, C. C. C., van de Beek, C., & Berenbaum, S. A. (2005). Prenatal sex hormone effects on child and adult sex-typed behavior: Methods and findings. *Neuroscience and Biobehavioral Reviews, 29,* 353–384.

Cohn, L. D. (1991). Sex differences in the course of personality development: A meta-analysis. *Psychological Bulletin, 109,* 252–266.

Cohn, L. D., & Westenberg, P. M. (2004). Intelligence and maturity: Meta-analytic evidence for the incremental and discriminant validity of Loevinger's Measure of Ego Development. *Journal of Personality and Social Psychology, 86,* 760–772.

Collier, P. J., & Callero, P. J. (2005). Role theory and social cognition: Learning to think like a recycler. *Self and Identity, 4,* 45–58.

Collins, N. L., Ford, M. B., Guichard, A. C., Feeney, B. C. (2006). Responding to need in intimate relationships: Normative processes and individual differences. In M. Mikulincer & G. Goodman (Eds.), *The dynamics of love: Attachment, caregiving, and sex* (pp. 149–189). New York: Guilford.

Collins, N. L., & Read, S. J. (1990). Adult attachment, working models, and relationship quality in dating couples. *Journal of Personality and Social Psychology, 58,* 644–663.

Conklin, C. A., & Tiffany, S. T. (2001). The impact of imagining personalized versus standardized urge scenarios on cigarette craving and autonomic reactivity. *Experimental and Clinical Psychopharmacology, 9,* 399–408.

Conklin, C. A., & Tiffany, S. T. (2002). Applying extinction research and theory to cue-exposure addiction treatments. *Addiction, 97,* 155–167.

Conley, J. J. (1985). Longitudinal stability of personality traits: A multitrait-multimethod-multioccasion analysis. *Journal of Personality and Social Psychology, 49,* 1266–1282.

Conner, T., & Barrett, L. (2005). Implicit self-attitudes predict spontaneous affect in daily life. *Emotion, 5,* 476–488.

Constantian, C. A. (1981). *Attitudes, beliefs, and behavior in regard to spending time alone.* Unpublished doctoral dissertation, Harvard University, Cambridge, MA.

Converse, J., & Presser, S. (1986). *Survey questions: Handcrafting the standardized questionnaire.* Newbury Park, CA: Sage.

Conway, M., & Giannopoulos, C. (1993). Dysphoria and decision making: Limited information use for evaluations of multiattribute targets. *Journal of Personality and Social Psychology, 64,* 613–623.

Cook, M. L., & Peterson, C. (1986). Depressive irrationality. *Cognitive Therapy and Research, 10,* 293–298.

Cook, W. L. (2000). Understanding attachment security in a family context. *Journal of Personality and Social Psychology, 78,* 285–294.

Cooley, E. J., & Spiegler, M. D. (1980). Cognitive versus emotional coping responses as alternatives to test anxiety. *Cognitive Therapy and Research, 4,* 159–166.

Coolidge, F. L., Moor, C. J., Yamazaki, T. G., Stewart, S. E., & Segal, D. L. (2001). On the relationship between Karen Horney's tripartite neurotic type theory and personality disorder features. *Personality and Individual Differences, 30,* 1387–1400.

Cooper, M. L., Shapiro, C. M., & Powers, A. M. (1998). Motivations for sex and risky sexual behavior among adolescents and young adults: A functional perspective. *Journal of Personality and Social Psychology, 75,* 1528–1558.

Corr, P. J., Pickering, A. D., & Gray, J. A. (1997). Personality, punishment, and procedural learning: A test of J. A. Gray's anxiety theory. *Journal of Personality and Social Psychology, 73,* 337–344.

Cortes, J. B., & Gatti, F. M. (1965). Physique and self-descriptions of temperament. *Journal of Consulting Psychology, 29,* 432–439.

Costa, P. T., Jr., & McCrae, R. R. (1980). Influence of extraversion and neuroticism on subjective well-being: Happy and unhappy people. *Journal of Personality and Social Psychology, 38,* 668–678.

Costa, P. T., Jr., & McCrae, R. R. (1985). *The NEO Personality Inventory manual.* Odessa, FL: Psychological Assessment Resources.

Costa, P. T., Jr., & McCrae, R. R. (1988a). From catalog to classification: Murray's needs and the five-factor model. *Journal of Personality and Social Psychology, 55,* 258–265.

Costa, P. T., Jr., & McCrae, R. R. (1988b). Personality in adulthood: A six-year longitudinal study of self-reports and spouse ratings on the NEO personality inventory. *Journal of Personality and Social Psychology, 54,* 853–863.

Costa, P. T., Jr., & McCrae, R. R. (1989). Personality continuity and the changes of adult life. In M. Storandt & G. R. VandenBos (Eds.), *The adult years: Continuity and change* (pp. 45–77). Washington, DC: American Psychological Association.

Costa, P. T., Jr., & McCrae, R. R. (1992). *Revised NEO Personality Inventory (NEO-PI-R) and NEO Five-Factor Inventory (NEO-FFI) professional manual.* Odessa, FL: Psychological Assessment Resources.

Costa, P. T., Jr., & McCrae, R. R. (1995). Domains and facets: Hierarchical personality assessment using the revised NEO Pesonality Inventory. *Journal of Personality Assessment, 64,* 21–50.

Costa, P. T., Jr., & Widiger, T. A. (Eds.). (2002). *Personality disorders and the five-factor model of personality* (2nd ed.). Washington, DC: American Psychological Association.

Couch, A., & Keniston, K. (1960). Yeasayers and naysayers: Agreeing response set as a personality variable. *Journal of Abnormal and Social Psychology, 60,* 151–174.

Cozzarelli, C. (1993). Personality and self-efficacy as predictors of coping with abortion. *Journal of Personality and Social Psychology, 65,* 1224–1236.

Craig, K. D., & Weinstein, M. S. (1965). Conditioning vicarious affective arousal. *Psychological Reports, 17,* 955–963.

Craighead, W. E., Kazdin, A. E., & Mahoney, M. J. (1981). *Behavior modification: Principles, issues, and applications.* Boston: Houghton Mifflin.

Cramer, P. (2000). Defense mechanisms in psychology today: Further processes for adaptation. *American Psychologist, 55,* 637–646.

Cramer, P., & Tracy, A. (2005). The pathway from child personality to adult adjustment: The road is not straight. *Journal of Research in Personality, 39,* 369–394.

Crandall, R., McCown, D. A., & Robb, Z. (1988). The effects of assertiveness training on self-actualization. *Small Group Behavior, 19,* 134–145.

Crawford, C. B. (1989). The theory of evolution: Of what value to psychology? *Journal of Comparative Psychology, 103,* 4–22.

Crawford, C. B., Smith, M. S., & Krebs, D. (Eds.). (1987). *Sociobiology and psychology: Ideas, issues and applications.* Hillsdale, NJ: Erlbaum.

Crawford, L. E., & Cacioppo, J. T. (2002). Learning where to look for danger: Integrating affective and spatial information. *Psychological Science, 13,* 449–453.

Crews, F. (1996). The verdict on Freud. *Psychological Science, 7,* 63.

Crick, N. R., & Dodge, K. A. (1994). A review and reformulation of social information-processing mechanisms in children's social adjustment. *Psychological Bulletin, 115,* 74–101.

Cristóbal-Azkarate, J., Chavira, R., Boeck, L., Rodríguez-Luna, E., & Veà, J. J. (2006). Testosterone levels of free-ranging resident mantled howler monkey males in relation to the number and density of solitary males: A test of the challenge hypothesis. *Hormones and Behavior, 49,* 261–267.

Crittenden, P. M. (1990). Internal representational models of attachment relationships. *Infant Mental Health Journal, 11,* 259–277.

Crocker, J. (1981). Judgment of covariation by social perceivers. *Psychological Bulletin, 90,* 272–292.

Crocker, J., & Knight, K. M. (2005). Contingencies of self-worth. *Current Directions in Psychological Science, 14,* 200–203.

Crocker, J., Luhtanen, R. K., Cooper, M. L., & Bouvrette, A. (2003). Contingencies of self-worth in college students: Theory and measurement. *Journal of Personality and Social Psychology, 85,* 894–908.

Crocker, J., & Park, L. E. (2004). The costly pursuit of self-esteem. *Psychological Bulletin, 130,* 392–414.

Crocker, J., & Wolfe, C. T. (2001). Contingencies of self-worth. *Psychological Review, 108,* 593–623.

Cronbach, L. J., & Meehl, P. E. (1955). Construct validity in psychological tests. *Psychological Bulletin, 52,* 281–302.

Crouse, B. B., & Mehrabian, A. (1977). Affiliation of opposite-sexed strangers. *Journal of Research in Personality, 11,* 38–47.

Crowne, D. P., & Marlowe, D. (1964). *The approval motive: Studies in evaluative dependence.* New York: Wiley.

Csikszentmihalyi, M. (1975). *Beyond boredom and anxiety.* San Francisco: Jossey-Bass.

Csikszentmihalyi, M. (1978). Attention and the holistic approach to behavior. In K. S. Pope & J. L. Singer (Eds.), *The stream of consciousness: Scientific investigations into the flow of human experience.* New York: Plenum.

Csikszentmihalyi, M. (1982). Toward a psychology of optimal experience. In L. Wheeler (Ed.), *Review of personality and social psychology* (Vol. 3, pp. 13–36). Beverly Hills, CA: Sage.

Csikszentmihalyi, M. (1990). *Flow: The psychology of optimal experience.* New York: Harper & Row.

Csikszentmihalyi, M., & Csikszentmihalyi, I. S. (Eds.). (1988). *Optimal experience: Psychological studies of flow in consciousness.* New York: Cambridge University Press.

Csikszentmihalyi, M., & LeFevre, J. (1989). Optimal experience in work and leisure. *Journal of Personality and Social Psychology, 56,* 815–822.

Cunningham, M. R., Barbee, A. P., & Pike, C. L. (1990). What do women want? Facialmetric assessment of multiple motives in the perception of male facial physical attractiveness. *Journal of Personality and Social Psychology, 59,* 61–72.

Cutter, H. S. G., Boyatzis, R. E., & Clancy, D. D. (1977). The effectiveness of power motivation training in rehabilitating alcoholics. *Journal of Studies on Alcohol, 38,* 131–141.

Dabbs, J. M., Jr. (1992a). Testosterone and occupational achievement. *Social Forces, 70,* 813–824.

Dabbs, J. M., Jr. (1992b). Testosterone measurements in social and clinical psychology. *Journal of Social and Clinical Psychology, 11,* 302–321.

Dabbs, J. M., Jr. (1997). Testosterone, smiling, and facial appearance. *Journal of Nonverbal Behavior, 21,* 45–55.

Dabbs, J. M., Jr. (1998). Testosterone and the concept of dominance. *Behavioral and Brain Sciences, 21,* 370–371.

Dabbs, J. M., Jr., Alford, E. C., & Fielden, J. A. (1998). Trial lawyers: Blue collar talent in a white collar world. *Journal of Applied Social Psychology, 28,* 84–94.

Dabbs, J. M., Jr., Bernieri, F. J., Strong, R. K., Campo, R., & Milun, R. (2001). Going on stage: Testosterone in greetings and meetings. *Journal of Research in Personality, 35,* 27–40.

Dabbs, J. M., Jr., & Dabbs, M. G. (2000). *Heroes, rogues and lovers: Testosterone and behavior.* New York: McGraw-Hill.

Dabbs, J. M., Jr., de La Rue, D., & Williams, P. M. (1990). Testosterone and occupational choice: Actors, ministers, and other men. *Journal of Personality and Social Psychology, 59,* 1261–1265.

Dabbs, J. M., Jr., Frady, R. L., Carr, T. S., & Besch, N. F. (1987). Saliva testosterone and criminal violence in young adult prison inmates. *Psychosomatic Medicine, 49,* 174–182.

Dabbs, J. M., Jr., Hargrove, M. F., & Heusel, C. (1996). Testosterone differences among college fraternities: Well-behaved vs. rambunctious. *Personality and Individual Differences, 290,* 157–161.

Dabbs, J. M., Jr., & Mallinger, A. (1999). High testosterone levels predict low voice pitch among men. *Personality and Individual Differences, 27,* 801–804.

Dabbs, J. M., Jr., & Mohammed, S. (1992). Male and female salivary testosterone concentrations before and after sexual activity. *Physiology and Behavior, 52,* 195–197.

Dabbs, J. M., Jr., & Morris, R. (1990). Testosterone, social class, and antisocial behavior in a sample of 4,462 men. *Psychological Science, 1,* 209–211.

Dabbs, J. M., Jr., Riad, J. K., & Chance, S. E. (2001). Testosterone and ruthless homicide. *Personality and Individual Differences, 31,* 599–603.

Dabbs, J. M., Jr., Ruback, R. B., Frady, R. L., Hopper, C. H., & Sgoutas, D. S. (1988). Saliva testosterone and criminal violence among women. *Personality and Individual Differences, 9,* 269–275.

Daitzman, R., & Zuckerman, M. (1980). Disinhibitory sensation seeking, personality and gonadal hormones. *Personality and Individual Differences, 1,* 103–110.

Daly, M., & Wilson, M. I. (1988). *Homicide.* New York: Aldine de Gruyter.

Daly, M., & Wilson, M. I. (1990). Killing the competition: Female/female and male/male homicide. *Human Nature, 1,* 81–107.

Daly, M., & Wilson, M. I. (1996). Violence against stepchildren. *Current Directions in Psychological Science, 5,* 77–81.

Daniels, D. (1986). Differential experiences of siblings in the same family as predictors of adolescent sibling personality differences. *Journal of Personality and Social Psychology, 51,* 339–346.

Daniels, D., & Plomin, R. (1985). Differential experience of siblings in the same family. *Developmental Psychology, 21,* 747–760.

Darley, J. M., & Goethals, G. R. (1980). People's analyses of the causes of ability-linked performances. In L. Berkowitz (Ed.), *Advances in experimental social psychology* (Vol. 13). New York: Academic.

Davidson, M. A., McInnes, R. G., & Parnell, R. W. (1957). The distribution of personality traits in seven-year-old children: A combined psychological, psychiatric, and somatotype study. *British Journal of Educational Psychology, 27,* 48–61.

Davidson, R. J. (1988). EEG measures of cerebral asymmetry: Conceptual and methodological issues. *International Journal of Neuroscience, 39,* 71–89.

Davidson, R. J. (1992). Prolegomenon to the structure of emotion: Gleanings from neuropsychology. *Cognition and Emotion, 6,* 245–268.

Davidson, R. J. (1995). Cerebral asymmetry, emotion, and affective style. In R. J. Davidson & K. Hugdahl (Eds.), *Brain asymmetry* (pp. 361–387). Cambridge, MA: MIT Press.

Davidson, R. J., Ekman, P., Saron, C. D., Senulis, J. A., & Friesen, W. V. (1990). Approach–withdrawal and cerebral asymmetry: Emotional expression and brain physiology I. *Journal of Personality and Social Psychology, 58,* 330–341.

Davidson, R. J., Jackson, D. C., & Kalin, N. H. (2000). Emotion, plasticity, context, and regulation: Perspectives from affective neuroscience. *Psychological Bulletin, 126,* 890–909.

Davidson, R. J., Pizzagalli, D., Nitschke, J. B., & Putnam, K. (2002). Depression: Perspectives from affective neuroscience. *Annual Review of Psychology, 53,* 545–574.

Davidson, R. J., & Sutton, S. K. (1995). Affective neuroscience: The emergence of a discipline. *Current Opinion in Neurobiology, 5,* 217–224.

Davila, J., Burge, D., & Hammen, C. (1997). Why does attachment style change? *Journal of Personality and Social Psychology, 73,* 826–838.

Davis, C. G., Nolen-Hoeksema, S., & Larson, J. (1998). Making sense of loss and benefiting from the experience:

Two construals of meaning. *Journal of Personality and Social Psychology, 75,* 561–574.

Davis, D., Shaver, P. R., & Vernon, M. L. (2003). Physical, emotional, and behavioral reactions to breaking up: The roles of gender, age, emotional involvement, and attachment style. *Personality and Social Psychology Bulletin, 29,* 871–884.

Davis, P. J. (1987). Repression and the inaccessibility of affective memories. *Journal of Personality and Social Psychology, 53,* 585–593.

Davis, P. J., & Schwartz, G. E. (1987). Repression and the inaccessibility of affective memories. *Journal of Personality and Social Psychology, 52,* 155–162.

Davison, G. C., & Wilson, G. T. (1973). Processes of fear reduction in systematic desensitization: Cognitive and social reinforcement factors in humans. *Behavior Therapy, 4,* 1–21.

Dawkins, R. (1976). *The selfish gene.* New York: Oxford University Press.

Dawson, M. E., & Furedy, J. J. (1976). The role of awareness in human differential autonomic classical conditioning: The necessary-gate hypothesis. *Psychophysiology, 13,* 50–53.

Dawson, M. R. W. (2004). *Minds and machines.* Malden, MA: Blackwell.

Dawson, M. R. W. (2005). *Connectionism: A hands-on approach.* Malden, MA: Blackwell.

Deaux, K., & Lewis, L. L. (1984). Structure of gender stereotypes: Interrelationships among components and gender label. *Journal of Personality and Social Psychology, 46,* 991–1004.

Deci, E. L. (1975). *Intrinsic motivation.* New York: Plenum.

Deci, E. L., Koestner, R., & Ryan, R. M. (1999). A meta-analytic review of experiments examining the effects of extrinsic rewards on intrinsic motivation. *Psychological Bulletin, 125,* 627–668.

Deci, E. L., La Guardia, J. G., Moller, A. C., Scheiner, M. J., & Ryan, R. M. (2006). On the benefits of giving as well as receiving autonomy support: Mutuality in close friendships. *Personality and Social Psychology Bulletin, 32,* 313–327.

Deci, E. L., & Ryan, R. M. (1980). The empirical exploration of intrinsic motivational processes. In L. Berkowitz (Ed.), *Advances in experimental social psychology* (Vol. 13). New York: Academic.

Deci, E. L., & Ryan, R. M. (1985). *Intrinsic motivation and self-determination in human behavior.* New York: Plenum.

Deci, E. L., & Ryan, R. M. (1991). A motivational approach to self: Integration in personality. In R. Dienstbier (Ed.), *Nebraska symposium on motivation: Perspectives on motivation* (Vol. 38, pp. 237–288). Lincoln: University of Nebraska Press.

Deci, E. L., & Ryan, R. M. (2000). The "what" and "why" of goal pursuits: Human needs and the self-determination of behavior. *Psychological Inquiry, 11,* 227–268.

DeHart, T., Pelham, B. W., & Tennen, H. (2006). What lies beneath: Parenting style and implicit self-esteem. *Journal of Experimental Social Psychology, 42,* 1–17.

De Houwer, J., Thomas, S., & Baeyens, F. (2001). Associative learning of likes and dislikes: A review of 25 years of research on human evaluative conditioning. *Psychological Bulletin, 127,* 853–869.

DeLisi, L. E., Shaw, S. H., Crow, T. J., et al. (2002). A genome-wide scan for linkage to chromosomal regions in 382 sibling pairs with schizophrenia or schizoaffective disorder. *American Journal of Psychiatry, 159,* 803–812.

Della Libera, C., & Chelazzi, L. (2006). Visual selective attention and the effects of monetary rewards. *Psychological Science, 17,* 222–227.

Deluty, R. H. (1985). Consistency of assertive, aggressive, and submissive behavior for children. *Journal of Personality and Social Psychology, 49,* 1054–1065.

Demorest, A. (2005). *Psychology's grand theories: How personal experiences shaped professional ideas.* Mahwah, NJ: Erlbaum.

De Neys, W. (2006). Dual processing in reasoning: Two systems but one reasoner. *Psychological Science, 17,* 428–433.

Depue, R. A. (1979). *The psychobiology of the depressive disorders: Implications for the effect of stress.* New York: Academic.

Depue, R. A. (1995). Neurobiological factors in personality and depression. *European Journal of Personality, 9,* 413–439.

Depue, R. A., & Collins, P. F. (1999). Neurobiology of the structure of personality: Dopamine, facilitation of incentive motivation, and extraversion. *Behavioral and Brain Sciences, 22,* 491–517.

Depue, R. A., & Iacono, W. G. (1989). Neurobehavioral aspects of affective disorders. *Annual Review of Psychology, 40,* 457–492.

Depue, R. A., Krauss, S. P., & Spoont, M. R. (1987). A two-dimensional threshold model of seasonal bipolar affective disorder. In D. Magnusson & A. Öhman (Eds.), *Psychopathology: An interactional perspective* (pp. 95–123). Orlando, FL: Academic.

Depue, R. A., Luciana, M., Arbisi, P., Collins, P., & Leon, A. (1994). Dopamine and the structure of personality: Relation of agonist-induced dopamine activity to positive emotionality. *Journal of Personality and Social Psychology, 67,* 485–498.

Depue, R. A., & Morrone-Strupinksy, J. V. (2005). A neurobehavioral model of affiliative bonding: Implications for conceptualizing a human trait of affiliation. *Behavioral and Brain Sciences, 28,* 313–395.

Depue, R. A., & Spoont, M. R. (1986). Conceptualizing a serotonin trait: A behavioral dimension of constraint. *Annals of the New York Academy of Sciences, 487,* 47–62.

Derryberry, D., & Rothbart, M. K. (1997). Reactive and effortful processes in the organization of temperament. *Development and Psychopathology, 9,* 633–652.

DeRubeis, R. J., Tang, T. Z., & Beck, A. T. (2001). Cognitive therapy. In Dobson, K. S. (Ed.), *Handbook of cognitive-behavioral therapies* (2nd ed., pp. 349–392). New York: Guilford.

de St. Aubin, E., McAdams, D. P., & Kim, T. (2004). *The generative society: Caring for future generations.* Washington DC: American Psychological Association.

DeSteno, D., Bartlett, M. Y., Braverman, J., & Salovey, P. (2002). Sex differences in jealousy: Evolutionary mechanism or artifact of measurement? *Journal of Personality and Social Psychology, 83,* 1103–1116.

Detera-Wadleigh, S. D., Berrettini, W. H., Goldin, L. R., Boorman, D., Anderson, S., & Gershon, E. S. (1987). Close linkage of c-harvey-ras-1 and the insulin gene to affective disorder is ruled out in three North American pedigrees. *Nature, 325,* 806–808.

Deutsch, F. M., Ruble, D. N., Fleming, A., Brooks-Gunn, J., & Stangor, C. (1988). Information-seeking and maternal self-definition during the transition to motherhood. *Journal of Personality and Social Psychology, 55,* 420–431.

DeVellis, R. F., DeVellis, B. M., & McCauley, C. (1978). Vicarious acquisition of learned helplessness. *Journal of Personality and Social Psychology, 36,* 894–899.

DeVito, A. J. (1985). Review of Myers–Briggs Type Indicator. In J. V. Mitchell (Ed.), *The ninth mental measurements yearbook* (pp. 1029–1032). Lincoln, NE: Buros Institute of Mental Measurements.

Di Blas, L., & Forzi, M. (1999). Refining a descriptive structure of personality attibutes in the Italian language: The abridged big three circumplex structure. *Journal of Personality and Social Psychology, 76,* 451–481.

Dick, D. M., & Rose, R. J. (2002). Behavior genetics: What's new? What's next? *Current Directions in Psychological Science, 11,* 70–74.

Dickens, W. T., & Flynn, J. R. (2001). Heritability estimates versus large environmental effects: The IQ paradox resolved. *Psychological Review, 108,* 346–369.

Dickerson, S. S., & Kemeny, M. E. (2004). Acute stressors and cortisol responses: A theoretical integration and synthesis of laboratory research. *Psychological Bulletin, 130,* 355–391.

DiClemente, C. C. (1981). Self-efficacy and smoking cessation. *Cognitive Therapy and Research, 5,* 175–187.

Diener, C. I., & Dweck, C. S. (1978). An analysis of learned helplessness: Continuous changes in performance, strategy, and achievement cognitions following failure. *Journal of Personality and Social Psychology, 36,* 451–462.

Diener, E. (1979). Deindividuation, self-awareness, and disinhibition. *Journal of Personality and Social Psychology, 37,* 1160–1171.

Digman, J. M. (1990). Personality structure: Emergence of the five-factor model. *Annual Review of Psychology, 41,* 417–440.

Digman, J. M. (1997). Higher-order factors of the Big Five. *Journal of Personality and Social Psychology, 73,* 1246–1256.

Digman, J. M., & Inouye, J. (1986). Further specification of the five robust factors of personality. *Journal of Personality and Social Psychology, 50,* 116–123.

Digman, J. M., & Shmelyov, A. G. (1996). The structure of temperament and personality in Russian children. *Journal of Personality and Social Psychology, 71,* 341–351.

Digman, J. M., & Takemoto-Chock, N. K. (1981). Factors in the natural language of personality: Re-analysis, comparison, and interpretation of six major studies. *Multivariate Behavioral Research, 16,* 149–170.

Dijksterhuis, A., & Bargh, J. A. (2001). The perception–behavior expressway. In M. P. Zanna (Ed.), *Advances in experimental social psychology* (Vol. 33, pp. 1–40). San Diego: Academic.

Dijkstra, P., & Buunk, B. P. (1998). Jealousy as a function of rival characteristics: An evolutionary perspective. *Personality and Social Psychology Bulletin, 24,* 1158–1166.

DiLalla, L. F., & Gottesman, I. I. (1991). Biological and genetic contributors to violence—Widom's untold tale. *Psychological Bulletin, 109,* 125–129.

Diven, K. (1936). Certain determinants in the conditioning of anxiety reactions. *Journal of Psychology, 3,* 291–308.

Dixon, N. F. (1981). *Preconscious processing.* Chichester, England: Wiley.

Dodge, K. A. (1986). A social information-processing model of social competence in children. In M. Perlmutter (Ed.), *Minnesota symposium on child psychology* (Vol. 18). Hillsdale, NJ: Erlbaum.

Dodge, K. A., & Crick, N. R. (1990). Social information-processing bases of aggressive behavior in children. *Personality and Social Psychology Bulletin, 16,* 8–22.

Dollard, J., & Miller, N. E. (1950). *Personality and psychotherapy: An analysis in terms of learning, thinking, and culture.* New York: McGraw-Hill.

Dollinger, S. J., & Orf, L. A. (1991). Personality and performance in "personality": Conscientiousness and openness. *Journal of Research in Personality, 25,* 276–284.

Domhoff, G. W. (2003). *The scientific study of dreams: Neural networks, cognitive development, and content analysis.* Washington, DC: American Psychological Association.

Donnellan, M. B., Conger, R. D., & Bryant, C. M. (2004). The big five and enduring marriages. *Journal of Research in Personality, 38,* 481–504.

Donnerstein, E. (1980). Aggressive erotica and violence against women. *Journal of Personality and Social Psychology, 39,* 269–277.

Donnerstein, E. (1983). Erotica and human aggression. In R. G. Geen & E. Donnerstein (Eds.), *Aggression: Theoretical and empirical reviews.* New York: Academic.

Donnerstein, E., Donnerstein, M., & Evans, R. (1975). Erotic stimuli and aggression: Facilitation or inhibition? *Journal of Personality and Social Psychology, 32,* 237–244.

Donnerstein, E., & Hallam, J. (1978). The facilitating effects of erotica on aggression toward females. *Journal of Personality and Social Psychology, 36,* 1270–1277.

Doob, A. N. (1970). Catharsis and aggression: The effect of hurting one's enemy. *Journal of Experimental Research in Personality, 4,* 291–296.

Dosamantes-Alperson, E., & Merrill, N. (1980). Growth effects of experiential movement psychotherapy. *Psychotherapy: Theory, Research, and Practice, 17,* 63–68.

Douglas, C. (1993). *Translate this darkness: The life of Christiana Morgan.* New York: Simon & Schuster.

Drabman, R. S., & Spitalnik, R. (1973). Training a retarded child as a behavioral teaching assistant. *Journal of Behavior Therapy and Experimental Psychiatry, 4,* 269–272.

Dreisbach, G., & Goschke, T. (2004). How positive affect modulates cognitive control: Reduced perseveration at the cost of increased distractibility. *Journal of Experimental Psychology: Learning, Memory, and Cognition, 30,* 343–353.

Duck, S. W. (1973). *Personal relationships and personal constructs.* London, England: Wiley.

Duck, S. W. (1977). Inquiry, hypothesis, and the quest for validation: Personal construct systems in the development of acquaintance. In S. W. Duck (Ed.), *Theories of interpersonal attraction.* London, England: Academic.

Duck, S. W., & Allison, D. (1978). I liked you but I can't live with you: A study of lapsed friendships. *Social Behavior and Personality, 8,* 43–47.

Dulany, D. E. (1968). Awareness, rules and propositional control: A confrontation with S-R behavior theory. In T. R. Dixon & D. L. Horton (Eds.), *Verbal behavior and general behavior theory.* Englewood Cliffs, NJ: Prentice-Hall.

Dunn, J., & Plomin, R. (1990). *Separate lives: Why siblings are so different.* New York: Basic Books.

Dunning, D., & McElwee, R. O. (1995). Idiosyncratic trait definitions: Implications for self-description and social judgment. *Journal of Personality and Social Psychology, 68,* 936–946.

Dweck, C. S., & Leggett, E. L. (1988). A social-cognitive approach to motivation and personality. *Psychological Review, 95,* 256–273.

Eagle, M. N. (1984). *Recent developments in psychoanalysis: A critical evaluation.* New York: McGraw-Hill.

Eagly, A. H. (1987). *Sex differences in social behavior: A social-role interpretation.* Hillsdale, NJ: Erlbaum.

Eagly, A. H., & Wood, W. (1999). The origins of sex differences in human behavior: Evolved dispositions versus social roles. *American Psychologist, 54,* 408–423.

Eaves, L. J., Eysenck, H. J., & Martin, N. G. (1989). *Genes, culture, and personality: An empirical approach.* San Diego: Academic.

Ebbesen, E. B., Duncan, B., & Konecni, V. J. (1975). Effects of content of verbal aggression on future verbal aggression: A field experiment. *Journal of Experimental Social Psychology, 11,* 192–204.

Ebrecht, M., Hextall, J., Kirtley, L., Taylor, A., Dyson, M., & Weinman, J. (2004). Perceived stress and cortisol levels predict speed of wound healing in healthy male adults. *Psychoneuroendocrinology, 29,* 798–809.

Ebstein, R. P. (2006). The molecular genetic architecture of human personality: Beyond self-report questionnaires. *Molecular Psychiatry, 11,* 427–445.

Ebstein, R. P., Novick, O., Umansky, R., Priel, B., Osher, Y., Blaine, D., Bennett, E. R., Nemanov, L., Katz, M., & Belmaker, R. H. (1996). Dopamine D4 receptor (D4DR) exon III polymorphism associated with the human personality trait of novelty seeking. *Nature Genetics, 12,* 78–80.

Edwards, A. L. (1957). *The social desirability variable in personality assessment and research.* New York: Dryden.

Edwards, A. L. (1959). *Edwards Personal Preference Schedule manual.* New York: Psychological Corporation.

Egeland, J. A., Gerhard, D. S., Pauls, D. L., Sussex, J. N., & Kidd, K. K. (1987). Bipolar affective disorders linked to DNA markers on chromosome 11. *Nature, 325,* 783–787.

Einstein, D., & Lanning, K. (1998). Shame, guilt, ego development, and the five-factor model of personality. *Journal of Personality, 66,* 555–582.

Eisenberg, N. (2002). Emotion-related regulation and its relation to quality of social functioning, In W. W. Hartup & R. A. Weinberg (Eds.), *Child psychology in retrospect and prospect: The Minnesota symposium on child psychology* (Vol. 32, pp. 133–171). Mahwah, NJ: Erlbaum.

Eisenberg, N., Fabes, R. A., Guthrie, I. K., & Reiser, M. (2000). Dispositional emotionality and regulation: Their role in predicting quality of social functioning. *Journal of Personality and Social Psychology, 78,* 136–157.

Eisenberg, N., Fabes, R. A., Murphy, B., Karbon, M., Maszk, P., Smith, M., O'Boyle, C., & Suh, K. (1994). The relations of emotionality and regulation to dispositional and situational empathy-related responding. *Journal of Personality and Social Psychology, 66,* 776–797.

Eisenberg, N., Spinrad, T. L., Fabes, R. A., Reiser, M., Cumberland, A., Shepard, S. A., Valiente, C., Losoya, S. H., Guthrie, I. K., & Thompson, M. (2004). The relations of effortful control and impulsivity to children's resiliency and adjustment. *Child Development, 75,* 25–46.

Eisenberger, R. (1992). Learned industriousness. *Psychological Review, 99,* 248–267.

Eisenberger, R., Armeli, S., & Pretz, J. (1998). Can the promise of reward increase creativity? *Journal of Personality and Social Psychology, 74,* 704–714.

Eisenberger, R., & Rhoades, L. (2001). Incremental effects of reward on creativity. *Journal of Personality and Social Psychology, 81,* 728–741.

Eisenberger, R., & Selbst, M. (1994). Does reward increase or decrease creativity? *Journal of Personality and Social Psychology, 66,* 1116–1127.

Ekehammar, B. (1974). Interactionism in personality from a historical perspective. *Psychological Bulletin, 81,* 1026–1048.

Elder, G. H., Jr., Caspi, A., & Downey, G. (1986). Problem behavior and family relationships: Life course and intergenerational themes. In A. B. Sorenson, F. Weinert, & L. R. Sherrod (Eds.), *Human development and the life course: Multidisciplinary perspectives* (pp. 293–340). Hillsdale, NJ: Erlbaum.

Elder, G. H., Jr., & MacInnis, D. J. (1983). Achievement imagery in women's lives from adolescence to adulthood. *Journal of Personality and Social Psychology, 45,* 394–404.

Ellenberger, H. F. (1970). *The discovery of the unconscious.* New York: Basic Books.

Elliot, A. J. (2005). A conceptual history of the achievement goal construct. In A. J. Elliot & C. S. Dweck (Eds.), *Handbook of competence and motivation* (pp. 52–72). New York: Guilford.

Elliot, A. J., Gable, S. L., & Mapes, R. R. (2006). Approach and avoidance motivation in the social domain. *Personality and Social Psychology Bulletin, 32,* 378–391.

Elliot, A. J., & Harackiewicz, J. M. (1994). Goal setting, achievement orientation, and intrinsic motivation: A mediational analysis. *Journal of Personality and Social Psychology, 66,* 968–980.

Elliot, A. J., & Harackiewicz, J. M. (1996). Approach and avoidance achievement goals and intrinsic motivation: A mediational analysis. *Journal of Personality and Social Psychology, 70,* 461–475.

Elliot, A. J., & McGregor, H. A. (2001). A 2 × 2 achievement goal framework. *Journal of Personality and Social Psychology, 80,* 501–519.

Elliot, A. J., & Sheldon, K. M. (1997). Avoidance achievement motivation: A personal goals analysis. *Journal of Personality and Social Psychology, 73,* 171–185.

Elliot, A. J., & Thrash, T. M. (2002). Approach–avoidance motivation in personality: Approach and avoidance temperaments and goals. *Journal of Personality and Social Psychology, 82,* 804–818.

Elliott, E. S., & Dweck, C. S. (1988). Goals: An approach to motivation and achievement. *Journal of Personality and Social Psychology, 54,* 5–12.

Ellis, A. E. (1987). The impossibility of achieving consistently good mental health. *American Psychologist, 42,* 364–375.

Elman, J. L. (2005). Connectionist models of cognitive development: Where next? *Trends in Cognitive Sciences, 9,* 112–117.

Elmore, A. M., & Tursky, B. (1981). A comparison of two psychophysiological approaches to the treatment of migraine. *Headache, 21,* 93–101.

Emmons, R. A. (1986). Personal strivings: An approach to personality and subjective well-being. *Journal of Personality and Social Psychology, 51,* 1058–1068.

Emmons, R. A., & Diener, E. (1986). Situation selection as a moderator of response consistency and stability. *Journal of Personality and Social Psychology, 51,* 1013–1019.

Emmons, R. A., Diener, E., & Larsen, R. J. (1986). Choice and avoidance of everyday situations and affect congruence: Two

models of reciprocal interactionism. *Journal of Personality and Social Psychology, 51,* 815–826.

Emmons, R. A., & King, L. A. (1988). Conflict among personal strivings: Immediate and long-term implications for psychological and physical well-being. *Journal of Personality and Social Psychology, 54,* 1040–1048.

Emmons, R. A., King, L. A., & Sheldon, K. (1993). Goal conflict and the self-regulation of action. In D. M. Wegner & J. W. Pennebaker (Eds.), *Handbook of mental control* (pp. 528–551). Englewood Cliffs, NJ: Prentice-Hall.

Endler, N. S., & Magnusson, D. (1976). *Interactional psychology and personality.* Washington, DC: Hemisphere.

Entwisle, D. R. (1972). To dispel fantasies about fantasy-based measures of achievement motivation. *Psychological Bulletin, 77,* 377–391.

Epstein, L. H., Saelens, B. E., Myers, M. D., & Vito, D. (1997). Effects of decreasing sedentary behaviors on activity choice in obese children. *Health Psychology, 16,* 107–113.

Epstein, S. (1983). The unconscious, the preconscious, and the self-concept. In J. Suls & A. G. Greenwald (Eds.), *Psychological perspectives on the self* (Vol. 2). Hillsdale, NJ: Erlbaum.

Epstein, S. (1985). The implications of cognitive-experiential self theory for research in social psychology and personality. *Journal for the Theory of Social Behavior, 15,* 283–310.

Epstein, S. (1990). Cognitive–experiential self-theory. In L. Pervin (Ed.), *Handbook of personality: Theory and research* (pp. 165–192). New York: Guilford.

Epstein, S. (1994). Integration of the cognitive and the psychodynamic unconscious. *American Psychologist, 49,* 709–724.

Epstein, S., Lipson, A., Holstein, C., & Huh, E. (1992). Irrational reactions to negative outcomes: Evidence for two conceptual systems. *Journal of Personality and Social Psychology, 62,* 328–339.

Epting, F. R. (1972). The stability of cognitive complexity in construing social issues. *British Journal of Social and Clinical Psychology, 11,* 122–125.

Epting, F. R. (1980). *Personal construct theory psychotherapy.* New York: Wiley.

Erdelyi, M. H. (1985). *Psychoanalysis: Freud's cognitive psychology.* New York: Freeman.

Erdelyi, M. H. (in press). The unified theory of repression. *Behavioral and Brain Science.*

Ericsson, K. A., & Simon, H. A. (1993). *Protocol analysis: Verbal reports as data* (Rev. ed.). Cambridge, MA: MIT Press.

Erikson, E. H. (1950). *Childhood and society.* New York: Norton.

Erikson, E. H. (1963). *Childhood and society* (2nd ed.). New York: Norton.

Erikson, E. H. (1964). *Insight and responsibility.* New York: Norton.

Erikson, E. H. (1968). *Identity: Youth and crisis.* New York: Norton.

Erikson, E. H. (1974). *Dimensions of a new identity.* New York: Norton.

Erikson, E. H. (1982). *The life cycle completed: A review.* New York: Norton.

Ernst, C., & Angst, J. (1983). *Birth order: Its influence on personality.* Berlin, Germany: Springer-Verlag.

Esterson, A. (1993). *Seductive mirage: An exploration of the work of Sigmund Freud.* Chicago: Open Court.

Esterson, A. (1998). Jeffrey Masson and Freud's seduction theory: A new fable based on old myths. *History of the Human Sciences, 11,* 1–21.

Esterson, A. (2001). The mythologizing of psychoanalytic history: Deception and self-deception in Freud's accounts of the seduction theory episode. *History of Psychiatry, 12,* 329–352.

Esterson, A. (2002). The myth of Freud's ostracism by the medical community in 1896–1905: Jeffrey Masson's assault on truth. *History of Psychology, 5,* 115–134.

Evans, R. I. (1989). *Albert Bandura: The man and his ideas— A dialogue.* New York: Praeger.

Ewart, C. K. (1978). Self-observation in natural environments: Reactive effects of behavior desirability and goal-setting. *Cognitive Therapy and Research, 2,* 39–56.

Exner, J. E., Jr. (1974). *The Rorschach systems.* New York: Grune & Stratton.

Exner, J. E., Jr. (1993). *The Rorschach: A comprehensive system: Vol. 1. Basic foundations* (3rd ed.). New York: Wiley.

Exner, J. E., Jr. (1996). A comment on "The comprehensive system for the Rorschach: A critical examination." *Psychological Science, 7,* 11–13.

Eysenck, H. J. (1952). *The scientific study of personality.* New York: Macmillan.

Eysenck, H. J. (1961). The effects of psychotherapy. In H. J. Eysenck (Ed.), *Handbook of abnormal psychology.* New York: Basic Books.

Eysenck, H. J. (1964a). *Crime and personality.* Boston: Houghton Mifflin.

Eysenck, H. J. (1964b). Involuntary rest pauses in tapping as a function of drive and personality. *Perceptual and Motor Skills, 18,* 173–174.

Eysenck, H. J. (1967). *The biological basis of personality.* Springfield, IL: Charles C. Thomas.

Eysenck, H. J. (1970). *The structure of human personality* (3rd ed.). London, England: Methuen.

Eysenck, H. J. (1975). *The inequality of man.* San Diego: EdITS.

Eysenck, H. J. (Ed.). (1981). *A model for personality.* Berlin: Springer-Verlag.

Eysenck, H. J. (1983). Psychopharmacology and personality. In W. Janke (Ed.), *Response variability to psychotropic drugs.* London, England: Pergamon.

Eysenck, H. J. (1986). Models and paradigms in personality research. In A. Angleitner, A. Furnham, & G. Van Heck (Eds.), *Personality psychology in Europe, Vol. 2: Current trends and controversies* (pp. 213–223). Lisse, Holland: Swets & Zeitlinger.

Eysenck, H. J. (1992). Four ways five factors are *not* basic. *Personality and Individual Differences, 13,* 667–673.

Eysenck, H. J. (1993). Comment on Goldberg. *American Psychologist, 48,* 1299–1300.

Eysenck, H. J., & Eysenck, M. W. (1985). *Personality and individual differences: A natural science approach.* New York: Plenum.

Eysenck, H. J., & Eysenck, S. B. G. (1975). *Manual of the Eysenck Personality Questionnaire.* San Diego: EdITS.

Eysenck, H. J., & Eysenck, S. B. G. (1976). *Psychoticism as a dimension of personality.* London, England: Hodder & Stoughton.

Fadiga, L., Fogassi, L., Gallese, V., & Rizzolatti, G. (2000). Visuomotor neurons: Ambiguity of the discharge or "motor" perception? *International Journal of Psychophysiology, 35,* 165–177.

Fagot, B. I. (1977). Consequences of moderate cross-gender behavior in preschool children. *Child Development, 48,* 902–907.

Fairbairn, W. R. D. (1952). *Psycho-analytic studies of the personality.* New York: Basic Books.

Fairbairn, W. R. D. (1954). *An object relations theory of personality.* New York: Basic Books.

Fairbanks, L. A. (2001). Individual differences in response to a stranger: Social impulsivity as a dimension of temperament in vervet monkeys (*Cercopithecus aethiops sabaeus*). *Journal of Comparative Psychology, 115,* 22–28.

Falbo, T. (1981). Relationships between birth category, achievement, and interpersonal orientation. *Journal of Personality and Social Psychology, 41,* 121–131.

Faraone, S. V., Taylor, L., & Tsuang, M. (2002). The molecular genetics of schizophrenia: An emerging consensus. *Expert reviews in molecular medicine, 23.* Retrieved from http://www.expertreviews.org/02004751h.htm

Feather, N. T. (1961). The relationship of persistence at a task to expectations of success and achievement-related motivation. *Journal of Abnormal and Social Psychology, 63,* 552–561.

Feather, N. T. (Ed.). (1982). *Expectations and actions: Expectancy–value models in psychology.* Hillsdale, NJ: Erlbaum.

Feeney, B. C. (2004). A secure base: Responsive support of goal strivings and exploration in adult intimate relationships. *Journal of Personality and Social Psychology, 87,* 631–648.

Feeney, B. C. (2006). An attachment theory perspective on the interplay between intrapersonal and interpersonal processes. In K. D. Vohs & E. J. Finkel (Eds.), *Self and relationships* (pp. 133–159). New York: Guilford.

Feeney, B. C., & Cassidy, J. A. (2003). Reconstructive memory related to adolescent-parent conflict interactions: The influence of attachment-related representations on immediate perceptions and changes in perceptions over time. *Journal of Personality and Social Psychology, 85,* 945–955.

Feeney, B. C., & Collins, N. C. (2003). Motivations for caregiving in adult intimate relationships: Influences on caregiving behavior and relationship functioning. *Personality and Social Psychology Bulletin, 29,* 950–968.

Feeney, B. C., & Collins, N. L. (2001). Predictors of caregiving in adult intimate relationships: An attachment theoretical perspective. *Journal of Personality and Social Psychology, 80,* 972–994.

Feeney, J. A., & Noller, P. (1990). Attachment style as a predictor of adult romantic relationships. *Journal of Personality and Social Psychology, 58,* 281–291.

Fehr, E., & Gächter, S. (2002). Altruistic punishment in humans. *Nature, 415,* 137–140.

Feingold, A. (1992). Gender differences in mate selection preferences: A test of the parental investment model. *Psychological Bulletin, 112,* 125–139.

Fekken, G. C., & Holden, R. R. (1992). Response latency evidence for viewing personality traits as schema indicators. *Journal of Research in Personality, 26,* 103–120.

Feldman, F. (1968). Results of psychoanalysis in clinic case assignments. *Journal of the American Psychoanalytic Association, 16,* 274–300.

Fellous, J. -M., & Arbib, M. A. (Eds.). (2005). *Who needs emotions? The brain meets the robot.* New York: Oxford University Press.

Fenichel, O. (1945). *The psychoanalytic theory of neurosis.* New York: Norton.

Fenigstein, A., & Buss, A. H. (1974). Association and affect as determinants of displaced aggression. *Journal of Research in Personality, 7,* 306–313.

Fenigstein, A., Scheier, M. F., & Buss, A. H. (1975). Public and private self-consciousness: Assessment and theory. *Journal of Consulting and Clinical Psychology, 43,* 522–527.

Ferguson, M. J., Bargh, J. A., & Nayak, D. A. (2005). Aftereffects: How automatic evaluations influence the interpretation of subsequent, unrelated stimuli. *Journal of Experimental Social Psychology, 41,* 182–191.

Festinger, L., Pepitone, A., & Newcomb, T. (1952). Some consequences of deindividuation in a group. *Journal of Abnormal and Social Psychology, 47,* 382–389.

Findley, M. J., & Cooper, H. M. (1983). Locus of control and academic achievement: A literature review. *Journal of Personality and Social Psychology, 44,* 419–427.

Finkel, E. J., & Campbell, W. K. (2001). Self-control and accommodation in close relationships: An interdependence analysis. *Journal of Personality and Social Psychology, 81,* 263–277.

Fisher, S. (1973). *The female orgasm.* New York: Basic Books.

Fisher, S., & Greenberg, R. P. (1977). *The scientific credibility of Freud's theories and therapy.* New York: Basic Books.

Fiske, D. W. (1949). Consistency of the factorial structures of personality ratings from different sources. *Journal of Abnormal and Social Psychology, 44,* 329–344.

Fiske, S. T., & Taylor, S. E. (1984). *Social cognition.* Reading, MA: Addison-Wesley.

Fitzsimons, G. M., & Bargh, J. A. (2003). Thinking of you: Nonconscious pursuit of interpersonal goals associated with relationship partners. *Journal of Personality and Social Psychology, 84,* 148–164.

Fitzsimons, G. M., & Bargh, J. A. (2004). Automatic self-regulation. In R. F. Baumeister & K. D. Vohs (Eds.), *Handbook of self-regulation: Research, theory, and applications* (pp. 151–170). New York: Guilford.

Flanders, J. P. (1968). A review of research on imitative behavior. *Psychological Bulletin, 69,* 316–337.

Fleeson, W. (2001). Toward a structure- and process-integrated view of personality: Traits as density distributions of states. *Journal of Personality and Social Psychology, 80,* 1011–1027.

Fleeson, W. (2004). Moving personality beyond the person-situation debate. *Current Directions in Psychological Science, 13,* 83–87.

Fleeson, W., Leicht, C. (2006). On delineating and integrating the study of variability and stability in personality psychology: Interpersonal trust as illustration. *Journal of Research in Personality, 40,* 5–20.

Fleeson, W., Malanos, A. B., & Achille, N. M. (2002). An intraindividual process approach to the relationship between extraversion and positive affect: Is acting extraverted as "good" as being extraverted? *Journal of Personality and Social Psychology, 83,* 1409–1422.

Fletcher, G. J. O., Danilovics, P., Fernandez, G., Peterson, D., & Reeder, G. D. (1986). Attributional complexity: An individual differences measure. *Journal of Personality and Social Psychology, 51,* 875–884.

Flink, C., Boggiano, A. K., & Barrett, M. (1990). Controlling teaching strategies: Undermining children's self-determination and performance. *Journal of Personality and Social Psychology, 59,* 916–924.

Florian, V., Mikulincer, M., & Hirschberger, G. (2002). The anxiety-buffering function of close relationships: Evidence that relationship commitment acts as a terror management mechanism. *Journal of Personality and Social Psychology, 82,* 527–542.

Flory, J. D., Matthews, K. A., & Owens, J. F. (1998). A social information processing approach to dispositional hostility: Relationships with negative mood and blood pressure elevations at work. *Journal of Social and Clinical Psychology, 17,* 491–504.

Flynn, F. J. (2005). Having an open mind: The impact of openness to experience on interracial attitudes and impression formation. *Journal of Personality and Social Psychology, 88,* 816–826.

Foa, E. B., & Meadows, E. A. (1997). Psychosocial treatments for posttraumatic stress disorder: A critical review. *Annual Review of Psychology, 48,* 449–480.

Fodor, E. M. (1984). The power motive and reactivity to power stresses. *Journal of Personality and Social Psychology, 47,* 853–859.

Folkman, S., & Moskowitz, J. T. (2004). Coping: Pitfalls and promise. *Annual Review of Psychology, 55,* 745–774.

Fowles, D. C. (1980). The three arousal model: Implications of Gray's two-factor learning theory for heart rate, electrodermal activity, and psychopathy. *Psychophysiology, 17,* 87–104.

Fox, N. A., & Davidson, R. J. (1988). Patterns of brain electrical activity during facial signs of emotion in 10-month-old infants. *Developmental Psychology, 24,* 230–236.

Fraley, R. C. (2002). Attachment stability from infancy to adulthood: Meta-analysis and dynamic modeling of developmental mechanisms. *Personality and Social Psychology Review, 6,* 123–151.

Fraley, R. C., Garner, J. P., & Shaver, P. R. (2000). Adult attachment and the defensive regulation of attention and memory: Examining the role of preemptive and postemptive defensive processes. *Journal of Personality and Social Psychology, 79,* 816–826.

Fraley, R. C., & Shaver, P. R. (1998). Airport separations: A naturalistic study of adult attachment dynamics in separating couples. *Journal of Personality and Social Psychology, 75,* 1198–1212.

Frank, E., & Brandstätter, V. (2002). Approach versus avoidance: Different types of commitment in intimate relationships. *Journal of Personality and Social Psychology, 82,* 208–221.

Frank, L. K. (1939). Projective methods for the study of personality. *Journal of Psychology, 8,* 389–413.

Frank, M. J., & Claus, E. D. (2006). Anatomy of a decision: Striato-orbitofrontal interactions in reinforcement learning, decision making, and reversal. *Psychological Review, 113,* 300–326.

Frank, M. J., & O'Reilly, R. C. (2006). A mechanistic account of striatal dopamine function in human cognition: Psychopharmacological studies with cabergoline and haloperidol. *Behavioral Neuroscience, 120,* 497–517.

Frank, M. J., Seeberger, L. C., & O'Reilly, R. C. (2004). By carrot or by stick: Cognitive reinforcement learning in Parkinsonism. *Science, 306,* 1940–1943.

Frank, S., & Quinlan, D. M. (1976). Ego development and female delinquency: A cognitive-developmental approach. *Journal of Abnormal Psychology, 85,* 505–510.

Frankel, A., & Snyder, M. L. (1978). Poor performance following unsolvable problems: Learned helplessness or egotism? *Journal of Personality and Social Psychology, 36,* 1415–1423.

Frankl, V. E. (1969). *The doctor and the soul.* New York: Bantam.

Fransella, F. (1972). *Personal change and reconstruction.* New York: Academic.

Freedman, J. L. (1986). Television violence and aggression: A rejoinder. *Psychological Bulletin, 100,* 372–378.

French, E. G. (1955). Some characteristics of achievement motivation. *Journal of Experimental Psychology, 50,* 232–236.

Freud, A. (1966). *The ego and the mechanisms of defense* (Rev. ed.). New York: International Universities Press.

Freud, S. (1933). *New introductory lectures on psychoanalysis.* New York: Norton. (Translated by W. J. H. Sprott)

Freud, S. (1936). *The problem of anxiety.* New York: Norton. (Translated by H. A. Bunker; originally published, 1926)

Freud, S. (1949). *An outline of psychoanalysis.* New York: Norton. (Translated by J. Strachey; originally published, 1940)

Freud, S. (1953a). Three essays on sexuality. In J. Strachey (Ed.), *The standard edition of the complete psychological works of Sigmund Freud* (Vol. 7). London, England: Hogarth. (Originally published, 1905)

Freud, S. (1953b). The interpretation of dreams. In J. Strachey (Ed.), *The standard edition of the complete psychological works of Sigmund Freud* (Vols. 4 and 5). London: Hogarth Press. (Originally published, 1900)

Freud, S. (1955). Beyond the pleasure principle. In J. Strachey (Ed.), *The standard edition of the complete psychological works of Sigmund Freud* (Vol. 18). London, England: Hogarth. (Originally published, 1920)

Freud, S. (1959). Inhibitions, symptoms and anxiety. In J. Strachey (Ed.), *The standard edition of the complete psychological works of Sigmund Freud* (Vol. 20). London, England: Hogarth. (Originally published, 1926)

Freud, S. (1960a). *Jokes and their relation to the unconscious.* New York: Norton. (Translated by J. Strachey, originally published, 1905)

Freud, S. (1960b). Psychopathology of everyday life. In J. Strachey (Ed.), *The standard edition of the complete psychological works of Sigmund Freud* (Vol. 6). London, England: Hogarth. (Originally published, 1901)

Freud, S. (1961). The unconscious. In J. Strachey (Ed.), *The standard edition of the complete psychological works of Sigmund Freud* (Vol. 14). London, England: Hogarth. (Originally published, 1915)

Freud, S. (1962). *The ego and the id.* New York: Norton. (Originally published, 1923)

Freund, A. M., & Baltes, P. B. (2002). Life-management strategies of selection, optimization, and compensation. Measurement by self-report and construct validity. *Journal of Personality and Social Psychology, 82,* 642–662.

Freyd, J. J. (1987). Dynamic mental representations. *Psychological Review, 94,* 427–438.

Freyd, J. J. (1996). *Betrayal trauma: The logic of forgetting childhood abuse.* Cambridge, MA: Harvard.

Friedman, H. S., Tucker, J. S., Schwartz, J. E., Martin, L. R., Tomlinson-Keasey, C., Wingard, D. L., & Criqui, M. H. (1995). Childhood conscientiousness and longevity: Health behaviors and cause of death. *Journal of Personality and Social Psychology, 68,* 696–701.

Friedman, L. J. (1999). *Identity's architect: A biography of Erik H. Erikson.* New York: Scribner.

Fritz, H. L., & Helgeson, V. S. (1998). Distinctions of unmitigated communion from communion: Self-neglect and overinvolvement with others. *Journal of Personality and Social Psychology, 75,* 121–140.

Frodi, A. (1977). Sexual arousal, situational restrictiveness, and aggressive behavior. *Journal of Research in Personality, 11,* 48–58.

Fujita, K., Trope, Y., Liberman, N., & Leven-Sagi, M. (2006). Construal levels and self-control. *Journal of Personality and Social Psychology, 90,* 351–567.

Fukuyama, F. (2002). *Our posthuman future: Consequences of the biotechnology revolution.* New York: Farrar, Straus, & Giroux.

Fultz, J., Schaller, M., & Cialdini, R. B. (1988). Empathy, sadness, and distress: Three related but distinct vicarious affective responses to another's suffering. *Personality and Social Psychology Bulletin, 14,* 312–325.

Funder, D. C. (1991). Global traits: A neo-Allportian approach to personality. *Psychological Science, 2,* 31–39.

Funder, D. C. (2001). Personality. *Annual Review of Psychology, 52,* 197–221.

Funder, D. C., & Block, J. (1989). The role of ego-control, ego-resiliency, and IQ in delay of gratification in adolescence. *Journal of Personality and Social Psychology, 57,* 1041–1050.

Funder, D. C., Block, J. H., & Block, J. (1983). Delay of gratification: Some longitudinal personality correlates. *Journal of Personality and Social Psychology, 44,* 1198–1213.

Funder, D. C., & Colvin, C. R. (1991). Explorations in behavioral consistency: Properties of persons, situations, and behaviors. *Journal of Personality and Social Psychology, 60,* 773–794.

Funder, D. C., & Ozer, D. J. (1983). Behavior as a function of the situation. *Journal of Personality and Social Psychology, 44,* 107–112.

Furr, R. M., & Funder, D. C. (2004). Situational similarity and behavioral consistency: Subjective, objective, variable-centered, and person-centered approaches. *Journal of Research in Personality, 38,* 421–447.

Gable, S. L. (2006). Approach and avoidance social motives and goals. *Journal of Personality, 74,* 175–222.

Gable, S. L., Reis, H. T., & Elliot, A. J. (2000). Behavioral activation and inhibition in everyday life. *Journal of Personality and Social Psychology, 78,* 1135–1149.

Gacsaly, S. A., & Borges, C. A. (1979). The male physique and behavioral expectancies. *Journal of Psychology, 101,* 97–102.

Gallagher, W. (1994). How we become what we are. *Atlantic Monthly, 274,* 39–55.

Gallese, V. (2001). The "shared manifold" hypothesis: From mirror neurons to empathy. *Journal of Consciousness Studies, 8,* 33–50.

Gallistel, C. R. (1980). *The organization of action: A new synthesis.* Hillsdale, NJ: Erlbaum.

Ganellen, R. J. (1996a). Comparing the diagnostic efficiency of the MMPMI, MCMI-II, and Rorschach: A review. *Journal of Personality Assessment, 67,* 219–243.

Ganellen, R. J. (1996b). *Integrating the Rorschach and MMPI-2 in personality assessment.* Hillsdale, NJ: Erlbaum.

Gangestad, S. W., & Simpson, J. A. (2000). The evolution of human mating: Trade-offs and strategic pluralism. *Behavioral and Brain Sciences, 23,* 573–587.

Gangestad, S. W., & Snyder, M. (1985). "To carve nature at its joints": On the existence of discrete classes in personality. *Psychological Review, 92,* 317–349.

Garcia, J., & Koelling, R. A. (1966). Relation of cue to consequence in avoidance learning. *Psychonomic Science, 4,* 123–124.

Gardner, H. (1985). *The mind's new science: A history of the cognitive revolution.* New York: Basic Books.

Gauthier, J., & Ladouceur, R. (1981). The influence of self-efficacy reports on performance. *Behavior Therapy, 12,* 436–439.

Geen, R. G. (1981). Behavioral and physiological reactions to observed violence: Effects of prior exposure to aggressive stimuli. *Journal of Personality and Social Psychology, 40,* 868–875.

Geen, R. G. (1984). Preferred stimulation levels in introverts and extraverts: Effects on arousal and performance. *Journal of Personality and Social Psychology, 46,* 1303–1312.

Geen, R. G. (1998). Aggression and antisocial behavior. In D. T. Gilbert, S. T. Fiske, & G. Lindzey (Eds.), *The handbook of social psychology* (Vol. 2, 4th ed., pp. 317–356). Boston: McGraw-Hill.

Geen, R. G., Stonner, D., & Shope, G. L. (1975). The facilitation of aggression by aggression: Evidence against the catharsis hypothesis. *Journal of Personality and Social Psychology, 31,* 721–726.

George, D. T., Umhau, J. C., Phillips, M. J., Emmela, D., Ragan, P. W., Shoaf, S. E., & Rawlings, R. R. (2001). Serotonin, testosterone, and alcohol in the etiology of domestic violence. *Psychiatry Research, 104,* 27–37.

Gerst, M. S. (1971). Symbolic coding processes in observational learning. *Journal of Personality and Social Psychology, 19,* 7–27.

Giancola, P. R. (2004). Executive functioning and alcohol-related aggression. *Journal of Abnormal Psychology, 113,* 541–555.

Gibson, H. B. (1981). *Hans Eysenck: The man and his work.* London, England: Peter Owen.

Gigerenzer, G., & Goldstein, D. G. (1996). Reasoning the fast and frugal way: Models of bounded rationality. *Psychological Review, 103,* 650–669.

Gill, M. M. (1959). The present state of psychoanalytic theory. *Journal of Abnormal and Social Psychology, 58,* 1–8.

Gilovich, T. (1990). Differential construal and the false consensus effect. *Journal of Personality and Social Psychology, 59,* 623–634.

Giltay, E. J., Kamphuis, M. H., Kalmijn, S., Zitman, F. G., & Kromhout, D. (2006). Dispositional optimism and the risk of cardiovascular death: The Zutphen elderly study. *Archives of Internal Medicine, 166,* 431–436.

Glassman, N. S., & Andersen, S. M. (1999). Activating transference without consciousness: Using significant-other representations to go beyond what is subliminally given. *Journal of Personality and Social Psychology, 77,* 1146–1162.

Glue, P., Wilson, S., Coupland, N., Ball, D., & Nutt, D. (1995). The relationship between benzodiazepine receptor sensitivity and neuroticism. *Journal of Anxiety Disorders, 9,* 33–45.

Glueck, S., & Glueck, E. (1956). *Physique and delinquency.* New York: Harper.

Goddard, A. W., Mason, G. F., Almai, A., Rothman, D. L., Behar, K. L., Petroff, O. A. C., Charney, D. S., & Krystal, J. H. (2001). Reductions in occipital cortex GABA levels in panic disorder detected with H-Magnetic resonance spectroscopy. *Archives of General Psychiatry, 58,* 556–561.

Goldberg, A. (Ed.). (1985). *Progress in self psychology* (Vol. 1). New York: Guilford.

Goldberg, L. R. (1981). Language and individual differences: The search for universals in personality lexicons. In L. Wheeler (Ed.), *Review of personality and social psychology* (Vol. 2, pp. 141–165). Beverly Hills, CA: Sage.

Goldberg, L. R. (1982). From ace to zombie: Some explorations in the language of personality. In C. D. Spielberger & J. N. Butcher (Eds.), *Advances in personality assessment* (Vol. 1). Hillsdale, NJ: Erlbaum.

Goldberg, L. R. (1993a). The structure of personality traits: Vertical and horizontal aspects. In D. C. Funder, R. Parke, C. Tomlinson-Keasey, & K. Widaman (Eds.), *Studying lives through time: Approaches to personality and development* (pp. 169–188). Washington, DC: American Psychological Association.

Goldberg, L. R. (1993b). The structure of phenotypic personality traits. *American Psychologist, 48,* 26–34.

Goldenberg, J. L., Pyszczynski, T., Greenberg, J., & Solomon, S. (2000). Fleeing the body: A terror management perspective on the problem of human corporeality. *Personality and Social Psychology Review, 4,* 200–218.

Goldenberg, J. L., Pyszczynski, T., Greenberg, J., Solomon, S., Kluck, B., & Cornwell, R. (2001). I am *not* an animal: Mortality salience, disgust, and the denial of human creatureliness. *Journal of Experimental Psychology: General, 130,* 427–435.

Goldfield, G. S., & Epstein, L. H. (2002). Can fruits and vegetables and activities substitute for snack foods? *Health Psychology, 21,* 299–303.

Goldfried, M. R. (1971). Systematic desensitization as training in self-control. *Journal of Consulting and Clinical Psychology, 37,* 228–234.

Goldfried, M. R., & Davison, G. C. (1976). *Clinical behavior therapy.* New York: Holt, Rinehart, & Winston.

Goldfried, M. R., & Merbaum, M. (Eds.). (1973). *Behavior change through self-control.* New York: Holt, Rinehart, & Winston.

Goldiamond, I. (1976). Self-reinforcement. *Journal of Applied Behavior Analysis, 9,* 509–514.

Goldstein, J. H., & Arms, R. L. (1971). Effects of observing athletic contests on hostility. *Sociometry, 34,* 90–93.

Gollwitzer, P. M. (1999). Implementation intentions: Strong effects of simple plans. *American Psychologist, 54,* 493–503.

Gollwitzer, P. M, & Brandstätter, V. (1997). Implementation intentions and effective goal pursuit. *Journal of Personality and Social Psychology, 73,* 186–199.

Goranson, R. E. (1970). Media violence and aggressive behavior: A review of experimental research. In L. Berkowitz (Ed.), *Advances in experimental social psychology* (Vol. 5). New York: Academic.

Gosling, S. D. (2001). From mice to men: What can we learn about personality from animal research? *Psychological Bulletin, 127,* 45–86.

Gotlib, I. H. (1983). Perception and recall of interpersonal feedback: Negative bias in depression. *Cognitive Therapy and Research, 7,* 399–412.

Gottesman, I. I., & Shields, J. (1972). *Schizophrenia and genetics.* New York: Academic.

Gould, R. L. (1980). Transformations during early and middle adult years. In N. J. Smelser & E. H. Erikson (Eds.), *Themes of work and love in adulthood* (pp. 213–237). Cambridge, MA: Harvard University Press.

Govorun, O., Fuegen, K., & Payne, B. K. (2006). Stereotypes focus defensive projection. *Personality and Social Psychology Bulletin, 32,* 781–793.

Grammer, K., & Thornhill, R. (1994). Human facial attractiveness and sexual selection: The role of symmetry and averageness. *Journal of Comparative Psychology, 108,* 233–242.

Gray, J. (1992). *Men are from Mars, women are from Venus: A practical guide for improving communication and getting what you want in your relationships.* New York: HarperCollins.

Gray, J. A. (1982). *The neuropsychology of anxiety: An enquiry into the functions of the septo-hippocampal system.* New York: Oxford University Press.

Gray, J. A. (1987). Perspectives on anxiety and impulsivity: A commentary. *Journal of Research in Personality, 21,* 493–509.

Gray, J. A. (1990). Brain systems that mediate both emotion and cognition. *Cognition and Emotion, 4,* 269–288.

Gray, J. A. (1991). The neuropsychology of temperament. In J. Strelau & A. Angleitner (Eds.), *Explorations in temperament: International perspectives on theory and measurement* (pp. 105–128). New York: Plenum.

Gray, J. A. (1994a). Personality dimensions and emotion systems. In P. Ekman & R. J. Davidson (Eds.), *The nature of emotion: Fundamental questions* (pp. 329–331). New York: Oxford University Press.

Gray, J. A. (1994b). Three fundamental emotion systems. In P. Ekman & R. J. Davidson (Eds.), *The nature of emotion: Fundamental questions* (pp. 243–247). New York: Oxford University Press.

Gray, J. A., & McNaughton, N. (2000). *The neuropsychology of anxiety: An enquiry into the functions of the septo-hippocampal system* (2nd ed.). Oxford, England: Oxford University Press.

Gray, J. D., & Silver, R. C. (1990). Opposite sides of the same coin: Former spouses' divergent perspectives in coping with their divorce. *Journal of Personality and Social Psychology, 59,* 1180–1191.

Gray, J. R., & Braver, T. S. (2002). Personality predicts working-memory-related activation in the caudal anterior cingulate cortex. *Cognitive, Affective, & Behavioral Neuroscience, 2,* 64–75.

Graziano, W. G., & Eisenberg, N. H. (1999). Agreeableness as a dimension of personality. In R. Hogan, J. Johnson, & S. Briggs (Eds.), *Handbook of personality* (pp. 795–825). San Diego: Academic.

Graziano, W. G., Jensen-Campbell, L. A., & Hair, E. C. (1996). Perceiving interpersonal conflict and reacting to it: The case for agreeableness. *Journal of Personality and Social Psychology, 70,* 820–835.

Green, J. D., & Campbell, W. K. (2000). Attachment and exploration in adults: Chronic and contextual accessibility. *Personality and Social Psychology Bulletin, 26,* 452–461.

Greenberg, B. D., Li, Q., Lucas, F. R., Hu, S., Sirota, L. A., Benjamin, J., Lesch, K.-P., Hamer, D., & Murphy, D. L. (2000). Association between the serotonin transporter promoter polymorphism and personality traits in a primarily female population sample. *American Journal of Medical Genetics (Neuropsychiatric Genetics), 96,* 202–216.

Greenberg, G. (2005). The limitations of behavior-genetic analyses: Comment on McGue, Elkins, Walden, and Ianoco. *Developmental Psychology, 41,* 989–992.

Greenberg, J., Pyszczynski, T., & Solomon, S. (1982). The self-serving attributional bias: Beyond self-presentation. *Journal of Experimental Social Psychology, 18,* 56–67.

Greenberg, J., Pyszczynski, T., & Solomon, S. (1986). The causes and consequences of a need for self-esteem: A terror management theory. In R. F. Baumeister (Ed.), *Public self and private self* (pp. 189–212). New York: Springer-Verlag.

Greenberg, J., Solomon, S., & Pyszczynski, T. (1997). Terror management theory of self-esteem and social behavior: Empirical assessments and conceptual refinements. In M. P. Zanna (Ed.), *Advances in experimental social psychology* (Vol. 29, pp. 61–139). New York: Academic.

Greene, D. L., & Winter, D. G. (1971). Motives, involvements, and leadership among black college students. *Journal of Personality, 39,* 319–332.

Greenfield, N. S., & Sternbach, R. A. (1972). *Handbook of psychophysiology.* New York: Holt, Rinehart, & Winston.

Greenwald, A. G., & Banaji, M. R. (1989). The self as a memory system: Powerful, but ordinary. *Journal of Personality and Social Psychology, 57,* 41–54.

Greenwald, A. G., Banaji, M. R., Rudman, L. A., Farnham, S. D., Nosek, B. A., & Mellott, D. S. (2002). A unified theory of implicit attitudes, stereotypes, self-esteem, and self-concept. *Psychological Review, 109,* 3–25.

Greenwald, A. G., McGhee, D. E., & Schwartz, J. L. K. (1998). Measuring individual differences in implicit cognition: The implicit association test. *Journal of Personality and Social Psychology, 74,* 1464–1480.

Greenwald, A. G., & Pratkanis, R. A. (1984). The self. In R. S. Wyer, Jr., & T. K. Srull (Eds.), *Handbook of social cognition* (Vol. 3). Hillsdale, NJ: Erlbaum.

Greer, S., & Morris, T. (1975). Psychological attributes of women who develop breast cancer: A controlled study. *Journal of Psychosomatic Research, 19,* 147–153.

Grewen, K. M., Gridler, S. S., Amico, J., & Light, K. C. (2005). Effects of partner support on resting oxytocin, cortisol, norepinephrine, and blood pressure before and after warm partner contact. *Psychosomatic Medicine, 67,* 531–538.

Griffin, D., & Bartholomew, K. (1994). Models of the self and other: Fundamental dimensions underlying measures of adult attachment. *Journal of Personality and Social Psychology, 67,* 430–445.

Grigsby, J., & Stevens, D. (2000). *Neurodynamics of personality.* New York: Guilford.

Grimes, J. M., Ricci, L. A., & Melloni, R. H., Jr. (2006). Plasticity in anterior hypothalamic vasopressin correlates with aggression during anabolic-androgenic steroid withdrawal in hamsters. *Behavioral Neuroscience, 120,* 115–124.

Grings, W. W. (1973). The role of consciousness and cognition in autonomic behavior change. In F. J. McGuigan & R. Schoonover (Eds.), *The psychophysiology of thinking.* New York: Academic.

Grolnick, W. S., & Ryan, R. M. (1989). Parent styles associated with children's self-regulation and competence in school. *Journal of Educational Psychology, 81,* 143–154.

Grossmann, K. E., Grossmann, K., & Waters, E. (2005). *Attachment from infancy to adulthood: The major longitudinal studies.* New York: Guilford.

Grouzet, F. M. E., Kasser, T., Ahuvia, A., Fernández Dols, J. M., Kim, Y., Lau, S., Ryan, R. M., Saunders, S., Schmuck, P., & Sheldon, K. M. (2005). The structure of goal contents across 15 cultures. *Journal of Personality and Social Psychology, 89,* 800–816.

Gruber, A. J., & Pope, H. G., Jr. (2000). Psychiatric and medical effects of anabolic-androgenic steroid use in women. *Psychotherapy and Psychosomatics, 69,* 19–26.

Gruen, R. J., & Mendelsohn, G. (1986). Emotional responses to affective displays in others: The distinction between empathy and sympathy. *Journal of Personality and Social Psychology, 51,* 609–614.

Guisinger, S., & Blatt, S. J. (1994). Individuality and relatedness: Evolution of a fundamental dialectic. *American Psychologist, 49,* 104–111.

Gurin, P., Gurin, G., Lao, R. C., & Beattie, M. (1969). Internal-external control in the motivational dynamics of Negro youth. *Journal of Social Issues, 25,* 29–53.

Gutierres, S. E., Kenrick, D. T., & Partch, J. J. (1999). Beauty, dominance, and the mating game: Contrast effects in self-assessment reflect gender differences in mate selection. *Personality and Social Psychology Bulletin, 25,* 1126–1134.

Haaga, D. A. F., Dyck, M. J., & Ernst, D. (1991). Empirical status of cognitive theory of depression. *Psychological Bulletin, 110,* 215–236.

Haan, N. (1981). Common dimensions of personality development: Early adolescence to middle life. In D. H. Eichorn, J. A. Clausen, N. Haan, M. P. Honzik, & P. H. Mussen (Eds.), *Present and past in middle life* (pp. 117–151). New York: Academic.

Haas, H. A. (2002). Extending the search for folk personality constructs: The dimensionality of the personality-relevant proverb domain. *Journal of Personality and Social Psychology, 82,* 594–609.

Hackett, G., & Horan, J. J. (1979). Partial component analysis of a comprehensive smoking program. *Addictive Behaviors, 4,* 259–262.

Haemmerlie, F. M., & Montgomery, R. L. (1984). Purposefully biased interactions: Reducing heterosocial anxiety through self-perception theory. *Journal of Personality and Social Psychology, 47,* 900–908.

Hall, R. V., Lund, D., & Jackson, D. (1968). Effects of teacher attention on study behavior. *Journal of Applied Behavior Analysis, 1,* 1–12.

Halpern, J. (1977). Projection: A test of the psychoanalytic hypothesis. *Journal of Abnormal Psychology, 86,* 536–542.

Halverson, C. F., Jr., Kohnstamm, G. A., & Martin, R. P. (Eds.). (1994). *The developing structure of temperament and personality from infancy to adulthood.* Hillsdale, NJ: Erlbaum.

Hamilton, J. C., Greenberg, J., Pyszczynski, T., & Cather, C. (1993). A self-regulatory perspective on psychopathology and psychotherapy. *Journal of Psychotherapy Integration, 3,* 205–248.

Hamilton, W. D. (1964). The genetical evolution of social behavior. *Journal of Theoretical Biology, 7,* 1–52.

Hampson, S. E., Andrews, J. A., Barckley, M., Lichtenstein, E., & Lee, M. E. (2000). Conscientiousness, perceived risk, and risk-reduction behaviors: A preliminary study. *Health Psychology, 19,* 496–500.

Hampson, S. E., Goldberg, L. R., Vogt, T. M., & Dubanoski, J. P. (2006). Forty years on: Teachers' assessments of children's personality traits predict self-reported health behaviors and outcomes at midlife. *Health Psychology, 25,* 57–64.

Handley, S. L. (1995). 5-Hydroxytryptamine pathways in anxiety and its treatment. *Pharmacology & Therapeutics, 66,* 103–148.

Hankin, B. L., Kassel, J. D., & Abela, J. R. Z. (2005). Adult attachment dimensions and specificity of emotional distress symptoms: Prospective investigations of cognitive risk and interpersonal stress generation as mediating mechanisms. *Personality and Social Psychology Bulletin, 31,* 136–151.

Hansenne, M., Pinto, E., Pitchot, W., Reggers, J., Scantamburlo, G., Moor, M., & Ansseau, M. (2002). Further evidence on the relationship between dopamine and novelty seeking: A neuroendocrine study. *Personality and Individual Differences, 33,* 967–977.

Harackiewicz, J. M. (1979). The effects of reward contingency and performance feedback on intrinsic motivation. *Journal of Personality and Social Psychology, 37,* 1352–1363.

Hardy, K. R. (1957). Determinants of conformity and attitude change. *Journal of Abnormal and Social Psychology, 54,* 289–294.

Harmon-Jones, E., & Allen, J. J. (1997). Behavioral activation sensitivity and resting frontal EEG asymmetry: Covariation of putative indicators related to risk for mood disorders. *Journal of Abnormal Psychology, 106,* 159–163.

Harmon-Jones, E., Lueck, L., Fearn, M., & Harmon-Jones, C. (2006). The effect of personal relevance and approach-related action expectation on relative left frontal cortical activity. *Psychological Science, 17,* 434–440.

Harmon-Jones, E., & Sigelman, J. D. (2001). State anger and prefrontal brain activity: Evidence that insult-related relative left-prefrontal activation is associated with experienced anger and aggression. *Journal of Personality and Social Psychology, 80,* 797–803.

Harmon-Jones, E., Vaughn-Scott, K., Mohr, S., Sigelman, J., & Harmon-Jones, C. (2004). The effect of manipulated sympathy and anger on left and right frontal cortical activity. *Emotion, 4,* 95–101.

Harris, C. R. (2002). Sexual and romantic jealousy in heterosexual and homosexual adults. *Psychological Science, 13,* 7–12.

Harris, C. R. (2003). A review of sex differences in sexual jealousy, including self-report data, psychophysiological responses, interpersonal violence, and morbid jealousy. *Personality and Social Psychology Review, 7,* 102–128.

Harris, J. R. (1995). Where is the child's environment? A group socialization theory of development. *Psychological Review, 102,* 458–489.

Harrison, R. J., Connor, D. F., Nowak, C., Nash, K., & Melloni, R. H., Jr. (2000). Chronic anabolic-androgenic steroid treatment during adolescence increases anterior hypothalamic vasopressin and aggression in intact hamsters. *Psychoneuroendocrinology, 25,* 317–338.

Hart, D., Keller, M., Edelstein, W., & Hofmann, V. (1998). Childhood personality influences on social-cognitive development: A longitudinal study. *Journal of Personality and Social Psychology, 74,* 1278–1289.

Hart, H. M., McAdams, D. P., Hirsch, B. J., & Bauer, J. J. (2001). Generativity and social involvement among African Americans and white adults. *Journal of Research in Personality, 35,* 208–230.

Hartmann, H. (1958). *Ego psychology and the problem of adaptation.* New York: International Universities Press. (Originally published, 1939)

Hartmann, H. (1964). *Essays on ego psychology: Selected problems in psychoanalytic theory.* New York: International Universities Press.

Hassin, R. R., Bargh, J. A., & Uleman, J. S. (2002). Spontaneous causal inferences. *Journal of Experimental Social Psychology, 38,* 515–522.

Hassin, R. R., Uleman, J. S., & Bargh, J. A. (Eds.). (2005). *The new unconscious.* New York: Oxford University Press.

Hathaway, S. R., & McKinley, J. C. (1943). *MMPI manual.* New York: Psychological Corporation.

Hauser, S. T. (1976). Loevinger's model and measure of ego development: A critical review. *Psychological Bulletin, 83,* 928–955.

Haviland, J. M., McGuire, T. R., & Rothbaum, P. A. (1983). A critique of Plomin and Foch's "A twin study of objectively assessed personality in childhood." *Journal of Personality and Social Psychology, 45,* 633–640.

Hayes, S. C., Rincover, A., & Volosin, D. (1980). Variables influencing the acquisition and maintenance of aggressive behavior: Modeling versus sensory reinforcement. *Journal of Abnormal Psychology, 89,* 254–262.

Hayes-Roth, B., & Hayes-Roth, F. (1979). A cognitive model of planning. *Cognitive Science, 3,* 275–310.

Haynes, S. N., & O'Brien, W. H. (2000). *Principles and practice of behavioral assessment.* Amsterdam, The Netherlands: Kluwer.

Hazan, C., & Shaver, P. R. (1987). Romantic love conceptualized as an attachment process. *Journal of Personality and Social Psychology, 52,* 511–524.

Hazan, C., & Shaver, P. R. (1990). Love and work: An attachment-theoretical perspective. *Journal of Personality and Social Psychology, 59,* 270–280.

Hazan, C., & Shaver, P. R. (1994). Attachment as an organizational framework for research on close relationships. *Psychological Inquiry, 5,* 1–22.

Hazen, N. L., & Durrett, M. E. (1982). Relationship of security of attachment to exploration and cognitive mapping abilities in 2-year-olds. *Developmental Psychology, 18,* 751–759.

Heath, A. C., Neale, M. C., Kessler, R. C., Eaves, L. J., & Kendler, K. S. (1992). Evidence for genetic influences on personality from self-reports and informant ratings. *Journal of Personality and Social Psychology, 63,* 85–96.

Heckhausen, H. (1967). *The anatomy of achievement motivation.* New York: Academic.

Heckhausen, H., & Gollwitzer, P. M. (1987). Thought contents and cognitive functioning in motivational versus volitional states of mind. *Motivation and Emotion, 11,* 101–120.

Heckhausen, H., Schmalt, H. D., & Schneider, K. (1985). *Achievement motivation in perspective.* New York: Academic.

Heiby, E. M. (1982). A self-reinforcement questionnaire. *Behaviour Research and Therapy, 20,* 397–401.

Heider, F. (1944). Social perception and phenomenal causation. *Psychological Review, 51,* 358–374.

Heider, F. (1958). *The psychology of interpersonal relations.* New York: Wiley.

Heilbrun, K. S. (1980). Silverman's psychodynamic activation: A failure to replicate. *Journal of Abnormal Psychology, 89,* 560–566.

Helgeson, V. S. (1994). Relation of agency and communion to well-being: Evidence and potential explanations. *Psychological Bulletin, 116,* 412–428.

Helgeson, V. S. (2003). Gender-related traits and health. In J. Suls & K. A. Wallston (Eds.), *Social psychological foundations of health and illness* (pp. 367–394). Oxford, England: Blackwell.

Helgeson, V. S., & Fritz, H. L. (1998). A theory of unmitigated communion. *Personality and Social Psychology Review, 2,* 173–183.

Helgeson, V. S., & Fritz, H. L. (1999). Unmitigated agency and unmitigated communion: Distinctions from agency and communion. *Journal of Research in Personality, 33,* 131–158.

Helgeson, V. S., Reynolds, K. A., & Tomich, P. L. (2006). A meta-analytic approach to benefit finding and health. *Journal of Consulting and Clinical Psychology, 74,* 797–816.

Heller, M. S., & Polsky, S. (1975). *Studies in violence and television.* New York: American Broadcasting Companies.

Helmreich, R. L., LeFan, J. H., Bakeman, R., Wilhelm, J., & Radloff, R. (1972). The Tektite 2 human behavior program. *JSAS Catalog of Selected Documents in Psychology, 2,* 13 (MS no. 70).

Helson, R., & Moane, G. (1987). Personality change in women from college to midlife. *Journal of Personality and Social Psychology, 53,* 176–186.

Helson, R., & Roberts, B. W. (1994). Ego development and personality change in adulthood. *Journal of Personality and Social Psychology, 66,* 911–920.

Helson, R., Jones, C., & Kwan, V. S. Y. (2002). Personality change over 40 years of adulthood: Hierarchical linear modeling analyses of two longitudinal samples. *Journal of Personality and Social Psychology, 83,* 752–766.

Helson, R., Kwan, V. S. Y., John, O. P., & Jones, C. (2002). The growing evidence for personality change in adulthood: Findings from research with personality inventories. *Journal of Research in Personality, 36,* 287–306.

Helson, R., & Srivastava, S. (2002). Creative and wise people: Similarities, differences, and how they develop. *Personality and Social Psychology Bulletin, 28,* 1430–1440.

Henderlong, J., & Lepper, M. R. (2002). The effects of praise on children's intrinsic motivation: A review and synthesis. *Psychological Bulletin, 128,* 774–795.

Hennig, J., Reuter, M., Netter, P., Burk, C., & Landt, O. (2005). Two types of aggression are differentially related to serotonergic activity and the A779C TPH polymorphism. *Behavioral Neuroscience, 119,* 16–25.

Henriques, J. B., & Davidson, R. J. (1990). Asymmetrical brain electrical activity discriminates between previously depressed subjects and healthy controls. *Journal of Abnormal Psychology, 99,* 22–31.

Henriques, J. B., & Davidson, R. J. (1991). Left frontal hypoactivation in depression. *Journal of Abnormal Psychology, 100,* 535–545.

Hersch, P. D., & Scheibe, K. E. (1967). Reliability and validity of internal-external control as personality dimensions. *Journal of Consulting Psychology, 31,* 609–613.

Hersen, M., & Bellack, A. (Eds.). (1976). *Behavioral assessment.* New York: Pergamon.

Heschl, A. (2002). *The intelligent genome: On the origin of the human mind by mutation and selection.* New York: Springer-Verlag.

Hess, E. H. (1973). *Imprinting.* New York: Van Nostrand Reinhold.

Hewitt, P. L., & Genest, M. (1990). The ideal self: Schematic processing of perfectionistic content in dysphoric university students. *Journal of Personality and Social Psychology, 59,* 802–808.

Higgins, E. T. (1987). Self-discrepancy: A theory relating self and affect. *Psychological Review, 94,* 319–340.

Higgins, E. T. (1990). Personality, social psychology, and person–situation relations: Standards and knowledge activation as a common language. In L. A. Pervin (Ed.), *Handbook of personality: Theory and research* (pp. 301–338). New York: Guilford.

Higgins, E. T. (1997). Beyond pleasure and pain. *American Psychologist, 52,* 1280–1300.

Higgins, E. T., & Bargh, J. A. (1987). Social cognition and social perception. *Annual Review of Psychology, 38,* 369–425.

Higgins, E. T., Bond, R. N., Klein, R., & Strauman, T. (1986). Self-discrepancies and emotional vulnerability: How magnitude, accessibility and type of discrepancy influence affect. *Journal of Personality and Social Psychology, 51,* 1–15.

Higgins, E. T., & Brendl, C. M. (1995). Accessibility and applicability: Some "activation rules" influencing judgment. *Journal of Experimental Social Psychology, 31,* 218–243.

Higgins, E. T., King, G. A., & Mavin, G. H. (1982). Individual construct accessibility and subjective impressions and recall. *Journal of Personality and Social Psychology, 43,* 35–47.

Higgins, R. L., Snyder, C. R., & Berglas, S. (Eds.). (1990). *Self-handicapping: The paradox that isn't.* New York: Plenum.

Higgins, S. T., Wong, C. J., Badger, G. J., Haug Ogden, D. E., & Dantona, R. L. (2000). Contingent reinforcement increases cocaine abstinence during outpatient treatment and 1 year of follow-up. *Journal of Consulting and Clinical Psychology, 68,* 64–72.

Hill, C. A. (1987). Affiliation motivation: People who need people . . . but in different ways. *Journal of Personality and Social Psychology, 52,* 1008–1018.

Hill, C. A. (1991). Seeking emotional support: The influence of affiliative need and partner warmth. *Journal of Personality and Social Psychology, 60,* 112–121.

Hill, T., Lewicki, P., Czyzewska, M., & Boss, A. (1989). Self-perpetuating development of encoding biases in person perception. *Journal of Personality and Social Psychology, 57,* 373–387.

Hillix, W. A., & Marx, M. H. (1960). Response strengthening by information and effect on human learning. *Journal of Experimental Psychology, 60,* 97–102.

Hilton, N. Z., Harris, G. T., & Rice, M. E. (2000). The functions of aggression by male teenagers. *Journal of Personality and Social Psychology, 79,* 988–994.

Hinkley, K., & Andersen, S. M. (1996). The working self-concept in transference: Significant-other activation and self change. *Journal of Personality and Social Psychology, 71,* 1279–1295.

Hiroto, D. S., & Seligman, M. E. P. (1975). Generality of learned helplessness in man. *Journal of Personality and Social Psychology, 31,* 311–327.

Hirt, E. R., McCrea, S. M., & Boris, H. I. (2003). "I know you self-handicapped last exam": Gender differences in reactions to self-handicapping. *Journal of Personality and Social Psychology, 84,* 177–193.

Hobfoll, S. E., Rom, T., & Segal, B. (1989). Sensation seeking, anxiety, and risk taking in the Israeli context. In S. Einstein (Ed.), *Drugs and alcohol use: Issues and factors* (pp. 53–59). New York: Plenum.

Hobson, J. A. (1988). *The dreaming brain.* New York: Basic Books.

Hodgins, H. S., Koestner, R., & Duncan, N. (1996). On the compatibility of autonomy and relatedness. *Personality and Social Psychology Bulletin, 22,* 227–237.

Hodgkinson, S., Sherrington, R., Gurling, H., Marchbanks, R., & Reeders, S. (1987). Molecular genetic evidence for heterogeneity in manic depression. *Nature, 325,* 805–806.

Hoffman, E. (1988). *The right to be human: A biography of Abraham Maslow.* Los Angeles: Jeremy P. Tarcher.

Hoffman, E. (1994). *The drive for self: Alfred Adler and the founding of individual psychology.* Reading, MA: Addison-Wesley.

Hoffman, L. W. (1991). The influence of the family environment on personality: Accounting for sibling differences. *Psychological Bulletin, 110,* 187–203.

Hofstee, W. K. B., de Raad, B., & Goldberg, L. R. (1992). Integration of the big five and circumplex approaches to trait structure. *Journal of Personality and Social Psychology, 63,* 146–163.

Hogan, R., & Nicholson, R. A. (1988). The meaning of personality test scores. *American Psychologist, 43,* 621–626.

Hogan, R., DeSoto, C. B., & Solano, C. (1977). Traits, tests, and personality research. *American Psychologist, 32,* 255–264.

Hogansen, J., & Lanning, K. (2001). Five factors in sentence-completion test categories: Toward rapprochement between trait and maturational approaches to personality. *Journal of Research in Personality, 35,* 449–462.

Hokanson, J. E., & Burgess, M. (1962a). The effects of status, type of frustration, and aggression on vascular processes. *Journal of Abnormal and Social Psychology, 65,* 232–237.

Hokanson, J. E., & Burgess, M. (1962b). The effects of three types of aggression on vascular processes. *Journal of Abnormal and Social Psychology, 64,* 446–449.

Hokanson, J. E., Burgess, M., & Cohen, M. F. (1963). Effects of displaced aggression on systolic blood pressure. *Journal of Abnormal and Social Psychology, 67,* 214–218.

Hokanson, J. E., & Edelman, R. (1966). Effects of three social responses on vascular processes. *Journal of Personality and Social Psychology, 3,* 442–447.

Hokanson, J. E., & Shetler, S. (1961). The effect of overt aggression on physiological arousal. *Journal of Abnormal and Social Psychology, 63,* 446–448.

Hokanson, J. E., Willers, K. R., & Koropsak, E. (1968). The modification of autonomic responses during aggressive interchanges. *Journal of Personality, 36,* 386–404.

Holahan, C. J., Moos, R. H., Holahan, C. K., Cronkite, R. C., & Randall, P. K. (2003). Drinking to cope and alcohol use and abuse in unipolar depression: A 10-year model. *Journal of Abnormal Psychology, 112,* 159–165.

Holden, K. B., & Rotter, J. B. (1962). A nonverbal measure of extinction in skill and chance situations. *Journal of Experimental Psychology, 63,* 519–520.

Holmes, D. (1972). Aggression, displacement and guilt. *Journal of Personality and Social Psychology, 21,* 296–301.

Holmes, D. S. (1981). Existence of classical projection and the stress-reducing function of attribution projection: A reply to Sherwood. *Psychological Bulletin, 90,* 460–466.

Holroyd, C. B., & Coles, M. G. H. (2002). The neural basis of human error processing: Reinforcement learning, dopamine, and the error-related negativity. *Psychological Review, 109,* 679–709.

Holt, R. (1966). Measuring libidinal and aggressive motives and their controls by means of the Rorschach test. In D. Levine (Ed.), *Nebraska symposium on motivation.* Lincoln: University of Nebraska Press.

Holt, R. R. (1980). Loevinger's measure of ego development: Reliability and national norms for male and female short forms. *Journal of Personality and Social Psychology, 39,* 909–920.

Holtzworth-Munroe, A. (1992). Social skill deficits in maritally violent men: Interpreting the data using a social information processing model. *Clinical Psychology Review, 12,* 605–617.

Holyoak, K. J., Koh, K., & Nisbett, R. E. (1989). A theory of conditioning: Inductive learning within rule-based default hierarchies. *Psychological Review, 96,* 315–340.

Holyoak, K. J., & Spellman, B. A. (1993). Thinking. *Annual Review of Psychology, 44,* 265–315.

Hopkin, K. (1995). Programmed cell death: A switch to the cytoplasm? *Journal of NIH Research, 7,* 39–41.

Hoppe, C. (1972). *Ego development and conformity behavior.* Unpublished doctoral dissertation, Washington University, St. Louis, MO.

Hormuth, S. E. (1990). *The ecology of the self: Relocation and self-concept change.* Cambridge, England: Cambridge University Press.

Horney, K. (1937). *Neurotic personality of our times.* New York: Norton.

Horney, K. (1939). *New ways in psychoanalysis.* New York: Norton.

Horney, K. (1942). *Self-analysis.* New York: Norton.

Horney, K. (1945). *Our inner conflicts.* New York: Norton.

Horney, K. (1950). *Neurosis and human growth.* New York: Norton.

Horney, K. (1967). *Feminine psychology.* New York: Norton.

Horowitz, M. J. (1986). *Stress response syndromes* (2nd ed.). New York: Aronson.

Horvath, P., & Zuckerman, M. (1993). Sensation seeking, risk appraisal, and risky behavior. *Personality and Individual Differences, 14,* 41–52.

Hovland, C. I. (1937). The generalization of conditioning responses. I. The sensory generalization of conditioned responses with varying frequencies of tone. *Journal of General Psychology, 17,* 125–148.

Howard, G. S. (1990). On the construct validity of self-reports: What do the data say? *American Psychologist, 45,* 292–294.

Howard, G. S., Maxwell, S. E., Weiner, R. L., Boynton, K. S., & Rooney, W. M. (1980). Is a behavioral measure the best estimate of behavioral parameters? Perhaps not. *Applied Psychological Measurement, 4,* 293–311.

Hsee, C. K., & Abelson, R. P. (1991). The velocity relation: Satisfaction as a function of the first derivative of outcome over time. *Journal of Personality and Social Psychology, 60*, 341–347.

Hubbard, J. A., Dodge, K. A., Cillessen, A. H. N., Coie, J. D., & Schwartz, D. (2001). The dyadic nature of social information processing in boys' reactive and proactive aggression. *Journal of Personality and Social Psychology, 80*, 268–280.

Hull, C. L. (1943). *Principles of behavior.* New York: Appleton-Century-Crofts.

Hull, J. G. (1981). A self-awareness model of the causes and effects of alcohol consumption. *Journal of Abnormal Psychology, 90*, 586–600.

Hull, J. G., & Rielly, N. P. (1986). An information-processing approach to alcohol use and its consequences. In R. E. Ingram (Ed.), *Information processing approaches to clinical psychology.* New York: Academic.

Hull, J. G., Slone, L. B., Meteyer, K. B., & Matthews, A. R. (2002). The nonconsciousness of self-consciousness. *Journal of Personality and Social Psychology, 83*, 406–424.

Humphreys, L. G. (1939). The effect of random alteration of reinforcement on the acquisition and extinction of conditioned eyelid reactions. *Journal of Experimental Psychology, 15*, 141–158.

Hutchison, K. E., McGeary, J., Smolen, A., Bryan, A., & Swift, R. M. (2002). The DRD4 VNTR polymorphism moderates craving after alcohol consumption. *Health Psychology, 21*, 139–146.

Hy, L. X., & Loevinger, J. (1996). *Measuring ego development* (2nd ed.). Mahwah, NJ: Erlbaum.

Hyman, I. E., Husband, T. H., & Billings, F. J. (1995). False memories of childhood experiences. *Applied Cognitive Psychology, 9*, 181–197.

Hymbaugh, K., & Garrett, J. (1974). Sensation seeking among skydivers. *Perceptual and Motor Skills, 38*, 118.

Ilgen, M., McKellar, J., & Tiet, Q. (2005). Abstinence self-efficacy and abstinence 1 year after substance use disorder treatment. *Journal of Consulting and Clinical Psychology, 73*, 1175–1180.

Ingram, R. E. (Ed.). (1986). *Information-processing approaches to clinical psychology.* New York: Academic.

Isaacs, E. A., & Clark, H. H. (1987). References in conversation between experts and novices. *Journal of Experimental Psychology: General, 116*, 26–37.

Isabella, R. A., Belsky, J., & von Eye, A. (1989). Origins of infant–mother attachment: An examination of interactional synchrony during the infant's first year. *Developmental Psychology, 25*, 12–21.

Jacklin, C. N., Maccoby, E. E., & Doering, C. H. (1983). Neonatal sex-steroid hormones and timidity in 6–18-month-old boys and girls. *Developmental Psychobiology, 16*, 163–168.

Jackson, D. N. (1984). *Personality Research Form manual* (3rd ed.). Port Huron, MI: Research Psychologists.

Jackson, D. N., & Messick, S. (Eds.). (1967). *Problems in assessment.* New York: McGraw-Hill.

Jacob, S., McClintock, M. K., Zelano, B., & Ober, C. (2002). Paternally inherited HLA alleles are associated with women's choice of male odor. *Nature Genetics, 30*, 175–179.

James, W. (1890). *The principles of psychology* (Vol. 2). New York: Holt.

Jang, K. L., Hu, S., Livesley, W. J., Angleitner, A., Riemann, R., Ando, J., Ono, Y., Vernon, P. A., & Hamer, D. H. (2001). Covariance structure of neuroticism and agreeableness: A twin and molecular genetic analysis of the role of the serotonin transporter gene. *Journal of Personality and Social Psychology, 81*, 295–304.

Jang, K. L., Livesley, W. J., Angleitner, A., Riemann, R., & Vernon, P. A. (2002). Genetic and environmental influences on the covariance of facets defining the domains of the five-factor model of personality. *Personality and Individual Differences, 33*, 83–101.

Jang, K. L., Livesley, W. J., & Vernon, P. A. (1996). Heritability of the big five personality dimensions and their facets: A twin study. *Journal of Personality, 64*, 577–591.

Jang, K. L., McCrae, R. R., Angleitner, A., Riemann, R., & Livesley, W. J. (1998). Heritability of facet-level traits in a cross-cultural twin sample: Support for a hierarchical model of personality. *Journal of Personality and Social Psychology, 74*, 1556–1565.

Janoff-Bulman, R. (1992). *Shattered assumptions: Towards a new psychology of trauma.* New York: Free Press.

Janoff-Bulman, R., & Leggatt, H. K. (2002). Culture and social obligation: When "shoulds" are perceived as "wants." *Journal of Research in Personality, 36*, 260–270.

Jeffery, R. W. (1976). The influence of symbolic and motor rehearsal on observational learning. *Journal of Research in Personality, 10*, 116–127.

Jenkins, H. M. (1962). Resistance to extinction when partial reinforcement is followed by regular reinforcement. *Journal of Experimental Psychology, 64*, 441–450.

Jenkins, S. R. (1987). Need for achievement and women's careers over 14 years: Evidence for occupational structure effects. *Journal of Personality and Social Psychology, 53*, 922–932.

Jenkins, S. R. (1994). Need for power and women's careers over 14 years: Structural power, job satisfaction, and motive change. *Journal of Personality and Social Psychology, 66*, 155–165.

Jensen, M. B. (1987). Psychobiological factors predicting the course of breast cancer. *Journal of Personality, 55*, 317–342.

Jensen-Campbell, L. A., Adams, R., Perry, D. G., Workman, K. A., Furdella, J. Q., & Egan, S. K. (2002). Agreeableness, extraversion, and peer relations in early adolescence: Winning friends and deflecting aggression. *Journal of Research in Personality, 36*, 224–251.

Jensen-Campbell, L. A., Gleason, K. A., Adams, R., & Malcolm, K. T. (2003). Interpersonal conflict, agreeableness, and personality development. *Journal of Personality, 71,* 1059–1086.

Jensen-Campbell, L. A., & Graziano, W. G. (2001). Agreeableness as a moderator of interpersonal conflict. *Journal of Personality, 69,* 323–362.

Jensen-Campbell, L. A., Graziano, W. G., & West, S. G. (1995). Dominance, prosocial orientation, and female preferences: Do nice guys really finish last? *Journal of Personality and Social Psychology, 68,* 427–440.

Jessor, R., Costa, F., Jessor, L., & Donovan, J. E. (1983). Time of first intercourse: A prospective study. *Journal of Personality and Social Psychology, 44,* 608–626.

Jessor, S. L., & Jessor, R. (1975). Transition from virginity to nonvirginity among youth: A social-psychological study over time. *Developmental Psychology, 11,* 473–484.

Jockin, V., McGue, M., & Lykken, D. T. (1996). Personality and divorce: A genetic analysis. *Journal of Personality and Social Psychology, 71,* 288–299.

John, O. P. (1990). The big-five factor taxonomy: Dimensions of personality in the natural language and in questionnaires. In L. Pervin (Ed.), *Handbook of personality theory and research* (pp. 66–100). New York: Guilford.

John, O. P., & Robins, R. W. (1994). Accuracy and bias in self-perception: Individual differences in self-enhancement and the role of narcissism. *Journal of Personality and Social Psychology, 66,* 206–219.

Johnson, D. J., & Rusbult, C. E. (1989). Resisting temptation: Devaluation of alternative partners as a means of maintaining commitment in close relationships. *Journal of Personality and Social Psychology, 57,* 967–980.

Johnson, J. A., Germer, C. K., Efran, J. S., & Overton, W. F. (1988). Personality as the basis for theoretical predilections. *Journal of Personality and Social Psychology, 55,* 824–835.

Johnson, J. A., & Ostendorf, F. (1993). Clarification of the five-factor model with the abridged big five dimensional circumplex. *Journal of Personality and Social Psychology, 65,* 563–576.

Johnson, S. L. (2005). Mania and goal regulation: A review. *Clinical Psychology Review, 25,* 241–262.

Johnson, S. L., & Leahy, R. L. (Eds.). (2003). *Psychological treatment of bipolar disorder.* New York: Guilford.

Johnson, S. L., Sandrow, D., Meyer, B., Winters, R., Miller, I., Solomon, D., & Keitner, G. (2000). Increases in manic symptoms after life events involving goal attainment. *Journal of Abnormal Psychology, 109,* 721–727.

Johnson, W., & Kieras, D. (1983). Representation-saving effects of prior knowledge in memory for simple technical prose. *Memory & Cognition, 11,* 456–466.

Joireman, J., Anderson, J., & Strathman, A. (2003). The aggression paradox: Understanding links among aggression, sensation seeking, and the consideration of future consequences. *Journal of Personality and Social Psychology, 84,* 1287–1302.

Jonas, K. J., & Sassenberg, K. (2006). Knowing how to react: Automatic response priming from social categories. *Journal of Personality and Social Psychology, 90,* 709–721.

Jonas, E., Schimel, J., Greenberg, J., & Pyszczynski, T. (2002). The Scrooge effect: Evidence that mortality salience increases prosocial attitudes and behavior. *Personality and Social Psychology Bulletin, 28,* 1342–1353.

Jones, A., & Crandall, R. (1986). Validation of a short index of self-actualization. *Personality and Social Psychology Bulletin, 12,* 63–73.

Jones, E. E., & Berglas, S. (1978). Control of attributions about the self through self-handicapping strategies: The appeal of alcohol and the role of underachievement. *Personality and Social Psychology Bulletin, 4,* 200–206.

Jones, E. E., & Nisbett, R. E. (1971). The actor and the observer: Divergent perceptions of the causes of behavior. In E. E. Jones et al. (Eds.), *Attribution: Perceiving the causes of behavior.* Morristown, NJ: General Learning.

Jones, E. E., & Pittman, T. S. (1982). Toward a general theory of strategic self-presentation. In J. Suls (Ed.), *Psychological perspectives on the self* (Vol. 1). Hillsdale, NJ: Erlbaum.

Jones, J. T., Pelham, B. W., Carvallo, M., & Mirenberg, M. C. (2004). How do I love thee? Let me count the Js: Implicit egotism and interpersonal attraction. *Journal of Personality and Social Psychology, 87,* 665–683.

Jones, M. C. (1968). Personality correlates and antecedents of drinking patterns in adult males. *Journal of Consulting and Clinical Psychology, 32,* 2–12.

Jones, M. C. (1971). Personality antecedents and correlates of drinking patterns in women. *Journal of Consulting and Clinical Psychology, 36,* 61–69.

Jones, W. H., Hobbes, S. A., & Hockenberg, D. (1982). Loneliness and social skills deficits. *Journal of Personality and Social Psychology, 42,* 682–689.

Jöreskog, K. G., & Sörbom, D. (1979). *Advances in factor analysis and structural equations.* Cambridge, MA: Abt Associates.

Josephs, R. A., Sellers, J. G., Newman, M. L., & Mehta, P. H. (2006). The mismatch effect: When testosterone and status are at odds. *Journal of Personality and Social Psychology, 90,* 999–1013.

Jourard, S. M. (1974). *Healthy personality: An approach from the viewpoint of humanistic psychology.* New York: Macmillan.

Jung, C. G. (1933). *Psychological types.* New York: Harcourt, Brace, & World.

Jung, C. G. (1960). *The structure and dynamics of the psyche, Collected works* (Vol. 8). Princeton, NJ: Princeton University Press. (Originally published in German, 1926)

Jung, C. G. (1968). *Analytical psychology: Its theory and practice.* New York: Pantheon.

Juni, S. (1981). Maintaining anonymity vs. requesting feedback as a function of oral dependency. *Perceptual and Motor Skills, 52,* 239–242.

Juni, S., & Fischer, R. E. (1985). Religiosity and preoedipal fixation. *Journal of Genetic Psychology, 146,* 27–35.

Juni, S., & Lo Cascio, R. (1985). Preference for counseling and psychotherapy as related to preoedipal fixation. *Psychological Reports, 56,* 431–438.

Juni, S., Masling, J., & Brannon, R. (1979). Interpersonal touching and orality. *Journal of Personality Assessment, 43,* 235–237.

Jussim, L. (1991). Social perception and social reality: A reflection–construction model. *Psychology Review, 98,* 54–73.

Kagan, J. (1994). *Galen's prophecy: Temperament in human nature.* New York: Basic Books.

Kahn, M. (2002). *Basic Freud: Psychoanalytic thought for the 21st century.* New York: Basic Books.

Kahn, S., Zimmerman, G., Csikszentmihalyi, M., & Getzels, J. W. (1985). Relations between identity in young adulthood and intimacy at midlife. *Journal of Personality and Social Psychology, 49,* 1316–1322.

Kamin, L. J. (1968). Attention-like processes in classical conditioning. In M. R. Jones (Ed.), *Miami symposium on the prediction of behavior: Aversive stimuli* (pp. 9–32). Coral Gables, FL: University of Miami Press.

Kanayama, G., Gruber, A. J., Pope, H. G., Jr., Borowiecki, J. J., & Hudson, J. I. (2001). Over-the-counter drug use in gymnasiums: An underrecognized substance abuse problem? *Psychotherapy and Psychosomatics, 70,* 137–140.

Kanfer, F. H. (1977). The many faces of self-control, or behavior modification changes its focus. In R. B. Stuart (Ed.), *Behavioral self-management: Strategies, techniques, and outcomes.* New York: Brunner/Mazel.

Kanfer, F. H., & Busemeyer, J. R. (1982). The use of problem-solving and decision-making in behavior therapy. *Clinical Psychology Review, 2,* 239–266.

Kanfer, F. H., & Hagerman, S. M. (1981). The role of self-regulation. In L. P. Rehm (Ed.), *Behavior therapy for depression: Present status and future directions.* New York: Academic.

Kanfer, F. H., & Hagerman, S. M. (1985). Behavior therapy and the information-processing paradigm. In S. Reiss & R. R. Bootzin (Eds.), *Theoretical issues in behavior therapy.* New York: Academic.

Kanfer, F. H., Karoly, P., & Newman, A. (1975). Reduction of children's fear of the dark by competence-related and situational threat-related verbal cues. *Journal of Consulting and Clinical Psychology, 43,* 251–258.

Kanfer, F. H., & Marston, A. R. (1963). Human reinforcement: Vicarious and direct. *Journal of Experimental Psychology, 65,* 292–296.

Kanfer, F. H., & Saslow, G. (1965). Behavioral analysis: An alternative to diagnostic classification. *Archives of General Psychiatry, 12,* 519–538.

Kanfer, F. H., & Schefft, B. K. (1988). *Guiding the process of therapeutic change.* Champaign, IL: Research Press.

Kaplan, A. G., & Bean, J. P. (1976). *Beyond sex-role stereotypes: Readings toward a psychology of androgyny.* Boston: Little, Brown.

Kaplan, A. G., & Sedney, M. A. (1980). *Psychology and sex roles: An androgynous perspective.* Boston: Little, Brown.

Kaplan, J. R., Manuck, S. B., Fontenot, M. B., & Mann, J. J. (2002). Central nervous system monoamine correlates of social dominance in cynomolgus monkeys (*Macaca fascicularis*). *Neuropsychopharmacology, 26,* 431–443.

Karylowski, J. J. (1990). Social reference points and accessibility of trait-related information in self–other similarity judgments. *Journal of Personality and Social Psychology, 58,* 975–983.

Kasser, T. (2002). *The high price of materialism.* Cambridge, MA: Bradford Books.

Kasser, T., Koestner, R., & Lekes, N. (2002). Early family experiences and adult values: A 26-year, prospective longitudinal study. *Personality and Social Psychology Bulletin, 28,* 826–835.

Kasser, T., & Ryan, R. M. (1993). A dark side of the American dream: Correlates of financial success as a central life aspiration. *Journal of Personality and Social Psychology, 65,* 410–422.

Katigbak, M. S., Church, A. T., Guanzon-Lapeña, M. A., Carlota, A. J., & del Pilar, G. H. (2002). Are indigenous personality dimensions culture specific? Philippine inventories and the five-factor model. *Journal of Personality and Social Psychology, 82,* 89–101.

Kawada, C. L. K., Oettingen, G., Gollwiter, P. M., & Bargh, J. A. (2004). The projection of implicit and explicit goals. *Journal of Personality and Social Psychology, 86,* 545–559.

Kazdin, A. E. (1974). Effects of covert modeling and reinforcement on assertive behavior. *Journal of Abnormal Psychology, 83,* 240–252.

Kazdin, A. E. (1975). Covert modeling, imagery assessment, and assertive behavior. *Journal of Consulting and Clinical Psychology, 43,* 716–724.

Keane, T. M., Kolb, L. C., Kaloupek, D. G., Orr, S. P., Blanchard, E. B., Thomas, R. G., Hsieh, F. Y., & Lavori, P. W. (1998). Utility of psychophysiological measurement in the diagnosis of posttraumatic stress disorder: Results from a Department of Veteran Affairs cooperative study. *Journal of Consulting and Clinical Psychology, 66,* 914–923.

Keller, P. E., Wascher, E., Prinz, W., Waszak, F., Koch, I., & Rosenbaum, D. A. (2006). Differences between intention-based and stimulus-based actions. *Journal of Psychophysiology, 20,* 9–20.

Kelly, A. E., Klusas, J. A., von Weiss, R. T., & Kenny, C. (2001). What is it about revealing secrets that is beneficial? *Personality and Social Psychology Bulletin, 27,* 651–665.

Kelly, G. A. (1955). *The psychology of personal constructs* (Vols. 1 and 2). New York: Norton.

Kelly, G. A. (1962). Europe's matrix of decisions. In M. R. Jones (Ed.), *Nebraska symposium on motivation* (Vol. 10). Lincoln: University of Nebraska Press.

Kelly, G. A. (1969). In whom confide: On whom depend for what? In B. Maher (Ed.), *Clinical psychology and personality.* New York: Wiley.

Kendler, K. S. (1997). Social support: A genetic–epidemiological analysis. *American Journal of Psychiatry, 154,* 1398–1404.

Kendler, K. S. (2005). "A gene for . . .": The nature of gene action in psychiatric disorders. *American Journal of Psychiatry, 162,* 1243–1252.

Kenford, S. L., Fiore, M. C., Jorenby, D. E., & Smith, S. S. (1994). Predicting smoking cessation: Who will quit with and without the nicotine patch. *Journal of the American Medical Association, 217,* 589–594.

Kenrick, D. T., Groth, G. E., Trost, M. R., & Sadalla, E. K. (1993). Integrating evolutionary and social exchange perspectives on relationships: Effects of gender, self-appraisal, and involvement level on mate selection criteria. *Journal of Personality and Social Psychology, 64,* 951–969.

Kenrick, D. T., & Keefe, R. C. (1992). Age preferences in mates reflect sex differences in human reproductive strategies. *Behavioral and Brain Sciences, 15,* 75–91.

Kenrick, D. T., Neuberg, S. L., Zierk, K. L., & Krones, J. M. (1994). Evolution and social cognition: Contrast effects as a function of sex, dominance, and physical attractiveness. *Personality and Social Psychology Bulletin, 20,* 210–217.

Kenrick, D. T., Sadalla, E. K., Groth, G., & Trost, M. R. (1990). Evolution, traits, and the stages of human courtship: Qualifying the parental investment model. *Journal of Personality, 58,* 97–116.

Kenrick, D. T., & Stringfield, D. O. (1980). Personality traits and the eye of the beholder: Crossing some traditional philosophical boundaries in the search for consistency in all of the people. *Psychological Review, 87,* 88–104.

Kenrick, D. T., Sundie, J. M., Nicastle, L. D., & Stone, G. O. (2001). Can one ever be too wealthy or too chaste? Searching for nonlinearities in mate judgment. *Journal of Personality and Social Psychology, 80,* 462–471.

Kernberg, O. (1976). *Borderline conditions and pathological narcissism.* New York: Jason Aronson.

Kernberg, O. (1980). *Internal world and external reality.* New York: Jason Aronson.

Kessler, R. C., Kendler, K. S., Heath, A., Neale, M. C., & Eaves, L. J. (1992). Social support, depressed mood, and adjustment to stress: A genetic epidemiologic investigation. *Journal of Personality and Social Psychology, 62,* 257–272.

Keyes, C. L. M., Shmotkin, D., & Ryff, C. D. (2002). Optimizing well-being: The empirical encounter of two traditions. *Journal of Personality and Social Psychology, 82,* 1007–1022.

Kiecolt-Glaser, J. K., Bane, C., Glaser, R., & Malarkey, W. B. (2003). Love, marriage, and divorce: Newlyweds' stress hormones foreshadow relationship changes. *Journal of Consulting and Clinical Psychology, 71,* 176–188.

Kiecolt-Glaser, J. K., McGuire, L., Robles, T. F., & Glaser, R. (2002). Emotions, morbidity, and mortality: New perspectives from psychoneuroimmunology. *Annual Reviews of Psychology, 53,* 83–107.

Kieras, J. E., Tobin, R. M., Graziano, W. G., & Rothbart, M. K. (2005). You can't always get what you want: Effortful control and children's responses to undesirable gifts. *Psychological Science, 16,* 391–396.

Kihlstrom, J. F. (1987). The cognitive unconscious. *Science, 237,* 1445–1452.

Kimura, D. (1999). *Sex and cognition.* Cambridge, MA: MIT Press.

Kinder, L. S., Kamarck, T. W., Baum, A., & Orchard, T. J. (2002). Depressive symptomatology and coronary heart disease in type 1 diabetes mellitus: A study of possible mechanisms. *Health Psychology, 21,* 542–552.

Kirkpatrick, L. A. (1998). God as a substitute attachment figure: A longitudinal study of adult attachment style and religious change in college students. *Personality and Social Psychology Bulletin, 24,* 961–973.

Kirkpatrick, L. A., & Davis, K. E. (1994). Attachment style, gender, and relationship stability: A longitudinal analysis. *Journal of Personality and Social Psychology, 66,* 502–512.

Kirsch, I. (1985). Response expectancy as a determinant of experience and behavior. *American Psychologist, 40,* 1189–1202.

Kirsch, I. (1990). *Changing expectations: A key to effective psychotherapy.* Pacific Grove, CA: Brooks/Cole.

Kirsch, I., Mearns, J., & Catanzaro, S. J. (1990). Mood-regulation expectancies as determinants of dysphoria in college students. *Journal of Counseling Psychology, 37,* 306–312.

Kirschenbaum, D. S. (1987). Self-regulatory failure: A review with clinical implications. *Clinical Psychology Review, 7,* 77–104.

Kitcher, P. (1987). Précis of *Vaulting ambition: Sociobiology and the quest for human nature. Behavioral and Brain Sciences, 10,* 61–100.

Klein, G. S. (1970). *Perception, motives, and personality.* New York: Knopf.

Klein, J. (1987). *Our need for others and its roots in infancy.* London, England: Tavistock.

Klein, M. (1935). *The psychoanalysis of children.* New York: Norton.

Klein, M. (1955a). The psychoanalytic play technique. *American Journal of Orthopsychiatry, 112,* 418–422.

Klein, M. (1955b). The psychoanalytic play technique, its history and significance. In M. Klein, P. Heiman, & R. Money-Kyrle (Eds.), *New directions in psychoanalysis: The significance of infant conflict in the pattern of adult behavior.* New York: Basic Books.

Klinesmith, J., Kasser, T., & McAndrew, F. T. (2006). Guns, testosterone, and aggression: An experimental test of a mediational hypothesis. *Psychological Science, 17,* 568–571.

Klinger, E. (1975). Consequences of commitment to and disengagement from incentives. *Psychological Review, 82,* 1–25.

Klinger, E. (1987). Current concerns and disengagement from incentives. In F. Halisch & J. Kuhl (Eds.), *Motivation, intention, and volition* (pp. 337–347). Berlin, Germany: Springer-Verlag.

Klion, R. E., & Leitner, L. M. (1991). Impression formation and construct system organization. *Social Behavior and Personality, 19,* 87–98.

Klohnen, E. C. (1996). Conceptual analysis and measurement of the construct of ego-resiliency. *Journal of Personality and Social Psychology, 70,* 1067–1079.

Klohnen, E. C., Vandewater, E. A., & Young, A. (1996). Negotiating the middle years: Ego-resiliency and successful midlife adjustment in women. *Psychology and Aging, 11,* 431–442.

Knapp, R. R. (1976). *Handbook for the Personal Orientation Inventory.* San Diego: EdITS.

Knee, C. R., Lonsbary, C., Canevello, A., & Patrick, H. (2005). Self-determination and conflict in romantic relationships. *Journal of Personality and Social Psychology, 89,* 997–1009.

Knee, C. R., Patrick, H., Vietor, N. A., Nanayakkara, A., & Neighbors, C. (2002). Self-determination as growth motivation in romantic relationships. *Personality and Social Psychology Bulletin, 28,* 609–619.

Knickmeyer, R., Baron-Cohen, S., Raggatt, P., Taylor, K., & Hackett, G. (2006). Fetal testosterone and empathy. *Hormones and Behavior, 49,* 282–292.

Knutson, B., Wolkowitz, O. M., Cole, S. W., Chan, T., Moore, E. A., Johnson, R. C., Terpstra, J., Turner, R. A., & Reus, V. I. (1998). Selective alteration of personality and social behavior by serotonergic intervention. *American Journal of Psychiatry, 155,* 373–379.

Kobak, R. R., & Hazan, C. (1991). Attachment in marriage: Effects of security and accuracy of working models. *Journal of Personality and Social Psychology, 60,* 861–869.

Kochanska, G., Friesenborg, A. E., Lange, L. A., & Martel, M. M. (2004). Parents' personality and infants' temperament as contributors to their emerging relationship. *Journal of Personality and Social Psychology, 86,* 744–759.

Kochanska, G., & Knaack, A. (2003). Effortful control as a personality characteristic of young children: Antecedents, correlates, and consequences. *Journal of Personality, 71,* 1087–1112.

Koestner, R., Lekes, N., Powers, T. A., & Chicoine, E. (2002). Attaining personal goals: Self-concordance plus implementation intentions equals success. *Journal of Personality and Social Psychology, 83,* 231–244.

Koestner, R., Zuckerman, M., & Koestner, J. (1987). Praise, involvement, and intrinsic motivation. *Journal of Personality and Social Psychology, 53,* 383–390.

Koffka, K. (1935). *Principles of Gestalt psychology.* New York: Harcourt, Brace.

Kohler, E., Keysers, C., Umiltà, M. A., Fogassi, L., Gallese, V., & Rizzolatti, G. (2002). Hearing sounds, understanding actions: Action representation in mirror neurons. *Science, 297,* 846–848.

Köhler, W. (1947). *Gestalt psychology.* New York: Liveright.

Kohut, H. (1977). *The restoration of the self.* New York: International Universities Press.

Konecni, V. J. (1975). Annoyance, type and duration of postannoyance activity, and aggression: The "cathartic effect." *Journal of Experimental Psychology: General, 104,* 76–102.

Koole, S. L., Jager, W., van den Berg, A. E., Vlek, C. A. J., & Hofstee, W. K. B. (2001). On the social nature of personality: Effects of extraversion, agreeableness, and feedback about collective resource use on cooperation in a resource dilemma. *Personality and Social Psychology Bulletin, 27,* 289–301.

Korchmaros, J. D., & Kenny, D. A. (2001). Emotional closeness as a mediator of the effect of genetic relatedness on altruism. *Psychological Science, 12,* 262–265.

Kornhaber, R. C., & Schroeder, H. E. (1975). Importance of model similarity on extinction of avoidance behavior in children. *Journal of Consulting and Clinical Psychology, 43,* 601–607.

Kosfeld, M., Heinrichs, M., Zack, P. J., Fischbacher, U., & Fehr, E. (2005). Oxytocin increases trust in humans. *Nature, 435,* 673–676.

Kotler, M., Cohen, H., Segman, R., Gritsenko, L., Nemanov, L., Lerer, B., Kramer, I., Zer-Zion, M., Kletz, I., & Ebstein, R. P. (1997). Excess dopamine D_4 receptor (D4DR) exon III seven repeat allele in opioid-dependent subjects. *Molecular Psychiatry, 2,* 251–254.

Kotre, J. (1984). *Outliving the self: Generativity and the interpretation of lives.* Baltimore: Johns Hopkins University Press.

Kowaz, A. M., & Marcia, J. E. (1991). Development and validation of a measure of Eriksonian industry. *Journal of Personality and Social Psychology, 60,* 390–396.

Kramer, P. D. (1993). *Listening to Prozac: A psychiatrist explores anti-depressant drugs and the remaking of the self.* New York: Viking.

Krantz, D. S., & McCeney, M. K. (2002). Effects of psychological and social factors on organic disease: A critical assessment of research on coronary heart disease. *Annual Reviews of Psychology, 53,* 341–369.

Kretschmer, E. (1925). *Physique and character.* New York: Harcourt, Brace.

Krieger, S. R., Epting, F. R., & Leitner, L. (1974). Personal constructs and attitudes toward death. *Omega, 5,* 299.

Kriegman, D., & Knight, C. (1988). Social evolution, psychoanalysis, and human nature. *Social Policy, 19,* 49–55.

Krueger, R. F. (2002). Personality from a realist's perspective: Personality traits, criminal behaviors, and the externalizing spectrum. *Journal of Research in Personality, 36,* 564–572.

Krueger, R. F., Schmutte, P. S., Caspi, A., Moffitt, T. E., Campbell, K., & Silva, P. A. (1994). Personality traits are linked to crime among men and women: Evidence from a birth cohort. *Journal of Abnormal Psychology, 103,* 328–338.

Krueger, R. F., Watson, D., & Barlow, D. H. (Eds.). (2005). Toward a dimensionally based taxonomy of psychopathology [Special section]. *Journal of Abnormal Psychology, 114,* 491–569.

Kuhl, J. (2000). The volitional basis of Personality Systems Interaction Theory: Applications in learning and treatment contexts. *International Journal of Educational Research, 33,* 665–703.

Kuhl, J., & Helle, P. (1986). Motivational and volitional determinants of depression: The degenerated-intention hypothesis. *Journal of Abnormal Psychology, 95,* 247–251.

Kuiper, N. A., & Derry, P. A. (1981). The self as a cognitive prototype: An application to person perception and depression. In N. Cantor & J. Kihlstrom (Eds.), *Cognition, social interaction, and personality.* Hillsdale, NJ: Erlbaum.

Kukla, A. (1972). Foundations of an attributional theory of performance. *Psychological Review, 79,* 454–470.

Kulhavy, R. W., & Stock, W. A. (1989). Feedback in written instruction: The place of response certitude. *Educational Psychology Review, 1,* 279–308.

Kunda, Z. (1999). *Social cognition: Making sense of people.* Cambridge, MA: MIT Press.

Kunda, Z., & Thagard, P. (1996). Forming impressions from stereotypes, traits, and behaviors: A parallel-constraint-satisfaction theory. *Psychological Review, 103,* 284–308.

Kunzmann, U., & Baltes, P. B. (2003). Wisdom-related knowledge: Affective, motivational, and interpersonal correlates. *Personality and Social Psychology Bulletin, 29,* 1104–1119.

La Greca, A. M., & Santogrossi, D. A. (1980). Social skills training with elementary school students: A behavioral group approach. *Journal of Consulting and Clinical Psychology, 48,* 220–227.

La Greca, A. M., Stone, W. L., & Bell, C. R., III (1983). Facilitating the vocational–interpersonal skills of mentally retarded individuals. *American Journal of Mental Deficiency, 88,* 270–278.

La Guardia, J. G., Ryan, R. M., Couchman, C. E., & Deci, E. L. (2000). Within-person variation in security of attachment: A self-determination theory perspective on attachment, need fulfillment, and well-being. *Journal of Personality and Social Psychology, 79,* 367–384.

Lakoff, G. (1987). *Women, fire, and dangerous things: What categories reveal about the mind.* Chicago: University of Chicago Press.

Lamiell, J. T. (1981). Toward an idiothetic psychology of personality. *American Psychologist, 36,* 276–289.

Landreth, G. L. (1991). *Play therapy: The art of the relationship.* Muncie, IN: Accelerated Development.

Landy, F. J. (1986). Stamp collecting versus science: Validation as hypothesis testing. *American Psychologist, 41,* 1183–1192.

Lane, R. D., & Nadel, L. (Eds.). (2000). *Cognitive neuroscience of emotion.* New York: Oxford University Press.

Lang, P. J., & Lazovik, A. D. (1963). Experimental desensitization of a phobic. *Journal of Abnormal and Social Psychology, 66,* 519–525.

Langens, T. A., & Schmalt, H.-D. (2002). Emotional consequences of positive daydreaming: The moderating role of fear of failure. *Personality and Social Psychology Bulletin, 28,* 1725–1735.

Langner, C. A., & Winter, D. G. (2001). The motivational basis of concessions and compromise: Archival and laboratory studies. *Journal of Personality and Social Psychology, 81,* 711–727.

Langston, C., & Cantor, N. (1989). Social anxiety and social constraint: When "making friends" is hard. *Journal of Personality and Social Psychology, 56,* 649–661.

Lanning, K. (1994). Dimensionality of observer ratings on the California Adult Q-set. *Journal of Personality and Social Psychology, 67,* 151–160.

Lansing, J. B., & Heyns, R. W. (1959). Need affiliation and frequency of four types of communication. *Journal of Abnormal and Social Psychology, 58,* 365–372.

Larsen, R. J., & Ketelaar, T. (1991). Personality and susceptibility to positive and negative emotional states. *Journal of Personality and Social Psychology, 61,* 132–140.

Larstone, R. M., Jang, K. L., Livesley, W. J., Vernon, P. A., & Wolf, H. (2002). The relationship between Eysenck's P-E-N model of personality, the five-factor model of personality, and traits delineating personality dysfunction. *Personality and Individual Differences, 33,* 25–37.

Lassiter, G. D., Briggs, M. A., & Bowman, R. E. (1991). Need for cognition and the perception of ongoing behavior. *Personality and Social Psychology Bulletin, 17,* 156–160.

Lassiter, G. D., Briggs, M. A., & Slaw, R. D. (1991). Need for cognition, causal processing, and memory for behavior. *Personality and Social Psychology Bulletin, 17,* 694–700.

Lau, R. R. (1989). Construct accessibility and electoral choice. *Political Behavior, 11,* 5–32.

Laurenceau, J.-P., Barrett, L. F., & Pietromonaco, P. R. (1998). Intimacy as an interpersonal process: The importance of self-disclosure, and perceived partner responsiveness in interpersonal exchanges. *Journal of Personality and Social Psychology, 74,* 1238–1251.

Lazarus, R. S. (1966). *Psychological stress and the coping process.* New York: McGraw-Hill.

Lazarus, R. S., & Folkman, S. (1984). *Stress, appraisal, and coping.* New York: Springer.

Le Vay, S. (1991). A difference in hypothalamic structure between heterosexual and homosexual men. *Science, 253,* 1034–1037.

Le Vay, S. (1993). *The sexual brain.* Cambridge, MA: MIT Press.

Leak, G. K., & Christopher, S. B. (1982). Freudian psychoanalysis and sociobiology: A synthesis. *American Psychologist, 37,* 313–322.

Leary, M. R., & Baumeister, R. F. (2000). The nature and function of self-esteem: Sociometer theory. In M. P. Zanna (Ed.), *Advances in experimental social psychology* (Vol. 32, pp. 1–62). San Diego: Academic.

Lee, L., & Snarey, J. (1988). The relationship between ego and moral development: A theoretical review and empirical analysis. In D. K. Lapsley & F. C. Power (Eds.), *Self, ego, and identity: Integrative approaches* (pp. 151–178). New York: Springer-Verlag.

Lefcourt, H. M. (1976). *Locus of control: Current trends in theory and research.* Hillsdale, NJ: Erlbaum.

Lefcourt, H. M. (Ed.). (1981). *Research with the locus of control construct. Vol. 1, Assessment methods.* New York: Academic.

Lefcourt, H. M., Martin, R. A., Fick, C. M., & Saleh, W. E. (1985). Locus of control for affiliation and behavior in social interactions. *Journal of Personality and Social Psychology, 48,* 755–759.

Lefcourt, H. M., Von Baeyer, C. I., Ware, E. E., & Cox, D. J. (1979). The Multidimensional-Multiattributional Causality scale: The development of a goal specific locus of control scale. *Canadian Journal of Behavioral Science, 11,* 286–304.

Leit, R. A., Pope, H. G., Jr., & Gray, J. J. (2001). Cultural expectations of muscularity in men: The evolution of playgirl centerfolds. *International Journal of Eating Disorders, 29,* 90–93.

Leitner, L. M., & Cado, S. (1982). Personal constructs and homosexual stress. *Journal of Personality and Social Psychology, 43,* 869–872.

Lemann, N. (1994). Is there a science of success? *Atlantic Monthly, 273,* 83–98.

Lengfelder, A., & Gollwitzer, P. M. (2001). Reflective and reflexive action control in patients with frontal brain lesions. *Neuropsychology, 15,* 80–100.

Lepper, M. R., & Greene, D. (1975). Turning play into work: Effects of adult surveillance and extrinsic rewards on children's intrinsic motivation. *Journal of Personality and Social Psychology, 31,* 479–486.

Lepper, M. R., & Greene, D. (1978). *The hidden costs of reward.* Hillsdale, NJ: Erlbaum.

Lesch, K.-P., Bengel, D., Heils, A., Sabol, S. Z., Greenberg, B. D., Petri, S., et al. (1996). Association of anxiety-related traits with a polymorphism in the serotonin transporter gene regulatory region. *Science, 274,* 1527–1531.

Lesch, K.-P., & Mössner, R. (1998). Genetically driven variation in serotonin uptake: Is there a link to affective spectrum, neurodevelopmental, and neurodegenerative disorders? *Biological Psychiatry, 44,* 179–192.

Levenson, H. (1973). Multidimensional locus of control in psychiatric patients. *Journal of Consulting and Clinical Psychology, 41,* 397–404.

Levenson, H. (1981). Differentiating among internality, powerful others, and chance. In H. F. Lefcourt (Ed.), *Research with the locus of control construct. Vol. 1, Assessment methods.* New York: Academic.

Levenson, R. W., & Ruef, A. M. (1992). Empathy: A physiological substrate. *Journal of Personality and Social Psychology, 63,* 234–246.

Levine, D. S., & Leven, S. J. (Eds.). (1992). *Motivation, emotion, and goal direction in neural networks.* Hillsdale, NJ: Erlbaum.

Levinson, D. J. (1978). *The seasons of a man's life.* New York: Knopf.

Lewin, D. I. (1990). Gene therapy nears starting gate. *Journal of NIH Research, 2,* 36–38.

Lewin, K. (1951a). *Field theory in social science.* New York: Harper.

Lewin, K. (1951b). The nature of field theory. In M. H. Marx (Ed.), *Psychological theory.* New York: Macmillan.

Lewinsohn, P. M., Mischel, W., Chaplin, W., & Barton, R. (1980). Social competence and depression: The role of illusory self-perceptions. *Journal of Abnormal Psychology, 89,* 203–212.

Lewis, D. J., & Duncan, C. P. (1956). Effect of different percentages of money reward on extinction of a lever pulling response. *Journal of Experimental Psychology, 52,* 23–27.

Lewontin, R. C., Rose, S., & Kamin, L. J. (1984). *Not in our genes: Biology, ideology, and human nature.* New York: Penguin.

Li, N. P., Bailey, J. M., Kenrick, D. T., & Linsenmeier, J. A. W. (2002). The necessities and luxuries of mate preferences: Testing the tradeoffs. *Journal of Personality and Social Psychology, 82,* 947–955.

Li, T., Xu, K., Deng, H., Cai, G., Liu, J., Liu, X., Wang, R., Xiang, X., Zhao, J., Murray, R. M., Sham, P. C., & Collier, D. A. (1997). Association analysis of the dopamine D_4 gene exon III VNTR and heroin abuse in Chinese subjects. *Molecular Psychiatry, 2,* 413–416.

Libera, C. D., & Chelazzi, L. (2006). Visual selective attention and the effects of monetary rewards. *Psychological Science, 17,* 222–227.

Lichtenstein, E., & Danaher, B. G. (1976). Modification of smoking behavior: A critical analysis of theory, research, and practice. In M. Hersen, R. M. Eisler, & P. M. Miller (Eds.), *Progress in behavior modification* (Vol. 3). New York: Academic.

Lieberman, M. D., Gaunt, R., Gilbert, D. T., & Trope, Y. (2002). Reflection and reflexion: A social cognitive neuroscience approach to attributional inference. In M.

Zanna (Ed.), *Advances in Experimental Social Psychology* (pp. 199–249). San Diego: Academic.

Liebert, R. M., & Baron, R. A. (1972). Some immediate effects of televised violence on children's behavior. *Developmental Psychology, 6,* 469–475.

Liebert, R. M., & Fernandez, L. E. (1970). Effects of vicarious consequences on imitative performance. *Child Development, 41,* 841–852.

Light, K. C., Smith, T. E., Johns, J. M., Brownley, K. A., Hofheimer, J. A., & Amico, J. A. (2000). Oxytocin responsivity in mothers of infants: A preliminary study of relationships with blood pressure during laboratory stress and normal ambulatory activity. *Health Psychology, 19,* 560–567.

Lilienfeld, S. O., Wood, J. M., & Garb, H. N. (2000). The scientific status of projective techniques. *Psychological Science in the Public Interest, 1,* 27–66.

Linville, P. W. (1987). Self-complexity as a cognitive buffer against stress-related illness and depression. *Journal of Personality and Social Psychology, 52,* 663–676.

Litt, M. D. (1988). Self-efficacy and perceived control: Cognitive mediators of pain tolerance. *Journal of Personality and Social Psychology, 54,* 149–160.

Little, B. R. (1989). Personal projects analysis: Trivial pursuits, magnificent obsessions, and the search for coherence. In D. M. Buss & N. Cantor (Eds.), *Personality psychology: Recent trends and emerging directions* (pp. 15–31). New York: Springer-Verlag.

Locke, E. A., & Latham, G. P. (1990). *A theory of goal setting and task performance.* Englewood Cliffs, NJ: Prentice-Hall.

Locurto, C. M., Terrace, H. S., & Gibbon, J. (Eds.). (1980). *Autoshaping and conditioning theory.* New York: Academic.

Loehlin, J. C. (1992). *Genes and environment in personality development.* Newbury Park, CA: Sage.

Loehlin, J. C., & Nichols, R. C. (1976). *Heredity, environment, and personality.* Austin: University of Texas Press.

Loehlin, J. C., Willerman, L., & Horn, J. M. (1985). Personality resemblances in adoptive families when the children are late-adolescent or adult. *Journal of Personality and Social Psychology, 48,* 376–392.

Loehlin, J. C., Willerman, L., & Horn, J. M. (1988). Human behavior genetics. *Annual Review of Psychology, 38,* 101–133.

Loevinger, J. (1966). The meaning and measurement of ego development. *American Psychologist, 21,* 195–206.

Loevinger, J. (1969). Theories of ego development. In L. Breger (Ed.), *Clinical–cognitive psychology: Models and integrations.* Englewood Cliffs, NJ: Prentice-Hall.

Loevinger, J. (1976). *Ego development: Conceptions and theories.* San Francisco: Jossey-Bass.

Loevinger, J. (1987). *Paradigms of personality.* New York: W. H. Freeman.

Loevinger, J. (1993). Measurement of personality: True or false? *Psychological Inquiry, 4,* 1–16.

Loevinger, J., & Knoll, E. (1983). Personality: Stages, traits, and the self. *Annual Review of Psychology, 34,* 195–222.

Loevinger, J., & Wessler, R. (1970). *Measuring ego development 1. Construction and use of a sentence-completion test.* San Francisco: Jossey-Bass.

Loftus, E. F. (1997). Creating false memories. *Scientific American, 277,* 70–75.

Loftus, E. F., Coan, J. A., & Pickrell, J. E. (1996). Manufacturing false memories using bits of reality. In L. Reder (Ed.), *Implicit memory and metacognition* (pp. 195–220). Mahwah, NJ: Erlbaum.

Loftus, E. F., & Pickrell, J. E. (1995). The formation of false memories. *Psychiatric Annals, 25,* 720–725.

Lord, C. G. (1982). Predicting behavioral consistency from an individual's perception of situational similarities. *Journal of Personality and Social Psychology, 42,* 1076–1088.

Lovaas, O. I., Freitag, G., Gold, V. J., & Kassorla, I. C. (1965). Recording apparatus for observation of behaviors of children in free play settings. *Journal of Experimental Child Psychology, 2,* 108–120.

Lowell, E. L. (1952). The effect of need for achievement on learning and speed of performance. *Journal of Psychology, 33,* 31–40.

Lucas, R. E., & Diener, E. (2001). Understanding extraverts' enjoyment of social situations: The importance of pleasantness. *Journal of Personality and Social Psychology, 81,* 343–356.

Lucas, R. E., Diener, E., Grob, A., Suh, E. M., & Shao, L. (2000). Cross-cultural evidence for the fundamental features of extraversion. *Journal of Personality and Social Psychology, 79,* 452–468.

Lumsden, C., & Wilson, E. O. (1981). *Genes, mind, and culture.* Cambridge, MA: Harvard University Press.

Lundy, A. C. (1985). The reliability of the Thematic Apperception Test. *Journal of Personality Assessment, 49,* 141–145.

Lütkenhaus, P., Grossmann, K. E., & Grossmann, K. (1985). Infant-mother attachment at twelve months and style of interaction with a stranger at the age of three years. *Child Development, 56,* 1538–1542.

Lykken, D. T., & Tellegen, A. (1993). Is human mating adventitious or the result of lawful choice? A twin study of mate selection. *Journal of Personality and Social Psychology, 65,* 56–68.

Lynam, D. R., Leukefeld, C., & Clayton, R. R. (2003). The contribution of personality to the overlap between antisocial behavior and substance use/misuse. *Aggressive Behavior, 29,* 316–331.

Lynn, R. (2001). *Eugenics: A reassessment.* Westport, CT: Praeger.

Lynn, S. J., Myers, B., & Malinoski, P. (1997). Hypnosis, pseudomemories, and clinical guidelines: A sociocognitive perspective. In J. D. Read & D. S. Lindsay (Eds.),

Recollections of trauma: Scientific studies and clinical practice. New York: Plenum.

Maccoby, E. E., & Wilson, W. C. (1957). Identification and observational learning from films. *Journal of Abnormal and Social Psychology, 55,* 76–87.

MacKay, D. M. (1963). Mindlike behavior in artefacts. In K. M. Sayre & F. J. Crosson (Eds.), *The modeling of mind: Computers and intelligence.* Notre Dame, IN: University of Notre Dame Press.

MacKay, D. M. (1966). Cerebral organization and the conscious control of action. In J. C. Eccles (Ed.), *Brain and conscious experience.* Berlin, Germany: Springer-Verlag.

Macrae, C. N., & Boderhausen, G. V. (2000). Social cognition: Thinking categorically. *Annual Review of Psychology, 51,* 93–120.

Macrae, C. N., Milne, A. B., & Bodenhausen, G. V. (1994). Stereotypes as energy-saving devices: A peek inside the cognitive toolbox. *Journal of Personality and Social Psychology, 66,* 37–47.

Maddi, S. R. (1980). *Personality theories: A comparative analysis.* Homewood, IL: Dorsey.

Magnus, K., Diener, E., Fujita, F., & Pavot, W. (1993). Extraversion and neuroticism as predictors of objective life events: A longitudinal analysis. *Journal of Personality and Social Psychology, 65,* 1046–1053.

Magnusson, D., & Endler, N. S. (Eds.). (1977). *Personality at the crossroads: Current issues in interactional psychology.* Hillsdale, NJ: Erlbaum.

Mahler, M. S. (1968). *On human symbiosis and the vicissitudes of individuation: Infantile psychosis.* New York: International Universities Press.

Mahler, M. S., Pine, F., & Bergman, A. (1975). *The psychological birth of the human infant: Symbiosis and individuation.* New York: Basic Books.

Mahoney, M. J. (1977). Some applied issues in self-monitoring. In J. D. Cone & R. P. Hawkins (Eds.), *Behavioral assessment: New directions in clinical psychology.* New York: Brunner/Mazel.

Main, M., & Cassidy, J. (1988). Categories of response to reunion with the parent at age 6: Predictable from infant attachment classifications and stable over a 1-month period. *Developmental Psychology, 24,* 415–426.

Major, B., Cozzarelli, C., Sciacchitano, A. M., Cooper, M. L., Testa, M., & Mueller, P. M. (1990). Perceived social support, self-efficacy, and adjustment to abortion. *Journal of Personality and Social Psychology, 59,* 452–463.

Major, B., Richards, C., Cooper, M. L., Cozzarelli, C., & Zubek, J. (1998). Personal resilience, cognitive appraisals, and coping: An integrative model of adjustment to abortion. *Journal of Personality and Social Psychology, 74,* 735–752.

Malamuth, N. M., & Donnerstein, E. (Eds.). (1984). *Pornography and sexual aggression.* New York: Academic.

Malec, J., Park, T., & Watkins, J. T. (1976). Modeling with role playing as a treatment for test anxiety. *Journal of Consulting and Clinical Psychology, 44,* 679.

Mallick, S. K., & McCandless, B. R. (1966). A study of catharsis of aggression. *Journal of Personality and Social Psychology, 4,* 591–596.

Maltzman, I. (1968). Theoretical conceptions of semantic conditioning and generalization. In T. R. Dixon & D. L. Horton (Eds.), *Verbal behavior and general behavior theory.* Englewood Cliffs, NJ: Prentice-Hall.

Mancuso, J. C., & Adams-Webber, J. R. (Eds.). (1982). *The construing person.* New York: Praeger.

Maner, J. K., Luce, C. L., Neuberg, S. L., Cialdini, R. B., Brown, S., & Sagarin, B. J. (2002). The effects of perspective taking on motivations for helping: Still no evidence for altruism. *Personality and Social Psychology Bulletin, 28,* 1601–1610.

Manning, M. M., & Wright, T. L. (1983). Self-efficacy expectancies, outcome expectancies, and the persistence of pain control in childbirth. *Journal of Personality and Social Psychology, 45,* 421–431.

Mansfield, E. D., & McAdams, D. P. (1996). Generativity and themes of agency and communion in adult autobiography. *Personality and Social Psychology Bulletin, 22,* 721–731.

Manuck, S. B., Flory, J. D., Ferrell, R. E., Mann, J. J., & Muldoon, M. F. (2000). A regulatory polymorphism of the monoamine oxidase-A gene may be associated with variability in aggression, impulsivity, and central nervous system serotonergic responsivity. *Psychiatry Research, 95,* 9–23.

Manuck, S. B., Flory, J. D., McCaffery, J. M., Matthews, K. A., Mann, J. J., & Muldoon, M. F. (1998). Aggression, impulsivity, and central nervous system serotonergic responsivity in a nonpatient sample. *Neuropsychopharmacology, 19,* 287–299.

Manuck, S. B., Flory, J. D., Muldoon, M. F., & Ferrell, R. E. (2003). A neurobiology of intertemporal choice. In G. Loewenstein, D. Read, & R. F. Baumeister (Eds.), *Time and decision: Economic and psychological perspectives on intertemporal choice* (pp. 139–172). New York: Russell Sage Foundation.

Marangoni, C., Garcia, S., Ickes, W., & Teng, G. (1995). Empathic accuracy in a clinically relevant setting. *Journal of Personality and Social Psychology, 68,* 854–869.

Marcia, J. E. (1966). Development and validation of ego identity statuses. *Journal of Personality and Social Psychology, 3,* 551–558.

Marcia, J. E. (1976). Identity six years after: A follow-up study. *Journal of Youth and Adolescence, 5,* 145–160.

Marcia, J. E. (1980). Identity in adolescence. In J. Adelson (Ed.), *Handbook of adolescent psychology.* New York: Wiley.

Marcus, G. F. (1996). Why do children say "breaked"? *Current Directions in Psychological Science, 5,* 81–85.

Marcus-Newhall, A., Pedersen, W. C., Carlson, M., & Miller, N. (2000). Displaced aggression is alive and well: A meta-analytic review. *Journal of Personality and Social Psychology, 78,* 670–689.

Markey, C. N., Markey, P. M., & Tinsley, B. J. (2003). Personality, puberty, and preadolescent girls' risky behaviors: Examining the predictive value of the five-factor model of personality. *Journal of Research in Personality, 37,* 405–419.

Markon, K. E., Krueger, R. F., & Watson, D. (2005). Delineating the structure of normal and abnormal personality: An integrative hierarchical approach. *Journal of Personality and Social Psychology, 88,* 139–157.

Markus, H. (1977). Self-schemata and processing information about the self. *Journal of Personality and Social Psychology, 35,* 63–78.

Markus, H., & Nurius, P. (1986). Possible selves. *American Psychologist, 41,* 954–969.

Markus, H., & Sentis, K. (1982). The self and social information processing. In J. Suls (Ed.), *Psychological perspectives on the self* (Vol. 1, pp. 41–70). Hillsdale, NJ: Erlbaum.

Markus, H., & Wurf, E. (1987). The dynamic self-concept: A social psychological perspective. *Annual Review of Psychology, 38,* 299–337.

Martin, L. L., & Tesser, A. (1996). Some ruminative thoughts. In R. S. Wyer, Jr. (Ed.), *Advances in social cognition* (Vol. 9, pp. 1–47). Mahwah, NJ: Erlbaum.

Masling, J. M., & Bornstein, R. F. (Eds.). (1994). *Empirical perspectives on object relations theory.* Washington, DC: American Psychological Association.

Masling, J. M., Johnson, C., & Saturansky, C. (1974). Oral imagery, accuracy of perceiving others, and performance in Peace Corps training. *Journal of Personality and Social Psychology, 30,* 414–419.

Masling, J. M., O'Neill, R., & Jayne, C. (1981). Orality and latency of volunteering to serve as experimental subjects. *Journal of Personality Assessment, 45,* 20–22.

Masling, J. M., O'Neill, R., & Katkin, E. S. (1982). Autonomic arousal, interpersonal climate, and orality. *Journal of Personality and Social Psychology, 42,* 529–534.

Masling, J. M., Price, J., Goldband, S., & Katkin, E. S. (1981). Oral imagery and autonomic arousal in social isolation. *Journal of Personality and Social Psychology, 40,* 395–400.

Masling, J. M., Rabie, L., & Blondheim, S. H. (1967). Obesity, level of aspiration, and Rorschach and TAT measures of oral dependence. *Journal of Consulting Psychology, 31,* 233–239.

Masling, J. M., Weiss, L., & Rothschild, B. (1968). Relationships of oral imagery to yielding behavior and birth order. *Journal of Consulting and Clinical Psychology, 32,* 38–81.

Maslow, A. H. (1955). Deficiency motivation and growth motivation. In M. R. Jones (Ed.), *Nebraska symposium on motivation.* Lincoln: University of Nebraska Press.

Maslow, A. H. (1962). *Toward a psychology of being.* Princeton, NJ: Van Nostrand.

Maslow, A. H. (1968). *Toward a psychology of being* (2nd ed.). New York: Van Nostrand.

Maslow, A. H. (1970). *Motivation and personality* (Rev. ed.). New York: Harper & Row.

Maslow, A. H. (1971). *The farther reaches of human nature.* New York: Viking.

Maslow, A. H. (1979). *The journals of A. H. Maslow* (2 vols.). R. J. Lowry (Ed.). Monterey, CA: Brooks/Cole.

Mason, A., & Blankenship, V. (1987). Power and affiliation motivation, stress, and abuse in intimate relationships. *Journal of Personality and Social Psychology, 52,* 203–210.

Masson, J. M. (1984). *The assault on truth.* New York: Farrar, Straus, & Giroux.

Matas, L., Arend, R. A., & Sroufe, L. A. (1978). Continuity of adaptation in the second year: The relationship between quality of attachment and later competence. *Child Development, 49,* 547–556.

Matthews, K. A., Batson, C. D., Horn, J., & Rosenman, R. (1981). "Principles in his nature which interest him in the fortune of others . . .": The heritability of empathic concern for others. *Journal of Personality, 49,* 237–247.

Matthews, K. A., Owens, J. F., Kuller, L. H., Sutton-Tyrrell, K., & Jansen-McWilliams, L. (1998). Are hostility and anxiety associated with carotid atherosclerosis in healthy postmenopausal women? *Psychosomatic Medicine, 60,* 633–638.

Matthiesen, A.-S., Ransjö-Arvidson, A.-B., Nissen, E., & Uvnäs-Moberg, K. (2001). Postpartum maternal oxytocin release by newborns: Effects of infant hand massage and sucking. *Birth, 28,* 13–19.

May, R. (1953). *Man's search for himself.* New York: Norton.

May, R. (1958). The origins and significance of the existential movement in psychology. In R. May, E. Angel, & H. F. Ellenberger (Eds.), *Existence: A new dimension in psychiatry and psychology.* New York: Basic Books.

May, R. (Ed.). (1969). *Existential psychology* (2nd ed.). New York: Random House.

Mazur, A. (1985). A biosocial model of status in face-to-face primate groups. *Social Forces, 64,* 377–402.

Mazur, A., & Booth, A. (1998). Testosterone and dominance in men. *Behavior and Brain Sciences, 21,* 353–397.

Mazur, A., Booth, A., & Dabbs, J. M., Jr. (1992). Testosterone and chess competition. *Social Psychology Quarterly, 55,* 70–77.

McAdams, D. P. (1982). Experiences of intimacy and power: Relationships between social motives and autobiographical memory. *Journal of Personality and Social Psychology, 42,* 292–302.

McAdams, D. P. (1984). Human motives and personal relationships. In V. J. Derlaga (Ed.), *Communication, intimacy, and close relationships.* New York: Academic.

McAdams, D. P. (1985). *Power, intimacy, and the life story: Personological inquiries into identity.* New York: Guilford.

McAdams, D. P. (1989). *Intimacy: The need to be close.* New York: Doubleday.

McAdams, D. P. (1992). The five-factor model *in* personality: A critical appraisal. *Journal of Personality, 60,* 329–361.

McAdams, D. P. (1993). *The stories we live by: Personal myths and the making of the self.* New York: Morrow.

McAdams, D. P. (2001). The psychology of life stories. *Review of General Psychology, 5,* 100–122.

McAdams, D. P. (2006). *The redemptive self: Stories Americans live by.* New York: Oxford University Press.

McAdams, D. P., Anyidoho, N. A., Brown, C., Huang, Y. T., Kaplan, B., & Machado, M. A. (2004). Traits and stories: Links between dispositional and narrative features of personality. *Journal of Personality, 72,* 761–784.

McAdams, D. P., & Bryant, F. B. (1987). Intimacy motivation and subjective mental health in a nationwide sample. *Journal of Personality, 55,* 395–413.

McAdams, D. P., & Constantian, C. A. (1983). Intimacy and affiliation motives in daily living: An experience sampling analysis. *Journal of Personality and Social Psychology, 45,* 851–861.

McAdams, D. P., & de St. Aubin, E. (1992). A theory of generativity and its assessment through self-report, behavioral acts, and narrative themes in autobiography. *Journal of Personality and Social Psychology, 62,* 1003–1015.

McAdams, D. P., Diamond, A., de St. Aubin, E., & Mansfield, E. (1997). Stories of commitment: The psychosocial construction of generative lives. *Journal of Personality and Social Psychology, 72,* 678–694.

McAdams, D. P., Healy, S., & Krause, S. (1984). Social motives and patterns of friendship. *Journal of Personality and Social Psychology, 47,* 828–838.

McAdams, D. P., Jackson, R. J., & Kirshnit, C. (1984). Looking, laughing, and smiling in dyads as a function of intimacy motivation and reciprocity. *Journal of Personality, 52,* 261–273.

McAdams, D. P., & Pals, J. L. (2006). A new big five: Fundamental principles for an integrative science of personality. *American Psychologist, 61,* 204–217.

McAdams, D. P., & Powers, J. (1981). Themes of intimacy in behavior and thought. *Journal of Personality and Social Psychology, 40,* 573–587.

McAdams, D. P., Reynolds, J., Lewis, M., Patten, A. H., & Bowman, P. J. (2001). When bad things turn good and good things turn bad: Sequences of redemption and contamination in life narrative and their relation to psychosocial adaptation in midlife adults and in students. *Personality and Social Psychology Bulletin, 27,* 474–485.

McAdams, D. P., & Vaillant, G. E. (1982). Intimacy motivation and psychosocial adjustment: A longitudinal study. *Journal of Personality Assessment, 46,* 586–593.

McArthur, L. Z. (1981). The role of attention in impression formation and causal attribution. In E. T. Higgins, C. P.

Herman, & M. P. Zanna (Eds.), *Social cognition: The Ontario Symposium* (Vol. 1). Hillsdale, NJ: Erlbaum.

McClelland, D. C. (1961). *The achieving society.* Princeton, NJ: Van Nostrand.

McClelland, D. C. (1965). Toward a theory of motive acquisition. *American Psychologist, 20,* 321–333.

McClelland, D. C. (1979). Inhibited power motivation and high blood pressure in men. *Journal of Abnormal Psychology, 88,* 182–190.

McClelland, D. C. (1984). *Human motivation.* Glenview, IL: Scott, Foresman.

McClelland, D. C. (1985). How motives, skills, and values determine what people do. *American Psychologist, 40,* 812–825.

McClelland, D. C. (1989). Motivational factors in health and disease. *American Psychologist, 44,* 675–683.

McClelland, D. C., Atkinson, J. W., Clark, R. A., & Lowell, E. L. (1953). *The achievement motive.* New York: Appleton-Century-Crofts.

McClelland, D. C., & Boyatzis, R. E. (1982). Leadership motive pattern and long-term success in management. *Journal of Applied Psychology, 67,* 737–743.

McClelland, D. C., Davis, W. N., Kalin, R., & Wanner, E. (Eds.). (1972). *The drinking man.* New York: Free Press.

McClelland, D. C., Koestner, R., & Weinberger, J. (1989). How do self-attributed and implicit motives differ? *Psychological Review, 96,* 690–702.

McClelland, D. C., & Winter, D. G. (1969). *Motivating economic achievement.* New York: Free Press.

McClelland, J. L. (1999). Cognitive modeling, connectionist. In R. W. Wilson & F. C. Keil (Eds.), *The MIT encyclopedia of the cognitive sciences* (pp. 137–139). Cambridge, MA: MIT Press.

McClelland, J. L., Rumelhart, D. E., & PDP Research Group. (Eds.). (1986). *Parallel distributed processing: Explorations in the microstructure of cognition: Vol. 2. Psychological and biological models.* Cambridge, MA: MIT Press.

McCrae, R. R. (1993). Moderated analyses of longitudinal personality stability. *Journal of Personality and Social Psychology, 65,* 577–585.

McCrae, R. R. (1996). Social consequences of experiential openness. *Psychological Bulletin, 120,* 323–337.

McCrae, R. R., & Costa, P. T., Jr. (1987). Validation of the five-factor model of personality across instruments and observers. *Journal of Personality and Social Psychology, 52,* 81–90.

McCrae, R. R., & Costa, P. T., Jr. (1989a). Reinterpreting the Myers–Briggs type indicator from the perspective of the five-factor model of personality. *Journal of Personality, 57,* 17–40.

McCrae, R. R., & Costa, P. T., Jr. (1989b). The structure of interpersonal traits: Wiggins's circumplex and the five-factor model. *Journal of Personality and Social Psychology, 56,* 586–595.

McCrae, R. R., & Costa, P. T., Jr. (1997). Personality trait structure as a human universal. *American Psychologist, 52,* 509–516.

McCrae, R. R., & Costa, P. T., Jr. (2003). *Personality in adulthood: A five-factor theory perspective* (2nd ed.). New York: Guilford.

McCrae, R. R., Costa, P. T., Jr., & Busch, C. M. (1986). Evaluating comprehensiveness in personality systems: The California Q-Set and the five factor model. *Journal of Personality, 54,* 430–446.

McCrae, R. R., & John, O. P. (1992). An introduction to the five-factor model and its implications. *Journal of Personality, 60,* 175–215.

McCrae, R. R., Terracciano, A., et al. (2005). Universal features of personality traits from the observer's perspective: Data from 50 cultures. *Journal of Personality and Social Psychology, 88,* 547–561.

McCrae, R. R., Zonderman, A. B., Costa, P. J., Jr., Bond, M. H., & Paunonen, S. V. (1996). Evaluating replicability of factors in the Revised NEO Personality Inventory: Confirmatory factor analysis versus Procrustes rotation. *Journal of Personality and Social Psychology, 70,* 552–566.

McCullough, M. (2001). Freud's seduction theory and its rehabilitation: A saga of one mistake after another. *Review of General Psychology, 5,* 3–22.

McCullough, M. E., Emmons, R. A., Kilpatrick, S. D., & Mooney, C. N. (2003). Narcissists as "victims": The role of narcissism in the perception of transgressions. *Personality and Social Psychology Bulletin, 29,* 885–893.

McCullough, M. E., & Hoyt, W. T. (2002). Transgression-related motivational dispositions: Personality substrates of forgiveness and their links to the big five. *Personality and Social Psychology Bulletin, 28,* 1556–1573.

McCullough, M. E., Tsang, J., & Brion, S. (2003). Personality traits in adolescence as predictors of religiousness in early adulthood: Findings from the Terman longitudinal study. *Personality and Social Psychology Bulletin, 29,* 980–991.

McFall, R., & Twentyman, C. T. (1973). Four experiments on relative contributions of rehearsal, modeling and coaching to assertion training. *Journal of Abnormal Psychology, 81,* 199–218.

McGregor, H. A., & Elliot, A. J. (2005). The shame of failure: Examining the link between fear of failure and shame. *Personality and Social Psychology Bulletin, 31,* 218–231.

McGregor, I., & Marigold, D. C. (2003). Defensive zeal and the uncertain self: What makes you so sure? *Journal of Personality and Social Psychology, 85,* 838–852.

McGregor, I., Zanna, M. P., Holmes, J. G., & Spencer, S. J. (2001). Compensatory conviction in the face of personal uncertainty: Going to extremes and being oneself. *Journal of Personality and Social Psychology, 80,* 472–488.

McGue, M., & Lykken, D. T. (1992). Genetic influence on risk of divorce. *Psychological Science, 3,* 368–373.

McGuffin, P., Rijsdijk, F., Andrew, M., Sham, P., Katz, R., & Cardno, A. (2003). The heritability of bipolar affective disorder and the genetic relationship to unipolar depression. *Archives of General Psychiatry, 60,* 497–502.

McGuire, W. (Ed.). (1974). *The Freud/Jung letters: The correspondence between Sigmund Freud and C. G. Jung.* Princeton, NJ: Princeton University Press.

McGuire, W. J., & McGuire, C. V. (1986). Differences in conceptualizing self versus conceptualizing other people as manifested in contrasting verb types used in natural speech. *Journal of Personality and Social Psychology, 51,* 1135–1143.

McMahan, I. D. (1973). Relationships between causal attributions and expectancy of success. *Journal of Personality and Social Psychology, 28,* 108–114.

McNamara, P., McLaren, D., Smith, D., Brown, A., & Stickgold, R. (2005). A "Jekyll and Hyde" within: Aggressive versus friendly interactions in REM and non-REM dreams. *Psychological Science, 16,* 130.

Medin, D. L. (1989). Concepts and conceptual structure. *American Psychologist, 44,* 1469–1481.

Meehl, P. E. (1962). Schizotaxia, schizotypy, schizophrenia. *American Psychologist, 17,* 827–838.

Meehl, P. E. (1992). Factors and taxa, traits and types, differences of degree and differences in kind. *Journal of Personality, 60,* 117–174.

Megargee, E. I. (1966). Undercontrolled and overcontrolled personality types in extreme antisocial aggression. In E. I. Megargee & J. E. Moranson (Eds.), *Psychological Monographs.* New York: Harper & Row.

Megargee, E. I. (1971). The role of inhibition in the assessment and understanding of violence. In J. L. Singer (Ed.), *The control of aggression and violence.* New York: Academic.

Megargee, E. I., Cook, P. E., & Mendelsohn, G. A. (1967). Development and evaluation of an MMPI scale of assaultiveness in overcontrolled individuals. *Journal of Abnormal Psychology, 72,* 519–528.

Meichenbaum, D. (1971). Examination of model characteristics in reducing avoidance behavior. *Journal of Personality and Social Psychology, 17,* 298–307.

Meichenbaum, D. (1972). Cognitive modification of test anxious college students. *Journal of Consulting and Clinical Psychology, 39,* 370–379.

Meichenbaum, D. (1974). *Cognitive behavior modification.* Morristown, NJ: General Learning.

Meichenbaum, D. (1977). *Cognitive-behavior modification: An integrative approach.* New York: Plenum.

Meichenbaum, D. (1985). *Stress inoculation training.* New York: Pergamon.

Meichenbaum, D., & Goodman, J. (1971). Training impulsive children to talk to themselves: A means of developing self-control. *Journal of Abnormal Psychology, 77,* 115–126.

Meier, B. P., & Robinson, M. D. (2004). Does quick to blame mean quick to anger? The role of agreeableness in dissociating blame and anger. *Personality and Social Psychology Bulletin, 30,* 856–867.

Meier, B. P., Robinson, M. D., & Wilkowski, B. M. (2006). Turning the other cheek: Agreeableness and the regulation of aggression-related primes. *Psychological Science, 17,* 136–142.

Melamed, B. G., & Siegel, L. J. (1975). Reduction of anxiety in children facing hospitalization and surgery by use of filmed modeling. *Journal of Consulting and Clinical Psychology, 43,* 511–521.

Melamed, B. G., Weinstein, D., Hawes, R., & Katin-Borland, M. (1975). Reduction of fear-related dental management problems using filmed modeling. *Journal of the American Dental Association, 90,* 822–826.

Meltzoff, A. N. (1985). Immediate and deferred imitation in fourteen- and twenty-four-month-old infants. *Child Development, 56,* 62–72.

Mendoza-Denton, R., Ayduk, O., Mischel, W., Shoda, Y., & Testa, A. (2001). Person x situation interactionism in self-encoding (*I am . . . when . . .*): Implications for affect regulation and social information processing. *Journal of Personality and Social Psychology, 80,* 533–544.

Merluzzi, T. V., Glass, C. R., & Genest, M. (Eds.). (1981). *Cognitive assessment.* New York: Guilford.

Merluzzi, T. V., Rudy, T. E., & Glass, C. R. (1981). The information-processing paradigm: Implications for clinical science. In T. V. Merluzzi, C. R. Glass, & M. Genest (Eds.), *Cognitive assessment.* New York: Guilford.

Mershon, B., & Gorsuch, R. L. (1988). Number of factors in the personality sphere: Does increase in factors increase predictability of real-life criteria? *Journal of Personality and Social Psychology, 55,* 675–680.

Metcalfe, J., & Mischel, W. (1999). A hot/cool-system analysis of delay of gratification: Dynamics of willpower. *Psychological Review, 106,* 3–19.

Meyer, D., Leventhal, H., & Gutmann, M. (1985). Common-sense models of illness: The example of hypertension. *Health Psychology, 4,* 115–135.

Meyer, J. P. (1980). Causal attribution for success and failure: A multivariate investigation of dimensionality, formation, and consequences. *Journal of Personality and Social Psychology, 38,* 708–718.

Meyer, J. P., & Pepper, S. (1977). Need compatibility and marital adjustment in young married couples. *Journal of Personality and Social Psychology, 35,* 331–342.

Michalski, R. L., & Shackelford, T. K. (2002). An attempted replication of the relationships between birth order and personality. *Journal of Research in Personality, 36,* 182–188.

Mickelson, K. D., Kessler, R. C., & Shaver, P. R. (1997). Adult attachment in a nationally representative sample. *Journal of Personality and Social Psychology, 73,* 1092–1106.

Mikulincer, M. (1998). Adult attachment style and individual differences in functional versus dysfunctional experiences of anger. *Journal of Personality and Social Psychology, 74,* 513–524.

Mikulincer, M., Florian, V., & Hirschberger, G. (2003). The existential function of close relationships: Introducing death into the science of love. *Personality and Social Psychology Review, 7,* 20–40.

Mikulincer, M., Florian, V., & Weller, A. (1993). Attachment styles, coping strategies, and posttraumatic psychological distress: The impact of the Gulf War in Israel. *Journal of Personality and Social Psychology, 64,* 817–826.

Mikulincer, M., & Goodman, G. S. (2006). *Dynamics of romantic love: Attachment, caregiving, and sex.* New York: Guilford.

Mikulincer, M., Hirschberger, G., Nachmias, O., & Gillath, O. (2001). The affective component of the secure base schema: Affective priming with representations of attachment security. *Journal of Personality and Social Psychology, 81,* 305–321.

Mikulincer, M., & Horesh, N. (1999). Adult attachment style and the perception of others: The role of projective mechanisms. *Journal of Personality and Social Psychology, 76,* 1022–1034.

Mikulincer, M., & Nachshon, O. (1991). Attachment styles and patterns of self-disclosure. *Journal of Personality and Social Psychology, 61,* 321–331.

Mikulincer, M., & Shaver, P. R. (2001). Attachment theory and intergroup bias: Evidence that priming the secure base schema attenuates negative reactions to out-groups. *Journal of Personality and Social Psychology, 81,* 97–115.

Mikulincer, M., & Shaver, P. R. (2005). Attachment security, compassion, and altruism. *Current Directions in Psychological Science, 14,* 34–38.

Mikulincer, M., & Shaver, P. R. (2007). *Attachment in adulthood: Structure, dynamics, and change.* New York: Guilford.

Mikulincer, M., Shaver, P. R., Gillath, O., & Nitzberg, R. A. (2005). Attachment, caregiving, and altruism: Boosting attachment security increases compassion and helping. *Journal of Personality and Social Psychology, 89,* 817–839.

Mill, J. S. (1962). "On liberty." In M. Warnock (Ed.), *John Stuart Mill: Utilitarianism, On liberty, Essay on Bentham, together with selected writings of Jeremy Bentham and John Austin.* Cleveland, OH: World. (Originally published, 1859)

Miller, G. A., Galanter, E., & Pribram, K. H. (1960). *Plans and the structure of behavior.* New York: Holt, Rinehart, & Winston.

Miller, G. E., Cohen, S., & Ritchey, A. K. (2002). Chronic psychological stress and the regulation of pro-inflammatory cytokines: A glucocorticoid-resistance model. *Health Psychology, 21,* 531–541.

Miller, I. W., & Norman, W. H. (1979). Learned helplessness in humans: A review and attribution-theory model. *Psychological Bulletin, 86,* 93–119.

Miller, J. D., Lynam, D., & Leukefeld, C. (2003). Examining antisocial behavior through the lens of the five factor model of personality. *Aggressive Behavior, 29,* 497–514.

Miller, L. C., Putcha-Bhagavatula, A., & Pedersen, W. C. (2002). Men's and women's mating preferences: Distinct evolutionary mechanisms? *Current Directions in Psychological Science, 11,* 88–93.

Miller, N. E. (1944). Experimental studies of conflict. In J. McVicker Hunt (Ed.), *Personality and the behavior disorders* (Vol. 1, pp. 431–465). New York: Ronald.

Miller, N. E. (1948). Theory and experiment relating psychoanalytic displacement to stimulus–response generalization. *Journal of Abnormal and Social Psychology, 43,* 155–178.

Miller, N. E. (1951). Learnable drives and rewards. In S. S. Stevens (Ed.), *Handbook of experimental psychology.* New York: Wiley.

Miller, N. E., & Dollard, J. (1941). *Social learning and imitation.* New Haven, CT: Yale University Press.

Miller, N., Pedersen, W. C., Earleywine, M., & Pollock, V. E. (2003). A theoretical model of triggered displaced aggression. *Personality and Social Psychology Review, 7,* 75–97.

Miller, R. S. (1987). Empathic embarrassment: Situational and personal determinants of reactions to the embarrassment of another. *Journal of Personality and Social Psychology, 53,* 1061–1069.

Miller, S., Saccuzzo, D., & Braff, D. (1979). Information-processing deficits in remitted schizophrenics. *Journal of Abnormal Psychology, 88,* 446–449.

Mineka, S., & Zinbarg, R. (2006). A contemporary learning theory perspective on the etiology of anxiety disorders. *American Psychologist, 61,* 10–26.

Mirels, H. (1970). Dimensions of internal versus external control. *Journal of Consulting and Clinical Psychology, 34,* 226–228.

Mischel, W. (1961). Delay of gratification, need for achievement, and acquiescence in another culture. *Journal of Abnormal and Social Psychology, 62,* 543–552.

Mischel, W. (1966). Theory and research on the antecedents of self-imposed delay of reward. In B. A. Maher (Ed.), *Progress in experimental personality research* (Vol. 3). New York: Academic.

Mischel, W. (1968). *Personality and assessment.* New York: Wiley.

Mischel, W. (1970). Sex typing and socialization. In P. H. Mussen (Ed.), *Carmichael's manual of child psychology* (Rev. ed.). New York: Wiley.

Mischel, W. (1973). Toward a cognitive social learning reconceptualization of personality. *Psychological Review, 80,* 252–283.

Mischel, W. (1974). Processes in delay of gratification. In L. Berkowitz (Ed.), *Advances in experimental social psychology* (Vol. 7). New York: Academic.

Mischel, W. (1977). The interaction of person and situation. In D. Magnusson & N. S. Endler (Eds.), *Personality at the crossroads: Current issues in interactional psychology.* Hillsdale, NJ: Erlbaum.

Mischel, W. (1979). On the interface of cognition and personality: Beyond the person–situation debate. *American Psychologist, 34,* 740–754.

Mischel, W. (1990). Personality dispositions revisited and revised: A view after three decades. In L. A. Pervin (Ed.), *Handbook of personality: Theory and research* (pp. 111–134). New York: Guilford.

Mischel, W., & Baker, N. (1975). Cognitive transformations of reward objects through instructions. *Journal of Personality and Social Psychology, 31,* 254–261.

Mischel, W., & Ebbesen, E. (1970). Attention in delay of gratification. *Journal of Personality and Social Psychology, 16,* 329–337.

Mischel, W., Ebbesen, E., & Zeiss, A. (1973). Selective attention to the self: Situational and dispositional determinants. *Journal of Personality and Social Psychology, 27,* 129–142.

Mischel, W., & Liebert, R. M. (1966). Effects of discrepancies between observed and imposed reward criteria on their acquisition and transmission. *Journal of Personality and Social Psychology, 3,* 45–53.

Mischel, W., & Metzner, R. (1962). Preference for delayed reward as a function of age, intelligence, and length of delay interval. *Journal of Abnormal and Social Psychology, 64,* 425–431.

Mischel, W., & Moore, B. (1973). Effects of attention to symbolically presented rewards upon self-control. *Journal of Personality and Social Psychology, 28,* 172–179.

Mischel, W., & Shoda, Y. (1995). A cognitive–affective system theory of personality: Reconceptualizing situations, dispositions, and invariance in personality structure. *Psychological Review, 102,* 246–268.

Mischel, W., Shoda, Y., & Mendoza-Denton, R. (2002). Situation–behavior profiles as a locus of consistency in personality. *Current Directions in Psychological Science, 11,* 50–54.

Moffitt, T. E. (2005a). The new look of behavioral genetics in developmental psychopathology: Gene-environment interplay in antisocial behaviors. *Psychological Bulletin, 131,* 533–554.

Moffitt, T. E. (2005b). Genetic and environmental influences on antisocial behaviors: Evidence from behavioral-genetic research. *Advances in genetics, 55,* 41–104.

Moffitt, T. E., Caspi, A., & Rutter, M. (2006). Measured gene-environment interactions in psychopathology: Concepts, research strategies, and implications for research, intervention, and public understanding of genetics. *Perspectives on Psychological Science, 1,* 5–27.

Monson, T., Hesley, J., & Chernick, L. (1982). Specifying when personality traits can and cannot predict behavior: An alternative to abandoning the attempt to predict single-act criteria. *Journal of Personality and Social Psychology, 43,* 385–399.

Moore, B., Mischel, W., & Zeiss, A. (1976). Comparative effects of the reward stimulus and its cognitive representation in voluntary delay. *Journal of Personality and Social Psychology, 34,* 419–424.

Moore, J. W. (1972). Stimulus control: Studies of auditory generalization in rabbits. In A. H. Black & W. F. Prokasy (Eds.), *Classical conditioning II: Current research and theory.* New York: Appleton-Century-Crofts.

Moors, A., & De Hower, J. (2006). Automaticity: A theoretical and conceptual analysis. *Psychological Bulletin, 132,* 297–326.

Morf, C. C., & Rhodewalt, F. (1993). Narcissism and self-evaluation maintenance: Explorations in object relations. *Personality and Social Psychology Bulletin, 19,* 668–676.

Morgan, C. D., & Murray, H. A. (1935). A method for investigating fantasies. *Archives of Neurology and Psychiatry, 34,* 289–306.

Morilak, D. A., Barrera, G., Echevarria, D. J., Garcia, A. S., Hernandez, A., Ma, S., & Petre, C. O. (2005). Role of brain norepinephrine in the behavioral response to stress. *Biological Psychiatry, 29,* 1214–1224.

Morris, L. W., Davis, M. A., & Hutchings, C. H. (1981). Cognitive and emotional components of anxiety: Literature review and a revised worry–emotionality scale. *Journal of Educational Psychology, 73,* 541–555.

Morrone, J. V., Depue, R. A., Scherer, A. J., & White, T. L. (2000). Film-induced incentive motivation and positive activation in relation to agentic and affiliative components of extraversion. *Personality and Individual Differences, 29,* 199–216.

Moskowitz, D. S. (1994). Cross-situational generality and the interpersonal circumplex. *Journal of Personality and Social Psychology, 66,* 921–933.

Moskowitz, G. B. (1993). Individual differences in social categorization: The influence of personal need for structure on spontaneous trait inferences. *Journal of Personality and Social Psychology, 65,* 132–142.

Motley, M. T. (1985). Slips of the tongue. *Scientific American, 253,* 116–127.

Mowrer, R. R., & Klein, S. B. (Eds.). (2001). *Handbook of contemporary learning theories.* Mahwah, NJ: Erlbaum.

Mueller, C. M., & Dweck, C. S. (1998). Praise for intelligence can undermine children's motivation and performance. *Journal of Personality and Social Psychology, 75,* 33–52.

Mullen, B. (1986). Atrocity as a function of lynch mob composition: A self-attention perspective. *Personality and Social Psychology Bulletin, 12,* 187–197.

Muraven, M., & Baumeister, R. F. (2000). Self-regulation and depletion of limited resources: Does self-control resemble a muscle? *Psychological Bulletin, 126,* 247–259.

Muraven, M., Tice, D. M., & Baumeister, R. F. (1998). Self-control as a limited resource: Regulatory depletion patterns. *Journal of Personality and Social Psychology, 74,* 774–789.

Murray, E. J. (1985). Coping and anger. In T. M. Field, P. M. McCabe, & N. Schneiderman (Eds.), *Stress and coping.* Hillsdale, NJ: Erlbaum.

Murray, H. A. (1938). *Explorations in personality.* New York: Oxford University Press.

Murray, S. L., & Holmes, J. G. (1993). Seeing virtues in faults: Negativity and the transformation of interpersonal narratives in close relationships. *Journal of Personality and Social Psychology, 65,* 707–722.

Murray, S. L., Holmes, J. G., & Griffin, D. W. (2000). Self-esteem and the quest for felt security: How perceived regard regulates attachment processes. *Journal of Personality and Social Psychology, 78,* 478–498.

Murray, S. L., Holmes, J. G., Griffin, D. W., Bellavia, G., & Rose, P. (2001). The mismeasure of love: How self-doubt contaminates relationship beliefs. *Personality and Social Psychology Bulletin, 27,* 423–436.

Mussweiler, T. (2006). Doing is for thinking! Stereotype activation by stereotypic movements. *Psychological Science, 17,* 17–21.

Mustanski, B. S., Dupree, M. G., Nievergelt, C. M., Bocklandt, S., Schork, N. J., & Hamer, D. H. (2005). A genome-wide scan of male sexual orientation. *Human Genetics, 116,* 272–278.

Myers, M. B., & McCaulley, M. H. (1985). *Manual: A guide to the development and use of the Myers–Briggs Type Indicator.* Palo Alto, CA: Consulting Psychologists.

Nasby, W. (1985). Private self-consciousness, articulation of the self-schema, and the recognition memory of trait adjectives. *Journal of Personality and Social Psychology, 49,* 704–709.

Neale, M. C., & Stevenson, J. (1989). Rater bias in the EASI temperament scales: A twin study. *Journal of Personality and Social Psychology, 56,* 446–455.

Neimeyer, G. J., & Neimeyer, R. A. (1981). Personal construct perspectives on cognitive assessment. In T. V. Merluzzi, C. R. Glass, & M. Genest (Eds.), *Cognitive assessment.* New York: Guilford.

Neimeyer, R. A. (1985). Personal constructs in clinical practice. In P. C. Kendall (Ed.), *Advances in cognitive-behavioral research and therapy* (Vol. 4, pp. 275–339). New York: Academic.

Nell, V. (2002). Why young men drive dangerously: Implications for injury prevention. *Current Directions in Psychological Science, 11,* 75–79.

Nelson, R. O. (1977). Methodological issues in assessment via self-monitoring. In J. D. Cone & R. P. Hawkins (Eds.),

Behavioral assessment: New directions in clinical psychology. New York: Brunner/Mazel.

Netter, P., Hennig, J., & Rohrmann, S. (1999). Psychobiological differences between the aggression and psychoticism dimension. *Pharmacopsychiatry, 32,* 5–12.

Neuberg, S. L., & Newsom, J. T. (1993). Personal need for structure: Individual differences in the desire for simple structure. *Journal of Personality and Social Psychology, 65,* 113–131.

Neuringer, A. (2004). Reinforced variability in animals and people: Implications for adaptive action. *American Psychologist, 59,* 891–906.

Newcomb, M. D., & McGee, L. (1991). Influence of sensation seeking on general deviance and specific problem behaviors from adolescence to young adulthood. *Journal of Personality and Social Psychology, 61,* 614–628.

Newell, A., & Simon, H. A. (1972). *Human problem solving.* Englewood Cliffs, NJ: Prentice-Hall.

Newman, D. L., Tellegen, A., & Bouchard, T. J., Jr. (1998). Individual differences in adult ego development: Sources of influence in twins reared apart. *Journal of Personality and Social Psychology, 74,* 985–995.

Newman, J. P., Wallace, J. F., Strauman, T. J., Skolaski, R. L., Oreland, K. M., Mattek, P. W., Elder, K. A., & McNeeley, J. (1993). Effects of motivationally significant stimuli on the regulation of dominant responses. *Journal of Personality and Social Psychology, 65,* 165–175.

Newman, L. S., Duff, K. J., & Baumeister, R. F. (1997). A new look at defensive projection: Thought suppression, accessibility, and biased person perception. *Journal of Personality and Social Psychology, 72,* 980–1001.

Nezu, A. M. (1987). A problem-solving formulation of depression: A literature review and proposal of a pluralistic model. *Clinical Psychology Review, 7,* 121–144.

Niedenthal, P. M., Halberstadt, J. B., & Innes-Ker, A. H. (1999). Emotional response categorization. *Psychological Review, 106,* 337–361.

Niedenthal, P. M., Setterlund, M. B., & Wherry, M. B. (1992). Possible self-complexity and affective reactions to goal-relevant evaluation. *Journal of Personality and Social Psychology, 63,* 5–16.

Nielsen, T. A. (2000). A review of mentation in REM and NREM sleep: "Covert" REM sleep as a possible reconciliation of two opposing models. *Behavioral and Brain Sciences, 23,* 851–866.

Nigg, J. T. (2000). On inhibition/disinhibition in developmental pychopathology: Views from cognitive and personality psychology as a working inhibition taxonomy. *Psychological Bulletin, 126,* 220–246.

Nigg, J. T., John, O. P., Blaskey, L. G., Huang-Pollock, C. L., Willcutt, E. G., Hinshaw, S. P., & Pennington, B. (2002). Big five dimensions and ADHD symptoms: Links between personality traits and clinical symptoms. *Journal of Personality and Social Psychology, 83,* 451–469.

Nisbett, R. E., & Cohen, D. (1996). *Culture of honor.* Boulder, CO: Westview.

Nisbett, R. E., & Ross, L. (1980). *Human inference: Strategies and shortcomings of social judgment.* Englewood Cliffs, NJ: Prentice-Hall.

Nisbett, R. E., & Wilson, T. D. (1977). Telling more than we can know: Verbal reports on mental processes. *Psychological Review, 84,* 231–259.

Nolen-Hoeksema, S., Morrow, J., & Frederickson, B. L. (1993). Response styles and the duration of episodes of depressed mood. *Journal of Abnormal Psychology, 102,* 20–28.

Nolen-Hoeksema, S., Parker, L., & Larson, J. (1994). Ruminative coping with depressed mood following loss. *Journal of Personality and Social Psychology, 67,* 92–104.

Norman, D. A. (1981). Categorization of action slips. *Psychological Review, 88,* 1–15.

Norman, W. T. (1963). Toward an adequate taxonomy of personality attributes: Replicated factor structure in peer nomination personality ratings. *Journal of Abnormal and Social Psychology, 66,* 574–583.

Novaco, R. W. (1978). Anger and coping with stress: Cognitive behavioral interventions. In J. P. Foreyt & D. P. Rathjen (Eds.), *Cognitive behavior therapy: Research and application.* New York: Plenum.

Nowak, A., Vallacher, R. R., Tesser, A., & Borkowski, W. (2000). Society of self: The emergence of collective properties in self-structure. *Psychological Review, 107,* 39–61.

O'Connor, B. P. (2002). The search for dimensional structure differences between normality and abnormality: A statistical review of published data on personality and psychopathology. *Journal of Personality and Social Psychology, 83,* 962–982.

O'Connor, B. P., & Dyce, J. A. (2001). Rigid and extreme: A geometric representation of personality disorders in five-factor model space. *Journal of Personality and Social Psychology, 81,* 1119–1130.

O'Connor, S. C., & Rosenblood, L. K. (1996). Affiliation motivation in everyday experience: A theoretical comparison. *Journal of Personality and Social Psychology, 70,* 513–522.

O'Donnell, M. C., Fisher, R., Rickard, M., & McConaghy, N. (2000). Emotional suppression: Can it predict cancer outcome in women with suspicious screening mammograms? *Psychological Medicine, 30,* 1079–1088.

O'Donohue, W., & Kitchener, R. (Eds.). (1999). *Handbook of behaviorism.* San Diego: Academic.

O'Leary, K. D., & Becker, W. C. (1967). Behavior modification of an adjustment class: A token reinforcement program. *Exceptional Children, 33,* 637–642.

Ogilvie, D. M. (1987). The undesired self: A neglected variable in personality research. *Journal of Personality and Social Psychology, 52,* 379–385.

Öhman, A., & Mineka, S. (2001). Fears, phobias, and preparedness: Toward an evolved module of fear and fear learning. *Psychological Review, 108,* 483–522.

Oliver, M. B., & Hyde, J. S. (1993). Gender differences in sexuality: A meta-analysis. *Psychological Bulletin, 114,* 29–51.

Olson, J. M., Vernon, P. A., Harris, J. A., & Jang, K. L. (2001). The heritability of attitudes: A study of twins. *Journal of Personality and Social Psychology, 80,* 845–860.

Oreland, L. (2004). Platelet monoamine oxidase, personality and alcoholism: The rise, fall and resurrection. *Neurotoxicology, 25,* 79–89.

Oring, E. (1984). *The jokes of Sigmund Freud: A study in humor and Jewish identity.* Philadelphia: University of Pennsylvania Press.

Orlofsky, J. L., Marcia, J. E., & Lesser, I. M. (1973). Ego identity states and the intimacy versus isolation crisis of young adulthood. *Journal of Youth and Adolescence, 27,* 211–219.

Orr, S. P., Lasko, N. B., Metzger, L. J., Berry, N. J., Ahern, C. E., & Pitman, R. K. (1998). Psychophysiologic assessment of women with posttraumatic stress disorder resulting from childhood sexual abuse. *Journal of Consulting and Clinical Psychology, 66,* 906–913.

Öst, L. G., Ferebee, I., & Furmark, T. (1997). One-session group therapy of spider phobia: Direct versus indirect treatments. *Behavior Research and Therapy, 35,* 721–732.

Overall, N. C., Fletcher, G. J. O., & Friesen, M. D. (2003). Mapping the intimate relationship mind: Comparisons between three models of attachment representations. *Personality and Social Psychology Bulletin, 29,* 1479–1493.

Overmier, J. B., & Seligman, M. E. P. (1967). Effects of inescapable shock upon subsequent escape and avoidance learning. *Journal of Comparative and Physiological Psychology, 63,* 28–33.

Overwalle, F. V., & Siebler, F. (2005). A connectionist model of attitude formation and change. *Personality and Social Psychology Review, 9,* 231–274.

Owen, M. J., Williams, N. M., & O'Donovan, M. C. (2004). The molecular genetics of schizophrenia: New findings promise new insights. *Molecular Psychiatry, 9,* 14–27.

Oyserman, D., Bybee, D., & Terry, K. (2006). Possible selves and academic outcomes: How and when possible selves impel action. *Journal of Personality and Social Psychology.*

Oyserman, D., Bybee, D., Terry, K., & Hart-Johnson, T. (2004). Possible selves as roadmaps. *Journal of Research in Personality, 38,* 130–149.

Oyserman, D., Terry, K., & Bybee, D. (2002). A possible selves intervention to enhance school involvement. *Journal of Adolescence, 25,* 313–326.

Ozer, D. J. (1986). *Consistency in personality: A methodological framework.* New York: Springer-Verlag.

Ozer, D. J., & Benet-Martínez, V. (2006). Personality and the prediction of consequential outcomes. *Annual Review of Psychology, 57,* 401–421.

Ozer, D. J., & Reise, S. P. (1994). Personality assessment. *Annual Review of Psychology, 45,* 357–388.

Ozer, E. M., & Bandura, A. (1990). Mechanisms governing empowerment effects: A self-efficacy analysis. *Journal of Personality and Social Psychology, 58,* 472–486.

Paaver, M., Eensoo, D., Pulver, A., & Harro, J. (2006). Adaptive and maladaptive impulsivity, platelet monoamine oxidase (MAO) activity and risk-admitting in different types of risky drivers. *Psychopharmacology, 186,* 32–40.

Pang, J. S., & Schultheiss, O. C. (2005). Assessing implicit motives in U.S. college students: Effects of picture type and position, gender and ethnicity, and cross-cultural comparisons. *Journal of Personality Assessment, 85,* 280–294.

Panksepp, J. (1998). *Affective neuroscience: The foundations of human and animal emotions.* New York: Oxford University Press.

Panksepp, J., & Cox, J. (1986). An overdue burial for the serotonin theory of anxiety. *Behavioral and Brain Sciences, 9,* 340–341.

Park, C. L., Armeli, S., & Tennen, H. (2004). Appraisal-coping goodness of fit: A daily internet study. *Personality and Social Psychology Bulletin, 30,* 558–569.

Park, J.-W., Yoon, S.-O., Kim, K.-H., & Wyer, R. S., Jr. (2001). Effects of priming a bipolar attribute concept on dimension versus concept-specific accessibility of semantic memory. *Journal of Personality and Social Psychology, 81,* 405–420.

Parke, R. D. (1969). Effectiveness of punishment as an interaction of intensity, timing, agent nurturance, and cognitive structuring. *Child Development, 40,* 211–235.

Parnell, R. W. (1957). Physique and mental breakdown in young adults. *British Medical Journal, 1,* 1485–1490.

Partridge, T. (2005). Are genetically informed designs genetically informative? Comment on McGue, Elkins, Walden, and Iacono (2005) and quantitative behavioral genetics. *Developmental Psychology, 41,* 985–988.

Patterson, C. M., & Newman, J. P. (1993). Reflectivity and learning from aversive events: Toward a psychological mechanism for the syndromes of disinhibition. *Psychological Review, 100,* 716–736.

Paul, G. L. (1966). *Insight vs. desensitization in psychotherapy: An experiment in anxiety reduction.* Stanford, CA: Stanford University Press.

Paulhus, D. L. (1983). Sphere-specific measures of perceived control. *Journal of Personality and Social Psychology, 44,* 1253–1265.

Paulhus, D. L. (1998). Interpersonal and intrapsychic adaptiveness of trait self-enhancement: A mixed blessing? *Journal of Personality and Social Psychology, 74,* 1197–1208.

Paulhus, D. L., & Christie, R. (1981). Spheres of control: An interactionist approach to assessment and perceived control. In H. F. Lefcourt (Ed.), *Research with the locus of control construct. Vol. 1, Assessment methods.* New York: Academic.

Paulhus, D. L., & Suedfeld, P. (1988). A dynamic complexity model of self-deception. In J. S. Lockard & D. L. Paulhus (Eds.), *Self-deception: An adaptive mechanism?* Englewood Cliffs, NJ: Prentice-Hall.

Paulhus, D. L., Trapnell, P. D., & Chen, D. (1999). Birth order effects on personality and achievement within families. *Psychological Science, 10,* 482–488.

Paunonen, S. V. (1989). Consensus in personality judgments: Moderating effects of target–rater acquaintanceship and behavior observability. *Journal of Personality and Social Psychology, 56,* 823–833.

Paunonen, S. V. (1998). Hierarchical organization of personality and prediction of behavior. *Journal of Personality and Social Psychology, 74,* 538–556.

Paunonen, S. V., & Ashton, M. C. (2001a). Big five factors and facets and the prediction of behavior. *Journal of Personality and Social Psychology, 81,* 524–539.

Paunonen, S. V., & Ashton, M. C. (2001b). Big five predictors of academic achievement. *Journal of Research in Personality, 35,* 78–90.

Paunonen, S. V., & Jackson, D. N. (2000). What is beyond the big five? Plenty! *Journal of Personality, 68,* 821–835.

Paunonen, S. V., Jackson, D. N., Trzebinski, J., & Forsterling, F. (1992). Personality structure across cultures: A multimethod evaluation. *Journal of Personality and Social Psychology, 62,* 447–456.

Pavlov, I. P. (1927). *Conditioned reflexes.* Oxford, England: Oxford University Press.

Pavlov, I. P. (1955). *Selected works.* New York: Foreign Languages.

Payne, B. K. (2005). Conceptualizing control in social cognition: How executive functioning modulates the expression of automatic stereotyping. *Journal of Personality and Social Psychology, 89,* 488–503.

Peabody, D. (1984). Personality dimensions through trait inferences. *Journal of Personality and Social Psychology, 46,* 384–403.

Peabody, D., & De Raad, B. (2002). The substantive nature of psycholexical personality factors: A comparison across languages. *Journal of Personality and Social Psychology, 83,* 983–997.

Peabody, D., & Goldberg, L. R. (1989). Some determinants of factor structures from personality-trait descriptors. *Journal of Personality and Social Psychology, 57,* 552–567.

Peciña, S., Cagniard, B., Berridge, K. C., Aldridge, J. W., & Zhuang, X. (2003). Hyperdopaminergic mutant mice have higher "wanting" but not "liking" for sweet rewards. *Journal of Neuroscience, 23,* 9395–9402.

Pedersen, N. L., Plomin, R., McClearn, G. E., & Friberg, L. (1988). Neuroticism, extraversion, and related traits in adult twins reared apart and reared together. *Journal of Personality and Social Psychology, 55,* 950–957.

Pelham, B. W., Mirenberg, M. C., & Jones, J. T. (2002). Why Susie sells seashells by the seashore: Implicit egotism and major life decisions. *Journal of Personality and Social Psychology, 82,* 469–487.

Pennebaker, J. W. (1989). Confession, inhibition, and disease. In L. Berkowitz (Ed.), *Advances in Experimental Social Psychology* (Vol. 22, pp. 211–244). San Diego: Academic.

Pennebaker, J. W. (1993). Putting stress into words: Health, linguistic, and therapeutic implications. *Behaviour Research and Therapy, 31,* 539–548.

Pennebaker, J. W., & Beall, S. K. (1986). Confronting a traumatic event: Toward an understanding of inhibition and disease. *Journal of Abnormal Psychology, 95,* 274–281.

Pennebaker, J. W., & Chung, C. K. (2007). Expressive writing, emotional upheavals, and health. In H. Friedman & R. Silver (Eds.), *Foundations of health psychology* (pp. 263–284). New York: Oxford University Press.

Pennebaker, J. W., & Graybeal, A. (2001). Patterns of natural language use: Disclosure, personality, and social integration. *Current Directions in Psychological Science, 10,* 90–93.

Pennebaker, J. W., Kiecolt-Glaser, J. K., & Glaser, R. (1988). Disclosure of traumas and immune function: Health implications for psychotherapy. *Journal of Consulting and Clinical Psychology, 56,* 239–245.

Peplau, L. A., & Perlman, D. (Eds.). (1982). *Loneliness: A sourcebook of current theory, research, and therapy.* New York: Wiley.

Perkins, K. A. (1999). Nicotine self-administration. *Nicotine and Tobacco Research, 1* (suppl.), 133–137.

Pervin, L. A. (1983). The stasis and flow of behavior: Toward a theory of goals. In M. M. Page & R. Dienstbier (Eds.), *Nebraska symposium on motivation* (Vol. 31). Lincoln: University of Nebraska Press.

Pervin, L. A. (1985). Personality: Current controversies, issues, and directions. *Annual Review of Psychology, 36,* 83–114.

Pervin, L. A. (Ed.). (1989). *Goal concepts in personality and social psychology.* Hillsdale, NJ: Erlbaum.

Pervin, L. A. (1994). A critical analysis of current trait theory. *Psychological Inquiry, 5,* 103–113.

Peterson, C. (1995). Explanatory style. In G. M. Buchanan & M. E. P. Seligman (Eds.), *Explanatory style* (pp. 233–246). Hillsdale, NJ: Erlbaum.

Peterson, L. M. (1980). Why men have pockets in their pants: A feminist insight (or, If Freud had been a woman). *Society for the Advancement of Social Psychology Newsletter, 6,* 19.

Petri, H. L., & Mishkin, M. (1994). Behaviorism, cognitivism, and the neuropsychology of memory. *American Scientist, 82,* 30–37.

Petry, N. M., Martin, B., Cooney, J. L., & Kranzler, H. R. (2000). Give them prizes, and they will come: Contingency management for treatment of alcohol dependence. *Journal of Consulting and Clinical Psychology, 68,* 250–257.

Phares, E. J. (1957). Expectancy changes in skill and chance situations. *Journal of Abnormal and Social Psychology, 54,* 339–342.

Phares, E. J. (1976). *Locus of control in personality.* Morristown, NJ: General Learning.

Piedmont, R. L., McCrae, R. R., & Costa, P. T., Jr. (1992). An assessment of the Edwards Personal Preference Schedule from the perspective of the five-factor model. *Journal of Personality Assessment, 58,* 67–78.

Pierce, T., & Lydon, J. E. (2001). Global and specific relational models in the experience of social interactions. *Journal of Personality and Social Psychology, 80,* 613–631.

Pietromonaco, P. R., & Carnelley, K. B. (1994). Gender and working models of attachment: Consequences for perception of self and romantic relationships. *Personal Relationships, 1,* 3–26.

Pietromonaco, P. R., & Barrett, L. F. (1997). Working models of attachment and daily social interactions. *Journal of Personality and Social Psychology, 73,* 1409–1423.

Plaks, J. E., Stroessner, S. J., Dweck, C. S., & Sherman, J. W. (2001). Person theories and attention allocation: Preferences for stereotypic versus counterstereotypic information. *Journal of Personality and Social Psychology, 80,* 876–893.

Plomin, R. (1974). *A temperament theory of personality development: Parent–child interactions.* Unpublished doctoral dissertation, University of Texas at Austin.

Plomin, R. (1981). Ethnological behavioral genetics and development. In K. Immelmann, G. W. Barlow, L. Petrinovich, & M. Main (Eds.), *Behavioral development: The Bielefeld interdisciplinary project.* Cambridge, England: Cambridge University Press.

Plomin, R. (1989). Environment and genes: Determinants of behavior. *American Psychologist, 44,* 105–111.

Plomin, R. (1995). Molecular genetics and psychology. *Current Directions in Psychological Science, 4,* 114–117.

Plomin, R. (1997). *Behavioral Genetics.* New York: Freeman.

Plomin, R., & Crabbe, J. (2000). DNA. *Psychological Bulletin, 126,* 806–828.

Plomin, R., & Daniels, D. (1987). Why are children in the same family so different from one another? *Behavioral and Brain Sciences, 10,* 1–60.

Plomin, R., DeFries, J. C., Craig, I. W., & McGuffin, P. (Eds.). (2003). *Behavioral genetics in the postgenomic era.* Washington, DC: American Psychological Association.

Plomin, R., DeFries, J. C., & Loehlin, J. C. (1977). Genotype–environment interaction and correlation in the analysis of human behavior. *Psychological Bulletin, 84,* 309–322.

Plomin, R., DeFries, J. C., & McClearn, G. E. (1990). *Behavioral genetics: A primer* (2nd ed.). New York: W. H. Freeman.

Plomin, R., & Foch, T. T. (1980). A twin study of objectively assessed personality in childhood. *Journal of Personality and Social Psychology, 39,* 680–688.

Plomin, R., & Rende, R. (1991). Human behavioral genetics. *Annual Review of Psychology, 42,* 161–190.

Plomin, R., & Rowe, D. C. (1977). A twin study of temperament in young children. *Journal of Psychology, 97,* 107–113.

Plomin, R., Scheier, M. F., Bergeman, C. S., Pedersen, N. L., Nesselroade, J. R., & McClearn, G. E. (1992). Optimism, pessimism, and mental health: A twin/adoption analysis. *Personality and Individual Differences, 13,* 921–930.

Pollak, S., & Gilligan, C. (1982). Images of violence in Thematic Apperception Test stories. *Journal of Personality and Social Psychology, 42,* 159–167.

Pool, R. (1993). Evidence for homosexuality gene. *Science, 261,* 291–292

Posner, M. I., & DiGirolamo, G. J. (2000). Cognitive neuroscience: Origins and promise. *Psychological Bulletin, 126,* 873–889.

Postman, L. (1951). Toward a general theory of cognition. In J. H. Rohrer & M. Sherif (Eds.), *Social psychology at the crossroads.* New York: Harper.

Powell, J., & Azrin, N. (1968). The effects of shock as a punisher for cigarette smoking. *Journal of Applied Behavior Analysis, 1,* 63–71.

Powell, R. A., & Boer, D. P. (1994). Did Freud mislead patients to confabulate memories of abuse? *Psychological Reports, 74,* 1283–1298.

Powers, S. I., Pietromonaco, P. R., Gunlicks, M., & Sayer, A. (2006). Dating couples' attachment styles and patterns of cortisol reactivity and recovery in response to a relationship conflict. *Journal of Personality and Social Psychology, 90,* 613–628.

Powers, W. T. (1973). *Behavior: The control of perception.* Chicago: Aldine.

Prager, K. J. (1982). Identity development and self-esteem in young women. *Journal of Genetic Psychology, 141,* 177–182.

Pratt, M. W., Danso, H. A., Arnold, M. L., Norris, J. E., & Filyer, R. (2001). Adult generativity and the socialization of adolescents: Relations to mothers' and fathers' parenting beliefs, styles, and practices. *Journal of Personality, 69,* 89–120.

Pratto, F., & Hegarty, P. (2000). The political psychology of reproductive strategies. *Psychological Science, 11,* 57–62.

Prentice-Dunn, S., & Rogers, R. W. (1980). Effects of deindividuating situational cues and aggressive models on subjective deindividuation and aggression. *Journal of Personality and Social Psychology, 39,* 104–113.

Prentice-Dunn, S., & Rogers, R. W. (1982). Effects of public and private self-awareness on deindividuation and aggression. *Journal of Personality and Social Psychology, 43,* 503–513.

Prentice-Dunn, S., & Rogers, R. W. (1989). Deindividua-
tion and the self-regulation of behavior. In P. B. Paulus
(Ed.), *Psychology of group influence* (2nd ed., pp. 87–109).
Hillsdale, NJ: Erlbaum.

Pressman, S. D., & Cohen, S. (2005). Does positive affect
influence health? *Psychological Bulletin, 131,* 925–971.

Preston, K. L., Umbricht, A., Wong, C. J., & Epstein, D. H.
(2001). Shaping cocaine abstinence by successive approximation. *Journal of Consulting and Clinical Psychology, 69,*
643–654.

Price, M. A., Tennant, C. C., Smith, R. C., Butow, P. N.,
Kennedy, S. J., Kossoff, M. B., & Dunn, S. M. (2001). The
role of psychosocial factors in the development of breast
carcinoma: Part I. The cancer-prone personality. *Cancer,
91,* 679–685.

Privette, G., & Landsman, T. (1983). Factor analysis of peak
performance: The full use of potential. *Journal of Personality and Social Psychology, 44,* 195–200.

Pronin, E., Steele, C. M., & Ross, L. (2004). Identity bifur-
cation in response to stereotype threat: Women and math-
ematics. *Journal of Experimental Social Psychology, 40,*
152–168.

Pruessner, J. C., Champagne, F., Meaney, M. J., & Dagher, A.
(2004). Dopamine release in response to a psychological
stress in humans and its relationship to early life maternal
care: A positron emission tomography study using [11C]
raclopride. *The Journal of Neuroscience, 24,* 2825–2831.

Pryor, J. B., Reeder, G. D., Yeadon, C., & Hesson-McInnis,
M. (2004). A dual-process model of reactions to perceived
stigma. *Journal of Personality and Social Psychology, 87,*
436–452.

Pyszczynski, T., & Greenberg, J. (1985). Depression and
preference for self-focusing stimuli after success and
failure. *Journal of Personality and Social Psychology, 49,*
1066–1075.

Pyszczynski, T., & Greenberg, J. (1987). Self-regulatory
perseveration and the depressive self-focusing style: A self-
awareness theory of reactive depression. *Psychological Bulletin, 102,* 122–138.

Pyszczynski, T., Greenberg, J., & Solomon, S. (2000).
Proximal and distal defense: A new perspective on
unconscious motivation. *Current Directions in Psychological
Science, 9,* 156–160.

Pyszczynski, T., Greenberg, J., Solomon, S., Arndt, J., &
Schimel, J. (2004). Why do people need self-esteem? A
theoretical and empirical review. *Psychological Bulletin,
130,* 435–468.

Pyszczynski, T., Solomon, S., & Greenberg, J. (2002). *In the
wake of 9/11: The psychology of terror.* Washington, DC:
American Psychological Association.

Pytlik Zillig, L. M., Hemenover, S. H., & Dienstbier, R. A.
(2002). What do we assess when we assess a big 5 trait? A
content analysis of the affective, behavioral, and cognitive

processes represented in big 5 personality inventories. *Personality and Social Psychology Bulletin, 28,* 847–858.

Quinn, S. (1987). *A mind of her own: The life of Karen Horney.*
New York: Summit.

Rabin, A. I., Zucker, R. A., Emmons, R. A., & Frank, S.
(Eds.). (1990). *Studying persons and lives.* New York:
Springer.

Rachlin, H. (1977). Reinforcing and punishing thoughts.
Behavior Therapy, 8, 659–665.

Rachman, J., & Teasdale, J. (1969). *Aversion therapy and
behaviour disorders: An analysis.* Coral Gables, FL: University
of Miami Press.

Rachman, S. (Ed.). (1978). *Advances in behaviour research and
therapy* (Vol. 1). Oxford, England: Pergamon.

Rapaport, D. (1960). *The structure of psychoanalytic theory: A
systematizing attempt* (Psychological Issues Monograph 6).
New York: International Universities Press.

Raskin, P. A., & Israel, A. C. (1981). Sex-role imitation in
children: Effects of sex of child, sex of model, and sex-
role appropriateness of modeled behavior. *Sex Roles, 7,*
1067–1076.

Razran, G. H. S. (1940). Conditioned response changes in
rating and appraising sociopolitical slogans. *Psychological
Bulletin, 37,* 481.

Read, S. J. (1987). Constructing causal scenarios: A knowledge structure approach to causal reasoning. *Journal of Personality and Social Psychology, 52,* 288–302.

Read, S. J., Jones, D. K., & Miller, L. C. (1990). Traits as
goal-based categories: The importance of goals in the
coherence of dispositional categories. *Journal of Personality
and Social Psychology, 58,* 1048–1061.

Read, S. J., & Miller, L. C. (Eds.). (1998). *Connectionist models
of social reasoning and social behavior.* Mahwah, NJ: Erlbaum.

Read, S. J., & Miller, L. C. (2002). Virtual personalities: A
neural network model of personality. *Personality and Social
Psychology Review, 6,* 357–369.

Read, S. J., Vanman, E. J., & Miller, L. C. (1997). Connectionism, parallel constraint satisfaction processes, and
Gestalt principles: (Re)introducing cognitive dynamics to
social psychology. *Review of Personality and Social Psychology, 1,* 26–53.

Reason, J., & Mycielska, K. (1982). *Absent-minded? The psychology of mental lapses and everyday errors.* Englewood
Cliffs, NJ: Prentice-Hall.

Redmore, C., & Waldman, K. (1975). Reliability of a sentence completion measure of ego development. *Journal of
Personality Assessment, 39,* 236–243.

Reese, E. P. (1966). The analysis of human operant behavior. In J. A. Vernon (Ed.), *Introduction to psychology: A self-
selection textbook.* Dubuque, IA: Brown.

Reinisch, J. M. (1981). Prenatal exposure to synthetic pro-
gestins increases potential for aggression in humans. *Science, 211,* 1171–1173.

Repetti, R. L. (1989). Effects of daily workload on subsequent behavior during marital interactions: The role of social withdrawal and spouse support. *Journal of Personality and Social Psychology, 57,* 651–659.

Rescorla, R. A. (1972). Informational variables in Pavlovian conditioning. In G. H. Bower (Ed.), *The psychology of learning and motivation* (Vol. 6, pp. 1–46). New York: Academic.

Rescorla, R. A. (1987). A Pavlovian analysis of goal-directed behavior. *American Psychologist, 42,* 119–129.

Rescorla, R. A. (1988). Pavlovian conditioning: It's not what you think it is. *American Psychologist, 43,* 151–160.

Rescorla, R. A. (1997). Response-inhibition in extinction. *Quarterly Journal of Experimental Psychology: Comparative and Physiological Psychology, 50B,* 238–252.

Rescorla, R. A. (1998). Instrumental learning: Nature and persistence. In M. Sabourin, F. Craik, et al. (Eds.), *Advances in psychological science, Vol. 2: Biological and cognitive aspects* (pp. 239–257). Hove, England: Psychology Press.

Reuter, M., Schmitz, A., Corr, P., & Hennig, J. (2005). Molecular genetics support Gray's personality theory: The interaction of COMT and DRD2 polymorphisms predicts the behavioural approach system. *International Journal of Neuropsychopharmacology, 9,* 155–166.

Revonsuo, A. (2000). The reinterpretation of dreams: An evolutionary hypothesis of the function of dreaming. *Behavioral and Brain Sciences, 23,* 877–901.

Reyna, C., Henry, P. J., Korfmacher, W., & Tucker, A. (2005). Examining the principles in principled conservatism: The role of responsibility stereotypes as cues for deservingness in racial policy decisions. *Journal of Personality and Social Psychology, 90,* 109–128.

Reynolds, S. K., & Clark, L. A. (2001). Predicting dimensions of personality disorder from domains and facets of the five-factor model. *Journal of Personality, 69,* 199–222.

Rhawn, J. (1980). Awareness, the origin of thought, and the role of conscious self-deception in resistance and repression. *Psychological Reports, 46,* 767–781.

Rhee, S. H., & Waldman, I. D. (2002). Genetic and environmental influences on antisocial behavior: A meta-analysis of twin and adoption studies. *Psychological Bulletin, 128,* 490–529.

Rhodewalt, F., & Morf, C. C. (1998). On self-aggrandizement and anger: A temporal analysis of narcissism and affective reactions to success and failure. *Journal of Personality and Social Psychology, 74,* 672–685.

Rholes, W. S., & Simpson, J. A. (2004). *Adult attachment: Theory, research, and clinical implications.* New York: Guilford.

Rholes, W. S., Simpson, J. A., & Friedman, M. (2006). Avoidant attachment and the experience of parenting. *Personality and Social Psychology Bulletin, 32,* 275–285.

Rholes, W. S., Simpson, J. A., & Oriña, M. M. (1999). Attachment and anger in an anxiety-provoking situation. *Journal of Personality and Social Psychology, 76,* 940–957.

Riedel, W. (1970). An investigation of personal constructs through nonverbal tasks. *Journal of Abnormal Psychology, 76,* 173–179.

Riordan, C. A., & Tedeschi, J. T. (1983). Attraction in aversive environments: Some evidence for classical conditioning and negative reinforcement. *Journal of Personality and Social Psychology, 44,* 683–692.

Risley, T. R. (1968). The effects and side effects of punishing the autistic behaviors of a deviant child. *Journal of Applied Behavior Analysis, 1,* 21–34.

Ritvo, L. B. (1990). *Darwin's influence on Freud: A tale of two sciences.* New Haven, CT: Yale University Press.

Rizzolatti, G., Fogassi, L., & Gallese, V. (2002). Motor and cognitive functions of the ventral premotor cortex. *Current Opinion in Neurobiology, 12,* 149–154.

Roberts, B. W., & Bogg, T. (2004). A longitudinal study of the relationships between conscientiousness and the social-environmental factors and substance-use behaviors that influence health. *Journal of Personality, 72,* 325–354.

Roberts, B. W., Caspi, A., & Moffitt, T. E. (2001). The kids are alright: Growth and stability in personality development from adolescence to adulthood. *Journal of Personality and Social Psychology, 81,* 670–683.

Roberts, B. W., & Del Vecchio, W. F. (2000). The rank-order consistency of personality traits from childhood to old age: A quantitative review of longitudinal studies. *Psychological Bulletin, 126,* 3–25.

Roberts, B. W., & Robins, R. W. (2000). Broad dispositions, broad aspirations: The intersection of personality traits and major life goals. *Personality and Social Psychology Bulletin, 26,* 1284–1296.

Roberts, B. W., Walton, K. E., & Bogg, T. (2005). Conscientiousness and health across the life course. *Review of General Psychology, 9,* 156–168.

Roberts, J. E., Gotlib, I. H., & Kassel, J. D. (1996). Adult attachment security and symptoms of depression: The mediating roles of dysfunctional attitudes and low self-esteem. *Journal of Personality and Social Psychology, 70,* 310–320.

Roberts, J. E., & Monroe, S. M. (1994). A multidimensional model of self-esteem in depression. *Clinical Psychology Review, 14,* 161–181.

Robins, R. W., Fraley, R. C., Roberts, B. W., & Trzesniewski, K. H. (2001). A longitudinal study of personality change in young adulthood. *Journal of Personality, 69,* 617–640.

Robins, R. W., John, O. P., Caspi, A., Moffitt, T. E., & Stouthamer-Loeber, M. (1996). Resilient, overcontrolled, and undercontrolled boys: Three replicable personality types. *Journal of Personality and Social Psychology, 70,* 157–171.

Robins, R. W., Noftle, E. E., Trzesniewski, K. H., & Roberts, B. W. (2005). Do people know how their personality has changed? Correlates of perceived and actual personality change in young adulthood. *Journal of Personality, 73,* 489–522.

Robins, R. W., & Pals, J. L. (2002). Implicit self-theories in the academic domain: Implications for goal orientation, attributions, affect, and self-esteem change. *Self and Identity, 1,* 313–336.

Robinson, F. G. (1992). *Love's story told: A life of Henry A. Murray.* Cambridge, MA: Harvard University Press.

Robinson, S., Sandstrom, S. M., Denenberg, V. H., & Palmiter, R. D. (2005). Distinguishing whether dopamine regulates liking, wanting, and/or learning about rewards. *Behavioral Neuroscience, 119,* 5–15.

Robles, T. F., Glaser, R., & Kiecolt-Glaser, J. K. (2005). Out of balance: A new look at chronic stress, depression, and immunity. *Current Directions in Psychological Science, 14,* 111–115.

Roccas, S., Sagiv, L., Schwartz, S. H., & Knafo, A. (2002). The big five personality factors and personal values. *Personality and Social Psychology Bulletin, 28,* 789–801.

Rogers, C. R. (1951). *Client-centered therapy: Its current practice, implications and theory.* Boston: Houghton Mifflin.

Rogers, C. R. (1959). A theory of therapy, personality and interpersonal relationships, as developed in the client-centered framework. In S. Koch (Ed.), *Psychology: A study of a science* (Vol. 3). New York: McGraw-Hill.

Rogers, C. R. (1961). *On becoming a person.* Boston: Houghton Mifflin.

Rogers, C. R. (1965). *Client-centered therapy: Its current practice, implication, and theory.* Boston: Houghton Mifflin.

Rogers, C. R., & Dymond, R. F. (Eds.). (1954). *Psychotherapy and personality change: Coordinated research studies in the client-centered approach.* Chicago: University of Chicago Press.

Rogers, C. R., & Stevens, B. (1967). *Person to person: The problem of being human.* New York: Simon & Schuster.

Rogers, T. B. (1981). A model of the self as an aspect of the human information-processing system. In N. Cantor & J. F. Kihlstrom (Eds.), *Personality, cognition and social interaction.* Hillsdale, NJ: Erlbaum.

Rogers, T. B., Kuiper, N. A., & Kirker, W. S. (1977). Self-reference and the encoding of personal information. *Journal of Personality and Social Psychology, 35,* 677–688.

Roney, J. R. (2003). Effects of visual exposure to the opposite sex: Cognitive aspects of mate attraction in human males. *Personality and Social Psychology Bulletin, 29,* 393–404.

Rorer, L. G. (1965). The great response-style myth. *Psychological Bulletin, 63,* 129–156.

Rorschach, H. (1942). *Psychodiagnostics.* Berne, Switzerland: Huber.

Rosch, E., & Mervis, C. (1975). Family resemblances: Studies in the internal structure of categories. *Cognitive Psychology, 7,* 573–605.

Rosekrans, M. A. (1967). Imitation in children as a function of perceived similarity and vicarious reinforcement. *Journal of Personality and Social Psychology, 7,* 307–315.

Roseman, I. J. (1991). Appraisal determinants of discrete emotions. *Cognition and Emotion, 5,* 161–200.

Rosen, C. M. (1987). The eerie world of reunited twins. *Discover, 8,* 36–46.

Rosenbaum, D. A. (1987). Hierarchical organization of motor programs. In S. Wise (Ed.), *Neural and behaviorial approaches to higher brain function* (pp. 45–66). New York: Wiley.

Rosenbaum, D. A. (1990). *Human motor control.* San Diego: Academic.

Rosenbaum, D. A. (2005). The Cinderella of psychology: The neglect of motor control in the science of mental life and behavior. *American Psychologist, 60,* 308–317.

Rosenthal, T. L., & Reese, S. L. (1976). The effects of covert and overt modeling on assertive behavior. *Behavior Research and Therapy, 14,* 463–469.

Rosenwald, G. C. (1972). Effectiveness of defenses against anal impulse arousal. *Journal of Consulting and Clinical Psychology, 39,* 292–298.

Ross, D. M., Ross, S. A., & Evans, T. A. (1971). The modification of extreme social withdrawal by modeling with guided participation. *Journal of Behavior Therapy and Experimental Psychiatry, 2,* 273–279.

Ross, M. (1989). Relation of implicit theories to the construction of personal histories. *Psychological Review, 96,* 341–357.

Ross, M., & Fletcher, G. J. O. (1985). Attribution and social perception. In G. Lindzey & E. Aronson (Eds.), *The handbook of social psychology* (3rd ed., pp. 73–122). Reading, MA: Addison-Wesley.

Roth, S. (1980). A revised model of learned helplessness in humans. *Journal of Personality, 48,* 103–133.

Rothbart, M. K., Ahadi, S. A., & Evans, D. E. (2000). Temperament and personality: Origins and outcomes. *Journal of Personality and Social Psychology, 78,* 122–135.

Rothbart, M. K., Ahadi, S. A., Hershey, K., & Fisher, P. (2001). Investigations of temperament at three to seven years: The Children's Behavior Questionnaire. *Child Development, 72,* 1394–1408.

Rothbart, M. K., & Bates, J. E. (1998). Temperament. In W. Damon (Series Ed.) and N. Eisenberg (Vol. Ed.), *Handbook of child psychology: Vol 3. Social, emotional and personality development* (5th ed., pp. 105–176). New York: Wiley.

Rothbart, M. K., Ellis, L. K., Rueda, M. R., & Posner, M. I. (2003). Developing mechanisms of temperamental effortful control. *Journal of Personality, 71,* 1113–1143.

Rothbart, M. K., & Posner, M. (1985). Temperament and the development of self-regulation. In L. C. Hartlage & C. F. Telzrow (Eds.), *The neuropsychology of individual differences: A developmental perspective* (pp. 93–123). New York: Plenum.

Rotter, J. B. (1954). *Social learning and clinical psychology.* New York: Prentice-Hall.

Rotter, J. B. (1966). Generalized expectancies for internal versus external control of reinforcement. *Psychological Monographs, 80* (1, Whole No. 609).

Rotter, J. B. (1982). *The development and applications of social learning theory: Selected papers.* New York: Praeger.

Rotter, J. B. (1990). Internal versus external control of reinforcement: A case history of a variable. *American Psychologist, 45,* 489–493.

Rotter, J. B., Seeman, M., & Liverant, S. (1962). Internal versus external control of reinforcement: A major variable in behavior theory. In N. F. Washburne (Ed.), *Decisions, values, and groups* (Vol. 2). New York: Pergamon.

Rowe, D. C. (1994). *The limits of family influence: Genes, experience, and behavior.* New York: Guilford.

Rowe, D. C. (2001). *Biology and crime.* Los Angeles: Roxbury.

Roy-Byrne, P. (2005). The GABA-benzodiazepine receptor complex: Structure, function, and role in anxiety. *Journal of Clinical Psychiatry, 66,* 14–20.

Roy-Byrne, P., Russo, J., Pollack, M., Stewart, R., Bystrisky, A., Bell, J., Rosenbaum, J., Corrigan, M. H., Stolk, J., Rush, A. J., & Ballenger, J. (2003). Personality and symptom sensitivity predictors of alprazolam withdrawal in panic disorder. *Psychological Medicine, 33,* 511–518.

Rozsnafszky, J. (1981). The relationship of level of ego development to Q-sort personality ratings. *Journal of Personality and Social Psychology, 41,* 99–120.

Rubin, R. T., Reinisch, J. M., & Haskett, R. F. (1981). Postnatal gonadal steroid effects on human behavior. *Science, 211,* 1318–1324.

Ruchkin, V., Koposov, R. A., af Klinteberg, B., Oreland, L., & Grigorenko, E. L. (2005). Platelet MAO-B, personality, and psychopathology. *Journal of Abnormal Psychology, 114,* 477–482.

Rushton, J. P. (1988). Genetic similarity, mate choice, and fecundity in humans. *Ethology and Sociobiology, 9,* 329–335.

Rushton, J. P. (1989a). Genetic similarity, human altruism, and group selection. *Behavioral and Brain Sciences, 12,* 503–559.

Rushton, J. P. (1989b). Genetic similarity in male friendships. *Ethology and Sociobiology, 10,* 361–373.

Rushton, J. P., & Bons, T. A. (2005). Mate choice and friendship in twins. *Psychological Science, 16,* 555–559.

Rushton, J. P., Brainerd, C. J., & Pressley, M. (1983). Behavioral development and construct validity: The principle of aggregation. *Psychological Bulletin, 94,* 18–38.

Rushton, J. P., Fulker, D. W., Neale, M. C., Nias, D. K. B., & Eysenck, H. J. (1986). Altruism and aggression: The heritability of individual differences. *Journal of Personality and Social Psychology, 50,* 1192–1198.

Rushton, J. P., Russell, R. J. H., & Wells, P. A. (1984). Genetic similarity theory: Beyond kin selection. *Behavior Genetics, 14,* 179–193.

Ryan, R. M. (1982). Control and information in the intrapersonal sphere: An extension of cognitive evaluation theory. *Journal of Personality and Social Psychology, 43,* 450–461.

Ryan, R. M. (1993). Agency and organization: Intrinsic motivation, autonomy, and the self in psychological development. In J. Jacobs (Ed.), *Nebraska symposium on motivation: Developmental perspectives on motivation* (Vol. 40, pp. 1–56). Lincoln: University of Nebraska Press.

Ryan, R. M., & Connell, J. P. (1989). Perceived locus of causality and internalization: Examining reasons for acting in two domains. *Journal of Personality and Social Psychology, 57,* 749–761.

Ryan, R. M., & Deci, E. L. (2001). On happiness and human potentials: A review of research on hedonic and eudaimonic well-being. *Annual Review of Psychology, 52,* 141–166.

Ryan, R. M., Rigby, S., & King, K. (1993). Two types of religious internalization and their relations to religious orientations and mental health. *Journal of Personality and Social Psychology, 65,* 586–596.

Ryan, R. M., Sheldon, K. M., Kasser, T., & Deci, E. L. (1996). All goals are not created equal: An organismic perspective on the nature of goals and their regulation. In P. M. Gollwitzer & J. A. Bargh (Eds.), *The psychology of action: Linking cognition and motivation to behavior* (pp. 7–26). New York: Guilford.

Sabini, J., & Green, M. C. (2004). Emotional responses to sexual and emotional infidelity: Constants and differences across genders, samples, and methods. *Personality and Social Psychology Bulletin, 30,* 1375–1388.

Sadalla, E. K., Kenrick, D. T., & Vershure, B. (1987). Dominance and heterosexual attraction. *Journal of Personality and Social Psychology, 52,* 730–738.

Samuel, D. B., & Widiger, T. A. (2006). Clinicians' judgments of clinical utility: A comparison of the DSM-IV and five-factor models. *Journal of Abnormal Psychology, 115,* 298–308.

Sarason, I. G. (1975). Test anxiety and the self-disclosing coping model. *Journal of Consulting and Clinical Psychology, 43,* 148–153.

Saucier, G. (1992). Benchmarks: Integrating affective and interpersonal circles with the big-five personality factors. *Journal of Personality and Social Psychology, 62,* 1025–1035.

Saucier, G., & Goldberg, L. R. (1998). What is beyond the big five? *Journal of Personality, 66,* 495–524.

Saucier, G., & Goldberg, L. R. (2001). Lexical studies of indigenous personality factors: Premises, products, and prospects. *Journal of Personality, 69,* 847–879.

Saucier, G., & Ostendorf, F. (1999). Hierarchical subcomponents of the big five personality factors: A cross-language replication. *Journal of Personality and Social Psychology, 76,* 613–627.

Saucier, G., & Simonds, J. (2006). The structure of personality and temperament. In D. K. Mroczek & T. D. Little (Eds.), *Handbook of Personality Development* (pp. 109–128). Mahwah, NJ: Erlbaum.

Saudino, K. J., McGuire, S., Reiss, D., Hetherington, E. M., & Plomin, R. (1995). Parent ratings of EAS temperaments in twins, full siblings, half siblings, and step siblings. *Journal of Personality and Social Psychology, 68,* 723–733.

Saudino, K. J., Pedersen, N. L., Lichtenstein, P., McClearn, G. E., & Plomin, R. (1997). Can personality explain genetic influences on life events? *Journal of Personality and Social Psychology, 72,* 196–206.

Scarr, S. (1985). Constructing psychology: Making facts and fables for our time. *American Psychologist, 40,* 499–512.

Scarr, S., & Carter-Saltzman, L. (1979). Twin method: Defense of a critical assumption. *Behavior Genetics, 9,* 527–542.

Scarr, S., & McCartney, K. (1983). How people make their own environments: A theory of genotype -> environment effects. *Child Development, 54,* 424–435.

Schank, R. C., & Abelson, R. P. (1977). *Scripts, plans, goals, and understanding.* Hillsdale, NJ: Erlbaum.

Schefft, B. K., & Lehr, B. K. (1985). A self-regulatory model of adjunctive behavior change. *Behavior Modification, 9,* 458–476.

Scheier, M. F., & Carver, C. S. (1983). Self-directed attention and the comparison of self with standards. *Journal of Experimental Social Psychology, 19,* 205–222.

Scheier, M. F., & Carver, C. S. (1988). A model of behavioral self-regulation: Translating intention into action. In L. Berkowitz (Ed.), *Advances in experimental social psychology* (Vol. 21, pp. 303–346). New York: Academic.

Scheier, M. F., & Carver, C. S. (1992). Effects of optimism on psychological and physical well-being: Theoretical overview and empirical update. *Cognitive Therapy and Research, 16,* 201–228.

Scheier, M. F., Carver, C. S., & Bridges, M. W. (2001). Optimism, pessimism, and psychological well-being. In E. C. Chang (Ed.), *Optimism and pessimism: Implications for theory, research, and practice* (pp. 189–216). Washington, DC: American Psychological Association.

Scheier, M. F., Matthews, K. A., Owens, J. F., Magovern, G. J., Lefebvre, R. C., Abbott, R. A., & Carver, C. S. (1989). Dispositional optimism and recovery from coronary artery bypass surgery: The beneficial effects on physical and psychological well-being. *Journal of Personality and Social Psychology, 57,* 1024–1040.

Scheier, M. F., Matthews, K. A., Owens, J. F., Schulz, R., Bridges, M. W., Magovern, G. J., Sr., & Carver, C. S. (1999). Optimism and rehospitalization following coronary artery bypass graft surgery. *Archives of Internal Medicine, 159,* 829–835.

Scheirer, M. A., & Kraut, R. E. (1979). Increasing educational achievement via self-concept change. *Review of Educational Research, 49,* 131–150.

Schell, T. L., Klein, S. B., & Babey, S. H. (1996). Testing a hierarchical model of self-knowledge. *Psychological Science, 7,* 170–173.

Schiedel, D. G., & Marcia, J. E. (1985). Ego identity, intimacy, sex-role orientation, and gender. *Journal of Personality and Social Psychology, 21,* 149–160.

Schimek, J. G. (1987). Fact and fantasy in the seduction theory: A historical review. *Journal of the American Psychoanalytic Association, 35,* 937–965.

Schimel, J., Arndt, J., Pyszczynski, T., & Greenberg, J. (2001). Being accepted for who we are: Evidence that social validation of the intrinsic self reduces general defensiveness. *Journal of Personality and Social Psychology, 80,* 35–52.

Schimel, J., Greenberg, J., & Martens, A. (2003). Evidence that projection of a feared trait can serve a defensive function. *Personality and Social Psychology Bulletin, 29,* 969–979.

Schimmack, U., Oishi, S., Furr, R. M., & Funder, D. C. (2004). Personality and life satisfaction: A facet-level analysis. *Personality and Social Psychology Bulletin, 30,* 1062–1075.

Schmidt, L. A. (1999). Frontal brain electrical activity in shyness and sociability. *Psychological Science, 10,* 316–320.

Schmidt, R. A. (1976). The schema as a solution to some persistent problems in motor learning theory. In G. E. Stelmach (Ed.), *Motor control: Issues and trends.* New York: Academic.

Schmidt, R. A. (1988). *Motor control and learning: A behavioral emphasis* (2nd ed.). Champaign, IL: Human Kinetics Publishers.

Schmitt, D. P. (2003). Universal sex differences in the desire for sexual variety: Tests from 52 nations, 6 continents, and 13 islands. *Journal of Personality and Social Psychology, 85,* 85–104.

Schmitt, D. P. (2004). Patterns and universals of mate poaching across 53 nations: The effects of sex, culture and personality on romantically attracting another person's partner. *Journal of Personality and Social Psychology, 86,* 560–584.

Schmitt, D. P., & Buss, D. M. (1996). Strategic self-promotion and competitor derogation: Sex and context effects on the perceived effectiveness of mate attraction tactics. *Journal of Personality and Social Psychology, 70,* 1185–1204.

Schmitt, D. P., & Buss, D. M. (2001). Human mate poaching: Tactics and temptations for infiltrating existing mateships. *Journal of Personality and Social Psychology, 80,* 894–917.

Schmitt, W. A., Brinkley, C. A., & Newman, J. P. (1999). Testing Damasio's somatic marker hypothesis with psychopathic individuals: Risk takers or risk averse? *Journal of Abnormal Psychology, 108,* 538–543.

Schneider, D. J. (1991). Social cognition. *Annual Review of Psychology, 42,* 527–561.

Schneider, K. J., Bugental, J. F. T., & Pierson, J. F. (Eds.). (2001). *The handbook of humanistic psychology: Leading edges in theory, research, and practice.* Thousand Oaks, CA: Sage.

Schneiderman, N., & Gormezano, I. (1964). Conditioning of the nictitating membrane of the rabbit as a function of the CS–US interval. *Journal of Comparative and Physiological Psychology, 57,* 188–195.

Schober, M. F., & Clark, H. H. (1989). Understanding by addressees and overhearers. *Cognitive Psychology, 21,* 211–232.

Schriesheim, C. A., & Hill, K. D. (1981). Controlling acquiescence response bias by item reversals: The effect on questionnaire validity. *Educational and Psychological Measurement, 41,* 1101–1114.

Schuckit, M. A., & Rayses, V. (1979). Ethanol ingestion: Differences in blood acetaldehyde concentrations in relatives of alcoholics and controls. *Science, 203,* 54–55.

Schultheiss, O. C. (2002). An information-processing account of implicit motive arousal. In P. R. Pintrich & M. L. Maehr (Eds.), *Advances in motivation and achievement: New directions in measures and methods* (Vol. 12, pp. 1–41). Amsterdam, The Netherlands: Elsevier.

Schultheiss, O. C., & Brunstein, J. C. (2001). Assessment of implicit motives with a research version of the TAT: Picture profiles, gender differences, and relations to other personality measures. *Journal of Personality Assessment, 77,* 71–86.

Schultheiss, O. C., & Brunstein, J. C. (2002). Inhibited power motivation and persuasive communication: A lens model analysis. *Journal of Personality, 70,* 553–582.

Schultheiss, O. C., Campbell, K. L., & McClelland, D. C. (1999). Implicit power motivation moderates men's testosterone responses to imagined and real dominance success. *Hormones and Behavior, 36,* 234–241.

Schultheiss, O. C., Dargel, A., & Rohde, W. (2003). Implicit motives and sexual motivation and behavior. *Journal of Research in Personality, 37,* 224–230.

Schultheiss, O. C., & Hale, J. A. (in press). Implicit motives modulate attentional orienting to facial expressions of emotion. *Motivation and Emotion.*

Schultheiss, O. C., & Pang, J. S. (in press). Measuring implicit motives. In R. W. Robins, R. C. Fraley, & R. Krueger (Eds.), *Handbook of Research Methods in Personality Psychology.* New York: Guilford.

Schultheiss, O. C., Pang, J. S., Torges, C. M., Wirth, M. M., & Treynor, W. (2005). Perceived facial expressions of emotion as motivational incentives: Evidence from a differential implicit learning paradigm. *Emotion, 5,* 41–54.

Schultheiss, O. C., & Rohde, W. (2002). Implicit power motivation predicts men's testosterone changes and implicit learning in a contest situation. *Hormones and Behavior, 41,* 195–202.

Schultheiss, O. C., Wirth, M. M., Torges, C. M., Pang, J. S., Villacorta, M. A., & Welsh, K. M. (2005). Effects of implicit power motivation on men's and women's implicit learning and testosterone changes after social victory or defeat. *Journal of Personality and Social Psychology, 88,* 174–188.

Schultz, C. B., & Pomerantz, M. (1976). Achievement motivation, locus of control, and academic achievement behavior. *Journal of Personality, 44,* 38–51.

Schultz, T. R., & Lepper, M. R. (1996). Cognitive dissonance reduction as constraint satisfaction. *Psychological Review, 103,* 219–240.

Schultz, W. (2000). Multiple reward signals in the brain. *Nature Reviews, 1,* 199–207.

Schultz, W. (2006). Behavioral theories and the neurophysiology of reward. *Annual Reviews of Psychology, 57,* 87–115.

Schutte, N. S., Kenrick, D. T., & Sadalla, E. K. (1985). The search for predictable settings: Situational prototypes, constraint, and behavioral variation. *Journal of Personality and Social Psychology, 49,* 121–128.

Schwartz, B. (1989). *Psychology of learning and behavior* (3rd ed.). New York: Norton.

Schwarz, N. (1990). Feelings as information: Informational and motivational functions of affective states. In E. T. Higgins & R. M. Sorrentino (Eds.), *Handbook of motivation and cognition: Foundations of social behavior* (Vol. 2, pp. 527–561). New York: Guilford.

Seamans, J. K. & Yang, C. R. (2004). The principal features and mechanisms of dopamine modulation in the prefrontal cortex. *Progress in Neurobiology, 74,* 1–57.

Sears, R. R. (1943). *Survey of objective studies of psychoanalytic concepts* (Bulletin 51). New York: Social Sciences Research Council.

Sears, R. R., Rau, L., & Alpert, R. (1965). *Identification and child rearing.* Stanford, CA: Stanford University Press.

Sechrest, L. (1977). Personal constructs theory. In R. J. Corsini (Ed.), *Current personality theories.* Itasca, IL: Peacock.

Sederer, L., & Seidenberg, R. (1976). Heiress to an empty throne: Ego-ideal problems of contemporary women. *Contemporary Psychoanalysis, 12,* 240–251.

Segal, N. L. (1993). Twin, sibling, and adoption methods: Tests of evolutionary hypotheses. *American Psychologist, 48,* 943–956.

Segal, N. L. (1999). *Entwined lives: Twins and what they tell us about human behavior.* New York: Dutton.

Segal, Z. V. (1988). Appraisal of the self-schema construct in cognitive models of depression. *Psychological Bulletin, 103,* 147–162.

Segerstorm, S. C., Miller, G. E. (2004). Psychological stress and the human immune system: A meta-analytic study of 30 years of inquiry. *Psychological Bulletin, 130,* 601–641.

Seidenberg, M. S. (2005). Connectionist models of word reading. *Current Directions in Psychological Science, 14,* 238–242.

Seifer, R., Sameroff, A. J., Barrett, L. C., & Krafchuk, E. (1994). Infant temperament measured by multiple observations and mother report. *Child Development, 65,* 1478–1490.

Seligman, M. E. P., & Hager, J. L. (Eds.). (1972). *Biological boundaries of learning.* New York: Appleton-Century-Crofts.

Seligman, M. E. P., & Maier, S. F. (1967). Failure to escape traumatic shock. *Journal of Experimental Psychology, 74,* 1–9.

Seltzer, R. A. (1973). Simulation of the dynamics of action. *Psychological Reports, 32,* 859–872.

Semmer, N., & Frese, M. (1985). Action theory in clinical psychology. In M. Frese & J. Sabini (Eds.), *Goal directed behavior: The concept of action in psychology.* Hillsdale, NJ: Erlbaum.

Sen, S., Villafuerte, S., Nesse, R., Stoltenberg, S. F., Hopcian, J., Gleiberman, L., Weder, A., & Burmeister, M. (2004). Serotonin transporter and GABA(A) alpha 6 receptor variants are associated with neuroticism. *Biological Psychiatry, 55,* 244–249.

Shane, M. S., & Peterson, J. B. (2004). Self-induced memory distortions and the allocation of processing resources at encoding and retrieval. *Cognition and Emotion, 18,* 533–558.

Shao, C., Li, Y., Jiang, K., Zhang, D., Xu, Y., Lin, L., Wang, Q., Zhao, M., & Jin, L. (2006). Dopamine D4 receptor polymorphism modulates cue-elicited heroin craving in Chinese. *Psychopharmacology, 186,* 185–190.

Shapiro, D., & Surwit, R. S. (1979). Biofeedback. In O. F. Pomerleau & J. P. Brady (Eds.), *Behavioral medicine: Theory and practice.* Baltimore: Williams & Wilkins.

Shaver, P. R., & Brennan, K. A. (1992). Attachment styles and the "big five" personality traits: Their connections with each other and with romantic relationship outcomes. *Personality and Social Psychology Bulletin, 18,* 536–545.

Shaver, P. R., & Rubenstein, C. (1980). *Childhood attachment experience and adult loneliness.* In L. Wheeler (Ed.), *Review of personality and social psychology* (Vol. 1, pp. 42–73). Beverly Hills, CA: Sage.

Shedler, J., & Block, J. (1990). Adolescent drug use and psychological health: A longitudinal inquiry. *American Psychologist, 45,* 612–630.

Shedler, J., Mayman, M., & Manis, M. (1993). The *illusion of mental health. American Psychologist, 48,* 1117–1131.

Sheeran, P., Webb, T. L., & Gollwitzer, P. M. (2005). The interplay between goal intentions and implementation intentions. *Personality and Social Psychology Bulletin, 31,* 87–98.

Sheldon, K. M. (2005). Positive value change during college: Normative trends and individual differences. *Journal of Research in Personality, 39,* 209–223.

Sheldon, K. M., & Elliot, A. J. (1998). Not all personal goals are personal: Comparing autonomous and controlled reasons for goals as predictors of effort and attainment. *Personality and Social Psychology Bulletin, 24,* 546–557.

Sheldon, K. M., & Elliot, A. J. (1999). Goal striving, need satisfaction, and longitudinal well-being: The self-concordance model. *Journal of Personality and Social Psychology, 76,* 482–497.

Sheldon, K. M., Elliot, A. J., Kim, Y., & Kasser, T. (2001). What is satisfying about satisfying events? Testing 10 candidate psychological needs. *Journal of Personality and Social Psychology, 80,* 325–339.

Sheldon, K. M., & Houser-Marko, L. (2001). Self-concordance, goal attainment, and the pursuit of happiness: Can there be an upward spiral? *Journal of Personality and Social Psychology, 80,* 152–165.

Sheldon, K. M., & Kasser, T. (1998). Pursuing personal goals: Skills enable progress but not all progress is beneficial. *Personality and Social Psychology Bulletin, 24,* 1319–1331.

Sheldon, K. M., Ryan, R. M., & Reis, H. (1996). What makes for a good day? Competence and autonomy in the day and in the person. *Personality and Social Psychology Bulletin, 22,* 1270–1279.

Sheldon, W. H. (with the collaboration of S. S. Stevens). (1942). *The varieties of temperament: A psychology of constitutional differences.* New York: Harper.

Sher, K. J., Bartholow, B. D., & Wood, M. D. (2000). Personality and substance use disorders: A prospective study. *Journal of Consulting and Clinical Psychology, 68,* 818–829.

Sherwood, G. G. (1981). Self-serving biases in person perception: An examination of projection as a mechanism of defense. *Psychological Bulletin, 90,* 445–459.

Shiner, R. L., Masten, A. S., & Tellegen, A. (2002). A developmental perspective on personality in emerging adulthood: Childhood antecedents and concurrent adaptation. *Journal of Personality and Social Psychology, 83,* 1165–1177.

Shoal, G. D., & Giancola, P. R. (2003). Negative affectivity and drug use in adolescent boys: Moderating and mediating mechanisms. *Journal of Personality and Social Psychology, 84,* 221–233.

Shoda, Y., Mischel, W., & Wright, J. C. (1989). Intuitive interactionism in person perception: Effects of situation–behavior relations on dispositional judgments. *Journal of Personality and Social Psychology, 56,* 41–53.

Shoda, Y., Mischel, W., & Wright, J. C. (1993). The role of situational demands and cognitive competencies in behavior organization and personality coherence. *Journal of Personality and Social Psychology, 65,* 1023–1035.

Shoda, Y., Mischel, W., & Wright, J. C. (1994). Intraindividual stability in the organization and patterning of behavior: Incorporating psychological situations into the idiographic analysis of personality. *Journal of Personality and Social Psychology, 67,* 674–687.

Shostrom, E. L. (1964). An inventory for the measurement of self-actualization. *Educational and Psychological Measurement, 24,* 207–218.

Shostrom, E. L. (1974). *Manual for the Personal Orientation Inventory.* San Diego: EdITS.

Showers, C. J., & Ryff, C. D. (1996). Self-differentiation and well-being in a life transition. *Personality and Social Psychology Bulletin, 22,* 448–460.

Shubsachs, A. P. W. (1975). To repeat or not to repeat? Are frequently used constructs more important to the subject? *British Journal of Medical Psychology, 48,* 31–37.

Sidanius, J., Pratto, F., & Bobo, L. (1994). Social dominance orientation and the political psychology of gender: A case of invariance? *Journal of Personality and Social Psychology, 67,* 998–1011.

Silverman, L. H. (1976). Psychoanalytic theory: "The reports of my death are greatly exaggerated." *American Psychologist, 31,* 621–637.

Silverman, L. H. (1983). The subliminal psychodynamic activation method: Overview and comprehensive listing of studies. In J. Masling (Ed.), *Empirical studies of psychoanalytic theories* (Vol. 1, pp. 69–100). Hillsdale, NJ: Erlbaum.

Silverman, L. H., Ross, D. L., Adler, J. M., & Lustig, D. A. (1978). Simple research paradigm for demonstrating subliminal psychodynamic activation: Effects of Oedipal stimuli on dart-throwing accuracy in college men. *Journal of Abnormal Psychology, 87,* 341–357.

Simon, D., Snow, C. J., & Read, S. J. (2004). The redux of cognitive consistency theories: Evidence judgments by constraint satisfaction. *Journal of Personality and Social Psychology, 86,* 814–837.

Simon, D. P., & Simon, H. A. (1978). Individual differences in solving physics problems. In R. S. Siegler (Ed.), *Children's thinking: What develops?* (pp. 325–348). Hillsdale, NJ: Erlbaum.

Simon, H. A. (1967). Motivational and emotional controls of cognition. *Psychological Review, 74,* 29–39.

Simpson, J. A. (1990). Influence of attachment styles on romantic relationships. *Journal of Personality and Social Psychology, 59,* 971–980.

Simpson, J. A., & Rholes, W. S. (Eds.). (1998). *Attachment theory and close relationships.* New York: Guilford.

Simpson, J. A., Rholes, W. S., & Nelligan, J. S. (1992). Support seeking and support giving within couples in an anxiety-provoking situation: The role of attachment styles. *Journal of Personality and Social Psychology, 62,* 434–446.

Simpson, J. A., Rholes, W. S., Oriña, M. M., & Grich, J. (2002). Working models of attachment, support giving, and support seeking in a stressful situation. *Personality and Social Psychology Bulletin, 28,* 598–608.

Simpson, J. A., Winterheld, H. A., & Chen, J. Y. (2006). Personality and relationships: A temperament perspective. In A. L Vangelisti & D. Perlman (Eds.), *The Cambridge handbook of personal relationships* (pp. 231–250). New York: Cambridge University Press.

Singer, J. A. (2004). Narrative identity and meaning making across the adult lifespan: An introduction. *Journal of Personality, 72,* 437–459.

Singer, J. A. (2005). *Personality and psychotherapy: Treating the whole person.* New York: Guilford.

Singh, D. (1995). Female judgment of male attractiveness and desirability for relationships: Role of waist-to-hip ratio and financial status. *Journal of Personality and Social Psychology, 69,* 1089–1101.

Skinner, B. F. (1938). *The behavior of organisms.* New York: Appleton-Century-Crofts.

Skinner, B. F. (1948). "Superstition" in the pigeon. *Journal of Experimental Psychology, 38,* 168–172.

Skinner, B. F. (1953). *Science and human behavior.* New York: Macmillan.

Skinner, B. F. (1974). *About behaviorism.* New York: Knopf.

Skinner, B. F. (1987). Whatever happened to psychology as the science of behavior? *American Psychologist, 42,* 780–786.

Skinner, B. F. (1989). The origins of cognitive thought. *American Psychologist, 44,* 13–18.

Skowronski, J. J., Carlston, D. E., Mae, L., & Crawford, M. T. (1998). Spontaneous trait transference: Communicators take on the qualities they describe in others. *Journal of Personality and Social Psychology, 74,* 837–848.

Sloman, S. A. (1996). The empirical case for two forms of reasoning. *Psychological Bulletin, 119,* 3–22.

Small, M. F. (1993). *Female choices: Sexual behavior of female primates.* Ithaca, NY: Cornell University Press.

Smith, A. (1969). *The theory of moral sentiments.* New Rochelle, NY: Arlington House. (Originally published in 1759)

Smith, C. P. (Ed.). (1992). *Motivation and personality: Handbook of thematic content analysis.* New York: Cambridge University Press.

Smith, E. E., Shoben, E. J., & Rips, L. J. (1974). Structure and process in semantic memory: A featural model for semantic decisions. *Psychological Review, 81,* 214–241.

Smith, E. R. (1996). What do connectionism and social psychology offer each other? *Journal of Personality and Social Psychology, 70,* 893–912.

Smith, E. R., Murphy, J., & Coats, S. (1999). Attachment to groups: Theory and measurement. *Journal of Personality and Social Psychology, 77,* 94–110.

Smith, G. M. (1967). Usefulness of peer ratings of personality in educational resarch. *Educational and Psychological Measurement, 27,* 967–984.

Smith, K. D., Keating, J. P., & Stotland, E. (1989). Altruism reconsidered: The effect of denying feedback on a victim's status to empathic witnesses. *Journal of Personality and Social Psychology, 57,* 641–650.

Smith, M. L., & Glass, G. V. (1977). Meta-analysis of psychotherapy outcome studies. *American Psychologist, 32,* 752–760.

Smith, M. L., Glass, G. V., & Miller, T. I. (1980). *The benefits of psychotherapy.* Baltimore: Johns Hopkins Press.

Smith, R. E. (1989). Effects of coping skills training on generalized self-efficacy and locus of control. *Journal of Personality and Social Psychology, 56,* 228–233.

Smolensky, P. (1988). On the proper treatment of connectionism. *Behavioral and Brain Sciences, 11,* 1–23.

Smolensky, P., Mozer, M. C., & Rumelhart, D. E. (Eds.). (1996). *Mathematical perspectives on neural networks.* Mahwah, NJ: Erlbaum.

Smyth, J. M. (1998). Written emotional expression: Effect sizes, outcome types, and moderating variables. *Journal of Consulting and Clinical Psychology, 66,* 174–184.

Snyder, C. R., & Higgins, R. L. (1988). Excuses: Their effective role in the negotiation of reality. *Psychological Bulletin, 104,* 23–35.

Snyder, M. (1974). The self-monitoring of expressive behavior. *Journal of Personality and Social Psychology, 30,* 526–537.

Snyder, M. (1987). *Public appearances/private realities: The psychology of self-monitoring.* New York: W. H. Freeman.

Snyder, M., & Gangestad, S. (1982). Choosing social situations: Two investigations of the self-monitoring process. *Journal of Personality and Social Psychology, 43,* 123–135.

Snyder, M. L., Stephan, W. G., & Rosenfield, D. (1976). Egotism and attribution. *Journal of Personality and Social Psychology, 33,* 435–441.

Snyder, M. L., Stephan, W. G., & Rosenfield, D. (1978). Attributional egotism. In J. H. Harvey, W. Ickes, & R. F. Kidd (Eds.), *New directions in attributional research* (Vol. 2). Hillsdale, NJ: Erlbaum.

Sobotka, S. S., Davidson, R. J., & Senulis, J. A. (1992). Anterior brain electrical asymmetries in response to reward and punishment. *Electroencephalography and Clinical Neurophysiology, 83,* 236–247.

Solms, M. (2000). Dreaming and REM sleep are controlled by different brain mechanisms. *Behavioral and Brain Sciences, 23,* 843–850.

Solomon, R. L. (1964). Punishment. *American Psychologist, 19,* 239–253.

Somer, O., & Goldberg, L. R. (1999). The structure of Turkish trait-descriptive adjectives. *Journal of Personality and Social Psychology, 76,* 431–450.

Sorg, B. A., & Whitney, P. (1992). The effect of trait anxiety and situational stress on working memory capacity. *Journal of Research in Personality, 26,* 235–241.

Sorrentino, R. M., & Field, N. (1986). Emergent leadership over time: The functional value of positive motivation. *Journal of Personality and Social Psychology, 50,* 1091–1099.

Soubrié, P. (1986). Reconciling the role of central serotonin neurons in human and animal behavior. *Behavioral and Brain Sciences, 9,* 319–364.

Spacapan, S., & Cohen, S. (1983). Effects and aftereffects of stressor expectations. *Journal of Personality and Social Psychology, 45,* 1243–1254.

Spangler, W. D., & House, R. J. (1991). Presidential effectiveness and the leadership motive profile. *Journal of Personality and Social Psychology, 60,* 439–455.

Spanos, N. P. (1996). *Multiple identities and false memories.* Washington, DC: American Psychological Association.

Spetch, M. L., Wilkie, D. M., & Pinel, J. P. J. (1981). Backward conditioning: A reevaluation of the empirical evidence. *Psychological Bulletin, 89,* 163–175.

Spielberger, C. D., & DeNike, L. D. (1966). Descriptive behaviorism versus cognitive theory in verbal operant conditioning. *Psychological Review, 73,* 309–326.

Spooner, A., & Kellogg, W. N. (1947). The backward conditioning curve. *American Journal of Psychology, 60,* 321–334.

Sprecher, S., Sullivan, Q., & Hatfield, E. (1994). Mate selection preferences: Gender differences examined in a national sample. *Journal of Personality and Social Psychology, 66,* 1074–1080.

Srivastava, S., McGonigal, K. M., Richards, J. M., Butler, E. A., & Gross, J. J. (2006). Optimism in close relationships: How seeing things in a positive light makes them so. *Journal of Personality and Social Psychology, 91,* 143–153.

Sroufe, L. A., & Fleeson, J. (1986). Attachment and the construction of relationships. In W. W. Hartup & Z. Rubin (Eds.), *Relationships and development* (pp. 51–71). Hillsdale, NJ: Erlbaum.

Srull, T. K., & Wyer, R. S., Jr. (1979). The role of category accessibility in the interpretation of information about persons: Some determinants and implications. *Journal of Personality and Social Psychology, 37,* 1660–1672.

St. Clair, M. (1986). *Object relations and self psychology: An introduction.* Monterey, CA: Brooks/Cole.

Staats, A. W. (1996). *Behavior and personality: Psychological behaviorism.* New York: Springer.

Staats, A. W., & Burns, G. L. (1982). Emotional personality repertoire as cause of behavior. *Journal of Personality and Social Psychology, 43,* 873–881.

Staats, A. W., & Staats, C. K. (1958). Attitudes established by classical conditioning. *Journal of Abnormal and Social Psychology, 57,* 37–40.

Staats, A. W., Staats, C. K., & Crawford, H. L. (1962). First-order conditioning of meaning and the parallel conditioning of a GSR. *Journal of General Psychology, 67,* 159–167.

Staats, C. K., & Staats, A. W. (1957). Meaning established by classical conditioning. *Journal of Experimental Psychology, 54,* 74–80.

Stanton, A. L., Danoff-Burg, S., Sworowski, L. A., Collins, C. A., Branstetter, A. D., Rodriguez-Hanley, A., Kirk, S. B., & Austenfeld, J. L. (2002). Randomized, controlled trial of written emotional expression and benefit finding in breast cancer patients. *Journal of Clinical Oncology, 20,* 4160–4168.

Stanton, A. L., & Snider, P. R. (1993). Coping with a breast cancer diagnosis: A prospective study. *Health Psychology, 12,* 16–23.

Steele, C. M. (1988). The psychology of self-affirmation: Sustaining the integrity of the self. In L. Berkowitz (Ed.), *Advances in experimental social psychology* (Vol. 21, pp. 261–302). New York: Academic.

Steele, C. M. (1997). A threat in the air: How stereotypes shape intellectual identity and performance. *American Psychologist, 52,* 613–629.

Steele, C. M., & Aronson, J. (1995). Stereotype threat and the intellectual test performance of African Americans. *Journal of Personality and Social Psychology, 69,* 797–811.

Sternberg, R. J. (Ed.). (1982). *Handbook of human intelligence.* New York: Cambridge University Press.

Steronko, R. J., & Woods, D. J. (1978). Impairment in early stages of visual information processing in nonpsychotic schizotypic individuals. *Journal of Abnormal Psychology, 87,* 481–490.

Stevens, R. (1983). *Erik Erikson: An introduction.* New York: St. Martin's.

Stevenson, H. W., Hale, G. A., Hill, K. T., & Moely, B. E. (1967). Determinants of children's preferences for adults. *Child Development, 38,* 1–14.

Stewart, A. J. (1980). Personality and situation in the prediction of women's life patterns. *Psychology of Women Quarterly, 5,* 195–206.

Stewart, A. J., & Vandewater, E. A. (1999). "If I had it to do over again. . ." Midlife review, midcourse corrections, and women's well-being in midlife. *Journal of Personality and Social Psychology, 76,* 270–283.

Stock, G. (2002). *Redesigning humans: Our inevitable genetic future.* Boston: Houghton Mifflin.

Stolberg, S. (1994, March 27). Genetic bias: Held hostage by heredity. *Los Angeles Times,* p. 1A.

Stone, L. J., & Hokanson, J. E. (1969). Arousal reduction via self-punitive behavior. *Journal of Personality and Social Psychology, 12,* 72–79.

Stotland, E. (1969). Exploratory investigation of empathy. In L. Berkowitz (Ed.), *Advances in experimental social psychology* (Vol. 4). New York: Academic.

Strack, F., & Deutsch, R. (2004). Reflective and impulsive determinants of social behavior. *Personality and Social Psychology Review, 8,* 220–247.

Straub, R. E., Jiang, Y., MacLean, C. J., Ma, Y., Webb, B. T., et al. (2002). Genetic variation in the 6p22.3 gene *DTNBP1,* the human ortholog of the mouse dysbindin gene, is associated with schizophrenia. *American Journal of Human Genetics, 71,* 337–348.

Strauman, T. J. (1989). Self-discrepancies in clinical depression and social phobia: Cognitive structures that underlie emotional disorders? *Journal of Abnormal Psychology, 53,* 14–22.

Strauman, T. J., & Higgins, E. T. (1987). Automatic activation of self-discrepancies and emotional syndromes: When cognitive structures influence affect. *Journal of Personality and Social Psychology, 53,* 1004–1014.

Strong, R. K., & Dabbs, J. M., Jr. (2000). Testosterone and behavior in normal young children. *Personality and Individual Differences, 28,* 909–915.

Strube, M. J. (1989). Evidence for the *type* in Type A behavior: A taxometric analysis. *Journal of Personality and Social Psychology, 56,* 972–987.

Stucke, T. S., & Sporer, S. L. (2002). When a grandiose self-image is threatened: Narcissism and self-concept clarity as predictors of negative emotions and aggression following ego-threat. *Journal of Personality, 70,* 509–532.

Stumpf, H. (1993). The factor structure of the Personality Research Form: A cross-national evaluation. *Journal of Personality, 61,* 27–48.

Stumphauzer, J. S. (1972). Increased delay of gratification in young prison inmates through imitation of high delay peer models. *Journal of Personality and Social Psychology, 21,* 10–17.

Sulloway, F. J. (1996). *Born to rebel: Birth order, family dynamics, and creative lives.* New York: Pantheon.

Sutton, S. K., & Davidson, R. J. (1997). Prefrontal brain asymmetry: A biological substrate of the behavioral approach and inhibition systems. *Psychological Science, 8,* 204–210.

Swann, W. B., Jr. (1987). Identity negotiation: Where two roads meet. *Journal of Personality and Social Psychology, 53,* 1038–1051.

Swann, W. B., Jr. (1990). To be adored or to be known: The interplay of self-enhancement and self-verification. In E. T. Higgins & R. M. Sorrentino (Eds.), *Handbook of motivation and cognition* (Vol. 2, pp. 408–448). New York: Guilford.

Swann, W. B., Jr., Bosson, J. K., & Pelham, B. W. (2002). Different partners, different selves: Strategic verification of circumscribed identities. *Personality and Social Psychology Bulletin, 28,* 1215–1228.

Swann, W. B., Jr., Pelham, B. W., & Krull, D. S. (1989). Agreeable fancy or disagreeable truth? Reconciling self-enhancement and self-verification. *Journal of Personality and Social Psychology, 57,* 782–791.

Swann, W. B., Jr., Wenzlaff, R. M., & Tafarodi, R. W. (1992). Depression and the search for negative evaluations: More evidence of the role of self-verification strivings. *Journal of Abnormal Psychology, 101,* 314–317.

Tajfel, H., & Turner, J. C. (1986). The social identity theory of intergroup behavior. In S. Worchel & W. G. Austin (Eds.), *Psychology of intergroup relations* (2nd ed., pp. 7–24). Chicago: Nelson-Hall.

Tangney, J. P., Baumeister, R. F., & Boone, A. L. (2004). High self-control predicts good adjustment, less pathology, better grades, and interpersonal success. *Journal of Personality, 72,* 271–324.

Tannen, D. (1990). *You just don't understand: Women and men in conversation.* New York: Ballantine.

Tavris, C., & Wade, C. (1984). *The longest war: Sex differences in perspective* (2nd ed.). New York: Harcourt Brace Jovanovich.

Taylor, M. C., & Hall, J. A. (1982). Psychological androgyny: Theories, methods and conclusions. *Psychological Bulletin, 92,* 347–366.

Taylor, S. E. (1983). Adjustment to threatening events: A theory of cognitive adaptation. *American Psychologist, 38,* 1161–1173.

Taylor, S. E. (2002). *The tending instinct: How nurturing is essential to who we are and how we live.* New York: Henry Holt.

Taylor, S. E., & Brown, J. D. (1988). Illusion and well-being: A social psychological perspective on mental health. *Psychological Bulletin, 103,* 193–210.

Taylor, S. E., & Fiske, S. T. (1978). Salience, attention, and attribution: Top of the head phenomena. In L. Berkowitz (Ed.), *Advances in experimental social psychology* (Vol. 11). New York: Academic.

Taylor, S. E., & Gollwitzer, P. M. (1995). Effects of mindset on positive illusions. *Journal of Personality and Social Psychology, 69,* 213–226.

Taylor, S. E., Klein, L. C., Lewis, B. P., Gruenewald, T. L., Gurung, R. A. R., & Updegraff, J. A. (2000). Biobehavioral responses to stress in females: Tend-and-befriend, not fight-or-flight. *Psychological Review, 107,* 411–429.

Taylor, S. E., Lichtman, R. R., & Wood, J. V. (1984). Attributions, beliefs in control, and adjustment to breast cancer. *Journal of Personality and Social Psychology, 46,* 489–502.

Tedeschi, R. G., & Calhoun, L. G. (1995). *Trauma and transformation: Growing in the aftermath of suffering.* Thousand Oaks, CA: Sage.

Tellegen, A. (1985). Structure of mood and personality and their relevance to assessing anxiety, with an emphasis on self-report. In A. H. Tuma & J. D. Maser (Eds.), *Anxiety and the anxiety disorders* (pp. 681–706). Hillsdale, NJ: Erlbaum.

Tellegen, A., Lykken, D. T., Bouchard, T. J., Jr., Wilcox, K. J., Segal, N. L., & Rich, S. (1988). Personality similarity in twins reared apart and together. *Journal of Personality and Social Psychology, 54,* 1031–1039.

Tesch, S. A., & Whitbourne, S. K. (1982). Intimacy status and identity status in young adults. *Journal of Personality and Social Psychology, 43,* 1041–1051.

Tesser, A. (1971). Evaluative and structural similarity of attitudes as determinants of interpersonal attraction. *Journal of Personality and Social Psychology, 18,* 92–96.

Tesser, A. (1986). Some effects of self-evaluation maintenance on cognition and action. In R. M. Sorrentino & E. T. Higgins (Eds.), *The handbook of motivation and cognition: Foundations of social behavior.* New York: Guilford.

Tesser, A. (1988). Toward a self-evaluation maintenance model of social behavior. In L. Berkowitz (Ed.), *Advances in experimental social psychology* (Vol. 21, pp. 181–227). New York: Academic.

Tesser, A. (1991). Social vs. clinical approaches to self psychology: The self-evaluation maintenance model and Kohutian object relations theory. In R. Curtis (Ed.), *The relational self: Theoretical convergences in psychoanalysis and social psychology* (pp. 257–281). New York: Guilford.

Tesser, A. (1993). The importance of heritability in psychological research: The case of attitudes. *Psychological Review, 100,* 129–142.

Tesser, A., & Campbell, J. (1983). Self-definition and self-evaluation maintenance. In J. Suls & A. G. Greenwald (Eds.), *Psychological perspectives on the self* (Vol. 2). Hillsdale, NJ: Erlbaum.

Thagard, P. (1989). Explanatory coherence. *Behavioral and Brain Sciences, 12,* 435–467.

Thagard, P., & Millgram, E. (1995). Inference to the best plan: A coherence theory of decision. In A. Ram & D. B. Leake (Eds.), *Goal-driven learning* (pp. 439–454). Cambridge, MA: MIT Press.

Theios, J. (1962). The partial reinforcement effect sustained through blocks of continuous reinforcement. *Journal of Experimental Psychology, 64,* 1–6.

Thelen, M. H., & Rennie, D. L. (1972). The effect of vicarious reinforcement on imitation: A review of the literature. In B. Maher (Ed.), *Progress in experimental personality research* (Vol. 6). New York: Academic.

Thiessen, D., & Gregg, B. (1980). Human assortative mating and genetic equilibrium: An evolutionary perspective. *Ethology and Sociobiology, 1,* 111–140.

Thomas, M. H., Horton, R. W., Lippincott, E. C., & Drabman, R. S. (1977). Desensitization to portrayals of real-life aggression as a function of exposure to television violence. *Journal of Personality and Social Psychology, 35,* 450–458.

Thompson, G. C. (1968). George Alexander Kelly (1905–1967). *Journal of General Psychology, 79,* 19–24.

Thompson, S. C. (1985). Finding positive meaning in a stressful event and coping. *Basic and Applied Social Psychology, 6,* 279–295.

Thompson, S. C. (1991). The search for meaning following a stroke. *Basic and Applied Social Psychology, 12,* 81–96.

Thompson, S. C., & Janigian, A. S. (1988). Life schemes: A framework for understanding the search for meaning. *Journal of Social and Clinical Psychology, 7,* 260–280.

Thorndike, E. L. (1898). Animal intelligence: An experimental study of the associative processes in animals. *Psychological Monographs, 2* (Whole No. 8).

Thorndike, E. L. (1905). *The elements of psychology.* New York: A. G. Seiler.

Thorndike, E. L. (1933). *An experimental study of rewards.* New York: Teachers College Press.

Thorne, A. (1987). The press of personality: A study of conversations between introverts and extraverts. *Journal of Personality and Social Psychology, 53,* 718–726.

Thrash, T. M., & Elliot, A. J. (2002). Implicit and self-attributed achievement motives: Concordance and predictive validity. *Journal of Personality, 70,* 729–755.

Thronquist, M. H., Zuckerman, M., & Exline, R. V. (1991). Loving, liking, looking, and sensation seeking in unmarried college couples. *Personality and Individual Differences, 12,* 1283–1292.

Timberlake, W. (1993). Behavior systems and reinforcement: An integrative approach. *Journal of the Experimental Analysis of Behavior, 60,* 105–128.

Toates, F. (2006). A model of the hierarchy of behaviour, cognition, and consciousness. *Consciousness and Cognition, 15,* 75–118.

Tobin, R. M., Graziano, W. G., Vanman, E. J., & Tassinary, L. G. (2000). Personality, emotional experience, and efforts to control emotions. *Journal of Personality and Social Psychology, 79,* 656–669.

Todd, M., Tennen, H., Carney, M. A., Armeli, S., & Affleck, G. (2004). Do we know how we cope? Relating daily coping reports to global and time-limited retrospective assessments. *Journal of Personality and Social Psychology, 86,* 310–319.

Tolman, E. C. (1932). *Purposive behavior in animals and men.* New York: Appleton-Century-Crofts.

Tolman, E. C. (1959). Principles of purposive behavior. In S. Koch (Ed.), *Psychology: A study of a science* (Vol. 2, pp. 92–157). New York: McGraw-Hill.

Tomich, P. T., & Helgeson, V. S. (2002). Five years later: A cross-sectional comparison of breast cancer survivors with healthy women. *Psycho-Oncology, 11,* 154–169.

Tomich, P. T., & Helgeson, V. S. (2004). Is finding something good in the bad always good? Benefit finding among women with breast cancer. *Health Psychology, 23,* 16–23.

Toner, I. J., & Smith, R. A. (1977). Age and overt verbalization in delay-maintenance behavior in children. *Journal of Experimental Child Psychology, 24,* 123–128.

Tooby, J., & Cosmides, L. (1989). Evolutionary psychology and the generation of culture, Part I. *Ethology and Sociobiology, 10,* 29–49.

Tooby, J., & Cosmides, L. (1990). On the universality of human nature and the uniqueness of the individual. *Journal of Personality, 58,* 17–67.

Trapnell, P. D., & Campbell, J. D. (1999). Private self-consciousness and the five-factor model of personality: Distinguishing rumination from reflection. *Journal of Personality and Social Psychology, 76,* 284–304.

Trapnell, P. D., & Wiggins, J. S. (1990). Extension of the interpersonal adjective scales to include the big five dimensions of personality. *Journal of Personality and Social Psychology, 59,* 781–790.

Triandis, H. C., Hui, H., Albert, R. D., Leung, S., Lisansky, J., Diaz-Loving, R., Plascencia, L., Marin, G., Betancourt, H., & Loyola-Cintron, L. (1984). Individual models of social behavior. *Journal of Personality and Social Psychology, 46,* 1389–1404.

Trivers, R. L. (1971). The evolution of reciprocal altruism. *Quarterly Review of Biology, 46,* 35–57.

Trivers, R. L. (1972). Parental investment and sexual selection. In B. Campbell (Ed.), *Sexual selection and the descent of man: 1871–1971* (pp. 136–179). Chicago: Aldine.

Trobst, K. K., Herbst, J. H., Masters, H. L., III, & Costa, P. T., Jr. (2002). Personality pathways to unsafe sex: Personality, condom use, and HIV risk behaviors. *Journal of Research in Personality, 36,* 117–133.

Trope, Y. (1975). Seeking information about one's own ability as a determinant of choice among tasks. *Journal of Personality and Social Psychology, 32,* 1004–1013.

Trope, Y. (1979). Uncertainty-reducing properties of achievement tasks. *Journal of Personality and Social Psychology, 37,* 1505–1518.

Trope, Y. (1980). Self-assessment, self-enhancement, and task preference. *Journal of Experimental Social Psychology, 16,* 116–129.

Trope, Y., & Fishbach, A. (2000). Counteractive self-control in overcoming temptation. *Journal of Personality and Social Psychology, 79,* 493–506.

Trope, Y., & Fishbach, A. (2005). Going beyond the motivation given: Self-control and situational control over behavior. In R. R. Hassin, J. S. Uleman, & J. A. Bargh (Eds.), *The new unconscious* (pp. 537–563). New York: Oxford University Press.

Truax, C. B., & Mitchell, K. M. (1971). Research on certain therapist interpersonal skills in relation to process and outcome. In A. E. Bergin & S. L. Garfield (Eds.), *Handbook of psychotherapy and behavior change.* New York: Wiley.

Tse, W. S., & Bond, A. J. (2001). Serotonergic involvement in the psychosocial dimension of personality. *Journal of Psychopharmacology, 15,* 195–198.

Tulving, E. (1972). Episodic and semantic memory. In E. Tulving & W. Donaldson (Eds.), *Organization of memory.* New York: Academic.

Tulving, E. (1993). What is episodic memory? *Current Directions in Psychological Science, 2,* 67–70.

Turk, D. (1978). Cognitive behavioral techniques in the management of pain. In J. P. Foreyt & D. P. Rathjen (Eds.), *Cognitive behavior therapy: Research and application.* New York: Plenum.

Turkheimer, E. (1998). Heritability and biological explanation. *Psychological Review, 105,* 782–791.

Turner, J. L., Foa, E. B., & Foa, U. G. (1971). Interpersonal reinforcers: Classification, interrelationship, and some differential properties. *Journal of Personality and Social Psychology, 19,* 168–170.

Turner, R. A., Altemus, M., Enos, T., Cooper, B., & McGuinness, T. (1999). Preliminary research on plasma oxytocin in normal cycling women: Investigating emotion and interpersonal distress. *Psychiatry, 62,* 97–113.

Twenge, J. M. (2000). The age of anxiety? Birth cohort change in anxiety and neuroticism, 1952–1993. *Journal of Personality and Social Psychology, 79,* 1007–1021.

Twenge, J. M. (2001). Birth cohort changes in extraversion: A cross-temporal meta-analysis, 1966–1993. *Personality and Individual Differences, 30,* 735–748.

Twenge, J. M. (2002). Birth cohort, social change, and personality: The interplay of dysphoria and individualism in the 20th century. In D. Cervone & W. Mischel (Eds.), *Advances in personality science* (pp. 196–218). New York: Guilford.

Twenge, J. M., Baumeister, R. F., Tice, D. M., & Stucke, T. S. (2001). If you can't join them, beat them: Effects of social exclusion on aggressive behavior. *Journal of Personality and Social Psychology, 81,* 1058–1069.

Twenge, J. M., & Campbell, W. K. (2001). Age and birth cohort differences in self-esteem: A cross-temporal meta-analysis. *Personality and Social Psychology Review, 5,* 321–344.

Twenge, J. M., & Campbell, W. K. (2003). "Isn't it fun to get the respect that we're going to deserve?" Narcissism, social rejection, and aggression. *Personality and Social Psychology Bulletin, 29,* 261–272.

Tyner, S. D., Venkatachalam, S., Choi, J., Jones, S., Ghebranious, N., Igelmann, H., Lu, X., Soron, G., Cooper, B., Brayton, C., Park, S. H., Thompson, T., Karsenty, G., Bradley, A., & Donehower, L. A. (2002). p53 mutant mice that display early ageing-associated phenotypes. *Nature, 415,* 45–53.

Udry, J. R., & Talbert, L. M. (1988). Sex hormone effects on personality at puberty. *Journal of Personality and Social Psychology, 54,* 291–295.

Underwood, B. J. (1975). Individual differences as a crucible in theory construction. *American Psychologist, 30,* 128–134.

Vaillant, G. E. (1977). *Adaptation to life.* Boston: Little, Brown.

Vallacher, R. R., & Nowak, A. (1997). The emergence of dynamical social psychology. *Psychological Inquiry, 8,* 73–99.

Vallacher, R. R., Read, S. J., & Nowak, A. (Eds.). (2002). The dynamical perspective in personality and social psychology [Special issue]. *Personality and Social Psychology Review, 6* (4).

Vallacher, R. R., & Wegner, D. M. (1985). *A theory of action identification.* Hillsdale, NJ: Erlbaum.

Vallacher, R. R., & Wegner, D. M. (1987). Action identification theory: The representation and control of behavior. *Psychological Review, 94,* 3–15.

Vallacher, R. R., & Wegner, D. M. (1989). Levels of personal agency: Individual variation in action identification. *Journal of Personality and Social Psychology, 57,* 660–671.

Vallerand, R. J. (1997). Toward a hierarchical model of intrinsic and extrinsic motivation. In M. P. Zanna (Ed.), *Advances in experimental social psychology* (Vol. 29, pp. 271–360). San Diego: Academic.

Van Honk, J., Schutter, D. J. L. G., Hermans, E. J., Putman, P., Tuiten, A., & Koppeschaar, H. (2004). Testosterone shifts the balance between sensitivity for punishment and reward in healthy young women. *Psychoneuroendocrinology, 29,* 937–943.

Van Maanen, J. (1973). Observations on the making of policemen. *Human Organization, 32,* 407–418.

Van Maanen, J. (1975). Police socialization: A longitudinal examination of job attitudes in an urban police department. *Administrative Science Quarterly, 20,* 207–228.

Vandenberg, S. G., Singer, S. M., & Pauls, D. L. (1986). *The heredity of behavior disorders in adults and children.* New York: Plenum.

Vandewater, E. A., Ostrove, J. M., & Stewart, A. J. (1997). Predicting women's well-being in midlife: The importance of personality development and social role involvements. *Journal of Personality and Social Psychology, 72,* 1147–1160.

Vaughan, K. B., & Lanzetta, J. T. (1980). Vicarious instigation and conditioning of facial expressive and autonomic responses to a model's expressive display of pain. *Journal of Personality and Social Psychology, 38,* 909–923.

Vernon, D. T. A. (1974). Modeling and birth order in responses to painful stimuli. *Journal of Personality and Social Psychology, 29,* 794–799.

Vernon, P. E. (1964). *Personality assessment: A critical survey.* New York: Wiley.

Veroff, J. (1957). Development and validation of a projective measure of power motivation. *Journal of Abnormal and Social Psychology, 54,* 1–8.

Verplanken, B., & Holland, R. W. (2002). Motivated decision making: Effects of activation and self-centrality of values on choices and behavior. *Journal of Personality and Social Psychology, 82,* 434–447.

Vertes, R. P. (2004). Memory consolidation in sleep: Dream or reality. *Neuron, 44,* 135–148.

Viken, R. J., & McFall, R. M. (1994). Paradox lost: Implications of contemporary reinforcement theory for behavior therapy. *Current Directions in Psychological Science, 3,* 121–125.

Viken, R. J., Rose, R. J., Kaprio, J., & Koskenvuo, M. (1994). A developmental genetic analysis of adult personality: Extraversion and neuroticism from 18 to 59 years of age. *Journal of Personality and Social Psychology, 66,* 722–730.

Vohs, K. D., & Baumeister, R. F. (2005). Self-regulation and self-presentation: Regulatory resource depletion impairs impression management and effortful self-presentation depletes regulatory resources. *Journal of Personality and Social Psychology, 88,* 632–657.

Vohs, K. D., Baumeister, R. F., & Ciarocco, N. J. (2005). Self-regulation and self-presentation: Regulatory resource depletion impairs impression management and effortful self-presentation depletes regulatory resources. *Journal of Personality and Social Psychology, 88,* 632–657.

Wacker, J., Chavanon, M., & Stemmler, G. (2006). Investigating the dopaminergic basis of extraversion in humans: A multilevel approach. *Journal of Personality and Social Psychology.*

Wade, S. L., Borawski, E. A., Taylor, H. G., Drotar, D., Yeates, L. O., & Stancin, T. (2001). The relationship of caregiver coping to family outcomes during the initial year following pediatric traumatic injury. *Journal of Consulting and Clinical Psychology, 69,* 406–415.

Wagner, A. R., Siegel, S., Thomas, E., & Ellison, G. D. (1964). Reinforcement history and the extinction of a conditioned salivary response. *Journal of Comparative and Physiological Psychology, 58,* 354–358.

Wahlsten, D. (1990). Insensitivity of the analysis of variance to heredity–environment interaction. *Behavioral and Brain Sciences, 13,* 100–161.

Wahlsten, D. (1999). Single-gene influences on brain and behavior. *Annual Review of Psychology, 50,* 599–624.

Walker, E. F., & Diforio, D. (1997). Schizophrenia: A neural diathesis-stress model. *Psychological Review, 104,* 667–685.

Walker, M. P. (2005). A refined model of sleep and the time course of memory formation. *Behavioral and Brain Sciences, 28,* 51–104.

Walker, R. N. (1962). Body build and behavior in young children. Body build and nursery school teacher ratings. *Monographs of the Society for Research on Child Development, 27* (Serial No. 84).

Wallace, H. M., & Baumeister, R. F. (2002). The performance of narcissists rises and falls with perceived opportunity for glory. *Journal of Personality and Social Psychology, 82,* 819–834.

Walls, R. T., & Cox, J. (1971). Expectancy of reinforcement in chance and skills tasks under motor handicaps. *Journal of Clinical Psychology, 27,* 436–438.

Wallston, B. S., & Wallston, K. A. (1978). Locus of control and health: A review of the literature. *Health Education Monographs, 6,* 107–117.

Wallston, K. A., & Wallston, B. S. (1981). Health locus of control scales. In H. F. Lefcourt (Ed.), *Research with the locus of control construct. Vol. 1, Assessment methods.* New York: Academic.

Walters, R. H., & Parke, R. D. (1964). Influence of response consequences to a social model on resistance to deviation. *Journal of Experimental Child Psychology, 1,* 269–280.

Walther, E. (2002). Guilty by mere association: Evaluative conditioning and the spreading attitude effect. *Journal of Personality and Social Psychology, 82,* 919–934.

Walton, K. E., & Roberts, B. W. (2004). On the relationship between substance use and personality traits: Abstainers are not maladjusted. *Journal of Research in Personality, 38,* 515–535.

Watson, D., & Clark, L. A. (1984). Negative affectivity: The disposition to experience aversive emotional states. *Psychological Bulletin, 96,* 465–490.

Watson, D., & Clark, L. A. (1994). Introduction to the special issue on personality and psychopathology. *Journal of Abnormal Psychology, 103,* 3–5.

Watson, D., Clark, L. A., McIntyre, C. W., & Hamaker, S. (1992). Affect, personality, and social activity. *Journal of Personality and Social Psychology, 63,* 1011–1025.

Watson, D., & Tellegen, A. (1985). Toward a consensual structure of mood. *Psychological Bulletin, 98,* 219–235.

Watson, D., Wiese, D., Vaidya, J., & Tellegen, A. (1999). The two general activation systems of affect: Structural findings, evolutionary considerations, and psychobiological evidence. *Journal of Personality and Social Psychology, 76,* 820–838.

Watson, J. B., & Raynor, R. (1920). Conditioned emotional reactions. *Journal of Experimental Psychology, 3,* 1–14.

Watt, J. D., & Blanchard, M. J. (1994). Boredom proneness and the need for cognition. *Journal of Research in Personality, 28,* 44–51.

Webb, T., & Sheeran, P. (2003). Can implementation intentions help to overcome ego-depletion? *Journal of Experimental Social Psychology, 39,* 279–286.

Wegner, D. M. (1989). *White bears and other unwanted thoughts: Suppression, obsession, and the psychology of mental control.* New York: Viking Penguin.

Wegner, D. M. (1994). Ironic processes of mental control. *Psychological Review, 101,* 34–52.

Wegner, D. M. (2002). *The illusion of conscious will.* Cambridge, MA: MIT Press.

Wegner, D. M., Schneider, D. J., Carter, S. R., III, & White, T. L. (1987). Paradoxical effects of thought suppression. *Journal of Personality and Social Psychology, 53,* 5–13.

Wegner, D. M., Shortt, J. W., Blake, A. W., & Page, M. S. (1990). The suppression of exciting thoughts. *Journal of Personality and Social Psychology, 58,* 409–418.

Wegner, D. M., Wenzlaff, R. M., & Kozak, M. (2004). Dream rebound: The return of suppressed thoughts in dreams. *Psychological Science, 15,* 232–236.

Wegner, D. M., & Wheatley, T. (1999). Apparent mental causation: Sources of the experience of will. *American Psychologist, 54,* 480–492.

Weinberger, D. A., Schwartz, G. E., & Davidson, R. J. (1979). Low-anxious, high-anxious, and repressive coping styles: Psychometric patterns and behavioral and physiological responses to stress. *Journal of Abnormal Psychology, 88,* 369–380.

Weinberger, J. L., & Hardaway, R. (1990). Separating science from myth in subliminal psychodynamic activation. *Clinical Psychology Review, 10,* 727–756.

Weinberger, J. L., & Silverman, L. H. (1987). Subliminal psychodynamic activation: A method for studying psychoanalytic dynamic propositions. In R. Hogan & W. H. Jones (Eds.), *Perspectives in personality* (Vol. 2, pp. 251–287). Greenwich, CT: JAI.

Weiner, B. (1979). A theory of motivation for some classroom experiences. *Journal of Educational Psychology, 71,* 3–25.

Weiner, B. (1986). *An attributional theory of motivation and emotion.* New York: Springer-Verlag.

Weiner, B. (1990). Attribution in personality psychology. In L. A. Pervin (Ed.), *Handbook of personality: Theory and research* (pp. 465–485). New York: Guilford.

Weiner, B., & Litman-Adizes, T. (1980). An attributional, expectancy–value analysis of learned helplessness and depression. In J. Garber & M. E. P. Seligman (Eds.), *Human helplessness: Theory and applications.* New York: Academic.

Weiner, B., Heckhausen, H., Meyer, W., & Cook, R. E. (1972). Causal ascriptions and achievement behaviors: A conceptual analysis of effort and reanalysis of locus of control. *Journal of Personality and Social Psychology, 21,* 239–248.

Weiner, B., Nierenberg, R., & Goldstein, M. (1976). Social learning (locus of control) versus attributional (causal stability) interpretations of expectancy of success. *Journal of Personality, 44,* 52–68.

Weinstein, N. D. (1989). Optimistic biases about personal risks. *Science, 246,* 1232–1233.

Weisberg, P., & Waldrop, P. B. (1972). Fixed-interval work habits of congress. *Journal of Applied Behavioral Analysis, 5,* 93–97.

Weiss, L., & Masling, J. (1970). Further validation of a Rorschach measure of oral imagery: A study of six clinical groups. *Journal of Abnormal Psychology, 76,* 83–87.

Weiss, R. S. (Ed.). (1973). *Loneliness: The experience of emotional and social isolation.* Cambridge, MA: MIT Press.

Wendelken, C., & Shastri, L. (2005). Connectionist mechanisms for cognitive control. *Neurocomputing: An International Journal, 65–66,* 663–672.

Wenzlaff, R. M., & Wegner, D. M. (2000). Thought suppression. *Annual Review of Psychology, 51,* 59–91.

Wenzlaff, R. M., Wegner, D. M., & Roper, D. W. (1988). Depression and mental control: The resurgence of unwanted negative thoughts. *Journal of Personality and Social Psychology, 55,* 1–11.

Westen, D. (1991). Social cognition and object relations. *Psychological Bulletin, 109,* 429–455.

Westen, D. (1998). The scientific legacy of Sigmund Freud: Toward a psychodynamically informed psychological science. *Psychological Bulletin, 124,* 333–371.

Westenberg, P. M., & Block, J. (1993). Ego development and individual differences in personality. *Journal of Personality and Social Psychology, 65,* 792–800.

Westmaas, J. L., & Silver, R. C. (2001). The role of attachment in responses to victims of life crises. *Journal of Personality and Social Psychology, 80,* 425–438.

Wheeler, R. E., Davidson, R. J., & Tomarken, A. J. (1993). Frontal brain asymmetry and emotional reactivity: A biological substrate of affective style. *Psychophysiology, 30,* 82–89.

Whitam, F. L., Diamond, M., & Martin, J. (1993). Homosexual orientation in twins: A report on 61 pairs and three triplet sets. *Archives of Sexual Behavior, 22,* 187–206.

Whitbeck, L. B., Hoyt, D. R., Simons, R. L., Conger, R. D., Elder, G. H., Jr., Lorenz, F. O., & Huck, S. (1992). Intergenerational continuity of parental rejection and depressed affect. *Journal of Personality and Social Psychology, 63,* 1036–1045.

Whitbourne, S. K., Zuschlag, M. K., Elliot, L. B., & Waterman, A. S. (1992). Psychosocial development in adulthood: A 22-year sequential study. *Journal of Personality and Social Psychology, 63,* 260–271.

White, K. M., Houlihan, J., Costos, D., & Speisman, J. C. (1990). Adult development in individuals and relationships. *Journal of Research in Personality, 24,* 371–386.

White, R. W. (1959). Motivation reconsidered: The concept of competence. *Psychological Review, 66,* 297–333.

White, R. W. (1963). *Ego and reality in psychoanalytic theory: A proposal regarding independent ego energies* (Psychological Issues Monograph 11). New York: International Universities Press.

Wickelgren, W. A. (1977). *Learning and memory.* Englewood Cliffs, NJ: Prentice-Hall.

Wicker, F. W., Brown, G., Wiehe, J. A., Hagen, A. S., & Reed, J. L. (1993). On reconsidering Maslow: An examination of the deprivation/domination proposition. *Journal of Research in Personality, 27,* 118–133.

Widiger, T. A., Trull, T. J., Clarkin, J. F., Sanderson, C., & Costa, P. T., Jr. (2002). A description of the DSM-IV personality disorders with the five-factor model. In P. T.

Costa, Jr. & T. A. Widiger (Eds.), *Personality disorders and the five-factor model of personality* (2nd ed., pp. 89–99). Washington, DC: American Psychological Association.

Wiedenfeld, S. A., O'Leary, A., Bandura, A., Brown, S., Levine, S., & Raska, K. (1990). Impact of perceived self-efficacy in coping with stressors on components of the immune system. *Journal of Personality and Social Psychology, 59,* 1082–1094.

Wiener, N. (1948). *Cybernetics: Control and communication in the animal and the machine.* Cambridge, MA: MIT Press.

Wiggins, J. S. (1973). *Personality and prediction: Principles of personality assessment.* Reading, MA: Addison-Wesley.

Wiggins, J. S. (1979). A psychological taxonomy of trait-descriptive terms: The interpersonal domain. *Journal of Personality and Social Psychology, 37,* 395–412.

Wiggins, J. S. (Ed.). (1996). *The five-factor model of personality: Theoretical perspectives.* New York: Guilford.

Wiggins, J. S., Phillips, N., & Trapnell, P. (1989). Circular reasoning about interpersonal behavior: Evidence concerning some untested assumptions underlying diagnostic classification. *Journal of Personality and Social Psychology, 56,* 296–305.

Willerman, L., Loehlin, J. C., & Horn, J. M. (1992). An adoption and a cross-fostering study of the Minnesota Multiphasic Personality Inventory (MMPI) Psychopathic Deviate scale. *Behavior Genetics, 22,* 515–529.

Williams, G. C., & Deci, E. L. (1996). Internalization of biopsychosocial values by medical students: A test of self-determination theory. *Journal of Personality and Social Psychology, 70,* 767–779.

Williams, G. C., Grow, V. M., Freedman, Z. R., Ryan, R. M., & Deci, E. L. (1996). Motivational predictors of weight loss and weight-loss maintenance. *Journal of Personality and Social Psychology, 70,* 115–126.

Williams, R. L., Moore, C. A., Pettibone, T. J., & Thomas, S. P. (1992). Construction and validation of a brief self-report scale of self-management practices. *Journal of Research in Personality, 26,* 216–234.

Wilson, E. O. (1975). *Sociobiology: The new synthesis.* Cambridge, MA: Harvard University Press.

Wilson, J. Q., & Herrnstein, R. J. (1985). *Crime and human nature.* New York: Simon & Schuster.

Wilson, M. I., & Daly, M. (1985). Competitiveness, risk-taking, and violence: The young male syndrome. *Ethology and Sociobiology, 6,* 59–73.

Wilson, M. I., & Daly, M. (1996). Male sexual proprietariness and violence against wives. *Current Directions in Psychological Science, 5,* 2–7.

Wink, P., & Helson, R. (1993). Personality change in women and their partners. *Journal of Personality and Social Psychology, 65,* 597–605.

Winson, J. (1985). *Brain and psyche: The biology of the unconscious.* Garden City, NY: Doubleday.

Winson, J. (1990). The meaning of dreams. *Scientific American, 263,* 86–96.

Winter, D. G. (1972). The need for power in college men: Action correlates and relationship to drinking. In D. C. McClelland, W. N. Davis, R. Kalin, & E. Wanner (Eds.), *The drinking man.* New York: Free Press.

Winter, D. G. (1973). *The power motive.* New York: Free Press.

Winter, D. G. (1988). The power motive in women—and men. *Journal of Personality and Social Psychology, 54,* 510–519.

Winter, D. G. (1993). Power, affiliation, and war: Three tests of a motivational model. *Journal of Personality and Social Psychology, 65,* 532–545.

Winter, D. G. (1994). *Manual for scoring motive imagery in running text.* University of Michigan, Ann Arbor: Unpublished manuscript.

Winter, D. G. (1996). *Personality: Analysis and interpretation of lives.* New York: McGraw-Hill.

Winter, D. G., & Barenbaum, N. B. (1985). Responsibility and the power motive in women and men. *Journal of Personality, 53,* 335–355.

Winter, D. G., John, O. P., Stewart, A. J., Klohnen, E. C., & Duncan, L. E. (1998). Traits and motives: Toward an integration of two traditions in personality research. *Psychological Bulletin, 105,* 230–250.

Winter, D. G., Stewart, A. J., & McClelland, D.C. (1977). Husband's motives and wife's career level. *Journal of Personality and Social Psychology, 35,* 159–166.

Wirth, M. M., Welsh, K., & Schultheiss, O. C. (2006). Salivary cortisol changes in humans after winning or losing a dominance contest depend on implicit power motivation. *Hormones and Behavior, 49,* 346–352.

Wise, R. A. (2004). Dopamine, learning and motivation. *Nature Reviews Neuroscience, 5,* 1–10.

Wisman, A., & Koole, S. L. (2003). Hiding in the crowd: Can mortality salience promote affiliation with others who oppose one's worldviews? *Journal of Personality and Social Psychology, 84,* 511–526.

Wispé, L. (1986). The distinction between sympathy and empathy: To call forth a concept, a word is needed. *Journal of Personality and Social Psychology, 50,* 314–321.

Woike, B. A. (1995). Most-memorable experiences: Evidence for a link between implicit and explicit motives and social cognitive processes in everyday life. *Journal of Personality and Social Psychology, 68,* 1081–1091.

Woike, B., Mcleod, S., & Goggin, M. (2003). Implicit and explicit motives influence accessibility to different autobiographical knowledge. *Personality and Social Psychology Bulletin, 29,* 1046–1055.

Wolberg, L. R. (1967). *The technique of psychotherapy.* New York: Grune & Stratton.

Wolfe, J. B. (1936). Effectiveness of token-rewards for chimpanzees. *Comparative Psychology Monographs, 12* (Whole No. 60).

Wolfe, R. N., & Kasmer, J. A. (1988). Type versus trait: Extraversion, impulsivity, sociability, and preferences for cooperative and competitive activities. *Journal of Personality and Social Psychology, 54,* 864–871.

Wolpe, J. (1981). Behavior therapy versus psychoanalysis: Therapeutic and social implications. *American Psychologist, 36,* 159–164.

Wong, M. M., & Csikszentmihalyi, M. (1991). Affiliation motivation and daily experience: Some issues on gender differences. *Journal of Personality and Social Psychology, 60,* 154–164.

Wood, J. M., Nezworski, M. T., & Stejskal, W. J. (1996a). The comprehensive system for the Rorschach: A critical examination. *Psychological Science, 7,* 3–10.

Wood, J. M., Nezworski, M. T., & Stejskal, W. J. (1996b). Thinking critically about the comprehensive system for the Rorschach: A reply to Exner. *Psychological Science, 7,* 14–17.

Wood, R., & Bandura, A. (1989). Impact of conceptions of ability on self-regulatory mechanisms and complex decision making. *Journal of Personality and Social Psychology, 56,* 407–415.

Wood, W., & Eagly, A. H. (2002). A cross-cultural analysis of the behavior of women and men: Implications for the origins of sex differences. *Psychological Bulletin, 128,* 699–727.

Wood, W., Quinn, F. M., & Kashy, D. A. (2002). Habits in everyday life: Thought, emotion, and action. *Journal of Personality and Social Psychology, 83,* 1281–1297.

Wood, W., Tam, L., & Guerrero Witt, M. (2005). Changing circumstances, disrupting habits. *Journal of Personality and Social Psychology, 88,* 918–933.

Woodruffe, C. (1985). Consensual validation of personality traits: Additional evidence and individual differences. *Journal of Personality and Social Psychology, 48,* 1240–1252.

Wortman, C. B., & Brehm, J. W. (1975). Responses to uncontrollable outcomes: An integration of reactance theory and the learned helplessness model. In L. Berkowitz (Ed.), *Advances in experimental social psychology* (Vol. 8). New York: Academic.

Wright, J. C., & Mischel, W. (1988). Conditional hedges and the intuitive psychology of traits. *Journal of Personality and Social Psychology, 55,* 454–469.

Wright, J. C., Lindgren, K. P., & Zakriski, A. L. (2001). Syndromal versus contextualized personality assessment: Differentiating environmental and dispositional determinants of boys' aggression. *Journal of Personality and Social Psychology, 81,* 1176–1189.

Wright, J. C., & Zakriski, A. L. (2003). When syndromal similarity obscures functional dissimilarity: Distinctive evoked environments of externalizing and mixed syndrome boys. *Journal of Consulting and Clinical Psychology, 71,* 516–527.

Wright, J. C., Zakriski, A. L., & Drinkwater, M. (1999). Developmental psychopathology and the reciprocal patterning of behavior and environment: Distinctive situational and behavioral signatures of internalizing, externalizing, and mixed-syndrome children. *Journal of Consulting and Clinical Psychology, 67,* 95–107.

Wright, R. A. (1996). Brehm's theory of motivation as a model of effort and cardiovascular response. In P. M. Gollwitzer & J. A. Bargh (Eds.), *The psychology of action: Linking cognition and motivation to behavior* (pp. 424–453). New York: Guilford.

Wrosch, C., Dunne, E., Scheier, M. F., & Schulz, R. (2006). *Journal of Behavioral Medicine, 29,* 299–306.

Wrosch, C., Scheier, M. F., Carver, C. S., & Schulz, R. (2003). The importance of goal disengagement in adaptive self-regulation: When giving up is beneficial. *Self and Identity, 2,* 1–20.

Wulfert, E., Block, J. A., Santa Ana, E., Rodriguez, M. L., & Colsman, M. (2002). Delay of gratification: Impulsive choices and problem behaviors in early and late adolescence. *Journal of Personality, 70,* 533–552.

Wyer, R. S., Jr., & Srull, T. K. (1986). Human cognition in its social context. *Psychology Review, 93,* 322–359.

Wylie, R. (1979). *The self concept* (Vol. 2). Lincoln: University of Nebraska Press.

Yates, B. T., & Mischel, W. (1979). Young children's preferred attentional strategies for delaying gratification. *Journal of Personality and Social Psychology, 37,* 286–300.

Yates, J., & Taylor, J. (1978). Stereotypes for somatotypes: Shared beliefs about Sheldon's physiques. *Psychological Reports, 43,* 777–778.

York, K. L., & John, O. P. (1992). The four faces of Eve: A typological analysis of women's personality at midlife. *Journal of Personality and Social Psychology, 63,* 494–508.

Young, J. E., & Klosko, J. S. (1993). *Reinventing your life.* New York: Plume.

Zald, D. H., & Depue, R. A. (2001). Serotonergic functioning correlates with positive and negative affect in psychiatrically healthy males. *Personality and Individual Differences, 30,* 71–86.

Zeidner, M., & Hammer, A. L. (1992). Coping with missile attack: Resources, strategies, and outcomes. *Journal of Personality, 60,* 709–746.

Zeldow, P. B., Daugherty, S. R., & McAdams, D. P. (1988). Intimacy, power, and psychological well-being in medical students. *Journal of Nervous and Mental Disease, 176,* 182–187.

Zelenski, J. M., & Larsen, R. J. (1999). Susceptibility to affect: A comparison of three personality taxonomies. *Journal of Personality, 67,* 761–791.

Zener, K. (1937). The significance of behavior accompanying conditioned salivary secretion for theories of the conditioned response. *American Journal of Psychology, 50,* 384–403.

Zentall, T. R., Sutton, J. E., & Sherburne, L. M. (1996). True imitative learning in pigeons. *Psychological Science, 7,* 343–346.

Zillmann, D. (1971). Excitation transfer in communication-mediated aggressive behavior. *Journal of Experimental Social Psychology, 7,* 419–434.

Zillmann, D. (1998). *Connections between sexuality and aggression* (2nd ed.). Mahwah, NJ: Erlbaum.

Zimmerman, D. W. (1957). Durable secondary reinforcement: Method and theory. *Psychological Review, 14,* 373–383.

Zinbarg, R. E., & Mohlman, J. (1998). Individual differences in the acquisition of affectively valenced associations. *Journal of Personality and Social Psychology, 74,* 1024–1040.

Zucker, A. N., Ostrove, J. M., & Stewart, A. J. (2002). College-educated women's personality development in adulthood: Perceptions and age differences. *Psychology & Aging, 17,* 236–244.

Zuckerman, M. (1971). Dimensions of sensation seeking. *Journal of Consulting and Clinical Psychology, 36,* 45–52.

Zuckerman, M. (1979). *Sensation seeking: Beyond the optimal level of arousal.* Hillsdale, NJ: Erlbaum.

Zuckerman, M. (1985). Biological foundations of the sensation-seeking temperament. In J. Strelau, F. H. Farley, & A. Gale (Eds.), *The biological bases of personality and behavior. Vol. 1. Theories, measurement techniques, and development.* Washington, DC: Hemisphere.

Zuckerman, M. (1991). *The psychobiology of personality.* New York: Cambridge University Press.

Zuckerman, M. (1992). What is a basic factor and which factors are basic? Turtles all the way down. *Personality and Individual Differences, 13,* 675–681.

Zuckerman, M. (1993). P-impulsive sensation seeking and its behavioral, psychophysiological and biochemical correlates. *Neuropsychobiology, 28,* 30–36.

Zuckerman, M. (1994). *Behavioral expression and biosocial bases of sensation seeking.* New York: Cambridge University Press.

Zuckerman, M. (1995). Good and bad humors: Biochemical bases of personality and its disorders. *Psychological Science, 6,* 325–332.

Zuckerman, M. (1996). The psychobiological model for impulsive unsocialized sensation seeking: A comparative approach. *Neuropsychobiology, 34,* 125–129.

Zuckerman, M. (2005). *Psychobiology of Personality.* New York: Cambridge University Press.

Zuckerman, M., Bernieri, F., Koestner, R., & Rosenthal, R. (1989). To predict some of the people some of the time: In search of moderators. *Journal of Personality and Social Psychology, 57,* 279–293.

Zuckerman, M., Kieffer, S. C., & Knee, C. R. (1998). Consequences of self-handicapping: Effects on coping, academic performance, and adjustment. *Journal of Personality and Social Psychology, 74,* 1619–1628.

Zuckerman, M., Koestner, R., DeBoy, T., Garcia, T., Maresca, B. C., & Sartoris, J. M. (1988). To predict some of the people some of the time: A reexamination of the moderator variable approach in personality theory. *Journal of Personality and Social Psychology, 54,* 1006–1019.

Zuckerman, M., Kuhlman, D. M., Joireman, J., Teta, P., & Kraft, M. (1993). A comparison of three structural models for personality: The big three, the big five, and the alternative five. *Journal of Personality and Social Psychology, 65,* 757–768.

Zuckerman, M., & Neeb, M. (1980). Demographic influences in sensation seeking and expressions of sensation seeking in religion, smoking, and driving habits. *Personality and Individual Differences, 1,* 197–206.

Zuckerman, M., & Tsai, F. Costs of self-handicapping. *Journal of Personality, 73,* 411–442.

Zuroff, D. C. (1986). Was Gordon Allport a trait theorist? *Journal of Personality and Social Psychology, 51,* 993–1000.

Zwanzger, P., & Rupprecht, R. (2005). Selective GABA-ergic treatment for panic? Investigations in experimental panic induction and panic disorder. *Journal of Psychiatry & Neuroscience, 30,* 167–175.